Microsoft

Programming Microsoft® Visual C#® 2005: The Base Class Library

Francesco Balena
(Code Architects)

PUBLISHED BY
Microsoft Press
A Division of Microsoft Corporation
One Microsoft Way
Redmond, Washington 98052-6399

Library of Congress Control Number 2006922557

Printed and bound in the United States of America.

1 2 3 4 5 6 7 8 9   QWT   8 7 6

Distributed in Canada by H.B. Fenn and Company Ltd.

A CIP catalogue record for this book is available from the British Library.

Microsoft Press books are available through booksellers and distributors worldwide. For further information about international editions, contact your local Microsoft Corporation office or contact Microsoft Press International directly at fax (425) 936-7329. Visit our Web site at www.microsoft.com/mspress. Send comments to mspinput@microsoft.com.

Acquisitions Editor: Ben Ryan
Project Editor: Kathleen Atkins
Technical Editor: Jack Beaudry
Copy Editor: Christina Palaia
Indexer Editor: Julie Bess

Body Part No. X12-21116

To Adriana

my wife, my friend, my love

Contents at a Glance

Table of Contents

What do you think of this book?
We want to hear from you!

Microsoft is interested in hearing your feedback about this publication so we can continually improve our books and learning resources for you. To participate in a brief online survey, please visit: *www.microsoft.com/learning/booksurvey/*

Acknowledgments

First of all, I am glad to have the opportunity to thank my friend Giuseppe Dimauro, for helping me to better understand the many secrets behind the Microsoft Windows and .NET Framework platforms.

Enrico Sabbadin is a true expert in N-tier enterprise applications, COM+, and security, and I feel very lucky he could review all the chapters while I was writing them. He provided many valuable suggestions.

I'd like to thank Marco Bellinaso and Alberto Falossi, two pillars of the Code Architects team. While I was busy on this book, Marco did a marvelous job with our U.S. site (*http://www.dotnet2themax.com*), and Alberto did the same with our Italian Web site (*http://www.dotnet2themax.it*).

Next come all the wonderful people at Microsoft Press. Kathleen Atkins has taken care of all my books, and she is so marvelous that I can't even think of writing a book with another editor. Jack Beaudry helped in finding typos and mistakes in code, whereas Christina Palaia did the same with my prose. English isn't my mother tongue, so you can imagine the job she had to face.

This book would be very different—or it wouldn't exist at all—if it weren't for Ben Ryan, my acquisitions editor, who accepted the proposal and provided many suggestions before, during, and after the writing of the book.

Introduction

The majority of the developers I know are convinced that all they need to write great applications is in-depth knowledge of high-level programming technologies such as Microsoft Windows Forms, ADO.NET, and ASP.NET, plus "good enough" familiarity with their programming language of choice. After all, the language is just the glue used to bind together the objects provided by the .NET Framework, right?

Well, not exactly. There is a sort of gray area between the language and high-level objects of the Microsoft .NET Framework, such as forms or ASP.NET Web pages. For example, the .NET classes that represent primitive data types, such as numeric and date values, arrays, and collections, fall into this gray area, as do generic collections. The same holds true for the types that allow you to deal with files and streams, create legacy COM components, and work with string and binary resources. If you aren't familiar with these types, you are missing much of the potential offered by the .NET Framework. Most of the types in this area belong to the .NET Framework Base Class Library (BCL).

If you aren't familiar with an important low-level mechanism at the BCL level, you might create sloppy and bugged applications. This can happen, for example, if you fail to account for the undeterministic finalization process, or fail to consider the issues that can arise when working with multiple threads in a Windows Forms application. Or when you don't account for versioning when serializing an object, a thorny issue because serialization can occur transparently when you work with serviced components or remoting. Questions about these topics appear frequently in forums, a clue that many developers aren't as familiar with these issues as they should be.

A quick look at bookstore shelves shows that you can find tons of books on mainstream areas such as Windows Forms, ASP.NET, ADO.NET, Web services, XML, and security, but it's harder to find books that cover the BCL. Even more difficult is finding information sources that cover these topics from the perspective of the application developer, as opposed to that of the system developer. You can find magazine and online articles that explain all the low-level details of, say, memory management and the garbage collector, but when it's time to apply these concepts to real-world applications, you're on your own.

The goal of this book is to fill this gap. It covers all the previously mentioned areas from the point of view of developers who want to create better, faster, and more robust applications in less time and using less code.

Take regular expressions, for example, which I cover in Chapter 6. In addition to providing a complete reference of the search patterns you can use with the Regex class, I illustrate many real-world techniques for solving recurring programming tasks—such as reading fixed-length and comma-delimited data files, parsing HTML pages, and validating user input—with a fraction of the code you'd have to write using a different approach. After many years, I continue to be surprised by the time and effort that regular expressions save me virtually every day, and I am equally surprised by the fact that so few developers are familiar with them.

The chapters on reflection and custom attributes are two more examples of the point I am making. Taken together, these features can revolutionize the way you write applications because they allow you to write code that is more generic and therefore more easily reused. Yet, I estimate that less than 1 percent of .NET Framework developers use them effectively in their applications. You can appreciate their potential in Chapter 10, "Custom Attributes," which includes the full source code of a plug-in architecture for a Windows Forms application and an N-tier enterprise-level framework.

The material included in this book is taken from the fourth edition of my *Programming Microsoft Visual Basic 2005: The Language* in the Programming Microsoft Visual Basic series from Microsoft Press. But it isn't a mere language-to-language translation because I completely revised the text and the code with the intent of being closer to the "C# way" of solving problems. For example, I rewrote several code portions to use new C# features, such as anonymous methods and iterators.

Live Updates and Feedback

Even though I have been working with Visual Basic, C#, and the .NET Framework for so many years, I continue to learn something new almost every day. You can learn more about my discoveries by visiting my Web site, where I maintain the home page for this and all my other books, at this URL:

http://www.dotnet2themax.com

You can also subscribe to the site's newsletter and receive information about new articles and code snippets available online. Or you can read my English blog, where I post updates about this book, comments from readers, plans for future Microsoft Press books, and so forth:

http://www.dotnet2themax.com/blogs/fbalena

(Tip: Select the Books category to read all posts related to this and forthcoming books.) Writing this book has been a challenge. I think (and hope) I did a good job, but I surely look forward to reading your comments, reactions, and suggestions for improvements. You can leave a comment at my blog (shown in Figure I-1) or write me at *fbalena@codearchitects.com*.

Figure A-1   My blog

Who Is This Book For?

The short answer is that this book is for all Microsoft Visual C# 2005 developers.

A more articulated answer is that this book is addressed to the following people:

- Expert Visual C# developers who want to learn more about advanced .NET Framework programming techniques, such as memory optimization, object serialization, and threading

- Developers who are familiar with features in .NET Framework 1.1 and want to learn about the new BCL features in version 2.0

- Programmers of any expertise level who want to write robust and maintainable applications by taking advantage of object-oriented features of Visual C# and other .NET Framework techniques, such as reflection and custom attributes

 Sections marked with this icon describe features that have been added in version 2.0 of the .NET Framework or in version 2005 of Visual C#.

Organization of This Book

Programming Microsoft Visual C# 2005: The Base Class Library is broadly divided into two parts.

The first seven chapters are about basic types in the .NET Framework, including primitive types, interfaces, and generic classes. Chapter 2, "Object Lifetime," illustrates several programming techniques to use the .NET Framework garbage collector, and Chapter 5, "Arrays and

Collections," shows you how to work wonders with .NET Framework complex data structures (including the generics collection). In my favorite chapter, Chapter 6, "Regular Expressions," I describe all I've learned about this exciting .NET Framework feature.

The remaining chapters cover more advanced programming topics, such as threading, serialization, PInvoke, and COM Interop. These features can make your applications more powerful, but failing to use them properly can introduce many hard-to-find bugs; thus, read these chapters carefully. Chapter 9, "Reflection," and Chapter 10, "Custom Attributes," are actually one very long chapter split into two: in the former, I offer a very complete reference on reflection; in the latter, I offer a few real-world (and quite complex) examples of the wonders custom attributes can do for you.

System Requirements

You need the following hardware and software to build and run the code samples in this book:

- Microsoft Windows XP with Service Pack 2, Microsoft Windows Server 2003 with Service Pack 1, or Microsoft Windows 2000 with Service Pack 4
- Microsoft Visual Studio 2005 Standard Edition or Microsoft Visual Studio 2005 Professional Edition
- 1-GHz Pentium or compatible processor
- 384 MB RAM (512 MB or more recommended)
- Video (800 × 600 or higher resolution) monitor with at least 256 colors (1,024 × 768 High Color 16-bit recommended)
- Microsoft mouse or compatible pointing device

Technology Updates

As technologies related to this book are updated, links to additional information will be added to the Microsoft Press Technology Updates Web page. Visit this page periodically for updates on Visual Studio 2005 and other technologies:

http://www.microsoft.com/mspress/updates/

Code Samples

All of the code samples discussed in this book can be downloaded from the book's companion content page at the following address:

http://www.microsoft.com/mspress/companion/0-7356-2308-2

Support for This Book

Every effort has been made to ensure the accuracy of the information in this book and in the companion content. Microsoft Press provides support for books and companion content at the following Web site:

http://www.microsoft.com/learning/support/books/

I provide support for this book, including an errata page and updated code samples, at my Web site:

http://www.dotnet2themax.com/

and through my blog:

http://www.dotnet2themax.com/blogs/fbalena

Questions and Comments

If you have comments, questions, or ideas regarding the book or the companion content, or questions that are not answered by visiting the preceding sites, please send them to Microsoft Press by e-mail:

mspinput@microsoft.com

Or by postal mail:

Microsoft Press

Attn: *Programming Microsoft Visual C# 2005: The Base Class Library* Editor

One Microsoft Way

Redmond, WA 98052-6399

Please note that Microsoft software product support is not offered through the preceding addresses.

Chapter 1
.NET Framework Basic Types

The Microsoft .NET Framework exposes hundreds of different classes to accomplish such jobs as opening files, parsing XML, and updating databases, but it is more than just a collection of useful objects. It's a well-structured object tree that also provides objects to store values, such as numbers, dates, and strings. Everything in the .NET Framework is a class, and at the top of the object hierarchy sits the System.Object class.

Note   To avoid long lines, code samples in this chapter assume that the following using statements are used at the top of each source file:

```
using System;
using System.Diagnostics;
using System.Globalization;
using System.IO;
using System.Runtime.InteropServices;
using System.Security;
using System.Text;
using System.Threading;
using System.Windows.Forms;
```

The System.Object Type

All classes inherit—directly or indirectly—from System.Object, which means that you can always assign any object to a System.Object variable and never get a compilation or runtime error when you do so:

```
// The object C# type is a synonym for System.Object.
object o = new AnyOtherType();
```

Incidentally, note that interfaces are the only things in the .NET Framework that do not derive from System.Object.

Public and Protected Methods

Because .NET types inherit from System.Object (see Figure 1-1), they all expose the four instance methods that System.Object exposes, namely the following:

- **Equals** An overridable method that checks whether the current object has the same value as the object passed as an argument. It returns true when two object references point to the same object instance, but many classes override this method to implement a different type of equality. For example, numeric types override this method so that it returns true if the objects being compared have the same numeric value.

- **GetHashCode** An overridable method that returns a hash code for the object. This method is used when the object is a key for collections and hash tables. Ideally, the hash code should be unique for any given object instance so that you can verify that two objects are "equal" by comparing their hash codes. However, implementing a hash function that provides unique values is seldom possible, and different objects might return the same hash code, so you should *never* infer that two instances with the same hash code are equal, whatever "equal" might mean for that specific type. A class can override this method to implement a different hash algorithm to improve performance when its objects are used as keys in collections. A class that overrides the Equals method should always override the GetHashCode method as well, so that two objects considered to be equal also return the same hash code.

- **GetType** A method that returns a value that identifies the type of the object. The returned value is typically used in reflection operations, as explained in Chapter 9, "Reflection."

- **ToString** An overridable method that returns the complete name of the class, for example, MyNamespace.MyClass. However, most classes redefine this method so that it returns a string that better describes the value of the object. For example, basic types such as int, double, and string override this method to return the object's numeric or string value. The ToString method is implicitly called when you pass an object to the Console.Write and Debug.Write methods. Interestingly, ToString is culturally aware. For example, when applied to a numeric type, it uses a comma as the decimal separator if the current culture requires it.

The System.Object class also exposes two static methods:

- **Equals** A static member that takes two object arguments and returns true if they can be considered to be equal. It is similar to, and often used in lieu of, the instance method with the same name, which would fail if invoked on a variable reference that is null.

- **ReferenceEquals** A static method that takes two object arguments and returns true if they reference the same instance; thus, it corresponds to the == operator in Microsoft Visual C# when applied to object references. This method is similar to the Equals method except that derived classes can't override it.

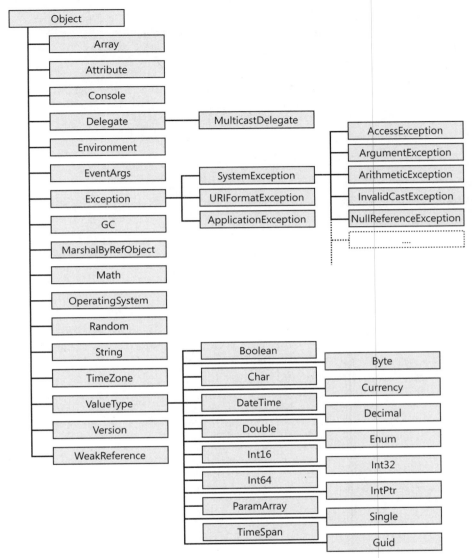

Figure 1-1 The most important classes in the System namespace

The System.Object class also exposes two protected methods. Because everything in the .NET Framework derives directly or indirectly from System.Object, all the classes you write can invoke the following methods in their base class and override them:

- **MemberwiseClone** A method that returns a new object of the same type and initializes the new object's fields and properties so that the new object can be considered a copy (a clone) of the current object.

■ **Finalize**   An overridable method that the .NET Framework calls when the object is taken by the garbage collector. (For more information about this method, see the sections titled "The Finalize Method" and "The Dispose Method" in Chapter 2, "Object Lifetime.")

The System class hierarchy includes all the most common and useful objects in the .NET Framework, including all the basic data types. The most important classes are depicted in Figure 1-1.

Value Types and Reference Types

Most basic data types (numbers, dates, and so on) in the .NET hierarchy inherit from System.ValueType and so have a common behavior. For example, System.ValueType overrides the Equals method and redefines equality so that two object references are considered equal if they have the same value (which is the way we usually compare numbers and dates), rather than if they point to the same instance. In addition, all classes deriving from System.ValueType override the GetHashCode method so that the hash code is created by taking into account the object's fields.

Classes that inherit from System.ValueType are commonly referred to as *value types*, to distinguish them from other classes, which are collectively named *reference types*. All numeric and Enum types are value types, as are types that work with dates. The .NET documentation uses the term *type* to encompass the meaning of value and reference types. I follow that convention in this book and reserve the word *class* for reference types only.

C# prevents you from explicitly inheriting from System.ValueType. The only way you can create a value type is by creating a struct block:

```
struct Position
{
    double X;
    double Y;
    // Add here other fields, properties, methods, and interfaces.
    …
}
```

Broadly speaking, value types are more efficient than are reference types because their data isn't allocated in the managed heap and therefore isn't subject to garbage collection. More precisely, a value type declared as a local variable in a procedure is allocated on the stack; when the procedure is exited, the value is simply discarded without making any extra work for the garbage collector. (The destructor method is invalid in structures.) This description isn't strictly accurate, however, if the structure includes a member of a reference type.

Consider this new version of the Position type:

```
struct Position
{
    double X;
    double Y;
    string Description;        // String is a reference type.
    …
}
```

The garbage collector has to reclaim the memory used for the Description string member when such a structure is destroyed. In other words, value types are significantly faster than reference types only if they don't expose any members of a reference type.

Many technical articles explain that value types are allocated on the stack and don't take memory from the managed heap, but this description isn't 100 percent correct: if a value type is used in the definition of a reference type, it does take room in the heap, as in this case:

```
public class Square
{
    // These two members go in the heap, in the slot allocated for the Square object.
    double Side;
    Position Position;
    // The pointer to the Name string is allocated in the slot for the Square
    // object, but its characters go in *another* slot of the heap.
    string Name;
}
```

Other factors might affect your choice of a value type or a reference type. Value types are implicitly sealed; thus, you should use a structure if your object functions like a primitive type and doesn't need to inherit special behaviors from other types, and other types don't need to derive from it. Also, structures can't be abstract and can't contain virtual methods, other than those inherited from System.Object.

A detail that might confuse many developers is that the String class is a reference type, not a value type, as shown in Figure 1-1. You can easily demonstrate this point by assigning a string variable to another variable, and then testing whether both variables point to the same object:

```
string s1 = "ABCD";
string s2 = s1;
// Prove that both variables point to the same object.
Console.WriteLine(string.ReferenceEquals(s1, s2));      // => True
```

.NET arrays are reference types, too, and assigning an array to an Array variable copies only the object's reference, not the array contents. The Array class exposes the Clone method to enable you to make a shallow copy of its elements. (A shallow copy is a copy operation that creates a copy of an object but not of its child objects.)

Boxing and Unboxing

Even if performance is your primary concern, you shouldn't always opt for value types because sometimes reference types are faster. For example, an assignment between value types involves the copy of every field in the object, whereas assigning a reference value to a variable requires only the copy of the object's address (4 bytes in 32-bit versions of the Microsoft Windows operating system).

When you pass a value type to a method that expects an object argument, a different kind of performance hit occurs because the value must be boxed in this case. *Boxing a value* means that the compiler creates a copy of it in the managed heap and assigns the address of this copy to an object variable or argument so that the type can then be used as a reference type. A boxed value doesn't maintain a link to the original value, which means you can modify either one without affecting the other.

If this boxed value is later assigned to a variable of the original (value) type, the object is said to be *unboxed* and data is copied from the managed heap into the memory allocated to the variable (for example, on the stack if it's a local variable). Not surprisingly, boxing and unboxing take CPU time and eventually require some memory to be reclaimed during a garbage collection. The bottom line: if you carry out many assignments or frequently perform operations that result in a boxing and unboxing sequence, implementing a reference type might be a wiser choice.

Boxing occurs transparently in most cases, whereas you require an explicit cast or as operator to convert back from an object to a value type. You can determine whether a call causes a boxing operation by looking at the method declaration in the object browser or in the class documentation. If the method takes an argument of the type you're passing, no boxing occurs; if it takes a generic object argument, your argument will be boxed. When you create your own methods, you might consider including overloaded variations that take arguments of different types as well as a catchall procedure that takes an object argument.

In general, it doesn't make sense to compare the performance of a method that uses boxing with a similar method that doesn't. An informal benchmark shows that a tight loop that calls a function that requires boxing can be up to 30 times slower than a loop that doesn't use boxing. However, you must repeat the loop 10 million times to see a meaningful difference in absolute terms, so in practice you should worry about boxing only in time-critical code sections.

You might be using boxing sometimes without knowing it. First, you implicitly box a structure if you call one of the virtual methods that the structure inherits from System.Object—for example, ToString. Second, you implicitly box a structure if you call a method of an interface that the structure exposes.

Knowing about boxing enables you to optimize your code in ways that are out of reach for the C# compiler. For example, consider the following code:

```
object res;
for (i = 1; i <= 1000; i++)
{
   for (j = 1; j <= 100000; j++)
   {
      // GetObject takes two Object arguments, and therefore causes
      // the boxing of both i and j.
      res = GetObject(i, j);
   }
}
```

The value of the i variable doesn't change in the inner loop, yet the code that the C# compiler produces boxes this value each time the GetObject method is invoked. By boxing the value yourself, you can double the speed of this code:

```
for (i = 1; i <= 1000; i++)
{
   // Cache the value type in an object variable.
   object o = i;
   for (j = 1; j <= 100000; j++)
   {
      res = GetObject(o, j);        // Only j is boxed.
   }
}
```

String Types

C# supports the string data type, which maps to the System.String class. Because System .String is a full-featured type, you can manipulate strings by means of the many methods it exposes.

To begin with, the String class exposes many overloaded constructor methods, so you can create a string in a variety of ways—for example, as a sequence of N same characters:

```
// A sequence of <N> characters
string s = new string('A', 10);                    // => AAAAAAAAAA
```

Properties and Methods

The only properties of the String class are Length and Chars. The former returns the number of characters in the string; the latter is the indexer of the String type and returns the character at a given zero-based index:

```
string s = "ABCDEFGHIJ";
Console.WriteLine(s.Length);          // => 10
// Index is zero-based.
Console.WriteLine(s[3]);              // => D
```

You can tap the power of the String class by invoking one of its many methods. For example, see how simple and readable the operation of inserting a substring is:

```
s = s.Insert(3, "1234");                     // => ABC1234DEFGHIJ
```

Here's another example of the compactness that you can get by using the String methods. Let's say you want to trim all the space and tab characters from the beginning of a string. In C#, you simply have to load all the characters to be trimmed in an array of Chars and pass the array to the TrimStart function:

```
char[] cArr = new char[]{' ', '\t'};
s = s.TrimStart(cArr);
```

(You can use the same pattern with the TrimEnd and Trim functions.) In many cases, String methods can deliver great performance because you can state more precisely what you're after. For example, see how you can determine whether a string begins or ends with a given sequence of characters:

```
// Check whether the string starts with "abc" and ends with "xyz."
if ( s.StartsWith("abc") && s.EndsWith("xyz") )
{
   ok = true;
}
```

You can iterate over all the characters of a string by using a foreach loop:

```
string s = "ABCDE";
foreach ( char c in s )
{
   Console.Write(c + ".");              // => A.B.C.D.E.
}
```

Here's an interesting detail: the C# compiler automatically translates the foreach loop into the following more efficient for loop:

```
// This is how C# actually compiles a foreach loop over a string.
for ( int index = 0; index < s.Length; index++ )
{
   char c = s[index];
   ...
}
```

Comparing and Searching Strings

Many methods in the String type enable you to compare strings or search a substring inside the current string. In version 2.0 of the .NET Framework, the String type overloads both the instance and the static version of the Equals method to take an additional String-Comparison enum type that specifies the locale to be used for the comparison and whether the comparison is case sensitive. In general, it is recommended that you use the static version of this method because it works well even if one or both the strings to be compared are null:

```
// Compare two strings in case-sensitive mode, using Unicode values.
bool match = string.Equals(s1, s2);
// Compare two strings in case-insensitive mode, using the current locale.
match = string.Equals(s1, s2, StringComparison.CurrentCultureIgnoreCase);
// Compare two strings in case-sensitive mode, using the invariant locale.
match = string.Equals(s1, s2, StringComparison.InvariantCulture);
// Compare the numeric Unicode values of all the characters in the two strings.
match = string.Equals(s1, s2, StringComparison.Ordinal);
```

(Read on for more information about locales and the CultureInfo type.) In general, you should use the Ordinal and OrdinalIgnoreCase enumerated values, if possible, because they are more efficient. For example, these values can be fine when comparing file paths, registry keys, and XML and HTML tags.

The InvariantCulture and InvariantCultureIgnoreCase values are arguably the least useful ones and should be used in the rare cases when you compare strings that are linguistically meaningful but don't have a cultural meaning; using these values ensures that comparisons yield the same results on all machines, regardless of the culture of the current thread.

If you need to detect whether a string is less than or greater than another string, you should use the static Compare method, which can also compare substrings, in either case-sensitive or case-insensitive mode. The return value is −1, 0, or 1 depending on whether the first string is less than, equal to, or greater than the second string:

```
// Compare two strings in case-sensitive mode, using the current culture.
int res = string.Compare(s1, s2);
if ( res < 0 )
{
    Console.WriteLine("s1 < s2");
}
else if ( res > 0 )
{
    Console.WriteLine("s1 > s2");
}
else
{
    Console.WriteLine("s1 = s2");
}
// Compare the first 10 characters of two strings in case-insensitive mode.
// (Second and fourth arguments are the index of first char to compare.)
res = string.Compare(s1, 0, s2, 0, 10, true);
```

In .NET Framework version 2.0, you can also pass a StringComparison enum value to specify whether you want to use the invariant locale, the current locale, or the numeric Unicode value of individual characters, and whether you want the comparison to be in case-insensitive mode:

```
// Compare two strings using the local culture in case-insensitive mode.
res = string.Compare(s1, s2, StringComparison.CurrentCultureIgnoreCase);
// Compare two substrings using the invariant culture in case-sensitive mode.
res = string.Compare(s1, 0, s2, 0, 10, StringComparison.InvariantCulture);
// Compare two strings by the numeric code of their characters.
res = string.Compare(s1, s2, StringComparison.Ordinal);
```

The StringComparer type (also new in .NET Framework 2.0) offers an alternative technique for doing string comparisons. The static properties of this type return an IComparer object able to perform a specific type of comparison on strings. For example, here's how you can perform a case-insensitive comparison according to the current culture:

```
// Compare two strings using the local culture in case-insensitive mode.
res = StringComparer.CurrentCultureIgnoreCase.Compare(s1, s2);
// Compare two strings using the invariant culture in case-sensitive mode.
res = StringComparer.InvariantCulture.Compare(s1, s2);
```

The StringComparer object has the added advantage that you can pass it to methods that take an IComparer argument, such as the Array.Sort method, but it has some short-comings, too; for one, you can't use the StringComparer.Compare method to compare substrings.

The String type also exposes the CompareTo instance method, which compares the current string to the passed argument and returns −1, 0, or 1, exactly as the static Compare method does. However, the CompareTo method doesn't offer any of the options of the Compare method and therefore should be avoided unless you intend to compare using the current culture's rules. In addition, because it is an instance method, you should always check that the instance isn't null before invoking the method:

```
// This statement throws an exception if s1 is null.
if ( s1.CompareTo(s2) > 0 )
{
    Console.WriteLine("s1 > s2");
}
```

When comparing just the numeric Unicode value of individual characters, you can save a few CPU cycles by using the CompareOrdinal static method; in general, however, you should use this method only to test equality because it seldom makes sense to decide whether a string is greater than or less than another string based on Unicode numeric values:

```
if ( string.CompareOrdinal(s1, s2) == 0 )
{
    Console.WriteLine("s1 = s2");
}
```

A .NET string variable is considered to be *null* if it is null and is considered to be *empty* if it points to a zero-character string. In earlier versions of C#, you must test these two conditions separately, but .NET Framework 2.0 introduces the handy IsNullOrEmpty static method:

```
// These two statements are equivalent, but only the latter works in .NET 2.0.
string s = "ABCDE";
if ( s == null || s.Length == 0 )
{
   Console.WriteLine("Empty string");
}
if ( string.IsNullOrEmpty(s) )
{
   Console.WriteLine("Empty string");
}
```

The simplest way to check whether a string appears inside another string is by means of the Contains method, also new in .NET Framework 2.0:

```
// The Contains method works only in case-sensitive mode.
s = "ABCDEFGHI ABCDEF";
bool found = s.Contains("BCD");                        // => True
found = s.Contains("bcd");                             // => False
```

You can detect the actual position of a substring inside a string by means of the IndexOf and LastIndexOf methods, which return the index of the first and last occurrence of a substring, respectively, or −1 if the search fails:

```
int pos = s.IndexOf("CDE");                                      // => 2
pos = s.LastIndexOf("CDE");                                      // => 12
// Both IndexOf and LastIndexOf are case sensitive by default...
pos = s.IndexOf("cde");                                          // => -1
// ...but they offer an overload that can specify case-insensitiveness.
pos = s.LastIndexOf("cde", StringComparison.CurrentCultureIgnoreCase);   // => 12
```

The StartsWith and EndsWith methods enable you to check quickly whether a string starts with or ends with a given substring. By default, these methods perform a case-sensitive comparison using the current culture:

```
match = s.StartsWith("ABC");                          // => True
match = s.EndsWith("def");                            // => False
```

In .NET Framework 2.0, these two methods have been expanded to support a StringComparison argument and can take a CultureInfo object as a third argument so that you can specify the locale to be used when comparing characters and whether the comparison is case insensitive:

```
// Both these statements assign true to the variable.
match = s.StartsWith("abc", StringComparison.CurrentCultureIgnoreCase);
match = s.EndsWith("CDE", true, CultureInfo.InvariantCulture);
```

The IndexOfAny and LastIndexOfAny methods return the first and last occurrence, respectively, of a character among those in the specified array. Both these methods can take an optional starting index in the second argument and a character count in the third argument:

```
char[] chars = new char[]{'D', 'F', 'I'};
pos = s.IndexOfAny(chars);              // => 3
pos = s.LastIndexOfAny(chars);          // => 15
pos = s.IndexOfAny(chars, 6);           // => 8
pos = s.IndexOfAny(chars, 6, 2);        // => -1
```

Modifying and Extracting Strings

The simplest way to create a new string from an existing string is by means of the Substring method, which extracts a substring starting at a given index and with the specified number of arguments:

```
string s = "ABCDEFGHI ABCDEF";
// Extract the substring after the 11th character.
string result = s.Substring(10);         // => ABCDEF
// Extract 4 characters after the 11th character.
result = s.Substring(10, 4);             // => ABCD
// Extract the last 4 characters.
result = s.Substring(s.Length - 4);      // => CDEF
```

The Insert method returns the new string created by inserting a substring at the specified index, whereas the Remove method removes a given number of characters, starting at the specified index:

```
result = s.Insert(4, "-123-");           // => ABCD-123-EFGHI ABCDEF
result = s.Remove(4, 3);                 // => ABCDHI ABCDEF
```

In .NET Framework 2.0, the Remove method has been overloaded with a version that takes only the start index:

```
// Extract the first 4 characters.
result = s.Remove(4);                    // => ABCD
```

I hinted at the TrimStart method earlier. This method, used with the TrimEnd and Trim methods, enables you to discard spaces and other characters that are found at the left side, the right side, or both sides of a string. By default, these methods trim white-space characters (that is, spaces, tabs, and newlines), but you can pass one or more arguments to specify which characters have to be trimmed:

```
string t = "  001234.560   ";
result = t.Trim();                       // => "001234.560"
result = t.TrimStart(' ', '0');          // => "1234.560   "
result = t.TrimEnd(' ', '0');            // => "  001234.56"
result = t.Trim(' ', '0');               // => "1234.56"
```

The opposite operation of trimming is padding. You can pad a string with a given character, either to the left or the right, to bring the string to the specified length, by means of the PadLeft and PadRight methods. The most obvious reason for using these methods is to align strings and numbers:

```
// Right-align a number in a field that is 8-char wide.
int number = 1234;
result = number.ToString().PadLeft(8);          // => "    1234"
```

As their name suggests, the ToLower and ToUpper methods return a new string obtained by converting all the characters of a string to lowercase or uppercase. Version 2.0 of the .NET Framework also provides the new ToLowerInvariant and ToUpperInvariant methods, which convert a string by using the casing rules of the invariant culture:

```
// Convert the s string to lowercase, using the current culture's rules.
result = s.ToLower();
// Convert the s string to uppercase, using the invariant culture's rules.
result = s.ToUpperInvariant();
```

Microsoft guidelines suggest that you use the ToUpperInvariant method when preparing a normalized string for comparison in case-insensitive mode because this is the way the Compare method works internally when you use the StringComparison.InvariantCultureIgnoreCase. As odd as it might sound, under certain cultures converting two strings to uppercase and then comparing them might deliver a different result from the one you receive if you convert them to lowercase before the comparison.

The Replace method replaces all the occurrences of a single character or a substring with another character or substring. All the searches are performed in case-sensitive mode:

```
string k = "ABCDEFGHI ABCDEF";
result = k.Replace("BCDE", "--");               // => A--FGHI A--F
```

Working with String and Char Arrays

A few methods take or return an array of String or Char elements. For example, the ToCharArray method returns an array containing all the characters in the string. You typically use this method when it is more efficient to process the characters separately than it is to extract them from the string. For example, consider the problem of checking whether two strings contain the same characters, regardless of their order (in other words, whether one string is the anagram of the other).

```
string s1 = "file";
string s2 = "life";
// Transform both strings to an array of characters.
char[] chars1 = s1.ToCharArray();
char[] chars2 = s2.ToCharArray();
// Sort both arrays.
Array.Sort(chars1);
Array.Sort(chars2);
```

```
// Build two new strings from the sorted arrays, and compare them.
string sorted1 = new string(chars1);
string sorted2 = new string(chars2);
// Compare them. (You can use case-insensitive comparison, if necessary.)
bool match = (string.Compare(sorted1, sorted2) == 0);        // => True
```

You can split a string into an array of substrings by using the Split method, which takes a list of separators and an optional maximum number of elements in the result array. This method has been improved in .NET Framework 2.0, and it can now process separators of any length and optionally drop empty elements in the result array:

```
string x = "Hey, Visual C# Rocks!";
string[] arr = x.Split(' ', ',', '.');
// The result contains the words "Hey", "", "Visual", "C#", "Rocks!"
int numOfWords = arr.Length;                    // => 5
// Same as before, but no more than 100 elements, and drop empty items.
char[] separators = {' ', ',', '.'};
string[] arr2 = x.Split(separators, 100, StringSplitOptions.RemoveEmptyEntries);
// The result contains the words "Hey", "Visual", "C#", "Rocks!"
numOfWords = arr2.Length;                        // => 4
```

The new ability to use multicharacter strings as a separator is quite useful when you need to retrieve the individual lines of a string containing pairs of carriage return–line feeds (CR-LF):

```
// Count the number of nonempty lines in a text file.
string[] crlfs = {"\r\n"};
string[] lines = File.ReadAllText("data.txt").Split(crlfs, StringSplitOptions.None);
int numOfLines = lines.Length;
```

You can perform the opposite operation (that is, concatenating all the elements of a string array) by using the Join static method. This method optionally takes the initial index and the maximum number of elements to be considered.

```
// (Continuing the previous example…)
// Reassemble the string by adding CR-LF pairs, but skip the first array element.
string newText = string.Join("\r\n", lines, 1, lines.Length - 1);
```

The Missing Methods

Despite the large number of methods exposed by the String type, at times you must write your own function to accomplish recurring tasks. For example, there is no built-in method similar to PadLeft or PadRight but capable of centering a string in a field of a given size. Here's the code that performs this task:

```
public static string PadCenter(string s, int width, char padChar, bool truncate)
{
   int diff = width - s.Length;
   if ( diff == 0 || (diff < 0 && !(truncate)) )
   {
      // Return the string as is.
      return s;
   }
}
```

```
   else if (diff < 0)
   {
       // Truncate the string.
       return s.Substring(0, width);
   }
   else
   {
       // Half of the extra chars go to the left, the remaining ones go to the right.
       return s.PadLeft(width - diff / 2, padChar).PadRight(width, padChar);
   }
}
```

Just for fun, here's a method that also enables you to reverse all the characters in a string or in only a portion of it:

```
public static string StringReverse(string s, int startIndex, int count)
{
   char[] chars = s.ToCharArray();
   if (count < 0)
   {
       count = s.Length - startIndex;
   }
   Array.Reverse(chars, startIndex, count);
   return new string(chars);
}
```

Here's a method based on the CopyTo method that enables you to duplicate a string a given number of times:

```
public static string StringDuplicate(string s, int count)
{
   // Prepare a character array of given length.
   char[] chars = new char[s.Length * count - 1 + 1];
   // Copy the string into the array multiple times.
   for (int i = 0; i <= count - 1; i++)
   {
       s.CopyTo(0, chars, i * s.Length, s.Length);
   }
   return new string(chars);
}
```

Or you can use the following one-liner, which builds a string of spaces that has a length equal to the number of repetitions, and then replaces each space with the string to be repeated:

```
// Repeat the Text string a number of times equal to Count.
string dupstring = new string(' ', Count).Replace(" ", Text);
```

You can build on the IndexOf method to count the number of occurrences of a substring:

```
public static int CountSubstrings(string source, string search)
{
   int count = -1;
   int index = -1;
   do
```

```
   {
      count += 1;
      index = source.IndexOf(search, index + 1);
   }
   while ( index >= 0 );
   return count;
}
```

You can also calculate the number of occurrences of a substring with the following technique, which is more concise but slightly less efficient than the previous method because it creates two temporary strings:

```
count = source.Replace(search, search + "*").Length - source.Length;
```

String Optimizations

An important detail to keep in mind is that a String object is *immutable*: once you create a string, its contents can never change. In fact, all the methods shown so far don't modify the original String; rather, they return another String object that you might or might not assign to the same String variable. Understanding this detail enables you to avoid a common programming mistake:

```
string s = "abcde";
// You *might* believe that the next statement changes the string...
s.ToUpper();
// ...but it doesn't because the result wasn't assigned back to s.
Console.WriteLine(s);                        // => abcde
// This is the correct way to invoke string methods.
s = s.ToUpper();
```

If you do assign the result to the same variable, the original string becomes unreachable from the application (unless there are other variables pointing to it) and is eventually discarded by the garbage collector. Because string values are immutable, the compiler can optimize the resulting code in ways that wouldn't be possible otherwise. For example, consider this code fragment:

```
string s1 = "1234" + "5678";
string s2 = "12345678";
Console.WriteLine(object.ReferenceEquals(s1, s2));          // => True
```

The compiler computes the concatenation (+) operator at compile time and realizes that both variables contain the same sequence of characters, so it can allocate only one block of memory for the string and have the two variables pointing to it. Because the string is immutable, a new object is created behind the scenes as soon as you attempt to modify the characters in that string.

Because of this behavior, you never really need to invoke the Clone method to explicitly create a copy of the string. Simply use the string as you would normally, and the compiler creates a copy for you if and when necessary.

The CLR can optimize string management by maintaining an internal pool of string values known as an *intern pool* for each .NET application. If the value being assigned to a string variable coincides with one of the strings already in the intern pool, no additional memory is created and the variable receives the address of the string value in the pool. As shown earlier, the compiler is capable of using the intern pool to optimize string initialization and have two string variables pointing to the same String object in memory. This optimization step isn't performed at run time, though, because the search in the pool takes time and in most cases it would fail, adding overhead to the application without bringing any benefit.

```
// Prove that no optimization is performed at run time.
s1 = "1234";
s1 += "5678";
s2 = "12345678";
// These two variables point to different String objects.
Console.WriteLine(object.ReferenceEquals(s1, s2));          // => False
```

You can optimize string management by using the Intern static method. This method searches a string value in the intern pool and returns a reference to the pool element that contains the value if the value is already in the pool. If the search fails, the string is added to the pool and a reference to it is returned. Notice how you can manually optimize the preceding code snippet by using the String.Intern method:

```
s1 = "ABCD";
s1 += "EFGH";
// Move S1 to the intern pool.
s1 = String.Intern(s1);
// Assign S2 a string constant (that we know is in the pool).
s2 = "ABCDEFGH";
// These two variables point to the same String object.
Console.WriteLine(object.ReferenceEquals(s1, s2));          // => True
```

This optimization technique makes sense only if you're working with long strings that appear in multiple portions of the applications. Another good time to use this technique is when you have many instances of a server-side component that contain similar string variables, such as a database connection string. Even if these strings don't change during the program's lifetime, they're usually read from a file, and, therefore, the compiler can't optimize their memory allocation automatically. By using the Intern method, you can help your application produce a smaller memory footprint. You can also use the IsInterned static method to check whether a string is in the intern pool (in which case the string itself is returned) or not (in which case the method returns null):

```
// Continuing previous example…
if ( string.IsInterned(s1) != null )
{
    // This block is executed because s1 is in the intern pool.
}
```

Here's another simple performance tip: try to gather multiple string concatenations in the same statement instead of spreading them across separate lines. The C# compiler can optimize multiple concatenation operations only if they're in the same statement.

The CultureInfo Type

The System.Globalization.CultureInfo class defines an object that you can inspect to determine some key properties of any installed languages. You can also use the object as an argument in many methods of the String and other types. The class exposes the CurrentCulture static property, which returns the CultureInfo object for the current language:

```
// Get information about the current locale.
CultureInfo ci = CultureInfo.CurrentCulture;
// Assuming that the current language is Italian, we get:
Console.WriteLine(ci.Name);                              // => it
Console.WriteLine(ci.EnglishName);                       // => Italian
Console.WriteLine(ci.NativeName);                        // => italiano
Console.WriteLine(ci.LCID);                              // => 16
Console.WriteLine(ci.TwoLetterISOLanguageName);          // => it
Console.WriteLine(ci.ThreeLetterISOLanguageName);        // => ita
Console.WriteLine(ci.ThreeLetterWindowsLanguageName);    // => ITA
```

You can get additional information about the locale through the TextInfo object, exposed by the property with the same name:

```
TextInfo ti = ci.TextInfo;
Console.WriteLine(ti.ANSICodePage);                      // => 1252
Console.WriteLine(ti.EBCDICCodePage);                    // => 20280
Console.WriteLine(ti.OEMCodePage);                       // => 850
Console.WriteLine(ti.ListSeparator);                     // => ;
```

The CultureInfo object exposes two properties, NumberFormat and DateTimeFormat, which return information about how numbers and dates are formatted according to a given locale. For example, consider this code:

```
// How do you spell "Sunday" in German?
// First create a CultureInfo object for German/Germany.
// (Note that you must pass a string in the form "locale-COUNTRY" if
// a given language is spoken in multiple countries.)
CultureInfo ciDe = new CultureInfo("de-DE");
// Next get the corresponding DateTimeFormatInfo object.
DateTimeFormatInfo dtfi = ciDe.DateTimeFormat;
// Here's the answer.
Console.WriteLine(dtfi.GetDayName(DayOfWeek.Sunday));    // => Sonntag
```

You'll find the "locale-COUNTRY" strings in many places of the .NET Framework. The Get-Cultures static method returns an array of all the installed cultures, so you can inspect all the languages that your operating system supports:

```
// Get info on all the installed cultures.
CultureInfo[] ciArr = CultureInfo.GetCultures(CultureTypes.AllCultures);
// Print abbreviation and English name of each culture.
foreach ( CultureInfo c in ciArr )
{
   Console.WriteLine("{0} ({1})", c.Name, c.EnglishName);
}
```

The GetCultureInfo static method, new in .NET Framework 2.0, enables you to retrieve a cached, read-only version of a CultureInfo object. When you repeatedly use this method to ask for the same culture, the same cached CultureInfo object is returned, thus saving instantiation time:

```
CultureInfo ci1 = CultureInfo.GetCultureInfo("it-IT");
CultureInfo ci2 = CultureInfo.GetCultureInfo("it-IT");
// Prove that the second call returned a cached object.
Console.WriteLine(object.ReferenceEquals(ci1,ci2));     // => True
```

The auxiliary TextInfo object permits you to convert a string to uppercase, lowercase, or title case (for example, "These Are Four Words") for a given language:

```
// Create a CultureInfo object for Canadian French. (Use a cached object if possible.)
CultureInfo ciFr = CultureInfo.GetCultureInfo("fr-CA");
// Convert a string to title case using Canadian French rules.
s = ciFr.TextInfo.ToTitleCase(s);
```

Most of the string methods whose result depends on the locale accept a CultureInfo object as an argument, namely, Compare, StartsWith, EndsWith, ToLower, and ToUpper. (This feature is new to .NET Framework 2.0 for the last four methods.) Let's see how you can pass this object to the String.Compare method so that you can compare strings according to the collation rules defined by a given language. One overloaded version of the Compare method takes four arguments: the two strings to be compared, a Boolean value that indicates whether the comparison is case insensitive, and a CultureInfo object that specifies the language to be used:

```
string s1 = "cioè";
string s2 = "CIOÈ";
// You can create a CultureInfo object on the fly.
if ( string.Compare(s1, s2, true, new CultureInfo("it")) == 0 )
{
   Console.WriteLine("s1 = s2");
}
```

There is also an overloaded version that compares two substrings:

```
if (string.Compare(s1, 1, s2, 1, 4, true, new CultureInfo("it")) == 1)
{
   Console.WriteLine("s1's first four chars are greater than s2's");
}
```

If you don't pass any CultureInfo object to the Compare method, the comparison is performed using the locale associated with the current thread. You can change this locale value by assigning a CultureInfo object to the CurrentCulture property of the current thread, as follows:

```
// Use Italian culture for all string operations and comparisons.
Thread.CurrentThread.CurrentCulture = new CultureInfo("it-IT");
```

You can also compare values according to an invariant culture so that the order in which your results are evaluated is the same regardless of the locale of the current thread. In this case, you can pass the return value of the CultureInfo.InvariantCulture static property:

```
if ( string.Compare(s1, s2, true, CultureInfo.InvariantCulture) == 0 )
{ … }
```

.NET Framework 2.0 offers the new StringComparison enumerated type that enables you to perform comparisons and equality tests using the current culture, the invariant culture, and the numeric values of individual characters, both in case-sensitive and case-insensitive ways. For more details and examples, read the section titled "Comparing and Searching Strings" earlier in this chapter.

The Encoding Class

All .NET strings store their characters in Unicode format, so sometimes you might need to convert them to and from other formats—for example, ASCII or the UCS Transformation Format 7 (UTF-7) or UTF-8 variants of the Unicode format. You can do this by using the Encoding class in the System.Text namespace.

The first thing to do when converting a .NET Unicode string to or from another format is create the proper encoding object. The Encoding class opportunely exposes the most common encoding objects through the following static properties: ASCII, Unicode (little-endian byte order), BigEndianUnicode, UTF7, UTF8, UTF32, and Default (the system's current ANSI code page). Here's an example of how you can convert a Unicode string to a sequence of bytes that represents the same string in ASCII format:

```
string text = "A Unicode string with accented vowels: àèéìòù";
Encoding uni = Encoding.Unicode;
byte[] uniBytes = uni.GetBytes(text);
Encoding ascii = Encoding.ASCII;
byte[] asciiBytes = Encoding.Convert(uni, ascii, uniBytes);

// Convert the ASCII bytes back to a string.
string asciiText = new string(ascii.GetChars(asciiBytes));
Console.WriteLine(asciiText);          // => A Unicode string with accented vowels: ??????
```

You can also create other Encoding objects with the GetEncoding static method, which takes either a code page number or code page name and throws a NotSupportedException if the code page isn't supported:

```
// Get the encoding object for code page 1252.
Encoding enc = Encoding.GetEncoding(1252);
```

The GetEncodings method (new in .NET Framework 2.0) returns an array of EncodingInfo objects, which provide information on all the Encoding objects and code pages installed on the computer:

```
foreach ( EncodingInfo ei in Encoding.GetEncodings() )
{
   Console.WriteLine("Name={0}, DisplayName={1}, CodePage={2}", ei.Name,
      ei.DisplayName, ei.CodePage);
}
```

The GetChars method expects that the byte array you feed it contains an integer number of characters. (For example, it must end with the second byte of a two-byte character.) This requirement can be a problem when you read the byte array from a file or from another type of stream, and you're working with a string format that allows one, two, or three bytes per character. In such cases, you should use a Decoder object, which remembers the state between consecutive calls. For more information, read the MSDN documentation.

Formatting Numeric Values

The Format static method of the String class enables you to format a string and include one or more numeric or date values in it, in a way similar to the Console.Write method. The string being formatted can contain placeholders for arguments, in the format {N} where *N* is an index that starts at 0:

```
// Print the value of a string variable.
string xyz = "foobar";
string msg = msg = string.Format("The value of {0} variable is {1}.", "XYZ", xyz);
   // => The value of XYZ variable is foobar.
```

If the argument is numeric, you can add a colon after the argument index and then a character that indicates what kind of formatting you're requesting. The available characters are G (general), N (number), C (currency), D (decimal), E (scientific), F (fixed-point), P (percent), R (round-trip), and X (hexadecimal):

```
// Format a Currency according to current locale.
msg = string.Format("Total is {0:C}, balance is {1:C}", 123.45, -67);
   // => Total is $123.45, balance is ($67.00)
```

The number format uses commas—or to put it more precisely, the thousands separator defined by the current locale—to group digits:

```
msg = string.Format("Total is {0:N}", 123456.78);   // => Total is 123,456.78
```

You can append an integer after the N character to round or extend the number of digits after the decimal point:

```
msg = string.Format("Total is {0:N4}", 123456.785555);   // => Total is 123,456.7856
```

The decimal format works with integer values only and throws a FormatException if you pass a noninteger argument; you can specify a length that, if longer than the result, causes one or more leading zeros to be added:

```
msg = string.Format("Total is {0:D8}", 123456);          // => Total is 00123456
```

The fixed-point format is useful with decimal values, and you can indicate how many decimal digits should be displayed (two if you omit the length):

```
msg = string.Format("Total is {0:F3}", 123.45678);       // => Total is 123.457
```

The scientific (or exponential) format displays numbers as *n.mmmE+eeee*, and you can control how many decimal digits are used in the mantissa portion:

```
msg = string.Format("Total is {0:E}", 123456.789);    // => Total is 1.234568E+005
msg = string.Format("Total is {0:E3}", 123456.789);   // => Total is 1.235E+005
```

The general format converts to either fixed-point or exponential format, depending on which format delivers the most compact result:

```
msg = string.Format("Total is {0:G}", 123456);        // => Total is 123456
msg = string.Format("Total is {0:G4}", 123456);       // => Total is 1.235E+05
```

The percent format converts a number to a percentage with two decimal digits by default, using the format specified for the current culture:

```
msg = string.Format("Percentage is {0:P}", 0.123);    // => Total is 12.30 %
```

The round-trip format converts a number to a string containing all significant digits so that the string can be converted back to a number later without any loss of precision:

```
// The number of digits you pass after the "R" character is ignored.
msg = string.Format("Value of PI is {0:R}", Math.PI);
   // => Value of PI is 3.1415926535897931
```

Finally, the hexadecimal format converts numbers to hexadecimal strings. If you specify a length, the number is padded with leading zeros if necessary:

```
msg = string.Format("Total is {0:X8}", 65535);        // => Total is 0000FFFF
```

You can build custom format strings by using a few special characters; Table 1-1 summarizes the meaning of these characters. Here are a few examples:

```
msg = string.Format("Total is {0:##,###.00}", 1234.567);    // => Total is 1,234.57
msg = string.Format("Percentage is {0:##.000%}", .3456);    // => Percentage is 34.560%
```

```
// An example of prescaler
msg = string.Format("Length in {0:###,.00 }", 12344);       // => Total is 12.34

// Two examples of exponential format
msg = string.Format("Total is {0:#.#####E+00}", 1234567); // => Total is 1.23457E+06
msg = string.Format("Total is {0:#.#####E0}", 1234567);    // => Total is 1.23457E6

// Two examples with separate sections
msg = string.Format("Total is {0:##;<##>}", -123);          // => Total is <123>
msg = string.Format("Total is {0:#;(#);zero}", 1234567);    // => Total is 1234567
```

In some cases, you can use two or three sections to avoid if or switch blocks. For example, you can replace the following code:

```
if (n1 > n2)
{
    msg = "n1 is greater than n2";
}
else if (n1 < n2)
{
    msg = "n1 is less than n2";
}
else
{
    msg = "n1 is equal to n2";
}
```

with the more concise but somewhat more cryptic code:

```
msg = string.Format("n1 is {0:greater than;less than;equal to} n2", n1 - n2);
```

A little-known feature of the String.Format method—as well as all the methods that use it internally, such as the Console.Write method—is that it enables you to specify the width of a field and decide to align the value to the right or the left:

```
// Build a table of numbers, their square, and their square root.
// This prints the header of the table.
Console.WriteLine("{0,-5} | {1,7} | {2,10:N2}", "N", "N^2", "Sqrt(N)");
for ( int n = 1; n <= 100; n++ )
{
    // N is left-aligned in a field 5 char wide,
    // N^2 is right-aligned in a field 7 char wide, and Sqrt(N) is displayed with
    // 2 decimal digits and is right-aligned in a field 10 char wide.
    Console.WriteLine("{0,-5} | {1,7} | {2,10:N2}", n, Math.Pow(n, 2), Math.Sqrt(n));
}
```

You specify the field width after the comma; use a positive width for right-aligned values and a negative width for left-aligned values. If you want to provide a predefined format, use a colon as a separator after the width value. As shown in the previous example, field widths are also supported with numeric, string, and date values.

Finally, you can insert literal braces by doubling them in the format string:

```
Console.WriteLine(" {{{0}}}", 123);              // => {123}
```

Table 1-1 Special Formatting Characters in Custom Formatting Strings

Format	Description
#	Placeholder for a digit or a space.
0	Placeholder for a digit or a zero.
.	Decimal separator.
,	Thousands separator; if used immediately before the decimal separator, it works as a prescaler. (For each comma in this position, the value is divided by 1,000 before formatting.)
%	Displays the number as a percentage value.
E+000	Displays the number in exponential format, that is, with an E followed by the sign of the exponent, and then a number of exponent digits equal to the number of zeros after the plus sign.
E-000	Like the previous exponent symbol, but the exponent sign is displayed only if negative.
;	Section separator. The format string can contain one, two, or three sections. If there are two sections, the first applies to positive and zero values, and the second applies to negative values. If there are three sections, they are used for positive, negative, and zero values, respectively.
\char	Escape character, to insert characters that otherwise would be taken as special characters (for example, \; to insert a semicolon and \\ to insert a backslash).
'...' "..."	A group of literal characters. You can add a sequence of literal characters by enclosing them in single or double quotation marks.
Other	Any other character is taken literally and inserted in the result string as is.

Formatting Date Values

The String.Format method also supports date and time values with both standard and custom formats. Table 1-2 summarizes all the standard date and time formats and makes it easy to find the format you're looking for at a glance.

```
DateTime aDate = new DateTime(2005, 5, 17, 15, 54, 0);
string msg = string.Format("Event Date/Time is {0:f}", aDate);
   // => Event Date Time is Tuesday, May 17, 2005 3:54 PM
```

If you can't find a standard date and time format that suits your needs, you can create a custom format by putting together the special characters listed in Table 1-3:

```
msg = string.Format("Current year is {0:yyyy}", DateTime.Now);  // => Current year is 2005
```

The default date separator (/) and default time separator (:) formatting characters are particularly elusive because they're replaced by the default date and time separator defined for the current locale. In some cases—most notably when formatting dates for a structured query language (SQL) SELECT or INSERT command—you want to be sure that a given separator is used on all occasions. In this case, you must use the backslash escape character to force a specific separator:

```
// Format a date in the format mm/dd/yyyy, regardless of current locale.
msg = string.Format(@"{0:MM\/dd\/yyyy}", aDate);    // => 05/17/2005
```

Table 1-2   Standard Formats for Date and Time Values[1]

Format	Description	Pattern	Example
d	ShortDatePattern	MM/dd/yyyy	1/6/2005
D	LongDatePattern	dddd, MMMM dd, yyyy	Thursday, January 06, 2005
f	Full date and time (long date and short time)	dddd, MMMM dd, yyyy HH:mm	Thursday, January 06, 2005 3:54 PM
F	FullDateTimePattern (long date and long time)	dddd, MMMM dd, yyyy HH:mm:ss	Thursday, January 06, 2005 3:54:20 PM
g	general (short date and short time)	MM/dd/yyyy HH:mm	1/6/2005 3:54 PM
G	General (short date and long time)	MM/dd/yyyy HH:mm:ss	1/6/2005 3:54:20 PM
M,m	MonthDayPattern	MMMM dd	January 06
Y,y	YearMonthPattern	MMMM, yyyy	January, 2005
t	ShortTimePattern	HH:mm	3:54 PM
T	LongTimePattern	HH:mm:ss	3:54:20 PM
s	SortableDateTime Pattern (conforms to ISO 8601) using current culture	yyyy-MM-dd HH:mm:ss	2005-01-06T15:54:20
u	UniversalSortable DateTimePattern (conforms to ISO 8601), unaffected by current culture	yyyy-MM-dd HH:mm:ss	2002-01-06 20:54:20Z
U	UniversalSortable DateTimePattern	dddd, MMMM dd, yyyy HH:mm:ss	Thursday, January 06, 2005 5:54:20 PM
R,r	RFC1123Pattern	ddd, dd MMM yyyy HH':'mm':'ss 'GMT'	Thu, 06 Jan 2005 15:54:20 GMT
O,o	RoundtripKind (useful to restore all properties when parsing)	yyyy-MM-dd HH:mm:ss.fffffffK	2005-01-06T15:54:20.0000000-08:00

[1.] Notice that formats U, u, R, and r use Universal (Greenwich) Time, regardless of the local time zone, so example values for these formats are 5 hours ahead of example values for other formats (which assume local time to be U.S. Eastern time). The Pattern column specifies the corresponding custom format string made up of the characters listed in Table 1-3.

Table 1-3   Character Sequences That Can Be Used in Custom Date and Time Formats

Format	Description
d	Day of month (one or two digits as required).
dd	Day of month (always two digits, with a leading zero if required).
ddd	Day of week (three-character abbreviation).
dddd	Day of week (full name).
M	Month number (one or two digits as required).
MM	Month number (always two digits, with a leading zero if required).
MMM	Month name (three-character abbreviation).
MMMM	Month name (full name).
y	Year (last one or two digits, no leading zero).
yy	Year (last two digits).
yyyy	Year (four digits).
H	Hour in 24-hour format (one or two digits as required).
HH	Hour in 24-hour format (always two digits, with a leading zero if required).
h	Hour in 12-hour format (one or two digits as required).
hh	Hour in 12-hour format.
m	Minutes (one or two digits as required).
mm	Minutes (always two digits, with a leading zero if required).
s	Seconds (one or two digits as required).
ss	Seconds.
t	The first character in the AM/PM designator.
f	Second fractions, represented in one digit. (ff means second fractions in two digits, fff in three digits, and so on up to 7 fs in a row.)
F	Second fractions, represented in an optional digit. Similar to f, except it can be used with DateTime.ParseExact without throwing an exception if there are fewer digits than expected (new in .NET Framework 2.0).
tt	The AM/PM designator.
z	Time zone offset, hour only (one or two digits as required).
zz	Time zone offset, hour only (always two digits, with a leading zero if required).
zzz	Time zone offset, hour and minute (hour and minute values always have two digits, with a leading zero if required).
K	The Z character if the Kind property of the DateTime value is Utc; the time zone offset (e.g., "−8:00") if the Kind property is Local; an empty character if the Kind property is Unspecified (new in .NET Framework 2.0).
/	Default date separator.
:	Default time separator.
\char	Escape character, to include literal characters that would be otherwise considered special characters.
%format	Includes a predefined date/time format in the result string.

Table 1-3   Character Sequences That Can Be Used in Custom Date and Time Formats

Format	Description
'...' "..."	A group of literal characters. You can add a sequence of literal characters by enclosing them in single or double quotation marks.
other	Any other character is taken literally and inserted in the result string as is.

The Char Type

The Char class represents a single character. There isn't much to say about this data type, other than it exposes a number of useful static methods that enable you to test whether a single character meets a given criterion. All these methods are overloaded and take either a single Char or a String plus an index in the string. For example, you check whether a character is a digit as follows:

```
// Check an individual Char value.
bool ok = char.IsDigit('1');          // => True
// Check the Nth character in a string.
ok = char.IsDigit("A123", 0);         // => False
```

This is the list of the most useful static methods that test single characters: IsControl, IsDigit, IsLetter, IsLetterOrDigit, IsLower, IsNumber, IsPunctuation, IsSeparator, IsSymbol, IsUpper, and IsWhiteSpace.

You can convert a character to uppercase and lowercase with the ToUpper and ToLower static methods. By default these methods work according to the current thread's locale, but you can pass them an optional CultureInfo object, or you can use the culture-invariant versions ToUpperInvariant and ToLowerInvariant:

```
char newChar = char.ToUpper('a');                      // => A
newChar = char.ToLower('H', new CultureInfo("it-IT")); // => h
char loChar = char.ToLowerInvariant('G');              // => g
```

You can convert a string into a Char by means of the CChar operator or the Char.Parse method. Or you can use the new TryParse static method (added in .NET Framework 2.0) to check whether the conversion is possible and perform it in one operation:

```
if ( char.TryParse("a", out newChar) )
{
    // newChar contains the 'a' character.
}
```

The StringBuilder Type

As you know, a String object is immutable, and its value never changes after the string has been created. This means that any time you apply a method that changes its value, you're actually creating a new String object. For example, the following statement:

```
S = S.Insert(3, "1234");
```

doesn't modify the original string in memory. Instead, the Insert method creates a new String object, which is then assigned to the S string variable. The original string object in memory is eventually reclaimed during the next garbage collection unless another variable points to it. The superior memory allocation scheme of .NET ensures that this mechanism adds a relatively low overhead; nevertheless, too many allocate and release operations can degrade your application's performance. The System.Text.StringBuilder object offers a solution to this problem.

You can think of a StringBuilder object as a buffer that can contain a string with the ability to grow from zero characters to the buffer's current capacity. Until you exceed that capacity, the string is assembled in the buffer and no memory is allocated or released. If the string becomes longer than the current capacity, the StringBuilder object transparently creates a larger buffer. The default buffer initially contains 16 characters, but you can change this by assigning a different capacity in the StringBuilder constructor or by assigning a value to the Capacity property:

```
// Create a StringBuilder object with initial capacity of 1,000 characters.
StringBuilder sb = new StringBuilder(1000);
```

You can process the string held in the StringBuilder object with several methods, most of which have the same name as and work similarly to methods exposed by the String class—for example, the Insert, Remove, and Replace methods. The most common way to build a string inside a StringBuilder object is by means of its Append method, which takes an argument of any type and appends it to the current internal string:

```
// Create a comma-delimited list of the first 100 integers.
for ( int n = 1; n <= 100; n++ )
{
    // Note that two Append methods are faster than a single Append,
    // whose argument is the concatenation of N and ",".
    sb.Append(n);
    sb.Append(",");
}
// Insert a string at the beginning of the buffer.
sb.Insert(0, "List of numbers: ");
Console.WriteLine(sb);          // => List of numbers: 1,2,3,4,5,6,
```

The Length property returns the current length of the internal string:

```
// Continuing previous example…
Console.WriteLine("Length is {0}.", sb.Length);     // => Length is 309.
```

There's also an AppendFormat method, which enables you to specify a format string, much like the String.Format method, and an AppendLine method (new in .NET Framework 2.0), which appends a string and the default line terminator:

```
for ( int n = 1; n <= 100; n++ )
{
    sb.AppendLine(n.ToString());
}
```

The following procedure compares how quickly the String and StringBuilder classes perform a large number of string concatenations:

```
string s = "";
const int TIMES = 10000;
Stopwatch sw = new Stopwatch();
sw.Start();
for ( int i = 1; i <= TIMES; i++ )
{
    s += i.ToString() + ",";
}
sw.Stop();
Console.WriteLine("Regular string: {0} milliseconds", sw.ElapsedMilliseconds);

sw = new Stopwatch();
sw.Start();
StringBuilder sb = new StringBuilder(TIMES * 4);
for ( int i = 1; i <= TIMES; i++ )
{
    // Notice how you can merge two Append methods.
    sb.Append(i).Append(",");
}
sw.Stop();
Console.WriteLine("StringBuilder: {0} milliseconds.", sw.ElapsedMilliseconds);
```

The results of this benchmark can be astonishing because they show that the StringBuilder object can be more than 100 times faster than the regular String class is. The actual ratio depends on how many iterations you have and how long the involved strings are. For example, when TIMES is set to 20,000 on my computer, the standard string takes 5 seconds to complete the loop, whereas the StringBuilder type takes only 8 milliseconds!

The SecureString Type

The way .NET strings are implemented has some serious implications related to security. In fact, if you store confidential information in a string—for example, a password or a credit card number—another process that can read your application's address space can also read your data. Although getting access to a process's address space isn't really a trivial task, consider that some portions of your address space are often saved in the operating system's swap file, where reading them is much easier.

The fact that strings are immutable means that you can't really clear a string after using it. Worse, because a string is subject to garbage collection, there might be several copies of it in memory, which in turn increases the probability that one of them goes in the swap file. A Microsoft .NET Framework version 1.1 application that wants to ensure the highest degree of confidentiality should stay clear of standard strings and use some other technique, for example, an encrypted Char or Byte array, which is decrypted only one instant before using the string and cleared immediately afterward.

Version 2.0 of the .NET Framework makes this process easier with the introduction of the SecureString type, in the System.Security namespace. Basically, a SecureString instance is an array of characters that is encrypted using the Data Protection API (DPAPI). Unlike the standard string, and similar to the StringBuilder type, the SecureString type is mutable: you build it one character at a time by means of the AppendChar method, similar to what you do with the StringBuilder type, and you can also insert, remove, and modify individual characters by means of the InsertAt, SetAt, and RemoveAt methods. Optionally, you can make the string immutable by invoking the MakeReadOnly method. Finally, to reduce the number of copies that float in memory, SecureString instances are *pinned*, which means that they can't be moved around by the garbage collector.

The SecureString type is so secure that it exposes neither a method to initialize it from a string nor a method that returns its contents as clear text: the former task requires a series of calls to AppendChar, the latter can be performed with the help of the Marshal type, as I'll explain shortly. A SecureString isn't serializable and therefore you can't even save to file for later retrieval. And of course you can't initialize it from a string burnt into your code, which would defy the intended purpose of this type. What are your options for correctly initializing a SecureString object, then?

A first option is to store the password as clear text in an access control list (ACL)–protected file and read it one char at a time. This option isn't bulletproof, though, and in some cases it can't be applied anyway because the confidential data is entered by the user at run time.

Another option—actually the only option that you can adopt when the user enters the confidential data at run time—is to have the user enter the text one character at a time, and then encrypt it on the fly. The following code snippet shows how you can fake a password-protected TextBox control in a Windows Forms application that never stores its contents in a regular string:

```
public SecureString password = new SecureString();

private void txtPassword_KeyPress(object sender, KeyPressEventArgs e)
{
   if ( (int) e.KeyChar == 8)
   {
      // Backspace: remove the char from the secure string.
      if (txtPassword.SelectionStart > 0)
      {
         password.RemoveAt(txtPassword.SelectionStart - 1);
      }
   }
   else if ( (int)e.KeyChar >= 32)
   {
      // Delete current selection.
      if (txtPassword.SelectionLength > 0)
      {
         for ( int i = txtPassword.SelectionStart +  txtPassword.SelectionLength - 1;
            i >= txtPassword.SelectionStart; i--)
```

```
        {
            password.RemoveAt(i);
        }
    }
    // Regular character: insert it in the secure string.
    if ( txtPassword.SelectionStart == txtPassword.TextLength )
    {
        password.AppendChar(e.KeyChar);
    }
    else
    {
        password.InsertAt(txtPassword.SelectionStart, e.KeyChar);
    }
    // Display (and store) an asterisk in the text box.
    e.KeyChar = '*';
    }
}
```

As I mentioned before, the SecureString object doesn't expose any method that returns its contents as clear text. Instead, you must use a couple of methods of the Marshal type, in the System.Runtime.InteropServices namespace:

```
// Convert the password into an unmanaged BSTR.
IntPtr ptr = Marshal.SecureStringToBSTR(password);
// For demo purposes, convert the BSTR into a regular string and use it.
string pw = Marshal.PtrToStringBSTR(ptr);
...
// Clear the unmanaged BSTR used for the password.
Marshal.ZeroFreeBSTR(ptr);
```

Of course, the previous code isn't really secure because at one point you have assigned the password to a regular string. In some cases, this is unavoidable, but at least this approach ensures that the clear text string exists for a shorter amount of time. An alternative, better approach is to have the unmanaged Basic string (BSTR) processed by a piece of unmanaged code.

You really see the benefits of this technique when you use a member that accepts a SecureString instance, for example, the Password property of the ProcessStartInfo type:

```
// Run Notepad under a different user account.
ProcessStartInfo psi = new ProcessStartInfo("notepad.exe");
psi.UseShellExecute = false;
psi.UserName = "Francesco";
psi.Password = password;
Process.Start(psi);
```

Numeric Types

As you know, short, int, and long types are just aliases for the Int16, Int32, and Int64 .NET classes. By recognizing their true nature and by using their methods and properties, you can better exploit these types. This section applies to all the numeric types in the .NET Framework, namely Boolean, Byte, SByte, Int16, Int32, Int64, UInt16, UInt32, UInt64, Single, Double, and Decimal.

Properties and Methods

All numeric types—and all .NET classes, for that matter—expose the ToString method, which converts their numeric value to a string. This method is especially useful when you're appending the number value to another string:

```
double myValue = 123.45;
string res = "The final value is " + myValue.ToString();
```

The ToString method is culturally aware and by default uses the culture associated with the current thread. For example, it uses a comma as a decimal separator if the current thread's culture is Italian or German. Numeric types overload the ToString method to take either a format string or a custom formatter object. (For more detail, refer to the section titled "Formatting Numeric Values" earlier in this chapter.)

```
// Convert an integer to hexadecimal.
res = 1234.ToString("X");              // => 4D2
// Display PI with 6 digits (in all).
double d = Math.PI;
res = d.ToString("G6");                // => 3.14159
```

You can use the CompareTo method to compare a number with another numeric value of the same type. This method returns 1, 0, or −1, depending on whether the current instance is greater than, equal to, or less than the value passed as an argument:

```
float sngValue = (float) 1.23;
// Compare the float variable sngValue with 1.
int res = sngValue.CompareTo(1);
if ( res > 0 )
{
    Console.WriteLine("sngValue is > 1");
}
else if ( res < 0 )
{
    Console.WriteLine("sngValue is < 1");
}
else
{
    Console.WriteLine("sngValue is = 1");
}
```

The argument must be the same type as the value to which you're applying the CompareTo method, so you must convert it if necessary.

All the numeric classes expose the MinValue and MaxValue static fields, which return the smallest and greatest value that you can express with the corresponding type:

```
// Display the greatest value you can store in a Double variable.
Console.WriteLine(Double.MaxValue);       // => 1.79769313486232E+308
```

The numeric classes that support floating-point values—namely, Single and Double classes—expose a few additional read-only static properties. The Epsilon property returns the smallest positive (nonzero) number that can be stored in a variable of that type:

```
Console.WriteLine(Single.Epsilon);        // => 1.401298E-45
Console.WriteLine(Double.Epsilon);        // => 4.94065645841247E-324
```

The NegativeInfinity and PositiveInfinity fields return a constant that represents an infinite value, whereas the NaN field returns a constant that represents the Not-a-Number value (NaN is the value you obtain, for example, when evaluating the square root of a negative number). In some cases, you can use infinite values in expressions:

```
// Any number divided by infinity gives 0.
Console.WriteLine(1 / Double.PositiveInfinity);        // => 0
```

The Single and Double classes also expose static methods that enable you to test whether they contain special values, such as IsInfinity, IsNegativeInfinity, IsPositiveInfinity, and IsNaN.

Formatting Numbers

All the numeric classes support an overloaded form of the ToString method that enables you to apply a format string:

```
int intValue = 12345;
string res = intValue.ToString("##,##0.00");    // => 12,345.00
```

The method uses the current locale to interpret the formatting string. For example, in the preceding code it uses the comma as the thousands separator and the period as the decimal separator if running on a U.S. system, but reverses the two separators on an Italian system. You can also pass a CultureInfo object to format a number for a given culture:

```
CultureInfo ci = new CultureInfo("it-IT");
res = intValue.ToString("##,##0.00", ci);    // => 12.345,00
```

The previous statement works because the ToString takes an IFormatProvider object to format the current value, and the CultureInfo object exposes this interface. In this section, I show you how you can take advantage of another .NET object that implements this interface, the NumberFormatInfo object.

The NumberFormatInfo class exposes many properties that determine how a numeric value is formatted, such as NumberDecimalSeparator (the decimal separator character), NumberGroupSeparator (the thousands separator character), NumberDecimalDigits (number of decimal digits), CurrencySymbol (the character used for currency), and many others. The simplest way to create a valid NumberFormatInfo object is by means of the CurrentInfo static method of the NumberFormatInfo class; the returned value is a read-only NumberFormatInfo object based on the current locale:

```
NumberFormatInfo nfi = NumberFormatInfo.CurrentInfo;
```

(You can also use the InvariantInfo property, which returns a NumberFormatInfo object that is culturally independent.)

The problem with the preceding code is that the returned NumberFormatInfo object is read-only, so you can't modify any of its properties. This object is therefore virtually useless because the ToString method implicitly uses the current locale anyway when formatting a value. The solution is to create a clone of the default NumberFormatInfo object and then modify its properties, as in the following snippet:

```
// Format a number with current locale formatting options, but use a comma
// for the decimal separator and a space for the thousands separator.
// (You need a cast because the Clone method returns an Object.)
NumberFormatInfo nfi = (NumberFormatInfo) NumberFormatInfo.CurrentInfo.Clone();
// The nfi object is writable, so you can change its properties.
nfi.NumberDecimalSeparator = ",";
nfi.NumberGroupSeparator = " ";
// You can now format a value with the custom NumberFormatInfo object.
float sngValue = 12345.5F;
Console.WriteLine(sngValue.ToString("##,##0.00", nfi));     // => 12 345,50
```

For the complete list of NumberFormatInfo properties and methods, see the MSDN documentation.

Parsing Strings into Numbers

All numeric types support the Parse static method, which parses the string passed as an argument and returns the corresponding numeric value. The simplest form of the Parse method takes one string argument:

```
// Next line assigns 1234 to the variable.
short shoValue = short.Parse("1234");
```

An overloaded form of the Parse method takes a NumberStyle enumerated value as its second argument. NumberStyle is a bit-coded value that specifies which portions of the number are allowed in the string being parsed. Valid NumberStyle values are AllowLeadingWhite (1), AllowTrailingWhite (2), AllowLeadingSign (4), AllowTrailingSign (8), AllowParentheses (16), AllowDecimalPoint (32), AllowThousand (64), AllowExponent (128), AllowCurrencySymbol (256), and AllowHexSpecifier (512). You can specify which portions of the strings are valid by using the Or bitwise operator on these values, or you can use some predefined compound values, such as Any (511, allows everything), Integer (7, allows trailing sign and leading/trailing white spaces), Number (111, like Integer but allows thousands separator and decimal point), Float (167, like Integer but allows decimal separator and exponent), and Currency (383, allows everything except exponent).

The following example extracts a Double value from a string and recognizes white spaces and all the supported formats:

```
double dblValue = double.Parse(" 1,234.56E6 ", NumberStyles.Any);
   // dblValue is assigned the value 1234560000.
```

You can be more specific about what is valid and what isn't:

```
NumberStyles style = NumberStyles.AllowDecimalPoint | NumberStyles.AllowLeadingSign;
// This works and assigns -123.45 to sngValue.
float sngValue = float.Parse("-123.45", style);
// This throws a FormatException because of the thousands separator.
sngValue = float.Parse("12,345.67", style);
```

A third overloaded form of the Parse method takes any IFormatProvider object; thus, you can pass it a CultureInfo object:

```
// Parse a string according to Italian rules.
sngValue = float.Parse("12.345,67", new CultureInfo("it-IT"));
```

 All the numeric types in .NET Framework 2.0 expose a new method named TryParse, which enables you to avoid time-consuming exceptions if a string doesn't contain a number in a valid format. (This method is available in .NET Framework 1.1 only for the Double type.) The TryParse method takes a variable by reference in its second argument and returns true if the parsing operation is successful:

```
int intValue = 0;
if ( int.TryParse("12345", out intValue) )
{
    // intValue contains the result of the parse operation.
}
else
{
    // The string doesn't contain an integer value in a valid format.
}
```

A second overload of the TryParse method takes a NumberStyles enumerated value and an IFormatProvider object in its second and third arguments:

```
NumberStyles style = NumberStyles.AllowDecimalPoint |
    NumberStyles.AllowLeadingSign | NumberStyles.AllowThousands;
float aValue = 0;
if ( float.TryParse("-12345.67", style, new CultureInfo("it-IT"), out aValue) )
{
    // aValue contains a valid number
}
```

The Convert Type

The System.Convert class exposes several static methods that help in converting to and from the many data types available in .NET. In their simplest form, these methods can convert any base type to another type:

```
// Convert the string "123.45" to a Double.
double dblValue = Convert.ToDouble("123.45");
```

The Convert class exposes many To*Xxxx* methods, one for each base type: ToBoolean, ToByte, ToChar, ToDateTime, ToDecimal, ToDouble, ToInt16, ToInt32, ToInt64, ToSByte, ToSingle, ToString, ToUInt16, ToUInt32, and ToUInt64:

```
// Convert a Double value to an integer.
int intValue = Convert.ToInt32(dblValue);
```

The To*Xxxx* methods that return an integer type—namely, ToByte, ToSByte, ToInt16, ToInt32, ToInt64, ToUInt16, ToUInt32, and ToUInt64—expose an overload that takes a string and a base and convert a string holding a number in that base. The base can only be 2, 8, 10, or 16:

```
// Convert from a string holding a binary representation of a number.
int result = Convert.ToInt32("11011", 2);            // => 27
// Convert from an octal number.
result = Convert.ToInt32("777", 8);                  // => 511
// Convert from a hexadecimal number.
result = Convert.ToInt32("AC", 16);                  // => 172
```

You can perform the conversion in the opposite direction—that is, from an integer into the string representation of a number in a different base—by means of overloads of the ToString method:

```
// Determine the binary representation of a number.
string text = Convert.ToString(27, 2);               // => 11011
// Determine the hexadecimal representation of a number. (Note: result is lowercase.)
text = Convert.ToString(172, 16);                    // => ac
```

The Convert class exposes two methods that convert to and from Base64-encoded strings, which is the format used for Multipurpose Internet Mail Extensions (MIME) e-mail attachments. The ToBase64String method takes an array of bytes and encodes it as a Base64 string. The FromBase64String method does the conversion in the opposite direction:

```
// An array of 16 bytes (two identical sequences of 8 bytes)
byte[] b1 = new byte[]{12, 45, 213, 88, 11, 220, 34, 0, 12, 45, 213, 88, 11, 220, 34, 0};
// Convert it to a Base64 string.
string s64 = Convert.ToBase64String(b1);
Console.WriteLine(s64);
// Convert it back to an array of bytes, and display it.
byte[] b2 = Convert.FromBase64String(s64);
foreach ( byte b in b2 )
{
    Console.Write("{0} ", b);
}
```

A new option in .NET Framework 2.0 enables you to insert a line separator automatically every 76 characters in the value returned by a ToBase64String method:

```
s64 = Convert.ToBase64String(b1, Base64FormattingOptions.InsertLineBreaks);
```

In addition, the Convert class exposes the ToBase64CharArray and FromBase64CharArray methods, which convert a Byte array to and from a Char array instead of a String. Finally, the class also exposes a generic ChangeType method that can convert (or at least attempt to convert) a value to any other type. You must use the typeof operator to create the System.Type object to pass in the method's second argument:

```
// Convert a value to Double.
Console.WriteLine(Convert.ChangeType(value, typeof(double)));
```

Random Number Generator

The System.Random type enables you to generate a series of random values. You can set the seed for random number generation in this class's constructor method:

```
// The argument must be a 32-bit integer.
Random rand = new Random(12345);
```

When you pass a given seed number, you always get the same random sequence. To get different sequences each time you run the application, you can have the seed depend on the current time:

```
// You need these conversions because the Ticks property
// returns a 64-bit value that must be truncated to a 32-bit integer.
int seed = (int) (DateTime.Now.Ticks & int.MaxValue);
rand = new Random(seed);
```

Once you have an initialized Random object, you can extract random positive 32-bit integer values each time you query its Next method:

```
for ( int i = 1; i <= 10; i++ )
{
    Console.WriteLine(rand.Next());
}
```

You can also pass one or two arguments to keep the return value in the desired range:

```
// Get a value in the range 0 to 1,000.
int intValue = rand.Next(1000);
// Get a value in the range 100 to 1,000.
intValue = rand.Next(100, 1000);
```

The NextDouble method returns a random floating-point number between 0 and 1:

```
double dblValue = rand.NextDouble();
```

Finally, you can fill a Byte array with random values with the NextBytes method:

```
// Get an array of 100 random byte values.
byte[] buffer = new byte[100];
rand.NextBytes(buffer);
```

Note   Although the Random type is OK in most kinds of applications, for example, when developing card games, the values it generates are easily reproducible and aren't random enough to be used in cryptography. For a more robust random value generator you should use the RNGCryptoServiceProvider class, in the System.Security.Cryptography namespace.

The DateTime Type

System.DateTime is the main .NET class for working with date and time values. Not only does it offer a place to store data values, it also exposes many useful methods for working with date and time values. You can initialize a DateTime value in several ways:

```
// Create a Date value by providing year, month, and day values.
DateTime dt = new DateTime(2005, 1, 6);           // January 6, 2005

// Provide hour, minute, and second values also.
dt = new DateTime(2005, 1, 6, 18, 30, 20);        // January 6, 2005 6:30:20 PM

// Add millisecond value (half a second in this example).
dt = new DateTime(2005, 1, 6, 18, 30, 20, 500);

// Create a time value from ticks (10 million ticks = 1 second).
long ticks = 20000000;                            // 2 seconds
// This is considered the time elapsed from Jan. 1 of year 1.
dt = new DateTime(ticks);                         // 1/1/0001 12:00:02 AM
```

You can use the Now and Today static properties:

```
// The Now property returns the system date and time.
dt = DateTime.Now;                 // For example, October 17, 2005 3:54:20 PM
// The Today property returns the system date only.
dt = DateTime.Today;               // For example, October 17, 2005 12:00:00 AM
```

The UtcNow static property returns the current time expressed as a Universal Time Coordinate (UTC) value and enables you to compare time values originated in different time zones; this property ignores the Daylight Saving Time if currently active for the current time zone:

```
dt = DateTime.UtcNow;
```

Once you have an initialized DateTime value, you can retrieve individual portions by using one of its read-only properties, namely, Date (the date portion), TimeOfDay (the time portion), Year, Month, Day, DayOfYear, DayOfWeek, Hour, Minute, Second, Millisecond, and Ticks:

```
// Is today the first day of the current month?
if ( DateTime.Today.Day == 1 )
{
   Console.WriteLine("First day of month");
}
// How many days have passed since January 1?
Console.WriteLine(DateTime.Today.DayOfYear);
// Get current time-note that ticks are included.
Console.WriteLine(DateTime.Now.TimeOfDay);      // => 10:39:28.3063680
```

The TimeOfDay property is peculiar in that it returns a TimeSpan object, which represents a difference between dates. Although this class is distinct from the DateTime class, it shares many of the DateTime class properties and methods and almost always works together with DateTime values, as you'll see shortly.

A note for the curious programmer: a DateTime value is stored as the number of ticks (1 tick = 100 nanoseconds) elapsed since January 1, 0001; this storage format can work for any date between 1/1/0001 and 12/12/9999. In .NET Framework 2.0, this tick value takes 62 bits, and the remaining 2 bits are used to preserve the information whether the date/time is expressed in Daylight Saving Time and whether the date/time is relative to the current time zone (the default) or is expressed as a UTC value.

Adding and Subtracting Dates

The DateTime class exposes several instance methods that enable you to add and subtract a number of years, months, days, hours, minutes, or seconds to or from a DateTime value. The names of these methods leave no doubt about their function: AddYears, AddMonths, AddDays, AddHours, AddMinutes, AddSeconds, AddMilliseconds, AddTicks. You can add an integer value when you're using AddYears and AddMonths and a decimal value in all other cases. In all cases, you can pass a negative argument to subtract rather than add a value:

```
// Tomorrow's date
dt = DateTime.Today.AddDays(1);
// Yesterday's date
dt = DateTime.Today.AddDays(-1);
// What time will it be 2 hours and 30 minutes from now?
dt = DateTime.Now.AddHours(2.5);

// A CPU-intensive way to pause for 5 seconds.
DateTime endTime = DateTime.Now.AddSeconds(5);
do {} while ( DateTime.Now < endTime );
```

The Add method takes a TimeSpan object as an argument. Before you can use it, you must learn to create a TimeSpan object, choosing one of its overloaded constructor methods:

```
// One 64-bit value is interpreted as a Ticks value.
TimeSpan ts = new TimeSpan(13500000);                  // 1.35 seconds
// Three integer values are interpreted as hours, minutes, seconds.
ts = new TimeSpan(0, 32, 20);                          // 32 minutes, 20 seconds
// Four integer values are interpreted as days, hours, minutes, seconds.
ts = new TimeSpan(1, 12, 0, 0);                        // 1 day and a half
// (Note that arguments aren't checked for out-of-range errors; therefore,
//  the next statement delivers the same result as the previous one.)
ts = new TimeSpan(0, 36, 0, 0);                        // 1 day and a half
// A fifth argument is interpreted as a millisecond value.
ts = new TimeSpan(0, 0, 1, 30, 500);                   // 90 seconds and a half
```

Now you're ready to add an arbitrary date or time interval to a DateTime value:

```
// What will be the time 2 days, 10 hours, and 30 minutes from now?
dt = DateTime.Now.Add(new TimeSpan(2, 10, 30, 0));
```

The DateTime class also exposes a Subtract instance method that works in a similar way:

```
// What was the time 1 day, 12 hours, and 20 minutes ago?
dt = DateTime.Now.Subtract(new TimeSpan(1, 12, 20, 0));
```

The Subtract method is overloaded to take another DateTime object as an argument, in which case it returns the TimeSpan object that represents the difference between the two dates:

```
// How many days, hours, minutes, and seconds have elapsed
// since the beginning of the third millennium?
DateTime startDate = new DateTime(2001, 1, 1);
TimeSpan diff = DateTime.Now.Subtract(startDate);
```

Once you have a TimeSpan object, you can extract the information buried in it by using one of its many properties, whose names are self-explanatory: Days, Hours, Minutes, Seconds, Milliseconds, Ticks, TotalDays, TotalHours, TotalMinutes, TotalSeconds, and TotalMilliseconds. The TimeSpan class also exposes methods such as Add, Subtract, Negate, and CompareTo.

The CompareTo method enables you to determine whether a DateTime value is greater or less than another DateTime value:

```
// Is current date later than October 30, 2005?
int res = DateTime.Today.CompareTo(new DateTime(2005, 10, 30));
if ( res > 0 )
{
    // Later than Oct. 30, 2005
}
else if ( res < 0 )
{
    // Earlier than Oct. 30, 2005
}
else
{
    // Today is Oct. 30, 2005.
}
```

By default, DateTime values are relative to the current time zone and you should never compare values coming from different time zones, unless they are in UTC format (see the section titled "Working with Time Zones" later in this chapter). Also, when evaluating the difference between two dates in the same time zone, you might get a wrong result if a transition to or from Daylight Saving Time has occurred between the two dates. This is one more reason to use dates in UTC format.

The IsDaylightSavingTime method (new in .NET Framework 2.0) enables you to detect whether Daylight Saving Time is active for the current time zone:

```
if ( DateTime.Now.IsDaylightSavingTime() )
{
    Console.Write("Daylight Saving Time is active");
}
```

Finally, the DateTime class exposes two static methods that can be handy in many applications:

```
// Test for a leap year.
Console.WriteLine(DateTime.IsLeapYear(2000));          // => true
// Retrieve the number of days in a given month.
Console.WriteLine(DateTime.DaysInMonth(2000, 2));      // => 29
```

Despite the abundance of date and time methods, the DateTime type doesn't offer a simple way to calculate the whole number of years or months elapsed between two dates. For example, you can't calculate the age of a person using this statement:

```
int age = DateTime.Now.Year - aPerson.BirthDate.Year;
```

because the result would be one unit greater than the correct value if the person hasn't celebrated a birthday in the current year. I have prepared a couple of reusable routines that provide the missing functionality:

```
// Return the whole number of years between two dates.

public static int YearDiff(DateTime startDate, DateTime endDate)
{
   int result = endDate.Year - startDate.Year;
   if ( endDate.Month < startDate.Month ||
      (endDate.Month == startDate.Month && endDate.Day < startDate.Day))
   {
      result--;
   }
   return result;
}

// Return the whole number of months between two dates.
public static int MonthDiff(DateTime startDate, DateTime endDate)
{
   int result = endDate.Year * 12 + endDate.Month -
      (startDate.Year * 12 + startDate.Month);
   if ( endDate.Month == startDate.Month && endDate.Day < startDate.Day )
   {
      result--;
   }
   return result;
}
```

Formatting Dates

The DateTime type overrides the ToString method to accept a standard date format among those specified in Table 1-2 or a user-defined format created by assembling the characters listed in Table 1-3:

```
// This is January 6, 2005 6:30:20.500 PMU.S. Eastern Time.
DateTime dt = new DateTime(2005, 1, 6, 18, 30, 20, 500);
```

```
// Display a date using the LongDatePattern standard format.
string dateText = dt.ToString("D");      // => Thursday, January 06, 2005
// Display a date using a custom format.
dateText = dt.ToString("d-MMM-yyyy");    // => 6-Jan-2005
```

You can format a DateTime value in other ways by using some peculiar methods that only this type exposes:

```
Console.WriteLine(dt.ToShortDateString());     // => 1/6/2005
Console.WriteLine(dt.ToLongDateString());      // => Thursday, January 06, 2005
Console.WriteLine(dt.ToShortTimeString());     // => 6:30 PM
Console.WriteLine(dt.ToLongTimeString());      // => 6:30:20 PM
Console.WriteLine(dt.ToFileTime());            // => 127495062205000000
Console.WriteLine(dt.ToOADate());              // => 38358.7710706019
// The next two results vary depending on the time zone you're in.
Console.WriteLine(dt.ToUniversalTime());       // => 1/7/2005 12:30:20 PM
Console.WriteLine(dt.ToLocalTime());           // => 1/6/2005 12:30:20 PM
```

A few of these formats might require additional explanation:

- The ToFileTime method returns an unsigned 8-byte value representing the date and time as the number of 100-nanosecond intervals that have elapsed since 1/1/1601 12:00 A.M. The DateTime type also supports the ToFileTimeUtc method, which ignores the local time zone.

- The ToOADate method converts to an OLE Automation–compatible value. (This is a Double value similar to date values used in Microsoft Visual Basic 6.)

- The ToUniversalTime method considers the DateTime value a local time and converts it to UTC format.

- The ToLocalTime method considers the DateTime value a UTC value and converts it to a local time.

The DateTime class exposes two static methods, FromOADate and FromFileTime, to parse an OLE Automation date value or a date formatted as a file time.

Parsing Dates

The operation complementary to date formatting is date parsing. The DateTime class provides a Parse static method for parsing jobs of any degree of complexity:

```
DateTime dt = DateTime.Parse("2005/1/6 12:30:20");
```

The flexibility of this method becomes apparent when you pass an IFormatProvider object as a second argument to it—for example, a CultureInfo object or a DateTimeFormatInfo object. The DateTimeFormatInfo object is conceptually similar to the NumberFormatInfo object described earlier (see the section titled "Formatting Numbers" earlier in this chapter), except that it holds information about separators and formats allowed in date and time values:

```
// Get a writable copy of the current locale's DateTimeFormatInfo object.
DateTimeFormatInfo dtfi = (DateTimeFormatInfo) DateTimeFormatInfo.CurrentInfo.Clone();
// Change date and time separators.
dtfi.DateSeparator = "-";
dtfi.TimeSeparator = ".";
// Now we're ready to parse a date formatted in a nonstandard way.
dt = DateTime.Parse("2005-1-6 12.30.20", dtfi);
```

Many non-U.S. developers will appreciate the ability to parse dates in formats other than month/day/year. In this case, you have to assign a correctly formatted pattern to the DateTimeFormatInfo object's ShortDatePattern, LongDatePattern, ShortTimePattern, Long-TimePattern, or FullDateTimePattern property before doing the parse:

```
// Prepare to parse (dd/mm/yy) dates, in short or long format.
dtfi.ShortDatePattern = "d/M/yyyy";
dtfi.LongDatePattern = "dddd, dd MMMM, yyyy";

// Both these statements assign the date "January 6, 2005."
dt = DateTime.Parse("6-1-2005 12.30.44", dtfi);
dt = DateTime.Parse("Thursday, 6 January, 2005", dtfi);
```

You can use the DateTimeFormatInfo object to retrieve standard or abbreviated names for weekdays and months, according to the current locale or any locale:

```
// Display the abbreviated names of months.
foreach ( string s in DateTimeFormatInfo.CurrentInfo.AbbreviatedMonthNames )
{
   Console.WriteLine(s);
}
```

Even more interesting, you can set weekday and month names with arbitrary strings if you have a writable DateTimeFormatInfo object, and then you can use the object to parse a date written in any language, including invented ones. (Yes, including Klingon!)

Another way to parse strings in formats other than month/day/year is to use the ParseExact static method. In this case, you pass the format string as the second argument, and you can pass null to the third argument if you don't need a DateTimeFormatInfo object to further qualify the string being parsed:

```
// This statements assigns the date "January 6, 2005."
dt = DateTime.ParseExact("6-1-2005", "d-M-yyyy", null);
```

The second argument can be any of the supported DateTime formats listed in Table 1-2. In .NET Framework 2.0, the new format F has been added to support the ParseExact method when there are a variable number of fractional digits.

Both the Parse and ParseExact methods throw an exception if the input string doesn't comply with the expected format. As you know, exceptions can add a lot of overhead to your applications and you should avoid them if possible. Version 2.0 of the .NET Framework extends the DateTime class with the TryParse and the TryParseExact methods, which return true if the parsing succeeds and store the result of the parsing in a DateTime variable passed a second argument:

```
DateTime aDate;
if ( DateTime.TryParse("January 6, 2005", out aDate) )
{
   // aDate contains the parsed date.
}
```

Another overload of the TryParse method takes an IFormatProvider object (for example, a CultureInfo instance) and a DateTimeStyles bit-coded value; the latter argument enables you to specify whether leading or trailing spaces are accepted and whether local or universal time is assumed:

```
CultureInfo ci = new CultureInfo("en-US");
if ( DateTime.TryParse(" 6/1/2005 14:26 ", ci,
  DateTimeStyles.AllowWhiteSpaces | DateTimeStyles.AssumeUniversal, out aDate) )
{
   // aDate contains the parsed date.
}
```

If you specify the DateTimesStyles.AssumeUniversal enumerated value (new in .NET Framework 2.0), the parsed time is assumed to be in UTC format and is automatically converted to the local time zone. By default, date values are assumed to be relative to the current time zone.

Working with Time Zones

DateTime values in version 1.1 of the .NET Framework have a serious limitation: they are always expected to store a local time, rather than a normalized UTC time. This assumption causes a few hard-to-solve problems, the most serious of which is a problem that manifests itself when a date value is serialized in one time zone and deserialized in a different zone, using either the SoapFormatter or the XmlSerializer object. These two objects, in fact, store information about the time zone together with the actual date value: when the object is deserialized in a different time zone, the time portion of the date is automatically adjusted to reflect the new geographical location.

In most cases, this behavior is correct, but at times it causes the application to malfunction. Let's say that a person was born in Italy on January 1, 1970, at 2 A.M.; if this date value is serialized as XML and sent to a computer in New York—for example, by using a Web service or by saving the information in a file that is later transferred using FTP or HTTP—the person would appear to have been born on December 31, 1969, at 8 P.M. As you can see, the issue with dates in .NET Framework 1.1 originates from the fact that you can't specify whether a value stored in a DateTime variable is to be considered relative to the current time zone or an absolute UTC value.

This problem has been solved quite effectively in .NET Framework 2.0 by the addition of a new Kind property to the DateTime type. This property is a DateTimeKind enumerated value that can be Local, Utc, or Unspecified. For backward compatibility with .NET Framework 1.1 applications, by default a DateTime value has a Kind property set to DateTimeKind.Local, unless you specify a different value in the constructor:

```
// February 14, 2005, at 12:00 AM, UTC value
DateTime aDate = new DateTime(2005, 2, 14, 12, 0, 0, DateTimeKind.Utc);
// Test the Kind property.
Console.WriteLine(aDate.Kind.ToString());                    // Utc
```

The Kind property is read-only, but you can use the SpecifyKind static method to create a different DateTime value if you want to pass from local to UTC time or vice versa:

```
// Next statement changes the Kind property (but doesn't change the date/time value!).
DateTime newDate = DateTime.SpecifyKind(aDate, DateTimeKind.Utc);
```

An important note: the Kind property is accounted for only when serializing and deserializing a date value and is ignored when doing comparisons.

In .NET Framework 1.1, DateTime values are serialized as 64-bit numbers by means of the Ticks property. In .NET Framework 2.0, however, when saving a DateTime value to a file or a database field, you should save the new Kind property as well; otherwise, the deserialization mechanism would suffer from the same problems you see in .NET Framework 1.1. The simplest way to do so is by means of the new ToBinary instance method (which converts the DateTime object to a 64-bit value) and the new FromBinary static method (which converts a 64-bit value to a DateTime value):

```
// Convert to an Int64 value.
long lngValue = aDate.ToBinary();
…
// Convert back from an Int64 to a DateTime value.
newDate = DateTime.FromBinary(lngValue);
```

You can also serialize a DateTime value as text. In this case, you should use the ToString method with the o format (new in .NET Framework 2.0). This format serializes all the information related to a date, including the Kind property and the time zone (if the date isn't in UTC format), and you can read it back by means of a ParseExact method if you specify the new DateTimeStyles.RoundtripKind enumerated value:

```
// Serialize a date in UTC format.
string text = aDate.ToString("o", CultureInfo.InvariantCulture);

// Deserialize it into a new DateTime value.
newDate = DateTime.ParseExact(text, "o", CultureInfo.InvariantCulture,
DateTimeStyles.RoundtripKind);
```

The TimeZone Type

The .NET Framework supports time zone information through the System.TimeZone object, which you can use to retrieve information about the time zone set in Windows regional settings:

```
// Get the TimeZone object for the current time zone.
TimeZone tz = TimeZone.CurrentTimeZone;
// Display name of time zone, without and with Daylight Saving Time.
// (I got these results by running this code in Italy.)
Console.WriteLine(tz.StandardName);        // => W. Europe Standard Time
Console.WriteLine(tz.DaylightName);        // => W. Europe Daylight Time
```

The most interesting piece of information here is the offset from UTC format, which you retrieve by means of the GetUTCOffset method. You must pass a date argument to this method because the offset depends on whether Daylight Saving Time is in effect. The returned value is in ticks:

```
// Display the time offset of W. Europe time zone in March 2005,
// when Daylight Saving Time is not active.
Console.WriteLine(tz.GetUtcOffset(new DateTime(2005, 3, 1)));   // => 01:00:00
// Display the time offset of W. Europe time zone in July,
// when Daylight Saving Time is active.
Console.WriteLine(tz.GetUtcOffset(new DateTime(2005, 7, 1)));   // => 02:00:00
```

The IsDaylightSavingTime method returns true if Daylight Saving Time is in effect:

```
// No Daylight Saving Time in March
Console.WriteLine(tz.IsDaylightSavingTime(new DateTime(2005, 3, 1)));
// => False
```

Finally, you can determine when Daylight Saving Time starts and ends in a given year by retrieving an array of DaylightTime objects with the TimeZone's GetDaylightChanges method:

```
// Retrieve the DaylightTime object for year 2005.
DaylightTime dlc = tz.GetDaylightChanges(2005);
// Note that you might get different start and end dates if you
// run this code in a country other than the United States.
Console.WriteLine("Starts at {0}, Ends at {1}, Delta is {2} minutes",
    dlc.Start, dlc.End, dlc.Delta.TotalMinutes);
    // => Starts at 3/27/2005 2:00:00 A.M., ends at 10/30/2005 3:00:00 A.M.
    //    Delta is 60 minutes.
```

The Guid Type

The System.Guid type exposes several static and instance methods that can help you work with globally unique identifiers (GUIDs), that is, those 128-bit numbers that serve to uniquely identify elements and that are ubiquitous in Windows programming. The NewGuid static method is useful for generating a new unique identifier:

```
// Create a new GUID.
Guid guid1 = Guid.NewGuid();
// By definition, you'll surely get a different output here.
Console.WriteLine(guid1.ToString());       // => 3f5f1d42-2d92-474d-a2a4-1e707c7e2a37
```

If you already have a GUID—for example, a GUID you have read from a database field—you can initialize a Guid variable by passing the GUID representation as a string or as an array of bytes to the type's constructor:

```
// Initialize from a string.
Guid guid2 = new Guid("45FA3B49-3D66-AB33-BB21-1E3B447A6621");
```

You can do only two more things with a Guid object: you can convert it to a Byte array with the ToByteArray method, and you can compare two Guid values for equality using the Equals method (inherited from System.Object):

```
// Convert to an array of bytes.
byte[] bytes = guid1.ToByteArray();
foreach (byte b in bytes)
{
    Console.Write("{0} ", b);
// => 239 1 161 57 143 200 172 70 185 64 222 29 59 15 190 205
}

// Compare two GUIDs.
if ( !guid1.Equals(guid2) )
{
    Console.WriteLine("GUIDs are different.");
}
```

Enums

Any Enum you define in your application derives from System.Enum, which in turn inherits from System.ValueType. Ultimately, therefore, user-defined Enums are value types, but they are special in that you can't define additional properties, methods, or events. All the methods they expose are inherited from System.Enum. (It's illegal to explicitly inherit a class from System.Enum in C#.)

All the examples in this section refer to the following Enum block:

```
// This Enum defines the data type accepted for a value entered by the end user.
public enum DataEntry
{
    IntegerNumber,
    FloatingNumber,
    CharString,
    DateTime,
}
```

By default, the first enumerated type is assigned the value 0. You can change this initial value if you want, but you aren't encouraged to do so. In fact, it is advisable that 0 be a valid value for any Enum blocks you define; otherwise, a noninitialized Enum variable would contain an invalid value.

The .NET documentation defines a few guidelines for Enum values:

- Use names without the Enum suffix; use singular names for regular Enum types and plural for bit-coded Enum types.

- Use PascalCase for the name of both the Enum and its members. (An exception is constants from the Windows API, which are usually all uppercase.)

- Use 32-bit integers unless you need a larger range, which normally happens only when you have a bit-coded Enum with more than 32 possible values.

- Don't use Enums for open sets, that is, sets that you might need to expand in the future (for example, operating system versions).

Displaying and Parsing Enum Values

The Enum class overrides the ToString method to return the value as a readable string format. This method is useful when you want to expose a (nonlocalized) string to the end user:

```
DataEntry de = DataEntry.DateTime;
// Display the numeric value.
Console.WriteLine(Convert.ToDecimal(de));      // => 3
// Display the symbolic value.
Console.WriteLine(de.ToString());              // => DateTime
```

Or you can use the capability to pass a format character to an overloaded version of the ToString method. The only supported format characters are G, g (general), X, x (hexadecimal), F, f (fixed-point), and D, d (decimal):

```
// General and fixed formats display the Enum name.
Console.WriteLine(de.ToString("F"));           // => DateTime
// Decimal format displays Enum value.
Console.WriteLine(de.ToString("D"));           // => 3
// Hexadecimal format displays eight hex digits.
Console.WriteLine(de.ToString("X"));           // => 00000003
```

The opposite of ToString is the Parse static method, which takes a string and converts it to the corresponding enumerated value. Being inherited from the generic Enum class, the Parse method returns a generic object, so you have to explicitly cast it to a specific enumerated variable:

```
de = (DataEntry) Enum.Parse(typeof(DataEntry), "CharString");
```

The Parse method throws an ArgumentException if the name doesn't correspond to a defined enumerated value. Names are compared in a case-sensitive way, but you can pass a true optional argument if you don't want to take the string case into account:

```
// *** This statement throws an exception.
Console.WriteLine(Enum.Parse(de.GetType(), "charstring"));
// This works well because case-insensitive comparison is used.
Console.WriteLine(Enum.Parse(de.GetType(), "charstring", true));
```

Other Enum Methods

The GetUnderlyingType static method returns the base type for an enumerated class:

```
Console.WriteLine(Enum.GetUnderlyingType(de.GetType()));        // => System.Int32
```

The IsDefined method enables you to check whether a numeric value is acceptable as an enumerated value of a given class:

```
if ( Enum.IsDefined(typeof(DataEntry), 3) )
{
    // 3 is a valid value for the DataEntry class.
    de = (DataEntry) 3;
}
```

The IsDefined method is useful because the cast operator doesn't check whether the value being converted is in the valid range for the target enumerated type. In other words, the following statement doesn't throw an exception:

```
// This code produces an invalid result, yet it doesn't throw an exception.
de = (DataEntry) 123;
```

Another way to check whether a numeric value is acceptable for an Enum object is by using the GetName method, which returns the name of the enumerated value or returns null if the value is invalid:

```
if ( Enum.GetName(typeof(DataEntry), 3) != null )
{
    de = (DataEntry) 3;
}
```

You can quickly list all the values of an enumerated type with the GetNames and GetValues methods. The former returns a String array holding the individual names (sorted by the corresponding values); the latter returns an object array that holds the numeric values:

```
// List all the values in DataEntry.
string[] names = Enum.GetNames(typeof(DataEntry));
Array values = Enum.GetValues(typeof(DataEntry));
for ( int i = 0; i <= names.Length - 1; i++ )
{
    Console.WriteLine("{0} = {1}", names[i], (int) values.GetValue(i));
}
```

Here's the output of the preceding code snippet:

```
IntegerNumber = 0
FloatingNumber = 1
CharString = 2
DateTime = 3
```

Bit-Coded Values

The .NET Framework supports a special Flags attribute that you can use to specify that an Enum object represents a bit-coded value. For example, let's create a new class named ValidDataEntry class, which enables the developer to specify two or more valid data types for values entered by an end user:

```
[Flags]
public enum ValidDataEntry
{
    None = 0,            // Always define an Enum value equal to 0.
    IntegerNumber = 1,
    FloatingNumber = 2,
    CharString = 4,
    DateTime = 8
}
```

The FlagAttribute class doesn't expose any property, and its constructor takes no arguments: the presence of this attribute is sufficient to label this Enum type as bit-coded.

Bit-coded enumerated types behave exactly like regular Enum values do except their ToString method recognizes the Flags attribute. When an enumerated type is composed of two or more flag values, this method returns the list of all the corresponding values, separated by commas:

```
ValidDataEntry vde = ValidDataEntry.IntegerNumber | ValidDataEntry.DateTime;
Console.WriteLine(vde.ToString());        // => IntegerNumber, DateTime
```

If no bit is set, the ToString method returns the name of the enumerated value corresponding to the zero value:

```
ValidDataEntry vde2 = 0;
Console.WriteLine(vde2.ToString());               // => None
```

If the value doesn't correspond to a valid combination of bits, the Format method returns the number unchanged:

```
vde = (ValidDataEntry) 123;
Console.WriteLine(vde.ToString());               // => 123
```

The Parse method is also affected by the Flags attribute:

```
vde = (ValidDataEntry) Enum.Parse(vde.GetType(), "IntegerNumber, FloatingNumber");
Console.WriteLine(Convert.ToInt32(vde));          // => 3
```

Chapter 2
Object Lifetime

An important facet of Microsoft .NET programming is understanding how the Common Language Runtime (CLR) allocates and releases memory and, above all, how objects are destroyed at the end of their life cycles. In this chapter, you'll learn how you can improve your applications' performance remarkably.

Note To avoid long lines, code samples in this chapter assume that the following using statements are used at the top of each source file:

```
using System;
using System.Collections;
using System.Diagnostics;
using System.IO;
using System.Runtime.InteropServices;
```

Memory Management in the .NET Framework

Microsoft Visual C# classes don't have destructor methods. In other words, no method or event in the class fires when the instance is destroyed. This is one of the more controversial features of the framework and was discussed for months in forums and newsgroups while the Microsoft .NET Framework was in beta version.

The Garbage Collection Process

The .NET Framework memory management relies on a sophisticated process known as *garbage collection*. When an application tries to allocate memory for a new object and the heap has insufficient free memory, the .NET Framework starts the garbage collection process, which is carried out by an internal object known as the *garbage collector*. Many technical articles use the GC abbreviation to indicate both the garbage collection and the garbage collector terms; strictly speaking, System.GC stands for garbage collector, even though in most cases it can indicate both terms.

The garbage collector visits all the objects in the heap and marks those objects that are pointed to by any variable in the application. (These variables are known as *roots* because they're at the top of the application's object graph.) The garbage collection process is quite sophisticated and recognizes objects referenced indirectly from other objects, such as when you have a Person object that references other Person instances through its Children property. After marking all the objects that can be reached from the application's code, the garbage collector can safely release the remaining (unmarked) objects because they're guaranteed to be unreachable by the application.

Next, the garbage collector compacts the heap and makes the resulting block of free memory available to new objects. Interestingly, this mechanism indirectly resolves any circular references existing among objects because the garbage collector doesn't mark unreachable objects. The garbage collector therefore correctly releases memory associated with objects pointed to by other objects in a circular reference fashion but not used by the main program.

In most real-world applications, the .NET way of dealing with object lifetime is significantly more efficient than the COM way is—and this is an all-important advantage because everything is an object in the .NET architecture. On the other hand, the garbage collection mechanism introduces a problem known as *nondeterministic finalization*: a .NET object is actually released sometime after the last variable pointing to it is set to null. For this reason, it's often necessary to distinguish between the *logical* destruction of an object (when the application clears the last variable pointing to the object) and its *physical* destruction (when the object is actually removed from memory). If the application doesn't create many objects, a .NET object might be collected only when the program terminates and there's no way for a .NET object to learn when it will become unreachable from the main application.

If memory is the only resource that an object uses, deferred destruction is never a problem. After all, if the application requires more memory, a garbage collection fires and a block of new memory is eventually made available. However, if the object allocates other types of resources—files, database connections, serial or parallel ports, internal Microsoft Windows objects—you want to make such releases as soon as possible so that another application can use them. In some cases, the problem isn't just a shortage of resources. For example, if the object opens a window to display the value of its properties, you surely want that window to be closed as soon as the object is logically destroyed so that a user can't look at outdated information. Thus, the problem is: how can you run your cleanup code when your .NET object is destroyed?

The previous question has no definitive answer. A partial solution comes in the form of two special methods: Finalize and Dispose.

The Finalize Method

The Finalize method is a special method that the garbage collector calls just before releasing the memory allocated to the object—that is, when the object is physically destroyed. It works more or less the same way the destructor method in C++ works, except that it can be called several seconds (or even minutes or hours) after the application has logically killed the object by setting the last variable pointing to the object to null (or by letting the variable go out of scope, which has the same effect).

All .NET objects inherit the Finalize protected method from the System.Object class; however, it is illegal to declare this method in C# as you would with a regular method. Instead, you must use the special syntax that is reminiscent of C++ destructors:

```
public class Person
{
    ...
    // C# syntax for the Finalize method
    ~Person()
    {
        Debug.WriteLine("A Person object is being destroyed.");
    }
}
```

The following application shows that the Finalize method isn't called immediately when all variables pointing to the object are set to null:

```
static void Main()
{
    Debug.WriteLine("About to create a Person object.");
    Person aPerson = new Person("John", "Evans");
    Debug.WriteLine("About to set the Person object to null.");
    aPerson = null;
    Debug.WriteLine("About to terminate the application.");
}
```

These are the messages that you'll see in the Debug pane of the Output window (interspersed among other diagnostic text):

```
About to create a Person object.
About to set the Person object to null.
About to terminate the application.
Person object is being destroyed.
```

The sequence of messages makes it apparent that the Person object isn't destroyed when the aPerson variable is set to null, but only later, when the application itself terminates.

Here's one important .NET programming guideline: never access any external object from a Finalize method because the external object might have been destroyed already. In fact, the object is being collected because it can't be reached from the main application, so a reference to another object isn't going to keep that object alive. The garbage collector can reclaim unreachable objects in any order, so the other object might be finalized before the current one. One of the few objects that can be safely accessed from a Finalize method is the base object of the current object, using the base keyword.

In general, it is safe to invoke static methods from inside the Finalize method, except when the application is shutting down. In the latter case, in fact, the .NET Framework might have already destroyed the System.Type object corresponding to the type that exposes the static method. For example, you shouldn't use the Console.WriteLine method because the Console object might be gone. The Debug object is one of the few objects that are guaranteed to stay alive until the very end, however, and that's why the previous code example uses Debug. WriteLine instead of Console.WriteLine. You can discern the two cases by querying the Environment.HasShutdownStarted method:

```
~Person()
{
    Debug.WriteLine("A Person object is being destroyed.");
    if ( !Environment.HasShutdownStarted )
    {
        Debug.WriteLine("Application is shutting down.");
    }
}
```

As I mentioned earlier, you can control the garbage collector by means of the System.GC type, which exposes only static members. For example, you can force a collection by means of its Collect method:

```
static void Main()
{
    Debug.WriteLine("About to create a Person object.");
    Person aPerson = new Person("John", "Evans");
    aPerson = null;
    Debug.WriteLine("About to fire a garbage collection.");
    GC.Collect();
    GC.WaitForPendingFinalizers();
    Debug.WriteLine("About to terminate the application.");
}
```

The WaitForPendingFinalizers method stops the current thread until all objects are correctly finalized; this action is necessary because the garbage collection process might run on a different thread. The sequence of messages in the Output window is now different:

```
About to create a Person object.
About to fire a garbage collection.
Person object is being destroyed.
Application is shutting down.
About to terminate the application.
```

However, calling the GC.Collect method to cause an *induced garbage collection* is usually a bad idea. If you run a garbage collection frequently, you're missing one of the most promising performance optimizations that the .NET Framework offers. The preceding code example, which uses the GC.Collect method only to fire the object's Finalize method, illustrates what you should *never* do in a real .NET application. In a server-side application—such as a Microsoft ASP.NET application—this rule has virtually no exceptions.

In a Windows Forms application, you can invoke the GC.Collect method, but only when the application is idle—for example, while it waits for user input—and only if you see that unexpected (that is, not explicitly requested) garbage collections are slowing the program noticeably during time-critical operations. For example, unexpected garbage collections might be a problem when your application is in charge of controlling hardware devices that require a short response time. By inducing a garbage collection when the program is idle, you decrease the probability that a standard garbage collection slows down the regular execution of your application.

Objects that expose the Finalize method aren't immediately reclaimed and usually require *at least* another garbage collection before they are swept out of the heap. The reason for this behavior is that the code in the Finalize method might store a reference to the current object in a global variable, an advanced technique known as *object resurrection* (discussed later in this chapter). If the object were garbage collected at this point, the reference in the global variable would become invalid; the CLR can't detect this special case until the subsequent garbage collection and must wait until then to definitively release the object's memory. If you also consider that the creation of objects using a Finalize method requires a few more CPU cycles, you see that object finalization doesn't come for free. In general, you should implement the Finalize method only if you have a very good reason to do so.

Another important guideline for .NET developers is that the Finalize method of a type should clean up all used resources and then invoke the base class's Finalize method. Unlike most other .NET developers—most notably, Microsoft Visual Basic programmers—C# developers can ignore this detail because the C# compiler enforces this rule behind the scenes. In fact, all the statements in a Finalize method are automatically wrapped in a try block, whose finally block contains the code that invokes the base class's Finalize method:

```
// This is how the C# compiler renders a finalizer....
try
{
    // The code in the finalizer goes here....
}
finally
{
    base.Finalize();
}
```

The Dispose Method

Because .NET objects don't have real destructors, well-designed classes should expose a method to let well-behaved clients manually release any resource such as files, database connections, and system objects as soon as they don't need the object any longer—that is, just before setting the reference to Nothing—rather than waiting for the subsequent garbage collection.

Classes that want to provide this feature should implement the IDisposable interface, which exposes only the Dispose method:

```
public class Widget : IDisposable
{
    public void Dispose()
    {
        // Close files and release other resources here.
        ...
    }
}
```

This is the usage pattern for an IDisposable object:

```
// Create the object.
Widget obj = new Widget();
// Use the object.
...
// Ask the object to release its resources, before setting it to null.
obj.Dispose();
obj = null;
```

Or you can use a using block:

```
// Create the object.
using ( Widget obj = new Widget() )
{
    // Use the object.
    ...
    // The object is disposed of and set to null here.
}
```

The using statement ensures that the Dispose method is called even if the code throws an exception, but it doesn't catch the exception. If you need to handle exceptions thrown while using the object, you must give up the convenience of the using keyword and use a regular try...catch...finally block:

```
Widget obj = null;
try
{
    // Create and use the object.
    obj = new Widget();
    ...
}
catch ( Exception ex )
{
    ...
}
finally
{
    // Ensure that the Dispose method is invoked.
    obj.Dispose();
}
```

Many stream- and connection-related objects in the .NET Framework, such as FileStream and all ADO.NET connection objects, have a public Close method that delegates to the private Dispose method. If you had to implement such types in C#, you would write code such as this:

```csharp
public class CustomStream : IDisposable
{
    // Implement the IDisposable interface explicitly.
    void IDisposable.Dispose()
    {
        // Close the stream here.
        …
    }

    public void Close()
    {
        this.Dispose();
    }
}
```

Interestingly, the using block works correctly with objects that implement a private Dispose method because behind the scenes it casts the object reference to an IDisposable variable. In some cases, you might need to have an explicit cast to this interface, as in the following generic cleanup routine:

```csharp
// Set an object to null and call its Dispose method if possible.
void ClearObject(ref object obj)
{
    IDisposable idisp = obj as IDisposable;
    if ( idisp != null )
    {
        idisp.Dispose();
    }
    // Next statement works because the object is passed by reference.
    obj = null;
}
```

.NET programming guidelines dictate that the Dispose method of an object should invoke the Dispose method of all the inner objects that the current object owns and that are hidden from the client code, and then it should call the base class's Dispose method (if the base class implements IDisposable). For example, if the Widget object has created a System.Timers .Timer object, the Widget.Dispose method should call the Timer.Dispose method. This suggestion and the fact that an object can be shared by multiple clients might cause a Dispose method to be called multiple times, and in fact a Dispose method shouldn't raise any errors when called more than once, even though all calls after the first one should be ignored. You can avoid releasing resources multiple times by using a class-level variable:

```csharp
private bool disposed = false;

public void Dispose()
{
```

```
     if ( ! disposed )
     {
        // Close files and release other resources here.
        ...
        // Ensure that further calls are ignored.
        disposed = true;
     }
  }
```

.NET programming guidelines also dictate that calling any method other than Dispose on an object that has already been disposed of should throw the special ObjectDisposedException. If you have implemented the class-level disposed field, implementing this guideline is trivial:

```
public void AnotherMethod()
{
    // Throw an exception if a client attempts to use a disposed object.
    if ( disposed )
    {
        throw new ObjectDisposedException("Widget");
    }
    ...
}
```

Combining the Dispose and Finalize Methods

Typically, you can allocate a resource other than memory in one of two ways: by invoking a piece of unmanaged code (for example, a Windows API function) or by creating an instance of a .NET class that wraps the resource. You need to understand this difference because the way you allocate a resource affects the decision about implementing the Dispose or the Finalize method.

You need to implement the IDisposable interface if a method in your type allocates resources other than memory, regardless of whether the resources are allocated directly (through a call to unmanaged code) or indirectly (through an object in the .NET Framework). Conversely, you need to implement the Finalize method only if your object allocates an unmanaged resource directly. Notice, however, that implementing IDisposable or the Finalize method is mandatory only if your code stores a reference to the resource in a class-level field: if a method allocates a resource and releases it before exiting, for example, by means of a using block, there's no need to implement either IDisposable or Finalize. In general, therefore, you must account for four different cases:

- **Neither the Dispose nor the Finalize method**   Your object uses only memory or other resources that don't require explicit deallocation, or the object releases any unmanaged resource before exiting the method that has allocated it. This is by far the most frequent case.

- **Dispose method only**   Your object allocates resources other than memory through other .NET objects, and you want to provide clients with a method to release those resources as soon as possible. This is the second most frequent case.

■ **Both the Dispose and the Finalize methods**   Your object directly allocates a resource (typically by calling a method in an unmanaged DLL) that requires explicit deallocation or cleanup. You do such explicit deallocation in the Finalize method, but provide the Dispose method as well to provide clients with the ability to release the resource before your object's finalization.

■ **Finalize method only**   You don't have any resources to release, but you need to perform a given action when your object is finalized. This is the least likely case and in practice it is useful only in a few uncommon scenarios.

The first case is simple, and I have already showed how to implement the second case, so we can focus on the third case and see how the Dispose and Finalize methods can cooperate with each other. Here's an example of a ClipboardWrapper object that opens and closes the system Clipboard:

```
public class ClipboardWrapper : IDisposable
{
    [DllImport("user32")]
    private static extern int OpenClipboard(int hwnd);
    [DllImport("user32")]
    private static extern int CloseClipboard();

    // Remember whether the Clipboard is currently open.
    public bool isOpen;

    // Open the Clipboard and associate it with a window.
    public void Open(int hWnd)
    {
        // OpenClipboard returns 0 if any error.
        if ( OpenClipboard(hWnd) == 0 )
        {
            throw new Exception("Unable to open Clipboard");
        }
        isOpen = true;
    }

    // Close the Clipboard—ignore the command if not open.
    public void Close()
    {
        if ( isOpen )
        {
            CloseClipboard();
            isOpen = false;
        }
    }

    public void Dispose()
    {
        Close();
    }
```

```
~ClipboardWrapper()
{
   Close();
}
}
```

What the OpenClipboard and CloseClipboard methods do isn't important in this context because I just selected two of the simplest Windows API procedures that allocate and release a system resource. What really matters in this example is that an application that opens the Clipboard and associates it with a window must also release the Clipboard as soon as possible because the Clipboard is a shared resource and no other window can access it in the meantime. (A real-world class would surely expose other useful methods to manipulate the Clipboard, but I want to keep this example as simple as possible.)

It's a good practice to have both the Dispose and the Finalize methods call the cleanup routine that performs the actual release operation (the Close method, in this example) so that you don't duplicate the code. Such a method can be public, as in this case, or it can be a private helper method. You also need a class-level variable (isOpen in the preceding code) to ensure that cleanup code doesn't run twice, once when the client invokes Dispose and once when the garbage collector calls the Finalize method. The same variable also ensures that nothing happens if clients call the Close or Dispose method multiple times.

A Better Dispose–Finalize Pattern

A problem with the technique just illustrated is that the garbage collector calls the Finalize method even if the client has already called the Dispose or Close method. As I explained previously, the Finalize method affects performance negatively because an additional garbage collection is required to destroy the object completely. Fortunately, you can control whether the Finalize method is invoked by using the GC.SuppressFinalize method. Using this method is straightforward. You typically call it from inside the Dispose method so that the garbage collector knows that it shouldn't call the Finalize method during the subsequent garbage collection.

Another problem that you might need to solve in a class that is more sophisticated than is the ClipboardWrapper demo shown earlier is that the cleanup code might access other objects referenced by the current object—for example, a control on a form—but you should never perform such access if the cleanup code runs in the finalization phase because those other objects might have been finalized already. You can resolve this issue by moving the actual cleanup code to an overloaded version of the Dispose method. This method takes a Boolean argument that specifies whether the object is being disposed of or finalized and avoids accessing external objects in the latter case. Here's a new version of the ClipboardWrapper class that uses this pattern to resolve these issues:

```
public class ClipboardWrapper2 : IDisposable
{
   [DllImport("user32")]
   private static extern int OpenClipboard(int hwnd);
   [DllImport("user32")]
```

```
private static extern int CloseClipboard();

// Remember whether the Clipboard is currently open.
public bool isOpen;
// Remember whether the object has already been disposed.
// (Protected makes it available to derived classes.)
protected bool disposed;

public ClipboardWrapper2()
{
    // Don't invoke the finalizer unless the Open method is actually invoked.
    GC.SuppressFinalize(this);
}

// Open the Clipboard and associate it with a window.
public void Open(int hWnd)
{
    // OpenClipboard returns 0 if any error.
    if ( OpenClipboard(hWnd) == 0 )
    {
        throw new Exception("Unable to open Clipboard");
    }
    isOpen = true;
    // Register the Finalize method, in case clients forget to call Close or Dispose.
    GC.ReRegisterForFinalize(this);
}

public void Close()
{
    Dispose();           // Delegate to the Dispose method.
}

public void Dispose()
{
    Dispose(true);
    // Remember that the object has been disposed.
    disposed = true;
    // Tell .NET not to call the Finalize method.
    GC.SuppressFinalize(this);
}

~ClipboardWrapper2()
{
    Dispose(false);
}

protected virtual void Dispose(bool disposing)
{
    // Exit if the object has already been disposed.
    if ( disposed )
    {
        return;
    }

    if ( disposing )
```

```
        {
            // The object is being disposed, not finalized. It is safe to access
            // other objects (other than the base object) only from inside this block.
            …
        }

        // Perform cleanup chores that have to be executed in either case.
        CloseClipboard();
        isOpen = false;
    }
}
```

Notice that the constructor method invokes GC.SuppressFinalize, which tells the CLR not to invoke the Finalize method; this call accounts for the case when a client creates a ClipboardWrapper2 object but never calls its Open method. The Finalize method is registered again by means of a call to the GC.ReRegisterForFinalize method in the Open method.

Finalization issues can become even more problematic if you consider that the Finalize method also runs if the object threw an exception in its constructor method. This means that the code in the Finalize method might access members that haven't been initialized correctly; thus, your finalization code should avoid accessing instance members if there is any chance that an error occurred in the constructor. Even better, the constructor method should use a try...catch block to trap errors, release any allocated resource, and then call GC.SuppressFinalize to prevent the standard finalization code from running on uninitialized members.

Finalizers in Derived Classes

I already explained that a well-written class that allocates and uses unmanaged resources (ODBC database connections, file and Windows object handles, and so on) should implement both a Finalize method and the IDisposable.Dispose method. If your application inherits from such a class, you must check whether your inherited class allocates any additional unmanaged resources. If not, you don't have to write any extra code because the derived class will inherit the base class implementation of both the Finalize and the Dispose methods. However, if the inherited class does allocate and use additional unmanaged resources, you should override the implementation of these methods, correctly release the unmanaged resources that the inherited class uses, and then call the corresponding method in the base class.

In the previous section, I illustrated a technique for correctly implementing these methods in a class, based on an overloaded Dispose method that contains the code for both the IDisposable.Dispose and the Finalize methods. As it happens, this overloaded Dispose method has a protected scope, so in practice you can correctly implement the Dispose–Finalize pattern in derived classes simply by overriding one method:

```
public class ClipboardWrapperEx : ClipboardWrapper2
{
    // Insert here regular methods, some of which might allocate additional
    // unmanaged resources.
    …
    // The only method we need to override to implement the Dispose-Finalize
```

```
    // pattern for this class
    protected override void Dispose(bool disposing)
    {
        // Exit now if the object has already been disposed.
        // (The disposed variable is declared as protected in the base class.)
        if ( disposed )
        {
            return;
        }

        try
        {
            if ( disposing )
            {
                // The object is being disposed, not finalized. It is safe to access
                // other objects (other than the base object) only from inside this block.
                ...
            }

            // Perform cleanup chores that have to be executed in either case.
            ...
        }
        finally
        {
            // Call the base class's Dispose method in all cases.
            base.Dispose(disposing);
        }
    }
}
```

If there is any chance that the code in the Dispose method might throw an exception, you should wrap it in a try block and invoke the base class's Dispose method from the finally block, as the previous code does. Failing to do so might result in the base class being prevented from releasing its own resources, which is something you should absolutely avoid for obvious reasons.

A Simplified Approach to Finalization

Authoring a class that correctly implements the Dispose and Finalize methods isn't a trivial task, as you've seen in previous sections. However, in most cases, you can take a shortcut and dramatically simplify the structure of your code by sticking to the following two guidelines. First, you wrap each unmanaged resource that requires finalization with a class whose only member is a field holding the handle of the unmanaged resource. Second, you nest this wrapper class inside another class that implements the Dispose method (but not the Finalize method). The nested class is marked as private; therefore, it can be accessed only by the class that encloses it.

To see in practice what these guidelines mean, consider the following sample code:

```
public class WinResource : IDisposable
{
    // A private field that creates a wrapper for the unmanaged resource
    private UnmanagedResourceWrapper wrapper = null;
    // True if the object has been disposed of
    private bool disposed = false;
```

```csharp
public WinResource(string someData)
{
    // Allocate the unmanaged resource here.
    wrapper = new UnmanagedResourceWrapper(someData);
}

// A public method that clients call to work with the unmanaged resource
public void DoSomething()
{
    // Throw an exception if the object has already been disposed of.
    if ( disposed )
    {
        throw new ObjectDisposedException("");
    }

    // This code can pass the wrapper.Handle value to API calls.
    ...
}

public void Dispose()
{
    // Avoid issues when multiple threads call Dispose at the same time.
    lock ( this )
    {
        // Do nothing if already disposed of.
        if ( disposed )
        {
            return;
        }

        // Dispose of all the disposable objects used by this instance,
        // including the one that wraps the unmanaged resource.
        ...
        wrapper.Dispose();
        // Remember this object has been disposed of.
        disposed = true;
    }
}

// The nested private class that allocates and releases the unmanaged resource
private sealed class UnmanagedResourceWrapper : IDisposable
{
    // An invalid handle value that the wrapper class can use to check
    // whether the handle is valid
    public static readonly IntPtr InvalidHandle = new IntPtr(-1);

    // A public field, but accessible only from inside the WinResource class
    public IntPtr Handle = InvalidHandle;

    // The constructor takes some data and allocates the unmanaged resource.
    public UnmanagedResourceWrapper(string someData)
    {
        // This is just a demo...
        this.Handle = new IntPtr(12345);
    }
```

```
public void Dispose()
{
    // Exit now if this object didn't complete its constructor correctly.
    if ( this.Handle == InvalidHandle )
    {
        return;
    }

    // Release the unmanaged resource here.
    // For example, CloseHandle(Handle)

    // Finally, invalidate the handle.
    this.Handle = InvalidHandle;
    // Tell the CLR not to call the Finalize method.
    GC.SuppressFinalize(this);
}

~UnmanagedResourceWrapper()
{
    Dispose();
}
    }
}
```

It's essential that the UnmanagedResourceWrapper class doesn't contain any fields, except the handle of the unmanaged resource, or methods, except those listed. If the unmanaged resource should interact with other resources, the code that implements this interaction should be located in the WinResource class. The WinResource class must coordinate all the resources (managed and unmanaged) that it has allocated and must release them in its Dispose method.

Let's discuss the advantages of this approach. First, and foremost, if the client code omits invoking the WinResource.Dispose method, all the memory used by the WinResource object will be cleared anyway at the first garbage collection. The inner UnmanagedResource-Wrapper object has a Finalize method and therefore will be released only during a subsequent garbage collection, but this object consumes very little memory and therefore this isn't a serious issue.

Second, the inner UnmanagedResourceWrapper is private and sealed, so you don't need to write any complex code that takes derived classes into account. (However, you can inherit from WinResource, if you need to, without any special caution.) Because the object is private, code outside the WinResource class can't get a reference to the UnmanagedResourceWrapper object and can't resurrect it.

Third, the UnmanagedResourceWrapper has only one field and this field is a value type; therefore, the code in the Dispose or Finalize method can't mistakenly access any reference type. (As you might recall, a reference type might already be disposed of when it's accessed during the finalization stage.) Because there is just one handle to account for, you don't have to write code that deals with errors in the UnmanagedResourceWrapper constructor. If the constructor fails, the value of the Handle field continues to be equal to the InvalidHandle constant; the Dispose method can detect this condition and skip the cleanup code.

Finally, the UnmanagedResourceWrapper class is so simple and generic that often you can copy and paste its code (with minor edits) inside other types that must manage unmanaged resources. Because it is nested inside another class, you don't even need to worry about name collisions.

> **Note**   Version 2.0 of the .NET Framework introduces the SafeHandle abstract class, which makes it simpler to author classes that use unmanaged resources. Basically, a SafeHandle object is a wrapper for a Windows handle and is vaguely similar to the UnmanagedResource-Wrapper in the previous example but with many additional features, such as the protection from a kind of attack known as *handle recycle attacks*. You can find more information in MSDN documentation and a few articles from the BCL Team, such as *https://blogs.msdn.com/bclteam/archive/2005/03/15/396335.aspx* and *http://blogs.msdn.com/cbrumme/archive/2004/02/20/77460.aspx*.

Advanced Techniques

As I promised at the beginning of this chapter, you can boost your application's performance if you understand the garbage collection process more thoroughly. In the remaining sections, you'll learn about generations, weak references, resurrections, and how these techniques can help you write better .NET software.

Generations

If the garbage collector had to visit all the objects referenced by an application, the garbage collection process might impose a severe overhead. Fortunately, some recurring patterns in object creation make it possible for the garbage collector to use heuristics that can significantly reduce the total execution time.

It has been observed that, from a statistical point of view, objects created early in the program's lifetime tend to stay alive longer than objects created later in a program do. Here's how you can intuitively justify this theory: objects created early are usually assigned to application-level variables and will be set to null only when the application ends, whereas objects created inside a class constructor method are usually released when the object is set to null. Finally, objects created inside a procedure are often destroyed when the procedure exits (unless they have been assigned to a variable defined outside the procedure, for example, an array or a collection).

The garbage collector has a simple way of determining how "old" an object is. Each object maintains a counter telling how many garbage collections that object has survived. The value of this counter is the object's *generation*. The higher this number is, the smaller the chances are that the object is collected during the next garbage collection.

The current version of the CLR supports only three distinct generation values. The generation value of an object that has never undergone a garbage collection is 0; if the object survives a garbage collection, its generation becomes 1; if it survives a second garbage collection, its generation becomes 2. Any subsequent garbage collection leaves the generation counter at 2 (or destroys the object). For example, an object that has a Finalize method always survives to the first garbage collection and is promoted to generation 1 because, as I explained earlier, the CLR can't sweep it out of the heap when the garbage collection occurs.

The CLR uses the generation counter to optimize the garbage collection process—for example, by moving the objects in generation 2 toward the beginning of the heap, where they are likely to stay until the program terminates; they are followed by objects in generation 1 and finally by objects in generation 0. This algorithm has proved to speed up the garbage collection process because it reduces the fragmentation of the managed heap.

You can learn the current generation of any object by passing it to the GC.GetGeneration method. The following code should give you a taste of how this method works:

```
string s = "dummy string";
// This is an object in generation 0.
Console.WriteLine(GC.GetGeneration(s));        // => 0
// Make it survive a first garbage collection.
GC.Collect(); GC.WaitForPendingFinalizers();
Console.WriteLine(GC.GetGeneration(s));        // => 1
// Make it survive a second garbage collection.
GC.Collect(); GC.WaitForPendingFinalizers();
Console.WriteLine(GC.GetGeneration(s));        // => 2
// Subsequent garbage collections don't increment the generation counter.
GC.Collect(); GC.WaitForPendingFinalizers();
Console.WriteLine(GC.GetGeneration(s));        // => 2
```

The GC.Collect method is overloaded to take a generation value as an argument, which results in the garbage collection of all the objects whose generation is lower than or equal to that value:

```
// Reclaim memory for unused objects in generation 0.
GC.Collect(0);
```

In general, the preceding statement is faster than running a complete garbage collection. To understand why, let's examine the three steps of the garbage collection process:

1. The garbage collector marks root objects and in general all the objects directly or indirectly reachable from the application.

2. The heap is compacted, and all the marked (that is, reachable) objects are moved toward the beginning of the managed heap to create a block of free memory near the end of the heap. Objects are sorted in the heap depending on their generation, with objects in generation 2 near the beginning of the heap and objects in generation 0 near the end of the heap, just before the free memory block. (To avoid time-consuming memory move operations, objects larger than approximately 85 KB are allocated in a separate heap that's never compacted.)

3. Root object variables in the main application are updated to point to the new positions of objects in the managed heap.

You speed up the second step (fewer objects must be moved in the heap) as well as the third step (because only a subset of all variables is updated) when you collect only generation-0 objects. Under certain conditions, even the first step is completed in less time, but this optimization technique might seem counterintuitive and requires an additional explanation.

Let's say that the garbage collector reaches a generation-1 object while traversing the object graph. Let's call this object A. In general, the collector can't simply ignore the portion of the object graph that has object A as its root because this object might point to one or more generation-0 objects that need to be marked. (For example, this might happen if object A is an array that contains objects created later in the program's lifetime.) However, the CLR can detect whether fields of object A have been modified since the previous garbage collection. If it turns out that object A hasn't been written to in the meantime, it means that object A can point only to generation-1 and generation-2 objects, so there is no reason for the collector to analyze that portion of the object graph because it was analyzed during the previous garbage collection and can't point to any generation-0 object. (Of course, similar reasoning applies when you use the GC.Collect(1) statement to collect only generation-0 and generation-1 objects.)

The CLR often attempts to collect only generation-0 objects to improve overall performance; if the garbage collection succeeds in freeing sufficient memory, no further steps are taken. Otherwise, the CLR attempts to collect generation-0 and generation-1 objects; if this second attempt fails to free enough memory, it collects all three generations. This means that older-generation objects might live undisturbed in the heap a long time after the application has logically killed them. The exact details of the type of garbage collection the CLR performs each time are vastly undocumented and might change over time.

 You can determine how many garbage collections of a given generation have occurred by querying the new CollectionCount method of the GC type:

```
// Determine how many gen-2 collections have occurred so far.
int count = GC.CollectionCount(2);
```

Garbage Collection and Performance

Before moving to a different topic, I want to show you how efficiently .NET manages memory. Let's again run a code snippet similar to the one I showed in the section titled "The Finalize Method" earlier in this chapter, but comment out the statement that explicitly sets the Person object to null:

```
// Compile this code with optimizations enabled.
static void Main()
{
    Debug.WriteLine("About to create a Person object.");
    Person aPerson = new Person("John", "Evans");
    // aPerson = null
    // After this point, aPerson is a candidate for garbage collection.
    Debug.WriteLine("About to fire a garbage collection.");
    GC.Collect();
    GC.WaitForPendingFinalizers();
    Debug.WriteLine("About to terminate the application.");
}
```

You might expect that the Person object is kept alive until the method exits. However, if optimizations are enabled, the JIT compiler is smart enough to detect that the object isn't used after the call to its constructor, so it marks it as a candidate for garbage collection. As a result, the code behaves exactly as if you explicitly set the variable to null after the last statement that references it. In other words, setting a variable to null as soon as you are done with an object doesn't necessarily make your code more efficient because the JIT compiler can apply this optimization technique automatically.

In at least one special case, however, explicitly setting a variable to null can affect performance positively. This happens when you destroy an object in the middle of a loop. In this case, the C# compiler can't automatically detect whether the variable is going to be used during subsequent iterations of the loop, and therefore the garbage collector can't automatically reclaim the memory used by the object. By clearing the object variable explicitly, you can help the garbage collector understand that the object can be reclaimed.

```
Person aPerson = new Person("John", "Evans");

// Use the aPerson object inside the loop.
for ( int i = 1; i <= 100; i++ )
{
    Console.WriteLine("Iteration #{0}", i);
    if ( i <= 50 )
    {
        // Use the object only in the first 50 iterations.
        ...
        // Explicitly set the variable to null after its last use.
        if ( i == 50 )
        {
            aPerson = null;
        }
    }
    else
    {
        // Do something else here, but don't use the aPerson variable.
        ...
```

```
    // Simulate a GC because of memory shortage
    if ( i == 99 )
    {
        GC.Collect(); GC.WaitForPendingFinalizers();
    }
  }
}
```

The fact that an object can be destroyed any time after the last time you reference it in code, and well before its reference goes out of scope, can have a surprisingly dangerous effect if the object wraps an unmanaged resource that is freed in the object's Finalize method. Say that you have authored a type named WinFile, which opens a file using the OpenFile API method and closes the file in the Finalize method:

```
void TestWinFile()
{
    WinFile wfile = new WinFile("data.txt");
    int handle = wfile.Handle;
    // Process the file by passing the handle to native Windows methods.
    ...
    // (The file is automatically closed in WinFile's finalizer.)
}
```

The problem here is that the garbage collector might collect the WinFile object and indirectly fire its Finalize method, which in turn would close the file before the procedure has completed its tasks. You might believe that adding a reference to the WinFile object at the end of the procedure would do the trick, but you'd be wrong. Consider this code:

```
void TestWinFile()
{
    ...
    // A failed attempt to keep the object alive until the end of the method
    DoNothingProc(wfile);
}

void DoNothingProc(object obj)
{
    // No code here
}
```

Surprisingly, the C# compiler is smart enough to realize that the DoNothingProc doesn't really use the object reference, and therefore passing the object to this procedure won't keep the WinFile object alive. The only method that is guaranteed to work in this case is the GC.KeepAlive method, whose name says it all:

```
void TestWinFile()
{
    ...
    // Keep the object alive until the end of the method.
    GC.KeepAlive(wfile);
}
```

In practice, however, you should never need the GC.KeepAlive method. In fact, if you authored the WinFile type correctly, it should expose the IDisposable interface, and therefore the actual code should look like this:

```
void TestWinFile()
{
    using ( WinFile wfile = new WinFile("data.txt") )
    {
        int handle = wfile.Handle;
        // Process the file by passing the handle to native Windows methods.
        ...
    }
}
```

The GC object in Microsoft .NET Framework version 2.0 has two new methods that enable you to let the garbage collector know that an unmanaged object consuming a lot of memory has been allocated or released so that the collector can fine-tune its performance and optimize its scheduling. You should invoke the AddMemoryPressure method to inform the garbage collector that the specified number of bytes has been allocated in the unmanaged memory; after releasing the object, you should invoke the RemoveMemoryPressure method to notify the CLR that an unmanaged object has been released and that the specified amount of memory is available again.

```
// Allocate an unmanaged object that takes approximately 1 MB of memory.
UnmanagedResource obj = new UnmanagedResource();
GC.AddMemoryPressure(1048576);                          // = 2^20
...
// Release the object here.
obj = null;
GC.RemoveMemoryPressure(1048576);
```

Even though .NET garbage collection is quite efficient, it can be a major source of overhead. In fact, not counting file and database operations, garbage collection is among the slowest activities that can take place during your application's lifetime; thus, it's your responsibility to keep the number of collections to a minimum. If you suspect that an application is running slowly because of too frequent garbage collections, use the Profile utility to monitor the following performance counters of the .NET CLR Memory object, as shown in Figure 2-1:

- # Gen 0 Collections, # Gen 1 Collections, # Gen 2 Collections (the number of garbage collections fired by the CLR)

- % Time In GC (the percentage of CPU time spent performing garbage collections)

- Gen 0 Heap Size, Gen 1 Heap Size, Gen 2 Heap Size, Large Object Heap Size (the size of the four heaps used by the garbage collector)

- # Bytes In All Heaps (the sum of the four heaps used by the application, that is, Generation-0, Generation-1, Generation-2, and Large Object heaps)

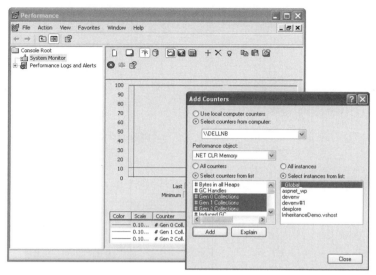

Figure 2-1   Using the Performance utility to monitor .NET memory performance counters

If the value of the first two sets of counters is suspiciously high, you can conclude that garbage collections are killing your application's performance and you should browse your source code looking for the causes of the higher-than-usual activity of the managed heap. I have compiled a list of issues you should pay attention to and which counters can help you solve your performance problem:

a.   Consider whether you can reduce the usage of the managed heap by defining structs instead of sealed classes. A local variable holding a struct is allocated on the stack and doesn't take space in the managed heap. On the other hand, the assignment of a structure to an object variable causes the structure to be boxed, which takes memory from the heap and adds overhead, so you should take this detail into account when opting for a structure. Also, don't use a struct if your type implements one or more interfaces because invoking a method through an interface variable forces the boxing of the structure.

b.   Use char variables instead of string variables if possible because char is a value type and char objects don't take space in the managed heap. More important, attempt to reduce the number of temporary strings used in expressions. When many concatenation operations are involved, use a StringBuilder object. (I cover the StringBuilder type in Chapter 1, ".NET Framework Basic Types.")

c.   Allocate disposable objects inside using blocks; if a using block can't be used, allocate the disposable object inside a try...catch block and invoke the Dispose method from inside the finally clause.

d. Allocate long-lasting objects earlier and assign them to variables that are never destroyed during the application life cycle, for example, static fields of a type that hold all the global variables in the application. This technique ensures that these objects will be moved near the beginning of the managed heap when the application starts and won't move from there during the application's lifetime. You can detect whether you have many objects that are candidates for this treatment by monitoring the Protected Memory From Gen 0 and Protected Memory From Gen 1 performance counters.

e. Avoid creating objects larger than about 85 KB if possible. An example of a large object is an array of Double numbers (8 bytes each) with more than about 10,880 elements. These large objects are stored in a separate area known as the large objects heap; moving these large objects in memory would add too much overhead, and therefore .NET never compacts this heap. As a result, the large object heap might become fragmented. You can detect whether you have many large objects by looking at the Large Object Heap Size performance counter.

f. As a rule, never fire a garbage collection by means of the GC.Collect method. In client applications, such as a Console or a Windows Forms application, you might start a collection only after an intensive user-interface action, for example, after loading or saving a file, so that the user won't perceive the extra overhead. Never use the GC.Collect method from inside a server-side application, such as an ASP.NET application or a COM+ library. You can detect whether you have too many GC.Collect methods in your code by monitoring the # Induced GC performance counter.

g. Never implement the Finalize method without a good reason to do so. If you do need a Finalize method, adopt the recommended pattern described earlier in this chapter. You can detect whether your finalizable objects can be the cause of a performance problem by looking at the Finalization Survivors performance counter.

h. If you must implement the Finalize method, ensure that the object doesn't take a significant amount of managed memory in addition to unmanaged resources. You can achieve this by wrapping the unmanaged resource in a nested class, as described in the section titled "A Simplified Approach to Finalization" earlier in this chapter.

Weak Object References

The .NET Framework provides a special type of object reference that doesn't keep an object alive: the *weak reference*. A weakly referenced object can be reclaimed during a garbage collection and must be re-created afterward if you want to use it again. Typical candidates for this technique are objects that take a lot of memory but whose state can be re-created with relatively little effort. For example, consider a class whose main purpose is to provide an optimized cache for the contents of text files. Traditionally, whenever you cache a large amount of data you must decide how much memory you set aside for the cache, but reserving too much memory for the cache might make the overall performance worse.

You don't have this dilemma if you use weak references. You can store as much data in the cache as you wish because you know that the system will automatically reclaim that memory when it needs it. Here's the complete source code for the CachedFile class:

```csharp
public class CachedFile
{
    // The name of the file cached
    public readonly string Filename;
    // A weak reference to the string that contains the text
    public WeakReference wrText;

    // The constructor takes the name of the file to read.
    public CachedFile(string filename)
    {
        this.Filename = filename;
    }

    // Read the contents of the file.
    private string ReadFile()
    {
        string text = File.ReadAllText(Filename);
        // Create a weak reference to this string.
        wrText = new WeakReference(text);
        return text;
    }

    // Return the textual content of the file.
    public string GetText()
    {
        object text = null;
        // Retrieve the target of the weak reference.
        if ( wrText != null )
        {
            text = wrText.Target;
        }

        if ( text != null )
        {
            // If nonnull, the data is still in the cache.
            return text.ToString();
        }
        else
        {
            // Otherwise, read it and put it in the cache again.
            return ReadFile();
        }
    }
}
```

There are two points of interest in this class. First, the ReadFile passes the value to be returned to the caller (the text variable) to the constructor of the WeakReference type and therefore creates a weak reference to the string. The second point of interest is in the GetText method, in which the code queries the WeakReference.Target property. If this property returns a non-null value, it means the weak reference hasn't been broken and still points to the original, cached string. Otherwise, the ReadFile method is invoked so that the file contents are read from disk and cached once again before being returned to the caller. Using the Cached-File type is easy:

```
// Read and cache the contents of the "book.txt" file.
CachedFile cf = new CachedFile("book.txt");
Console.WriteLine(cf.GetText());
…
// Uncomment next line to force a garbage collection.
// GC.Collect(); GC.WaitForPendingFinalizers();
…
// Read the contents again sometime later.
// (No disk access is performed, unless a GC has occurred in the meantime.)
Console.WriteLine(cf.GetText());
```

By tracing into the CachedFile class, you can easily prove that in most cases the file contents can be retrieved through the weak reference and that the disk isn't accessed again. By uncommenting the statement in the middle of the previous code snippet, however, you force a garbage collection, in which case the internal WeakReference object won't keep the string object alive and the code in the class will read the file again. The key point in this technique is that the client code doesn't know whether the cached data is used or a disk access is required. It just uses the CachedFile object as an optimized building block for dealing with large text files.

Remember that you create a weak reference by passing your object to the constructor of a System.WeakReference object. However, if the object is also pointed to by a regular, nonweak reference, it will survive any intervening garbage collection. In our example, this means that the code using the CachedFile class should not store the return value of the GetText method in a string variable because that would prevent the string from being garbage collected until that variable is explicitly set to null or goes out of scope:

```
// The wrong way to use the CachedFile class
CachedFile cf = new CachedFile("alargefile.txt");
string text = cf.GetText();
// The text string will survive any garbage collection.
```

Object Resurrection

Weak references are fine to create a cache of objects that are frequently used and that can be re-created in a relatively short time. The technique I illustrate in this section offers a slightly different solution to the same problem.

Earlier in this chapter, I briefly described the technique known as *object resurrection* through which an object being finalized can store a reference to itself in a variable defined outside the current instance so that this new reference keeps the object alive. Object resurrection is likely to be useful only in unusual scenarios, such as when you're implementing a pool of objects whose creation and destruction are time-consuming. For example, consider the following sample class, which implements an array containing a sequence of random Double values:

```csharp
public class RandomArray : IDisposable
{
    // This array stores the elements.
    public readonly double[] Values;

    // The constructor creates the random array.
    private RandomArray(int length)
    {
        Values = new double[length];
        Random rand = new Random();
        // This is a time-consuming operation.
        for ( int i = 0; i < length; i++ )
        {
            Values[i] = rand.NextDouble();
        }
    }
}
```

(Notice that you'll typically apply resurrection to objects that are far more complicated than this one and that use unmanaged resources as well. I am using RandomArray only for illustration purposes.)

If the main application creates and destroys thousands of RandomArray objects, it makes sense to implement a mechanism by which a RandomArray object is returned to an internal pool when the application doesn't need it any longer; if the application later requests another RandomArray object with the same number of elements, the object is taken from the pool instead of going through the relatively slow initialization process.

The internal pool is implemented as a static ArrayList object. To ensure that the application uses a pooled object, if available, the RandomArray class has a private constructor and a static public factory method named Create. Also, the class implements a finalizer to ensure that the instance is correctly returned to the pool when the application has finished with it. Here's the new version of the class:

```csharp
public class RandomArray : IDisposable
{
    // This array stores the elements.
    public readonly double[] Values;

    // The constructor creates the random array.
    private RandomArray(int length)
    {
        Values = new double[length];
        Random rand = new Random();
```

```
        // This is a time-consuming operation.
        for ( int i = 0; i < length; i++ )
        {
            Values[i] = rand.NextDouble();
        }
    }

    // Dispose and Finalize methods

    public void Dispose()
    {
        // Return this object to the pool.
        Pool.Add(this);
        GC.SuppressFinalize(this);
    }

    ~RandomArray()
    {
        Dispose();
    }

    // Static members

    // The pool of objects
    private static ArrayList Pool = new ArrayList();

    // The factory method
    public static RandomArray Create(int length)
    {
        // Check whether there is an element in the pool with the
        // requested number of elements.
        for ( int i = 0; i < Pool.Count; i++ )
        {
            RandomArray ra = (RandomArray) Pool[i];
            if ( ra.Values.Length == length )
            {
                // Remove the element from the pool.
                Pool.RemoveAt(i);
                // Reregister for finalization, in case no Dispose method is invoked.
                GC.ReRegisterForFinalize(ra);
                return ra;
            }
        }
        // If no suitable element is in the pool, create a new element.
        return new RandomArray(length);
    }
}
```

The key point in the previous code is the GC.ReRegisterForFinalize method call in the Create method. Without this call, the object handed to the application wouldn't execute the Finalize method, and therefore it would miss the chance of being returned to the pool when the application logically destroys the object. Also, the RandomArray class exposes the

IDisposable interface, and thus the client can explicitly return objects to the pool by invoking the Dispose method.

Here's a piece of code that uses the RandomArray object:

```
// Create a few RandomArray instances.
RandomArray ra1 = RandomArray.Create(10000);
RandomArray ra2 = RandomArray.Create(20000);
RandomArray ra3 = RandomArray.Create(30000);
// Clear some of them.
ra2 = null;
ra3 = null;
// Simulate a GC, which moves the objects to the pool.
GC.Collect(); GC.WaitForPendingFinalizers();

// Create a few more objects, which will be taken from the pool.
RandomArray ra4 = RandomArray.Create(20000);
RandomArray ra5 = RandomArray.Create(30000);
```

A pooled object might improve performance in other ways, for example, by creating a few instances in advance so that no initialization time is spent when the application asks for them. Object pooling can be useful in cases when performance isn't the main issue: for example, when you have a threshold for the number of objects that can be created.

Garbage Collection on Multiple-CPU Computers

When the .NET runtime is executing on a workstation, it's important that the user interface work as smoothly as possible, even at the cost of some loss of overall performance. On the other hand, performance becomes the top priority when an enterprise-level .NET application runs on a server machine. To account for these differences, the .NET Framework includes two types of garbage collectors: the workstation version and the multiple-CPU server version.

When running on a single-CPU machine, the collector always works in workstation mode. In this mode, the collector runs on a concurrent thread to minimize pauses, but the additional thread-switching activity can slow the application as a whole. When the workstation version is used on a multiple-CPU system, you have the option of running the garbage collector in concurrent mode: in this case, the GC thread runs on a separate CPU to minimize pauses. You activate concurrent mode by adding an entry to the configuration file:

```
<configuration>
   <runtime>
      <gcConcurrent enabled="true" />
   </runtime>
</configuration>
```

When the server version is used, objects are allocated from multiple heaps; the program freezes during a garbage collection, and each CPU works concurrently to compact one of the heaps. This technique improves overall performance and scales well when you install additional CPUs. The server version can be used only on multiple-CPU systems or on systems equipped with a hyperthreaded CPU.

In earlier versions of the .NET Framework, the server and the workstation versions of the garbage collector reside in different DLLs (mscorsvr.dll and mscorwks.dll) and you explicitly must select a different DLL to enable the server version. In .NET Framework 2.0, the two versions have been merged in the mscorwks.dll and you enable the server version by adding an entry to the configuration file:

```
<configuration>
   <runtime>
      <gcServer enabled="true" />
   </runtime>
</configuration>
```

Also new in .NET Framework 2.0 is the System.Runtime.GCSettings type, which exposes a static property that enables you to detect whether the server version of the garbage collector is used:

```
if ( System.Runtime.GCSettings.IsServerGC )
{
   Console.WriteLine("The server version of the garbage collector is used.");
}
```

Chapter 3
Interfaces

All developers should be very familiar with interfaces, for at least two reasons. First, you can often streamline the structure of your applications by defining your own interfaces. Second, the Microsoft .NET Framework defines many important interfaces and you should learn how to fully exploit their potential, either by invoking their methods or by implementing them in your own types. As a matter of fact, interfaces are one of the pillars on which the design of a .NET application can be based, together with other concepts such as inheritance and custom attributes.

Note To avoid long lines, code samples in this chapter assume that the following using statements are used at the top of each source file:

```
using System;
using System.Collections;
using System.Collections.Generic;
using System.Data;
using System.Diagnostics;
using System.IO;
using System.Runtime.Serialization;
using System.Windows.Forms;
```

Interfaces and Code Reuse

In my experience, many developers fail to grasp the potential that interfaces have in simplifying the structure of a .NET application and improving code reuse. Many books and introductory articles on interfaces, in fact, focus mainly on the syntactical details and omit explaining exactly *why* you should use interfaces in the first place.

To illustrate the power of interfaces, I must offer a moderately complex example. In general, you author an interface to define a group of methods and properties that, taken together, implement a specific feature or set of features. For example, you might define an IDataRowPersistable interface that contains the methods that enable an object to load and save its state to a row in a DataTable:

```
public interface IDataRowPersistable
{
    object PrimaryKey { get; }
    void Save(DataRow row);
    void Load(DataRow row);
}
```

As you can see, the interface is absolutely generic and can be used by any object that requires this capability. For example, a Student class might implement it as follows:

```
public class Student : IDataRowPersistable
{
    // These should be properties in a real-world class.
    public string FirstName;
    public string LastName;
    public DateTime BirthDate;
    // The primary key for this object is private.
    private Guid ID = Guid.Empty;

    // Two constructors
    public Student(string firstName, string lastName, DateTime birthDate)
    {
        this.FirstName = firstName;
        this.LastName = lastName;
        this.BirthDate = birthDate;
    }

    // A parameterless (default) constructor
    public Student()
    { }

    // Return the primary key of this object.
    public object PrimaryKey
    {
        get
        {
            // Generate the ID only when needed.
            if (this.ID.Equals(Guid.Empty))
            {
                this.ID = Guid.NewGuid();
            }
            return this.ID;
        }
    }

    public void Load(DataRow row)
    {
        this.ID = (Guid) row["ID"];
        this.FirstName = (string) row["FirstName"];
        this.LastName = (string) row["LastName"];
        this.BirthDate = (DateTime) row["BirthDate"];
    }
```

```
    public void Save(DataRow row)
    {
        // Save the ID only if the primary key field is null.
        if (DBNull.Value.Equals(row["ID"]))
        {
            row["ID"] = this.ID;
        }
        row["FirstName"] = this.FirstName;
        row["LastName"] = this.LastName;
        row["BirthDate"] = this.BirthDate;
    }

}
```

Here's an example of how a program might use the IDataRowPersistable interface to save an array of Student objects into a DataTable and load it back:

```
// Define a DataTable with four fields.
DataTable table = new DataTable();
// Create the ID column and make it the primary key for this table.
DataColumn idCol = table.Columns.Add("ID", typeof(Guid));
table.PrimaryKey = new DataColumn[] { idCol };
table.Columns.Add("FirstName", typeof(string));
table.Columns.Add("LastName", typeof(string));
table.Columns.Add("BirthDate", typeof(DateTime));

// Save an array of Student objects into the DataTable.
Student[] students = { new Student("John", "Evans", new DateTime(1965, 1, 2)),
    new Student("Ann", "Beebe", new DateTime(1972, 8, 17)),
    new Student("Robert", "Zare", new DateTime(1973, 11, 1)) };
Functions.SaveObjects(table, students);

// Load an array of Student objects from the DataTable.
Student[] newStudents = new Student[table.Rows.Count];
for (int i = 0; i < newStudents.Length; i++)
{
    newStudents[i] = new Student();
}
Functions.LoadObjects(table, newStudents);
```

The Functions class contains the helper methods that move an array of IDataRowPersistable objects to and from a DataTable:

```
public static void SaveObjects(DataTable table, IDataRowPersistable[] array)
{
    // Retrieve the primary key name. (Multiple column keys aren't supported.)
    string pkName = table.PrimaryKey[0].ColumnName;
    // Create a DataView sorted on the primary key.
    DataView dataView = new DataView(table);
    dataView.Sort = pkName;

    foreach ( IDataRowPersistable obj in array )
    {
        // Search for the corresponding DataRow in the table.
        DataRow row = null;
        int rowIndex = dataView.Find(obj.PrimaryKey);
```

```
        if ( rowIndex >= 0 )
        {
            // If found, get a reference to the corresponding DataRow.
            row = table.Rows[rowIndex];
        }
        else
        {
            // If not found, this is a new object.
            row = table.NewRow();
        }
        // Ask the object to save itself.
        obj.Save(row);
        // Add to the DataTable if it was a new row.
        if (rowIndex < 0)
        {
            table.Rows.Add(row);
        }
    }
}

public static void LoadObjects(DataTable table, IDataRowPersistable[] array)
{
    // Load each object with data from a DataRow.
    for ( int i = 0; i < table.Rows.Count; i++ )
    {
        DataRow row = table.Rows[i];
        array[i].Load(row);
    }
}
```

If you look carefully at the source code of the SaveObjects and LoadObjects methods, you won't see any reference to the Student type. In fact, these methods are absolutely generic and work with any type that implements the IDataRowPersistable interface and has a default constructor. Thanks to this interface, you created a piece of *polymorphic code* that you can reuse with many other types. For example, you might define an Employee type that implements the IDataRowPersistable interface and can still reuse much of the code that moves data to and from a DataTable (except you need a DataTable with a different schema).

At times it's difficult to understand whether a given set of features should be implemented by means of an interface or by inheriting from a base class. In general, inheriting from a base class is better in terms of code conciseness because you can implement common functionality right in the base class. However, inheritance wouldn't help much in the case just shown because each derived class would need to override the methods of the IDataRowPersistable interface to account for the different name and type of their members.

In other cases, you can't leverage inheritance because the types already have a base class. For example, all Microsoft Windows Forms controls inherit from the System.Windows.Forms .Control base class, so if you had defined a given functionality by means of a base class, you couldn't use it with a Microsoft Windows control because .NET doesn't support multiple inheritance.

In real-world applications, you can often mix interfaces and reflection techniques to make your code even more generic and reusable. For example, in Chapter 12, "Reflection," you'll see how you can implement the ISerializable interface with code that works well regardless of the type being serialized or deserialized.

Using .NET Interfaces

The .NET Framework defines and consumes dozens of different interfaces, and expert Microsoft Visual C# developers should learn how to use them profitably. In this section, you'll see how a few such system-wide interfaces can make your life simpler.

The IComparable Interface

The System.Array class exposes the Sort static method, which enables you to sort an array of simple data types, such as numbers or strings. However, this method can't directly sort more complex objects, such as Person, because it doesn't know how two Person objects compare with each other.

Implementing the IComparable interface makes your objects sortable by means of the Sort method exposed by many types in the .NET Framework, such as Array and ArrayList. This interface exposes only one method, CompareTo, which receives an object and is expected to return −1, 0, or 1, depending on whether the object on which CompareTo is called is less than, equal to, or greater than the object passed as an argument. Let's see how you can define a Person class that's sortable on its ReverseName property:

```
public class Person : IComparable
{
    // Public fields (should be properties in a real-world class)
    public string FirstName;
    public string LastName;

    // A simple constructor
    public Person(string firstName, string lastName)
    {
        this.FirstName = firstName;
        this.LastName = lastName;
    }

    // A property that returns the name in the format "Evans, John"
    public string ReverseName
    {
        get { return LastName + ", " + FirstName; }
    }

    // A property that returns a name in the format "John Evans"
    public string CompleteName
    {
        get { return FirstName + " " + LastName; }
    }
```

```
// This private procedure adds sorting capabilities to the class.
int IComparable.CompareTo(object obj)
{
    // Any nonnull object is greater than null.
    if ( obj == null )
    {
        return 1;
    }
    else
    {
        // Cast to Person; error if the argument is of a different type.
        Person other = (Person) obj;
        // Compare strings in case-insensitive mode.
        return string.Compare(this.ReverseName, other.ReverseName, true);
    }
}
}
```

Here's the client code that demonstrates how the IComparable interface works:

```
Person[] persons = { new Person("John", "Evans"),
    new Person("Robert", "Zare"), new Person("Robert", "Evans") };
Array.Sort(persons);
// Display all the elements in sorted order.
foreach ( Person p in persons )
{
    Console.WriteLine(p.ReverseName);
}
```

Notice that the implementation of CompareTo is less than optimal because it creates a lot of temporary strings (the results of calls to ReverseName), which can significantly slow down your application. Here's an implementation that's less concise and less linear, but faster:

```
int IComparable.CompareTo(object obj)
{
    // Any nonnull object is greater than null.
    if ( obj == null )
    {
        return 1;
    }

    // Cast to Person; error if the argument is of a different type.
    Person other = (Person) obj;
    // Compare LastName first.
    int result = string.Compare(this.LastName, other.LastName, true);
    if (result == 0)
    {
        // Compare FirstName only if the two persons have same last name.
        result = string.Compare(this.FirstName, other.FirstName, true);
    }
    return result;
}
```

The IComparer Interface

The IComparable interface is all you need when your objects can be compared in only one way. Most real-world objects, however, can be compared and sorted on different fields or field combinations; in such cases, you can use a variation of the Array.Sort method that takes an IComparer interface as its second argument. The IComparer interface exposes only one method, Compare, which receives two object references and returns −1, 0, or 1, depending on whether the first object is less than, equal to, or greater than the second object.

A class that can be sorted on different field combinations might expose two or more nested classes that implement the IComparer interface, one class for each possible sort method. For example, you might want to sort the Person class on either the (LastName, FirstName) or (FirstName, LastName) field combination; these combinations correspond to the ReverseName and CompleteName read-only properties in the code that follows. Here's a new version of the class that supports these features:

```csharp
public class Person : IComparable
{
   // (Definition of fields, properties, and constructor omitted)
   …

   // First nested class, to sort on CompleteName
   public class ComparerByName : IComparer
   {
      public int Compare(object o1, object o2)
      {
         // Two null objects are equal.
         if ( (o1 == null) && (o2 == null) )
         {
            return 0;
         }
         // Any nonnull object is greater than a null object.
         if (o1 == null )
         {
            return 1;
         }
         else if ( o2 == null )
         {
            return -1;
         }

         // Cast both objects to Person, and do the comparison.
         // (Throws an exception if arguments aren't Person objects.)
         Person p1 = (Person)o1;
         Person p2 = (Person)o2;
         return string.Compare(p1.CompleteName, p2.CompleteName, true);
      }
   }
}
```

```
// Second nested class, to sort on ReverseName
public class ComparerByReverseName : IComparer
{
    public int Compare(object o1, object o2)
    {
        // Two null objects are equal.
        if ( (o1 == null) && (o2 == null) )
        {
            return 0;
        }
        // Any nonnull object is greater than a null object.
        if ( o1 == null )
        {
            return 1;
        }
        else if ( o2 == null )
        {
            return -1;
        }

        // Save code by casting to Person objects on the fly.
        return string.Compare((o1 as Person).ReverseName,
            (o2 as Person).ReverseName, true);
    }
}
}
}
```

In a real-world class, you should avoid all the temporary strings created by calls to Complete-Name and ReverseName properties and compare the LastName and FirstName properties individually, as described at the end of the section titled "The IComparable Interface" earlier in this chapter. Using the two auxiliary classes is straightforward:

```
Person[] persons = { new Person("John", "Frum"),
    new Person("Robert", "Zare"), new Person("John", "Evans") };
// Sort the array on complete name.
Array.Sort(persons, new Person.ComparerByName());
// Sort the array on reversed name.
Array.Sort(persons, new Person.ComparerByReverseName());
```

When comparing strings, keep in mind that string comparisons are based on the current locale, or more precisely on the value of Thread.CurrentCulture. The StringComparer object exposes a few static read-only properties that return an IComparer object able to compare strings in a specific way. For example, you can use the StringComparer.Ordinal property to perform case-sensitive comparisons:

```
// arr is a string array.
Array.Sort<string>(arr, StringComparer.Ordinal);
```

The StringComparer.CurrentCultureIgnoreCase property returns an IComparer object that compares strings in case-insensitive mode according to the current culture, whereas the

InvariantCultureIgnoreCase does the same kind of comparison but according to the invariant culture. Read the section titled "Comparing and Searching Strings" in Chapter 1, ".NET Framework Basic Types," for more details.

Quite oddly, the .NET Framework doesn't allow you to sort an array in descending order; thus, the best you can do is sort the array as usual and then call the Array.Reverse method. A more efficient way to achieve this result would be to include a *reverse comparer*, that is, a comparer class that returns the negated result of the comparison. Instead of creating several reverse comparers, you're better off defining an adapter class that takes an IComparer object, uses it to do the comparison, but returns the negated result. The following ReverseComparer type implements this concept and, as an added touch, attempts to use the IComparable interface of either argument passed to the Compare method if the client didn't pass any IComparer object when instantiating the ReverseComparer object:

```
public class ReverseComparer : IComparer
{
    // The inner IComparer object
    private IComparer icomp;

    public ReverseComparer() : this(null)
    { }

    public ReverseComparer(IComparer icomp)
    {
        this.icomp = icomp;
    }

    public int Compare(object x, object y)
    {
        if ( icomp != null )
        {
            // Use inner IComparer object if possible; notice arguments in reverse order.
            return icomp.Compare(y, x);
        }
        else if (x != null && x is IComparable)
        {
            // Use x's IComparable interface; negate result to get the reverse effect.
            return -(x as IComparable).CompareTo(y);
        }
        else if (y != null && y is IComparable)
        {
            // Use y's IComparable interface. (No need to negate the result)
            return (y as IComparable).CompareTo(x);
        }
        else
        {
            throw new ArgumentException("Neither argument is IComparable");
        }
    }
}
```

Using the ReverseComparer is simple. Here's how you can sort a string array in reverse order, both in case-sensitive and case-insensitive modes:

```
string[] arr = { "a", "c", "f", "b", "z", "q" };
// Reverse sort of a string array in case-sensitive mode
Array.Sort(arr, new ReverseComparer());
// Reverse sort of a string array in case-insensitive mode
Array.Sort(arr, new ReverseComparer(StringComparer.CurrentCultureIgnoreCase));
```

The ICloneable Interface

Everything is an object under the .NET Framework. One consequence of this fact is that when you assign a variable to another variable, you get two variables pointing to the same object, rather than two distinct copies of the data. (In this discussion, I assume you're working with reference types, not value types.) Typically, you get a copy of the data by invoking a special method that the class exposes. In the .NET world, a class should implement the ICloneable interface and expose its only method, Clone, to let the outside world know that it can create a copy of its instances. Several objects in the framework implement this interface, including Array, ArrayList, BitArray, Font, Icon, Queue, and Stack.

Most of the time, implementing the ICloneable interface is straightforward, thanks to the MemberwiseClone protected method that all types inherit from System.Object. This method helps you clone an object without having to copy every property manually. See how you can use this method to implement a cloneable Employee class:

```
public class Employee : ICloneable
{
    public string FirstName;
    public string LastName;
    public Employee Boss;

    public Employee(string firstName, string lastName)
    {
        this.FirstName = firstName;
        this.LastName = lastName;
    }

    public object Clone()
    {
        return this.MemberwiseClone();
    }
}
```

The ICloneable interface is never called by the .NET runtime, and its only purpose is to provide a standardized way to let other developers know that your class supports cloning by means of a well-established syntax:

```
// Define an employee and his boss.
Employee john = new Employee("John", "Evans");
Employee robert = new Employee("Robert", "Zare");
```

```
john.Boss = robert;

// Clone it. The Clone method returns a generic object, so you need a cast.
Employee john2 = (Employee) john.Clone();
// Prove that all properties were copied.
Console.WriteLine("{0} {1}, whose boss is {2} {3}", john2.FirstName,
    john2.LastName, john2.Boss.FirstName, john2.Boss.LastName);
    // => John Evans, whose boss is Robert Zare
```

Shallow Copies and Deep Copies

You can perform two kinds of copy operations on an object. A *shallow copy* creates a copy of only the object in question. It doesn't make copies of secondary objects (or *child objects*) referenced by it. In contrast, a *deep copy* operation clones all secondary objects as well. The following code snippet makes this difference clear:

```
// Define an employee and his boss.
Employee john = new Employee("John", "Evans");
Employee robert = new Employee("Robert", "Zare");
john.Boss = robert;

// Clone it, and prove that the Employee object was cloned into a
// distinct instance, but his boss wasn't.
Employee john2 = (Employee) john.Clone();
Console.WriteLine(john == john2);            // => False
Console.WriteLine(john.Boss == john2.Boss);  // => True
```

You can see the difference between shallow and deep copies with arrays. Say that you have an array containing 100 references to Employee instances. A shallow copy of this array would create only one new object, that is, another array whose elements point to the same 100 Employee instances as the original array. A deep copy would create *at least* 101 objects, that is, a copy of the array and one copy for each of the 100 Employee objects (possibly plus other child objects of these Employee instances).

When shallow copying isn't enough and you really need to create a clone of the entire object graph that has the object at its root, you can't rely on the MemberwiseClone method alone; you must manually copy properties of each object. Here's a new Employee2 class that correctly clones the entire object graph:

```
public class Employee2 : ICloneable
{
    public Employee2 Boss;
    // (Other fields and constructor as in Employee …)

    public object Clone()
    {
        // Start with a shallow copy of this object.
        // (This copies all nonobject properties in one operation.)
        Employee2 em = (Employee2) this.MemberwiseClone();
```

```
        // Manually copy the Boss property, reusing its Clone method.
        if ( em.Boss != null )
        {
            em.Boss = (Employee2) this.Boss.Clone();
        }
        return em;
    }
}
```

This new version of the Clone method is still concise because it uses the MemberwiseClone method to copy all nonobject values, and it builds on the Clone method for the secondary objects (only Boss, in this case). This approach also works if the employee's boss has a boss.

However, most real-world object graphs are more complex than this example is, and exposing a Clone method that works correctly isn't a trivial task. For example, if the Employee2 class had a Colleagues property (a collection holding other Employee2 objects), the ensuing circular references would cause the Clone method to enter a recursion that would end with a stack overflow error. Fortunately, the .NET Framework offers a clean solution to this problem, as you can read about in the section titled "Deep Object Cloning" in Chapter 12.

One last note: the semantics of the ICloneable interface doesn't specify whether the Clone method should return a shallow copy or a deep copy of the object; thus, you are free to choose the behavior that fits your needs. However, it is essential that you clearly document this detail in the documentation that comes with your class.

The IDisposable Interface

I cover the IDisposable interface in Chapter 2, "Object Lifetime," so I won't repeat here why types that use other disposable objects should use this interface. In this section, however, I want to show how you can take advantage of this interface together with the using block to implement an interesting behavior. Consider the following class:

```
public class CurrentDirectory : IDisposable
{
    public string oldPath;

    public CurrentDirectory(string newPath)
    {
        // Remember the current directory, and then change it.
        oldPath = Directory.GetCurrentDirectory();
        Directory.SetCurrentDirectory(newPath);
    }

    public void Restore()
    {
        // Restore the original current directory.
        Directory.SetCurrentDirectory(oldPath);
    }
```

```
   // Explicit (private) interface implementation of IDisposable.Dispose
   void IDisposable.Dispose()
   {
      Restore();
   }
}
```

This simple class enables you to write the following code:

```
using ( CurrentDirectory dir = new CurrentDirectory(@"c:\temp"))
{
   // Current directory is now c:\temp.

   ...
   // The original current directory is restored when the using block is exited.
}
```

It's as if the IDisposable interface, together with the using keyword, enables you to "schedule" an operation for execution at the end of a block of code. Interestingly, you can even nest these blocks and you can avoid using an explicit variable to point to the IDisposable class because your code doesn't access any of its methods:

```
using ( new CurrentDirectory(@"c:\temp") )
{
   // Current directory is now c:\temp.

   ...
   using ( new CurrentDirectory(@"c:\windows") )
   {
      // Current directory is now c:\windows.

      ...
      // The next statement restores c:\temp as the current directory.
   }
   ...
   // The next statement restores the original current directory.
}
```

You can extend this concept further and create other types of disposable classes like Current-Directory. For example, the following MouseCursor class enables you to set a mouse cursor for a given Windows Forms control or form and automatically restore it at the end of a code block:

```
public class MouseCursor : IDisposable
{
   public Control control;
   public Cursor oldCursor;

   public MouseCursor(Control ctrl, Cursor newCursor)
   {
      // Remember control and old cursor, and then enforce new cursor.
      control = ctrl;
      oldCursor = ctrl.Cursor;
      control.Cursor = newCursor;
   }
```

```
public void Restore()
{
   // Restore the original cursor.
   control.Cursor = oldCursor;
}

// Explicit (private) implementation of IDisposable.Dispose
void IDisposable.Dispose()
{
   Restore();
}
}
```

Using this class is much easier than is manually setting and restoring the mouse cursor during a lengthy operation:

```
// This code must run inside a form class.
using ( new MouseCursor(this, Cursors.WaitCursor) )
{
   // Perform the lengthy operation here.
   ...
   // Next statement restores the original mouse cursor.
}
```

Writing Collection Classes

When C# compiles a foreach statement, it checks that the object following the in keyword supports the IEnumerable interface. When the foreach statement is executed, the code generated by the compiler invokes the only method in this interface, GetEnumerator. This function must return an object that supports the IEnumerator interface, which in turn exposes the following three members: MoveNext, Current, and Reset. The MoveNext method is called at each iteration: it should return true if a new value is available and false if there are no more elements. The Current read-only property returns the value to be used in the current iteration of the loop. The Reset method resets the internal pointer so that the next returned value is the first one in a new series. (The Reset method is currently unused by the code the C# compiler generates.)

> **Note**   I cover collections in more depth in Chapter 5, "Arrays and Collections." In this section, I quickly review the many ways the .NET Framework provides for creating a custom collection, and then I focus on collection classes that implement the IEnumerable interface directly.

Using Abstract Collection Types

You can define a class that supports iteration in a foreach loop by inheriting from one of the many base types provided by the .NET Framework, for example, the CollectionBase, ReadOnlyCollectionBase, and DictionaryBase abstract classes defined in System.Collections.

For example, the following type enables you to iterate over all the lines of a text file; it doesn't allow you to add to or remove items from the collection of text lines; therefore, it inherits from the ReadOnlyCollectionBase type:

```
public class TextLineCollection : ReadOnlyCollectionBase
{
    public TextLineCollection(string path)
    {
        // Load the inner list with text lines in the specified file.
        using ( StreamReader sr = new StreamReader(path) )
        {
            while (sr.Peek() >= 0)
            {
                this.InnerList.Add(sr.ReadLine());
            }
        }
    }

    public string this[int index]
    {
        get { return (string) this.InnerList[index]; }
    }
}
```

Here's how you can use the TextLineCollection class:

```
TextLineCollection lines = new TextLineCollection(@"c:\windows\win.ini");
// Display the last line.
Console.WriteLine(lines[lines.Count - 1]);
// Display all lines in a foreach loop.
foreach ( string s in lines )
{
    Console.WriteLine(s);
}
```

In this specific example, the property is read-only because a client isn't supposed to change individual lines once the collection has been initialized. But don't believe that this detail has to do with the fact that the collection inherits from ReadOnlyCollectionBase. When applied to a collection, read-only means that the collection has a fixed size, not that individual elements aren't writable.

Using Generics

Microsoft Visual C# 2005 supports generics, so you can implement a collection type with less code than you need to use under previous language versions. For example, this is all the code that you need to implement a collection object of Person objects:

```
public class PersonCollection : List<Person>
{ }
```

The PersonCollection class is strongly typed and exposes all the members you would expect from a collection, including Add, Insert, Remove, RemoveAt, Count, and many others; unlike a weakly typed collection, though, you can add only Person instances to this collection:

```
PersonCollection col = new PersonCollection();
col.Add(new Person("John", "Evans"));    // This statement works fine.
col.Add("a string");                     // *** This statement doesn't compile.
```

Of course, the PersonCollection class supports the foreach loop:

```
foreach ( Person p in col )
{
    Console.WriteLine(p.CompleteName);
}
```

You can learn more about generics in Chapter 4, "Generics."

Implementing the IEnumerable and IEnumerator Interfaces

So far, I've illustrated how you can create a collection class by inheriting from the abstract classes or the generic classes that the .NET Framework defines. All these classes provide a default implementation of IEnumerable, the interface that is implicitly queried for when the collection appears in a foreach loop. However, nothing prevents you from implementing this interface directly, a technique that requires a lot more code but provides the greatest flexibility.

To illustrate these interfaces in action using a specific example, I created a TextFileReader class that enables you to iterate over all the lines in a text file within a foreach loop, without using any additional memory because text lines are read from the file one at a time:

```
public class TextFileReader : IEnumerable
{
    public string path;

    public TextFileReader(string path)
    {
        this.path = path;        // Remember for later.
    }

    public IEnumerator GetEnumerator()
    {
        // Return an instance of the inner enumerator.
        return new FileReaderEnumerator(path);
    }

    // The private enumerator (nested inside TextFileReader)
    ...
}
```

The GetEnumerator function returns a FileReaderEnumerator object. You can implement this class as a nested type inside FileReader. Interestingly, if the enumerator object in a foreach loop exposes the IDisposable interface, the C# compiler automatically invokes the object's Dispose method when the loop terminates normally or exits because of a break keyword. The FileReaderEnumerator class takes advantage of this detail to ensure that the stream is correctly closed as soon as it is no longer necessary.

```csharp
private class FileReaderEnumerator : IEnumerator, IDisposable
{
    public StreamReader sr;           // The stream reader
    public string currLine;           // The text line just read

    public FileReaderEnumerator(string path)
    {
        sr = new StreamReader(path);
    }

    // The IEnumerator interface (three methods)

    public bool MoveNext()
    {
        if (sr.Peek() >= 0)
        {
            // If not at end of file, read the next line.
            currLine = sr.ReadLine();
            return true;
        }
        else
        {
            // Else, return false to stop enumeration.
            return false;
        }
    }

    public object Current
    {
        // Return the line read by MoveNext.
        get { return currLine; }
    }

    public void Reset()
    {
        // This method is never called and can be empty.
    }

    public void Dispose()
    {
        // Close the stream when this object is disposed.
        sr.Close();
    }
}
```

Here's how a client can read one line at a time from a text file:

```
foreach ( string s in new TextFileReader("document.txt") )
{
   Console.WriteLine(s);
}
```

Iterators in C# 2.0

You probably agree that you need to write a lot of code to correctly implement the IEnumerable interface and the corresponding IEnumerator class. To make coding much easier, C# 2.0 introduces a new feature named *iterators*. Thanks to iterators, you need to write the code only for the GetEnumerator method of the IEnumerable interface and don't have to worry about the IEnumerator class because C# synthesizes this class for you.

To show the power of iterators, let's write a new version of the TextFileReader class that leverages this new feature:

```
public class TextFileReader2 : IEnumerable
{
   public string path;

   public TextFileReader2(string path)
   {
      this.path = path;              // Remember for later.
   }

   public IEnumerator GetEnumerator()
   {
      using ( StreamReader sr = new StreamReader(path) )
      {
         // Loop while there's something to read.
         while ( sr.Peek() >= 0 )
         {
            // Return the next line.
            yield return sr.ReadLine();
         }
      }
   }
}
```

The key point in the preceding listing is the yield return keyword, which stops the processing of the current method and returns a value to the foreach statement in the caller code. At the next iteration of the loop, the GetEnumerator method reenters at the statement following the yield return keyword. It's really that easy, and you've saved the nearly 30 lines of code of the FileReaderEnumerator class that was necessary in the first version that explicitly implemented the IEnumerator interface.

The GetEnumerator method can also contain the yield break keyword, which allows you to interrupt enumeration before its natural end. For example, assume that the TextFileReader2 class is expected to stop enumeration when it reads a blank line. In this case, you should change the GetEnumerator method as follows:

```
public IEnumerator GetEnumerator()
{
    using ( StreamReader sr = new StreamReader(path) )
    {
        // Loop while there's something to read.
        while ( sr.Peek() >= 0 )
        {
            string line = sr.ReadLine();
            // Stop enumeration when a blank line is met.
            if ( line.Length == 0 )
            {
                yield break;
            }
            else
            {
                // Else return the text line just read.
                yield return line;
            }
        }
    }
}
```

Even if iterators enable you to save a lot of coding, you should be aware that the C# compiler still creates an IEnumerator class for you behind the scenes. You can prove this point easily by disassembling the executable using ILDASM, as shown in Figure 3-1: the C# compiler has created a nested class named <GetEnumerator>d_0, which implements both the IEnumerator and the IDisposable interfaces, plus several IL opcodes that transparently create an instance of this class when the main application executes the foreach loop.

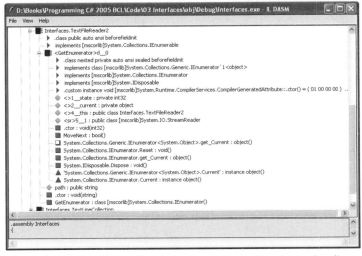

Figure 3-1   The effect of a yield return keyword as shown by disassembling the executable using ILDASM

The yield keyword can't appear inside an anonymous method, a block marked with the unsafe keyword, or a method that takes ref or out parameters. Also, a yield return keyword can't appear in a catch block or in a try block that has one or more catch clauses.

Interestingly, you can use the yield keyword in methods other than GetEnumerator. More precisely, you can use this keyword in any method that returns an IEnumerable object, even if the method is static or appears in a type that doesn't implement the IEnumerable interface. For example, the TextLineReader2 type might expose both the GetEnumerator method, which returns all the lines in the text file, and the GetLongLines method, which returns only the lines longer than the specified number of characters:

```
public IEnumerable GetLongLines(int minLength)
{
    using ( StreamReader sr = new StreamReader(path) )
    {
        // Loop while there's something to read.
        while ( sr.Peek() >= 0 )
        {
            string line = sr.ReadLine();
            // Return only lines longer than specified minimum.
            if ( line.Length >= minLength )
            {
                yield return line;
            }
        }
    }
}
```

You can then use the new method in a foreach block as follows:

```
TextFileReader2 reader = new TextFileReader2("document.txt");
// Display lines with 10 characters or more.
foreach ( string s in reader.GetLongLines(10) )
{
    Console.WriteLine(s);
}
```

Reusable Enumerable Adapters

A limitation of the foreach loop is that you can iterate over all the elements of a collection only in one direction, from the elements with lower indexes toward elements with higher indexes. It looks like you need a traditional, less elegant for loop to go in the opposite direction. However, now that you know the subtleties of the IEnumerable interface, you can create an adapter type that implements the IEnumerable interface and that wraps another IEnumerable object:

```
public class ReverseIterator : IEnumerable
{
    private ArrayList al = new ArrayList();

    public ReverseIterator(IEnumerable ienum)
```

```
   {
      // Read all the elements into the inner ArrayList.
      foreach (object o in ienum)
      {
         al.Add(o);
      }
      // Reverse the element order.
      al.Reverse();
   }

   // Return the GetEnumerator of the inner ArrayList.
   public IEnumerator GetEnumerator()
   {
      return al.GetEnumerator();
   }
}
```

Here's how you can use this adapter to iterate over the elements of a string array in reverse direction:

```
string[] arr = { "one", "two", "three", "four", "five", "six" };
foreach (string s in new ReverseIterator(arr))
{
   Console.WriteLine(s);      // => six five four three two one
}
```

This technique enables you to write code that is more elegant but far less efficient than a plain for with a negative step because the ReverseIterator type has to read all the elements of the array into an ArrayList object, reverse it, and pass the inner IEnumerator object back to the C# program, which traverses all the elements a second time.

Here's another example, which reuses the TextFileReader type to display all the lines in a text file in reverse order:

```
foreach (string s in new ReverseIterator(new TextFileReader("document.txt")))
{
   Console.WriteLine(s);
}
```

You can use the same principles to create other adapter classes. For example, the following RandomIterator class enables you to visit all the elements of an IEnumerable object in random order:

```
public class RandomIterator : IEnumerable
{
   private ArrayList al = new ArrayList();

   public RandomIterator(IEnumerable ienum)
   {
      // Read all the elements into the inner ArrayList.
      foreach (object o in ienum)
      {
         al.Add(o);
      }
```

```
    // Shuffle the ArrayList. (Use a truly random seed.)
    Random rand = new Random((int) (DateTime.Now.Ticks & int.MaxValue));
    for ( int i = al.Count - 1; i > 0; i-- )
    {
        // Swap i-th element with an element whose index is in the range [0, i].
        int j = rand.Next(0, i);
        object tmp = al[i];
        al[i] = al[j];
        al[j] = tmp;
    }
}

    // Return the GetEnumerator of the inner ArrayList.
    public IEnumerator GetEnumerator()
    {
        return al.GetEnumerator();
    }
}
```

The following code shows how you can apply the RandomIterator type to display the numbers in the range 0 to 9 in random order:

```
int[] arr = { 0, 1, 2, 3, 4, 5, 6, 7, 8, 9 };
foreach ( int n in new RandomIterator(arr) )
{
    Console.WriteLine(n);
}
```

You can provide even more flexibility by means of the yield keyword. The following adapter type enables you to both skip an initial number of elements and step over a given number of elements:

```
public class StepIterator : IEnumerable
{
    private IEnumerator ienum;
    private int stepValue;
    private int skipValue;

    // The constructor does nothing but remember values for later.
    public StepIterator(IEnumerable iEnumerable, int stepValue, int skipValue)
    {
        this.ienum = iEnumerable.GetEnumerator();
        this.stepValue = stepValue;
        this.skipValue = skipValue;
    }

    // Pass an instance of the inner enumerator.
    public IEnumerator GetEnumerator()
    {
        // Skip the desired number of elements.
        for ( int i = 1; i <= skipValue; i++ )
        {
            if ( !ienum.MoveNext() )
                yield break;
        }
```

```
        // The main enumerator loop
        while ( ienum.MoveNext() )
        {
            // Return the current value.
            yield return ienum.Current;
            // Step over the desired number of elements.
            for ( int i = 1; i < stepValue; i++ )
            {
                if ( !ienum.MoveNext() )
                {
                    yield break;
                }
            }
        }
    }
  }
}
```

The StepIterator class solves two of the most annoying limitations of the foreach loop by adding the ability to start with an element other than the first element and the ability to visit every N elements in the collection. For example, see how you can visit all the elements of a collection with even indexes:

```
int[] arr = { 0, 1, 2, 3, 4, 5, 6, 7, 8, 9 };
foreach (int n in new StepIterator(arr, 2, 0))
{
    Console.Write("{0} ", n);              // => 0 2 4 6 8
}
```

and the elements with odd indexes:

```
foreach (int n in new StepIterator(arr, 2, 1))
{
    Console.Write("{0} ", n);              // => 1 3 5 7 9
}
```

Here's another example. Say that you have a text file containing data in comma- or tab-delimited format, one record per line, but you need to skip over the very first line because this line contains the column headers (an arrangement that is typical of data files in this format). You can use the StepIterator together with the TextFileReader type to accomplish this task in a very elegant manner:

```
foreach (string s in new StepIterator(new TextFileReader("myfile.txt"), 1, 1))
{
    Console.WriteLine(s);
}
```

Notice that the StepIterator class doesn't suffer from the performance issue that affects the ReverseIterator and RandomIterator types because it doesn't have to read all the elements of the inner IEnumerable object in advance.

Chapter 4
Generics

Unless you are absolutely new to Microsoft .NET programming—or you're a .NET developer who has lived on a desert island for the last two years—you should have heard about generics and the fact that they are the most important addition to Microsoft Visual C# and other .NET languages. In this chapter, I show that generics are indeed a very important new feature of your favorite language, and I illustrate several examples of what generics can do to make your code faster, more concise, and more elegant.

In a nutshell, generics give you the ability to define a class that takes a type as an argument. Depending on the type argument, the generic definition generates a different concrete class. In this sense, generics add a degree of polymorphism, much like other techniques based on inheritance, interfaces, or late binding. But you'll soon discover that generics are much, much more powerful.

Before we dive into the topic, bear in mind that generics aren't a completely new concept in the programming world. In fact, .NET generics are similar to Microsoft Visual C++ templates, so you might already be familiar with the underlying concepts if you've worked in that language before. However, .NET generics have several features and advantages that C++ templates don't, for example, constraints.

 Note To avoid long lines, code samples in this chapter assume that the following using statements are used at the top of each source file:

```
using System;
using System.Collections;
using System.Collections.Generic;
using System.Diagnostics;
```

The Need for Generics

Let's start with a classic example that shows why generics can be so useful. Let's consider the ArrayList type, defined in the System.Collections namespace. I cover this and other collection-like types in Chapter 5, "Arrays and Collections," but for now it will suffice to see how you can define such a collection and add elements to it:

```
// This collection will contain only integer numbers.
ArrayList col = new ArrayList();
col.Add(11); col.Add(13); col.Add(19);
// foreach loops support casting from object to int.
foreach ( int n in col )
{
    Console.WriteLine(n);
}
// Reading an element requires an explicit cast operator.
int element = (int) col[0];
```

As simple as it is, this code has a couple of serious problems, one related to robustness and the other related to performance. The former problem is quite simple to demonstrate: the Array-List was designed to store values of any kind; hence, it stores its value internally inside System.Object slots. This means that a developer using the ArrayList can accidentally or purposely add an element that isn't an integer, an action that would make the foreach loop fail at run time:

```
// Adding a string to the collection doesn't raise any compile-time error...
col.Add("abc");
// ...but it makes the following statement fail at run time.
foreach ( int n in col )
{
    Console.WriteLine(n);
}
```

Also, the latter problem depends on the ArrayList using System.Object variables internally and manifests itself when you use the ArrayList to store value-typed elements, such as numbers, enumerated values, DataTime values, and any user-defined structure. In fact, when you store a value-typed element in an Object variable, the element must be boxed. A box operation takes both CPU cycles and memory from the managed heap, and therefore it should be avoided if possible.

The Traditional Solution

Under previous versions of the .NET Framework, you can solve the former problem and make the code more robust by defining a new class that inherits from the CollectionBase type, also in the System.Collections namespace. This type is one of the many abstract types provided in the .NET Framework with the purpose of enabling developers to define their own strong-typed collection classes. Here's a very simple implementation of a custom collection class that can store only integers:

```
public class IntegerCollection : CollectionBase
{
    public void Add(int item)
    {
        this.List.Add(item);
    }

    public void Remove(int item)
    {
        this.List.Remove(item);
    }

    public int this[int index]
    {
        get { return (int) this.List[index];}
        set { this.List[index] = value; }
    }
}
```

The code is quite simple: each method of the IntegerCollection class takes or returns an Int32 value and delegates to a method with the same name as the inner IList object named List. Despite its simplicity, this solution isn't exactly concise: a real-world class that exposes common methods such as Sort, Find, or Reverse (and all their overloads) would take about 100 lines. Worse, you would need a distinct class for each different type of strong-typed collection in your application; for example, a DoubleCollection class to hold double values, a DateTime-Collection class for DateTime values, and so forth. Granted, you can easily generate these collections by taking a template and performing a search-and-replace operation, but for sure you can think of many other, more pleasant ways to spend your time.

The IntegerCollection class enables you to write more robust and slightly less verbose code in the client application because any attempt to store a noninteger value in the collection is trapped at compile time and because reading an element doesn't require a cast operator any longer:

```
// This is the only statement that must be changed from the previous example.
IntegerCollection col = new IntegerCollection();
...
// Reading an element doesn't require any conversion operator.
int element = col[0];
// Adding anything but an integer raises a compile-time error.
col.Add("abc");                    // *** This statement doesn't compile.
```

However, the IntegerCollection type doesn't resolve the problem related to performance because integer values are still boxed when they are stored in the inner collection. In fact, this approach makes performance slightly worse because each call to a method in the Integer-Collection class must be routed to the method of the inner List collection.

The Generics-Based Solution

The .NET Framework comes with a new namespace named System.Collections.Generic, which contains several generics collections that can be specialized to contain only values of a given type. For example, see how you can define a collection containing only integer values by means of the new List type:

```
// This collection will contain only integer numbers.
List<int> col = new List<int>();
col.Add(11); col.Add(13); col.Add(19);
foreach ( int n in col )
{
    Console.WriteLine(n);
}
// Reading an element doesn't require any cast operator.
int element = col[0];
```

The type between angle brackets specifies that the generic List type must be specialized to work with elements of int type, and only with that type of element. In fact, any attempt to add elements of a different type raises a compile-time error:

```
// Adding a string causes a compile-time error.
col.Add("abc");                 // *** This statement doesn't compile.
```

Even if this isn't apparent when you look at the code, the solution based on generics also solves the performance problem because the List<int> collection stores its elements in Int32 slots—in general, in the variables typed after the type specified between angle brackets—and therefore no boxing occurs anywhere.

You can easily prove this point by compiling the following sample code:

```
ArrayList al = new ArrayList();
al.Add(9);
List<int> list = new List<int>();
list.Add(9);
```

Here's the corresponding IL code generated by the C# compiler:

```
//000015: ArrayList al = new ArrayList();
  IL_0000:  newobj      instance void
     [mscorlib]System.Collections.ArrayList::.ctor()
  IL_0005:  stloc.0
//000016: al.Add(9);
  IL_0006:  ldloc.0
  IL_0007:  ldc.i4.s    9
  IL_0009:  box         [mscorlib]System.Int32
  IL_000e:  callvirt    instance int32
     [mscorlib]System.Collections.ArrayList::Add(object)
  IL_0013:  pop
```

```
//000017: List<int> list = new List<int>();
  IL_0014:  newobj      instance void class
      [mscorlib]System.Collections.Generic.List`1<int32>::.ctor()
  IL_0019:  stloc.1
//000018: list.Add(9);
  IL_001a:  ldloc.1
  IL_001b:  ldc.i4.s    9
  IL_001d:  callvirt    instance void class
      [mscorlib]System.Collections.Generic.List`1<int32>::Add(!0)
```

It isn't essential that you understand the meaning of each IL statement here; the key point is that it requires a box IL opcode (shown in bold type) to prepare the integer value to be passed to the Add method of the ArrayList object, whereas no such opcode is used when calling the Add method of the List<int> object.

Because of the missing box operation, adding value-typed items to a generic collection is remarkably faster than adding the same items to a nongeneric collection is, even though the difference can go unnoticed until the repeated box operations cause a garbage collection. In an informal benchmark, adding one million integers to a List object is about six times faster than adding them to an ArrayList is.

You can extract elements from a generic collection and assign them to a strong-typed variable without having to convert them and without causing an unbox operation. This additional optimization can make your read operations faster by a factor of about 20 percent. This speed improvement isn't as impressive as the one that results when you add items, but on the other hand, it occurs even with small collections that don't stress the garbage collector.

The .NET Framework exposes many generic types in addition to the List object just shown: the Dictionary<K,V> and SortedDictionary<K,V> generic collections enable you to create strong-typed hash tables; the Stack<T>, Queue<T>, and LinkedList<T> are useful to create more robust and efficient versions of other common data structures. I cover these and other generic types later in this chapter and in Chapter 5.

Another important note: the type argument you pass when defining a generic instance can be any .NET type, including another generic or nongeneric collection. You can even pass a type that represents an array:

```
// A collection of generic dictionaries
List< Dictionary<string, int>> list = new List< Dictionary<string, int>>();
// A collection of arrays of integers
List<int[]> arrays = new List<int[]>();
// Add an array to the collection.
int[] arr = {1, 3, 5, 7, 9};
arrays.Add(arr);
// Display the second element of the first array, and then modify it.
Console.WriteLine(arrays[0][1]);            // => 3
arrays[0][1] = 999;
```

Authoring Generic Types

In addition to using generic types defined in the .NET Framework, Microsoft Visual C# 2005 also enables you to create your own generic types. As you'll see in a moment, the syntax for doing so is quite intuitive, even though you must account for some nonobvious details.

Generic Parameters

Let's begin with a very simple task: create a strong-typed collection that doesn't allow you to remove or modify an element after you've added it to the collection. The .NET Framework exposes many collection-like types, but none of them has exactly these features. The simplest thing to do is author a generic type named ReadOnlyList and reuse it to store elements of any sort. For simplicity's sake, the ReadOnlyList type uses a private array whose maximum number of elements must be defined when you instantiate a new collection:

```csharp
public class ReadOnlyList<T> : IEnumerable
{
    public T[] values;
    // The constructor takes the maximum number of elements.
    public ReadOnlyList(int elementCount)
    {
        values = new T[elementCount];
    }

    // The Count read-only property
    private int m_Count;

    public int Count
    {
        get { return m_Count;}
    }

    // Add a new element to the collection; error if too many elements.
    public void Add(T value)
    {
        values[m_Count++] = value;
    }

    // Return the N-th element; error if index is out of range.
    public T this[int index]
    {
        get
        {
            if (index < 0 || index >= m_Count)
            {
                throw new ArgumentException("Index out of range");
            }
            return values[index];
        }
    }
}

    // Support for IEnumerable interface
    public IEnumerator GetEnumerator()
```

```
    {
        // Create a sub array containing only the actual elements.
        T[] realValues = new T[this.Count];
        Array.Copy(values, realValues, this.Count);
        return realValues.GetEnumerator();
    }
}
```

The key point in the preceding code is the declaration of the generic parameter in the first line by means of the pair of angle brackets:

```
public class ReadOnlyList<T> : IEnumerable
```

Once you have defined the generic parameter, you can reuse it anywhere in the class (as well as in any nested class) as if it were a regular type name. For example, the generic parameter T appears in the declaration of the inner values array and in the signature of the Add and Item members (in bold type). You can use the ReadOnlyList generic type as you would use the List generic type, except that you must provide the maximum number of elements and you can't remove or modify any element after you've added it:

```
// This read-only list can contain up to 1,000 integer values.
ReadOnlyList<int> roList = new ReadOnlyList<int>(1000);
roList.Add(123);
Console.WriteLine(roList[0]);                    // => 123
// *** Next statement causes a compilation error: "Property is readonly."
// roList[0] = 234;
```

When you work with generics, you need a way to distinguish a generic type such as List<T>, which contains one or more type parameters, from a generic type such as List<int>, where the type parameter has been replaced (or *bound*) to a specific type. A type of the former kind is known as *generic type definition, open generic type,* or *unbound generic type,* whereas a type of the latter type is known as *bound generic type.*

Interestingly, the T generic parameter can be reused to define or instantiate other generic types. For example, you can simplify the ReadOnlyList class by using a private List<T> object instead of an array; incidentally, this change relieves you of the requirement of passing the maximum number of elements to the constructor:

```
public class ReadOnlyList2<T> : IEnumerable
{
    public List<T> values;

    public ReadOnlyList2()
    {
        values = new List<T>();
    }

    // Add a new element to the collection.
    public void Add(T value)
    {
        values.Add(value);
    }
```

```csharp
// Return the N-th element; error if index is out of range.
public T this[int index]
{
    get
    {
        if (index < 0 || index >= values.Count)
        {
            throw new ArgumentException("Index out of range");
        }
        return values[index];
    }
}

// Count, GetEnumerator, and other members as in ReadOnlyList class
...
}
```

The first problem you face when working with generics is that you can't really make any assumption about the type that will be passed to the generic type parameter. For example, the Add method receives an element of the generic type T, but it can't invoke any methods on this element except those inherited from System.Object. For the same reason, you can't use any operator on an element of type T, including math and comparison operators. For example, the simplest way to test a value against null is by means of the Object.Equals static method:

```csharp
public void Add(T value)
{
    // Add only nonnull elements to the collection.
    if ( !Object.Equals(value, null) )
    {
        values.Add(value);
    }
}
```

Notice that value types can't be equal to null; therefore, the Add statement is always executed if you pass a value type. To overcome this minor problem, the default operator has been added to the C# language. Read the section titled "Setting the Default Value" later in this chapter for more information about this operator.

Because of the inability to invoke methods in the type referenced by the parameter T, generics are best used as *containers* for objects that don't have an active role. Later in this chapter, you'll learn how you can use constraints to be able to invoke members on contained objects.

Multiple Generic Parameters

A generic class can also take multiple generic parameters. For example, consider the following Relation type, a simple class that enables you to create a one-to-one relation between two instances of a given type:

```csharp
public class Relation<T1, T2>
{
    public readonly T1 Object1;
    public readonly T2 Object2;
```

```
    public Relation(T1 obj1, T2 obj2)
    {
       this.Object1 = obj1;
       this.Object2 = obj2;
    }
}
```

Despite its simplicity, the Relation class can be quite useful to expand your object hierarchy with new features. For example, let's say that you have defined a Person class (which holds personal data about an individual) and a Company type (which holds information about a company). The Relation type enables you to indicate for which company a given person works:

```
Company ca = new Company("Code Architects");
Person john = new Person("John", "Evans");
Person ann = new Person("Ann", "Beebe");
Relation<Person, Company> relJohnCa = new Relation<Person, Company>(john, ca);
Relation<Person, Company> relAnnCa = new Relation<Person, Company>(ann, ca);
```

In a real program, you typically deal with many persons and many companies, so you would be better off creating a strong-typed list that can contain Relation objects. This can be achieved by using nested angle brackets keywords:

```
List<Relation<Person, Company>> relations = new List<Relation<Person, Company>>();
relations.Add(relJohnCa);
relations.Add(relAnnCa);
```

The ability to nest angle brackets extends the power of generics remarkably. For example, the following code extracts all the people who work for a given company:

```
private static List<Person> GetEmployees(
    List<Relation<Person, Company>> relations, Company company)
{
    List<Person> result = new List<Person>();
    foreach (Relation<Person, Company> rel in relations)
    {
        if ( rel.Object2 == company )
        {
            result.Add(rel.Object1);
        }
    }
    return result;
}
```

You might continue the previous example by extracting all the employees of the Code Architects company, as follows:

```
foreach ( Person p in GetEmployees(relations, ca) )
{
    Console.WriteLine(p.FirstName + " " + p.LastName);
}
```

As you can see, using nested angle brackets can make your code quite contorted and near unreadable. The following section shows how you can simplify things.

Generic Methods

You can also use angle brackets in the definition of a method. Consider the following procedure, which you can place inside a module:

```
// Exchange two arguments passed by address.
public static void Swap<T>(ref T x, ref T y)
{
   T tmp = x;
   x = y;
   y = tmp;
}
```

You can call the Swap method by passing two variables of the same type:

```
int n1 = 123;
int n2 = 456;
Swap<int>(ref n1, ref n2);
Console.WriteLine("n1={0}, n2={1}", n1, n2);     // => n1=456, n2=123
```

It's remarkable that in most cases the C# compiler doesn't even require the angle brackets in the method invocation:

```
// The following statement works correctly.
Swap(ref n1, ref n2);
```

Sometimes you do need to specify the angle brackets when invoking a generic method. Consider the following definition:

```
private static void DoSomething<T>(T x, T y)
{
   ...
}
```

The following client code works correctly even if no angle brackets are used because the compiler can determine the generic parameter to be passed behind the scenes by looking at the type of the first argument passed to the method:

```
DoSomething(123, 456);            // Same as DoSomething<int>
DoSomething(123.56, 456.78);      // Same as DoSomething<double>
```

However, you have a problem when the two arguments have a different type. For example, this code:

```
long l = 456;
int n = 123;
DoSomething(l, n);
```

fails to compile with the following error message:

```
The type arguments for method 'GenericsDemo.App.DoSomething' cannot be inferred from the usa
ge. Try specifying the type argument explicitly.
```

This error message is a bit surprising because if the compiler looks at the first value passed to the method and infers that type T stands for long, it should be able to automatically convert the second argument from int to long. However, it is evident that in this case the C# compiler isn't able to perform even a widening conversion automatically.

You can get rid of the compilation error in two ways: either by manually converting the second argument to the same type as the first one or by specifying the angle brackets in the method call:

```
// Both of these statements work correctly.
DoSomething(1, (long) n);
DoSomething<long>(1, n);
```

Finally, notice that only generic methods are supported; there is no such thing as a generic property, field, or event. In other words, C# refuses to compile this code:

```
public T Value<T>
{
   get { … }
   set { … }
}
```

However, you can have a property that reuses a generic parameter defined in the enclosing class:

```
public class Item<T>
{
   public T Value
   {
      get { … }
      set { … }
   }
}
```

Setting the Default Value

One interesting detail about C# generics is that you can deal with reference types and value types in the same way. To see what I mean, let's extend the implementation of the ReadOnly-List class with the ability to clear all the elements that are currently stored in the collection:

```
// (Inside the ReadOnlyList class …)
public void Reset()
{
   // Reset all existing elements to the type's default value.
   for (int i = 0; i < this.Count; i++)
   {
      values[i] = null;
   }
}
```

Unfortunately, the C# compiler rejects the statement in bold type with the following error:

```
Cannot convert null to type parameter 'T' because it could be a value type.
Consider using 'default(T)' instead.
```

It makes perfect sense, if you think about it: T might be a value type, and null values can't be assigned to value types. If we follow the compiler's suggestion and replace the statement as follows, the error message goes away:

```
values[i] = default(T);
```

In this case, the default value for that type—that is, zero for numeric types, a null globally unique identifier (GUID) for the System.Guid type, and so forth—is assigned instead. You can also use the default operator to check whether a given value is equal to the default value for a type:

```
if ( object.Equals(default(T), value) )
{
    // Value is null, zero, or whatever the default value for type T is.
}
```

Generic Interfaces

You can use generics with classes, structures, interfaces, and delegates, but not with Enum types. Generic structures work exactly the same way as generic classes do, but generic interfaces need some additional clarifications. The following code defines a generic interface and a class that implements that interface:

```
public interface IAdder<T>
{
    T Add(T n1, T n2);
}

public class Adder : IAdder<int>
{
    // Implementation of IAdder<int>.Add
    public int Add(int n1, int n2)
    {
        return n1 + n2;
    }
}
```

It is legal to implement multiple versions of the same generic interface, as in this code:

```
public class Adder : IAdder<int>, IAdder<double>
{
    // Implementation of IAdder<int>.Add
    public int Add(int n1, int n2)
    {
        return n1 + n2;
    }
```

```
   // Implementation of IAdder<double>.Add
   public double Add(double n1, double n2)
   {
      return n1 + n2;
   }
}
```

The most important difference between a standard (weakly typed) interface and a generic interface is that the latter can avoid a box operation when method arguments are of a value type. For example, before generics were introduced, the only way you could define a universal IAdder interface was to use object arguments, as in the following code:

```
public interface IAdder
{
   object Add(object n1, object n2);
}
```

Implementing such an interface in a class would require that both the arguments and the return value—all of which are numbers, and therefore value types—be boxed and unboxed. By comparison, no boxing occurs when you implement the IAdder<T> interface if T is a value type.

The .NET Framework defines several generic interfaces, most of which are the generic version of weakly typed interfaces. These are the most important ones:

- IComparable<T>, the strong-typed version of IComparable

- IComparer<T>, the strong-typed version of IComparer

- IEquatable<T>, which exposes an Equals method that takes an argument of a specific type

- IEnumerable<T> and IEnumerator<T>, which allow a class to support foreach loops

- ICollection<T>, a collection of elements of type T

- IList<T>, a series of elements of type T

- IDictionary<K, V>, a dictionary of elements of type V indexed by keys of type K

If the type that implements the interface is itself a generic type, the generic parameter can appear in the list of implemented interfaces, as in the following code:

```
public class TestComparer<T> : IComparer<T>
{
   public int Compare(T x, T y)
   {
      ...
   }
}
```

In practice, however, implementing generic interfaces in this way is difficult and sometimes impossible. For example, there is no simple way to implement the Compare method in the previous code snippet correctly because the code inside the method can't make any assumption about how two elements of type T can be compared to each other and can't use comparison operators with them. (You can sometimes work around this limitation by enforcing a constraint on the generic parameter, as you'll learn in a following section.)

Interestingly, many primitive .NET types have been expanded to implement the IEquatable<T> and IComparable<T> interfaces. For example, you can now invoke the strong-typed versions of the Equals and IComparable interfaces for all numeric types:

```
void TestInteger(int value)
{
   // These statements box their value in Microsoft .NET Framework 1.1
   // but not in version 2.0.
   if ( value.Equals(0) )
   {
      Console.WriteLine("It's zero");
   }
   else if ( value.CompareTo(0) > 0 )
   {
      Console.WriteLine("It's positive");
   }
}
```

You can't use the generic parameter directly as the base class or in the list of interfaces implemented by a type. In other words, the following statements don't compile:

```
public class TestClass<T> : T
{
   ...
}
```

> **Note**   A generic interface can inherit from the corresponding nongeneric one. For example, IEnumerable<T> inherits from IEnumerable; therefore, a class that implements the generic interface must implement both the IEnumerable<T>.GetEnumerator method and IEnumerator.GetEnumerator. Similarly, the IEnumerator<T> interface inherits from IEnumerator; therefore, a class that implements IEnumerator<T> must expose all three members of IEnumerator plus the strongly typed version of the Current property. (For more information about the IEnumerator interface, see Chapter 3, "Interfaces.")

Generics and Overloading

You can define generic types that have the same name but different numbers of generic parameters. For example, the following classes can coexist in the same namespace:

```
public class MyType
{
   ...
}
```

```
public class MyType<T>
{
    ...
}

public class MyType<T, K>
{
    ...
}
```

This feature is similar to method overloading in the sense that the compiler chooses the type whose number of generic parameters matches the number of generic arguments passed by the calling code:

```
MyType t1;                   // An instance of the first class
MyType<long> t2;             // An instance of the second class
MyType<long, double> t3;     // An instance of the third class
```

Similarly, you can define multiple methods that use the same name and different sets of generic parameters. In this case, however, the rules are slightly more complicated, and you must be aware of a few subtleties. Let's consider the following methods:

```
public static void DoTask<T, P>(T x, P y)
{
    Console.WriteLine("First version");
}

public static void DoTask<T>(T x, string y)
{
    Console.WriteLine("Second version");
}

public static void DoTask<T>(T x, T y)
{
    Console.WriteLine("Third version");
}
```

In most cases, the C# compiler is smart enough to generate code that invokes the most specific version, even if you omit the angle brackets in the method call:

```
DoTask(123, 456.78);         // Calls DoTask<int, double>
DoTask(123, "abc");          // Calls DoTask<int, string>
```

However, if you attempt to pass two arguments of the same type, for example, two integers, the compiler complains and explains that overload resolution failed because no method is specific to the arguments being passed:

```
// *** Next statement raises a compilation error.
DoTask(123, 123);
```

To solve the problem, you must give the compiler a hint about which version you want to be invoked:

```
// Next statement compiles correctly and invokes the third version of the method.
DoTask<int>(123, 123);
```

Generics and Inheritance

Earlier in this chapter, I state that you can use a generic parameter anywhere in a class, as if it were a regular type name. Well, that description isn't exactly accurate because a few exceptions exist:

- You can't inherit from a type passed as a generic parameter, and you can't use a generic parameter in the list of interfaces implemented by the type, as I explain at the end of the section titled "Generic Interfaces" earlier in this chapter.

- You can't use a generic parameter in an attribute declaration.

- You can't use a generic parameter in a method that is marked with the DllImport attribute, that is, in a method that runs unmanaged code.

Even if you can't inherit a type from a generic parameter, you can use a generic type as the base class, which is in fact a rather common case. For example, the following two classes are based on the Relation type defined in an earlier section:

```
public class PersonCompanyRelation : Relation<Person, Company>
{
    public PersonCompanyRelation(Person person, Company company)
        : base(person, company)
    {}
}

public class PersonCompanyRelationList : List<PersonCompanyRelation>
{}
```

Thanks to these two classes, the client code that puts Person and Company objects in relation to each other can be simplified as follows:

```
Company ca = new Company("Code Architects");
Person john = new Person("John", "Evans");
Person ann = new Person("Ann", "Beebe");

PersonCompanyRelationList relations = new PersonCompanyRelationList();
PersonCompanyRelation relJohnCa = new PersonCompanyRelation(john, ca);
relations.Add(relJohnCa);
relations.Add(new PersonCompanyRelation(ann, ca));
```

The GetEmployees method has a simpler and more readable declaration as well:

```
List<Person> GetEmployees(PersonCompanyRelationList relations, Company company)
{
    List<Person> result = new List<Person>();
    foreach ( Relation<Person, Company> rel in relations )
```

```
   {
      if (rel.Object2 == company)
      {
         result.Add(rel.Object1);
      }
   }
   return result;
}
```

The practice of defining and using a standard class that inherits from and wraps a generic type has a couple of advantages:

- The structure and the syntax of client code are simpler.

- The client code can be written in unmanaged code or in .NET languages that don't support generics.

Generics are fully CLS-compliant; therefore, all major .NET languages support them and you can freely expose them as parameters or return values of public methods. Even so, however, you might decide not to expose a generic type to the outside of your assembly to keep it fully interoperable with all .NET languages as well as unmanaged clients.

Generics and the is Operator

In general, a bound generic type can be used whenever you can use a regular type, as in this code:

```
if ( obj is List<string> )
{
   List<string> list = (List<string>) obj;
   ...
}
```

This rule holds true only for bound generic types, which represent real types, and isn't valid for open generic types, which represent a type definition rather than a real type. For example, the following code isn't valid (unless it appears inside a generic type that takes the T parameter):

```
void TestIsOperator(T obj)
{
   // *** This code causes the following compile error: Type T is not defined.
   if ( obj is List<T> )
   {
      List<string> list = (List<string>) obj;
      ...
   }
}
```

The previous test is rarely useful, because—even if it were a valid C# statement—you can't cast an object instance to a generic List<T> variable. As a matter of fact, you can't define such a variable:

```
// *** This statement causes two identical compile errors: Type T is not defined.
List<T> list = (List<T>) obj;
```

Let's see which options you have. If you simply must determine whether an object is an instance of a bound generic type, you can use this code:

```
if ( obj != null && obj.GetType().IsGenericType )
{
    // obj is an instance of a generic type.
}
```

However, if you need to check whether an object is an instance of a generic bound type that derives from a given open generic definition, such as a type of the form List<T>, you must use a different approach. The FullName of a generic type definition consists of the complete name of the generic class, followed by an inverse quote character, and then the number of type parameters. For example, the full name of the List<T> generic type definition is this:

```
System.Collections.Generic.List`1
```

The FullName of a bound generic type is obtained by concatenating the complete name of the type arguments (enclosed in brackets) to the previous string. For example, the full name of the List<int> type is

```
System.Collections.Generic.List`1[[System.Int32, mscorlib, Version=2.0.0.0,
    Culture=neutral, PublicKeyToken=b77a5c561934e089]]
```

Armed with this knowledge, you can test whether an object instance is a bound generic type of a List<T> type using this code:

```
if (obj != null && obj.GetType().FullName.StartsWith("System.Collections.Generic.List`1"))
{
    // obj is a generic type of the form List<T>.
}
```

The GetGenericTypeDefinition method returns the open generic type on which a generic type is based. For example, when applied to the List<int> type, this method returns a reference to the List<T> open generic type. You can use this knowledge to rewrite the previous code as follows:

```
if (obj != null && obj.GetType().IsGenericType &&
    obj.GetType().GetGenericTypeDefinition().FullName ==
    "System.Collections.Generic.List`1")
{
    // obj is a generic type of the form List<T>.
}
```

However, notice that the previous test isn't perfectly equivalent to the is operator, which also tests whether the first argument is an instance of any type derived from the type specified in the second argument. If you must perform this sort of test, you must adopt a technique based on reflection:

```
// Test whether obj is a List<T> or derives from a List<T> type.
if ( obj != null )
{
    Type type = obj.GetType();
```

```
   while ( type != null )
   {
      if ( type.FullName.StartsWith("System.Collections.Generic.List`1") )
      {
         Console.WriteLine("(obj is List<T>) is true!");
         break;
      }
      type = type.BaseType;
   }
}
```

You can read more about reflection, the GetType operator, and the methods of the System.Type class in Chapter 9, "Reflection."

Generic Constraints

Consider the following generic method, which returns the highest value among its arguments:

```
public static T Max<T>(params T[] values)
{
   T result = values[0];
   for ( int i = 1; i < values.Length; i++ )
   {
      // *** The next statement causes the following compilation error:
      //    Operator '>' cannot be applied to operands of type 'T' and 'T'.
      if ( values[i] > result )
      {
         result = values[i];
      }
   }
   return result;
}
```

As the remark in the preceding code indicates, the greater than sign (>) causes a compilation error because the compiler can't be sure that client code calls the method only with arguments that support this operator. This problem occurs quite frequently when you are working with generics, but you can work around it by enforcing a constraint for the T type. For example, you can require that the method be called only with types that support the IComparable interface:

```
public static T Max<T>(params T[] values) where T : IComparable
{
   ...
}
```

Because T surely exposes the IComparable interface, the code in the method can safely invoke the CompareTo method to calculate the highest value in the array:

```
public static T Max<T>(params T[] values) where T : IComparable
{
   T result = values[0];
   for (int i = 1; i < values.Length; i++)
```

```
      {
         if (result.CompareTo(values[i]) < 0)
         {
            result = values[i];
         }
      }
      return result;
}
```

Here's a piece of client code that uses the Max function:

```
// No need to specify angle brackets in calling the method.
Console.WriteLine(Max(12, 23, 6, -1));                    // => 23
```

C# supports five types of generic constraints:

- **Interface constraint**   The type argument must implement the specified interface.
- **Inheritance constraint**   The type argument must derive from the specified base class.
- **Class constraint**   The type argument must be a reference type.
- **Struct constraint**   The type argument must be a value type.
- **New constraint**   The type argument must expose a public parameterless (default) constructor.

Notice that you can't define a constraint specifying that a type must expose a constructor with a given signature; the new constraint ensures that one of the public constructors of the type has no arguments.

You can read more about these constraint types in the following sections.

The Interface Constraint

This kind of constraint is often used with the IComparable interface, as in the code example just shown. For instance, here's an interesting recursive method that returns the median value in a list. (The median of a list of N elements is the value that is greater than $N/2$ elements and less than the remaining $N/2$ elements.)

```
// Evaluate the median value of a list.
public static T MedianValue<T>(List<T> list) where T : IComparable
{
   // Call the other overload.
   return MedianValue<T>(list, -1);
}

public static T MedianValue<T>(List<T> list, int position) where T : IComparable
{
   // Provide a default value for the second argument.
   if ( position < 0 )
   {
      position = list.Count / 2;
   }
```

```
// If the list has just one element, we've found its median.
T guess = list[0];
if ( list.Count == 1 )
{
    return guess;
}

// These lists will contain values lower and higher than the current guess.
List<T> lowerList = new List<T>();
List<T> higherList = new List<T>();

for ( int i = 1; i < list.Count; i++ )
{
    T value = list[i];
    if (guess.CompareTo(value) <= 0)
    {
        // The value is higher than or equal to the current guess.
        higherList.Add(value);
    }
    else
    {
        // The value is lower than the current guess.
        lowerList.Add(value);
    }
}

if ( lowerList.Count > position )
{
    // The median value must be in the lower-than list.
    return MedianValue(lowerList, position);
}
else if ( lowerList.Count < position )
{
    // The median value must be in the higher-than list.
    return MedianValue(higherList, position - lowerList.Count - 1);
}
else
{
    // The guess is correct.
    return guess;
}
}
```

Of course, you can evaluate the median value of an array by sorting the array and then picking the element at index $N/2$, but the MedianValue is typically faster because it saves you the sort step.

You can retrieve other interesting values in a list by passing a second argument to the MedianValue method. For example, by passing the value 0, the method returns the lowest value in the list; by passing the value 1, the method returns the second-lowest value in the list; by passing the value $N - 1$, the method returns the highest value in a list of N elements; by passing the value $N - 2$, the method returns the second-highest value in the list, and so forth.

You can specify a generic interface as a constraint. For example, you can improve the Median-Value as follows:

```
public static T MedianValue<T>(List<T> list) where T : IComparable<T>
{
    ...
}
```

The advantage of using a generic interface instead of a weakly typed interface is that no boxing occurs when the new version of the MedianValue method invokes the CompareTo method of the interface:

```
// In the new version of MedianValue, this statement causes no boxing.
if ( guess.CompareTo(value) <= 0 )
{ ... }
```

All numeric types in the .NET Framework implement the IComparable<T> and IEquatable<T> interfaces; thus, the new version of the MedianValue method can work with all the integer and floating-point numeric types. If you define a new numeric data type, it is strongly recommended that you implement the IComparable<T> and IEquatable<T> generic interfaces.

You can use the interface constraint with any interface, not just IComparable. For example, a constraint for the ISerializable interface ensures that the generic type or method can be used only with types that can be serialized and deserialized from a file or a database field. (Read Chapter 12, "Object Serialization," for more information about the ISerializable interface.) In the remainder of this chapter, I provide other examples of interface constraints.

The Inheritance Constraint

The inheritance constraint tells the C# compiler that a generic argument can be only a type that derives from the specified class. The syntax is similar to the interface constraint:

```
// This generic class can be used only with types that derive
// from System.Windows.Forms.Control.
public class ControlCollection<T> where T: System.Windows.Forms.Control
{
    ...
}
```

Because of the inheritance constraint, you can use the ControlCollection class to create a collection of Button or TextBox controls, but not Person or Company objects. In addition to improved robustness, the inheritance constraint gives you the ability to invoke any public member of the type specified by the constraint. For example, the code in the ControlCollection class can safely access members of the Control type, such as the Text and ForeColor properties. Unfortunately, the presence of the inheritance constraint doesn't suffice to enable you to invoke the constructor of the class because classes that derive from the same base type can define a different set of constructors and even can have no public constructors at all. (See the section titled "The New Constraint" later in this chapter for more details.)

A few generics defined in the .NET Framework use the inheritance constraint. For example, the System.EventHandler<T> generic type is a delegate that can be used to define an event and mandates that the T type inherit from System.EventArgs. If EventHandler<T> were defined in C#, it would look like this:

```
delegate void EventHandler<T>(object sender, T e) where T : EventArgs;
```

(You can see this type in action in the section titled "Generics and Events" later in this chapter.) A few restrictions for the type follow the colon character in an inheritance constraint. For obvious reasons, the type can't be sealed, and therefore it can't be a structure. Also, you can't use the System.Object, System.ValueType, or System.Delegate types or any delegate type.

The Class and Struct Constraints

A generic parameter can be followed by the class clause, to specify that the type parameter is a reference type, or by the struct clause, to indicate that the type parameter is a value type:

```
public class ObjectCollection<T> where T : class
{
    ...
}

public class ValueCollection<T> where T : struct
{
    ...
}
```

> **Note**   In theory you might have two generic types with the same name that differ only by the class or struct constraint applied to their generic argument because the C# compiler should be able to use one or the other, depending on whether the generic argument is a class or a structure. However, the compiler isn't that smart, and the general rule still applies: a namespace can contain two generic types with the same name only if they take a different number of generic parameters.

The class constraint (but not the struct constraint) adds the ability to use null in assignments and comparisons that involve a variable typed after a generic type, and to compare variables using the == and != operators. For example, if you apply this constraint to the type parameters of the Relation generic class, you can define a Contains method that uses the == operator to check whether a given object is part of the relation:

```
public class Relation<T1, T2>
    where T1 : class
    where T2 : class
{
    public readonly T1 Object1;
    public readonly T2 Object2;

    public Relation(T1 obj1, T2 obj2)
    {
```

```
        this.Object1 = obj1;
        this.Object2 = obj2;
    }

    public bool Contains(object obj)
    {
        return this.Object1 == obj || this.Object2 == obj;
    }
}
```

Notice that you must define the Contains method so that it takes a generic Object argument. In this particular case, it doesn't really affect the quality of your code because the two objects passed to the constructor of the Relation class are reference types, and therefore no box operation occurs when the Contains method is used appropriately (unless you mistakenly pass this method a value-typed element that isn't part of the relation). You might believe that you can enforce a more robust code by offering two overloads for the Contains method, as in the following code:

```
public bool Contains(T1 obj)
{
    return this.Object1 == obj;
}
public bool Contains(T2 obj)
{
    return this.Object2 == obj;
}
```

This code compiles correctly, but only as long as the client code never creates a Relation object whose two generic parameters are the same type. For example, the following code doesn't compile:

```
Person john = new Person("John", "Evans");
Person ann = new Person("Ann", "Beebe");
Relation<Person, Person> rel = new Relation<Person, Person>(john, ann);
// Next statement raises the following compilation error:
//   The call is ambiguous between the following methods or properties…
bool found = rel.Contains(john);
```

Here's what has happened: when the compiler replaces both T1 and T2 with the Person type, it finds that two Contains methods are using the same signature. Oddly, the compiler should flag the statement that creates the Relation object as an error because the resulting bound generic class contains two overloaded methods with the same signature. Instead, the error is emitted only if the project actually contains a call to that method. Mysteries of .NET generics....

The New Constraint

The new constraint adds the requirement that the type passed as the generic parameter has a public parameterless constructor. This constraint enables you to create instances of the specified type, so you often use it in factory methods such as the following:

```
public static T CreateObject<T>() where T : new()
{
    return new T();
}
```

A better example shows how you can initialize an array of objects of a given type:

```
public static T[] CreateArray<T>(int numEls) where T : new()
{
   T[] values = new T[numEls];
   for ( int i = 0; i < numEls; i++ )
   {
      values[i] = new T();
   }
   return values;
}
```

The New constraint is often used in conjunction with other constraints, as explained in the following section.

Multiple Constraints

It is possible to enforce more than one constraint, on the same or on different generic parameters. This syntax is especially useful to combine the new constraint with the interface constraint or the inheritance constraint, or to enforce multiple interface constraints on the same generic parameter, as in this code:

```
class Widget<T,V> where T : IComparable, new() where V : IComparable, IConvertible
{
   ...
}
```

There are only a few rules to follow when multiple constraints are present. First, the class and struct constraints must come before any other constraint. Second, the new constraint must come after any other constraint. Needless to say, you can't specify both the class and the struct constraints in the same where clause.

The following example uses a compound constraint to implement a generic type that behaves like a sortable array:

```
public class SortableArray<T, C> where C : IComparer<T>, new()
{
   public T[] values;

   public SortableArray(int numElements)
   {
      values = new T[numElements];
   }

   public void Sort()
   {
      // Sort the array using the specified comparer object.
      Array.Sort(values, new C());
   }
```

```
    public T this[int index]
    {
        get { return values[index]; }
        set { values[index] = value; }
    }
}
```

To see the SortableArray class in action, you must define a suitable comparer class, which can be as simple as this one:

```
public class ReverseIntegerComparer : IComparer<int>
{
    public int Compare(int x, int y)
    {
        // Return -1 if x>y, +1 if x<y, 0 if x=y.
        return Math.Sign(y - x);
    }
}
```

Finally, you can define a SortableArray object that contains integers and that, when sorted, arranges elements in reverse order:

```
SortableArray<int, ReverseIntegerComparer> arr =
    new SortableArray<int, ReverseIntegerComparer>(10);
// Init the array here.
Random rand = new Random();
for ( int i = 0; i <= 9; i++ )
{
    arr[i] = rand.Next(1000);
}
arr.Sort();
```

Note You might wonder why the Compare method uses a Math.Sign function instead of a simpler call to the CompareTo method, exposed by the IComparable interface:

```
return (y as IComparable).CompareTo(x);
```

The reason is subtle and has to do with performance. The previous statement, in fact, causes two hidden box operations: first, the *y* variable is boxed when it is cast to the IComparable interface; second, the *x* Int32 value is passed to an object argument and therefore must be boxed as well. You can avoid the second box operation by casting to the IComparable<int> interface, as in this code:

```
return (y as IComparable<int>).CompareTo(x);
```

However, you can't avoid the first box operation, caused by the as operator, which in turn is necessary because the CompareTo method is private and can be accessed only through the IComparable interface.

In this particular case you can improve performance by passing the *y* − *x* difference to the Math.Sign method; when you have no other solution but to use the cast to invoke a private interface member, you can't avoid the extra box operation.

Checking a Constraint at Run Time

As sophisticated as it is, the constraint mechanism isn't perfect. For example, it isn't possible to request that a type passed as an argument implement *either* interface A or interface B (or both), or that it *not* implement an interface or inherit from a given base class, or that it be marked with a given attribute, or that it expose a method or a constructor with a given name and signature. And you can't check that *at least* one of the type arguments (but not necessarily all of them) implements a given interface. In cases like these, you can't specify a standard constraint; instead, the best you can do is check the condition at run time.

Provided that you know how to test the condition, it's easy to check the constraint in the type's constructor, as in this case:

```
public class ClassWithRuntimeConstraint<T>
{
   // Check that T is either IDisposable or ICloneable (or both).
   public ClassWithRuntimeConstraint()
   {
      if ( !typeof(IDisposable).IsAssignableFrom(typeof(T)) &&
         !typeof(ICloneable).IsAssignableFrom(typeof(T)) )
      {
         throw new ArgumentException("Invalid type argument");
      }
   }
}
```

Although this approach works, it is less than optimal because the condition is checked each time an instance of the class type is created. A better approach is to place the condition in the static constructor of the type, which is executed only once during the application's lifetime:

```
   // Check type constraint in the static type constructor.
   static ClassWithRuntimeConstraint()
   {
      if ( !typeof(IDisposable).IsAssignableFrom(typeof(T)) &&
         !typeof(ICloneable).IsAssignableFrom(typeof(T)) )
      {
         throw new ArgumentException("Invalid type argument");
      }
   }
```

Advanced Topics

Generic types are new, powerful tools in the hands of expert developers. As with all power tools, it takes some time to master them.

Nullable Types

Virtually all databases support the concept of nullable columns, namely, columns that can contain the special NULL value. Such a special value is often used as an alias for "unknown value" or "unassigned value." The use of nullable columns tends to make database-oriented applications more complicated than they need to be. For example, you can't move a value from a nullable numeric column into an Int32 or Double .NET variable without testing the value against the DBNull.Value special value. (The actual method or operation you must perform depends on the ADO.NET object you're using.)

Microsoft .NET Framework 2.0 introduces the concept of nullable types, that is, value types that can be assigned a special null value. Notice that only value types need to be treated in this way because reference types—such as strings and arrays—can use the null value as an alias for the "unknown" or "unassigned" state.

As you probably have already guessed by now, .NET nullable types are based on generics. For example, here's how you can define a nullable Integer value:

```
// Declare an "unassigned" nullable value.
Nullable<int> n;
// Assign it a value.
n = 123;
// Reset it to the "unassigned" state.
n = null;

// You can declare and assign a nullable value in these two ways.
Nullable<double> d1 = 123.45;
Nullable<double> d2 = new Nullable<double>(123.45);
```

Alternatively, you can declare a nullable type by appending the ? character to a value type's name, as in this code:

```
// Alternative, C#-specific syntax
double? d3 = 123.45;
```

The Nullable<T> generic type exposes two key properties, both of which are read-only. The HasValue property returns false if the element is in the unassigned state; the Value property returns the actual value if HasValue is true; otherwise, it throws an InvalidOperationException object:

```
if ( n.HasValue )
{
    Console.WriteLine("Value is {0}.", n.Value);
}
else
{
    Console.WriteLine("No value has been assigned yet.");
}
```

The Nullable<T> type supports conversions to and from the T type. For example, you can convert a double value to a Nullable<double> value and vice versa, but the latter conversion fails if the nullable element has no value; therefore, it is considered a narrowing conversion and requires an explicit cast operator:

```
double value = 123.45;
// This conversion can never fail.
```

```
double? value2 = value;
// The conversion in the opposite direction can fail, and thus it must be explicit.
double value3 = (double) value2;
```

Even though nullable types appear to be structures, they are given special treatment at the IL level and are often interchangeable with the underlying type they can contain. This special support becomes apparent in the way nullable values are boxed and unboxed. Consider this code:

```
// Create a null Nullable<int> value and box it.
int? n1 = null;
object obj = n1;
// obj contains something, yet next statement displays True.
Console.WriteLine(obj == null);              // => True
// You can unbox obj to a Nullable object or directly to an Int32 value.
int? n2 = (int?) obj;                        // n2 is assigned a null value.
int n3 = (int) obj;                          // Throws a NullReferenceException.
```

Even though you can use a nullable type in most of the places where the corresponding nonnullable type can appear, you have to account for one weird limitation: you can't pass a nullable type as a generic argument that has a structure constraint. In other words, assume you have the following generic class:

```
public class TestClass<T> where T : struct
{
    ...
}
```

If you now attempt to pass a nullable type to the T argument, as in this code:

```
// These statements are equivalent and both cause a compilation error.
TestClass<Nullable<int>> obj;
TestClass<int?> obj2;
```

you get the following error message:

```
The type 'int?' must be a non-nullable value type in order to use it as
parameter 'T' in the generic type or method 'GenericsDemo.App.TestClass<T>'
```

Math and Comparison Operators

Unfortunately, the Nullable<T> generic type doesn't support math operators. In other words, you can't directly add two nullable types. Instead, you must first convert them explicitly to the corresponding numeric type:

```
// This code assumes that d1 and d2 are Nullable<double> elements.
if ( d1.HasValue && d2.HasValue )
{
    double sum = d1.Value + d2.Value;
}
```

Another solution for this issue is based on the GetValueOrDefault method, which returns either the current value (if HasValue is true) or the default value:

```
// Add to nullable numbers, using zero if the value is null.
double sum = d1.GetValueOrDefault() + d2.GetValueOrDefault();
```

The GetValueOrDefault method can take one argument, which is used as the default value if HasValue is false:

```
// Assign the current value, or -1 if value is null.
double value = d1.GetValueOrDefault(-1);
```

The C# language has a new ?? operator, which can replace the GetValueOrDefault method:

```
// value2 is assigned the value of d1 if such value exists, else
// it is assigned -1. (Same as calling d1.GetValueOrDefault(-1).)
value = d1 ?? -1;
```

The Nullable<T> type supports all usual comparison operators, provided that the T type supports them. You can check whether two nullable values are equal by using the == and != operators, which work correctly also when both operands are null:

```
if ( d1 == d2 )
{
   // d1 is equal to d2.
}
```

Alternatively, you can use the Nullable.Equals<T> static method:

```
if ( Nullable.Equals(d1, d2) )
{
   // d1 is equal to d2.
}
```

Whereas the == and != operators behave as expected, you might be surprised by how other comparison operators evaluate their result. The <, <=, >, and >= operators, in fact, always return false if either operand is null. This behavior can bring quite inconsistent results. For example, you might discover that two Nullable<int> values are equal but that the greater than or equal (>=) or the less than or equal (<=) operator still returns false:

```
// Assuming that both d1 and d2 are null, the following statement displays True.
Console.WriteLine( d1 == d2 );
// But the following statement displays False.
Console.WriteLine( d1 >= d2 );
```

You can avoid this ambiguity by means of the Nullable.Compare static method; according to this method, a null value is always less than any nonnull value:

```
switch (Nullable.Compare(d1, d2))
{
   case -1:
     Console.WriteLine("d1 is null or is less than d2");
     break;
```

```
    case 1:
       Console.WriteLine("d2 is null or is less than d1");
       break;
    case 0:
       Console.WriteLine("d1 and d2 have same value or are both null.");
       break;
}
```

In some cases, you can work around the problem of whether to use the ?? operator or the GetValueOrDefault method and assign the lowest possible integer value to the "unknown" state:

```
Console.WriteLine(x1.GetValueOrDefault(int.MinValue) >=
   x2.GetValueOrDefault(int.MinValue));
```

A minor advantage of this technique is that it generates slightly less code and is slightly more efficient than a comparison operator applied directly to two Nullable<T> operands is. A comparison operator, in fact, always produces a call to the GetValueOrDefault method *and* the HasValue property.

Three-Valued Boolean Logic

Three-valued logic is quite common when you are dealing with Boolean expressions with operands that can take the true, false, or "unknown" value. For example, SQL makes extensive use of three-value logic because it must account for nullable fields. Consider the following SQL statement:

```
SELECT * FROM Customers WHERE City='Rome' Or Country='Vatican'
```

If the City field is NULL, the City='Rome' subexpression is also NULL; however, if Country is equal to Vatican, the second operand of the Or operator is true, which makes the entire WHERE clause true. In other words, a true operand makes the entire Or expression equal to true even if the other operand is NULL. Likewise, a false operand in an And expression makes the entire expression false, regardless of whether the other operand is known.

The &, |, and ~ operators comply with three-valued logic rules when applied to Nullable<bool> operands, as the following code demonstrates:

```
bool? fal = false;
bool? tru = true;
bool? unk = null;

Console.WriteLine(fal & unk);      // => False
Console.WriteLine(tru & unk);      // => (null)
Console.WriteLine(fal | unk);      // => (null)
Console.WriteLine(tru | unk);      // => True
Console.WriteLine(fal ^ unk);      // => (null)
Console.WriteLine(tru ^ unk);      // => (null)
Console.WriteLine(! unk);          // => (null)
```

Support for Math Operators

As I emphasize in previous sections, a generic type can't perform any math operation on objects with a type defined by using a generic parameter. In general, no operator can be used and no method can be invoked on such objects. (As a special case, you can work around the lack of support of relational operators by enforcing a constraint for either the IComparable or the IEquatable interfaces.)

In a perfect world, all .NET numeric types would support a common interface that would allow a generic type to perform math. For example, suppose that the following interface were defined in the .NET Framework:

```
public interface IMath<T>
{
    T Add(T n);
    T Subtract (T n);
    T Multiply (T n);
    T Divide (T n);
}
```

If all the .NET Framework numeric types supported the IMath<T> interface—in much the same way they support the IComparable<T> interface—a generic type could perform the four math operations on these types with no effort. Alas, this interface is neither defined in the .NET Framework nor implemented by any .NET type, so this approach isn't viable. It's a pity, and we can only hope that Microsoft will remedy this in a future version of the .NET Framework.

To understand how you can work around this issue, consider the relation between the IComparable<T> and the IComparer<T> interfaces. If you want to compare two objects that support the IComparable<T> interface, you can simply invoke the CompareTo method that these objects expose. However, if the objects don't expose this interface, you can define a type that supports the IComparer<T> interface and that is capable of comparing two objects of type T.

Along the same lines, you can work around the lack of support for math operators by defining an ICalculator<T> interface, and then create one or more types that implement this interface; these types provide the ability to perform math on elements of type T. Here's the definition of the ICalculator<T> interface:

```
public interface ICalculator<T>
{
    T Add(T n1, T n2);
    T Subtract(T n1, T n2);
    T Multiply(T n1, T n2);
    T Divide(T n1, T n2);
    T ConvertTo(object n);
}
```

Next, you need to implement one or more classes that implement this interface for all the numeric types in the .NET Framework and, optionally, for any custom type in your application that supports the four operators. You can adopt two strategies: you can have one separate class for each numeric type or an individual class that implements several versions of the interface, one of each numeric type you want to support.

The following NumericCalculator class implements the ICalculator interface for the Int32 and the Double types, but you can easily extend it to support all other primitive .NET numeric types. As you can see, it's a lot of code, but it's mostly a copy-and-paste job:

```
public class NumericCalculator : ICalculator<int>, ICalculator<double>
{
    // The ICalculator<int> interface

    int ICalculator<int>.Add(int n1, int n2)
    {
        return n1 + n2;
    }

    int ICalculator<int>.Subtract(int n1, int n2)
    {
        return n1 - n2;
    }

    int ICalculator<int>.Multiply(int n1, int n2)
    {
        return n1 * n2;
    }

    int ICalculator<int>.Divide(int n1, int n2)
    {
        return n1 / n2;
    }

    int ICalculator<int>.ConvertTo(object n)
    {
        return Convert.ToInt32(n);
    }

    // The ICalculator<double> interface

    double ICalculator<double>.Add(double n1, double n2)
    {
        return n1 + n2;
    }

    double ICalculator<double>.Subtract(double n1, double n2)
    {
        return n1 - n2;
    }
```

```csharp
double ICalculator<double>.Multiply(double n1, double n2)
{
    return n1 * n2;
}

double ICalculator<double>.Divide(double n1, double n2)
{
    return n1 / n2;
}

double ICalculator<double>.ConvertTo(object n)
{
    return Convert.ToDouble(n);
}
}
```

Let's now see how you can take advantage of the NumericCalculator class in a generic type that works as a list but is also capable of performing some basic statistical operations on its elements:

```csharp
public class StatsList<T, C> : List<T>
    where C : ICalculator<T>, new()
{
    // The object used as a calculator
    public C calc = new C();

    // Return the sum of all elements.
    public T Sum()
    {
        T result = default(T);
        foreach (T elem in this)
        {
            result = calc.Add(result, elem);
        }
        return result;
    }

    // Return the average of all elements.
    public T Avg()
    {
        return calc.Divide(this.Sum(), calc.ConvertTo(this.Count));
    }
}
```

Using the StatsList generic type is a breeze:

```csharp
StatsList<double, NumericCalculator> sl = new StatsList<double, NumericCalculator>();
for ( int i = 0; i <= 10; i++ )
{
    sl.Add(i);
}
Console.WriteLine("Sum = {0}", sl.Sum());        // => Sum = 55
Console.WriteLine("Average = {0}", sl.Avg());    // => Average = 5
```

Generics and Events

Generics can greatly simplify the structure of types that contain public events. As you might recall, all event handlers must receive two arguments: *sender* and *e*, where the latter is a System.Event-Args (if the event doesn't expose any additional property to subscribers) or an object that derives from System.EventArgs. To follow Microsoft guidelines closely, for each event that carries one or more arguments, you should define a type named *EventName*EventArgs that derives from Event-Args, the corresponding *EventName*EventHandler delegate, and (optionally) an On*EventName* overridable procedure that raises the event. It's a lot of work for just one event, and it's no surprise that most developers don't feel like writing all this code just to implement one event.

To see how the inheritance constraint can help you in streamlining the structure of events, let's suppose you are authoring an Employee class that exposes the Name and BirthDate properties and raises a *PropertyName*Changing event before either property is modified (so that subscribers can cancel the assignment) and a *PropertyName*Changed event after the property has been assigned. According to guidelines, you should define a class named NameChanging-EventArgs that exposes the ProposedValue read-only string property (the value about to be assigned to the Name property) and the Cancel read/write Boolean property (which can be set to true by event subscribers to cancel the assignment). Likewise, you should define a class named BirthDateChangingEventArgs class, which exposes the same properties, except that the ProposedValue property returns a DateTime value. Instead of defining two distinct classes, let's create a generic type named PropertyChangingEventArgs:

```
public class PropertyChangingEventArgs<T> : System.ComponentModle.CancelEventArgs
// Inheriting from CancelEventArgs adds support for the Cancel property.
{
    public PropertyChangingEventArgs(T proposedValue)
    {
        m_ProposedValue = proposedValue;
    }

    private T m_ProposedValue;

    public T ProposedValue
    {
        get { return m_ProposedValue; }
    }
}
```

You now have two options. First, you can use the PropertyChangingEventArgs<string> type for the NameChanging event and the PropertyChangingEventArgs<DateTime> type for the BirthDateChanging event; in this case, you'd need to edit the code slightly in the Employee class to account for these different names. Second, you can define two regular classes that inherit from the PropertyChangingEventArgs generic type:

```
public class NameChangingEventArgs : PropertyChangingEventArgs<string>
{
    ...
}
```

```
public class BirthDateChangingEventArgs : PropertyChangingEventArgs<DateTime>
{
   ...
}
```

In the remainder of this section, I assume that you've adopted the first approach and that all events are directly defined in terms of the PropertyChangingEventArgs<T> generic type.

The System.EventHandler<T> type is a generic delegate that can be passed any type that derives from System.EventArgs and that relieves you from defining a different delegate for each event. Thanks to this generic type and the nongeneric EventHandler type, you can define the four events in the Employee class as follows:

```
public class Employee
{
   public event EventHandler<PropertyChangingEventArgs<string>> NameChanging;
   public event EventHandler<PropertyChangingEventArgs<DateTime>> BirthDateChanging;
   public event EventHandler NameChanged;
   public event EventHandler BirthDateChanged;
   ...
```

Adding support for the Name and BirthDate properties, and corresponding *Xxxx*Changing and *Xxxx*Changed events, is now straightforward:

```
// (Continuing previous code snippet ...)
private string m_Name;

public string Name
{
   get
   {
      return m_Name;
   }
   set
   {
      if (m_Name != value)
      {
         PropertyChangingEventArgs<string> e =
            new PropertyChangingEventArgs<string>(value);
         OnNameChanging(e);
         if ( e.Cancel )
         {
            return;
         }
         m_Name = value;
         OnNameChanged(EventArgs.Empty);
      }
   }
}

private DateTime m_BirthDate;

public DateTime BirthDate
{
```

```
      get
      {
         return m_BirthDate;
      }
      set
      {
         if (m_BirthDate != value)
         {
            PropertyChangingEventArgs<DateTime> e =
               new PropertyChangingEventArgs<DateTime>(value);
            OnBirthDateChanging(e);
            if ( e.Cancel )
            {
               return;
            }
            m_BirthDate = value;
            OnBirthDateChanged(EventArgs.Empty);
         }
      }
   }

   // Protected OnXxxx methods
   protected virtual void OnNameChanging(PropertyChangingEventArgs<string> e)
   {
      if ( null != NameChanging )
      {
         NameChanging(this, e);
      }
   }

   protected virtual void OnNameChanged(EventArgs e)
   {
      if ( null != NameChanged )
      {
         NameChanged(this, e);
      }
   }

   protected virtual void OnBirthDateChanging(PropertyChangingEventArgs<DateTime> e)
   {
      if ( null != BirthDateChanging )
      {
         BirthDateChanging(this, e);
      }
   }

   protected virtual void OnBirthDateChanged(EventArgs e)
   {
      if ( null != BirthDateChanged )
      {
         BirthDateChanged(this, e);
      }
   }
}
```

Generics can help you reduce the amount of code needed to support events in one more way. The set blocks in the Name and BirthDate property procedures are almost identical, except for the name of the EventArgs-derived class and the On*Xxxx* methods. Even if the names of these On*Xxxx* methods are different, the syntax is similar, so you can invoke these methods through delegates. This technique enables you to move the common code into a separate module and reuse it for all the properties in all your types:

```
public static class EventHelper
{
    // Delegates declaration
    public delegate void OnPropertyChangingEventHandler<T>(PropertyChangingEventArgs<T> e);
    public delegate void OnPropertyChangedEventHandler(EventArgs e);

    public static void AssignProperty<T>(ref T oldValue, T proposedValue,
        OnPropertyChangingEventHandler<T> onChanging,
        OnPropertyChangedEventHandler onChanged)
    {
        // Nothing to do if the new value is the same as the old value.
        if ( object.Equals(oldValue, proposedValue) )
        {
            return;
        }
        // Invoke the OnChangingXXXX method. Exit if subscribers canceled the assignment.
        PropertyChangingEventArgs<T> e = new PropertyChangingEventArgs<T>(proposedValue);
        onChanging.DynamicInvoke(e);
        if (e.Cancel)
        {
            return;
        }
        // Proceed with assignment, and then invoke the OnChangedXXXX method.
        oldValue = proposedValue;
        onChanged.DynamicInvoke(EventArgs.Empty);
    }
}
```

Thanks to the EventHelper module, you can simplify the code in the Name and BirthDate properties significantly (changes are in bold type):

```
public string Name
{
    get
    {
        return m_Name;
    }
    set
    {
        EventHelper.AssignProperty<string>(ref m_Name, value,
            OnNameChanging, OnNameChanged);
    }
}

private DateTime m_BirthDate;

public DateTime BirthDate
{
    get
```

```
        {
            return m_BirthDate;
        }
        set
        {
            EventHelper.AssignProperty<DateTime>(ref m_BirthDate, value,
                OnBirthDateChanging, OnBirthDateChanged );
        }
    }
}
```

Object Pools

An *object pool* is a collection of objects that have been created and initialized in advance and are ready for the application to use them. Object pools are quite common in programming. For example, ADO.NET maintains a pool of connection objects: when the application asks for a connection to a database and a connection in the pool that already points to the specific database is available, ADO.NET takes a connection from the pool instead of instantiating it from scratch. When the application asks to close the connection, the physical connection isn't actually closed and the connection object is simply returned to the pool. When the same or another application asks for a connection to the same database, the connection object is taken from the pool, thus saving several seconds.

The following ObjectPool generic type implements a simple object pool. You can use this pool to create a new instance of a given type using the CreateObject method. When you don't need the object any longer, you can simply return it to the pool by using the DestroyObject method so that the next time the CreateObject method is invoked, no object is physically created:

```
public class ObjectPool<T> where T : new()
{
    public List<T> pool = new List<T>();

    // Create an object, taking it from the pool if possible.
    public T CreateObject()
    {
        if ( pool.Count == 0 )
        {
            return new T();
        }
        else
        {
            // Return the first object to the pool.
            T item = pool[0];
            pool.RemoveAt(0);
            return item;
        }
    }

    // Return an object to the pool.
    public void DestroyObject(T item)
    {
        pool.Add(item);
    }
}
```

The ObjectPool class is especially useful for types that require a nonnegligible amount of time to be instantiated; under such circumstances, the application can improve performance substantially by keeping these objects alive in the pool:

```
ObjectPool<Employee> pool = new ObjectPool<Employee>();
// These two elements are created when the method is invoked.
Employee e1 = pool.CreateObject();
Employee e2 = pool.CreateObject();
// Return one object to the pool, and then set its reference to null.
pool.DestroyObject(e1);
e1 = null;
// Now the pool contains one element, thus the next statement takes it from there.
Employee e3 = pool.CreateObject();
...
```

As I already explained, no form of generic constraint enables you to specify that a type must have a constructor with a given signature; thus, you can't pass arguments when instantiating a type that appears as a generic parameter. This issue severely limits the usefulness of the ObjectPool class.

The simplest way to work around this limitation and make the ObjectPool type more versatile is to define an interface that all poolable objects must implement:

```
public interface IPoolable
{
    void Initialize(params object[] propertyValues);
    bool IsEqual(params object[] propertyValues);
}
```

For each type, you should define a minimum set of properties that can distinguish individual instances of that type. For example, two Employee objects should be considered as equal when their Name and BirthDate properties have the same values; therefore, the Employee class might implement the IPoolable interface as follows:

```
public class Employee : IPoolable
{
    // The IPoolable interface

    public void Initialize(params object[] propertyValues)
    {
        this.Name = (string) propertyValues[0];
        this.BirthDate = (DateTime) propertyValues[1];
    }

    public bool IsEqual(params object[] propertyValues)
    {
        return (this.Name == (string) propertyValues[0])
            && (this.BirthDate == (DateTime) propertyValues[1]);
    }
    // (Implementation of Name and BirthDate properties is omitted....)
    ...
}
```

You can now improve the ObjectPool class to take advantage of the IPoolable interface and reuse an object in the pool only if its most important properties are equal to those of the object requested by the client:

```
public class ObjectPoolEx<T> where T : IPoolable, new()
{
    public List<T> pool = new List<T>();

    // Create an object, taking it from the pool if possible.
    public T CreateObject(params object[] propertyValues)
    {
        for ( int i = 0; i < pool.Count; i++ )
        {
            T item = pool[i];
            if ( item.IsEqual(propertyValues) )
            {
                // We've found an object with the required properties.
                pool.RemoveAt(i);
                return item;
            }
        }
        // Create and return a brand-new object.
        T obj = new T();
        obj.Initialize(propertyValues);
        return obj;
    }

    // Return an object to the pool.
    public void DestroyObject(T item)
    {
        pool.Add(item);
    }
}
```

The code that uses the ObjectPoolEx class to create a pool of Employee objects must provide an initial value for the Name and BirthDate properties:

```
ObjectPoolEx<Employee> pool = new ObjectPoolEx<Employee>();
// These two elements are created when the method is invoked.
Employee e1 = pool.CreateObject("Joe", new DateTime(1961, 1, 1));
Employee e2 = pool.CreateObject("Ann", new DateTime(1962, 2, 2));
// Return them to the pool and set their references to Nothing.
pool.DestroyObject(e1);
e1 = null;
pool.DestroyObject(e2);
e2 = null;
// This object can't be taken from the pool, because its
// properties don't match any of the objects in the pool.
Employee e3 = pool.CreateObject("Joe", new DateTime(1963, 3, 3));
// This object matches exactly one object in the pool, thus no new instance is created.
Employee e4 = pool.CreateObject("Ann", new DateTime(1962, 2, 2));
```

Once again, keep in mind that object pools are convenient only if the time you spend to instantiate an object is relevant; in all other cases, using an object pool is likely to degrade your performance without buying you any other benefit.

Chapter 5
Arrays and Collections

The Microsoft .NET Framework doesn't merely include classes for managing system objects, such as files, directories, processes, and threads. It also exposes objects, such as complex data structures (queues, stacks, lists, and hash tables), that help developers organize information and solve recurring problems. Many real-world applications use arrays and collections, and the .NET Framework support for arrays and collection-like objects is really outstanding. It can take you a while to get familiar with the many possibilities that the Common Language Runtime (CLR) offers, but this effort pays off nicely at coding time.

Arrays and collections have become even richer and more powerful in .NET Framework version 2.0 with the introduction of generics, both because many types have been extended with generics methods and because you can create strong-typed collections much more easily in this new version of the framework.

 Note To avoid long lines, code samples in this chapter assume that the following using statements are used at the top of each source file:

```
using System.Collections;
using System.Collections.Generic;
using System.Collections.ObjectModel;
using System.Collections.Specialized;
using System.Diagnostics;
using System.IO;
using System.Text.RegularExpressions;
```

The Array Type

By default, .NET arrays have a zero-based index. One-dimensional arrays with a zero lower index are known as *SZArrays* or *vectors* and are the fastest type of arrays available to developers. .NET also supports arrays with a different lower index, but they aren't CLS-compliant, aren't very efficient, and aren't recommended. In practice, you never need an array with a different lower index, and I won't cover them in this book.

The Array class constructor has a protected scope, so you can't directly use the new keyword with this class. This isn't a problem because you create an array using the standard Microsoft Visual C# syntax and you can even use initializers:

```
// An array initialized with the powers of 2
int[] intArr = new int[]{1, 2, 4, 8, 16, 32, 64, 128, 256, 512};
// Shortened syntax
int[] intArr = {1, 2, 4, 8, 16, 32, 64, 128, 256, 512};
// Noninitialized (empty) two-dimensional array
long[,] lngArr;
```

You can also create an array and initialize it on the fly, which is sometimes useful for passing an argument or assigning a property that takes an array without having to create a temporary array. To see why this feature can be useful, consider the following code:

```
// Create a temporary array.
int[] tmp = {2, 5, 9, 13};
// The obj.ValueArray property takes an array of Int32.
obj.ValueArray = tmp;
// Clear the temporary variable.
tmp = null;
```

The ability to create and initialize an array in a single statement can make the code more concise:

```
obj.ValueArray = new int[] {2, 5, 9, 13};
```

You get an error if you access a null array, which is an array variable that hasn't been initialized yet. You can test this condition using a plain == operator:

```
if ( lngArr == null )
{
    lngArr = new long[10,20];
}
```

You can query an array for its rank (that is, the number of dimensions) by using its Rank property, and you can query the total number of its elements by means of its Length property:

```
// …(Continuing the first example in this chapter)…
int res = lngArr.Rank;                      // => 2
// lngArr has 10*20 elements.
res = lngArr.Length;                        // => 200
```

Starting with version 1.1, the .NET Framework supports 64-bit array indexes, so an array index can also be a long value. To support these huge arrays, the Array class has been expanded with a LongLength property that returns the number of elements as an Int64 value.

The GetLength method returns the number of elements along a given dimension, whereas GetLowerBound and GetUpperBound return the lowest and highest indexes along the specified dimension. (For all the arrays you can create in C#, the GetLowerBound method returns 0.) As usual in the .NET Framework, the dimension number is zero-based:

```
// …(Continuing previous example)…
res = lngArr.GetLength(0);              // => 11
res = lngArr.GetLowerBound(1);          // => 0
res = lngArr.GetUpperBound(1);          // => 20
```

You can visit all the elements of an array using a single foreach loop and a strongly typed variable. This technique also works with multidimensional arrays, so you can process all the elements in a two-dimensional array with just one loop:

```
string[] strArr = {{"00", "01", "02"}, {"10", "11", "12"}};
foreach (string s in strArr)
{
    Console.Write(s + ",");        // => 00,01,02,10,11,12
}
```

Notice that a foreach loop on a multidimensional array visits array elements in a row-wise order (all the elements in the first row, then all the elements in the second row, and so on). Pay attention when migrating legacy applications because in most languages that preceded .NET this loop worked in column-wise order.

The Array class supports the ICloneable interface, so you can create a shallow copy of an array using the Clone instance method. (See the section titled "The ICloneable Interface" in Chapter 3, "Interfaces," for a discussion about shallow and deep copy operations.)

```
string[,] arr2 = (string[,]) strArr.Clone();
```

The CopyTo method enables you to copy a one-dimensional array to another one-dimensional array; you decide the starting index in the destination array:

```
// Create and initialize an array (10 elements).
int[] sourceArr = {1, 2, 3, 5, 7, 11, 13, 17, 19, 23};
// Create the destination array (must be same size or larger).
int[] destArr = new int[20];
// Copy the source array into the second half of the destination array.
sourceArr.CopyTo(destArr, 10);
```

Sorting Elements

The Array class offers several static methods for processing arrays quickly and easily. In Chapter 3, you learned that you can sort arrays of objects using an arbitrary group of keys by means of the Array.Sort method and the IComparable and IComparer interfaces. But the Array.Sort method is even more flexible than what you've seen so far. For example, it can sort just a portion of an array:

```
// Sort only elements [10,99] of the targetArray.
// Second argument is starting index; last argument is length of the subarray.
Array.Sort(targetArray, 10, 90);
```

You can also sort an array of values using another array that holds the sorting keys, which enables you to sort arrays of structures or objects even if they don't implement the IComparable interface. To see how this overloaded version of the Sort method works, let's start defining a structure:

```
public struct Employee
{
    public string FirstName;
    public string LastName;
    public DateTime HireDate;

    public Employee(string firstName, string lastName, DateTime hireDate)
    {
        this.FirstName = firstName;
        this.LastName = lastName;
        this.HireDate = hireDate;
    }

    // A function to display an element's properties easily
    public string Description()
    {
        return string.Format("{0} {1} (hired on {2})", FirstName, LastName,
            HireDate.ToShortDateString());
    }
}
```

The following code creates a main array of Employee structures, creates an auxiliary key array that holds the hiring date of each employee, and finally sorts the main array using the auxiliary array:

```
// Create a test array.
Employee[] employees = { new Employee("John", "Evans", new DateTime(2001, 3, 1)),
    new Employee("Robert", "Zare", new DateTime(2000, 8, 12)),
    new Employee("Ann", "Beebe", new DateTime(1999, 11, 1)) };
// Create a parallel array of hiring dates.
DateTime[] hireDates = new DateTime[employees.Length];
for ( int i = 0; i < employees.Length; i++ )
{
    hireDates[i] = employees[i].HireDate;
}
// Sort the array of Employees using HireDates to provide the keys.
Array.Sort(hireDates, employees);
// Prove that the array is sorted on the HireDate field.
foreach (Employee em in employees)
{
    Console.WriteLine(em.Description());
}
```

Interestingly, the key array is sorted as well, so you don't need to initialize it again when you add another element to the main array:

```
// Add a fourth employee.
Array.Resize<Employee>(ref employees, 4);
```

```
employees[3] = new Employee("Chris", "Cannon", new DateTime(2000, 5, 9));
// Extend the key array as well, no need to reinitialize it.
Array.Resize<DateTime>(ref hireDates, 4);
hireDates[3] = employees[3].HireDate;
// Re-sort the new, larger array.
Array.Sort(hireDates, employees);
```

(Read on for the description of the Array.Resize<T> generic method.) An overloaded version of the Sort method enables you to sort a portion of an array of values for which you provide an array of keys. This is especially useful when you start with a large array that you fill only partially:

```
// Create a test array with a lot of room.
Employee[] employees = new Employee[1000];
// Initialize only its first four elements.
...
// Sort only the portion actually used.
Array.Sort(hireDates, employees, 0, 4);
```

All the versions of the Array.Sort method that you've seen so far can take an additional IComparer object, which dictates how the array elements or keys are to be compared with one another. (See the section titled "The IComparer Interface" in Chapter 3.)

The Array.Reverse method reverses the order of elements in an array or in a portion of an array, so you can apply it immediately after a Sort method to sort in descending order:

```
// Sort an array of Int32 in reverse order.
Array.Sort(intArray);
Array.Reverse(intArray);
```

You pass the initial index and number of elements to reverse only a portion of an array:

```
// Reverse only the first 10 elements in intArray.
Array.Reverse(intArray, 0, 10);
```

You have a special case when you reverse only two elements, which is the same as swapping two consecutive elements, a frequent operation when you're working with arrays:

```
// Swap elements at indexes 5 and 6.
Array.Reverse(intArray, 5, 2);
```

Clearing, Copying, and Moving Elements

You can clear a portion of an array by using the Clear method, without a for loop:

```
// Clear elements [10,99] of an array.
Array.Clear(arr, 10, 90);
```

The Array.Copy method enables you to copy elements from a one-dimensional array to another. There are two overloaded versions for this method. The first version copies a given number of elements from the source array to the destination array:

```
int[] intArr = { 1, 2, 3, 4, 5, 6, 7, 8, 9, 10 };
int[] intArr2 = new int[20];
// Copy the entire source array into the first half of the target array.
Array.Copy(intArr, intArr2, 10);
for (int i = 0; i < 20; i++)
{
    Console.Write("{0} ", intArr2[i]);
       // => 1 2 3 4 5 6 7 8 9 10 0 0 0 0 0 0 0 0 0 0
}
```

The second version lets you decide the starting index in the source array, the starting index in the destination array (that is, the index of the first element that will be overwritten), and the number of elements to copy:

```
// Copy elements at indexes 5-9 to the end of intArr2.
Array.Copy(intArr, 5, intArr2, 15, 5);
// This is the first element that has been copied.
Console.WriteLine(intArr2[15]);                          // => 6
```

You get an exception of type ArgumentOutOfRangeException if you provide wrong values for the indexes or the destination array isn't large enough, and you get an exception of type RankException if either array has two or more dimensions.

The Copy method works correctly even when source and destination arrays have elements of different types, in which case it attempts to cast each individual source element to the corresponding element in the destination array. The actual behavior depends on many factors, though, such as whether the source or the destination is a value type or a reference type. For example, you can always copy from any array to an Object array, from an Int32 array to an Int64 array, and from a float array to a double array because they are widening conversions and can't fail. Copy throws an exception of type TypeMismatchException when you attempt a narrowing conversion between arrays of value types, even though individual elements in the source array might be successfully converted to the destination type:

```
int[] intArr3 = {1, 2, 3, 4, 5, 6, 7, 8, 9, 10};
// This Copy operation succeeds even if array types are different.
long[] lngArr3 = new long[20];
Array.Copy(intArr3, lngArr3, 10);

// This Copy operation fails with ArrayTypeMismatchException.
//    (But you can carry it out with an explicit for loop.)
short[] shoArr3 = new short[20];
Array.Copy(intArr3, shoArr3, 10);
```

Conversely, if you copy from and to an array of reference type, the Array.Copy method attempts the copy operation for each element; if an InvalidCastException object is thrown for an element, the method copies neither that element nor any of the values after the one that raised the error. This behavior can cause a problem because your code now has an array that is only partially filled.

The ConstrainedCopy method, new in .NET Framework 2.0, solves the issue I just mentioned, sort of. If an exception occurs when using this method, all changes to the destination array are undone in an orderly manner, so you can never end up with an array that has been copied or converted only partially. However, the ConstrainedCopy method can't really replace the Copy method in the previous code snippet because it requires that no form of boxing, unboxing, casting, widening conversion, or narrowing conversion occurs. In practice, you should use the ConstrainedCopy method only in critical regions where an unexpected exception, including a .NET internal error, might compromise your data.

The Array.Copy method can even copy a portion of an array over itself. In this case, the Copy method performs a "smart copy" in the sense that elements are copied correctly in ascending order when you're copying to a lower index and in reverse order when you're copying to a higher index. So you can use the Copy method to delete one or more elements and fill the hole that would result by shifting all subsequent elements one or more positions toward lower indexes:

```
long[] lngArr4 = {1, 2, 3, 4, 5, 6, 7, 8, 9, 10};
// Delete element at index 4.
Array.Copy(lngArr4, 5, lngArr4, 4, 5);
// Complete the delete operation by clearing the last element.
Array.Clear(lngArr4, lngArr4.Length - 1, 1);
// Now the array contains: {1, 2, 3, 4, 6, 7, 8, 9, 10, 0}
```

You can use this code as the basis for a reusable method that works with any type of array:

```
public static void ArrayDeleteElement(Array arr, int index)
{
    // This method works only with one-dimensional arrays.
    if (arr.Rank != 1)
    {
        throw new ArgumentException("Invalid rank");
    }
    // Shift elements from arr[index+1] to arr[index].
    Array.Copy(arr, index + 1, arr, index, arr.Length - index - 1);
    // Clear the last element.
    Array.Clear(arr, arr.Length - 1, 1);
}
```

Inserting an element is also easy, and again you can create a routine that works with arrays of any type:

```
public static void ArrayInsertElement(Array arr, int index, object newValue)
{
    // This method works only with one-dimensional arrays.
    if (arr.Rank != 1)
    {
```

```
            throw new ArgumentException("Invalid rank");
    }
    // Shift elements from arr[index] to arr[index+1] to make room.
    Array.Copy(arr, index, arr, index + 1, arr.Length - index - 1);
    // Assign the element using the SetValue method.
    arr.SetValue(newValue, index);
}
```

The Array class exposes the SetValue and GetValue methods to assign and read elements. You don't use these methods often in regular programming, but they turn out to be useful in methods that work with any type of array. You can also use generics to make your code even more concise, more robust, and faster:

```
public static void ArrayDeleteElement<T>(T[] arr, int index)
{
    Array.Copy(arr, index + 1, arr, index, arr.Length - index - 1);
    arr[index] = default(T);
}

public static void ArrayInsertElement<T>(T[] arr, int index, T newValue)
{
    Array.Copy(arr, index, arr, index + 1, arr.Length - index - 1);
    arr[index] = newValue;
}
```

You can also use the Copy method with multidimensional arrays, in which case the array is treated as if it were a one-dimensional array with all the rows laid down in memory, one after the other. This method works only if the source and destination arrays have the same rank, even if they can have a different number of rows and columns.

You can do some interesting tricks with the Buffer type, which exposes static methods that perform byte-by-byte operations on one-dimensional arrays. The elements in the two arrays don't need to be the same size; thus, for example, you can inspect the individual bytes of a Double array as follows:

```
// Inspecting the bytes of a Double array
double[] values = { 123, 456, 789 };          // 3 Doubles = 24 bytes
byte[] bytes = new byte[24];
Buffer.BlockCopy(values, 0, bytes, 0, 24);
foreach (byte b in bytes)
{
    Console.Write("{0} ", b);
    // => 0 0 0 0 0 192 94 64 0 0 0 0 0 128 124 64 0 0 0 0 0 168 136 64
}
```

Other methods of the Buffer type allow you to read and write individual bytes inside an array. For security reasons, the Buffer class works only with arrays of primitive types, such as Boolean, Char, and all numeric types. Arrays of other types cause an exception of type ArgumentException to be thrown.

Searching Values

The IndexOf method searches an array for a value and returns the index of the first element that matches or −1 if the search fails:

```
string[] strArr = {"Robert", "Joe", "Ann", "Chris", "Joe"};
int index = Array.IndexOf(strArr, "Ann");              // => 2
// Note that string searches are case sensitive.
index = Array.IndexOf(strArr, "ANN");                  // => -1
```

You can also specify a starting index and an optional ending index; if an ending index is omitted, the search continues until the end of the array. You can use the following approach to find all the values in the array with a given value:

```
// Search for all the occurrences of the "Joe" string.
index = Array.IndexOf(strArr, "Joe");
while ( index >= 0 )
{
   Console.WriteLine("Found at index {0}", index);
   // Search next occurrence.
   index = Array.IndexOf(strArr, "Joe", index + 1);
}
```

The LastIndexOf method is similar to IndexOf except that it returns the index of the last occurrence of the value. Because the search is backward, you must pass a start index equal to the end index:

```
// A revised version of the search loop, which searches
// from higher indexes toward the beginning of the array.
index = Array.LastIndexOf(strArr, "Joe", strArr.Length - 1);
while ( index >= 0 )
{
   Console.WriteLine("Found at index {0}", index);
   index = Array.LastIndexOf(strArr, "Joe", index - 1);
}
```

The IndexOf and LastIndexOf methods perform a linear search, so their performance degrades linearly with larger arrays. You deliver much faster code if the array is sorted and you use the BinarySearch method:

```
// Binary search on a sorted array
string[] strArr2 = {"Ann", "Chris", "Joe", "Robert", "Sam"};
index = Array.BinarySearch(strArr2, "Chris");          // => 1
```

If the binary search fails, the method returns a negative value that's the bitwise complement of the index of the first element that's larger than the value being searched for. This feature enables you to determine where the value should be inserted in the sorted array:

```
index = Array.BinarySearch(strArr2, "David");
if ( index >= 0 )
{
```

```
      Console.WriteLine("Found at index {0}", index);
}
else
{
   // Negate the result to get the index for the insertion point.
   index = ~index;
   Console.WriteLine("Not Found. Insert at index {0}", index);
      // => Not found. Insert at index 2
}
```

You can pass a start index and the length of the portion of the array in which you want to perform the search, which is useful when you're working with an array that's only partially filled:

```
index = Array.BinarySearch(strArr2, 0, 3, "Chris");        // => 1
```

Finally, both syntax forms for the BinarySearch method support an IComparer object at the end of the argument list; this argument lets you determine how array elements are to be compared. In practice, you can use the same IComparer object that you passed to the Sort method when you sorted the array.

Jagged Arrays

C# also supports arrays of arrays, that is, arrays whose elements are arrays. Arrays of arrays—also known as *jagged arrays*—are especially useful when you have a two-dimensional matrix with rows that don't have the same length. You can render this structure by using a standard two-dimensional array, but you'd have to size it to accommodate the row with the highest number of elements, which would result in wasted space. The arrays of arrays concept isn't limited to two dimensions only, and you might need three-dimensional or four-dimensional jagged arrays. Here is an example of a "triangular" matrix of strings:

```
"a00"
"a10"  "a11"
"a20"  "a21"  "a22"
"a30"  "a31"  "a32"  "a33"
```

The next code snippet shows how you can render the preceding structure as a jagged array, and then process it by expanding its rows:

```
// Initialize an array of arrays.
string[][] arr = { new string[] { "a00" },
   new string[] { "a10", "a11" },
   new string[] { "a20", "a21", "a22" },
   new string[] { "a30", "a31", "a32", "a33" } };

// Show how you can reference an element.
string elem = arr[3][1];                           // => a31
// Assign an entire row.
arr[0] = new string[] { "a00", "a01", "a02" };
// Read an element just added.
elem = arr[0][2];                                  // => a02
```

```
// Expand one of the rows.
Array.Resize<string>(ref arr[1], arr[1].Length + 2);
// Assign the new elements. (Currently they are null.)
arr[1][2] = "a12";
arr[1][3] = "a13";
// Read back one of them.
elem = arr[1][2];                                      // => a12
```

An obvious advantage of jagged arrays is that they can take less memory than regular multi-dimensional arrays do. Just as interesting, the JIT compiler produces code that is up to five or six times faster when accessing a jagged array than when accessing a multidimensional array. However, keep in mind that jagged arrays aren't CLS-compliant; thus, they shouldn't appear as arguments or return values in public methods.

A great way to take advantage of the higher speed of jagged arrays while continuing to use the standard multidimensional array syntax and hiding implementation details at the same time is by defining a generic type that wraps an array of arrays:

```
public class Matrix<T>
{
   private T[][] values;

   public Matrix(int rows, int cols)
   {
      values = new T[rows][];
      bounds = new int[] { rows - 1, cols - 1 };

      for (int i = 0; i < rows; i++)
      {
         T[] row = new T[cols];
      }
   }

   public T this[int row, int col]
   {
      get { return values[row][col]; }
      set { values[row][col] = value; }
   }
}
```

Using the Matrix class is almost identical to using a two-dimensional array, the only difference is in the way you create an instance of the array:

```
Matrix<double> mat = new Matrix<double>(100, 100);
mat[10, 1] = 123.45;
Console.WriteLine(mat[10, 1]);                         // => 123.45
```

Because of the way the CLR optimizes jagged arrays, the Matrix class is two to three times faster than a standard two-dimensional array is, while preserving the latter's standard syntax. Can you ask for more?

Generic Methods

In version 2.0 of the .NET Framework, the Array type has been extended with several generic methods. In general, these methods offer better type safety and, in most cases, better performance. For example, consider the following code:

```
// (Microsoft Visual C# .NET 2003 code)
// Create an array with a nonzero value in the last element.
short[] arr = new short[100000];
arr[100000] = -1;
// Search for the nonzero element.
int index = Array.IndexOf(arr, -1);
```

The standard IndexOf method must work with arrays of all kinds; thus, the search it performs isn't optimized for a specific element type. More specifically, the second argument must be boxed when you pass a value type, as in this case. To solve these issues, the Array class in .NET Framework 2.0 supports the IndexOf<T> generic method:

```
index = Array.IndexOf<short>(arr, -1);
```

The generic method appears to be from 15 to 100 times faster than the standard method is, depending on how many repetitions you execute. (Remember that each time you call the standard method, a boxing operation takes place and a temporary object is created behind the scenes.) Even with a few repetitions, the generic approach is clearly to be preferred, especially when you consider that it simply requires adding a pair of angle brackets to existing C# code. Notice that there is no significant performance gain in using this method with a reference type, for example, a string array.

Interestingly, the Microsoft Visual C# 2005 compiler automatically selects the generic version of a method, if possible—therefore, most of your Visual C# .NET 2003 code will perform better if you simply recompile it under the current Microsoft Visual Studio version. This behavior is a consequence of the fact that you can drop the <...> clause in generic methods if no ambiguity ensues, as I explained in the section titled "Generic Methods" in Chapter 4, "Generics." More specifically, the compiler selects the generic version of the second argument if it matches perfectly the type of the array passed in the first argument. For example, consider this code:

```
int arr = new int[100000];
arr[99999] = -1;
// Next statement is compiled using the IndexOf<int> generic method.
index = Array.IndexOf(arr, -1);

short search = -1;
// Next statement is compiled using the standard IndexOf, and boxing occurs.
index = Array.IndexOf(arr, search);
```

This undocumented behavior can lead to a serious loss of performance in some cases. For example, consider this code:

```
long[] lngArr = new long[100000];
lngArr(99999) = -1;
index = Array.IndexOf(lngArr, -1);
```

Quite surprisingly, the last statement in this code snippet is compiled using a standard IndexOf method instead of the more efficient IndexOf<long> method that you might expect. The reason: the −1 argument is considered a 32-bit value and therefore doesn't match the array of long values passed in the first argument. You therefore must either explicitly use the generic method or force the type of the second argument, as follows:

```
// Two techniques to force the compiler to use the generic method
index = Array.IndexOf<long>(lngArr, -1);
index = Array.IndexOf(lngArr, -1L);
```

If you think that this is just a syntax detail and that you shouldn't care about which method is actually chosen by the compiler, well, think again. If you force the compiler to select the IndexOf<long> method instead of the IndexOf standard method, your code can run *almost two orders of magnitude faster*! The actual ratio depends on how many times you invoke the method and becomes apparent when this number is high enough to fire one or more garbage collections.

> **Note**   The code examples in the remaining portion of this chapter use the generic syntax to emphasize the generic nature of methods, even if in most cases the <...> clause might be dropped. Although there aren't any established guidelines in this field, I recommend that you use explicit angle brackets in all cases, both to make your code more readable and to force the compiler to use the generic version when a standard version of the same method is available.

A few other generic methods that mirror existing methods have been added, including BinarySearch, LastIndexOf, and Sort. The generic sort method can take one or two generic parameters, depending on whether you pass a parallel array of keys:

```
// Sort an array of integers.
Array.Sort<int>(arr);
// Sort an array of integers using a parallel array of string keys.
string[] keys = new string[arr.Length];
// Fill the array of keys.
...
// Sort the integer array using the parallel key array.
Array.Sort<string>, Integer)(keys, arr);
```

The Resize<T> method changes the number of elements in a one-dimensional array while preserving existing elements. I have already used this method previously in this chapter:

```
int[] arr = {0, 1, 2, 3, 4};
...
// Extend the array to contain 10 elements, but preserve existing ones.
Array.Resize<int>(ref arr, 10);
```

There is no Resize method to resize two-dimensional arrays, but it's easy to create one:

```
public static void Resize<T>(ref T[,] arr, int rows, int cols)
{
```

```
    if ( rows <= 0 || cols <= 0 )
    {
        throw new ArgumentException("Invalid new size");
    }
    T[,] newArr = new T[rows, cols];
    for ( int r = 0; r <= Math.Min(arr.GetUpperBound(0), rows); r++ )
    {
        for ( int c = 0; c <= Math.Min(arr.GetUpperBound(1), cols); c++ )
        {
            newArr[r, c] = arr[r, c];
        }
    }
    arr = newArr;
}
```

All the remaining generic methods in the Array class take a delegate as an argument and enable you to perform a given operation without writing an explicit for or foreach loop. These methods are especially useful in C# when used together with anonymous methods. In fact, most of the generic methods exposed by the Array type take a Predicate<T> delegate; such delegates point to a function that takes an argument of type T and returns a bool value, which is typically the result of a test condition on the argument. For example, consider the code that you should write to find the first array element that meets a given criterion, for example, the first number that is positive and divisible by 10:

```
int[] arr()= {1, 3, 60, 4, 30, 66, -10, 79, 10, -4};
int result = 0;
for ( int i = 0; i < arr.Length; i++ )
{
    if ( arr[i] > 0 && (arr[i] % 10) == 0 )
    {
        result = arr[i];
        break;
    }
}
if ( result == 0 )
{
    Console.WriteLine("Not found");
}
else
{
    Console.WriteLine("Result = {0}", result);     // => Result = 60
}
```

You'll probably agree that it's a lot of code for such a simple task. Now, see how elegant the code becomes when you use the Find<T> generic method together with an anonymous method to get rid of the for loop:

```
int res = Array.Find<int>(arr, delegate(int n)
                              { return n > 0 && (n % 10) == 0; });
```

There is also a FindLast<T> generic method that, as its name implies, returns the last element in the array that matches the condition:

```
int res = Array.FindLast<int>(arr, delegate(int n)
                              { return n > 0 && (n % 10) == 0; });
```

Of course, the power of generics ensures that you can also use a similarly concise approach when looking for an element in a string array, a Double array, or an array of any type. If you simply want to check whether an element matching the condition exists, but you aren't interested in its value, you can use the new Exists generic method:

```
bool found = Array.Exists<int>(arr, delegate(int n)
                              { return n > 0 && (n % 10) == 0; });
if ( found )
{
    // The array contains at least one positive multiple of 10.
}
```

A limitation of the Find and FindLast methods is that they always return the default value of the type T if no match is found: null for strings and other reference types, zero for numbers, and so forth. In the preceding example, you know that the result—if found—is strictly positive, so a result equal to zero means that no match was found. If the zero or null value might be a valid match, however, you must opt for a different approach, based on the FindIndex<T> generic method:

```
int index = Array.FindIndex<int>(arr, delegate(int n)
                                 { return n > 0 && (n % 10) == 0; });
if ( index < 0 )
{
    Console.WriteLine("Element not found");
}
else
{
    Console.WriteLine("Element {0} found at index {1}", arr[index], index);
}
```

As you might expect, there is also a FindLastIndex<T> method that returns the last element that satisfies the condition:

```
index = Array.FindIndex<int>(arr, delegate(int n)
                             { return n > 0 && (n % 10) == 0; });
```

Unlike the Find and FindLast methods, both the FindIndex and FindLastIndex methods expose two overloads that enable you to indicate the starting index and the number of elements to be searched. If you are interested in gathering all the elements that match the condition, you might therefore use these methods in a loop, until they return −1, as in the following code:

```
int index = -1;
List<int> list = new List<int>();
while ( true )
```

```
{
   // Find the next match; exit the loop if not found.
   index = Array.FindIndex<int>(arr, index + 1, delegate(int n)
                                        { return n > 0 && (n % 10) == 0; });
   if ( index < 0 )
   {
      break;
   }
   // Remember the match in the List collection.
   list.Add(arr(index))
}
// Convert the List to a strong-typed array.
int[] matches = list.ToArray();
Console.WriteLine("Found {0} matches", matches.Length);    // => Found 3 matches
```

Once again, you'll surely appreciate the conciseness that the FindAll<T> method gives you:

```
// This statement is equivalent to the previous code snippet.
int[] matches = Array.FindAll<int>(arr, delegate(int n)
                                { return n > 0 && (n % 10) == 0; });
```

The TrueForAll<T> generic method enables you to quickly check whether all the elements in the array match the condition:

```
if ( Array.TrueForAll<int>(arr, delegate(int n)
                         { return n > 0 && (n % 10) == 0;}) )
{
   // All elements in the array are positive multiples of 10.
}
else
{
   // There is at least one element that isn't a positive multiple of 10.
}
```

(Note that there isn't a FalseForAll<T> generic method.) The ConvertAll<T, U> generic method provides a very powerful way to convert all the elements in an array into values of the same or different type. For example, here's how you can quickly convert all the elements in an Int32 array into their hexadecimal representation:

```
int[] arr = { 1, 3, 60, 4, 30, 66, -10, 79, 10, -4 };
string[] hexValues = Array.ConvertAll<int, string>(arr, delegate(int n)
                                        { return n.ToString("X2");  });
```

The second argument for the ConvertAll<T, U> method must be a delegate that points to a method that takes an argument of type T and returns a value of type U. In some cases, you don't even need to define a separate method because you can use a static method of a type defined in the .NET Framework. For example, here's how you can convert a numeric array into a string array:

```
string[] arrStr = Array.ConvertAll<int, string>(arr, Convert.ToString);
```

Many math transformations can be achieved by passing a delegate that points to one of the static methods of the Math type, for example, to round or truncate a Double or a Decimal value to an integer. You can use any of such methods, provided that the method takes only one argument.

The ForEach method, the last generic method in this overview, enables you to execute a given action or method for each element in the array; its second argument is an Action<T> delegate, which must point to a void procedure that takes an argument of type T. Here's an example that outputs all the elements of an array to the console window, without an explicit loop:

```
Array.ForEach<string>(arrStr, Console.WriteLine);
```

Please notice that I am providing these examples mainly as a demonstration of the power of generic methods in the Array type. I am not suggesting that you should always prefer these methods to simpler (and more readable) for or foreach loops. As a matter of fact, an explicit loop is often faster than an anonymous method used with a generic method of the Array class, so you should never use these generic methods in time-critical code.

The System.Collections Namespace

The System.Collections namespace exposes many classes that can work as data containers, such as collections and dictionaries. You can learn the features of all these objects individually, but a smarter approach is to learn about the underlying interfaces that these classes might implement.

The ICollection, IList, and IDictionary Interfaces

All the collection classes in the .NET Framework implement the ICollection interface, which inherits from IEnumerable and defines an object that supports enumeration through a foreach loop. The ICollection interface exposes a read-only Count property and a CopyTo method, which copies the elements from the collection object to an array.

The ICollection interface defines the minimum features that a collection-like object should have. The .NET Framework exposes two more interfaces whose methods add power and flexibility to a collection object: IList and IDictionary.

Many classes in the .NET Framework implement the IList interface. This interface inherits from ICollection, and therefore from IEnumerable, and represents a collection of objects that can be individually indexed. All the implementations of the IList interface fall into three categories: read-only (the collection's elements can't be modified or deleted, nor can new elements be inserted), fixed size (existing items can be modified, but elements can't be added or removed), and variable size (items can be modified, added, and removed).

The IList interface exposes several members in addition to the Count property and the CopyTo method inherited from IEnumerable. The names of these methods are quite self-explanatory: Add appends an element to the end of the collection; Insert adds a value between two existing elements; Remove deletes an element given its value; RemoveAt deletes an element at the specified index; Clear removes all the elements in one operation. You can access an element at a given index by means of the Item property (this is also the indexer of the class) and check whether an element with a given value exists with the Contains method (which returns a bool) or the IndexOf method (which returns the index where the element is found, or −1 if the element isn't found). You'll see all these methods and properties in action when I discuss the ArrayList type.

The IDictionary interface defines a collection-like object that contains one or more (key, value) pairs, where the key can be any object. As for the IList interface, implementations of the IDictionary interface can be read-only, fixed size, or variable size.

The IDictionary interface inherits the Count and CopyTo members from ICollection and extends it using the following methods: Add(key, value) adds a new element to the collection and associates it with a key; Remove removes an element with a given key; Clear removes all elements; Contains checks whether an element with a given key exists. You can access items in an IDictionary object with the Item(key) property, which C# clients see as the type's indexer; the Keys and Values read-only properties return an array containing all the keys and all the values in the collection, respectively.

For a class that implements the ICollection, IList, or IDictionary interface, it isn't mandatory that you expose all the interface's properties and methods as public members. For example, the Array class implements IList, but the Add, Insert, and Remove members don't appear in the Array class interface because arrays have a fixed size. You get an exception if you invoke these methods after casting an array to an IList variable.

A trait that all the classes in System.Collections—except the BitArray and BitVector32 types—have in common is that they store Object values. This means that you can store any type of value inside them and even store instances of different types inside the same collection. In some cases, this feature is useful, but when used with value types these collections cause a lot of boxing activity and their performance is less than optimal. Also, you often need to cast values to a typed variable when you unbox collection elements. As explained in Chapter 4, you should use a strong-typed generic collection to achieve type safety and more efficient code.

The ArrayList Type

You can think of the ArrayList class as a hybrid between an array and a collection. For example, you can address elements by their indexes, sort and reverse them, and search a value sequentially or by means of a binary search as you do with arrays; you can append elements, insert them in a given position, or remove them as you do with collections.

The ArrayList object has an initial capacity—in practice, the number of slots in the internal structure that holds the actual values—but you don't need to worry about that because an ArrayList is automatically expanded as needed, as are all collections. However, you can optimize your code by choosing an initial capability that offers a good compromise between used memory and the overhead that occurs whenever the ArrayList object has to expand:

```
// Create an ArrayList with default initial capacity of 4 elements.
ArrayList al = new ArrayList();
// Create an ArrayList with initial capacity of 1,000 elements.
ArrayList al2 = new ArrayList(1000);
```

(Notice that the initial capacity was 16 in .NET version 1.1 but has changed to 4 in version 2.0.) The ArrayList constructor can take an ICollection object and initialize its elements accordingly. You can pass another ArrayList or just a regular array:

```
// Create an array on the fly and pass it to the ArrayList constructor.
ArrayList al3 = new ArrayList(new string[]{"one", "two", "three"});
```

You can modify the capacity at any moment to enlarge the internal array or shrink it by assigning a value to the Capacity property. However, you can't make it smaller than the current number of elements actually stored in the array (which corresponds to the value returned by the Count property):

```
// Make the ArrayList take only the memory that it strictly needs.
al.Capacity = al.Count;
// Another way to achieve the same result
al.TrimToSize();
```

When the current capacity is exceeded, the ArrayList object doubles its capacity automatically. You can't control the growth factor of an ArrayList, so you should set the Capacity property to a suitable value to avoid time-consuming memory allocations.

Another way to create an ArrayList object is by means of its static Repeat method, which enables you to specify an initial value for the specified number of elements:

```
// Create an ArrayList with 100 elements equal to an empty string.
ArrayList al4 = ArrayList.Repeat("", 100);
```

The ArrayList class fully implements the IList interface. You add elements to an ArrayList object by using the Add method (which appends the new element after the last item) or the Insert method (which inserts the new element at the specified index). You remove a specific object by passing it to the Remove method, remove the element at a given index by using the RemoveAt method, or remove all elements with the Clear method:

```
// Be sure that you start with an empty ArrayList.
al.Clear();
// Append the elements "Joe" and "Ann" at the end of the ArrayList.
al.Add("Joe");
al.Add("Ann");
// Insert "Robert" item at the beginning of the list. (Index is zero-based.)
al.Insert(0, "Robert");
// Remove "Joe" from the list.
al.Remove("Joe");
// Remove the first element of the list ("Robert" in this case).
al.RemoveAt(0);
```

The Remove method removes only the first occurrence of a given object, so you need a loop to remove all the elements with a given value. You can't simply iterate through the loop until you get an error, however, because the Remove method doesn't throw an exception if the element isn't found. Therefore, you must use one of these two approaches:

```
// Using the Contains method is concise but not very efficient.
while ( al.Contains("element to remove") )
{
    al.Remove("element to remove");
}

// A more efficient technique: loop until the Count property becomes constant.
int saveCount = 0;
while ( al.Count == saveCount )
{
    saveCount = al.Count;
    al.Remove("element to remove");
}
```

You can read and write any ArrayList element using the Item property. This property is the type's indexer, so you can omit it and deal with this object as if it were a standard zero-based array:

```
al[0] = "first element";
```

Just remember that an element in an ArrayList object is created only when you call the Add method, so you can't reference an element whose index is equal to or higher than the Array-List's Count property. As with all collections, the preferred way to iterate over all elements is through the foreach loop, even though you can surely use a standard for loop:

```
// These two loops are equivalent.
foreach ( object o in al )
{
    Console.WriteLine(o);
}

for ( int i = 0; i < al.Count; i++ )
{
    Console.WriteLine(al[i]);
}
```

A good reason for using a for loop is that the controlling variable in a foreach loop is read-only, and thus you can't use a foreach loop if you need to modify elements in the ArrayList.

The ArrayList class exposes methods that enable you to manipulate ranges of elements in one operation. The AddRange method appends to the current ArrayList object all the elements contained in another object that implements the ICollection interface. Many .NET classes other than those described in this chapter implement ICollection, such as the collection of all the items in a ListBox control and the collection of nodes in a TreeView control. The following routine takes two ArrayList objects and returns a third ArrayList that contains all the items from both arguments:

```
public static ArrayList ArrayListJoin(ArrayList al1, ArrayList al2)
{
    // Note how we avoid time-consuming reallocations.
    ArrayList res = new ArrayList(al1.Count + al2.Count);
    // Append the items in the two ArrayList arguments.
    res.AddRange(al1);
    res.AddRange(al2);
    return res;
}
```

The InsertRange method works in a similar way but enables you to insert multiple elements at any index in the current ArrayList object:

```
// Insert all the items of al2 at the beginning of al.
al.InsertRange(0, al2);
// RemoveRange deletes multiple elements in the al object:
// Delete the last four elements (assumes there are at least four elements).
al.RemoveRange(al.Count - 4, 4);
```

Adding or removing elements from the beginning or the middle of an ArrayList is an expensive operation because all the elements with higher indexes must be shifted accordingly. In general, the Add method is faster than the Insert method is and should be used if possible.

You can read or write a group of contiguous elements by means of the GetRange and SetRange methods. The former takes an initial index and a count and returns a new ArrayList that contains only the elements in the selected range; the latter takes an initial index and an ICollection object:

```
// Display only the first 10 elements to the console window.
foreach ( object o in al.GetRange(0, 10) )
{
    Console.WriteLine(o);
}
// Copy the first 20 elements from al to al2.
al2.SetRange(0, al.GetRange(0, 20));
```

You can quickly extract all the items in the ArrayList object by using the ToArray method or the CopyTo method. Both of them support one-dimensional target arrays of any compatible type, but the latter also enables you to extract a subset of ArrayList:

```
// Extract elements to an Object array (never throws an exception).
object[] objArr = al.ToArray();
// Extract elements to a String array (might throw an InvalidCastException).
string[] strArr = (string[]) al.ToArray(typeof(string));

// Same as above but uses the CopyTo method.
// (Note that the target array must be large enough.)
string[] strArr2 = new string[al.Count];
al.CopyTo(strArr2);
```

```
// Copy only items [1,2], starting at element 4 in the target array.
string[] strArr3 = {"0", "1", "2", "3", "4", "5", "6", "7", "8", "9"};
// Syntax is: CopyTo(sourceIndex, target, destIndex, count).
al.CopyTo(0, strArr3, 4, 2);
```

The ArrayList class supports other useful methods, such as Sort, Reverse, BinarySearch, Contains, IndexOf, LastIndexOf, and Reverse. I described most of these methods in the section devoted to arrays, so I won't repeat their description here.

The TrimToSize method deserves a special mention. As I explained previously, the ArrayList automatically doubles its capacity whenever it needs room for a new element. After many insertions and deletions you might end up with an ArrayList that contains many unused slots; if you don't plan to add more elements to the ArrayList, you can reclaim the unused space by means of the TrimToSize method:

```
al.TrimToSize();
```

The last feature of the ArrayList class that's worth mentioning is its Adapter and ReadOnly static methods. The Adapter method takes an IList-derived object as its only argument and creates an ArrayList wrapper around that object. In other words, instead of creating a copy of the argument, the Adapter method creates an ArrayList object that "contains" the original collection. All the changes you make on the outer ArrayList object are duplicated in the original collection, and vice versa. You might want to use the Adapter method because the ArrayList class implements several methods—Reverse, Sort, BinarySearch, ToArray, IndexOf, and LastIndexOf, just to name a few—that are missing in a simpler IList object. The following code sample demonstrates how you can use this technique to reverse (or sort, and so on) all the items in a ListBox control:

```
// Create a wrapper around the ListBox.Items (IList) collection.
ArrayList lbAdapter = ArrayList.Adapter(listBox1.Items);
// Reverse their order.
lbAdapter.Reverse();
```

If you don't plan to reuse the ArrayList wrapper, you can make this code even more concise:

```
ArrayList.Adapter(listBox1.Items).Reverse();
```

The ReadOnly static method is similar to Adapter, except it returns a ArrayList that you can't modify in any way, including adding, removing, or assigning elements. This method can be useful when you want to pass your ArrayList to a method you didn't write yourself and you want to be sure that the method doesn't mistakenly modify the ArrayList or its elements.

The Hashtable Type

The Hashtable class implements the IDictionary interface, and it behaves much like the Scripting.Dictionary object that was available to COM developers. (The Dictionary object can be found in the Microsoft Scripting Runtime library.) All objects based on the IDictionary interface manage two internal series of data—values and keys—and you can use a key to retrieve the corresponding value. The actual implementation of the interface depends on the specific type. For example, the Hashtable type uses an internal hash table, a well-known data structure that has been studied for decades by computer scientists and has been thoroughly described in countless books on algorithms.

When a (key, value) pair is added to a Hashtable object, the position of an element in the internal array is based on the numeric hash code of the key. When you later search for that key, the key's hash code is used again to locate the associated value as quickly as possible, without sequentially visiting all the elements in the hash table. The .NET Hashtable type lets you use any object as a key. Behind the scenes, the Hashtable object uses the key's GetHashCode, a method that all objects inherit from System.Object.

Depending on how the hash code is evaluated, it frequently happens that multiple keys map to the same slot (or *bucket*) in the hash table. In this case, you have a *collision*. The .NET Hashtable object uses double hashing to minimize collisions, but it can't avoid collisions completely. Never fear—collisions are automatically dealt with transparently for the programmer, but you can get optimal performance by selecting an adequate initial capacity for the hash table. A larger table doesn't speed up searches remarkably, but it makes insertions faster.

You can also get better performance by selecting a correct load factor when you create a Hashtable object. This number determines the maximum ratio between values and buckets before the hash table is automatically expanded. The smaller this value is, the more memory is allocated to the internal table and the fewer collisions occur when you're inserting or searching for a value. The default load factor is 1.0, which in most cases delivers a good-enough performance, but you can set a smaller load factor when you create the Hashtable if you're willing to trade memory for better performance. You can initialize a Hashtable object in many ways:

```
// Default load factor and initial capacity
Hashtable ht = new Hashtable();
// Default load factor and specified initial capacity
Hashtable ht2 = new Hashtable(1000);
// Specified initial capacity and custom load factor
Hashtable ht3 = new Hashtable(1000, 0.8);
```

You can also initialize the Hashtable by loading it with the elements contained in any other object that implements the IDictionary interface (such as another Hashtable or a SortedList object). This technique is especially useful when you want to change the load factor of an existing hash table:

```
// Decrease the load factor of the current Hashtable.
ht = new HashTable(ht, 0.5);
```

Other, more sophisticated variants of the constructor let you pass an IComparer object to compare keys in a customized fashion, an IHashCodeProvider object to supply a custom algorithm for calculating hash codes of keys, or an IEqualityComparer object if you want to change the way keys are compared with each other. (More on this later.)

Once you've created a Hashtable, you can add a key and value pair, read or modify the value associated with a given key, and remove an item using the Remove method:

```
// Syntax for Add method is Add(key, value).
ht.Add("Joe", 12000);
ht.Add("Ann", 13000);
// Referencing a new key creates an element.
ht["Robert"] = 15000;
Console.Write(ht["Joe"]);                // => 12000
ht["Ann"] = (int) ht["Ann"] + 1000;
// By default keys are compared in case-insensitive mode,
// so the following statement creates a *new* element.
ht["ann"] = 15000;
// Reading a nonexistent element doesn't create it.
Console.WriteLine(ht["Lee"]);       // Doesn't display anything

// Remove an element given its key.
ht.Remove("Chris");
// How many elements are now in the Hashtable?
Console.WriteLine(ht.Count);        // => 4

// Adding an element that already exists throws an exception.
ht.Add("Joe", 11500);                   // Throws ArgumentException.
```

As I explained earlier, you can use virtually anything as a key, including a numeric value. When you're using numbers as keys, a Hashtable looks deceptively similar to an array:

```
ht[1] = 123;
ht[2] = 345;
```

But never forget that the expression between parentheses is just a key and not an index; thus, the ht[2] element isn't necessarily stored "after" the ht[1] element. As a matter of fact, the elements in a Hashtable object aren't stored in a particular order, and you should never write code that assumes that they are. This is the main difference between the Hashtable object and the SortedList object (which is described next).

The Hashtable object implements the IEnumerable interface, so you can iterate over all its elements using a foreach loop. Each element of a Hashtable is a DictionaryEntry object, which exposes a Key and a Value property:

```
foreach ( DictionaryEntry de in ht )
{
    Console.WriteLine("ht('{0}') = {1}", de.Key, de.Value);
}
```

The Hashtable's Keys and Values properties return an ICollection-based object that contains all the keys and all the values, respectively, so you can assign them to any object that implements the ICollection interface. Or you can use these properties directly in a foreach loop:

```
// Display all the keys in the Hashtable.
foreach ( object o in ht.Keys )      // Or use ht.Values for all the values.
{
   Console.WriteLine(o);
}
```

An important detail: the ICollection objects returned by the Keys and Values properties are "live" objects that continue to be linked to the Hashtable and reflect any additions and deletions performed subsequently, as this code demonstrates:

```
ht.Clear();
ICollection values = ht.Values;
ht.Add("Chris", 11000);
// Prove that the collection continues to be linked to the Hashtable.
Console.WriteLine(values.Count);            // => 1
```

By default, keys are compared in a case-sensitive way, so Joe, JOE, and joe are considered distinct keys. You can create case-insensitive instances of the Hashtable class through one of its many constructors, or you can use the CreateCaseInsensitiveHashtable static method of the System.Collections.Specialized.CollectionsUtil, as follows:

```
Hashtable ht4 = CollectionsUtil.CreateCaseInsensitiveHashtable();
```

Another way to implement a Hashtable that deals with keys in a nonstandard fashion is by providing an IEqualityComparer object to override the default comparison algorithm. For example, say that you want to create a Hashtable where all keys are Double (or convertible to Double) but are automatically rounded to the second decimal digit so that, for example, the keys 1.123 and 1.119 resolve to the same element in the Hashtable. You might perform the rounding each time you add or retrieve an element in the table, but the approach based on the IEqualityComparer interface is more elegant because it moves the responsibility into the Hashtable and away from the client:

```
public class FloatingPointKeyComparer : IEqualityComparer
{
   public int digits;

   public FloatingPointKeyComparer(int digits)
   {
      this.digits = digits;
   }

   public new bool Equals(object x, object y)
   {
      double d1 = Math.Round(Convert.ToDouble(x), digits);
      double d2 = Math.Round(Convert.ToDouble(y), digits);
      return d1 == d2;
   }
}
```

```
public int GetHashCode(object obj)
{
    double d = Math.Round(Convert.ToDouble(obj), digits);
    return d.GetHashCode();
}
}
```

The FloatingPointKeyComparer's constructor takes the number of digits used when rounding keys, so you can use it for any precision. The following example illustrates how to use it for keys rounded to the second decimal digit.

```
ht = new Hashtable(new FloatingPointKeyComparer(2));
ht.Add(1.123, "first");
ht.Add(1.456, "second");
// Prove that keys that round to the same Double number resolve to same item.
Console.WriteLine(ht[1.119]);                          // => first
```

The SortedList Type

The SortedList object is arguably the most versatile nongeneric collection-like object in the .NET Framework. It implements the IDictionary interface, like the Hashtable object, and also keeps its elements sorted. Alas, you pay for all this power in terms of performance, so you should use the SortedList object only when your programming logic requires an object with all this flexibility.

The SortedList object manages two internal arrays, one for the values and one for the companion keys. These arrays have an initial capacity, but they automatically grow when the need arises. Entries are kept sorted by their key, and you can even provide an IComparer object to affect how complex values (a Person object, for example) are compared and sorted. The SortedList class provides several constructor methods:

```
// A SortedList with default capacity (16 entries)
SortedList sl = new SortedList();
// A SortedList with specified initial capacity
SortedList sl2 = new SortedList(1000);

// A SortedList can be initialized with all the elements in an IDictionary.
Hashtable ht = new Hashtable();
ht.Add("Robert", 100);
ht.Add("Ann", 200);
ht.Add("Joe", 300);
SortedList sl3 = new SortedList(ht);
```

As soon as you add new elements to the SortedList, they're immediately sorted by their key. Like the Hashtable class, a SortedList contains DictionaryEntry elements:

```
foreach ( DictionaryEntry de in sl3 )
{
    Console.WriteLine("sl3('{0}') = {1}", de.Key, de.Value);
}
```

Here's the result that appears in the console window:

```
sl3('Ann') = 200
sl3('Joe') = 300
sl3('Robert') = 100
```

Keys are sorted according to the order implied by their IComparable interface, so numbers and strings are always sorted in ascending order. If you want a different order, you must create an object that implements the IComparer interface. For example, you can use the following class to invert the natural string ordering:

```
public class ReverseStringComparer : IComparer
{
   public int Compare(object x, object y)
   {
      // Just change the sign of the String.Compare result.
      return -string.Compare(x.ToString(), y.ToString());
   }
}
```

You can pass an instance of this object to one of the two overloaded constructors that take an IComparer object:

```
// A SortedList that loads all its elements from a Hashtable and
// sorts them with a custom IComparer object.
SortedList s15 = new SortedList(ht, new ReverseStringComparer());
foreach ( DictionaryEntry de in s15 )
{
   Console.WriteLine("sl3('{0}') = {1}", de.Key, de.Value);
}
```

Here are the elements of the resulting SortedList object:

```
s15('Robert') = 100
s15('Joe') = 300
s15('Ann') = 200
```

The SortedList class compares keys in case-sensitive mode, with lowercase characters coming before their uppercase versions (for example, Ann comes before ANN, which in turn comes before Bob). If you want to compare keys without taking case into account, you can create a case-insensitive SortedList object using the auxiliary CollectionsUtil object in the System .Collections.Specialized namespace:

```
SortedList s16 = CollectionsUtil.CreateCaseInsensitiveSortedList();
```

In this case, adding two elements whose keys differ only in case throws an Argument-Exception object.

You are already familiar with the majority of the members exposed by the SortedList type because they are also exposed by the Hashtable or ArrayList types: Capacity, Count, Keys, Values, Clear, Contains, CopyTo, Remove, RemoveAt, TrimToSize. The meaning of other methods should be self-explanatory: ContainsKey returns true if the SortedList contains a given key and is a synonym for Contains; ContainsValue returns true if the SortedList contains a given value; GetKey and GetByIndex return the key or the value at a given index; SetByIndex changes the value of an element at a given index; IndexOfKey and IndexOfValue return the index of a given key or value, or −1 if the key or the value isn't in the SortedList. All these methods work as intended, so I won't provide any code examples for them.

A couple of methods require further explanation, though: GetKeyList and GetValueList. These methods are similar to the Keys and Values properties, except they return an IList object rather than an ICollection object and therefore you can directly access an element at a given index. As for the Keys and Values properties, the returned object reflects any change in the SortedList.

```
sl = new SortedList();
// Get a live reference to key and value collections.
IList alKeys = sl.GetKeyList();
IList alValues = sl.GetValueList();
// Add some values out of order.
sl.Add(3, "three");
sl.Add(2, "two");
sl.Add(1, "one");
// Display values in sorted order.
for ( int i = 0; i <= sl.Count - 1; i++ )
{
    Console.WriteLine("{0} = '{1}'", alKeys[i], alValues[i]);
}
// Any attempt to modify the IList object throws an exception.
alValues.Insert(0, "four");              // Throws NotSupportedException error.
```

As I said before, the SortedList class is the most powerful collection-like object, but it's also the most demanding in terms of resources and CPU time. To see what kind of overhead you can expect when using a SortedList object, I created a routine that adds 100,000 elements to an ArrayList object, a Hashtable object, and a SortedList object. The results were pretty interesting: the ArrayList object was about 4 times faster than the Hashtable object, which in turn was from 8 to 100 times faster than the SortedList object was. Even though you can't take these ratios as reliable in all circumstances, they clearly show that you should never use a more powerful data structure if you don't really need its features.

In general, you should never use a SortedList if you can get along with a different data structure, unless you really need to keep elements sorted *always*. In most practical cases, however, you just need to sort elements after you've read them, so you can load them into a Hashtable and, when loading has completed, pass the Hashtable to the SortedList's constructor. To illustrate this concept and show how these types can cooperate with each other, I have prepared a short program that parses a long text string (for example, the contents of a text file) into individual words and loads them into an ArrayList; then it finds unique words by loading each word in a Hashtable and finally displays the sorted list of words in alphabetical order, together with the number of occurrences of that word:

```
// Read the contents of a text file. (Change file path as needed.)
string filetext = File.ReadAllText("foreword.txt");
// Use regular expressions to parse individual words, put them in an ArrayList.
ArrayList alWords = new ArrayList();
foreach ( Match m in Regex.Matches(filetext, @"\w+") )
{
    alWords.Add(m.Value);
}
Console.WriteLine("Found {0} words.", alWords.Count);

// Create a case-insensitive Hashtable.
Hashtable htWords = CollectionsUtil.CreateCaseInsensitiveHashtable();
// Process each word in the ArrayList.
foreach ( string word in alWords )
{
    // Search this word in the Hashtable.
    object elem = htWords[word];
    if ( elem == null )
    {
        // Not found: this is the first occurrence.
        htWords[word] = 1;
    }
    else
    {
        // Found: increment occurrence count.
        htWords[word] = (int) elem + 1;
    }
}
// Sort all elements alphabetically.
SortedList slWords = new SortedList(htWords);
// Display words and their occurrence count.
foreach ( DictionaryEntry de in slWords )
{
    Console.WriteLine("{0} ({1} occurrences)", de.Key, de.Value);
}
```

Read Chapter 6, "Regular Expressions," for more information about regular expressions.

Other Collections

Although the ArrayList, Hashtable, and SortedList types are collections you might need most frequently in your applications, the System.Collections namespace contains several other useful types. In this roundup section, I cover the Stack, Queue, BitArray, and BitVector32 types.

The Stack Type

The System.Collections.Stack type implements a last in, first out (LIFO) data structure, namely, a structure into which you can push objects and later pop them out. The last object pushed in is also the first one popped out. The three basic methods of a Stack object are Push, Pop, and Peek; the Count property returns the number of elements currently in the stack:

```
Stack st = new Stack();
// Push three values onto the stack.
st.Push(10);
st.Push(20);
st.Push(30);
// Pop the value on top of the stack, and display its value.
Console.WriteLine(st.Pop());              // => 30
// Read the value on top of the stack without popping it.
Console.WriteLine(st.Peek());             // => 20
// Now pop it.
Console.WriteLine(st.Pop());              // => 20
// Determine how many elements are now in the stack.
Console.WriteLine(st.Count);              // => 1
// Pop the only value still on the stack.
Console.WriteLine(st.Pop());              // => 10
// Check that the stack is now empty.
Console.WriteLine(st.Count);              // => 0
```

The only other methods that can prove useful are Contains, which returns true if a given value is currently on the stack; ToArray, which returns the contents of the stack as an array of the specified type; and Clear, which removes all the elements from the stack:

```
// Is the value 10 somewhere in the stack?
if ( st.Contains(10) )
{
   Console.Write("Found");
}

// Extract all the items to an array.
object[] values = st.ToArray();
// Clear the stack.
st.Clear();
```

The Stack object supports the IEnumerable interface, so you can iterate over its elements without popping them by means of a foreach loop:

```
foreach ( object o in st )
{
   Console.WriteLine(o);
}
```

The Queue Type

A first in, first out (FIFO) structure, also known as a *queue* or *circular buffer*, is often used to solve recurring programming problems. You need a queue structure when a portion of an application inserts elements at one end of a buffer and another piece of code extracts the first available element at the other end. This situation occurs whenever you have a series of elements that you must process sequentially but can't process immediately.

You can render a queue in C# by leveraging the System.Collections.Queue object. Queue objects have an initial capacity, but the internal buffer is automatically extended if the need arises. You create a Queue object by specifying its capacity and a growth factor, both of which are optional:

```
// A queue with initial capacity of 200 elements; a growth factor equal to 1.5
// (When new room is needed, the capacity will become 300, then 450, 675, etc.)
Queue qu1 = new Queue(200, 1.5F);
// A queue with 100 elements and a default growth factor of 2
Queue qu2 = new Queue(100);
// A queue with 32 initial elements and a default growth factor of 2
Queue qu3 = new Queue();
```

The key methods of a Queue object are Enqueue, Peek, and Dequeue. Check the output of the following code snippet, and compare it with the behavior of the Stack object:

```
Queue qu = new Queue(100);
// Insert three values in the queue.
qu.Enqueue(10);
qu.Enqueue(20);
qu.Enqueue(30);
// Extract the first value, and display it.
Console.WriteLine(qu.Dequeue());            // => 10
// Read the next value, but don't extract it.
Console.WriteLine(qu.Peek());               // => 20
// Extract it.
Console.WriteLine(qu.Dequeue());            // => 20
// Check how many items are still in the queue.
Console.WriteLine(qu.Count);                // => 1
// Extract the last element, and check that the queue is now empty.
Console.WriteLine(qu.Dequeue());            // => 30
Console.WriteLine(qu.Count);                // => 0
```

The Queue object also supports the Contains method, which checks whether an element is in the queue, and the Clear method, which clears the queue's contents. The Queue class implements IEnumerable and can be used in a foreach loop.

The BitArray Type

A BitArray object can hold a large number of Boolean values in a compact format, using a single bit for each element. This class implements IEnumerable (and thus supports foreach), ICollection, and ICloneable. You can create a BitArray object in many ways:

```
// Provide the number of elements (all initialized to false).
BitArray ba = new BitArray(1024);
// Provide the number of elements, and initialize them to a value.
BitArray ba2 = new BitArray(1024, true);

// Initialize the BitArray from an array of bool, byte, or int.
bool[] boolArr = new bool[1024];
```

```
// Initialize the boolArr array here.
...

BitArray ba3 = new BitArray(boolArr);

// Initialize the BitArray from another BitArray object.
BitArray ba4 = new BitArray(ba);
```

You can retrieve the number of elements in a BitArray by using either the Count property or the Length property. The Get method reads and the Set method modifies the element at the specified index:

```
// Set element at index 9, and read it back.
ba.Set(9, true);
Console.WriteLine(ba.Get(9));            // => True
```

The CopyTo method can move all elements back to an array of Booleans, or it can perform a bitwise copy of the BitArray to a zero-based Byte or Integer array:

```
// Bitwise copy to an array of Integers
int[] intArr = new int[32];              // 32 elements * 32 bits each = 1,024 bits
// Second argument is the index in which the copy begins in target array.
ba.CopyTo(intArr, 0);
// Check that bit 9 of first element in intArr is set.
Console.WriteLine(intArr[0]);            // => 512
```

The Not method complements all the bits in the BitArray object:

```
ba.Not();                                // No arguments
```

The And, Or, and Xor methods enable you to perform the corresponding operation on pairs of Boolean values stored in two BitArray objects:

```
// Perform an AND operation of all the bits in the first BitArray
// with the complement of all the bits in the second BitArray.
ba.And(ba2.Not);
```

Finally, you can set or reset all the bits in a BitArray class using the SetAll method:

```
// Set all the bits to true.
ba.SetAll(true);
```

The BitArray type doesn't expose any methods that enable you to quickly determine how many true (or false) elements are in the array. You can take advantage of the IEnumerator support of this class and use a foreach loop:

```
int bitCount = 0;
foreach ( bool b in ba )
{
    if ( b )
    {
        bitCount += 1;
    }
}
Console.WriteLine("Found {0} True values.", bitCount);
```

The BitVector32 Type

The BitVector32 class (in the System.Collections.Specialized namespace) is similar to the BitArray class in that it can hold a packed array of Boolean values, one per bit, but it's limited to 32 elements. However, a BitVector32 object can store a set of small integers that takes up to 32 consecutive bits and is therefore useful with bit-coded fields, such as those that you deal with when passing data to and from hardware devices.

```
BitVector32 bv = new BitVector32();
// Set one element and read it back.
bv[1] = true;
Console.WriteLine(bv[1]);                          // => True
```

You can also pass a 32-bit integer to the constructor to initialize all the elements in one pass:

```
// Initialize all elements to true.
bv = new BitVector32(-1);
```

To define a BitVector32 that is subdivided into sections that are longer than 1 bit, you must create one or more BitVector32.Section objects and use them when you later read and write individual elements. You define a section by means of the BitVector32.CreateSection static method, which takes the highest integer you want to store in that section and (for all sections after the first one) the previous section. Here's a complete example:

```
bv = new BitVector32();
// Create three sections, of 4, 5, and 6 bits each.
BitVector32.Section se1 = BitVector32.CreateSection(15);
BitVector32.Section se2 = BitVector32.CreateSection(31, se1);
BitVector32.Section se3 = BitVector32.CreateSection(63, se2);

// Assign a given value to each section.
bv[se1] = 10;
bv[se2] = 20;
bv[se3] = 40;
// Read values back.
Console.WriteLine(bv[se1]);            // => 10
Console.WriteLine(bv[se2]);            // => 20
Console.WriteLine(bv[se3]);            // => 40
```

The Data property sets or returns the internal 32-bit integer; you can use this property to save the bit-coded value into a database field or to pass it to a hardware device:

```
// Read the entire field as a 32-bit value.
Console.WriteLine(bv.Data);                   // => 20810
Console.WriteLine(bv.Data.ToString("X"));     // => 514A
```

Abstract Types for Strong-Typed Collections

As I have emphasized many times in earlier sections, all the types in the System.Collections namespace—with the exception of BitArray and BitVector32—are weakly typed collections that can contain objects of any kind. This feature makes them more flexible but less robust because any attempt to assign an object of the "wrong" type can't be flagged as an error by the compiler. You can overcome this limitation by creating a strong-typed collection class.

In Visual C# .NET 2003, you can implement custom strong-typed collection types by inheriting from one of the abstract base classes that the .NET Framework offers, namely these:

- **CollectionBase**   For strong-typed IList-based collections, that is, types that are functionally similar to ArrayList but capable of accepting objects of a specific type only.

- **ReadOnlyCollectionBase**   Like CollectionBase, except that the collection has a fixed size and you can't add elements to or remove elements from it after it has been instantiated. (Individual items can be either read-only or writable, depending on how you implement the collection.)

- **DictionaryBase**   For strong-typed IDictionary-based collections, that is, types that are functionally similar to Hashtable but capable of accepting objects of a specific type only.

- **NameObjectCollectionBase**   (In the System.Collections.Specialized namespace) For strong-typed collections whose elements can be accessed by either their index or the key associated with them. (You can think of these collections as a hybrid between the ArrayList and the Hashtable types.)

The importance of these base collection types has decreased in Visual C# 2005 because generics enable you to implement strong-typed collections in a much simpler and more efficient manner. However, in some scenarios you might need to use these base types in .NET Framework 2.0 as well, for example, when implementing a collection that must accept objects of two or more distinct types and these types don't share a common base class or interface. Another case when generics aren't very helpful is when you need to implement the IEnumerable interface directly, as I show in Chapter 3.

The CollectionBase Type

For the sake of illustration, I will show how you can inherit from CollectionBase to create an ArrayList-like collection that can host only Person objects. Consider the following definition of a Person:

```
public class Person
{
    // These should be properties in a real-world application.
    public string FirstName;
    public string LastName;
    public Person Spouse;
    public readonly ArrayList Children = new ArrayList();

    public Person(string firstName, string lastName)
    {
        this.FirstName = firstName;
        this.LastName = lastName;
```

```
    }

    public string ReverseName()
    {
        return LastName + ", " + FirstName;
    }
}
```

The Spouse member enables you to create a one-to-one relationship between two Person objects, whereas the Children member can implement a one-to-many relationship. The problem is that the Children collection is weakly typed; thus, a client program might mistakenly add to it an object of the wrong type without the compiler being able to spot the problem. You can solve this problem by creating a class that inherits from CollectionBase and that exposes a few strong-typed members that take or return Person objects:

```
public class PersonCollection : CollectionBase
{
    public void Add(Person item)
    {
        this.List.Add(item);
    }

    public void Remove(Person item)
    {
        this.List.Remove(item);
    }

    public Person this[int index]
    {
        get { return ((Person)this.List[index]); }
        set { this.List[index] = value; }
    }
}
```

The PersonCollection type inherits most of its public members from its base class, including Count, Clear, and RemoveAt; these are the members with signatures that don't mention the type of the specific objects you want to store in the collection (Person, in this case). Your job is to provide only the remaining members, which do nothing but delegate to the inner IList object by means of the protected List property.

To make the collection behave exactly as an ArrayList, you need to implement additional members, including Sort, IndexOf, and BinarySearch. These methods aren't exposed by the protected List property, but you can reach them by using the InnerList protected member (which returns the inner ArrayList):

```
public void Sort()
{
    this.InnerList.Sort();
}
```

When you've completed the PersonCollection type, you can replace the declaration of the Children member in the Person class to implement the one-to-many relationship in a more robust manner:

```
// (In the Person class…)
public readonly PersonCollection Children = new PersonCollection();

// (In the client application…)
Person john = new Person("John", "Evans");
john.Children.Add(new Person("Robert", "Evans"));        // This works.
// *** The next statement doesn't even compile.
john.Children.Add(new Object());
```

Quite surprisingly, however, the PersonCollection isn't very robust because an application can still add non-Person objects to it by accessing its IList interface:

```
// These statements raise neither a compiler warning nor a runtime error!
(john.Children as IList)[0] = new object();
(john.Children as IList).Add(new object());
```

Unfortunately, there is no way to tell the compiler to reject the preceding statement, but at least you can throw an exception at run time by checking the type of objects being assigned or added in the OnValidate protected method:

```
// (In the PersonCollection class…)
protected override void OnValidate(object value)
{
    if ( !(value is Person) )
    {
        throw new ArgumentException("Invalid item");
    }
}
```

The CollectionBase abstract class exposes other protected methods that can be overridden to execute a piece of custom code just before or after an operation is performed on the collection: OnClear and OnClearComplete methods run before and after a Clear method; OnInsert and OnInsertComplete methods run when an item is added to the collection; OnRemove and OnRemoveComplete run when an item is removed from the collection; OnSet and OnSet-Complete run when an item is assigned; OnGet runs when an item is read. For example, you might need to override these methods when the collection must notify another object when its contents change.

The ReadOnlyCollectionBase Type

The main difference between the CollectionBase type and the ReadOnlyCollectionBase type is that the latter doesn't expose any public member that would let clients add or remove items, such as Clear and RemoveAt. For a fixed-sized collection, you shouldn't expose methods such as Add and Remove, so in most cases your only responsibility is to implement the indexer. If you mark this property with the ReadOnly key, clients can't even assign a new value to the collection's elements:

```csharp
public class PersonCollection : ReadOnlyCollectionBase
{
    public PersonCollection()
    {
        // Initialize the inner collection here.
        …
    }

    public Person this[int index]
    {
        get { return (Person) this.List[index]; }
    }
}
```

The DictionaryBase Type

The technique to create a strong-typed dictionary is similar to what I've just showed for the CollectionBase type, except you inherit from DictionaryBase. This base class enables you to access an inner IDictionary object by means of the Dictionary protected property. Here's a PersonDictionary class that behaves much like the Hashtable object, but can contain only Person objects that are indexed by a string key:

```csharp
public class PersonDictionary : DictionaryBase
{
    public void Add(string key, Person item)
    {
        this.Dictionary.Add(key, item);
    }

    public void Remove(string key)
    {
        this.Dictionary.Remove(key);
    }

    public Person this[string key]
    {
        get { return (Person) this.Dictionary[key]; }
        set { this.Dictionary[key] = value; }
    }

    protected override void OnValidate(object key, object value)
    {
        if ( !(key is string) )
        {
            throw new ArgumentException("Invalid key");
        }
        else if ( !(value is Person) )
        {
            throw new ArgumentException("Invalid item");
        }
    }
}
```

The NameObjectCollectionBase Type

As I mentioned previously, you can inherit from the NameObjectCollectionBase type to implement a strong-typed collection that can refer to its elements by either a key or a numeric index. This type uses an internal Hashtable structure, but it doesn't expose it to inheritors. Instead, your public methods must perform their operation by delegating to a protected Base*Xxx* method, such as BaseAdd or BaseGet. Here's a complete example of a strong-typed collection based on the NameObjectCollectionBase abstract class:

```
public class PersonCollection2 : NameObjectCollectionBase
{
    public void Add(string key, Person p)
    {
        this.BaseAdd(key, p);
    }

    public void Clear()
    {
        this.BaseClear();
    }

    // The Remove method that takes a string key
    public void Remove(string key)
    {
        this.Remove(key);
    }

    // The Remove method that takes a numeric index
    public void Remove(int index)
    {
        this.Remove(index);
    }

    // The indexer property that takes a string key
    public Person this[string key]
    {
        get { return (Person) this.BaseGet(key); }
        set { this.BaseSet(key, value); }
    }

    // The indexer property that takes a numeric index
    public Person this[int index]
    {
        get { return (Person) this.BaseGet(index); }
        set { this.BaseSet(index, value); }
    }
}
```

Generic Collections

In Chapter 4, you saw how you can implement your own generic types. However, in most cases, you don't really need to go that far because you can simply use one of the many types defined in the System.Collections.Generic namespace, which contains both generic collection types and generic interfaces. You can use the generic collections both directly in your applications or inherit from them to extend them with additional methods. In either case, generics can make your programming much, much simpler.

For example, going back to the example in the section titled "The CollectionBase Type" earlier in this chapter, you can have the Person class expose a strong-typed collection of other Persons as easily as this code:

```
public class Person
{
    public readOnly List<Person> Children = new List<Person>();
    …
}
```

On the other hand, if you are migrating code from Visual C# .NET 2003 and don't want to break existing clients, you can use a different approach and replace the existing version of the PersonCollection strong-typed collection with this code:

```
public class PersonCollection : List<Person>
{
    // …and that's it!
}
```

Not only is the implementation of PersonCollection simpler, it is also more complete because it exposes all the methods you expect to find in a collection type, such as Sort and Reverse. Just as important, if the element type is a value type—such as a numeric type or a structure—the generic-based implementation is also far more efficient because values are never passed to an Object argument and therefore are never boxed.

The List Generic Type

If you are familiar with the ArrayList type, you already know how to use most of the functionality exposed by the List<T> type and its members: Add, Clear, Insert, Remove, RemoveAt, RemoveAll, IndexOf, LastIndexOf, Reverse, Sort, and BinarySearch. You can perform operations on multiple items by means of the GetRange, AddRange, InsertRange, and RemoveRange methods. The GetRange method returns another List<T> object, so you can assign its result in a strongly typed fashion:

```
// Create a list of persons
List<Person> persons = new List<Person>();
persons.Add(new Person("John", "Evans"));
persons.Add(new Person("Ann", "Beebe"));
persons.Add(new Person("Robert", "Zare"));
…
// Create a new collection and initialize it with 3 elements from first collection.
List<Person> persons2 = new List<Person>(persons.GetRange(0, 3));
// Add elements at indexes 10-14 from first collection.
persons2.AddRange(persons.GetRange(10, 5));
```

A List<T> collection can contain any object that derives from T; for example, a Person collection can also contain Employee objects if the Employee class derives from Person.

Interestingly, the AddRange and InsertRange methods take any object that implements the IEnumerable<T> interface; thus, you can pass them either another List object or a strong-typed array:

```
Person[] arr = new Person[] {new Person("John", "Evans"),
    new Person("Ann", "Beebe")};
// Insert these elements at the beginning of the collection.
persons.InsertRange(0, persons);
```

Because the arguments must implement the IEnumerable<T> interface, you can't pass them an Object array or a weakly typed ArrayList, even if you know for sure that the array or the ArrayList contains only objects of type T. In this case, you must write an explicit foreach loop:

```
// Add all the Person objects stored in an ArrayList.
foreach ( Person p in myArrayList )
{
    persons.Add(p);
}
```

The Remove method doesn't throw an exception if the specified element isn't in the collection; instead, it returns true if the element was successfully removed, false if the element wasn't found:

```
if ( persons.Remove(aPerson) )
{
    Console.WriteLine("The specified person was in the list and has been removed.");
}
```

The TrimExcess method enables you to reclaim the memory allocated to unused slots:

```
persons.TrimExcess();
```

This method does nothing if the list currently uses 90 percent or more of its current capability. The rationale behind this behavior is that trimming a list is an expensive operation and there is no point in performing it if the expected advantage is negligible.

Alternatively, you can assign the Capacity property directly. By default, the initial capacity is 4, unless you pass a different value to the constructor, but this value might change in future versions of the .NET Framework:

```
persons.Capacity = persons.Count;
```

Some generic methods of the List type might puzzle you initially. For example, the Sort method works as expected if the element type supports the IComparable interface; however, you can't provide an IComparer object to it to sort according to a user-defined order, as you'd do with a weak-typed ArrayList. Instead, you must define a class that implements the strong-typed IComparer<Person> interface. For example, the following class can work as a strong-typed comparer for the Person class:

```
public class PersonComparer : IComparer<Person>
{
    public int Compare(Person x, Person y)
    {
        return x.ReverseName().CompareTo(y.ReverseName());
    }
}
```

You can then use the PersonComparer class with the Sort method:

```
// Sort a collection of persons according to the ReverseName property.
persons.Sort(new PersonComparer());
```

(You can also use the same PersonComparer class with BinarySearch for superfast searches in a sorted collection.) A welcome addition to the Sort method in ArrayList is the ability to pass a delegate of type Comparison<T>, which must point to a function that compares two T objects and returns an integer that specifies which is greater. This feature means that you don't need to define a distinct comparer class for each possible kind of sort you want to implement:

```
// This function can be used to sort in the descending direction.
private static int ComparePersonsDesc(Person p1, Person p2)
{
    // Notice that the order of arguments is reversed.
    return p2.ReverseName().CompareTo(p1.ReverseName());
}

// Elsewhere in the program...
static void SortPersonList()
{
    List<Person> persons = new List<Person>();
    ...
    persons.Sort(ComparePersonsDesc);
}
```

Or you can avoid using an external method and use an anonymous method instead:

```
persons.Sort( delegate(Person p1, Person p2)
            { return p2.ReverseName().CompareTo(p1.ReverseName()); });
```

In addition to all the methods you can find in the ArrayList, the List type exposes all the new generic methods that have been added to the Array class in .NET Framework 2.0 and that expect a delegate as an argument, namely, ConvertAll, Exists, Find, FindAll, FindIndex, FindLastIndex, ForEach, and TrueForAll. For example, the TrueForAll method takes a Predicate<T> delegate, which must point to a function that tests a T object and returns a Boolean, so you can pass it the address of the String.IsNullOrEmpty static method to check whether all the elements of a List<string> object are null or empty:

```
List<string> list = new List<string>();
// Fill the list and process its elements...
...
if ( list.TrueForAll(string.IsNullOrEmpty) )
{
   Console.WriteLine("All elements are null or empty strings.");
}
```

You can also use the instance Equals method that the String type and most numeric types expose to check whether all elements are equal to a specific value:

```
string testValue = "ABC";
if ( list.TrueForAll(testValue.Equals) )
{
   Console.WriteLine("All elements are equal to 'ABC'");
}
```

Generic methods based on delegates often enable you to create unbelievably concise code, as in this example:

```
// Create two strong-typed collections of Double values.
List<double> list1 = new List<double>(new double[] { 1, 2, 3, 4, 5, 6, 7, 8, 9 });
List<double> list2 = new List<double>(new double[] { 0, 9, 12, 3, 6 });
// Check whether the second collection is a subset of the first one.
bool isSubset = list2.TrueForAll(list1.Contains);          // => False

// One statement to find all the elements in list2 that are contained in list1.
List<double> list3 = list2.FindAll(list1.Contains);
// Remove from list1 and list2 the elements that they have in common.
list1.RemoveAll(list3.Contains);
list2.RemoveAll(list3.Contains);

// Display the elements in the three lists.
list1.ForEach(Console.WriteLine);                   // => 1 2 4 5 7 8
list2.ForEach(Console.WriteLine);                   // => 0 12
list3.ForEach(Console.WriteLine);                   // => 9 3 6
```

The only method left to discuss is AsReadOnly. This method takes no arguments and returns a System.Collections.ObjectModel.ReadOnlyCollection<T> object, which, as its name suggests, is similar to the List type except you can neither add or remove objects nor modify existing items. Interestingly, the value returned by AsReadOnly is an adapter of the original list; thus, the elements in the returned list reflect any insertions and deletions performed on the original list. This feature enables you to pass a read-only reference to an external procedure that can read the most recent data added to the list but can't modify the list in any way:

```
// Get a read-only wrapper of the original list.
ReadOnlyCollection<double> roList = list1.AsReadOnly();
Console.WriteLine(roList.Count == list1.Count);          // => True
// Prove that roList reflects all the operations on the original list.
list1.Add(123);
Console.WriteLine(roList.Count == list1.Count);          // => True
```

The Dictionary Generic Type

The Dictionary<TKey,TValue> type is the generic counterpart of the Hashtable type, in that it can store (key, value) pairs in a strong-typed fashion. For example, here's a dictionary that can contain Person objects and index them by a string key (the person's complete name):

```
Dictionary<string,Person> dictPersons = new Dictionary<string,Person>();
dictPersons.Add("John Evans", new Person("John", "Evans"));
dictPersons.Add("Robert Zare", new Person("Robert", "Zare"));
```

The constructor of this generic class can take a capacity (the initial number of slots in the inner table), an object that implements the IDictionary<TKey,TValue> generic interface (such as another generic dictionary), an IEqualityComparer<T> object, or a few combinations of these three values. (In .NET Framework 2.0, the default capacity is just three elements, but might change in future versions of the .NET Framework.)

The constructor that takes an IEqualityComparer<T> object enables you to control how keys are compared. I demonstrated how to use the nongeneric IEqualityComparer interface in the section titled "The Hashtable Type" earlier in this chapter, so you should have no problem understanding how its generic counterpart works. The following class normalizes a person's name to the format "LastName,FirstName" and compares these strings in case-insensitive fashion:

```
public class NameEqualityComparer : IEqualityComparer<string>
{
    public bool Equals(string x, string y)
    {
        return string.Equals(NormalizedName(x), NormalizedName(y));
    }

    public int GetHashCode(string obj)
    {
        return NormalizedName(obj).GetHashCode();
    }

    // Helper method that returns a person name in upper case and in the
    // (LastName,FirstName) format, without any spaces.
    private string NormalizedName(string name)
    {
        // If there is a comma, assume that name is already in (last,first) format.
        if (name.IndexOf(',') < 0)
        {
            // Find first and last names.
            char[] separators = {' '};
            string[] parts = name.Split(separators, 2, StringSplitOptions.RemoveEmptyEntries);
            // Invert the two portions.
            name = parts[1] + "," + parts[0];
        }
        // Delete spaces, if any, convert to upper case, and return.
        return name.Replace(" ", "").ToUpper();
    }
}
```

You can use the NameEqualityComparer type to manage a dictionary of Persons whose elements can be retrieved by providing a name in several different formats:

```
dictPersons = new Dictionary<string, Person>(new NameEqualityComparer());
dictPersons.Add("John Evans", new Person("Joe", "Evans"));
dictPersons.Add("Robert Zare", new Person("Robert", "Zare"));
// Prove that the last element can be retrieved by providing a key in
// either the (last,first) format or the (first last) format, that spaces
// are ignored, and that character casing isn't significant.
string name;
name = dictPersons["robert zare"].ReverseName();      // => Zare, Robert
name = dictPersons["ZARE, robert"].ReverseName();     // => Zare, Robert
```

If necessary, you can retrieve a reference to the IEqualityComparer object by means of the dictionary's Comparer read-only property.

Unlike the Remove method in the Hashtable type, but similar to the Remove method in the List generic type, the Remove method of the Dictionary generic class returns true if the object was actually removed and false if no object with that key was found; therefore, you don't need to search the element before trying to remove it:

```
if (dictPersons.Remove("john evans"))
{
    Console.WriteLine("Element John Evans has been removed");
}
else
{
    Console.WriteLine("Element John Evans hasn't been found");
}
```

When a Dictionary object is used in a foreach loop, at each iteration you get an instance of the KeyValuePair<TKey,TValue> generic type, which enables you to access the dictionary elements in a strong-typed fashion:

```
foreach ( KeyValuePair<string, Person> kvp in dictPersons )
{
    // You can reference a member of the Person class in strong-typed fashion.
    Console.WriteLine("Key={0} FirstName={1}", kvp.Key, kvp.Value.FirstName);
}
```

The TryGetValue method takes a key and an object variable (which is taken by reference); if an element with that key is found, its value is assigned to the object and the method returns true. You can therefore test the presence of an element and retrieve it with a single operation by using this code:

```
Person p;
if ( dictPersons.TryGetValue("ann beebe", out p) )
{
    // The variable p contains a reference to the found element.
    Console.WriteLine("Found {0}", p.ReverseName());
}
```

```
else
{
    Console.WriteLine("Not found");
}
```

The remaining members of the Dictionary type are quite straightforward: the Keys and Values read-only properties, the Clear method, the ContainsKey and ContainsValue methods. They work exactly as do the methods with the same names of the Hashtable object (except that they are strong-typed) and I won't repeat their descriptions here.

The LinkedList Generic Type

Linked lists are data structures with elements that aren't stored in contiguous memory locations; you can visit all the elements of these lists because each element has a pointer to the next element (simple linked list) or to both the next and the previous elements (doubly linked list). Elements in such a structure are called *nodes* and cannot be referenced by means of an index or a key. You can reach a node only by following the chain of pointers, either starting at the first element and moving forward or starting at the last element and moving backward. Because there is no key, elements can have duplicate values. See Figure 5-1 for the .NET implementation of the double linked list data structure.

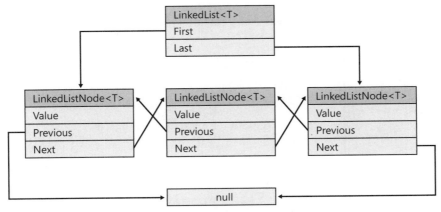

Figure 5-1   The LinkedList and LinkedListNode generic types

The LinkedList<T> type implements a strong-typed doubly linked list. Each node in a LinkedList structure is implemented as a LinkedListNode<T> object and exposes only four properties: Value (an object of type T), List (the list this node belongs to), Previous and Next (pointers to the previous and next nodes in the list). You can create a node by passing an object of type T to its constructor or by means of one of the methods in the parent LinkedList object, as you'll see in a moment. Two nodes in the list are special in that they represent the first and last nodes in the linked list. (These nodes are often called the *head* and the *tail* of the linked list.) You can get a reference to these nodes by means of the First and Last properties of the LinkedList type.

Enough theory for now. Let's see how to create and use a strong-typed generic linked list that can contain one or more Person objects. The remarks in code will help you to understand what happens inside the list:

```
LinkedList<Person> lnkList = new LinkedList<Person>();
// An empty linked list has no first or last node.
Console.WriteLine(lnkList.First == null);          // => True
Console.WriteLine(lnkList.Last == null);           // => True
```

The LinkedList type exposes four methods for adding a new node: AddFirst, AddLast, Add-Before, and AddAfter. All these methods have two overloads: the first overload takes an object of type T, wraps it into a LinkedListNode<T> object, inserts the node in the list, and returns it to the caller; the second overload takes a LinkedListNode<T> object and inserts it in the list at the desired position, but doesn't return anything. In most cases, you can write more concise code by using the former syntax and discarding the return value:

```
// Add the first node of the list.
Person p1 = new Person("John", "Evans");
lnkList.AddFirst(p1);
// When the list contains only one node, the first and last nodes coincide.
Console.WriteLine(lnkList.First == lnkList.Last);          // => True
```

Now the list isn't empty and you can add new elements using existing nodes as a reference for the AddBefore or AddAfter methods:

```
// Add a new node after the list head.
lnkList.AddAfter(lnkList.First, new Person("Ann", "Beebe"));
// The new node has become the list's tail node.
Console.WriteLine(lnkList.Last.Value.ReverseName());       // => Beebe, Ann
// Add a new node immediately before the list tail.
lnkList.AddBefore(lnkList.Last, new Person("Robert", "Zare"));
// Add a new node after the current list tail (it becomes the new tail).
lnkList.AddLast(new Person("James", "Hamilton"));
// Now the list contains four elements.
Console.WriteLine(lnkList.Count);                          // => 4
```

You can iterate over all the elements in a linked list in a couple of ways. First, you can use a traditional foreach loop:

```
foreach ( Person p in lnkList )
{
    Console.Write("{0} ", p.FirstName);        // => John Robert Ann James
}
```

Second, you can take advantage of the nature of the doubly linked list by following the chain of node pointers. This technique gives you more flexibility because you can traverse the list in both directions:

```
// Visit all nodes in reverse order.
LinkedListNode<Person> node = lnkList.Last;
while ( node != null )
```

```
{
    Console.WriteLine(node.Value.ReverseName());
    node = node.Previous;
}

// Change last name from Evans to Hamilton.
node = lnkList.First;
while ( node != null )
{
    if ( node.Value.LastName == "Evans" )
    {
        node.Value.LastName = "Hamilton";
    }
    node = node.Next;
}
```

Another good reason you might traverse the linked list manually is because you gain the ability to insert and delete nodes during the process. (Either operation would throw an exception if performed from inside a foreach loop.) Before I show how to perform this operation, let's take a step backward for a moment.

As I have already mentioned, the first thing to do on a freshly created LinkedList instance is create its first node (which also becomes its last node). This operation introduces an asymmetry between the first element added to the list and all the elements after it because adding the first element requires a different piece of code. This asymmetry makes programming a bit more complicated.

You can avoid the asymmetry and simplify programming by assuming that the first node in the linked list is a special node that is always present but contains no meaningful value:

```
LinkedList<Person> aList = new LinkedList<Person>();
aList.AddFirst(new LinkedListNode<Person>(null));
// You can now add all nodes with a plain AddLast method.
aList.AddLast(new Person("John", "Evans"));
aList.AddLast(new Person("Ann", "Beebe"));
aList.AddLast(new Person("Robert", "Zare"));
```

You must take the "dummy" first node into account when iterating over all the elements:

```
// We are sure that the first node exists; thus, the next statement can never throw.
LinkedListNode<Person> aNode = aList.First.Next;
while ( aNode != null )
{
    Console.WriteLine(aNode.Value.ReverseName());
    aNode = aNode.Next;
}
```

The first empty node simplifies programming remarkably because you don't need to take any special case into account. For example, here's a loop that removes all the persons that match a given criterion:

```
aNode = aList.First.Next;
while ( aNode != null )
```

```
{
   // Remove this node if the last name is Evans.
   if ( aNode.Value.LastName == "Evans" )
   {
      // Backtrack to previous node and remove the node that was current.
      // (We can be sure that the previous node exists.)
      aNode = aNode.Previous;
      aList.Remove(aNode.Next);
   }
   aNode = aNode.Next;
}
```

The LinkedList type also exposes the RemoveFirst and RemoveLast methods to remove the list's head and tail nodes, respectively. There is also an overload of the Remove method that takes an object of type T and returns true if the object was found and removed, false otherwise.

A last note about the technique based on the dummy first node: remember to take this dummy node into account when you display the number of elements in the list:

```
Console.WriteLine("The list contains {0} persons", aList.Count - 1);
```

The only methods I haven't covered yet are Find and FindLast, which take an object of type T and return the LinkedListNode<T> object that holds that object, or null if the search fails. Keep in mind, however, that searching a node is a relatively slow operation because these methods have to start at one of the list's ends and traverse each element until they find a match.

Other Generic Collections

The System.Collections.Generic namespace contains a few other generic collections, namely these:

- **Stack<T>**   The strong-typed version of the Stack collection class
- **Queue<T>**   The strong-typed version of the Queue collection class
- **SortedDictionary<TKey,TValue>**   The strong-typed version of the SortedList, which uses keys of type TKey associated with values of type TValue

The SortedDictionary type exposes many of the methods of the Dictionary type, but it also keeps all its elements in sorted order. To keep elements sorted, the constructor can take an object that implements the IComparer<TKey> generic interface. For example, suppose that your sorted list uses a filename as a key and you want to sort the elements according to file extension. First, define a comparer class that implements the IComparer<string> interface:

```
public class FileExtensionComparer : IComparer<string>
{
   public int Compare(string x, string y)
   {
```

```
        // Compare the extensions of filenames in case-insensitive mode.
        int res = string.Compare(Path.GetExtension(x), Path.GetExtension(y), true);
        if ( res == 0 )
        {
            // If extensions are equal, compare the entire filenames.
            res = string.Compare(Path.GetFileName(x), Path.GetFileName(y), true);
        }
        return res;
    }
}
```

You can then define a sorted dictionary that contains the text associated with a series of text files and keeps the entries sorted on the file extensions:

```
SortedDictionary<string, string> fileDict = new SortedDictionary<string, string>();
// Load some elements.
fileDict.Add("foo.txt", "contents of foo.txt...");
fileDict.Add("data.txt", "contents of data.txt...");
fileDict.Add("data.doc", "contents of data.doc...");
// Check that files have been sorted on their extension.
foreach ( KeyValuePair<string, string> kvp in fileDict )
{
    Console.Write("{0}, ", kvp.Key);         // => data.doc, data.txt, foo.txt,
}
```

Like the method with the same name of the Dictionary type, the TryGetValue method enables you to check whether an element with a given key exists and to read it using a single operation:

```
string text;
if ( fileDict.TryGetValue("foo.txt", out text) )
{
    // The text variable contains the value of the "foo.txt" element.
    Console.WriteLine(text);
}
```

Even if elements in a SortedDictionary can be accessed in order, you can't reference them by their index. If you need to read the key or the value of the Nth element, you must first copy the Keys or Values collection to a regular array:

```
// Display the value for the first item.
string[] values = new string[fileDict.Count];
fileDict.Values.CopyTo(values, 0);
Console.WriteLine(values[0]);
```

A Notable Example

I won't cover the Stack<T> and Queue<T> generic types: if you are familiar with their weak-typed counterparts, you already know how to use them. However, I do provide an example that demonstrates that these classes can help you write sophisticated algorithms in an efficient manner and with very little code. More precisely, I show you how to implement a complete Reverse Polish Notation (RPN) expression evaluator.

First a little background, for those new to RPN. An RPN expression is a sequence of operands and math operators in postfix notation. For example, the RPN expression "12 34 +" is equivalent to 12 + 34, whereas the expression "12 34 + 56 78 - *" is equivalent to (12 + 34) * (56 – 78). The RPN notation was used in programmable calculators in the 1980s and in programming languages such as Forth, but it is useful in many cases even today. (For example, a compiler must translate an expression to RPN to generate the actual IL or native code.) The beauty of the RPN notation is that you never need to assign a priority to operators and therefore you never need to use parentheses even for the most complex expressions. In fact, the rules for evaluating an RPN expression are quite simple:

1. Extract the tokens from the RPN expression one at a time.

2. If the token is a number, push it onto the stack.

3. If the token is an operator, pop as many numbers off the stack as required by the operator, execute the operation, and push the result onto the stack again.

4. When there are no more tokens, if the stack contains exactly one element, this is the result of the expression, else the expression is unbalanced.

Thanks to the String.Split method and the Stack<T> generic type, implementing this algorithm requires very few lines of code:

```csharp
public static double EvalRPN(string expression)
{
    Stack<double> stack = new Stack<double>();
    // Split the string expression into tokens.
    string[] operands = expression.ToLower().Split(
        new char[] {' '}, StringSplitOptions.RemoveEmptyEntries);
    foreach ( string op in operands )
    {
        switch ( op )
        {
            case "+":
                stack.Push(stack.Pop() + stack.Pop());
                break;
            case "-":
                stack.Push(-stack.Pop() + stack.Pop());
                break;
            case "*":
                stack.Push(stack.Pop() * stack.Pop());
                break;
            case "/":
                stack.Push( (1 / stack.Pop()) * stack.Pop() );
                break;
            case "sqrt":
                stack.Push( Math.Sqrt(stack.Pop()) );
                break;
            default:
                // Assume this token is a number, throw if the parse operation fails.
```

```
            stack.Push(double.Parse(op));
            break;
    }
}
// Throw if stack is unbalanced.
if ( stack.Count != 1 )
{
    throw new ArgumentException("Unbalanced expression");
}
return stack.Pop();
}
```

Here are a few usage examples:

```
double res = EvalRPN("12 34 + 56 78 - *");       // => -1012
res = EvalRPN("123 456 + 2 /");                  // => 289.5
res = EvalRPN("123 456 + 2 ");                   // => Exception: Unbalanced expression
res = EvalRPN("123 456 + 2 / *");                // => Exception: Stack empty
```

The System.Generic.ObjectModel Namespace

Previously, I showed that you can inherit from a generic type and implement either a standard class or another generic type. For example, the following code implements a typed collection of Person objects:

```
public class PersonCollection : List<Person>
{
}
```

The next code defines a new generic type that is similar to a sorted dictionary except it enables you to retrieve keys and values by their numeric index, thus solving one of the limitations of the SortedDictionary generic type:

```
public class IndexableDictionary<TKey, TValue> : SortedDictionary<TKey, TValue>
{
    // Retrieve a key by its index.
    public TKey GetKey(int index)
    {
        // Retrieve the N-th key.
        TKey[] keys = new TKey[this.Count - 1 + 1];
        this.Keys.CopyTo(keys, 0);
        return keys[index];
    }

    public TValue this[int index]
    {
        get { return this[GetKey(index)]; }
        set { this[GetKey(index)] = value; }
    }
}
```

(Notice that the IndexableDictionary class has suboptimal performance because finding the key with a given index is a relatively slow operation.) Here's how you can use the Indexable-Dictionary type:

```
IndexableDictionary<string, Person> idPersons =
   new IndexableDictionary<string, Person>();
idPersons.Add("Zare, Robert", new Person("Robert", "Zare"));
idPersons.Add("Beebe, Ann", new Person("Ann", "Beebe"));
Console.WriteLine(idPersons[0].ReverseName());          // => Beebe, Ann
```

Even if inheriting from concrete types such as List and Dictionary is OK in most cases, sometimes you can write better inherited classes by deriving from one of the abstract generic types defined in the System.Collections.ObjectModel namespace:

- **Collection<T>**   Provides a base class for generic collections that can be extended by adding or removing elements
- **ReadOnlyCollection<T>**   Provides a base class for generic read-only collections
- **KeyedCollection<TKey,TValue>**   Provides a base class for generic dictionaries

The main difference between regular generic types and the preceding abstract types is that the latter expose several protected methods that you can override to get more control of what happens when an element is modified or added to or removed from the collection. For example, the Collection<T> class exposes the following protected methods: ClearItems, InsertItem, RemoveItem, and SetItems, plus an Items protected property that enables you to access the inner collection of items.

Here's an example of a collection that can store a set of IComparable objects and that exposes an additional pair of read-only properties that returns the minimum and maximum values in the collection:

```
public class MinMaxCollection<T> : Collection<T>
   where T : IComparable
{
   private T min; private T max;
   private bool upToDate;

   public T MinValue
   {
      get
      {
         if ( !upToDate )
         {
            UpdateValues();
         }
         return min;
      }
   }

   public T MaxValue
   {
      get
```

```
      {
         if ( !upToDate )
         {
            UpdateValues();
         }
         return max;
      }
   }

   protected override void InsertItem(int index, T item)
   {
      base.InsertItem(index, item);
      if ( this.Count == 1 )
      {
         UpdateValues();
      }
      else if ( upToDate )
      {
         // If values are up-to-date, adjusting the min/max value is simple.
         if ( min.CompareTo(item) > 0 )
         {
            min = item;
         }
         if ( max.CompareTo(item) < 0 )
         {
            max = item;
         }
      }
   }

   protected override void SetItem(int index, T item)
   {
      // Check whether we're assigning the slot holding the min or max value.
      if ( min.CompareTo(this[index]) == 0 || max.CompareTo(this[index]) == 0 )
      {
         upToDate = false;
      }
      base.SetItem(index, item);
   }

   protected override void RemoveItem(int index)
   {
      // Check whether we're removing the min or max value.
      if ( min.CompareTo(this[index]) == 0 || max.CompareTo(this[index]) == 0 )
      {
         upToDate = false;
      }
      base.RemoveItem(index);
   }

   protected override void ClearItems()
   {
      base.ClearItems();
      upToDate = false;
   }

   // Helper method that updates the min/max values
```

```
    private void UpdateValues()
    {
        if ( this.Count == 0 )
        {
            // Assign default value of T if collection is empty.
            min = default(T); max = default(T);
        }
        else
        {
            // Else evaluate the min/max value.
            min = this[0]; max = this[0];
            foreach ( T item in this )
            {
                if ( min.CompareTo(item) > 0 )
                {
                    min = item;
                }
                if ( max.CompareTo(item) < 0 )
                {
                    max = item;
                }
            }
        }
        // Signal that min/max values are now up-to-date.
        upToDate = true;
    }
}
```

The noteworthy aspect of the MinMaxCollection is that it keeps an up-to-date value of the MinValue and MaxValue properties if possible, as long as the client program just adds new elements. If the client changes or removes an element that is currently the minimum or the maximum value, the upToDate variable is set to false so that the MinValue and MaxValue properties are recalculated the next time they are requested. This algorithm is quite optimized, yet it's generic enough to be used with any numeric type (more precisely: any type that supports the IComparable interface):

```
MinMaxCollection<double> col = new MinMaxCollection<double>();
// MinValue and MaxValue are updated during these insertions.
col.Add(123); col.Add(456); col.Add(789); col.Add(-33);
// This removal doesn't touch MinValue and MaxValue.
col.Remove(456);
Console.WriteLine("Min={0}, Max={1}", col.MinValue, col.MaxValue); // => Min=-33, Max=789

// This statement does affect MinValue and therefore sets upToDate=False.
col.Remove(-33);
// The next call to MinValue causes the properties to be recalculated.
Console.WriteLine("Min={0}, Max={1}", col.MinValue, col.MaxValue); // => Min=123, Max=789
```

The ReadOnlyCollection<T> abstract class is similar to Collection<T>, except that it doesn't expose any method for changing, adding, or removing elements after the collection has been created. (It is therefore the strong-typed counterpart of the ReadOnlyCollectionBase nongeneric abstract class.) Because the only operation that is supported after creation is enumeration, this base class doesn't expose any overridable protected methods.

Chapter 6

Regular Expressions

Regular expressions are a standard way to search for and optionally replace occurrences of substrings and text patterns. If you aren't familiar with regular expressions, just think of the wildcard characters you use at the command prompt to indicate a group of files (as in *.txt) or the special characters in LIKE clauses inside SQL queries:

```
SELECT name, city FROM customers WHERE name LIKE "A%"
```

Many computer scientists have thoroughly researched regular expressions, and a few programming languages—most notably Perl and Awk—are heavily based on regular expressions. Despite their usefulness in virtually every text-oriented task (including parsing log files and extracting information from HTML files), regular expressions are relatively rarely used by programmers, probably because they are based on a rather obscure syntax.

You can regard regular expressions as a highly specific programming language, and you know that all languages take time to learn and have idiosyncrasies. But when you see how much time regular expressions can save you—and I am talking about both coding time and CPU time—you'll probably agree that the effort you expend learning their contorted syntax is well worth it.

Note To avoid long lines, code samples in this chapter assume that the following using statements are used at the top of each source file:

```
using System;
using System.Collections;
using System.Diagnostics;
using System.Globalization;
using System.IO;
using System.Reflection;
using System.Text;
using System.Text.RegularExpressions;
```

Regular Expression Overview

The Microsoft .NET Framework comes with a very powerful regular expression engine that's accessible from any .NET language, so you can leverage the parsing power of languages such as Perl without having to switch away from your favorite language.

The Fundamentals

Regex is the most important class in this group, and any regular expression code instantiates at least an object of this class (or uses one of the Regex static methods). This object represents an immutable regular expression. You instantiate this object by passing to it the search pattern, written using the special regular expression language, which I describe later:

```
// This regular expression defines any group of 2 characters
// consisting of a vowel followed by a digit (\d).
Regex re = new Regex(@"[aeiou]\d");
```

Most regular expression patterns include the backslash (\) character because this character is used to insert special sequences; for this reason, patterns are usually specified as @-prefixed strings in Microsoft Visual C# source code.

The Matches method of the Regex object applies the regular expression to the string passed as an argument; it returns a MatchCollection object, a read-only collection that represents all the nonoverlapping matches:

```
Regex re = new Regex(@"[aeiou]\d");
// This source string contains 3 groups that match the Regex.
String text = "a1 = a1 + e2";
// Get the collection of matches.
MatchCollection mc = re.Matches(text);
// How many occurrences did we find?
Console.WriteLine(mc.Count);                         // => 3
```

You can also pass to the Matches method a second argument, which is interpreted as the index where the search begins.

The MatchCollection object contains individual Match objects, which expose properties such as Value (the matching string that was found), Index (the position of the matching string in the source string), and Length (the length of the matching string, which is useful when the regular expression can match strings of different lengths):

```
// …(Continuing the previous example)…
foreach ( Match m in mc )
{
   // Display text and position of this match.
   Console.WriteLine("'{0}' at position {1}", m.Value, m.Index);
}
```

The preceding code displays these lines in the console window:

```
'a1' at position 0
'a1' at position 5
'e2' at position 10
```

The Regex object can also modify a source string by searching for a given regular expression and replacing it with something else:

```
// Search for the "a" character followed by a digit.
Regex re2 = new Regex(@"a\d");
// Drop the digit that follows the "a" character.
string res = re2.Replace(text, "a"); // => a = a + e2
```

The Regex class also exposes static versions of the Match, Matches, and Replace methods. You can use these static methods when you don't want to instantiate a Regex object explicitly:

```
// This code snippet is equivalent to the previous one, but it doesn't
// instantiate a Regex object.
res = Regex.Replace(text, @"a\d", "a");
```

The best way to learn regular expressions is, not surprisingly, through practice. To help you in this process, I have created a RegexTester application that enables you to test any regular expression against any source string or text file. (See Figure 6-1.) This application has been a valuable tool for me in exploring regular expression intricacies, and I routinely use it whenever I have a doubt about how regular expressions work. See this book's companion source code. (This tool is written in Microsoft Visual Basic 2005.)

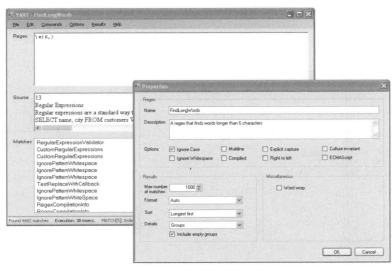

Figure 6-1   The RegexTester application, which enables you to experiment with all the most important methods and options of the Regex object

The Regular Expression Language

Table 6-1 lists all the constructs that are legal as regular expression patterns, grouped in the following categories:

- **Character escapes**   Used to match single characters. You need them to deal with non-printable characters (such as the newline and the tab characters) and to provide escaped versions for the characters that have a special meaning inside regular expression patterns. Together with substitutions, these are the only sequences that can appear in a replacement pattern.

- **Character classes**   Offer a means to match one character from a group that you specify between brackets, as in [aeiou]. You don't need to escape special characters when they appear in brackets except in the cases of the hyphen and the closing bracket, which are the only characters that have special meaning inside brackets. For example, [()[\]{}] matches opening and closing parentheses, brackets, and braces. (Notice that the] character is escaped, but the [character isn't.)

- **Atomic zero-width assertions**   Specify where the matching string should be, but don't consume characters. For example, the abc$ regular expression matches any abc word immediately before the end of a line without also matching the end of the line.

- **Quantifiers**   Specify that a subexpression must be repeated a given number of times. A particular quantifier applies to the character, character class, or group that immediately precedes it. For example, \w+ matches all the words with one or more characters, whereas \w{3,} matches all the words with at least three characters. Quantifiers can be divided in two categories: greedy and lazy. A *greedy* quantifier, such as * and +, always matches as many characters as possible, whereas a *lazy* quantifier, such as *? and +?, attempts to match as few characters as possible.

- **Grouping constructors**   Can capture and name groups of subexpressions as well as increase the efficiency of regular expressions with noncapturing look-ahead and look-behind modifiers. For example, (abc)+ matches repeated sequences of the "abc" string; (?<total>\d+) matches a group of one or more consecutive digits and assigns it the name total, which can be used later inside the same regular expression pattern or for substitution purposes.

- **Substitutions**   Can be used only inside a replacement pattern and, together with character escapes, are the only constructs that can be used inside replacement patterns. For example, when the sequence ${total} appears in a replacement pattern, it inserts the value of the group named total. Parentheses have no special meanings in replacement patterns, so you don't need to escape them.

- **Backreference constructs**   Enable you to reference a previous group of characters in the regular expression pattern by using its group number or name. You can use these constructs as a way to say "match the same thing again." For example, (?<value>\d+)=\k<value> matches identical numbers separated by an = sign, as in the "123=123" sequence.

- **Alternating constructs**   Provide a way to specify alternatives; for example, the sequence "I (am|have)" can match both the "I am" and "I have" strings.

- **Miscellaneous constructs**   Include constructs that allow you to modify one or more regular expression options in the middle of the pattern. For example, A(?i)BC matches all the variants of the ABC word that begin with uppercase *A* (such as Abc, ABc, AbC, and ABC). See Table 6-2 for a description of all the regular expression options.

Table 6-1   The Regular Expression Language

Category	Sequence	Description
Character escapes	Any character	Characters other than .$^{[(|)}*+?\ match themselves.
	\a	The bell alarm character (same as \x07).
	\b	The backspace (same as \x08), but only when used between brackets or in a replacement pattern. Otherwise, it matches a word boundary.
	\t	The tab character (same as \x09).
	\r	The carriage return (same as \x0D).
	\v	The vertical tab character (same as \x0B).
	\f	The form-feed character (same as \x0C).
	\n	The newline character (same as \x0A).
	\e	The escape character (same as \x1B).
	\040	An ASCII character expressed in octal notation (must have up to three octal digits). For example, \040 is a space.
	\x20	An ASCII character expressed in hexadecimal notation (must have exactly two digits). For example, \x20 is a space.
	\cC	An ASCII control character. For example, \cC is control+C.
	\u0020	A Unicode character in hexadecimal notation (must have exactly four digits). For example, \u0020 is a space.
	*	When the backslash is followed by a character in a way that doesn't form an escape sequence, it matches the character. For example, * matches the * character.
Character classes	.	The dot character matches any character except the newline character. It matches any character, including newline, if you're using the Singleline option.
	[aeiou]	Any character in the list between the opening and closing brackets; [aeiou] matches any vowel.
	[^aeiou]	Any character except those in the list between the opening and closing brackets; [^aeiou] matches any nonvowel.

Table 6-1   The Regular Expression Language

Category	Sequence	Description
	[a-zA-Z]	The - (hyphen) character enables you to specify ranges of characters: [a-zA-Z] matches any lower-case or uppercase character; [^0-9] matches any nondigit character. Notice, however, that accented letters aren't matched.
	[a-z-[aeiou]]	Character class subtraction: when a pair of brackets is nested in another pair of brackets and is pre-ceded by a minus sign, the regular expression matches all the characters in the outer pair except those in the inner pair. For example, [a-z-[aeiou]] matches any lowercase character that isn't a vowel. (Support for character class subtractions has been added in Microsoft .NET Framework version 2.0.)
	\w	A word character, which is an alphanumeric character or the underscore character; same as [a-zA-Z_0-9], but also matches accented letters and other alphabetical symbols.
	\W	A nonword character; same as [^a-zA-Z_0-9] but also excludes accented letters and other alphabeti-cal symbols.
	\s	A white-space character, which is a space, a tab, a form-feed, a newline, a carriage return, or a vertical-feed character; same as [\f\n\r\t\v].
	\S	A character other than a white-space character; same as [^ \f\n\r\t\v].
	\d	A decimal digit; same as [0-9].
	\D	A nondigit character; same as [^0-9].
	\p{name}	A character included in the named character class specified by {name}; supported names are Unicode groups and block ranges, for example, Ll, Nd, or Z.
	\P{name}	A character not included in groups and block ranges specified in {name}.
Atomic zero-width assertions	^	The beginning of the string (or the beginning of the line if you're using the Multiline option).
	$	The end of the string (or the end of the line if you're using the Multiline option).
	\A	The beginning of a string (like ^ but ignores the Multiline option).
	\Z	The end of the string or the position before the newline character at the end of the string (like $ but ignores the Multiline option).

Table 6-1   **The Regular Expression Language**

Category	Sequence	Description
	\z	Exactly the end of the string, whether or not there's a newline character (ignores the Multiline option).
	\G	The position at which the current search started—usually one character after the point at which the previous search ended.
	\b	The word boundary between \w (alphanumeric) and \W (nonalphanumeric) characters. It indicates the first and last characters of a word delimited by spaces or other punctuation symbols.
	\B	Not on a word boundary.
Quantifiers	*	Zero or more matches; for example, \bA\w* matches a word that begins with A and is followed by zero or more alphanumeric characters; same as {0,}.
	+	One or more matches; for example, \b[aeiou]+\b matches a word composed only of vowels; same as {1,}.
	?	Zero or one match; for example, \b[aeiou]\d?\b matches a word that starts with a vowel and is followed by zero or one digit; same as {0,1}.
	{N}	Exactly N matches; for example, [aeiou]{4} matches four consecutive vowels.
	{N,}	At least N matches; for example, \d{3,} matches groups of three or more digits.
	{N,M}	Between N and M matches; for example, \d{3,5} matches groups of three, four, or five digits.
	*?	Lazy *; the first match that consumes as few repeats as possible.
	+?	Lazy +; the first match that consumes as few repeats as possible, but at least one.
	??	Lazy ?; zero repeats if possible, or one.
	{N}?	Lazy {N}; equivalent to {N}.
	{N,}?	Lazy {N,}; as few repeats as possible, but at least N.
	{N,M}?	Lazy {N,M}; as few repeats as possible, but between N and M.
Grouping constructs	(substr)	Captures the matched substring. These captures are numbered automatically, based on the order of the left parenthesis, starting at 1. The zeroth capturing group is the text matched by the whole regular expression pattern.
	(?<name>expr) (?'name'expr)	Captures the subexpression and assigns it a name. The name must not contain any punctuation symbols.

Table 6-1   **The Regular Expression Language**

Category	Sequence	Description
	(?:expr)	Noncapturing group, that is, a group that doesn't appear in the Groups collection of the Match object.
	(?imnsx-imnsx: expr)	Enables or disables the options specified in the subexpression. For example, (?i-s) uses case-insensitive searches and disables single-line mode (see Table 6-2 for information about regular expression options).
	(?=expr)	Zero-width positive look-ahead assertion; continues match only if the subexpression matches at this position on the right. For example, \w+(?=,) matches a word followed by a comma, without matching the comma.
	(?!expr)	Zero-width negative look-ahead assertion; continues match only if the subexpression doesn't match at this position on the right. For example, \w+\b(?![,:;]) matches a word that isn't followed by a comma, a colon, or a semicolon.
	(?<=expr)	Zero-width positive look-behind assertion; continues match only if the subexpression matches at this position on the left. For example, (?<=[,;])\w+ matches a word that follows a comma or semicolon, without matching the comma or semicolon. This construct doesn't backtrack.
	(?<!expr>	Zero-width negative look-behind assertion; continues match only if the subexpression doesn't match at this position on the left. For example, (?<!,)\b\w+ matches a word that doesn't follow a comma.
	(?>expr)	Nonbacktracking subexpression; the subexpression is fully matched once, and it doesn't participate in backtracking. The subexpression matches only strings that would be matched by the subexpression alone.
	(?<name1-name2>expr) (?'name1-name2'expr)	Balancing group definition. Deletes the definition of the previously defined group name2 and stores in group name1 the interval between the previously defined name2 group and the current group. If no group name2 is defined, the match backtracks. Because deleting the last definition of name2 reveals the previous definition of name2, this construct allows the stack of captures for group name2 to be used as a counter for keeping track of nested constructs such as parentheses.

Table 6-1   **The Regular Expression Language**

Category	Sequence	Description
Substitutions	$N	Substitutes the last substring matched by group number N. ($0 replaces the entire match.)
	${name}	Substitutes the last substring matched by a (?<name>) group.
	$&	Substitutes the entire match (same as $0).
	$_	Substitutes the entire source string.
	$`	Substitutes the portion of the source string up to the match.
	$'	Substitutes the portion of the source string that follows the match.
	$+	Substitutes the last captured group.
	$$	A single dollar symbol (only when it appears in a substitution pattern).
Backreference constructs	\N \NN	Back reference to a previous group. For example, (\w)\1 finds doubled word characters, such as ss in expression. A backslash followed by a single digit is always considered a back reference (and throws a parsing exception if such a numbered reference is missing); a backslash followed by two digits is considered a numbered back reference if there's a corresponding numbered reference; otherwise, it's considered an octal code. In case of ambiguity, use the \k<name> construct.
	\k<name> \k'name'	Named back reference. (?<char>\w)\d\k<char> matches a word character followed by a digit and then by the same word character, as in the "B2B" string.
Alternating constructs	/	Either/or. For example, vb/c#/java. Leftmost successful match wins.
	(?(expr)yes/no)	Matches the yes part if the expression matches at this point; otherwise, matches the no part. The expression is turned into a zero-width assertion. If the expression is the name of a named group or a capturing group number, the alternation is interpreted as a capture test (see next case).
	(?(name)yes/no)	Matches the yes part if the named capture string has a match; otherwise, matches the no part. The no part can be omitted. If the given name doesn't correspond to the name or number of a capturing group used in this expression, the alternation is interpreted as an expression test (see previous case).

Table 6-1   The Regular Expression Language

Category	Sequence	Description
Miscellaneous constructs	(?imnsx-imnsx)	Enables or disables one or more regular expression options. For example, it allows case sensitivity to be turned on or off in the middle of a pattern. Option changes are effective until the closing parenthesis (see also the corresponding grouping construct, which is a cleaner form).
	(?# comment)	Inline comment inserted within a regular expression. The text that follows the # and continues until the first closing) character is ignored.
	#	X-mode comment; the text that follows an unescaped # until the end of line is ignored. This construct requires that the x option or the RegexOptions.IgnorePatternWhiteSpace enumerated option be activated.

Regular Expression Options

The Match, Matches, and Replace static methods of the Regex object support an optional argument, which enables you to specify one or more options to be applied to the regular expression search (see Table 6-2). For example, the following code searches for all occurrences of the abc word, regardless of its case:

```
string source = "ABC Abc abc";
MatchCollection mc = Regex.Matches(source, "abc");
Console.WriteLine(mc.Count);                                   // => 1
mc = Regex.Matches(source, "abc", RegexOptions.IgnoreCase);
Console.WriteLine(mc.Count);                                   // => 3
```

By default, the Regex class transforms the regular expression into a sequence of opcodes, which are then interpreted when the pattern is applied to a specific source string. If you specify the RegexOptions.Compiled option, however, the regular expression is compiled into IL rather than into regular expression opcodes. This feature enables the Just-In-Time (JIT) compiler to later convert the IL to native CPU instructions, which clearly delivers better performance:

```
// Create a compiled regular expression that searches
// words that start with uppercase or lowercase A.
Regex reComp = new Regex(@"\Aw+", RegexOptions.IgnoreCase | RegexOptions.Compiled);
```

The extra performance that the Compiled option can buy you varies depending on the specific regular expression, but you can reasonably expect a twofold increase in speed in most cases. However, the extra compilation step adds some overhead, so you should use this option only if you plan to use the regular expression multiple times. Another factor that you should take into account when using the RegexOptions.Compiled option is that the compiled IL code isn't unloaded when the Regex object is reclaimed by the garbage collector—it continues to take memory until the application terminates. So you should preferably limit the number of compiled regular expressions. Also, consider that the Regex class caches all regular expression opcodes in memory, so a regular expression isn't generally reparsed each time it's used. The caching mechanism also works when you use static methods and don't explicitly create Regex instances.

The RegexOptions.IgnorePatternWhitespace option tells the Regex object to ignore spaces, tabs, and newline characters in the pattern and to enable #-prefixed remarks. You see the usefulness of this option when you want to format the pattern with a more meaningful layout and to explain what each of its portions does:

```
// Match a string optionally enclosed in single or double quotation marks.
string pattern =
@"\s*        # ignore leading spaces
(            # two cases: quoted or unquoted string
(?<quote>    # case 1: define a group named 'quote' '
['""])      # the group is a single or double quote
.*?          # a sequence of characters (lazy matching)
\k<quote>    # followed by the same quote char
|            # end of case 1
[^'""]+     # case 2: a string without quotes
)            # end of case 2
\s*          # ignore trailing spaces";
Regex re = new Regex(pattern, RegexOptions.IgnorePatternWhitespace);
...
```

Because spaces are ignored, to match the space character you must use either the [ ] character class or the \x20 character escape (or another equivalent escape sequence) when the IgnorePatternWhitespace option is used.

The RegexOptions.Multiline option enables multiline mode, which is especially useful when you're parsing text files instead of plain strings. This option modifies the meaning and the behavior of the ^ and $ assertions so that they match the start and end of each line of text, respectively, rather than the start or end of the whole string. Thanks to this option, you need only a handful of statements to create a grep-like utility that displays how many occurrences of the regular expression passed in the first argument are found in the files indicated by the second argument:

```
// Compile this application and create the FileGrep.Exe executable.
static class FileGrep
{
    public static void Main(string[] args)
    {
        // Show syntax if too few arguments.
        if ( args.Length != 2 )
        {
            Console.WriteLine("Syntax: FILEGREP \"regex\" filespec");
            return;
        }
```

```
string pattern = args[0];
string filespec = args[1];
// Create the regular expression (throws if pattern is invalid).
Regex filePattern = new Regex(pattern, RegexOptions.IgnoreCase |
   RegexOptions.Multiline);

// Apply the regular expression to each file in specified or current directory.
string dirname = Path.GetDirectoryName(filespec);
if ( dirname.Length == 0 )
{
    dirname = Directory.GetCurrentDirectory();
}
string search = Path.GetFileName(filespec);
foreach ( string fname in Directory.GetFiles(dirname, search) )
{
    // Read file contents and apply the regular expression to it.
    string text = File.ReadAllText(fname);
    MatchCollection mc = filePattern.Matches(text);
    // Display filename if one or more matches.
    if ( mc.Count > 0 )
    {
        Console.WriteLine("{0} [{1} matches]", fname, mc.Count);
    }
}
    }
}
```

For example, you can use the FileGrep utility to find all .cs source files in the current directory that contain the definition of a public ArrayList variable or a public method that returns an ArrayList object:

```
FileGrep "^\s*public\s+(System.Collections.)?ArrayList\s+\w+" *.cs
```

It's easy to modify this code to display details about all occurrences or to extend the search to an entire directory tree.

 Note   The Windows operating system includes a little-known command-line utility named FindStr, which supports searches with regular expressions and recursion over subdirectories, case-insensitive matches, display of lines that do *not* include the pattern, and so forth. Learn more by typing FindStr /? at the command prompt.

Another way to specify a regular expression option is by means of the (?imnsx-imnsx) construct, which lets you enable or disable one or more options from the current position to the end of the pattern string. The following code snippet finds the names of a few countries, regardless of their case. Note that the regular expression options are specified inside the pattern string instead of as an argument of the Regex.Matches method:

```
string pattern = @"(?im)(USA|Germany|France|Italy)";
string source = File.ReadAllText("Test.txt");
MatchCollection ms = Regex.Matches(source, pattern);
```

Table 6-2   Regular Expression Options[1]

RegexOptions enum Value	Option	Description
None		No option
IgnoreCase	i	Case insensitivity match
Singleline	s	Singleline mode; changes the behavior of the . (dot) character so that it matches any character (instead of any character but the newline character).
Multiline	m	Multiline mode; changes the behavior of ^ and $ so that they match the beginning and end of individual lines, respectively, instead of the whole string.
ExplicitCapture	n	Captures only explicitly named or numbered groups of the form (?<name>) so that naked parentheses act as noncapturing groups without your having to use the (?:) construct.
IgnorePatternWhitespace	x	Ignores unescaped white space from the pattern and enables comments marked with #. Significant spaces in the pattern must be specified as [ ] or \x20.
CultureInvariant		Uses the culture implied by CultureInfo.InvariantCulture, instead of the locale assigned to the current thread.
Compiled		Compiles the regular expression and generates IL code; this option generates faster code at the expense of longer startup time.
ECMAScript		Enables ECMAScript-compliant behavior. This flag can be used only in conjunction with the IgnoreCase, Multiline, and Compiled flags.
RightToLeft		Specifies that the search is from right to left instead of from left to right. If a starting index is specified, it should point to the end of the string.

[1.] These regular expression options can be specified when you create the Regex object. If a character is provided in the middle column, they can be specified also from inside a (?) construct. All these options are turned off by default.

Regular Expression Types

Now that I have illustrated the fundamentals of regular expressions, it's time to examine all the types in the System.Text.RegularExpressions namespace.

The Regex Type

As discussed in the preceding section, the Regex type provides two overloaded constructors—one that takes only the pattern and another that also takes a bit-coded value that specifies the required regular expression options:

```
// This Regex object can search the word "USA" in a case-insensitive way.
Regex re = new Regex(@"\bUSA\b", RegexOptions.IgnoreCase);
```

The Regex class exposes only two properties, both of which are read-only. The Options property returns the second argument passed to the object constructor, while the RightToLeft property returns true if you specified the RightToLeft option. (The regular expression matches from right to left.) No property returns the regular expression pattern, but you can use the ToString method for this purpose.

Searching for Substrings

The Matches method searches the regular expression inside the string provided as an argument and returns a MatchCollection object that contains zero or more Match objects, one for each nonintersecting match. The Matches method is overloaded to take an optional starting index:

```
// Get the collection that contains all the matches.
MatchCollection mc = re.Matches(source);

// Print all the matches after the 100th character in the source string.
foreach ( Match m in re.Matches(source, 100) )
{
    Console.WriteLine(m.Value);
}
```

You can change the behavior of the Matches method (as well as the Match method, described later) by using a \G assertion to disable scanning. In this case, the match must be found exactly where the scan begins. This point is either at the index specified as an argument (or the first character if this argument is omitted) or immediately after the point where the previous match terminates. In other words, the \G assertion finds only *consecutive* matches:

```
// Finds consecutive groups of space-delimited numbers.
Regex re = new Regex(@"\G\s*\d+");
// Note that search stops at the first nonnumeric group.
Console.WriteLine(re.Matches("12 34 56 ab 78").Count);     // => 3
```

Sometimes, you don't really want to list all the occurrences of the pattern when determining whether the pattern is contained in the source string would suffice. For example, this is usually the case when you are checking that a value typed by the end user complies with the expected format (for example, it's a phone number or a social security number in a valid format). If that's your interest, the IsMatch method is more efficient than the Matches method is because it stops the scan as soon as the first match is found. You pass to this method the input string and an optional start index:

```
// Check whether the input string is a date in the format mm-dd-yy or
// mm-dd-yyyy. (The source string can use slashes as date separators and
// can contain leading or trailing white spaces.)
Regex re2 = new Regex(@"^\s*\d{1,2}(/|-)\d{1,2}\1(\d{4}|\d{2})\s*$");
if ( re2.IsMatch(" 12/10/2001 ") )
{
    Console.WriteLine("The date is formatted correctly.");
    // (We don't check whether month and day values are in valid range.)
}
```

The regular expression pattern in the preceding code requires an explanation:

1. The ^ and $ characters mean that the source string must contain one date value and nothing else. These characters must be used to check whether the source string *matches* the pattern, rather than *contains* it.

2. The \s* subexpression at the beginning and end of the string means that we accept leading and trailing white spaces.

3. The \d{1,2} subexpression means that the month and day numbers can have one or two digits, whereas the (\d{4}|\d{2}) subexpression means that the year number can have four or two digits. The four-digit case must be tested first; otherwise, only the first two digits are matched.

4. The (/|-) subexpression means that we take either the slash or the dash as the date separator between the month and day numbers.

5. The \1 subexpression means that the separator between day and year numbers must be the same separator used between month and day numbers.

The Matches method has an undocumented feature that becomes very handy when parsing very long strings. When you use the return value of this method in a foreach loop—as I did in the majority of examples shown so far—this method performs a sort of lazy evaluation: instead of processing the entire string, it stops the parsing process as soon as the first Match object can be returned to the calling program. When the next iteration of the loop begins, it restarts the parsing process where it had left previously, and so forth. If you exit the loop with a break statement, the remainder of the string is never parsed, which can be very convenient if you are looking for a specific match and don't need to list all of them. You can easily prove this feature with this code:

```
// Prepare to search for the "A" character.
Regex re = new Regex("A");
// Create a very long string with a match at its beginning and its end.
string text = "A" + new string(' ', 1000000) + "A";

Stopwatch sw = Stopwatch.StartNew();
foreach (Match m in re.Matches(text))
{
    // Show how long it took to find this match.
    Console.WriteLine("Elapsed {0} milliseconds", sw.ElapsedMilliseconds);
}
```

The output in the console window proves that the first Match object was returned almost instantaneously, whereas it took some millions of CPU cycles to locate the character at the end of the string:

```
Elapsed 0 milliseconds
Elapsed 80 milliseconds
```

Keep in mind that this lazy evaluation feature of the Matches method is disabled if you query other members of the returned MatchCollection object, for example, the Count property. It's quite obvious that the only way to count the occurrences of the pattern is to process the entire input string.

In some special cases you might want to have even more control on the parsing process, for example, to skip portions of the string that aren't of interest for your purposes. In these cases, you can use the Match method, which returns only the first Match object and lets you iterate over the remaining matches using the Match.NextMatch method, as this example demonstrates:

```
// Search all the dates in a source string.
string source = " 12-2-1999  10/23/2001 4/5/2001 ";
Regex re = new Regex(@"\s*\d{1,2}(/|-)\d{1,2}\1(\d{4}|\d{2})");
// Find the first match.
Match m = re.Match(source);
// Enter the following loop only if the search was successful.
while ( m.Success )
{
    // Display the match, but discard leading and trailing spaces.
    Console.WriteLine(m.ToString().Trim());
    // Find the next match; exit if not successful.
    m = m.NextMatch();
}
```

The Split method is similar to the String.Split method except it defines the delimiter by using a regular expression rather than a single character. For example, the following code prints all the elements in a comma-delimited list of numbers, ignoring leading and trailing white-space characters:

```
string source = "123, 456,,789";
Regex re = new Regex(@"\s*,\s*");
foreach ( string s in re.Split(source) )
{
    // Note that the third element is a null string.
    Console.Write(s + "-");                          // => 123-456--789-
}
```

(You can modify the pattern to \s*[,]+\s* to discard empty elements.) The Split method supports several overloaded variations, which enable you to define the maximum count of elements to be extracted and a starting index (if there are more elements than the given limit, the last element contains the remainder of the string):

```
// Split max 5 items.
string[] arr = re.Split(source, 5);
// Split max 5 items, starting at the 100th character.
string[] arr2 = re.Split(source, 5, 100);
```

The Replace Method

The Regex.Replace method enables you to replace portions of the source string selectively. This method requires that you create numbered or named groups of characters in the pattern and then use those groups in the replacement pattern. The following code example takes a string that contains one or more dates in the mm-dd-yy format (including variations with a / separator or a four-digit year number) and converts them to the dd-mm-yy format while preserving the original date separator:

```
string source = "12-2-1999   10/23/2001   4/5/2001 ";
string pattern =
    @"\b(?<mm>\d{1,2})(?<sep>(/|-))(?<dd>\d{1,2})\k<sep>(?<yy>(\d{4}|\d{2}))\b";
Regex re = new Regex(pattern);
Console.WriteLine(re.Replace(source, "${dd}${sep}${mm}${sep}${yy}"));
    // => 2-12-1999   23/10/2001   5/4/2001
```

The pattern string is similar to the one shown previously, with an important difference: it defines four groups—named mm, dd, yy, and sep—that are later rearranged in the replacement string. The \b assertion at the beginning and end of the pattern ensures that the date is a word of its own.

The Replace method supports other overloaded variants. For example, you can pass two additional numeric arguments, which are interpreted as the maximum number of substitutions and the starting index:

```
// Expand all "ms" abbreviations to "Microsoft" (regardless of their case).
string text = "Welcome to ms Ms ms MS";
Regex re2 = new Regex(@"\bMS\b", RegexOptions.IgnoreCase);
// Replace up to two occurrences, starting at the 12th character.
Console.WriteLine(re2.Replace(text, "Microsoft", 2, 12));
```

If the replacement operation does something more sophisticated than simply delete or change the order of named groups, you can use an overloaded version of the Replace function that takes a delegate argument pointing to a filter function you've defined elsewhere in the application. This feature gives you tremendous flexibility, as the following code demonstrates:

```
public static void TestReplaceWithCallback()
{
    // This pattern defines two integers separated by a plus sign.
    Regex re = new Regex(@"\d+\s*\+\s*\d+");
    string source = "a = 100 + 234: b = 200+345";
    // Replace all sum operations with their results.
    Console.WriteLine(re.Replace(source, DoSum));        // => a = 334: b = 545
}

// The callback method
private static string DoSum(Match m)
{
    // Parse the two operands.
    string[] args = m.Value.Split('+');
    long n1 = long.Parse(args[0]);
    long n2 = long.Parse(args[1]);
    // Return their sum, as a string.
    return (n1 + n2).ToString();
}
```

The delegate must point to a function that takes a Match object and returns a String object. The code inside this function can query the Match object properties to learn more about the match. For example, you can use the Index property to peek at what immediately precedes or follows in the source string so that you can make a more informed decision.

Callback functions are especially useful to convert individual matches to uppercase, lower-case, or proper case:

```
private static string ConvertToUpperCase(Match m)
{
    return m.Value.ToUpper();
}

private static string ConvertToLowerCase(Match m)
{
    return m.Value.ToLower();
}

private static string ConvertToProperCase(Match m)
{
    // We must convert to lowercase first, to ensure that ToTitleCase works as intended.
    return CultureInfo.CurrentCulture.TextInfo.ToTitleCase(m.Value.ToLower());
}
```

Here's an example:

```
// Convert country names in the text string to uppercase.
string text = "I visited italy, france, and then GERMANY";
Regex re2 = new Regex(@"\b(Usa|France|Germany|Italy|Great Britain)\b",
    RegexOptions.IgnoreCase);
text = re2.Replace(text, ConvertToProperCase);
Console.WriteLine(text);       // => I visited Italy, France, and then Germany
```

You might also want to use anonymous methods, as in this case:

```
// Convert all country names to uppercase.
text = re2.Replace(text, delegate(Match m)
    { return m.Value.ToUpper(); });
Console.WriteLine(text);       // => I visited ITALY, FRANCE, and then GERMANY
```

Static Methods

All the methods shown so far are also available as static methods; therefore, in many cases you don't need to create a Regex object explicitly. You generally pass the regular expression pattern to the static method as a second argument after the source string. For example, you can split a string into individual words as follows:

```
// \W means "any nonalphanumeric character."
string[] words = Regex.Split("Split these words", @"\W+");
```

The Regex class also exposes a few static methods that have no instance method counterpart. The Escape method takes a string and converts the special characters .$^{[(|)*+?\ to their equivalent escaped sequence. This method is especially useful when you let the end user enter the search pattern:

```
Console.WriteLine(Regex.Escape("(x)"));        // => \(x\)

// Check whether the character sequence the end user entered in
// the txtChars TextBox control is contained in the source string.
if ( Regex.IsMatch(source, Regex.Escape(txtChars.Text)) )
{ … }
```

The Unescape static method converts a string that contains escaped sequences back into its unescaped equivalent. This method has a limited usefulness in C# because you can directly embed unprintable characters in strings:

```
s = Regex.Unescape(@"First line\r\nSecond line ends with null char\x00")
```

The CompileToAssembly Method

When you use the RegexOptions.Compiled value in the Regex constructor, you can expect a slight delay for the regular expression to be compiled to IL. In most cases, this delay is negligible, but you can avoid it if you want by using the CompileToAssembly static method to precompile one or more regular expressions. The result of this precompilation is a separate assembly that contains one Regex-derived type for each regular expression you've precompiled. The following code shows how you can use the CompileToAssembly method to create an assembly that contains two precompiled regular expressions:

```
// The namespace for both compiled regex types in this sample
string nsName = "CustomRegex";
// The first regular expression compiles to a type named RegexWords.
// (The last argument means that the type is public.)
RegexCompilationInfo rci1 = new RegexCompilationInfo(@"\w+",
    RegexOptions.Compiled, "RegexWords", nsName, true);
// The second regular expression compiles to a type named RegexIntegers.
RegexCompilationInfo rci2 = new RegexCompilationInfo(@"\d+",
    RegexOptions.Compiled, "RegexIntegers", nsName, true);
// Create the array that defines all compiled regular expressions.
RegexCompilationInfo[] regexInfo = { rci1, rci2 };

// Compile these types to an assembly named "CustomRegularExpressions"
AssemblyName an = new AssemblyName();
an.Name = "CustomRegularExpressions";
Regex.CompileToAssembly(regexInfo, an);
```

The preceding code creates an assembly named CustomRegularExpressions.Dll in the same directory as the current application's executable. You can add a reference to this assembly from any Microsoft Visual Studio 2005 project and use the two RegexWords and RegexIntegers types, or you can load these types using reflection (see Chapter 9, "Reflection"). In the former case, you can use a strongly typed variable:

```
CustomRegex.RegexWords reWords = new CustomRegex.RegexWords();
foreach ( Match m in reWords.Matches("A string containing five words") )
{
    Console.WriteLine(m.Value);
}
```

The MatchCollection and Match Types

The MatchCollection class represents a set of matches. It has no constructor because you can create a MatchCollection object only by using the Regex.Matches method.

The Match class represents a single match. You can obtain an instance of this class either by iterating on a MatchCollection object or directly by means of the Match method of the Regex class. The Match object is immutable and has no public constructor.

The main properties of the Match class are Value, Length, and Index, which return the matched string, its length, and the index at which it appears in the source string. The ToString method returns the same string as the Value property does. I already showed you how to use the Success property of the Match class and its NextMatch method to iterate over all the matches in a string.

You must pay special attention when the search pattern matches an empty string, for example, \d* (which matches zero or more digits). When you apply such a pattern to a string, you typically get one or more empty matches, as you can see here:

```
Regex re = new Regex(@"\d*");
foreach ( Match m in re.Matches("1a23bc456de789") )
{
    // The output from this loop shows that some matches are empty.
    Console.Write(m.Value + ",");              // => 1,,23,,456,,,789,,
}
```

As I explained earlier, a search generally starts where the previous search ends. However, the rule is different when the engine finds an empty match because it advances by one character before repeating the search. You would get trapped in an endless loop if the engine didn't behave this way.

If the pattern contains one or more groups, you can access the corresponding Group object by means of the Match object's Groups collection, which you can index by the group number or group name. I discuss the Group object shortly, but you can already see how you can use the Groups collection to extract the variable names and values in a series of assignments:

```
string source = "a = 123: b=456";
Regex re2 = new Regex(@"(\s*)(?<name>\w+)\s*=\s*(?<value>\d+)");
foreach ( Match m in re2.Matches(source) )
```

```
{
    Console.WriteLine("Variable: {0}, Value: {1}", m.Groups["name"].Value,
        m.Groups["value"].Value);
}
```

This is the result displayed in the console window:

```
Variable: a, Value: 123
Variable: b, Value: 456
```

The Result method takes a replace pattern and returns the string that would result if the match were replaced by that pattern:

```
// This code produces exactly the same result as the preceding snippet.
foreach ( Match m in re2.Matches(source) )
{
    Console.WriteLine(m.Result("Variable: ${name}, Value: ${value}"));
}
```

The Group Type

The Group class represents a single group in a Match object and exposes a few properties whose meanings should be evident. The properties are Value (the text associated with the group), Index (its position in the source string), Length (the group's length), and Success (true if the group has been matched). This code sample is similar to the preceding example, but it also displays the index in the source string where each matched variable was found:

```
string text = "a = 123: b=456";
Regex re = new Regex(@"(\s*)(?<name>\w+)\s*=\s*(?<value>\d+)");
foreach ( Match m in re.Matches(text) )
{
    Group g = m.Groups["name"];
    // Get information on variable name and value.
    Console.Write("Variable '{0}' found at index {1}", g.Value, g.Index);
    Console.WriteLine(", value is {0}", m.Groups["value"].Value);
}
```

This is the result displayed in the console window:

```
Variable 'a' found at index 0, value is 123
Variable 'b' found at index 9, value is 456
```

The following example is more complex but also more useful. It shows how you can parse <A> tags in an HTML file and display the anchor text (the text that appears underlined on an HTML page) and the URL it points to. As you can see, it's just a matter of a few lines of code:

```
Regex re = new Regex(@"<A\s+HREF\s*=\s*("".+?""|.+?)>(.+?)</A>", RegexOptions.IgnoreCase);
// Load the contents of an HTML file.
string text = File.ReadAllText("test.htm");
```

```
// Display all occurrences.
Match m = re.Match(text);
while ( m.Success )
{
   Console.WriteLine("{0} => {1}", m.Groups[2].Value, m.Groups[1].Value);
   m = m.NextMatch();
}
```

To understand how the preceding code works, you must keep in mind that the <A> tag is followed by one or more spaces and then by an HREF attribute, which is followed by an equal sign and then the URL, which can be enclosed in quotation marks. All the text that follows the closing angle bracket up to the ending tag </A> is the anchor text. The regular expression uses the .+? lazy quantifier so as not to match too many characters and miss the delimiting quotation mark or the closing angle bracket.

The regular expression defined in the preceding code defines two unnamed groups—the URL and the anchor text—so displaying details for all the <A> tags in the HTML file is just a matter of looping over all the matches. The regular expression syntax is complicated by the fact that quotation mark characters must be doubled when they appear in an @-prefixed string constant.

A few methods in the Regex class can be useful to get information about the groups that the parser finds in the regular expression. The GetGroupNames method returns an array with the names of all groups; the GroupNameFromNumber returns the name of the group with a given index; and the GroupNumberFromName returns the index of a group with a given name. See the MSDN documentation for more information.

The CaptureCollection and Capture Types

The search pattern can include one or more capturing groups, which are named or unnamed subexpressions enclosed in parentheses. Capturing groups can be nested and can capture multiple substrings of the source strings because of quantifiers. For example, when you apply the (\w)+ pattern to the "abc" string, you get one match for the entire string and three captured substrings, one for each character.

Fortunately, in most cases you don't need to work with captures because analyzing the source string at the match and group levels is often sufficient. You can access the collection of capture substrings through the Captures method of either the Match or the Group object. This method returns a CaptureCollection object that in turn contains one or more Capture objects. Individual Capture objects enable you to determine where individual captured substrings appear in the source string. The following code displays all the captured strings in the "abc def" string:

```
string text = "abc def";
Regex re = new Regex(@"(\w)+");
// Get the name or numbers of all the groups.
string[] groups = re.GetGroupNames();
```

```
// Iterate over all matches.
foreach ( Match m in re.Matches(text) )
{
    // Display information on this match.
    Console.WriteLine("Match '{0}' at index {1}", m.Value, m.Index);
    // Iterate over the groups in each match.
    foreach ( string s in groups )
    {
        // Get a reference to the corresponding group.
        Group g = m.Groups[s];
        // Get the capture collection for this group.
        CaptureCollection cc = g.Captures;
        // Display the number of captures.
        Console.WriteLine("  Found {0} capture(s) for group {1}", cc.Count, s);
        // Display information on each capture.
        foreach ( Capture c in cc )
        {
            Console.WriteLine("    '{0}' at index {1}", c.Value, c.Index);
        }
    }
}
```

The text that follows is the result produced in the console window. (Notice that group 0 always refers to the match expression itself.)

```
Match 'abc' at index 0
  Found 1 capture(s) for group 0
    'abc' at index 0
  Found 3 capture(s) for group 1
    'a' at index 0
    'b' at index 1
    'c' at index 2
Match 'def' at index 4
  Found 1 capture(s) for group 0
    'def' at index 4
  Found 3 capture(s) for group 1
    'd' at index 4
    'e' at index 5
    'f' at index 6
```

Regular Expressions at Work

Most of the examples so far have showed many possible applications of regular expressions, yet they just scratch the surface of the power of regular expressions. In this last section, I illustrate more examples and provide hints of how to make the most of this powerful feature of the .NET Framework.

Common Regex Patterns

For your convenience, I have prepared a list of recurring patterns, which you can often use as is in your code (see Table 6-3). To help you find the pattern that suits your needs, the list includes some patterns that I covered earlier in this chapter as well as patterns that I discuss in following sections. You should enclose the pattern between a pair of \b sequences if you want to find individual words, or between the ^ and $ characters if you want to test whether the entire input string matches the pattern.

Table 6-3 Common Regular Expression Patterns

Sequence	Description
\d+	Positive integer.
[+-]?\d+	A positive or negative integer whose sign is optional.
[+-]?\d+(\.\d+)?	A floating-point number whose sign and decimal portion are optional.
[+-]?\d+(\.\d+)?(E[+-]?\d+)?	A floating-point number that can be optionally expressed in exponential format (e.g., 1.23E+12); the mantissa sign and the exponent sign are optional.
[0-9A-Fa-f]+	A hexadecimal number.
\w+	A sequence of alphanumeric and underscore characters; same as the [A–Za–z0–9_]+ sequence.
[A–Z]+	An all-uppercase word.
[A–Z][a–z]+	A proper name (the initial character is uppercase, and then all lowercase characters).
[A–Z][A–Za–z']+	A last name (the initial character is uppercase, and string can contain other uppercase characters and apostrophes, as in O'Brian).
[A–Za–z]{1,10}	A word of 10 characters or fewer.
[A–Za–z]{11,}	A word of 11 characters or more.
[A-Za–z_]\w*	A valid C# identifier that begins with a letter or underscores and optionally continues with letters, digits, or underscores.
(?<q>["']).*?\k<q>	A quoted string enclosed in either single or double quotation marks.
(10|11|12|0?[1–9])(?<sep>[-/])(30|31|2\d|1\d|0?[1–9])\k<sep>(\d{4}|\d{2})	A U.S. date in the mm-dd-yyyy or mm/dd/yyyy format. Month and day numbers can have a leading zero; month number must be in the range 1–12; day number must be in the range 1–31 (but invalid dates such as 2/30/2004 are matched); year number can have two or four digits and isn't validated.
(30|31|2\d|1\d|0?[1–9])(?<sep>[-/])(10|11|12|0?[1–9])\k<sep>(\d{4}|\d{2})	A European date in the dd-mm-yyyy or dd/mm/yyyy format. (See previous entry for more details.)
(2[0–3]|[01]\d|\d):[0–5]\d	A time value in the hh:mm 24-hour format; leading zero for hour value is optional.
\(\d{3}\)–\d{3}–\d{4}	A phone number such as (123)-456-7890.
\d{5}(-\d{4})?	A U.S. ZIP code.
\d{3}-\d{2}-\d{4}	A U.S. social security number (SSN).
((\d{16}|\d{4}(-\d{4}){3})|(\d{4}(\d{4}){3}))	A 16-digit credit card number that can embed optional dashes or spaces to define four groups of four digits, for example, 1234567812345678, 1234-5678-1234-5678, or 1234 5678 1234 5678. (Needless to say, it doesn't validate whether it is a valid credit card number.)

Table 6-3   Common Regular Expression Patterns

Sequence	Description
([0–9A–Fa–f]{32}|[0–9A–Fa–f]{8}-([0–9A–Fa–f]{4}-){3}[0–9A–Fa–f]{12})	A 32-digit GUID, with or without embedded dashes, as in 00000304-0000-0000-C000-000000000046.
([A–Za–z]:)?\\?([^/:*?<>"|\\]+\\)*[^/:*?<>"|\\]+	A Windows filename, with or without a drive and a directory name.
(http|https)://([\w-]+\.)+[\w-]+(/([\w- ./?%&=]*)?)?	An Internet URL; you should use the regular expression in case-insensitive mode to also match prefixes such as HTTP or Https.
\w+([-+.]\w+)*@\w+([-.]\w+)*\.\w+([-.]\w+)*	An Internet e-mail address.
((25[0-5]|2[0-4]\d|1\d\d|[1-9]\d|\d)\.){3}(25[0-5]|2[0-4]\d|1\d\d|[1-9]\d|\d)	A four-part IP address, such as 192.168.0.1; the pattern verifies that each number is in the range 0–255.
([1-5]\d{4}|6[0-4]\d{3}|65[0-4]\d{2}|655[0-2]\d|6553[0-4]|\d{1,4})	A 16-bit integer that can be assigned to an unsigned short variable, in the range of 0 to 65,535.
(-?[12]\d{4}|-?3[0-1]\d{3}|-?32[0-6]\d{2}|-?327[0-5]\d|-?3276[0-7]|-32768|-?\d{1,4})	A 16-bit integer that can be assigned to a signed short variable, in the range of −32,768 to 32,767.
^(?=.*\d)(?=.*[a-z])(?=.*[A-Z])\w{8,}$	A password of at least eight alphanumeric characters that contains at least one digit, one lowercase character, and one uppercase character. Replace the \w term with [0-9A-Za-z@.] to allow some symbols so that users can use their e-mail address as a password.

You can find more regular expressions in the Visual Studio Regular Expression Editor dialog box (see Figure 6-2) or by browsing the huge regular expression library you can find at *http://www.regexlib.com*. If you are very serious about regular expressions, don't miss The Regulator free utility, which you can download from *http://regex.osherove.com/*.

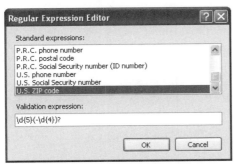

Figure 6-2   Setting the ValidationExpression property of a RegularExpressionValidator ASP.NET control by selecting one of the common regular expressions you find in the Regular Expression Editor dialog box

Searching for Words and Quoted Strings

A quite common operation with regular expressions is splitting a long string into words. Apparently, this is also the simplest task you can perform with regular expressions:

```
string text = "A word with àccéntèd vowels, and the 123 number.";
// This pattern includes words with accented characters and numbers.
string pattern = @"\w+";
foreach (Match m in Regex.Matches(text, pattern))
{
    Console.WriteLine(m.Value);
}
```

The problem with this oversimplified approach is that it also includes sequences of digits and underscores in the collection of results, and you might not want that. A better attempt is as follows:

```
pattern = @"[A-Za-z]+";
...
```

This works better, but fails to include entire words if they contain accented characters or characters from other alphabets, such as Greek or Cyrillic. Under previous versions of the .NET Framework, you could solve this issue by using the little-used \p sequence, which enables you to specify a Unicode character class. For example, the \p{Ll} sequence matches any lowercase character, whereas the \p{Lu} sequence matches any uppercase character. The solution to the problem is therefore as follows:

```
pattern = @"(\p{Lu}|\p{Ll})+";
...
```

The character class subtraction feature, introduced in .NET Framework 2.0, offers a new solution to the problem, based on the consideration that you can "subtract" the digits and the underscore from the range of characters expressed by the \w sequence:

```
pattern = @"[\w-[0-9_]]+";
...
```

When extracting words, you often want to discard *noise words*, such as articles (the, a, an), conjunctions (and, or), and so forth. You might discard these words inside the foreach loop, but it's more elegant to have the regular expression get rid of them:

```
pattern = @"\b(?!(the|a|an|and|or|on|with|of|but)\b)\w+";
text = "A fox and another animal on the lawn";
foreach ( Match m in Regex.Matches(text, pattern, RegexOptions.IgnoreCase) )
{
    Console.WriteLine("{0} ", m.Value);        // => fox another animal lawn
}
```

The \w+ in the previous pattern specifies that we are looking for a word, but the (?!...\b) expression specifies that the match must not begin with one of the noise words; the neat result is that the pattern matches all the words except those in the noise list.

Another common problem related to parsing is when you need to consider a quoted string as an individual word, such as when you parse the command passed to a command-line utility. (In this specific case, you might define a void Main that takes an array of strings as an argument and let the .NET Framework do the job for you, but it wouldn't work in the most general case.) The following regular expression matches an individual word or a string embedded in either single or double quotation marks:

```
// For simplicity's sake, use \w+ to match an individual word.
pattern = @"(?<q>["""']).*?\k<q>|\w+";
```

Notice that the .*? does a lazy matching so that it matches any character between the quotation marks, but won't match the closing quotation mark.

At times you might want to extract just *unique* words, such as when you want to make a dictionary of all the words in a text file or a set of text files. A possible solution is to extract all the words and use a Hashtable object to remember the words found so far:

```
string text = "one two three two zone four three";
Regex re = new Regex(@"\w+");
Hashtable words = new Hashtable();
foreach ( Match m in re.Matches(text) )
{
    if ( !words.Contains(m.Value) )
    {
        Console.Write("{0} ", m.Value);
        words.Add(m.Value, null);
    }
}
```

Quite surprisingly, you can achieve the same result with a single, albeit complex, regular expression:

```
string pattern = @"(?<word>\b\w+\b)(?!.+\b\k<word>\b)";
foreach ( Match m in Regex.Matches(text, pattern) )
{
    Console.Write("{0} ", m.Value);
}
```

The expression (?<word>\b\w+\b) matches a sequence of alphanumeric characters (\w) on a word boundary (\b) and assigns this sequence the name "word". The (?!) construct means that the word just matched must not be followed by the word already matched (the back reference \k<word>) even if there are other characters in the middle (represented by the .+ sequence). Translated into plain English, the regular expression means "match any word in the text that isn't followed by another instance of the same word" or, more simply, match all the words that appear only once in the document or the last occurrence of a repeated word. As you can see, all the unique words are found correctly, even though their order is different from the previous example:

```
one two zone four three
```

Notice that the \b characters in the regular expression prevent partial matches ("one" doesn't match the trailing portion of "zone"). A slightly different regular expression can find the duplicated words in a document:

```
pattern = @"(?<word>\b\w+\b)(?=.+\b\k<word>\b)";
```

where the (?=) construct means that the word match must be followed by another instance of itself. (Notice that this pattern finds all the duplicates; therefore, it finds two duplicates if there are three occurrences of a given word.) Although the regex-only techniques are very elegant, the look-ahead (?=) clause makes them relatively inefficient: for example, on a source text of about 1 million characters, the regex-only technique is approximately 8 times slower than is the technique that uses an auxiliary Hashtable to keep track of all the words already parsed.

One last type of word search I want to explain is the *proximity search*, which is when you search two strings that must be found close to each other in the source string, with no more than N words between them. For example, given the "one two three two zone four three" source string, a proximity search for the words "one" and "four" with N equal to 4 would be successful, whereas it would fail with N equal to 3. The pattern for such a proximity search is quite simple:

```
string text = "one two three two zone four three";
string pattern = @"\bone(\W+\w+){0,4}\W+\bfour\b";

// This technique uses regular expressions exclusively.
foreach ( Match m in Regex.Matches(text, pattern) )
{
    Console.Write("{0} ", m.Value);
}
```

You can also define a function that takes the input string, the two words, and the maximum distance between them and returns a MatchCollection object:

```
MatchCollection ProximityMatches(string text, string word1, string word2, int maxDistance)
{
    string pattern = @"\b" + word1 + @"(\W+\w+){0," + maxDistance.ToString()
        + @"}\" + @"W+\b" + word2 + @"\b";
    Regex re = new Regex(pattern, RegexOptions.IgnoreCase);
    return re.Matches(text);
}
```

Thus, the previous code snippet would become

```
MatchCollection mc = ProximityMatches(text, "one", "four", 4);
if ( mc.Count > 0 )
{ … }
```

Validating Strings, Numbers, and Dates

As I explained earlier in this chapter, typically you can use a search pattern as a validation pattern by simply enclosing it in the ^ and $ symbols and using the IsMatch method instead of the Matches method. For example, the following code checks that a string—presumably the Text property of a TextBox control—contains a five-digit U.S. ZIP code:

```
pattern = @"^\d{5}$";
if ( Regex.IsMatch(text, pattern) )
{
    // It's a string containing five digits.
}
```

Things become more interesting when you want to *exclude* a few combinations from the set of valid strings, which you can do with the (?!) clause. For example, the 00000 sequence isn't a valid ZIP code, and you can exclude it by using the following pattern:

```
pattern = @"^(?!00000)\d{5}$";
```

You can use the (?=) look-ahead assertion to check that the input string contains all characters in a given class, regardless of their position. For example, you can use the following pattern to enforce a robust password policy and ensure that the end user types a password of at least eight characters and that it contains a combination of digits and uppercase and lowercase letters:

```
pattern = @"^(?=.*\d)(?=.*[a-z])(?=.*[A-Z])\w{8,}$";
```

Let's see how this pattern works. The first (?=.*\d) clause makes the search fail at the very beginning if the portion of the input string to its right (and therefore, the entire input string) doesn't contain a digit. The (?=.*[a-z]) clause checks that the input string contains a lowercase character, and the (?=.*[A-Z]) clause does the same for uppercase characters. These three look-ahead clauses don't consume any characters, and therefore the remaining \w{8,} clause can check that the input string contains at least eight characters.

Validating a number in a given range poses a few interesting problems. In general, you might not want to use regular expressions to validate numbers or dates because the Parse and Try-Parse methods exposed by the DateTime type and all numeric types offer more flexibility and cause fewer headaches. However, in some cases, regular expressions can be a viable solution even for this task, for example, when you want to extract valid numbers and dates from a longer document.

Checking that an integer has up to the specified number of digits is a trivial problem, of course:

```
// Validate an integer in the range of 0 to 9,999; accept leading zeros.
pattern = @"^\d{1,4}$";
```

The negative (?!) look-ahead clause enables you to rule out a few cases, for example:

```
// Validate an integer in the range 1 to 9,999; reject leading zeros.
pattern = @"^(?!0)\d{1,4}$";
…
// Validate an integer in the range 0 to 9,999; reject leading zeros.
// (Same as previous one, but accept a single zero as a special case.)
pattern = @"^(0|(?!0)\d{1,4})$";
…
```

If the upper limit of the accepted range isn't a number in the form 99…999, you can still use regular expressions to do the validation, but the pattern becomes more complex. For example, the following pattern checks that a number is in the range 0 to 255 with no leading zeros:

```
pattern = @"^(25[0-5]|2[0-4]\d|1\d\d|[1-9]\d|\d)$";
```

The 25[0-5] clause validates numbers in the range 250 to 255; the 2[0-4]\d clause validates numbers in the range 200 to 249; the 1\d\d clause validates numbers in the range 100 to 199; the [1-9]\d clause takes care of the numbers 10 to 99; finally, the \d clause covers the range 0 to 9. A slight modification of this pattern enables you to validate a four-part IP address, such as 192.168.0.11:

```
pattern = @"^((25[0-5]|2[0-4]\d|1\d\d|[1-9]\d|\d)\.){3}"
    + @"(25[0-5]|2[0-4]\d|1\d\d|[1-9]\d|\d)$";
```

Things quickly become complicated with larger ranges:

```
// Validate an integer number in the range 0 to 65,535; leading zeros are OK.
pattern = @"^([1-5]\d{4}|6[0-4]\d{3}|65[0-4]\d{2}|655[0-2]\d|6553[0-4]|\d{1,4})$";
```

Numbers that can have a leading sign require special treatment:

```
// Validate an integer in the range -32,768 to 32,767; leading zeros are OK.
pattern = @"^(-?[12]\d{4}|-?3[0-1]\d{3}|-?32[0-6]\d{2}|-?327[0-5]\d|"
    + @"-?3276[0-7]|-32768|-?\d{1,4})$";
```

Notice in the previous pattern that the special case −32,768 must be dealt with separately; all the remaining clauses have an optional minus sign in front of them. You can use a similar technique to validate a time value:

```
// Validate a time value in the format hh:mm; the hour number can have a leading zero.
pattern = @"^(2[0-3]|[01]\d|\d):[0-5]\d$";
```

Validating a date value is much more difficult because each month has a different number of days and, above all, because the valid day range for February depends on whether the year is a leap year. Before I illustrate the complete pattern for solving this problem, let's see how we can use a regular expression to check whether a two-digit number is a multiple of 4:

```
// If the first digit is even, the second digit must be 0, 4, or 8.
// If the first digit is odd, the second digit must be 2 or 6.
pattern = @"^([02468][048]|[13579][26])$";
```

Under the simplified assumption that the year number has only two digits, and therefore the date refers to a year in the current century, we can simplify the regular expression significantly because year 2000 was a leap year, unlike 1900 and 2100. To better explain the final regular expression I have split the pattern onto four lines:

```
// This portion deals with months with 31 days.
string p1 = @"(0?[13578]|10|12)/(3[01]|[012]\d|\d)/\d{2}";
// This portion deals with months with 30 days.
string p2 = @"(0?[469]|11)/(30|[012]\d|\d)/\d{2}";
// This portion deals with February 29 in leap years.
string p3 = @"(0?2)/29/([02468][048]|[13579][26])";
// This portion deals with other days in February.
string p4 = @"(0?2)/(2[0-8]|[01]\d|\d)/\d{2}";
// Put all the patterns together.
pattern = string.Format("^({0}|{1}|{2}|{3})$", p1, p2, p3, p4);
// Check the date.
if ( Regex.IsMatch(text, pattern) )
{
    // Date is valid.
}
```

If the year number can have either two or four digits, we must take into account the fact that all years divisible by 100 are not leap years, except if they are divisible by 400. (For example, 1900 isn't a leap year, but 2000 is.) This constraint makes the regular expression more complicated, but by now you should be experienced enough to understand how the following code works:

```
// This portion deals with months with 31 days.
const string s1 = @"(0?[13578]|10|12)/(3[01]|[12]\d|0?[1-9])/(\d\d)?\d\d";
// This portion deals with months with 30 days.
const string s2 = @"(0?[469]|11)/(30|[12]\d|0?[1-9])/(\d\d)?\d\d ";
// This portion deals with days 1-28 in February in all years.
const string s3 = @"(0?2)/(2[0-8]|[01]\d|0?[1-9])/(\d\d)?\d\d";
// This portion deals with February 29 in years divisible by 400.
const string s4 = "(0?2)/29/(1600|2000|2400|2800|00)";
// This portion deals with February 29 in noncentury leap years.
const string s5 = @"(0?2)/29/(\d\d)?0[048]|[2468][048]|[13579][26])";
// Put all the patterns together.
pattern = string.Format("^({0}|{1}|{2}|{3}|{4})$", s1, s2, s3, s4, s5);
...
```

(Notice that I might have merged the portions s4 and s5 in a single subexpression that validates all leap years, but I kept the two expressions separate for clarity's sake.) It's easy to derive a similar regular expression for dates in dd/mm/yy (European) format and to account for separators other than the dash character.

Searching for Nested Tags

When you apply regular expressions to HTML or XML files, you must take the hierarchical natures of these files into account. For example, let's say that you want to extract the contents of <table>...</table> sections in an HTML file. You can't simply use a pattern such as this:

```
<table[\s>].*?</table>
```

because it would return bogus results when you apply it to a text that contains nested tables, such as:

`<table border=1><tr><td><table>...</table></td><td>...</td></tr></table>`

In cases like these, the balancing group definition construct shown in Table 6-1 can help because it enables you to take nested tags into account. (For a great example of how you can use this construct, read *http://blogs.msdn.com/bclteam/archive/2005/03/15/396452.aspx*.) However, this construct is quite difficult to use and has some limitations, the most notable of which is that it doesn't work well if you're looking for a series of nested tags, as when you want to display all <table>, <tr>, and <td> blocks regardless of their nesting level. In cases like these, you need two nested loops, as in the following code:

```csharp
// Find all nested HTML tags in a file. (e.g., <table>...</table>)
string text = File.ReadAllText("test.htm");
Regex re = new Regex(@"<(?<tag>(table|tr|td|div|span))[\s>]", RegexOptions.IgnoreCase);
foreach ( Match m in re.Matches(text) )
{
    // We've found an open tag. Lets look for open and close versions of this tag.
    string tag = m.Groups["tag"].Value;
    int openTags = 1;
    string pattern2 = string.Format(@"((?<open><{0})[\s>]|(?<close>)</{0}>)", tag);
    string found = null;
    Regex re2 = new Regex(pattern2, RegexOptions.IgnoreCase);

    foreach ( Match m2 in re2.Matches(text, m.Index + 1) )
    {
        if ( m2.Groups["open"].Success )
        {
            openTags++;
        }
        else if (m2.Groups["close"].Success)
        {
            if ( --openTags == 0 )
            {
                found = text.Substring(m.Index, m2.Index + m.Length + 1 - m.Index);
                break;
            }
        }
    }
    // Display this match.
    if ( found != null )
    {
        Console.WriteLine(found);
    }
    else
    {
        Console.WriteLine("Unmatched tag {0} at index {1}", tag, m.Index);
    }
}
```

Once you understand how this code works, you can easily modify it to match other hierarchical entities, for example, parentheses in math expressions or nested type definitions in .cs source files.

Parsing Data Files

Even though XML has emerged as the standard technology in exchange information, many legacy applications still output data in older and simpler formats. Two such formats are fixed-width text files and delimited text files. You can read these file types with regular expressions in a very elegant manner. Let's consider a fixed-width data file such as this one:

```
John   Evans   New York
Ann    Beebe   Los Angeles
```

Each text line contains information about first name (6 characters), last name (8 characters), and city. The largest city has 9 characters, but usually we can assume that the last field takes all the characters up to the end of the current line. Reading this file requires very few lines of code:

```
string pattern = "^(?<first>.{6})(?<last>.{8})(?<city>.+)$";
Regex re = new Regex(pattern);
using ( StreamReader sr = new StreamReader("data.txt") )
{
   while ( ! sr.EndOfStream )
   {
      Match m = re.Match(line);
      Console.WriteLine("First={0}, Last={1}, City={2}",
         m.Groups["first"].Value.TrimEnd(),
         m.Groups["last"].Value.TrimEnd(),
         m.Groups["city"].Value.TrimEnd());
   }
}
```

The expression (?<first>.{6}) creates a group named "first" that corresponds to the initial 6 characters. Likewise, (?<last>.{8}) creates a group named "last" that corresponds to the next 8 characters. Finally, (?<city>.+) creates a group for all the remaining characters on the line and names it "city." The ^ and $ characters stand for the beginning and the end of the line, respectively.

The beauty of this approach is that it is quite easy to adapt the code to different field widths and to work with delimited fields. For example, if the fixed-width fields are separated by semicolons, you simply modify the regular expression as follows, without touching the remaining code:

```
pattern = @"^(?<first>.{6});(?<last>.{8});(?<city>.+)$";
```

Let's now adapt the parsing program to another quite common exchange format: delimited text files. In this case, each field is separated from the next one by a comma, a semicolon, a tab, or another special character. To further complicate things, such files usually allow values embedded in single or double quotation marks; in this case, you can't just use the Split method of the String type to do the parsing because your result would be bogus if a quoted value happens to include the delimiter (as in "Evans, John").

In such cases, regular expressions are a real lifesaver. In fact, you just need to use a different regular expression pattern with the same parsing code used in previous examples. Let's start with the simplified assumption that there are no quoted strings in the file, as in the following:

```
John , Evans, New York
Ann, Beebe, Los Angeles
```

I threw in some extra white spaces to add interest to the discussion. These spaces should be ignored when you're parsing the text. Here is the regular expression that can be used to parse such a comma-delimited series of values:

```
pattern = @"^\s*(?<first>.*?)\s*,\s*(?<last>.*?)\s*,\s*(?<city>.*?)\s*$";
```

You don't need to modify other portions of the parsing code I showed previously. It is essential that \s* sequences and the delimiter character (the comma, in this specific case) are placed outside the (?) construct so that they aren't included in named groups. Also notice that we use the .*? sequence to avoid matching the delimiter character or the spaces that might surround it.

Next, let's see how to parse quoted fields, such as those found in the following text file:

```
'John, P.' , "Evans" , "New York"
'Robert "Zare"', "" , "Los Angeles, CA"
```

Text fields can be surrounded by both single and double quotation marks and they can contain commas as well as quotation marks not used as delimiters. The regular expression that can parse this text file is more complex:

```
pattern = @"^\s*(?<q1>[""'])(?<first>.*?)\k<q1>\s*,"
   + @"\s*(?<q2>[""'])(?<last>.*?)\k<q2>\s*,\s*(?<q3>[""'])(?<city>.*?)\k<q3>\s*$";
```

The (?<q1>[""']) subexpression matches either the single or the double leading quotation mark delimiter and assigns this group the name "q1." (The double quotation mark character is doubled because it appears in an @-prefixed string.) The \k<q1> subexpression is a back reference to whatever the q1 group found and therefore matches whichever quotation mark character was used at the beginning of the field. The q2 and q3 groups have the same role for the next two fields. Once again, you don't need to change any other statement in the parsing routine.

The previous pattern has a small defect, though. Many programs that output data in delimited format enclose a text field in quotation marks only if the field contains the delimiter character. For example, in the following data file the first and last fields in the first record are enclosed in quotation marks because they embed a comma, but the fields in the second record aren't.

```
"John, P." , Evans , "Los Angeles, CA"
Robert, Zare, New York
```

To solve this minor problem I need to introduce one of the most powerful features of regular expressions: conditional matching. Look closely at the following pattern:

```
pattern = @"^\s*(?<q1>[""']?)(?<first>.*?)(?(q1)\k<q1>)\s*"
    + @",\s*(?<q2>[""']?)(?<last>.*?)(?(q2)\k<q2>)\s*"
    + @",\s*(?<q3>[""']?)(?<city>.*?)(?(q3)\k<q3>)\s*$";
```

The (?<q1>["']?) is similar to the pattern used in the previous example, except it has a trailing ? character; therefore, it matches an optional single or double quotation mark character. Later in the same line you find the (?(q1)\k<q1>) clause, which tests whether the q1 group is defined and, if so, matches its value. In other words, if the q1 group actually matched the single or double quotation mark character, the expression (?(q1)\k<q1>) matches it again; otherwise, the expression is ignored. The same reasoning applies to the other two fields in the record.

The (?(expr)...) clause has an optional "no" portion (see Table 6-1), so you might even match a portion of a string if a previous group has *not* been matched.

Parsing and Evaluating Expressions

A nice and somewhat surprising application of regular expressions is in expression evaluation. In the section titled "The Replace Method" earlier in this chapter, you saw how you can evaluate the result of an addition operation embedded in a string such as "12+34" thanks to the overload of the Replace method that takes a callback function. Of course, you don't have to stop at addition, and in fact you can create a complete and quite versatile expression evaluator built on a single regular expression and some support code. Creating such a regular expression isn't a trivial task, though. Let's analyze the Evaluate method a piece at a time:

```
public static double Evaluate(string expr)
{
    // A floating-point number, with optional leading and trailing spaces
    const string num = @"\s*[+-]?\d+\.?\d*\b\s*";
    // A number inside a pair of parentheses
    const string nump = @"\s*\((?<nump>" + num + @")\)\s*";
    // Math operations
    const string add = @"(?<![*/^]\s*)(?<add1>" + num + @")\+(?<add2>" + num
        + @")(?!\s*[*/^])";
    const string subt = @"(?<![*/^]\s*)(?<sub1>" + num + @")\-(?<sub2>"
        + num + @")(?!\s*[*/^])";
    const string mul = @"(?<!\^\s*)(?<mul1>" + num + @")\*(?<mul2>" + num
        + @")(?!\s*\^)";
    const string div = @"(?<!\^\s*)(?<div1>" + num + @")\/(?<div2>" + num
        + @")(?!\s*\^)";
    const string modu = @"(?<!\^\s*)(?<mod1>" + num + @")\s+mod\s+(?<mod2>"
        + num + @")(?!\s*\^)";
    const string pow = "(?<pow1>" + num + @")\^(?<pow2>" + num + ")";
    // One-operand and two-operand functions
    const string fone = "(?<fone>(exp|log|log10|abs|sqr|sqrt|sin|cos|tan|asin|acos|atan))"
        + @"\s*\((?<fone1>" + num + @")\)";
    const string ftwo = "(?<ftwo>(min|max)\s*)\((?<ftwo1>" + num
        + "),(?<ftwo2>" + num + @")\)";
```

```
// Put everything in a single regular expression.
const string pattern = "(" + fone + "|" + ftwo + "|" + modu + "|" + pow
    + "|" + div + "|" + mul + "|" + subt + "|" + add + "|" + nump + ")";
Regex reEval = new Regex(pattern, RegexOptions.IgnoreCase);
...
```

The pattern corresponding to the num constant represents a floating-point number, option-ally preceded by a plus or minus sign. Let's now consider the regular expression that defines the addition operation: it consists of two numbers, each one forming a named group (add1 and add2); the two numbers are separated by the plus sign. Additionally, the pattern is pre-ceded by a (?<![*/^]\s*) negative look-behind assertion, which ensures that the first operand doesn't follow an operator with a higher priority than addition (that is, the multiplication, division, or raising to power operator). Similarly, the second operand is followed by the (?!\s*[*/^]) negative look-ahead assertion, which ensures that the addition isn't followed by an operation with higher priority. The patterns for other math operations are similar, so I won't describe them in detail. The body of the Evaluate function follows:

```
    ...
    // Ensure that +/- used for additions and subtractions doesn't precede a number.
    expr = Regex.Replace(expr, @"(?<=[0-9)]\s*)[+-](?=[0-9(])", "$0 ");
    Regex reNumber = new Regex("^" + num + "$");
    // Loop until the expression is reduced to a number.
    while ( !reNumber.IsMatch(expr) )
    {
        // Replace only the first subexpression that can be processed.
        string newExpr = reEval.Replace(expr, PerformOperation, 1);
        // If the expression hasn't been simplified, there must be a problem.
        if ( expr == newExpr )
        {
            throw new ArgumentException("Invalid expression");
        }
        // Reenter the loop with the new expression.
        expr = newExpr;
    }
    // Convert to a floating-point number and return.
    return double.Parse(expr);
}
```

At the top of the while loop, the reNumber regular expression checks whether the expression contains a number: in this case, the loop is exited and the value of the number is returned to the caller. If this isn't the case, the loop is repeated in the attempt to simplify the expres-sion using the reEval regular expression; if the expression doesn't change, it means that the expression can't be simplified further because it is malformed, and the method throws an exception. If the expression has been simplified, the loop is reentered.

The PerformOperation callback method is where the actual math operations are carried out. Detecting which operator has been matched is simple because all the groups defined by the various operators have different names:

```
private static string PerformOperation(Match m)
{
    double result = 0;
```

```
if ( m.Groups["nump"].Length > 0 )
{
    return m.Groups["nump"].Value.Trim();
}
else if ( m.Groups["add1"].Length > 0 )
{
    result = double.Parse(m.Groups["add1"].Value) + double.Parse(m.Groups["add2"].Value);
}
else if ( m.Groups["sub1"].Length > 0 )
{
    result = double.Parse(m.Groups["sub1"].Value) - double.Parse(m.Groups["sub2"].Value);
}
else if ( m.Groups["mul1"].Length > 0 )
{
    result = double.Parse(m.Groups["mul1"].Value) * double.Parse(m.Groups["mul2"].Value);
}
else if ( m.Groups["mod1"].Length > 0 )
{
    result = Math.IEEERemainder(double.Parse(m.Groups["mod1"].Value),
        double.Parse(m.Groups["mod2"].Value));
}
else if ( m.Groups["div1"].Length > 0 )
{
    result = double.Parse(m.Groups["div1"].Value) / double.Parse(m.Groups["div2"].Value);
}
else if ( m.Groups["pow1"].Length > 0 )
{
    result = Math.Pow(double.Parse(m.Groups["pow1"].Value),
        double.Parse(m.Groups["pow2"].Value));
}
else if ( m.Groups["fone"].Length > 0 )
{
    double operand = double.Parse(m.Groups["fone1"].Value);
    switch ( m.Groups["fone"].Value.ToLower() )
    {
        case "exp":
            result = Math.Exp(operand);
            break;
        case "log":
            result = Math.Log(operand);
            break;
        case "log10":
            result = Math.Log10(operand);
            break;
        case "abs":
            result = Math.Abs(operand);
            break;
        case "sqrt":
            result = Math.Sqrt(operand);
            break;
        case "sin":
            result = Math.Sin(operand);
            break;
        case "cos":
            result = Math.Cos(operand);
            break;
```

```
                    case "tan":
                        result = Math.Tan(operand);
                        break;
                    case "asin":
                        result = Math.Asin(operand);
                        break;
                    case "acos":
                        result = Math.Acos(operand);
                        break;
                    case "atan":
                        result = Math.Atan(operand);
                        break;
                }
            }
            else if ( m.Groups["ftwo"].Length > 0 )
            {
                double operand1 = double.Parse(m.Groups["ftwo1"].Value);
                double operand2 = double.Parse(m.Groups["ftwo2"].Value);
                switch ( m.Groups["ftwo"].Value.ToLower() )
                {
                    case "min":
                        result = Math.Min(operand1, operand2);
                        break;
                    case "max":
                        result = Math.Max(operand1, operand2);
                        break;
                }
            }
            return result.ToString();
        }
```

It's easy to create a Console application or a Windows Forms program that asks the user for an expression and displays the expression value. Figure 6-3 shows such a program in action. The only interesting piece of code is the method that runs when the user clicks the Eval button:

```
private void btnEval_Click( object sender, EventArgs e )
{
    // Evaluate the selected or entire portion of txtSource.
    string expr = txtExpression.Text;
    try
    {
        txtResult.Text = Functions.Evaluate(expr).ToString();
    }
    catch ( Exception ex )
    {
        txtResult.Text = ex.Message;
    }
}
```

The Evaluate function and the PerformOperation helper method have fewer than 90 executable statements, yet they implement a full-fledged expression evaluator that you can easily expand to support additional operators and functions. Such conciseness is possible thanks to the power of regular expressions and, in particular, to the ability to specify look-behind and look-ahead negative assertions, which ensures that the priority of the various operators is honored.

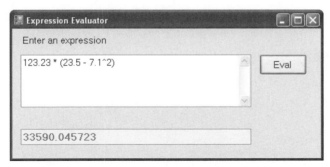

Figure 6-3   The demo application that tests the Evaluate method

Playing with Regular Expressions (Literally)

By now, you should be convinced that regular expressions are too powerful to be used only for plain text searches and substitutions. In this last example, I want to prove that regular expressions can be useful when you'd never suspect that searches are involved and that you can use them simply to perform pattern matching.

Let's consider the game of poker. I won't build an entire application that plays poker (nor encourage gambling in any way…), but I will focus on a very small programming problem that is related to this game. How would you write a method that evaluates the score corresponding to a hand of five cards? You can solve this problem in a variety of ways, with numerous if and switch statements, but the solution offered by regular expressions can hardly be beaten as far as elegance, performance, and conciseness are concerned.

The following method accepts five strings, each one corresponding to a card in the hand and each one consisting of a character pair; the first character stands for the card value and can be a digit 1–9, or T, J, Q, K (where T stands for Ten); the second character of the pair is the card's suit and can be C (clubs), D (diamonds), H (hearts), or S (spades). The code in the method sorts the five cards by their value, and then builds two separate strings—one containing the five values and the other containing the five suits—and tests them against suitable regular expressions, starting from the most complex and moving to the simpler ones. (Testing the regular expressions in this order is crucial; otherwise, a straight flush would be mistakenly reported as a plain straight and a full house would appear to be a pair.)

```
public static string EvalPokerScore( params string[] cards )
{
    // Sort the array and create the sequence of values and of suits.
    Array.Sort( cards );
    string values = string.Concat(cards[0][0], cards[1][0], cards[2][0],
        cards[3][0], cards[4][0]);
```

```
    string suits = string.Concat(cards[0][1], cards[1][1], cards[2][1],
        cards[3][1], cards[4][1]);
    // Check each sequence in order.
    if ( Regex.IsMatch( values, "12345|23456|34567|45678|56789|6789T|789JT|89JQT"
            + "|9JKQT|1JKQT" ) && Regex.IsMatch( suits, @"(.)\1\1\1\1" ) )
    {
        return "StraightFlush";
    }
    else if ( Regex.IsMatch( values, @"(.)\1\1\1" ) )
    {
        return "FourOfAKind";
    }
    else if ( Regex.IsMatch( values, @"(.)\1\1(.)\2|(.)\3(.)\4\4" ) )
    {
        return "FullHouse";
    }
    else if ( Regex.IsMatch( suits, @"(.)\1\1\1\1" ) )
    {
        return "Flush";
    }
    else if ( Regex.IsMatch( values, "12345|23456|34567|45678|56789|6789T|789JT|89JQT"
            + "|9JKQT|1JKQT" ) )
    {
        return "Straight";
    }
    else if ( Regex.IsMatch( values, @"(.)\1\1" ) )
    {
        return "ThreeOfAKind";
    }
    else if ( Regex.IsMatch( values, @"(.)\1(.)\2" ) )
    {
        return "TwoPairs";
    }
    else if ( Regex.IsMatch( values, @"(.)\1" ) )
    {
        return "OnePair";
    }
    else
    {
        return "HighCard";
    }
}
```

Here are a few examples of how you can call the method and the results it returns:

```
EvalPokerScore("1H", "4H", "3H", "5H", "2H");   // => StraightFlush
EvalPokerScore("9C", "9S", "8H", "TD", "9D");   // => ThreeOfAKind
EvalPokerScore("8C", "KC", "TC", "QC", "9C");   // => Flush
EvalPokerScore("TC", "KC", "QD", "8D", "9H");   // => HighCard
```

The EvalPokerScore method is so concise that you might be surprised to learn that you can simplify it further. The trick is simple and leverages the fact that patterns are just strings and can be stored in a data structure. In this case, you can use a two-dimensional array so that you can test each pattern in a for loop. (Use a pattern that always matches, such as a plain dot, if you aren't interested in matching either the values or the suits.)

```
public static string EvalPokerScore( params string[] cards )
{
    string[,] scores = { { "12345|23456|34567|45678|56789|6789T|789JT|89JQT|9JKQT|1JKQT",
        @"(.)\1\1\1\1", "StraightFlush" },
        { @"(.)\1\1\1", ".", "FourOfAKind" },
        { @"(.)\1\1(.)\2|(.)\3(.)\4\4", ".", "FullHouse" },
        { ".", @"(.)\1\1\1\1", "Flush" },
        { "12345|23456|34567|45678|56789|6789T|789JT|89JQT|9JKQT|1JKQT", ".", "Straight" },
        { @"(.)\1\1", ".", "ThreeOfAKind" },
        { @"(.)\1.?(.)\2", ".", "TwoPairs" },
        { @"(.)\1", ".", "OnePair" } };
    for ( int i=0; i<=scores.GetUpperBound( 0 ); i++ )
    {
        if ( Regex.IsMatch( values, scores[i, 0] ) && Regex.IsMatch( suits, scores[i, 1] ) )
        {
            return scores[i, 2];
        }
    }
    return "HighCard";
}
```

The preceding code highlights the fact that regular expressions have the ability to replace code with just data, in this case a series of if statements with strings stored in an array. In this particular example, this feature isn't especially useful (other than to make the code more concise). In many applications, however, this ability can make a big difference. For example, you can store all the validation patterns in a database or an XML file so that you can actually change the behavior of your application without even recompiling its code.

Chapter 7

Files, Directories, and Streams

The Microsoft .NET Framework offers excellent support for working with files and directories through the following classes in the System.IO namespace:

- **Path**   Contains static methods to manipulate path information.

- **Directory, File**   Contain static methods that enable you to enumerate and manipulate directories and files.

- **DirectoryInfo, FileInfo**   Represent individual directories or files and expose the methods to query their attributes and manipulate them.

- **DriveInfo**   Represents an individual drive and exposes the methods to query its attributes and manipulate them. (This class is new in .NET Framework version 2.0.)

- **FileSystemWatcher**   Can notify your program when a file or a directory is created, deleted, renamed, or modified in a folder or a folder tree.

The most important new feature in version 2.0 of the .NET Framework is the support for Microsoft Windows access control lists (ACLs) at the directory and file levels. ACLs are supported in a uniform way across the Directory, File, DirectoryInfo, and FileInfo types, so I gathered a detailed description of this new feature in a separate section titled "Working with Access Control Lists."

> **Note**   To avoid long lines, code samples in this chapter assume that the following using statements are used at the top of each source file:
>
> ```
> using System;
> using System.Collections;
> using System.Diagnostics;
> using System.Globalization;
> using System.IO;
> using System.IO.Compression;
> using System.Net;
> using System.Net.Sockets;
> using System.Security;
> using System.Security.AccessControl;
> using System.Security.Principal;
> using System.Text;
> ```

The Path Type

The Path class is the simplest type in the System.IO namespace. It exposes static fields and methods that can help you process file and directory paths. Four static fields return information about valid drive and filename separators; you might want to query them to prepare your programs to run on other operating systems if and when the .NET Framework is ported to platforms other than the Windows operating system:

```
Console.WriteLine(Path.AltDirectorySeparatorChar);   // => /
Console.WriteLine(Path.DirectorySeparatorChar);      // => \
Console.WriteLine(Path.PathSeparator);               // => ;
Console.WriteLine(Path.VolumeSeparatorChar);         // => :
```

The GetInvalidPathChars and GetInvalidFileNameChars methods return an array containing the characters that can't be used in path names and filenames, respectively:

```
// Note: the actual output from following methods includes unprintable characters.
Console.WriteLine(Path.GetInvalidPathChars());      // => <>|
Console.WriteLine(Path.GetInvalidFileNameChars());  // => <>|:*?\/
```

The GetTempPath and GetTempFileName methods take no arguments and return the location of the Windows temporary directory and the name of a temporary file, respectively:

```
Console.WriteLine(Path.GetTempPath());
    // => C:\Documents and Settings\Francesco\Local Settings\Temp
Console.WriteLine(Path.GetTempFileName());
    // => C:\Documents and Settings\Francesco\Local Settings\Temp\tmp1FC7.tmp
```

Other methods enable you to extract information from a file path, without your having to worry about whether the file or the directory exists:

```
string file = @"C:\MyApp\Bin\MyApp.exe";
Console.WriteLine(Path.GetDirectoryName(file));     // => C:\MyApp\Bin
Console.WriteLine(Path.GetFileName(file));          // => MyApp.exe
Console.WriteLine(Path.GetExtension(file));         // => .exe
```

```
Console.WriteLine(Path.GetFileNameWithoutExtension(file));  // => MyApp
Console.WriteLine(Path.GetPathRoot(file));                  // => C:\
Console.WriteLine(Path.HasExtension(file));                 // => True
Console.WriteLine(Path.IsPathRooted(file));                 // => True
```

You can use the GetDirectoryName on files and directory names; in the latter case, it returns the name of the parent directory. For example, you can use this technique to retrieve the name of the main Windows directory (which is the parent folder of the Windows System32 directory):

```
string winDir = Path.GetDirectoryName(Environment.SystemDirectory);
```

The GetFullPath method expands a relative path to an absolute path, taking the current directory into account:

```
// Next line assumes that current directory is C:\MyApp.
Console.WriteLine(Path.GetFullPath("MyApp.Exe"));           // => C:\MyApp\MyApp.Exe
```

The GetFullPath method has a nice feature: it normalizes paths that contain double dots and enables you to prevent attacks based on malformed paths. For example, let's say that you must allow access to the c:\public directory and prevent access to the c:\private folder. If you check the folder without normalizing the path, a malicious hacker might access a file in the private folder by providing a string such as c:\public\..\private*filename*.

The ChangeExtension method returns a filename with a different extension:

```
Console.WriteLine(Path.ChangeExtension("MyApp.Exe", "dat"));  // => MyApp.dat
```

Finally, the Combine method takes a path and a filename and combines them into a valid filename, adding or discarding backslash characters as required:

```
Console.WriteLine(Path.Combine(@"C:\MyApp", "MyApp.Dat"));    // => C:\MyApp\MyApp.Dat
```

The Directory and File Types

The Directory and File types contain only static methods that set or return information about entries in the file system. I cover both types in one section because they share most of their methods.

Enumerating Directories and Files

Thanks to the GetDirectories and GetFiles methods of the Directory type, you need very little code to iterate over all the directories and files of a directory tree. For example, the following code displays the structure of a directory tree and (optionally) the names of files in each folder:

```
// Display a directory tree, optionally showing files as well.
public static void DisplayDirTree(string dir, bool showFiles)
{
   // Call the private overload.
   DisplayDirTree(dir, showFiles, 0);
}
```

```csharp
// A private overload that accounts for nesting level
private static void DisplayDirTree(string dir, bool showFiles, int level)
{
   // Display the name of this directory with correct indentation.
   Console.WriteLine(new string('-', level * 2) + dir);

   try
   {
      // Display all files in this directory with correct indentation.
      if ( showFiles )
      {
         foreach ( string fname in Directory.GetFiles(dir) )
         {
            Console.WriteLine(new string(' ', level * 2 + 2) + fname);
         }
      }
      // A recursive call for all the subdirectories in this directory
      foreach ( string subdir in Directory.GetDirectories(dir) )
      {
         DisplayDirTree(subdir, showFiles, level + 1);
      }
   }
   catch
   {}    // Do nothing if any error (presumably "Drive not ready").
}
```

You can pass a directory name to the DisplayDirTree procedure or display the directory tree of all the drives in your system by using the GetLogicalDrives method of the Directory type:

```csharp
// Warning: this loop is going to take a *lot* of time.
foreach ( string rootDir in Directory.GetLogicalDrives() )
{
   DisplayDirTree(rootDir, true);
}
```

The GetFiles and GetDirectories methods can take a second argument containing wildcards to filter the result:

```csharp
// Display all the *.txt files in C:\DOCS.
foreach ( string fname in Directory.GetFiles(@"c:\docs", "*.txt") )
{
   Console.WriteLine(fname);
}
```

 A new, welcome addition to the GetFiles and GetDirectories methods is the ability to search in subdirectories automatically. For example, the following code displays all the DLLs in the c:\windows directory tree:

```csharp
foreach ( string file in Directory.GetFiles(@"c:\windows", "*.dll",
      SearchOption.AllDirectories) )
{
   Console.WriteLine(file);
}
```

Manipulating Directories and Files

As their names suggest, the SetCurrentDirectory and GetCurrentDirectory methods of the Directory type set and return the current directory:

```
// Save the current directory.
string currDir = Directory.GetCurrentDirectory();
// Change the current directory to something else.
Directory.SetCurrentDirectory(@"c:\temp");
…
// Restore the current directory.
Directory.SetCurrentDirectory(currDir);
```

The Directory.CreateDirectory method creates a directory and all the intermediate directories in the path if necessary:

```
// Next line works even if the C:\MyApp directory doesn't exist yet.
Directory.CreateDirectory(@"C:\MyApp\Data");
```

The Directory and File types have several methods in common. The Exists method checks whether a file or a directory exists, the Delete method removes it, and the Move method moves a file or an entire directory to a different folder and possibly renames it in the process:

```
if ( File.Exists(@"c:\data.txt") )
{
    File.Move(@"c:\data.txt", @"d:\data.txt");
}
```

By default, the Directory.Delete method can remove only an empty directory, but it has an overload that enables you to remove an entire directory tree:

```
// Delete the c:\tempdir folder and all its subfolders.
Directory.Delete(@"c:\tempdir", true);
```

You can use the GetCreationTime, GetLastAccessTime, GetLastWriteTime, and GetAttributes static methods to display information about a file or a directory or to filter files according to their attributes:

```
// Display only read-only .txt files in the c:\docs folder.
foreach ( string fname in Directory.GetFiles(@"c:\docs", "*.txt") )
{
    if ( (File.GetAttributes(fname) & FileAttributes.ReadOnly) != 0 )
    {
        Console.WriteLine(fname);
    }
}
```

The SetCreationTime, SetLastWriteTime, and SetLastAccessTime methods let you modify the date attributes of a file or directory:

```
// Change the access date and time of all files in c:\docs.
foreach ( string fname in Directory.GetFiles(@"c:\docs") )
```

```
{
    File.SetLastAccessTime(fname, DateTime.Now);
}
```

You can use the SetCreationTime method to create a "touch" utility that modifies the last write time of all the files specified on its command line:

```
// Change the access date/time of all files whose names are passed on the command line.
static void Main(string[] args)
{
    foreach ( string fname in args )
    {
        File.SetCreationTime(fname, DateTime.Now);
    }
}
```

Each Get*Xxxx*Time and Set*Xxxx*Time method that reads or modifies a date attribute has a matching Get*Xxxx*TimeUtc and Set*Xxxx*TimeUtc method that works with coordinated universal time (UTC), that is, an absolute DateTime value that isn't affected by the current time zone. These methods were added in .NET Framework version 1.1 to enable you to compare files that are scattered across the Internet. For example, you can use the File.GetLastWriteUtc method to implement a replication program that compares the files at two Internet sites in different time zones and overwrites the older one with the newer version.

The Directory type doesn't expose a GetAttributes method, but the File.GetAttributes method works also for directories, so this limitation isn't an issue. The SetAttributes and GetAttributes methods set or return a bit-coded FileAttributes value, which is a combination of Normal (no attributes), Archive, ReadOnly, Hidden, System, Directory, Compressed, Encrypted, Temporary, NotContentIndexed, and a few other values:

```
// Display system and hidden files in C:\.
foreach ( string fname in Directory.GetFiles(@"C:\") )
{
    FileAttributes attr = File.GetAttributes(fname);
    // Display the file if marked as hidden or system (or both).
    if ( (attr & FileAttributes.Hidden) != 0 | (attr & FileAttributes.System) != 0 )
    {
        Console.WriteLine(fname);
    }
}
```

The File type exposes a few methods that are missing in the Directory type. The Copy method can copy a file and overwrite the destination if necessary:

```
// true in the last argument means "overwrite the target file" if it exists already.
File.Copy(@"c:\data.bin", @"c:\backup\data.bin", true);
```

Three methods of the File type are new in .NET Framework 2.0. The Replace method performs a move+copy operation as a single command: it creates a backup copy of the destination file, and then copies the source file to the destination file. An optional fourth argument, if true, tells .NET to ignore any error that might occur when merging the attributes or the ACL of the two files involved in the command:

```
// Back up the current contents of c:\data.bin into c:\data.bak, and
// then copy the contents of c:\newdata.bin into c:\data.bin.
File.Replace(@"c:\data.bin", @"c:\newdata.bin", @"c:\data.bak", true);
```

The Encrypt method encrypts a file on an NTFS file system partition so that it can be read only by the current user; the process can be reversed by running the Decrypt method:

```
// Ensure that no other user account can read a file during a lengthy operation.
try
{
    File.Encrypt(@"c:\secretdata.txt");
    …
}
finally
{
    // Or just delete the file…
    File.Decrypt(@"c:\secretdata.txt");
}
```

Reading and Writing Files

In addition to the operations illustrated in the previous section, the File object can perform atomic read and write operations on text and binary files, in a very simple manner. All the methods that enable you to perform these tasks have been added in .NET Framework 2.0.

You read an entire text file by means of the ReadAllText method, and write it using the WriteAllText method:

```
// Read a text file, convert its contents to uppercase, and save it to another file.
string text = File.ReadAllText(@"c:\testfile.txt");
File.WriteAllText(@"c:\upper.txt", text.ToUpper());
```

Alternatively, you can read and write an array of strings by means of the ReadAllLines and WriteAllLines methods:

```
// Read the source file into an array of strings.
string[] lines = File.ReadAllLines("source.txt");
int count = 0;
// Delete empty lines, by moving non-empty lines towards lower indices.
for ( int i = 0; i < lines.Length ; i++ )
{
    if ( lines[i].Trim().Length > 0 )
    {
        lines[count++] = lines[i];
    }
}
// Trim lines in excess and write to destination file.
string[] lines2 = new string[count];
Array.Copy(lines, lines2, count);
File.WriteAllLines("source2.txt", lines2);
```

The AppendAllText method appends a string to an existing text file or creates a text file if the file doesn't exist yet:

```
// Append a message to a log file, creating the file if necessary.
string msg = string.Format("Application started at {0}\n", DateTime.Now);
File.AppendAllText(@"c:\log.txt", msg);
```

The five methods shown so far have an overloaded version that accepts a System.Text.Encoding object. (See Chapter 1, ".NET Framework Basic Types," for more details.) The ReadAllBytes and WriteAllBytes methods are similar, except they work with a Byte array and are therefore more useful with binary files:

```
// Very simple encryption of a binary file
byte[] bytes = File.ReadAllBytes("source.txt");
// Flip every other bit in each byte.
for ( int i = 0; i < bytes.Length; i++ )
{
   bytes[i] = (byte) (bytes[i] ^ 0x55);
}
// Write it to a different file
File.WriteAllBytes("source.enc", bytes);
```

In addition to the read and write methods that process the entire file, the File type exposes methods that open the file for reading, writing, or appending data and return a FileStream object. The most flexible of these methods is the Open method, which takes a filename and up to three additional arguments:

```
FileStream fs = File.Open(FileName, FileMode, FileAccess, FileShare);
```

Let's see these arguments in more detail:

- The FileMode argument can be Append, Create, CreateNew, Open, OpenOrCreate, or Truncate. Open and Append modes fail if the file doesn't exist; Create and CreateNew fail if the file already exists. Use OpenOrCreate to open a file or to create one if it doesn't exist yet.

- The FileAccess argument specifies what the application wants to do with the file and can be Read, Write, or ReadWrite.

- The FileShare argument tells which operations other FileStreams can perform on the open file. It can be None (all operations are prohibited), ReadWrite (all operations are allowed), Read, Write, Delete (new in .NET Framework 2.0), or Inheritable (not supported directly by Win32).

The File class exposes three variants of the Open method: Create, OpenRead, and OpenWrite. Like the generic Open method, these variants return a FileStream object. There are also three specific methods for working with text files (CreateText, OpenText, and AppendText), which return a StreamReader or StreamWriter object. I explain how to use the FileStream, the StreamReader, and the StreamWriter objects later in this chapter.

The DirectoryInfo and FileInfo Types

The DirectoryInfo and FileInfo types represent individual directories and files. Both types inherit from the FileSystemInfo abstract class and therefore have several properties in common, namely, Name, FullName, Extension, Exists, Attributes, CreationTime, CreationTimeUtc, LastWriteTime, LastWriteTimeUtc, LastAccessTime, and LastAccessTimeUtc. They also have two methods in common: Delete and Refresh, where the latter ensures that all properties are up-to-date.

You can get a reference to a DirectoryInfo or FileInfo object by using its constructor method, which takes the path of a specific directory or file:

```
// Create a DirectoryInfo object that points to C:\.
DirectoryInfo diRoot = new DirectoryInfo(@"c:\");
// Create a FileInfo object that points to c:\autoexec.bat.
FileInfo fiAutoexec = new FileInfo(@"c:\autoexec.bat");
```

Once you have a reference to a DirectoryInfo object, you can use its methods to enumerate the folder's contents and get other DirectoryInfo or FileInfo objects. (You can also apply filter criteria.)

```
// List the directories in c:\.
foreach ( DirectoryInfo di in diRoot.GetDirectories() )
{
    Console.WriteLine(di.Name);
}

// List all the *.txt files in c:\.
foreach ( FileInfo fi in diRoot.GetFiles("*.txt") )
{
    Console.WriteLine(fi.Name);
}
```

The DirectoryInfo.GetFileSystemInfos method returns an array of FileSystemInfo objects. Both the DirectoryInfo and FileInfo types inherit from the FileSystemInfo type, so you can process both files and subdirectories in a folder with a single loop:

```
// Show files and directories in one operation
foreach ( FileSystemInfo fsi in diRoot.GetFileSystemInfos() )
{
    // Use the "dir" or "file" prefix.
    string prefix;
    if ( (fsi.Attributes & FileAttributes.Directory) != 0 )
    {
        prefix = "dir";
    }
    else
    {
        prefix = "file";
    }
    // Print type, name and creation date.
    Console.WriteLine("[{0}] {1}  {2}", prefix, fsi.Name, fsi.CreationTime);
}
```

Most of the members of the DirectoryInfo and FileInfo types perform the same action as do the static methods with the same or similar names exposed by the Directory and File types. For example, the FileInfo.CreationTime property enables you to read and modify the creation date of a file, just like the File object's GetCreationTime and SetCreationTime methods do. Among the few exceptions is the FileInfo.Length property, which returns the length of a file:

```
// List all empty files in c:\.
foreach ( FileInfo fi in diRoot.GetFiles() )
{
    if ( fi.Length == 0 )
    {
        Console.WriteLine(fi.Name);
    }
}
```

You can get the parent directory of a file in two ways: the DirectoryName property returns the name of the directory, whereas the Directory property returns the DirectoryInfo object that represents that directory:

```
// List all the files in the same directory as the FileInfo object named fiDoc.
foreach ( FileInfo fi in fiDoc.Directory.GetFiles() )
{
    Console.WriteLine(fi.Name);
}
```

You can create a new folder by means of the CreateSubdirectory method of the DirectoryInfo object:

```
// Create a folder named Reports in the c:\tempdocs directory.
DirectoryInfo diDocs = new DirectoryInfo(@"c:\tempdocs");
diDocs.CreateSubdirectory("Reports");
```

Both the DirectoryInfo and the FileInfo types expose a MoveTo and a Delete method, but the DirectoryInfo.Delete method can take a Boolean argument, which, if true, causes the deletion of the entire subdirectory tree:

```
// (Continuing previous code snippet...)
// Delete the c:\tempdocs directory and its subfolders.
diDocs.Delete(true);
```

 In version 2.0 of the .NET Framework, the FileInfo object has been expanded with the IsReadOnly property (true if the file is read-only) and three methods: Encrypt, Decrypt, and Replace. For more details about these methods, read the description of methods with the same names in the section titled "The Directory and File Types" earlier in the chapter:

```
// Encrypt all the writable files in the c:\private directory.
DirectoryInfo diPrivate = new DirectoryInfo(@"c:\private");
foreach ( FileInfo fi in diPrivate.GetFiles() )
{
    if ( !fi.IsReadOnly )
```

```
    {
        fi.Encrypt();
    }
}
```

Finally, the FileInfo object exposes six methods that open a file, namely, Open, OpenRead, OpenWrite, OpenText, CreateText, and AppendText. They have the same purpose as the static methods with the same names exposed by the File type.

> **Note**   At the end of this overview of the DirectoryInfo and FileInfo objects, you might wonder whether you should use the instance methods of these types rather than the static methods with the same names exposed by the Directory and File types, respectively. In most cases, there is no "correct" decision, and it's mostly a matter of programming style and the specific needs that arise in a given program. For example, I find myself more comfortable with the Directory and File types, but I use the DirectoryInfo and FileInfo objects if I need to buffer the data about a directory or a file, or if I need to process files and directories in a uniform manner (as made possible by the FileSystemInfo base class). Interestingly, the FileInfo object doesn't expose some of the methods that have been added to the File type in .NET Framework 2.0, such as ReadAllText or WriteAllLines; thus, in general, using the File type gives you a little extra flexibility that is missing from the FileInfo class.

The DriveInfo Type

Previous versions of the .NET Framework exposed no classes for retrieving information about existing drives, so you had to use either PInvoke calls to the Windows API or Windows Management Instrumentation (WMI) classes. This gap has been filled in version 2.0 with the introduction of the DriveInfo type.

You can create a DriveInfo object in two ways: by passing a drive letter to its constructor or by means of the GetDrives static method, which returns an array containing information about all the installed drives:

```
// Display the volume label of drive C.
DriveInfo driveC = new DriveInfo("c:");
Console.WriteLine(driveC.VolumeLabel);
```

When enumerating drives, it's crucial that you don't attempt to read any member before testing the IsReady property:

```
// Display name and total size of all available drives.
foreach ( DriveInfo di in DriveInfo.GetDrives() )
{
    if ( di.IsReady )
    {
        Console.WriteLine("Drive {0}: {1:N} bytes", di.Name, di.TotalSize);
    }
}
```

The DriveInfo object exposes the following properties: Name, VolumeLabel, RootDirectory (the DirectoryInfo object that represents the root folder), DriveType (an enumerated value that can be Fixed, Removable, CDRom, Ram, Network, and Unknown), DriveFormat (a string such as NTFS or FAT32), TotalSize (the capacity of the drive in bytes), TotalFreeSpace (the total number of free bytes), and AvailableFreeSpace (the number of available free bytes; can be less than TotalFreeSpace if quotas are used). All the properties are read-only, which is quite understandable (even though I'd surely like to increase the amount of free space on a drive by simply setting a property!), except for the VolumeLabel property:

```
// Change the volume label of drive D.
DriveInfo driveD = new DriveInfo("d:");
driveD.VolumeLabel = "MyData";
```

The following loop displays information about all the installed drives in a tabular format, while skipping over the drives that aren't ready:

```
Console.WriteLine("{0,-6}{1,-10}{2,-8}{3,-16}{4,18}{5,18}", "Name",
    "Label", "Type", "Format", "TotalSize", "TotalFreeSpace");
Console.WriteLine(new string('-', 78));
foreach ( DriveInfo di in DriveInfo.GetDrives() )
{
    if ( di.IsReady )
    {
        Console.WriteLine("{0,-6}{1,-10}{2,-8}{3,-16}{4,18:N0}{5,18:N0}",
            di.Name, di.VolumeLabel, di.DriveType.ToString(), di.DriveFormat,
            di.TotalSize, di.TotalFreeSpace);
    }
    else
    {
        Console.WriteLine("{0,-6}(not ready)", di.Name);
    }
}
```

Here's an example of what you might see in the console window:

Name	Label	Type	Format	TotalSize	TotalFreeSpace
C:\		Fixed	NTFS	20,974,428,160	8,009,039,872
D:\	DATA	Fixed	NTFS	39,028,953,088	10,244,005,888
E:\	(not ready)				

The FileSystemWatcher Type

The FileSystemWatcher component enables you to monitor a directory or a directory tree so that you get a notification when something happens inside it—for example, when a file or a subdirectory is created, deleted, or renamed or when the folder's attributes are changed. This component can be useful in many circumstances. For example, say that you're creating an application that automatically encrypts all the files stored in a given directory. Without this component, you should poll the directory at regular intervals (typically using a Timer), but the FileSystemWatcher component makes this task easier. Another good example of how this component can be useful is when you cache a data file in memory to access its contents quickly, but need to reload it when another application modifies the data.

This component works on Microsoft Windows Millennium Edition (Me), Windows NT, Windows 2000, Windows XP, and Windows Server 2003.

Initializing a FileSystemWatcher Component

You can create a FileSystemWatcher component in either of two ways: by means of code or by dragging it from the Components tab of the Toolbox to the tray area of a Windows Forms class, a Web Forms page, or another Microsoft Visual Studio designer. There's no noticeable difference in performance or flexibility, so any method is fine. The demo application uses a component in a form's component tray area, which I have renamed fsw (see Figure 7-1), but creating it through code is equally simple:

```
FileSystemWatcher fsw = new FileSystemWatcher();
```

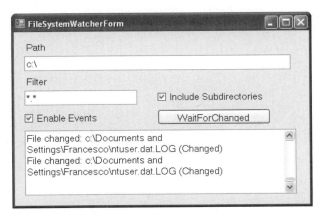

Figure 7-1   The demo application that enables you to experiment with the FileSystemWatcher component

Before you use this component, you must initialize at least its Path, IncludeSubdirectories, Filter, and NotifyFilter properties. The Path property is the name of the directory that you want to watch; notice that you're notified of changes occurring inside the directory, but not of changes to the directory's attributes (such as its Hidden or ReadOnly attribute).

The IncludeSubdirectories property should be set to false if you want to be notified of any change inside the specified directory only, or to true if you want to watch for changes in the entire directory tree whose root is the folder specified by the Path property.

The Filter property enables you to specify which files you're interested in; for example, use *.* to get notifications about all the files in the directory or *.txt to watch only files with the .txt extension. The default value for this property is a null string, which means all files (same as *.*).

The NotifyFilter property is a bit-coded value that specifies which kind of modifications are announced by means of the component's Changed event. This property can be a combination of one or more NotifyFilters enumerated values: Attributes, CreationTime, DirectoryName, FileName, LastAccess, LastWrite, Security, and Size. The initial value of this property is LastWrite | FileName | DirectoryName, so by default you don't get notifications when an attribute is changed.

Here's an example of how you can set up a FileSystemWatcher component to watch for events in the C:\Windows directory and its subdirectories:

```
FileSystemWatcher fsw = new FileSystemWatcher();
// Subscribe to events. (Event handlers are described later.)
fsw.Created += new FileSystemEventHandler(this.fsw_Created);
fsw.Deleted += new FileSystemEventHandler(this.fsw_Deleted);
fsw.Renamed += new RenamedEventHandler(this.fsw_Renamed);
fsw.Changed += new FileSystemEventHandler(this.fsw_Changed);
fsw.Error += new ErrorEventHandler(fsw_Error);

fsw.Path = @"c:\windows";
fsw.IncludeSubdirectories = true;          // Watch subdirectories.
fsw.Filter = "*.dll";                      // Watch only DLL files.
// Add attribute changes to the list of changes that can fire events.
fsw.NotifyFilter = fsw.NotifyFilter | NotifyFilters.Attributes;
// Enable event notification.
fsw.EnableRaisingEvents = true;
```

Getting Notifications

Once you've set up the component correctly, you can get a notification when something happens. You can achieve this by writing event handlers or using the WaitForChanged method.

Events

The simplest way to get a notification from the FileSystemWatcher component is by writing handlers for the component's events. However, events don't fire until you set EnableRaising-Events to true. The Created, Deleted, and Changed events receive a FileSystemEventArgs object, which exposes two important properties: Name (the name of the file that has been created, deleted, or changed) and FullPath (its complete path):

```
private void fsw_Created(object sender, FileSystemEventArgs e)
{
    Console.WriteLine("File created: {0}", e.FullPath);
}

private void fsw_Deleted(object sender, FileSystemEventArgs e)
{
    Console.WriteLine("File deleted: {0}", e.FullPath);
}

private void fsw_Changed(object sender, FileSystemEventArgs e)
{
    Console.WriteLine("File changed: {0}", e.FullPath);
}
```

The FileSystemEventArgs object also exposes a ChangeType enumerated property, which tells whether the event is a create, delete, or change event. You can use this property to use a single handler to manage all three events, as in this code:

```
private void fsw_EventHandler(object sender, FileSystemEventArgs e)
{
    Console.WriteLine("File changed: {0} ({1})", e.FullPath, e.ChangeType);
}
```

The Changed event receives no information about the type of change that fired the event, such as a change in the file's LastWrite date or attributes. Finally, the Renamed event receives a RenamedEventArgs object, which exposes two additional properties: OldName (the name of the file before being renamed) and OldFullPath (its complete path):

```
private void fsw_Renamed(object sender, System.IO.RenamedEventArgs e)
{
    Console.WriteLine("File renamed: {0} => {1}", e.OldFullPath, e.FullPath);
}
```

You can also have multiple FileSystemWatcher components forward their events to the same event handler. In this case, use the first argument to detect which specific component raised the event.

The FileSystemWatcher component raises one event for each file and for each action on the file. For example, if you delete 10 files, you receive 10 distinct Deleted events. If you move 10 files from one directory to another, you receive 10 Deleted events from the source directory and 10 Created events from the destination directory.

The WaitForChanged Method

If your application doesn't perform any operation other than waiting for changes in the specified path, or if you monitor file operations from a secondary thread, you can write simpler and more efficient code by using the WaitForChanged method. This method is synchronous and doesn't return until a file change is detected or the (optional) timeout expires. On return from this method, the application receives a WaitForChangedResult structure, whose fields enable you to determine whether the timeout elapsed, the type of event that occurred, and the name of the involved file:

```
// Create a *new* FileSystemWatcher component.
FileSystemWatcher tmpFsw = new FileSystemWatcher(path, filter);
// Wait max 10 seconds for an event.
WaitForChangedResult res = tmpFsw.WaitForChanged(WatcherChangeTypes.All, 10000);

if ( res.TimedOut )
{
    Console.WriteLine("10 seconds have elapsed without any event");
}
```

```
else
{
    string changeType = Enum.GetName(typeof(WatcherChangeTypes), res.ChangeType);
    Console.WriteLine("Event: {0} ({1})", res.Name, changeType);
}
```

The WaitForChanged method traps changes only in the directory the Path property points to and ignores the IncludeSubdirectories property. For this reason, the WaitForChangedResult structure includes a Name field but not a FullPath field. The first argument you pass to the WaitForChanged method lets you further restrict the kind of file operation you want to intercept:

```
// Pause the application until the c:\MyApp\temp.dat file is deleted.
tmpFsw = new FileSystemWatcher(@"c:\MyApp", "temp.dat");
tmpFsw.WaitForChanged(WatcherChangeTypes.Deleted);
```

Buffer Overflows

You should be aware of potential problems when too many events fire in a short time. The FileSystemWatcher component uses an internal buffer to keep track of file system actions so that events can be raised for each one of them, even if the application can't serve them fast enough. By default, this internal buffer is 8 KB long and can store about 160 events. Each event takes 16 bytes, plus 2 bytes for each character in the filename. (Filenames are stored as Unicode characters.) If you anticipate a lot of file activity, you should increase the size of the buffer by setting the InternalBufferSize property to a larger value. The size should be an integer multiple of the operating system's page size (4 KB under Windows 2000 and later versions). Alternatively, you can use the NotifyFilter property to limit the number of change operations that fire the Changed event or set IncludeSubdirectories to false if you don't need to monitor an entire directory tree. (Use multiple FileSystemWatcher components to monitor individual subdirectories if you aren't interested in monitoring all the subdirectories under a given path.)

You can't use the Filter property to prevent the internal buffer from overflowing because this property filters out files only after they've been added to the buffer. When the internal buffer overflows, you get an Error event:

```
private void fsw_Error(object sender, ErrorEventArgs e)
{
    Console.WriteLine("FileSystemWatcher error");
}
```

If you notice that your application receives this event, you should change your event-handling strategy. For example, you might store all the events in a queue and have them served by another thread.

Troubleshooting

By default, the Created, Deleted, Renamed, and Changed events run in a thread taken from the system thread pool. (See Chapter 11, "Threads," for more information about the thread pool.) Because Windows Forms controls aren't thread safe, you should avoid accessing any control or the form itself from inside the FileSystemWatcher component's event handlers. If you find this limitation unacceptable, you should assign a Windows Forms control to the component's SynchronizingObject property, as in this code:

```
// Use the current Form object as the synchronizing object.
fsw.SynchronizingObject = this;
```

The preceding code ensures that all event handlers run in the same thread that serves the form itself. When you create a FileSystemWatcher component using the Visual Studio 2005 designer, this property is automatically assigned the hosting form object.

Here are a few more tips about the FileSystemWatcher component and the problems you might need to solve when using it:

- The FileSystemWatcher component starts raising events when the Path property is non-empty and the EnableRaisingEvents property is true. You can also prevent the component from raising unwanted events during the initialization phase of a Form class by bracketing your setup statements between a call to the BeginInit method and a call to the EndInit method. (This is the approach used by the Visual Studio designer.)

- As I mentioned before, this component works only on Windows Me, Windows NT, Windows 2000, Windows XP, and Windows Server 2003. It raises an error when it points to a path on machines running earlier versions of the operating system. Remote machines must have one of these operating systems to work properly, but you can't monitor a remote Windows NT system from another Windows NT machine. You can use UNC-based directory names only on Windows 2000 or later systems. The FileSystemWatcher component doesn't work on CD-ROM and DVD drives because their contents can't change.

- In some cases, you might get multiple Created events, depending on how a file is created and on the application that creates it. For example, when you create a new file using Notepad, you see the following sequence of events: Created, Deleted, Created, and Changed. (The first event pair fires because Notepad checks whether the file exists by attempting to create it.)

- A change in a file can generate an extra event in its parent directory as well because the directory maintains information about the files it contains (their size, last write date, and so on).

- If the directory the Path property points to is renamed, the FileSystemWatcher component continues to work correctly. However, in this case, the Path property returns the old directory name, so you might get an error if you use it. (This happens because the component references the directory by its handle, which doesn't change if the directory is renamed.)

- If you create a directory inside the path being watched and the IncludeSubdirectories property is true, the new subdirectory is watched as well.

- When a large file is created in the directory, you might not be able to read the entire file immediately because it's still owned by the process that's writing data to it. You should protect any access to the original file with a try block and, if an exception is thrown, attempt the operation again some milliseconds later.

- When the user deletes a file in a directory, a new file is created in the Recycle Bin directory.

Working with Access Control Lists

 One of the most important new features in .NET Framework 2.0 is the support for reading and modifying Windows access control lists (ACLs) from managed code without having to call functions in the Windows API, as was necessary in previous .NET versions. To support this new feature, Microsoft introduced the System.Security.AccessControl namespace, added a few types to the System.Security.Principal namespace, and, above all, added several methods to all the .NET types that represent system resources to which an ACL can be associated. Examples of such resources are files, directories, the registry, Active Directory objects, and many types in the System.Threading namespace. In this chapter, I focus on file resources exclusively, but the concepts I introduce are valid for other resource types.

Account Names and Security Identifiers

Before you can see how to manipulate file ACLs, you must become familiar with three classes in System.Security.Principal namespace. The IdentityReference is an abstract type that represents a Windows identity and is the base class for the other two classes, NTAccount and SecurityIdentifier.

The IdentityReference type has one important property, Value, which returns the textual representation of the identity. The NTAccount type overrides this property to return an account or group name, such as BUILTIN\Users or NT AUTHORITY\SYSTEM, whereas the SecurityIdentifier class overrides the property to return the textual representation of a security identifier (SID), for example, S-1-5-21-583907252-1563985344-1957994488-1003. (This representation is also known as Security Descriptor Definition Language format, or SDDL.) The following code creates an NTAccount object and translates it to the security identifier (SID) format by means of the Translate method that the NTAccount type inherits from IdentityReference:

```
NTAccount nta = new NTAccount(@"BUILTIN\Administrators");
SecurityIdentifier sia = (SecurityIdentifier) nta.Translate(typeof(SecurityIdentifier));
Console.WriteLine("Name={0}, SID={1}", nta.Value, sia.Value);
    // => Name=BUILTIN\Administrators, SID=S-1-5-32-544
```

The NTAccount type also exposes a constructor that takes two arguments, the domain name and the account name:

```
nta = new NTAccount("CADomain", "Francesco");
```

Interestingly, Microsoft Visual C# supports the equal to (==) and not equal to (!=) operators to enable you to test two NTAccount or two SecurityIdentifier objects, but both operators require that the operators are of the same type; therefore, you must always convert an NTAccount to a SecurityIdentifier object (or vice versa) before comparing the objects:

```
// (Continuing previous code snippet…)
bool isSameAccount = nta.Equals(sia ) ;                              // => False
isSameAccount = ( nta.Translate(typeof(SecurityIdentifier)) == sia );   // => True
```

The constructor of the SecurityIdentifier type is overloaded to take either a SID in textual format or a WellKnownSidType enumerated value, such as AccountGuestSid (guest users), AnonymousSid (the anonymous account), and LocalSystemSid (the Local System account):

```
// Create the SecurityIdentifier corresponding to the Administrators group.
// (2nd argument must be non-null for some kinds of well-known SIDs.)
SecurityIdentifier sia2 = new
    SecurityIdentifier(WellKnownSidType.BuiltinAdministratorsSid, null);
Console.WriteLine(sia2.Value);                          // => S-1-5-32-544"
NTAccount nta2 = (NTAccount) sia2.Translate(typeof(NTAccount));
Console.WriteLine(nta2.Value);                          // => BUILTIN\Administrators

// Here's another way to get a reference to the same account.
sia2 = new SecurityIdentifier("S-1-5-32-544");
```

You can retrieve the SecurityIdentifier object corresponding to the current Windows user as follows:

```
SecurityIdentifier siUser = WindowsIdentity.GetCurrent().User;
```

Another common use of the SecurityIdentifier type is for checking whether a user is in a given group or role:

```
// Create the WindowsPrincipal corresponding to current user.
WindowsPrincipal wp = new WindowsPrincipal(WindowsIdentity.GetCurrent());
// Create the SecurityIdentifier for the BUILTIN\Administrators group.
SecurityIdentifier siAdmin =
    new SecurityIdentifier(WellKnownSidType.BuiltinAdministratorsSid, null);
// Check whether the current user is an administrator.
Console.WriteLine("Is a power user = {0}", wp.IsInRole(siAdmin));
```

The DirectorySecurity and FileSecurity Types

The System.Security.AccessControl namespace includes nearly all the types that enable you to control the ACLs associated with a Windows resource, such as the FileSecurity, Directory-Security, and RegistrySecurity types. (Only two ACL-related types aren't in this namespace, namely, System.DirectoryServices.ActiveDirectorySecurity and Microsoft.Iis.Metabase .MetaKeySecurity.) In this section, I focus on the FileSecurity and DirectorySecurity objects, which, not surprisingly, are very similar. In fact, both of them inherit from the FileSystem-Security class, which, in turn, inherits from NativeObjectSecurity.

You can get a reference to a FileSecurity or DirectorySecurity object in one of the following two ways. First, you can pass a path to its constructor, together with an AccessControlSection enumerated value that specifies which security information you're interested in:

```
string dirName = @"c:\windows";
string fileName = "data.txt";

// Retrieve only access information related to the folder.
DirectorySecurity dirSec = new DirectorySecurity(dirName, AccessControlSections.Access);
// Retrieve all security information related to the file.
FileSecurity fileSec = new FileSecurity(fileName, AccessControlSections.All);
```

(Valid values for AccessControlSections are Access, Owner, Audit, Group, All, and None.) Second, you can use the GetAccessControl method exposed by the Directory, File, DirectoryInfo, and FileInfo types:

```
// (This code is equivalent to previous snippet.)
dirSec = Directory.GetAccessControl(dirName, AccessControlSections.Access);
fileSec = File.GetAccessControl(fileName, AccessControlSections.All);
```

The simplest operation you can perform with a FileSecurity or a DirectorySecurity object is retrieving the discretionary access control list (DACL) or system access control list (SACL) associated with the resource in SDDL format:

```
// Get access-related security information for the data.txt file.
Console.WriteLine(fileSec.GetSecurityDescriptorSddlForm(AccessControlSections.Access));
        // => D:AI(D;;DCLCRPCR;;;SY)(A;ID;FA;;;BA)….
```

> **Note** A discretionary access control list (DACL) defines who is granted or denied access to an object. Each Windows object is associated with a DACL, which consists of a list of access control entries (ACEs); each ACE defines a trustee and specifies the access rights that are granted, denied, or audited for that trustee. If the object has no DACL, everyone can use the object; otherwise, each ACE is tested until the user (or the process that is impersonating the user) is granted the access to the object. If no ACE grants this permission, the user is prevented from using the object.
>
> A system access control list (SACL) enables administrators to log attempts to use a given object. A SACL contains one or more ACEs; each ACE specifies a trustee and the type of access (from that trustee) that causes the system to create an entry in the security event log. You can decide whether the entry in the log is generated in all cases, only if the access succeeds, or only if the access fails.

An SDDL string is rarely useful, though, or at least it is hard for humans to decode. To get the ACL in readable format you can use one of the following methods: GetOwner (to retrieve the owner of the resource), GetGroup (to retrieve the primary group associated with the owner), GetAccessRules (to retrieve the collection of access rules), and GetAuditRules (to retrieve the collection of audit rules). These three methods have similar syntax.

The GetOwner and GetGroup methods return a single object that derives from Identity-Reference, therefore either an NTAccount or a SecurityIdentifier object. You specify which object you want to be returned by passing a proper System.Type object as an argument:

```
// Get the owner of the data.txt as an NTAccount object.
NTAccount nta3 = (NTAccount) fileSec.GetOwner(typeof(NTAccount)) ;
// Get the primary group of the owner of data.txt as a SecurityIdentifier object.
SecurityIdentifier sia3 = (SecurityIdentifier) fileSec.GetGroup(typeof(SecurityIdentifier));
```

Once you have an NTAccount or a SecurityIdentifier object, you can query all its properties, as shown in the previous section.

The GetAccessRules method returns a collection of AccessRule objects, where each individual member in the collection tells whether a given action is granted to or denied a given user or group of users. Similar to the GetOwner and GetGroup methods, you must pass a System .Type object that specifies whether the user name or group is expressed by means of an NTAccount object or a SecurityIdentifier object:

```
// Display the header of the result table.
Console.WriteLine("{0,-25}{1,-30}{2,-8}{3,-6}", "User", "Rights", "Access", "Inherited");
Console.WriteLine(new string('-', 72));
// 1st argument tells whether to include access rules explicitly set for the object
// 2nd argument tells whether to include inherited rules.
foreach ( FileSystemAccessRule fsar in
   fileSec.GetAccessRules(true, true, typeof(NTAccount)) )
{
   Console.WriteLine("{0,-25}{1,-30}{2,-8}{3,-6}", fsar.IdentityReference.Value,
      fsar.FileSystemRights, fsar.AccessControlType, fsar.IsInherited);
}
```

The FileSystemAccessRule.FileSystemRights property returns a bit-coded FileSystemRights enumerated type that exposes values such as Read, Write, Modify, Delete, ReadAndExecute, FullControl, ReadAttributes, WriteAttributes, and many others. (See Table 7-1.) The FileSystemAccessRule.AccessControlType returns an enumerated value that can only be Allow or Deny. Here's the kind of output the previous code produces in the console window:

```
User                     Rights                        Access  Inherited
------------------------------------------------------------------------
BUILTIN\Administrators   FullControl                   Allow   True
NT AUTHORITY\SYSTEM      FullControl                   Allow   True
DESKTOP01\FrancescoB     Write                         Deny    False
BUILTIN\Users            ReadAndExecute, Synchronize   Allow   True
```

You can compare these results with the actual permissions set for the specific file. To do so, right-click the file in Windows Explorer, select the Properties command from the context menu, and switch to the Security tab, as shown in Figure 7-2. (If you don't see this tab, select the Folder Options command from the Tools menu in Windows Explorer, switch to the View tab, and ensure that the Use Simple File Sharing option is cleared.) Some attributes are visible in the Advanced Security Settings dialog box, which you display by clicking the Advanced button.

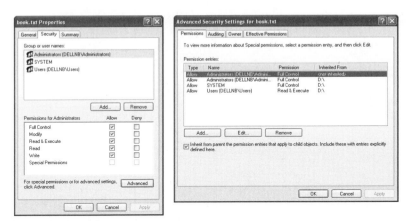

Figure 7-2   The Security tab of the Properties dialog box (left) and the Advanced Security Settings dialog box (right) of a file

Table 7-1   Values of the FileSystemRights Enumerated Type

Value	Description
AppendData	Specifies the right to append data to the end of a file.
ChangePermissions	Specifies the right to change the security and audit rules associated with a file or folder.
CreateDirectories	Specifies the right to create a folder. This right requires the Synchronize right. If you don't explicitly set the Synchronize right when creating a file or folder, the Synchronize right will be set automatically for you.
CreateFiles	Specifies the right to create a file. This right requires the Synchronize right. If you don't explicitly set the Synchronize right when creating a file or folder, the Synchronize right will be set automatically for you.
Delete	Specifies the right to delete a folder or file.
DeleteSubdirectories-AndFiles	Specifies the right to delete a folder and any files contained within that folder.
ExecuteFile	Specifies the right to run an application file.
FullControl	Specifies the right to exert full control over a folder or file and to modify access control and audit rules.
ListDirectory	Specifies the right to list the contents of a folder.
Modify	Specifies the right to read, write, list folder contents, delete folders and files, and run application files.
Read	Specifies the right to open and copy folders or files as read-only. It includes the right to read file system attributes, extended file system attributes, and access and audit rules.
ReadAndExecute	Specifies the right to open and copy folders or files as read-only and to run application files. It includes the right to read file system attributes, extended file system attributes, and access and audit rules.

Table 7-1   Values of the FileSystemRights Enumerated Type

Value	Description
ReadAttributes	Specifies the right to open and copy file system attributes from a folder or file. It doesn't include the right to read data, extended file system attributes, or access and audit rules.
ReadData	Specifies the right to open and copy a file or folder. It doesn't include the right to read file system attributes, extended file system attributes, or access and audit rules.
ReadExtendedAttributes	Specifies the right to open and copy extended file system attributes from a folder or file. It doesn't include the right to read data, file system attributes, or access and audit rules.
ReadPermissions	Specifies the right to open and copy access and audit rules from a folder or file. It doesn't include the right to read data, file system attributes, and extended file system attributes.
Synchronize	Specifies the right to synchronize a file or folder. The right to create a file or folder requires this right. If you don't explicitly set this right when creating a file, the right will be set automatically for you.
TakeOwnership	Specifies the right to change the owner of a folder or file.
Traverse	Specifies the right to list the contents of a folder and to run applications contained within that folder.
Write	Specifies the right to create folders and files and to add or remove data from files. It includes the ability to write file system attributes, extended file system attributes, and access and audit rules.
WriteAttributes	Specifies the right to open and write file system attributes to a folder or file. It doesn't include the ability to write data, extended attributes, or access and audit rules.
WriteData	Specifies the right to open and write to a file or folder. It doesn't include the right to open and write file system attributes, extended file system attributes, or access and audit rules.
WriteExtendedAttributes	Specifies the right to open and write extended file system attributes to a folder or file. It doesn't include the ability to write data, attributes, or access and audit rules.

You can change security-related information as well. For example, the FileSecurity object exposes the SetOwner method for changing the owner of a file:

```
// Transfer the ownership of the data.txt file to the System account.
NTAccount nta5 = new NTAccount(@"NT AUTHORITY\SYSTEM");
fileSec.SetOwner(nta5);
```

Modifying ACLs

You can do more than just change the owner of a file or directory object. In fact, you can specify exactly who can (or can't) do what, by creating or manipulating a FileSecurity or DirectorySecurity object and associating it with a file or directory. This is made possible by the SetAccessControl method exposed by the Directory, File, DirectoryInfo, and FileInfo types.

The simplest technique for changing the ACL of a file or a directory is by cloning the ACL obtained from another object, as in this code:

```
// Retrieve all security information related to the file.
FileSecurity fileSec = new FileSecurity("data.txt", AccessControlSections.All);
// Create a copy of the all permissions associated with the source file.
// (You can also copy just the access permissions, for example.)
string sddl = fileSec.GetSecurityDescriptorSddlForm(AccessControlSections.All);
FileSecurity fileSec2 = new FileSecurity();
fileSec2.SetSecurityDescriptorSddlForm(sddl);
// Enforce these permissions on the target file.
File.SetAccessControl("data.new", fileSec2);
```

For tasks that are more complex than just copying an existing ACL, you create individual FileSystemAccessRule objects and pass them to the FileSecurity.AddAccessRule method:

```
// Create an access rule that grants full control to administrators.
NTAccount ntAcc1 = new NTAccount(@"BUILTIN\Administrators");
FileSystemAccessRule fsar1 = new FileSystemAccessRule(ntAcc1,
    FileSystemRights.FullControl, AccessControlType.Allow);
// Create another access rule that denies write permissions to ASPNET user.
string aspnetUser = Environment.MachineName + @"\ASPNET";
NTAccount ntAcc2 = new NTAccount(aspnetUser);
FileSystemAccessRule fsar2 = new FileSystemAccessRule(ntAcc2,
    FileSystemRights.Write, AccessControlType.Deny);
// Create a FileSecurity object that contains these two access rules.
FileSecurity fsec = new FileSecurity();
fsec.AddAccessRule(fsar1);
fsec.AddAccessRule(fsar2);
// Assign these permissions to the data.txt file.
File.SetAccessControl("data.txt", fsec);
```

An overload of the constructor enables you to specify how permissions inherited from the parent object (the containing directory, in the case of the file system) should be dealt with.

```
FileSystemAccessRule fsar3 = new  FileSystemAccessRule(ntAcc2,
    FileSystemRights.Write | FileSystemRights.Read,
    InheritanceFlags.ContainerInherit | InheritanceFlags.ObjectInherit,
    PropagationFlags.None, AccessControlType.Allow);
```

The ContainerInherit flag means that the rule is propagated to all containers that are children of the current object, whereas the ObjectInherit flag means that the rule is propagated to all objects that are children of the current object. In the case of the file system, if the current object is a folder, the ContainerInherit flag affects its subdirectories and the ObjectInherit flag affects the files contained in the folder.

The PropagationFlags.None flag means that the rule applies to both the object and its children. The other two values for this flag are InheritOnly and NoPropagateInherit. The former value means that the rule applies to child objects but not to the object itself, thus you can enforce a rule for all the files and directories in a folder without affecting the folder itself; the latter value means that rule inheritance applies for only one level, therefore the rule affects the children of an object but not its grandchildren. In practice, these two flags aren't used often.

The FileSecurity type exposes other methods that enable you to modify the set of access rules contained in the object: ModifyAccessRule changes an existing access rule; PurgeAccessRules removes all the rules associated with a given IdentityReference object; RemoveAccessRule-Specific removes a specific access rule; ResetAccessRule adds the specified access rule and removes all the matching rules in one operation. Read MSDN documentation for details about these methods.

The FileSecurity object is also capable of reading and modifying the audit rules associated with a file or directory. (Audit rules specify which file operations on a file, either successful or not, are logged by the system.) For example, the following code displays all the audit rules associated with a file:

```
FileSecurity fsec = new FileSecurity("data.txt", AccessControlSections.All);

Console.WriteLine("{0,-25}{1,-30}{2,-8}{3,-6}", "User", "Rights", "Outcome", "Inherited");
Console.WriteLine(new string('-', 72));
foreach ( FileSystemAuditRule fsar in
    fsec.GetAuditRules(true, true, typeof(NTAccount)) )
{
    Console.WriteLine("{0,-25}{1,-30}{2,-8}{3,-6}", fsar.IdentityReference.Value,
        fsar.FileSystemRights, fsar.AuditFlags, fsar.IsInherited);
}
```

The AuditFlags property is an enumerated value that can be Success or Failure. You can use the AddAuditRule method to add an audit rule to the FileSecurity object, the ModifyAudit-Rule method to change an existing audit rule, and so forth.

The Stream Type

The Stream abstract type represents a sequence of bytes going to or coming from a storage medium (such as a file) or a physical or virtual device (such as a parallel port, an interprocess communication pipe, or a TCP/IP socket). Streams enable you to read from and write to a backing store, which can correspond to one of several storage mediums. For example, you can have file streams, memory streams, and network streams.

Because it's an abstract class, you don't create a Stream object directly, and you rarely use a Stream variable in your code. Rather, you typically work with types that inherit from it, such as the FileStream and the NetworkStream types.

Stream Operations

The fundamental operations you can perform on streams are read, write, and seek. Not all types of streams support all these operations—for example, the NetworkStream object doesn't support seeking. You can check which operations are allowed by using the stream's CanRead, CanWrite, and CanSeek properties.

Most stream objects perform data buffering in a transparent way. For example, data isn't immediately written to disk when you write to a file stream; instead, bytes are buffered and are eventually flushed when the stream is closed or when you issue an explicit Flush method. Buffering can improve performance remarkably. File streams are buffered, whereas memory streams aren't because there's no point in buffering a stream that maps to memory. You can use a BufferedStream object to add buffering capability to a stream object that doesn't offer it natively—for example, the NetworkStream object. Using BufferedStream in this fashion can improve performance remarkably if the application sends many small data packets rather than a few large ones.

Most of the properties of the Stream type—and of types that inherit from Stream—work as you would intuitively expect them to work:

- The Length property returns the total size of the stream, whereas the Position property determines the current position in the stream (that is, the offset of the next byte that will be read or written). You can change the stream's length using the SetLength method and change the position using the Seek method, but not all Stream types support these two methods.

- The Read method reads a number of bytes from the specified position into a Byte array, advances the stream pointer, and finally returns the number of bytes read. The ReadByte method reads and returns a single byte.

- The Write method writes a number of bytes from an array into the stream, and then advances the stream pointer. The WriteByte method writes a single byte to the stream.

- The Close method closes the stream and releases all the associated resources. The Flush method empties a buffered stream and ensures that all its contents are written to the underlying store. (It has no effect on nonbuffered streams.)

- In .NET Framework 2.0, you can use the CanTimeout read-only property to determine whether the stream supports timeouts in read and write operations; if this is the case, you can read or set these timeouts by means of the ReadTimeout and WriteTimeout properties. (These values are in milliseconds.)

Specific streams can implement additional methods and properties, such as the following:

- The FileStream class exposes the Handle property (which returns the operating system file handle) and the Lock and Unlock methods (which lock or unlock a portion of the file). When you're working with FileStream objects, the SetLength method actually trims or extends the underlying file.

- The MemoryStream class exposes the Capacity property (which returns the number of bytes allocated to the stream), the WriteTo method (which copies the entire contents to another stream), and the GetBuffer method (which returns the array of unsigned bytes from which the stream was created).

- The NetworkStream class exposes the DataAvailable property (which returns true when data is available on the stream for reading).

Stream Readers and Writers

Because the generic Stream object can read and write only individual bytes or groups of bytes, most of the time you use auxiliary stream reader and stream writer objects that enable you to work with more structured data, such as a line of text or a Double value. The .NET Framework offers several stream reader and writer pairs:

■ The BinaryReader and BinaryWriter types can work with primitive data in binary format, such as a float value or an encoded string.

■ The StreamReader and StreamWriter types can work with strings of text, such as the text you read from or write to a text file. These types can work in conjunction with an Encoder object, which determines how characters are encoded in the stream.

■ The StringReader type can read from a string; the StringWriter class can write to a String-Builder. (It can't write to a string because .NET strings are immutable.)

■ TextReader and TextWriter are abstract types that define how to work with strings of text in Unicode format. TextReader is the base type for the StreamReader and StringReader types; TextWriter is the base type for the StreamWriter and StringWriter types.

■ The XmlTextReader and XmlTextWriter types work with XML text.

■ The ResourceReader and ResourceWriter types work with resource files.

Reading and Writing Text Files

You typically use a StreamReader object to read from a text file. You can obtain a reference to such an object in many ways:

```
// With the File.OpenText static method
string fileName = @"c:\test.txt";
StreamReader sr = File.OpenText(fileName);

// With the OpenText instance method of a FileInfo object
FileInfo fi2 = new FileInfo(fileName);
StreamReader sr2 = fi2.OpenText();

// By passing a FileStream from the Open method of the File class to
// the StreamReader's constructor method
// (This technique lets you specify mode, access, and share mode.)
Stream st3 = File.Open(fileName, FileMode.Open, FileAccess.ReadWrite, FileShare.ReadWrite);
StreamReader sr3 = new StreamReader(st3);

// By opening a FileStream on the file and then passing it
// to the StreamReader's constructor method
FileStream fs4 = new FileStream(fileName, FileMode.Open);
StreamReader sr4 = new StreamReader(fs4);

// By getting a FileStream from the OpenRead method of the File class
// and passing it to the StreamReader's constructor
StreamReader sr5 = new StreamReader(File.OpenRead(fileName));
```

```
// By passing the filename to the StreamReader's constructor
StreamReader sr6 = new StreamReader(fileName);

// By passing the filename and encoding
StreamReader sr7 = new StreamReader(fileName, System.Text.Encoding.Unicode);
StreamReader sr8 = new StreamReader(fileName, System.Text.Encoding.ASCII);

// As before, but we let the system decide the best encoding.
StreamReader sr9 = new StreamReader(fileName, true);
```

The FileStream type in .NET Framework 2.0 has been expanded with new constructors to support two important new features. First, you can pass a FileSecurity object when you create a file, to specify the ACL associated with the file itself. Second, you can pass a FileOptions bit-coded value to specify additional options when opening a file. Supported values are None, SequentialScan (optimize caching for sequential access), RandomAccess (optimize caching for random access), WriteThrough (write data directly to disk, without buffering it), Encrypted (encrypt the file so that it can be read only by the same user account), Asynchronous (the file can be used for asynchronous reading and writing), and DeleteOnClose (the file is temporary and must be deleted when it's closed).

```
// Create a file for sequential reading and writing, with a 2K buffer;
// The file will be deleted when closed.
FileStream fs10 = new FileStream(@"c:\tryme.tmp", FileMode.CreateNew,
    FileAccess.ReadWrite, FileShare.Read, 2048,
    FileOptions.SequentialScan | FileOptions.DeleteOnClose);
```

After you get a reference to a StreamReader object, you can use one of its many methods to read one or more characters or whole text lines. The Peek method returns the code of the next character in the stream without actually extracting it, or it returns the special −1 value if there are no more characters. In practice, this method is used to test an end-of-file condition:

```
// Display all the text lines in a text file.
StreamReader sr = new StreamReader(fileName);
while ( sr.Peek() != -1 )
{
    Console.WriteLine(sr.ReadLine());
}
sr.Close();
```

Similarly to all stream-related objects, the StreamReader type implements the IDisposable interface, thus you can rewrite the previous code with a using block:

```
using ( StreamReader sr = new StreamReader(fileName) )
{
    while ( sr.Peek() != -1 )
    {
        Console.WriteLine(sr.ReadLine());
    }
}
```

In .NET Framework 2.0 you can rewrite the previous loop in a more readable style by means of the new EndOfStream read-only property:

```
while ( ! sr.EndOfStream )
{
    Console.WriteLine(sr.ReadLine());
}
```

You can also read one character at a time using the Read method, or you can read all the remaining characters using the ReadToEnd method:

```
// Read the entire contents of a file in one shot.
StreamReader sr = new StreamReader(fileName);
string fileContents = sr.ReadToEnd();
```

If you opened the StreamReader through a Stream object, you can use the Stream object's Seek method to move the pointer or read its current position. If you did not open the StreamReader through a Stream object, you can still access the inner Stream object that the .NET runtime creates anyway, through the StreamReader's BaseStream property:

```
// …(Continuing previous code example)…
// If the file is longer than 100 chars, process it again, one character at a
// time (admittedly a silly thing to do, but it's just a demo).
if ( fileContents.Length >= 100 )
{
    // Reset the stream's pointer to the beginning.
    sr.BaseStream.Seek(0, SeekOrigin.Begin);
    // Read individual characters until EOF is reached.
    while ( !sr.EndOfStream )
    {
        // Read method returns an integer, so convert it to Char.
        Console.Write((char) sr.Read());
    }
}
sr.Close();
```

You use a StreamWriter object to write to a text file. As with the StreamReader object, you can create a StreamWriter object in many ways:

```
// By means of the CreateText static method of the File type
string fileName = @"c:\test.dat";
StreamWriter sw1 = File.CreateText(fileName);

// By passing a FileStream from the Open method of the File type to
// the StreamWriter's constructor method
Stream st2 = File.Open(fileName, FileMode.Create, FileAccess.ReadWrite, FileShare.None);
StreamWriter sw2 = new StreamWriter(st2);

// By opening a FileStream on the file and then passing it
// to the StreamWriter's constructor
FileStream fs3 = new FileStream(fileName, FileMode.Open);
StreamWriter sw3 = new StreamWriter(fs3);
```

```
// By getting a FileStream from the OpenWrite method of the File type
// and passing it to the StreamWriter's constructor
StreamWriter sw4 = new StreamWriter(File.OpenWrite(fileName));

// By passing the filename to the StreamWriter's constructor
StreamWriter sw5 = new StreamWriter(fileName);
```

Other overloads of the StreamWriter's constructor enable you to specify whether the file is to be opened in append mode, the size of the buffer, and an Encoding object:

```
// Open the file in append mode, be prepared to output
// ASCII characters, and use a 2K buffer.
StreamWriter sw6 = new StreamWriter(fileName, true, Encoding.ASCII, 2024);
// Terminate each line with a null character followed by a newline character.
```

The NewLine property (new in .NET Framework 2.0) enables you to specify a nonstandard value for the line termination character:

```
// Terminate each line with a null character followed by a newline character.
sw6.NewLine = "\0\n";
```

The StreamWriter class exposes the Write and WriteLine methods: the Write method can write the textual representation of any basic data type (Int32, Double, and so on); the Write-Line method works only with strings and automatically appends a newline character. Leave the AutoFlush property set to false (the default value) if you want the StreamWriter to adopt a limited form of caching; you'll probably need to issue a Flush method periodically in this case. Set this property to true for those streams or devices, such as the console window, from which the user expects immediate feedback.

The following code uses a StreamReader object to read from a file and a StreamWriter object to copy the text to another file after converting the text to uppercase:

```
using ( StreamReader sr = new StreamReader("source.txt") )
{
    using ( StreamWriter sw = new StreamWriter("source.new") )
    {
        while ( ! sr.EndOfStream )
        {
            sw.WriteLine(sr.ReadLine().ToUpper());
        }
    }   // This actually writes data to the output file and closes it.
}       // This closes the input file.
```

If you're working with smaller text files, you can also trade some memory for speed and do without a loop. The following code keeps both the input and the output files entirely in memory:

```
// Notice that you don't strictly need curly braces for the outer using
// block, because it contains only one logical statement (the inner using block).
using ( StreamReader sr = new StreamReader("source.txt") )
```

```
using ( StreamWriter sw = new StreamWriter("source.new") )
{
    sw.Write(sr.ReadToEnd().ToUpper());
}
```

You should always close the Stream object after using it, either by means of a using block or explicitly with a Close method. If you fail to do so, the stream keeps the file open until the next garbage collection calls the Stream's Finalize method. There are at least two reasons why you'd rather close the stream manually. First, if the file is kept open longer than strictly necessary, you can't delete or move the underlying file, nor can another application open it for reading and/or writing (depending on the access mode you specified when opening the file). The second reason is performance: the code in the Stream's Close method calls the GC.Suppress-Finalize method, so the Stream object isn't finalized and therefore the resources it uses are released earlier.

Reading and Writing Binary Files

The BinaryReader and BinaryWriter types are suitable for working with binary streams; one such stream might be associated with a file containing data in native format. In this context, *native format* means the actual bits used to store the value in memory. You can't create a BinaryReader or BinaryWriter object directly from a filename as you can with the StreamReader and StreamWriter objects. Instead, you must create a Stream object explicitly and pass it to the constructor method of either the BinaryReader or the BinaryWriter class:

```
// Associate a stream with a new file opened with write access.
Stream st = File.Open(@"c:\values.dat", FileMode.Create, FileAccess.Write);
// Create a BinaryWriter associated with the output stream.
BinaryWriter bw = new BinaryWriter(st);
```

Working with the BinaryWriter object is especially simple because its Write method is overloaded to accept all the primitive .NET types, including signed and unsigned integers, floating-point numbers, and string values. The following code snippet writes 10 random Double values to a binary file:

```
// …(Continuing previous example)…
// Save 10 Double values to the file.
Random rand = new Random();
for ( int i = 1; i <= 10; i++ )
{
    bw.Write(rand.NextDouble());
}
// Flush the output data to the file.
bw.Close();
```

The BinaryReader class exposes many Read*Xxxx* methods, one for each possible native data type. Unlike the StreamReader type, which exposes an EndOfStream property, the

BinaryReader type requires that you use the PeekChar method to check whether other bytes are available:

```csharp
// Read back values written in previous example.

// Associate a stream with an existing file, opened with read access.
Stream st2 = File.Open(fileName, FileMode.Open, FileAccess.Read);
// Create a BinaryReader associated with the input stream.
using ( BinaryReader br2 = new BinaryReader(st2) )
{
    // Loop until data is available.
    while ( br2.PeekChar() != -1 )
    {
        // Read the next element. (We know it's a Double.)
        Console.WriteLine(br2.ReadDouble());
    }
    // Next statement closes both the BinaryReader and the underlying stream.
}
```

Outputting strings with a BinaryWriter requires some additional care, however. Passing a string to the Write method outputs a length-prefixed string to the stream. If you want to write only the actual characters (as happens when you're working with fixed-length strings), you must pass the Write method a Char array. The Write method is overloaded to take additional arguments that specify which portion of the array should be written.

Reading back strings requires different techniques as well, depending on how the string was written. You use the ReadString method for length-prefixed strings and the ReadChars method for fixed-length strings. You can see an example of these methods in action in the section titled "Memory Streams" shortly.

Note   File streams can be opened for asynchronous read and write operations, which can speed up your code's performance significantly. You'll learn about asynchronous file operations in Chapter 11.

Other Stream Types

Stream readers and writers aren't just for files, even though files are undoubtedly the most common kind of stream. In this last section, I cover other common types that derive from the Stream class.

Memory Streams

The MemoryStream object enables you to deal with memory as if it were a temporary file, a technique that usually delivers better performance than does using an actual file. The following code snippet shows how to write to and then read back 10 random numbers from a stream;

this example is similar to a code snippet illustrated earlier in this chapter, except this code uses a memory stream instead of a file stream:

```
// Create a memory stream with initial capacity of 1 KB.
MemoryStream st = new MemoryStream(1024);
BinaryWriter bw = new BinaryWriter(st);
Random rand = new Random();
// Write 10 random Double values to the stream.
for ( int i = 1; i <= 10; i++ )
{
    bw.Write(rand.NextDouble());
}

// Rewind the stream to the beginning and read back the data.
st.Seek(0, SeekOrigin.Begin);
BinaryReader br = new BinaryReader(st);
while ( br.PeekChar() != -1 )
{
    Console.WriteLine(br.ReadDouble());
}
bw.Close();
br.Close();
st.Close();
```

Of course, in this particular example you might have used an array to store random values and read them back. However, the approach based on streams enables you to move from a memory stream to a file-based stream by changing only one statement (the stream constructor).

This example writes three strings to a MemoryStream and then reads them back; it shows how to work with length-prefixed strings and two techniques for reading fixed-length strings:

```
MemoryStream st = new MemoryStream(1000);
BinaryWriter bw = new BinaryWriter(st);
// The BinaryWriter.Write method outputs a length-prefixed string.
bw.Write("a length-prefixed string");
// We'll use this 1-KB buffer for both reading and writing.
char[] buffer = new char[1024];

string s = "13 Characters";            // A fixed-length string
s.CopyTo(0, buffer, 0, s.Length);       // Copy into the buffer.
bw.Write(buffer, 0, s.Length);          // Output first 13 chars in buffer.
bw.Write(buffer, 0, s.Length);          // Do it a second time.

// Rewind the stream, and prepare to read from it.
st.Seek(0, SeekOrigin.Begin);
BinaryReader br = new BinaryReader(st);
// Reading the length-prefixed string is simple.
Console.WriteLine(br.ReadString());     // => a length-prefixed string

// Read the fixed-length string (13 characters) into the buffer.
br.Read(buffer, 0, 13);
s = new string(buffer, 0, 13);          // Convert to a string.
Console.WriteLine(s);                   // => 13 Characters
```

```
// Another way to read a fixed-length string (13 characters)
// (ReadChars returns a Char array that we can pass to the string constructor.)
s = new string(br.ReadChars(13));
Console.WriteLine(s);                    // => 13 Characters
```

String-Based Streams

If the data you want to read is already contained in a string variable, you can use a StringReader object to retrieve portions of it. For example, you can load the entire contents of a text file or a multiline text box control into a string and then extract the individual lines by using the StringReader.ReadLine method:

```
// The veryLongString variable contains the text to parse.
StringReader strReader = new StringReader(veryLongString);
// Display individual lines of text.
while ( strReader.Peek() != -1 )
{
    Console.WriteLine(strReader.ReadLine());
}
```

Of course, you can implement the same technique in other, equivalent ways—for example, by using the Split function to get an array with all the individual lines of code—but the solution based on the StringReader object is more resource-friendly because it doesn't duplicate the data in memory. As a matter of fact, the StringReader and StringWriter types don't even create an internal Stream object to store the characters; rather, they use the string itself as the backing store for the stream. (This fact explains why these two types don't expose the BaseStream property.)

You use a StringWriter object to output values to a string. However, you can't associate it with a String object because .NET strings are immutable. Instead, you have to create a StringBuilder and then associate it with a StringWriter object:

```
// Create a string with the space-separated abbreviated names of weekdays.
StringBuilder sb = new StringBuilder();
// The StringWriter associated with the StringBuilder
StringWriter strWriter = new StringWriter(sb);

// Output day names to the string.
foreach ( string d in DateTimeFormatInfo.CurrentInfo.AbbreviatedDayNames )
{
    strWriter.Write(d);
    strWriter.Write(" ");                // Append a space.
}
Console.WriteLine(sb);                   // => Sun Mon Tue Wed Thu Fri Sat
```

Network Streams

The .NET Framework supports exchanging data over the network using Transmission Control Protocol (TCP) by means of TcpClient and TcpListener types, both in the System.Net.Sockets namespace. TCP ensures that data is either correctly received or an exception is thrown, and for this reason it is the preferred protocol when you can't afford to lose data. The applications involved in data exchange can reside on the same computer or on different computers over the LAN or connected through the Internet. The actual data sent over the wire is read from and written to a NetworkStream object, also in the System.Net.Sockets namespace.

TCP assumes you have a server application that listens to requests coming from one or more clients. The client and the server applications must agree on the port number as well as the format of the data being sent over the wire. In the following example, the client application sends the name of a text file as a string terminated with a CR-LF character. The server application receives the filename sent from the client, searches the file in a specific directory, and sends the file's contents back to the client. Because the file contents can be of any length, the server application prefixes the actual data with a line containing the length of the data so that the client can read the exact number of bytes from NetworkStream. (In a real-world application, using a length prefix is important because a single server-side send operation can translate into multiple receive operations on the client side.) Both applications terminate when the client sends an empty filename to the server.

The server application must create a TcpListener object that listens to a given port and accepts incoming requests from clients. The AcceptTcpClient method waits until a connection is made and returns the TcpClient object that represents the client making the request. The GetStream method of this TcpClient object returns a NetworkStream that the server application can use to read data from clients and send them a result.

```
// The server application
sealed public class ServerApp
{
    public static void Main()
    {
        // Listen to port 2048.
        IPAddress localhostAddress = IPAddress.Loopback;
        TcpListener tcpList = new TcpListener(localhostAddress, 2048);
        tcpList.Start();

        while ( true )
        {
            // Wait for the next client to make a request.
            Console.WriteLine("Waiting for data from clients...");
            TcpClient tcpCli = tcpList.AcceptTcpClient();
            // Read data sent by the client (a CR-LF-separated string in this case).
            NetworkStream ns = tcpCli.GetStream();
            StreamReader sr = new StreamReader(ns);
            string receivedData = sr.ReadLine();

            if ( receivedData.Length > 0 )
            {
                // Read a file with this name from the c:\docs directory
                string fileName = Path.Combine(@"c:\docs", receivedData);
                Console.WriteLine("Reading file {0}...", fileName);
```

```
            string resultData = null;
            try
            {
                resultData = File.ReadAllText(fileName);
            }
            catch ( Exception ex )
            {
                resultData = "*** ERROR: " + ex.Message;
            }
            SendData(ns, resultData);
        }
        // Release resources and close the NetworkStream.
        sr.Close();
        ns.Close();
        tcpCli.Close();
        // Exit if the client sent an empty string.
        if ( receivedData.Length == 0 )
        {
            break;
        }
    }
    // Reject client requests from now on.
    tcpList.Stop();
}

// Send a length-prefixed string.
public static void SendData(NetworkStream ns, string data)
{
    // Send it back to the client.
    StreamWriter sw = new StreamWriter(ns);
    sw.WriteLine(data.Length);
    sw.Write(data);
    sw.Flush();                // This is VERY important.
    sw.Close();
}
}
```

The client code must instantiate a TcpClient object that references the server application by means of the server application's URL and port number. (The port number should be in the range of 1024 to 65535.) Next, the client invokes the TcpClient.GetStream method to retrieve the NetworkStream object that can be used to send and receive data from the server.

```
// The client application
sealed public class ClientApp
{
    public static void Main()
    {
        while ( true )
        {
            // Ask the end user for a filename.
            Console.Write("Enter a filename [an empty string to quit] >> ");
            string fileName = Console.ReadLine();
```

```
// This code assumes a server on local machine is listening to port 2048.
TcpClient tcpCli = new TcpClient("localhost", 2048);
// Retrieve the stream that can send and receive data.
NetworkStream ns = tcpCli.GetStream();
// Send a CR-LF-termined string to the server.

StreamWriter sw = new StreamWriter(ns);
sw.WriteLine(fileName);
sw.Flush();                            // This is VERY important!

if ( fileName.Length > 0 )
{
    // Receive data from the server application and display it.
    string resultData = ReadData(ns);
    Console.WriteLine(resultData);
}
// Release resources and close the NetworkStream.
sw.Close();
ns.Close();
if ( fileName.Length == 0 )
{
    break;
}
        }
    }
}

// Read a length-prefixed string.
public static string ReadData(NetworkStream ns)
{
    StreamReader sr = new StreamReader(ns);
    int dataLength = int.Parse(sr.ReadLine());
    char[] buffer = new char[dataLength];
    sr.Read(buffer, 0, dataLength);
    sr.Close();
    return new string(buffer);
    }
}
```

To test this code, create a directory named c:\docs and store a few text files in it. Compile the server and the client applications as separate Console projects and run both of them. Enter the name of a file in the client application and wait for the server to send back the textual content of the file.

Alternatively, you can create a solution that contains both these projects; then, right-click the solution item in the Solution Explorer window and select the Properties command. Select the Startup Project page in the dialog box that appears, click the Multiple Startup Projects radio button, and set the Action value to Start for both the server-side and client-side projects. (See Figure 7-3.) If you now press F5 or select the Start command from the Debug menu, both projects will be launched.

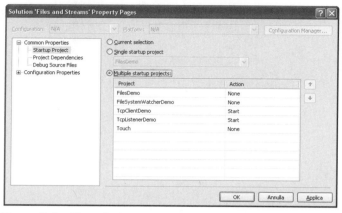

Figure 7-3   The solution's Property Pages dialog box, which enables you to decide which project to run when you press the F5 key

The NetworkStream type exposes a few other members of interest. For example, the DataAvailable property returns true if there is data waiting to be read. Network streams don't support the seek operation; thus, the CanSeek property always returns false and the Seek method throws an exception, as do the Length and Position properties.

The most important feature added in .NET Framework 2.0 is the support for timeouts through the ReadTimeout and WriteTimeout properties. By default, all read and write operations wait until data can be received or sent, but if you assign a value (in milliseconds) to these properties, any operation that doesn't complete within the specified timeout throws an IOException object.

Note   As with all the applications that exchange data using TCP, these sample applications (more precisely, the server application) might open a security hole on your computer because in theory a remote client might use the application to read the contents of a file on your computer. It is therefore essential that you protect your system by using other methods (for example, a firewall) and that you terminate the server application as soon as you're done with your experiments.

Buffered Streams

Most of the stream types in the .NET Framework provide a transparent mechanism for buffering, for example, the FileStream type, whereas other types never require buffering because they already map to a block of memory, as is the case with the MemoryStream, the StringReader, and StringWriter types. The remaining stream types, for example, the NetworkStream type, don't use any internal cache mechanism; thus, writing to and reading small pieces of data from them can be extremely inefficient. In such cases, you can improve performance by using an auxiliary BufferedStream object.

Using a BufferedStream object is quite simple and amounts to using this object to "wrap" another (unbuffered) stream. For example, let's say that you have the following piece of code:

```
// Initialize the array here (omitted).
string[] arr;
…
// Send the array of strings to a TCP server application.
TcpClient tcpCli = new TcpClient("localhost", 2048);
NetworkStream ns = tcpCli.GetStream();
StreamWriter sw = new StreamWriter(ns);
foreach ( string s in arr )
{
    sw.WriteLine(s);
}
```

You can make this code faster using a BufferedStream object by replacing the statement in bold type with these two lines:

```
BufferedStream bufStream = new BufferedStream(ns, 8192);
StreamWriter sw = new StreamWriter(bufStream);
```

The second argument passed to the BufferedStream's constructor is the size of the buffer; if omitted a default size of 4,096 bytes is used.

The great thing about the BufferedStream type is that it manages its internal buffer in a very smart way. If you read or write a piece of data larger than the buffer's size, the buffer isn't even used for that specific read or write operation; if you only read and write large pieces of data, the buffer isn't even allocated. You get the best performance with the BufferedStream if you perform a series of read or write operations, but don't alternate often between reads and writes.

Compressed Streams

 Two new types for compressing data have been added in version 2.0 of the .NET Framework: DeflateStream and GZipStream, both in the System.IO.Compression namespace. Both types enable you to compress and uncompress the bytes that flow through the stream; they expose a very similar interface and are virtually interchangeable; the only substantial difference is the format of their compressed output.

The DeflateStream type uses the Deflate compression algorithm, a patent-free algorithm that combines the LZ77 algorithm and Huffman coding; the main advantage of this algorithm is that data of any length can be compressed and uncompressed using an intermediate buffer of limited size. The GZipStream type uses the same compression algorithm, but it includes a cyclic redundancy check (CRC) value to detect data corruption.

The peculiarity of these two types is that they can work only together with another stream-based object. In fact, a DeflatedStream or GZipStream object "wraps" another stream that actually writes to the actual medium (if you are compressing data) or reads from the medium (if you are uncompressing data). Given the similarities between the two types, I show how to use just the DeflateStream type.

Compressing data is the easiest operation if you already have the data in a Byte array. For example, the following code uses the File.ReadAllBytes method to read the entire source file (that is, the uncompressed file) and compresses it into a new file:

```csharp
string uncompressedFile = "source.txt";
string compressedFile = "source.zip";
// Read the source (uncompressed) file in the buffer.
byte[] buffer = File.ReadAllBytes(uncompressedFile);
// Open the destination (compressed) file with a FileStream object.
FileStream outStream = new FileStream(compressedFile, FileMode.Create);
// Wrap a DeflateStream object around the output stream.
DeflateStream zipStream = new DeflateStream(outStream, CompressionMode.Compress);
// Write the contents of the buffer.
zipStream.Write(buffer, 0, buffer.Length);
// Flush compressed data and close all output streams.
zipStream.Flush();
zipStream.Close();
outStream.Close();
```

Things are slightly more complicated if the source file is too long to be read in memory and you must process it in chunks. The following reusable procedure adopts a more resource-savvy approach:

```csharp
public static void CompressFile(string uncompressedFile, string compressedFile)
{
    // Open the source (uncompressed) file, using a 4-KB input buffer.
    using ( FileStream inStream = new FileStream(uncompressedFile,
        FileMode.Open, FileAccess.Read, FileShare.None, 4096) )
    {
        // Open the destination (compressed) file by using a FileStream object.
        using ( FileStream outStream = new FileStream(compressedFile, FileMode.Create) )
        {
            // Wrap a DeflateStream object around the output stream.
            using ( DeflateStream zipStream = new DeflateStream(outStream,
                CompressionMode.Compress) )
            {
                // Prepare a 4K read buffer .
                byte[] buffer = new byte[4096];
                while ( true )
                {
                    // Read up to 4 KB from the input file; exit the loop if no more bytes.
                    int readBytes = inStream.Read(buffer, 0, buffer.Length);
                    if ( readBytes == 0 )
                    {
                        break;
                    }
```

```
                    // Write the contents of the buffer to the compressed stream.
                    zipStream.Write(buffer, 0, readBytes);
                }
                // Flush and close all streams.
                zipStream.Flush();
            }                            // Close the DeflateStream object.
        }                                // Close the output FileStream object.
    }                                    // Close the input FileStream object.
}
```

When decompressing a compressed file, you have no choice: you must process the incoming data in chunks. Here's the reason: when you read N compressed bytes, you don't know how many data bytes the decompress process will create. Here's a reusable method that implements all the necessary steps:

```
public static void UncompressFile(string compressedFile, string uncompressedFile)
{
    // Open the output (uncompressed) file, use a 4-KB output buffer.
    using ( FileStream outStream = new FileStream(uncompressedFile,
        FileMode.Create, FileAccess.Write, FileShare.None, 4096) )
    {
        // Open the source (compressed) file.
        using ( FileStream inStream = new FileStream(compressedFile, FileMode.Open) )
        {
            // Wrap the DeflateStream object around the input stream.
            using ( DeflateStream zipStream = new DeflateStream(inStream,
                CompressionMode.Decompress) )
            {
                // Prepare a 4K buffer.
                byte[] buffer = new byte[4096];
                while ( true )
                {
                    // Read enough compressed bytes to fill the 4-KB buffer.
                    int bytesRead = zipStream.Read(buffer, 0, 4096);
                    // Exit the loop if no more bytes were read.
                    if ( bytesRead == 0 )
                    {
                        break;
                    }
                    // Else, write these bytes to the uncompressed file, and loop.
                    outStream.Write(buffer, 0, bytesRead);
                }
                // Ensure that cached bytes are written correctly and close all streams.
                outStream.Flush();
            }                            // Close the DeflateStream object.
        }                                // Close the input FileStream object.
    }                                    // Close the output FileStream object.
}
```

Let's recap the rules for using the DeflateStream type correctly. When compressing data, you pass the output stream to the DeflateStream's constructor and specify CompressionMode .Compress in the second argument, and then you write the (uncompressed) bytes using the

DeflateStream.Write method. Conversely, when uncompressing data, you pass the input stream to the DeflateStream's constructor and specify CompressionMode.Decompress in the second argument, and then you read (compressed) bytes with the DeflateStream.Read method.

Finally, remember that you can use the DeflateStream and GZipStream types in a chain of streams; for example, you can output data to a BufferedStream object, which cascades to a DeflateStream object, which uses a NetworkStream object to send the compressed data across the wire. You can see a use for compressed streams in the section titled "A Practical Example: Compressed Serialization" in Chapter 12, "Object Serialization."

Chapter 8
Assemblies and Resources

All the Microsoft Visual C# applications you've seen so far were stand-alone executables, with all the code included in a single .exe file. Larger programs, however, are usually split into multiple executables—typically one .exe file and one or more DLLs. In this chapter, you'll see how easy creating a class library is and how you can be prepared to deal with versioning issues.

Note To avoid long lines, code samples in this chapter assume that the following using statements are used at the top of each source file:

```
using System;
using System.Collections;
using System.ComponentModel;
using System.Configuration;
using System.Diagnostics;
using System.Globalization;
using System.IO;
using System.Reflection;
using System.Resources;
using System.Runtime.CompilerServices;
using System.Runtime.InteropServices;
using System.Security.Permissions;
using System.Threading;
```

Assemblies

From a physical point of view, an assembly is just a collection of one or more executable and nonexecutable modules (examples of nonexecutable modules are resource, image, and HTML files). From a logical perspective, an assembly is the smallest unit of reuse, versioning, and deployment for .NET applications. For example, you can't assign different version numbers to the various files that make up an assembly.

When you're deciding which types should go in the same assembly, consider the following points:

- **Code reuse**   The assembly is the smallest unit of reuse, so you should keep together types that are normally used together.

- **Versioning**   The assembly is also the smallest unit of versioning, and all the modules in an assembly have the same versioning information.

- **Scoping**   The assembly scope (enforced by the internal keyword) lets you define which types are visible from outside the module in which they're defined, but not from the outside world.

In Microsoft .NET Framework version 2.0, you can have an assembly expose its internal types to other assemblies by means of the InternalsVisibleTo attribute, as I explain later in this chapter.

Private and Shared Assemblies

The .NET Framework supports two types of assemblies: private and shared. The latter type is also known as a *strong-named* or *signed* assembly for reasons that are explained in the next section.

A private assembly can be stored only in the main application's directory (or one of its subdirectories) and therefore can be used only by that application or another application installed in the same directory. Private assemblies are simpler to build and administer than shared assemblies are; they support XCOPY deployment and you can install a complete application simply by copying all its files and directories to the target computer's hard disk without having to register anything. (Of course, you still have to create shortcuts from the Start menu and other, similar amenities, but the concept should be clear.) In most circumstances, private assemblies are the best choice to make, even though you might end up with multiple identical copies of the same assembly in different directories. Private assemblies can help put an end to so-called DLL hell, and any developer or system administrator should be glad to trade some inexpensive disk space for more robust code.

A strong-named assembly is usually installed in a well-defined location of the hard disk, under the \Windows\Assembly directory. This location is known as the global assembly cache (GAC). The .NET Framework installs a special shell extension that lets you browse this directory with Windows Explorer and display information about all the assemblies installed in the GAC, including their version and culture. (See Figure 8-1.) You can also display more extensive version information by right-clicking an item and selecting Properties on the shortcut menu, an action that brings up the Properties dialog box for that assembly.

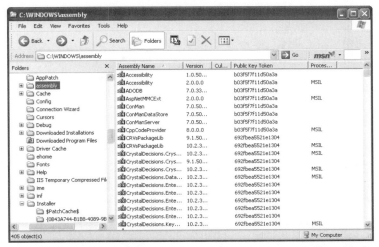

Figure 8-1   The global assembly cache as seen inside Windows Explorer

The assembly's public key token is a sort of signature of the software company that published the assembly. The public key token is a 64-bit hash value derived from the publisher's public key (which is 1,024 bits long, or 128 bytes); it isn't guaranteed to be universally unique like the public key, but it can be considered unique for most practical purposes.

What you see in Windows Explorer doesn't match the actual physical structure of the \Windows\Assembly directory. In fact, the GAC contains several directories, one for each assembly. In turn, each directory contains a subdirectory for each version of the assembly. For example, the System.dll assembly belonging to .NET Framework 2.0 is found in this directory:

```
C:\WINDOWS\assembly\GAC_MSIL\System\2.0.0.0__b77a5c561934e089
```

in which 2.0. 0.0 is the version of the assembly and b77a5c561934e089 is the Microsoft public key token.

 Starting with .NET Framework 2.0, there are actually several GAC directories: GAC_MSIL is for portable assemblies containing platform-independent IL code that will be JIT-compiled as needed; GAC_32 is for assemblies containing native 32-bit code, and GAC_64 is for assemblies containing native 64-bit code. If you've installed version 1.0 or 1.1 of the .NET Framework, you'll also find a directory named GAC.

This directory structure enables you to store different versions of the same assembly without any filename conflicts. You can bypass the Microsoft Windows shell extension and freely explore the real structure of the GAC by opening a command-prompt window and navigating to the C:\Windows\Assembly directory. Notice, however, that the GAC structure is an implementation detail and you shouldn't rely on this structure if you want to be compatible with future versions.

You can add to and delete assemblies from the GAC only if you have administrative rights on the system, which makes .NET applications that work with strong-named assemblies in the GAC inherently more robust than those that work with private assemblies. You can add to or remove assemblies from the GAC using a utility named GACUTIL, and you can remove an assembly from the GAC by selecting Uninstall on the shortcut menu inside Windows Explorer.

There are several key differences between private and shared assemblies:

- A signed (shared) assembly supports version information, and the GAC can keep different versions of the same assembly without any conflict so that each application can continue to work with the version it was compiled against (unless the administrator opts for a different binding policy). Private assemblies can be versioned, but version information is for your reference only, and the CLR doesn't use it. A private assembly is supposed to be deployed with the application itself, so the CLR doesn't enforce any special versioning policy.

- A signed assembly in the GAC makes your applications more robust in two ways. First, when the assembly is added to the cache, an integrity check is performed on all the files in the assembly to ensure that they haven't been altered after the compilation. Second, only the system administrator can install or remove an assembly from the GAC.

- A signed assembly in the GAC is more efficient than a private assembly is because the CLR can locate it faster and it doesn't need to be verified. Moreover, if multiple applications reference the same signed assembly, the CLR can load only one instance in memory in most circumstances (which saves resources and improves load time even more).

- Two (or more) versions of a signed assembly can run in the same process. For example, an application might use version 1.0 of an assembly named A and an assembly named B that uses version 1.1 of the A assembly. This important feature is called *side-by-side execution*, and it ensures that you won't have a compatibility problem when you mix components together.

- A signed assembly can be signed with an Authenticode digital signature. The signing mechanism uses a public key encryption schema, which guarantees that a particular assembly was created by a given manufacturer and that no one tampered with it.

Signed assemblies are usually stored in the GAC, but this isn't a requirement. For example, you might deploy a signed assembly in a known directory on the hard disk, where two or more applications can find it. However, only signed assemblies in the GAC benefit from all the advantages in the preceding list. (Signed assemblies deployed in other directories do support side-by-side execution and public key signing, though.)

As a rule, you write code for private and signed assemblies in the same way because the only difference between them is an attribute in your code (or an option that you set through Microsoft Visual Studio). However, the main goal in building signed assemblies is to share them among different applications, so you must take some constraints into account. For example, a shared assembly shouldn't create temporary files with fixed names and paths because calls from different clients might overwrite such files. Moreover, the .NET Framework supports side-by-side execution of shared assemblies in the same process (not just on the same machine), so a shared assembly shouldn't depend on process-wide resources.

Strong Names

The CLR looks for private assemblies only inside the caller application's directory tree, so the developer is in charge of avoiding naming conflicts for the private assemblies the application references. On the other hand, shared assemblies are typically deployed in the GAC, so it's vital for the CLR to distinguish shared assemblies that have the same name but that come from different publishers.

The .NET Framework ensures that a shared assembly's name is unique at the system level by assigning the assembly a strong name. You can think of a strong name as the combination of a textual name, a version number, a culture, a public key, and a value indicating the processor architecture. When displayed in a human-readable format, a strong name looks like the following text:

```
mscorlib, Version=2.0.0.0, Culture=neutral,
PublicKeyToken=b77a5c561934e089, ProcessorArchitecture=x86
```

The public key token is displayed in lieu of the longer public key. The previous string is always known as the *display name* of the assembly to distinguish it from the assembly's name, which is the filename without the .dll extension (as in mscorlib).

The ProcessorArchitecture value is new in .NET Framework 2.0 and is used to differentiate among versions of the same assembly that are compiled for specific processors. This value can be MSIL (processor-independent), x86 (all 32-bit processors), IA64 (Itanium 64-bit), or AMD64 (AMD 64-bit). This value helps the CLR bind the correct version of the assembly and prevents the installation of an assembly that is incompatible with the target system. Notice that a 64-bit machine can run assemblies marked for the x86 processor architecture: in this case, the assembly runs in the Windows-on-Windows (WOW) environment that emulates the 32-bit architecture.

In most cases, you create processor-independent assemblies, but you might need to compile a platform-specific assembly if your code must behave differently on different platforms. For example, this action is necessary when you use PInvoke to call a method in the Windows API and you know that the 32-bit and 64-bit versions of that method behave differently. Another time you might compile a platform-specific assembly is when you're using a COM component, which forces you to specify the x86 processor architecture so that your application will run in a WOW environment on 64-bit machines.

You can create platform-specific compiled assemblies by selecting an item in the Platform Target combo box on the Build page of the project designer. (See Figure 8-2.)

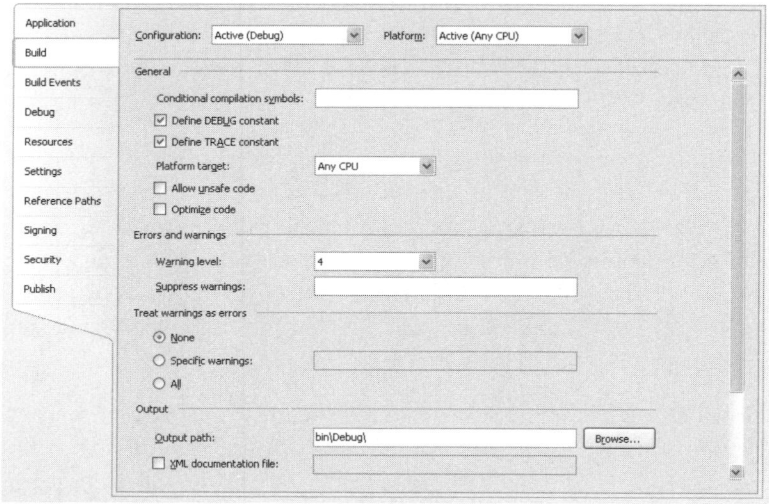

Figure 8-2   The Build page of the project designer

The security mechanism is based on a public key encryption method, but you don't have to be a cryptography wizard to create assemblies with strong names.

You generate strong-named assemblies in a two-step process. First, you run the Strong Name (SN) command-line utility to create an .snk file that contains a random-generated public and private key pair. Second, you add an assembly-level attribute to tell the compiler that the public key in that .snk file must be burned into the executable file. You can perform these steps manually, but in most cases you'll use Visual Studio 2005 for both of them.

You generate a random public and private key pair from the command line by using the –k option of the SN utility, which is located in the \Program Files\Microsoft Visual Studio 8\SDK\v2.0\Bin directory:

```
sn -k mykey.snk
```

This command creates the mykey.snk file, which contains the two keys. Store this file in a safe place (and make copies of it if necessary) because from now on you should use it to sign all the strong-named assemblies produced by your company.

After creating an .snk file, you can choose from several ways to produce an assembly with a strong name. If you're compiling from the command prompt, you use the CSC program with the /keyfile option for single-file assemblies, or you use the Assembly Linker utility (AL) with the /keyfile option for assemblies made of multiple files. The preferred way to create a signed assembly, however, is by inserting an AssemblyKeyFile attribute into the application's source code (typically into the AssemblyInfo.cs file):

```
[assembly: AssemblyKeyFile(@"c:\myapp\mykey.snk")]
```

The filename must be an absolute path so that it can reference the only .snk file that you use for all the strong assemblies you produce.

As I mentioned before, Visual Studio 2005 is capable of performing both these steps for you. Open the Signing page of the project designer, select the Sign The Assembly check box, select the <New...> element from the combo box below it, and then select a name for the .snk file that will be created and associated with the current project. (See Figure 8-3.) In most cases, however, you'll use the <Browse...> element from the combo box to point to the .snk file that contains the public and private keys of your company.

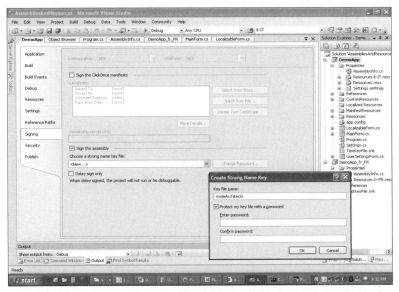

Figure 8-3   The Signing page of the project designer and the dialog box where you define a new .snk file

Note   Visual Studio gives you the ability to protect new publishers' key files with a password, which must be at least six characters long. It is strongly recommended that you use this option, which in fact is enabled by default. In this case, the file being produced has a .pfx extension (Personal Information Exchange), and users will be prompted for the password when they try to use this file. A .pfx file can be added to a certificate container.

Regardless of whether you're creating a new .snk file or are pointing to an existing file, Visual Studio copies the file in the project's folder, so you can copy your source files to another computer without any problem. To support this feature, Visual Studio doesn't generate an AssemblyKeyFile attribute (which requires an absolute path); instead, it uses the /keyfile option when it invokes the CSC compiler.

The AssemblyInfo.cs file that Visual Studio automatically creates in the Properties folder contains an AssemblyVersion attribute with an argument equal to 1.0.0.0:

```
[assembly: AssemblyVersion("1.0.0.0")]
```

The manifest section of any other assembly that references the signed assembly you've just signed will include the signed assembly's public key. When the caller assembly invokes one of the types in the signed assembly, the CLR compares the public key token in the manifest with the signed assembly's public key token so that the caller can be completely sure that the signed assembly hasn't been tampered with. (The CLR uses this 8-byte token instead of the entire public key to save space in the caller assembly manifest.) Notice that any .NET executable can reference a signed assembly, but a signed assembly can reference only other signed assemblies.

This mechanism just described ensures that the signed assembly hasn't been modified, but it doesn't ensure that the signed assembly actually comes from a specific software manufacturer. This latter issue is solved through full Authenticode signatures that can be applied to signed assemblies. These Authenticode signatures add a certificate that establishes trust. You can apply this Authenticode signature to an existing assembly by running the Signcode.exe utility.

Because strong names are a combination of a text name and a public key, they guarantee name uniqueness. If two companies use the same name for their (distinct) assemblies, their public keys are different and therefore the strong names are different as well. Name uniqueness extends to all versions of the same assembly, and the CLR ensures that—when it's opting for a given version of an assembly requested by a managed class—only assemblies coming from the same software company will be taken into account.

Installing in the GAC

The preferred way to install signed assemblies is to register them in the GAC. You can use a drag-and-drop operation or the GACUTIL command-line utility. Using a drag-and-drop operation is simple: use Windows Explorer to navigate to the \Windows\Assembly directory, and drop the DLL on the right-hand pane. (See Figure 8-1.) Running the GACUTIL utility is also straightforward and has the added benefit of being an action that you can include in an installation script:

```
gacutil /i testassembly.dll
```

You can add a command to the Tools menu in Visual Studio that runs this command on the current project by means of the External Tools command, or you can run it automatically after each successful build by means of a build event.

The /i command overwrites any assembly in the GAC with the same identity, but doesn't remove copies of the same assembly with a different version number because one of the goals of the GAC is to store multiple versions of the same assembly. Each new version that you install is added to the GAC, so you should periodically clear intermediate versions of the assembly from the GAC or run GACUTIL using the /u command to remove an outdated version of the assembly before installing a more recent one. You can list all the files in the GAC by means of the /l command.

The GACUTIL command can also specify an assembly trace reference, with the /r option. A *trace reference* maintains information about which application uses the assembly in the GAC so that the uninstall procedure for the application can determine whether it should remove the assembly GAC or should leave it there because it is being used by other applications. Applications installed with the Microsoft Installer (MSI) automatically add a trace reference and remove it when the application is uninstalled. Read MSDN documentation for more information about this option.

Adding an assembly to the GAC doesn't make your assembly visible in the Visual Studio Add Reference dialog box. This dialog box never parses the GAC and just displays assemblies located in the following two directories: C:\WINDOWS\Microsoft.NET\Framework*vx.y.zzzz* (the main .NET Framework directory) and C:\Program Files\Microsoft Visual Studio8\ Common7\IDE\.

PublicAssemblies. You might save your assemblies to the latter directory to make them quickly selectable from inside Visual Studio. Even better, you can add a new registry key under the HKEY_LOCAL_MACHINE\SOFTWARE\Microsoft\.

.NETFramework\AssemblyFolders key, name it MyAssemblies (or any name you like), and set the default value of this key equal to the directory that contains your assemblies (either private or shared). The next time you launch Visual Studio you'll see all the assemblies in this directory in the list of selectable ones.

 By default, Visual Studio doesn't take the version number into account when referencing a strong-named assembly that isn't part of the current solution. This behavior enables you to replace the referenced assembly with a newer version without having to update the reference. The application's manifest will point to the version of the reference at compilation time. You can disable this behavior by selecting the specific reference, pressing the F4 key to bring up the Properties window, and setting the Specific Version property to true. (See Figure 8-4.)

Figure 8-4   Properties of an assembly reference

Assembly-Level Attributes

You can set many assembly properties directly from inside your source code by using the many attribute classes in the System.Reflection namespace. All C# projects include a file named AssemblyInfo.cs, which contains template code for the attributes described in this section. Although you can place assembly-level attributes in any source file of your project—provided that they are outside a type definition—it is recommended that you define them in the AssemblyInfo.cs file, which is located in the Properties folder.

Here's the abridged version of the AssemblyInfo.cs file you can find in a newly created C# project:

```
using System.Reflection;
using System.Runtime.CompilerServices;
using System.Runtime.InteropServices;

[assembly: AssemblyTitle("DemoApp")]
[assembly: AssemblyDescription("")]
[assembly: AssemblyConfiguration("")]
[assembly: AssemblyCompany("Code Architects")]
[assembly: AssemblyProduct("DemoApp")]
[assembly: AssemblyCopyright("Copyright © Code Architects 2006")]
[assembly: AssemblyTrademark("")]
[assembly: AssemblyCulture("")]
[assembly: ComVisible(false)]

// The following GUID is for the ID of the typelib if this project is exposed to COM.
[assembly: Guid("533482ca-7480-4a4b-9333-b4142466cd8e")]

[assembly: AssemblyVersion("1.0.0.0")]
[assembly: AssemblyFileVersion("1.0.0.0")]
```

 Conveniently, Visual Studio 2005 lets you change these attributes without editing the AssemblyInfo.cs file directly. You simply have to display the project designer, select the Application page, and click the Assembly Information button (see Figure 8-5).

Figure 8-5   The Assembly Information dialog box

Table 8-1 lists the most important assembly-level attributes that the CLR supports. (Attributes related to COM Interop and security aren't included.)

Table 8-1   Assembly-Level Attributes

Attribute	Description
AssemblyCompany	The company name.
AssemblyConfiguration	A custom configuration setting to be stored in the assembly's manifest.
AssemblyCopyright	The copyright string.
AssemblyCulture	The supported culture. Passing a nonempty string marks the assembly as a satellite assembly, which is an assembly that contains only resources for a given culture; don't use a nonempty string for a regular assembly.
AssemblyDelaySign	Marks the assembly for partial or delayed signing. (Takes true or false; requires either AssemblyKeyFile or AssemblyKeyName.)
AssemblyDescription	The product description string.
AssemblyFileVersion	The Win32 version number, which doesn't have to be equal to the assembly version.
AssemblyFlags	Assembly flags, which tell which degree of side-by-side support the assembly offers.
AssemblyInformational Version	Informational version. A string version to be used in product and marketing literature.
AssemblyKeyFile	The file that contains the public/private key to make a signed assembly (or only the public key if partial signing).
AssemblyKeyName	The key container that holds the public/private key pair.
AssemblyProduct	The name of the product.
AssemblyTitle	The title for the assembly.
AssemblyTrademark	The trademark string.
AssemblyVersion	The assembly version number; can use the asterisk (*) for the revision and build or just for the build number to let the CLR generate version numbers using a time-based algorithm.
CLSCompliant	Whether the assembly is or isn't compliant with CLS guidelines.
InternalsVisibleTo	Nonpublic types in the assembly are visible to another assembly specified by the argument. (New in .NET Framework 2.0.)
NeutralResourcesLanguage	The neutral culture of the assembly.
ObfuscateAssembly	Instructs obfuscation tools to use their standard obfuscation rules for the appropriate assembly types. (New in .NET Framework 2.0.)
Obfuscation	Instructs obfuscation tools to apply obfuscation to this assembly. (New in .NET Framework 2.0.)
SatelliteContractVersion	The version of satellite assemblies, if different from version of main assembly.

The InternalsVisibleTo Attribute

 Version 2.0 of the .NET Framework supports the concept of *friend assemblies*, that is, assemblies that can reference nonpublic types defined in another assembly. Friend assemblies are important because they solve a frequent issue of Microsoft .NET Framework version 1.1 assemblies.

Let's say that you have two units of code that you must compile into separate assemblies A and B—for example, because they have different security settings or because they are written in different .NET languages. (As for the second requirement, you might use the Assembly Linker tool to create an assembly that combines modules written in different languages, but in practice this is a nuisance and few developers want to take that path.) Next, suppose that assembly B (and only assembly B) needs to access a few types in assembly A. Alas, if you mark those types with the public keyword, they will be visible to *all* external assemblies.

Version 1.1 of the .NET Framework doesn't offer an elegant solution to this recurring problem. The .NET Framework 1.1 technique that gets closer is based on the StrongNameIdentity-Permission attribute, which grants access to a type only to certain assemblies:

```
// Make the ConfidentialData type visible to all assemblies with a given public key.
[StrongNameIdentityPermission(SecurityAction.RequestMinimum,
    PublicKey="002400683011af5799aced238935f32ab125790aa787786343440023410" +
    "073958138838746ac86ef8732623f87978223aced6767169876acde74e59a6457be26ee0" +
    "045467467ce68a123cdef89648292518478536964ace47852361985636487523b7e0e25b" +
    "71ad39acef23457893574852568eac5863298de685de69124de56eded66978425008142e" +
    "f723bfe602345459574568790b365852cdead454585c6")]
public class ConfidentialData
{
    ...
}
```

The solution based on the StrongNameIdentityPermission attribute isn't optimal, however, because it requires that you use this attribute to mark each and every type in assembly A that you want to expose to assembly B. (You can use the attribute at the assembly level, but in that case you'd restrict the set of assemblies that can use *any* type in assembly A, which is rarely desirable.)

The .NET Framework 2.0 solution is straightforward because you simply need to have assembly A declare that assembly B is a friend assembly:

```
[assembly: InternalsVisibleTo("AssemblyB, PublicKey=002400683011af5799aced23…")]
```

(You can retrieve the public key token of an assembly by means of the -T option of the SN command-line utility.) If assembly B isn't strong named, you can drop the PublicKey portion from the attribute's argument:

```
[assembly: InternalsVisibleTo("AssemblyB")]
```

Microsoft IntelliSense recognizes this attribute and correctly displays all the internal types in an assembly as well as members with internal visibility when you browse them from a "friend" C# project. (See Figure 8-6.)

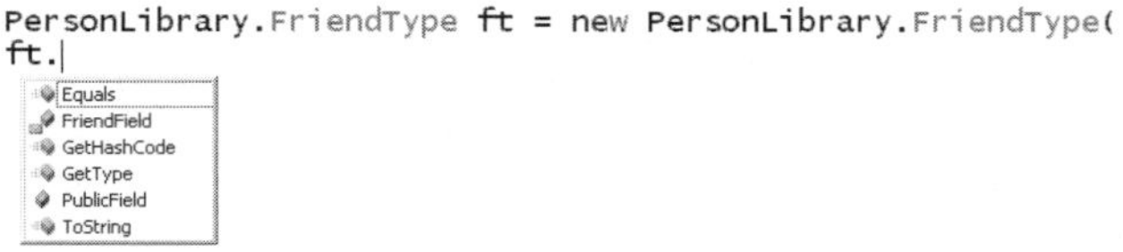

```
PersonLibrary.FriendType ft = new PersonLibrary.FriendType(
ft.|
```

Equals
FriendField
GetHashCode
GetType
PublicField
ToString

Figure 8-6   The InternalsVisibleTo attribute that enables a C# project to access internal types defined in other assemblies

Keep in mind that "assembly friendship" is neither reciprocal nor transitive: if A declares that B is a friend assembly, it doesn't mean that A is also a friend assembly of B and can peek into B's private types. Likewise, even if B is friend of A and C is a friend of B, you can't conclude that C is a friend of A. Instead, you'll need a specific InternalsVisibleTo attribute in A that grants friendship to C.

Note   If you write code in both Microsoft Visual C# 2005 and Microsoft Visual Basic 2005, keep in mind that this attribute is only partially supported by the latter language. A Visual Basic 2005 client can't access types in a friend assembly, regardless of the language used to create the assembly. More precisely, a friend assembly can be authored in both C# and Visual Basic, but only clients written in C# can access internal types in such a friend assembly.

Strong-Typed Settings

A good programming rule dictates that you should never hard code strings and other values in your code if there is a chance that such values might change in the future, for example, when you customize the application for a different customer or localize it for a different country. The classic example of this concept is user's color preferences, which should be stored in a separate file.

Visual Studio 2005 and C# provide two distinct answers to this need, in the form of custom strongly typed settings and resources. In this section, I illustrate custom settings, whereas I deal with resources later in this chapter.

The Properties.Settings Object

Microsoft .NET applications store their settings in an XML configuration that uses a name obtained by appending the .config extension to the executable filename (as in MyApp .exe.config). In .NET Framework 2.0, these configuration files have become even more flexible and powerful, thanks to the ability to store user-level settings (in addition to application-level settings) and to save these user settings when the application exits. These two features—both missing in .NET Framework 1.*x*—are actually related to each other: you need user-level settings (for example, preferences about color, fonts, window size and position) only if you have the ability to save these values when the user modifies them. Conversely, application-level settings (for example, the connection string to a database or the URL of a Web service) are set once and for all when the application is compiled or installed on the customer's machine and should be modified only by the administrator or personnel in the tech support department.

Visual Studio 2005 automatically generates the code of the Properties.Settings class, which in turn exposes all the application's settings as properties. You can add one or more settings on the Settings page of the project designer, select its type and value, and indicate whether it's an application-level read-only setting or a user-level writeable setting. (See Figure 8-7.)

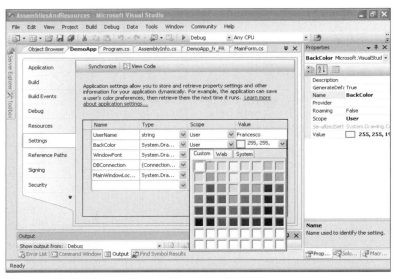

Figure 8-7 Editing settings in Visual Studio 2005

You aren't limited to settings of the String type or of another primitive .NET type, such as Int32 or Boolean. In fact, you can define a setting of any .NET type provided that the type is serializable. For example, you can create settings of type color, font, or point size, which are great for storing user preferences about the appearance of your application's windows. Additionally, Visual Studio supports two special setting types for database connection strings and Web service URLs.

If you don't see the type you need in the Type list, select the Browse element at the end of the list and select a type in the dialog box that Visual Studio displays. Notice that this dialog box doesn't display all .NET serializable types: it displays only the types for which a type UI designer exists; if this isn't the case, the value of the settings can't be edited in the Value column.

Once you have defined one or more settings, they appear as properties of the Properties
.Settings object and you can use them in a strong-typed fashion:

```
private void Form1_Load(object sender, EventArgs e)
{
   // Enforce user preferences when the form loads.
   this.BackColor = Properties.Settings.Default.BackColor;
   this.Font = Properties.Settings.Default.WindowFont;
}
```

If the setting is at the user level, you can assign it a new value:

```
Properties.Settings.Default.BackColor = Color.White;
// Change the current form's font to italic type.
Properties.Settings.Default.WindowFont = new Font(this.Font, FontStyle.Italics);
```

You can decide whether a user-level setting should roam when Windows roaming profiles are
enabled. (Roaming users are users that can connect from any computer in a LAN and still
find all their Windows preferences and settings.) To set this and a few other advanced properties of a setting, select an item on the Settings page of the project designer and switch to
the Properties window. You can rename a setting item and Visual Studio automatically
changes all occurrences in code to reflect the new name.

If the setting value is to be assigned to a property of a Windows Forms control when the
parent form is displayed, you can have Visual Studio generate the code automatically,
by following this procedure:

1. Select the control (or the form itself) and switch to the Properties window.

2. Expand the (ApplicationSettings) item, which appears at the top of the property list if
    properties are listed alphabetically. If the property that must be bound to the setting
    value isn't in the list, click the ellipsis button near the (PropertyBinding) subitem.

3. Select the property from the list that appears (see Figure 8-8), click the down arrow to its
    right, and select one of the settings from the list, or click the New element to create
    a new setting.

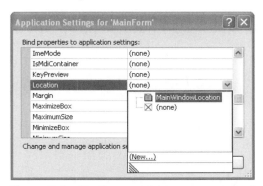

Figure 8-8   Binding a setting to a property of a control

A small icon appears in the Properties window to the right of all the properties that are bound to application or user settings.

Quite conveniently, Visual Studio also generates the code that automatically saves a control property to a user-level setting, which makes it very easy for users to reopen a form in the same state it was in the last time they worked with it, in the same or in the previous program session. Among the many properties you can save and reload automatically are the Location and Size of each individual form of your application; each user will find a form exactly where it was closed during the previous session.

Note Not all controls and not all properties on a control can be bound to a setting. More specifically, a component must implement the IBindableComponent interface and must implement an *Xxxx*Changed event for each property or implement the INotifyProperty-Changed interface to notify that a bound property's value has changed. If the component doesn't implement IBindableComponent, the property will be set when the form loads but won't be updated automatically; if the component doesn't notify when a property changes, the setting file isn't updated when the property changes. Some Windows Forms components, such as the ToolStripItem, don't support settings binding.

Properties.Settings Entries in Configuration Files

It is interesting to see where and how setting values are stored. The following listing is an example of a configuration file that contains one application-level and one user-level setting for an application named MyApp. (Longer entries have been rendered as multiple lines for typographical reasons.)

```xml
<?xml version="1.0" encoding="utf-8" ?>
<configuration>
   <configSections>
      <sectionGroup name="userSettings"
         type="System.Configuration.UserSettingsGroup, System,
         Version=2.0.0.0, Culture=neutral, PublicKeyToken=b77a5c561934e089" >
         <section name="MyApp.Properties.Settings"
            type="System.Configuration.ClientSettingsSection, System,
            Version=2.0.0.0, Culture=neutral, PublicKeyToken=b77a5c561934e089"
            allowExeDefinition="MachineToLocalUser" requirePermission="false" />
      </sectionGroup>
   </configSections>
   <connectionStrings>
      <add name=" MyApp.Properties.Settings.DBConnection" connectionString
         ="Data Source=MAINSVR; Initial Catalog=Northwind;Integrated Security=True" />
   </connectionStrings>
   <userSettings>
      <MyApp.Properties.Settings>
         <setting name="UserName" serializeAs="String">
            <value>Francesco</value>
         </setting>
         <setting name="BackColor" serializeAs="String">
            <value>255, 255, 192</value>
         </setting>
```

```
      <setting name="WindowFont" serializeAs="String">
          <value>Microsoft Sans Serif, 9.75pt</value>
      </setting>
    </MyApp.Properties.Settings>
  </userSettings>
</configuration>
```

The entries in the <configSections> section define the two sections that appear later in the same configuration file and the .NET types that are able to process the values these sections contain. The <userSettings> and <applicationSettings> sections are where the individual settings are defined. The <connectionStrings> section contains any connection string implicitly defined when you add a data source to the current project or when you select the (ConnectionString) type for a setting.

As you know, user-level settings can be modified by the application, and thus the entry in the application's configuration file is just the default value and doesn't necessarily reflect the current value for a given user. Here's an example of a configuration file that contains the setting values for a specific user:

```
<configuration>
  <userSettings>
    <MyApp.Properties.Settings>
      <setting name="BackColor" serializeAs="String">
          <value>180, 128, 128</value>
      </setting>
    </MyApp.Properties.Settings>
  </userSettings>
</configuration>
```

User-level settings are stored in a file named user.config in the following folder:

```
c:\Documents and Settings\Username\Local Settings\Application Data\CompanyName\
AppDomainName_Evidence_Hash\Version
```

where *CompanyName* is the value of the CompanyName attribute if available (otherwise, the element is ignored); *AppDomainName* is the FriendlyName of the current AppDomain (it usually defaults to the executable file's name); *Evidence* can be StrongName, URL, or Path and reflects the kind of evidence that identifies the assembly; *Hash* is the SHA1 hash of the evidence associated with the current AppDomain (the strong name if possible, else the URL, or the executable path); *Version* is the four-part version number of the executable. For example, the settings associated with the user named Francesco and related to version 1.1 of an application named MyApp.exe written by my company (Code Architects) might be stored in the following folder:

```
C:\Documents and Settings\Administrator\Local Settings\Application Data\
   Code_Architects\MyApp.exe_StrongName_vnvevct2pj1zeypy4yebywjdwvylgr3g
```

You can discover the folder where the .NET Framework stores the settings file for the current user and the current application by querying the Application.LocalUserAppDataPath. Unfortunately, this property is read-only and you can't change the location of the settings file.

(The location of the settings file is different for roaming users.) Interestingly, even if settings are stored on disk, they can be read and written to even when the application is partially trusted, as it happens with ClickOnce applications.

You can delete all the files used to store user-level settings by clicking the Synchronize button at the top of the Settings page of the project designer. (See Figure 8-7.)

Properties.Settings Properties and Methods

The Properties.Settings object exposes a few members in addition to those that correspond to the settings you've created in the project designer. The most important of these methods is Save, which saves all user-level settings:

```
Properties.Settings.Default.Save();
```

The Reload method rereads all settings from the configuration file; if the setting is bound to a property, the property is also affected:

```
Properties.Settings.Default.Reload();
```

The Reset method resets all settings to their default value using the data stored in the application's configuration file and ignoring any changes to user-level settings. Again, if the setting is bound to a property, the property is automatically assigned:

```
Properties.Settings.Default.Reset();
```

The indexer member of the Properties.Settings object allows you to retrieve the value of any property in a late-bound mode using code like this:

```
Color backColor = (Color) Properties.Settings.Default["BackColor"];
```

The Properties collection returns information about all the defined settings and enables you to iterate over all of them:

```
foreach ( SettingsProperty sp in Properties.Settings.Default.Properties )
{
    string desc = String.Format("{0} {1} = {2} (Default={3})",
        sp.PropertyType.FullName, sp.Name, Properties.Settings.Default[sp.Name],
            sp.DefaultValue);
    Debug.WriteLine(desc);
}
```

Here's an example of what might appear in the Debug window after running the previous code snippet:

```
System.String Username = Francesco (Default=unknownuser)
System.Boolean ShowStatusBar = True (Default=False)
System.Drawing.Point MainWindowLocation = Point [X=96, Y=60]
    (Default=Point [X=120, Y=100])
```

Properties.Settings Events

The Properties.Settings class also exposes four events that allow you to customize the default behavior:

- The SettingChanging event is raised before a user setting's value is changed; code in the event handler can inspect the value about to be assigned and optionally reject the assignment.

- The PropertyChanged event is raised after a user setting's value is changed.

- The SettingsLoaded event is raised when the application fills values of the Properties .Settings object at startup time and after a Reload or Reset method.

- The SettingsSaving event fires before the application saves user-level settings; code in the event handler can optionally cancel the save operation.

You can handle these events anywhere in the application, but the standard place for their handlers is in a file named Settings.cs. You can create and open this file by clicking the View Code button on the Settings page of the project designer.

The SettingChanging event is especially useful to reject invalid values for a given setting. For example, you might want to reject negative values for a property that indicates a position on the screen:

```
internal sealed partial class Settings
{
   public Settings()
   {
      this.SettingChanging += this.SettingChangingEventHandler;
      this.PropertyChanged += this.PropertyChangedEventHandler;
      this.SettingsSaving += this.SettingsSavingEventHandler;
   }

   private void SettingChangingEventHandler(object sender, SettingChangingEventArgs e)
   {
      switch ( e.SettingName )
      {
         case "MainWindowLocation":
            Point pt = (Point) e.NewValue;
            if ( pt.X < 0 || pt.Y < 0 )
            {
               // Cancel the assignment if either coordinate is negative.
               e.Cancel = true;
               // Ensure that the saved value isn't negative.
               Settings.Default.MainWindowLocation =
                  new Point(Math.Max(pt.X, 0), Math.Max(pt.Y, 0));
            }
            break;
         // Test other settings here.
      }
   }
}
```

The PropertyChanged event is useful for notifying other portions of the application that a setting has changed. For example, if the user modifies the BackColor property, you should enforce the new value for all the forms that are currently open:

```
private void PropertyChangedEventHandler(object sender, PropertyChangedEventArgs e)
{
    if ( e.PropertyName == "BackColor" )
    {
        // Change the BackColor property of all open forms.
    }
}
```

The SettingsSaving event enables you to give your user a chance to discard changes that were made during the current session:

```
// Inside the Settings partial class…
private void SettingsSavingEventHandler(object sender, CancelEventArgs e)
{
    if ( MessageBox.Show("Do you want to save new settings?", "Exiting the Application",
        MessageBoxButtons.YesNo, MessageBoxIcon.Question) == DialogResult.No )
    {
        e.Cancel = true;
    }
}
```

Resources and Satellite Assemblies

Resources offer a great way to include in the assembly's executable one or more pieces of information that would otherwise be provided as separate files. For example, you can embed a text file as a resource and then read the contents in that file from inside the application without having to distribute it as a separate file.

Strong-Typed Resources

The simplest way to create a resource is by means of the Resources page of the project designer. All the resources created in this designer appear as strong-typed properties. The designer supports strings, images, icons, .wav files, and any other kind of files.

Adding a string resource is straightforward, as shown in Figure 8-9: you just enter a resource name, the string value, and an optional comment. For all other resource types, you can just drop a file from Windows Explorer or use one of the commands on the Add Resource menu to create a new image, icon, or text file. Interestingly, you can author new images, icons, and text files by means of editors that are built into Visual Studio. (See Figure 8-10.)

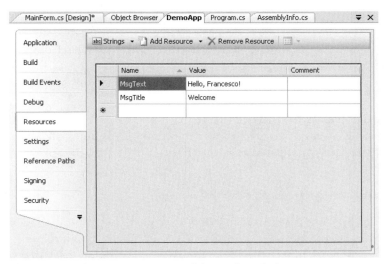

Figure 8-9   The Resources page of the project designer

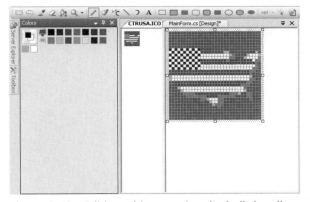

Figure 8-10   Editing a bitmap using the built-in editor

All the resources you create (other than strings) are stored in the Resources folder under the project folder. If you select a resource in the project designer and then switch to the Properties window, you can set a comment for the resource and use the Persistence property to decide whether the resource is linked or embedded. This property affects only how you deal with the resource from inside Visual Studio. In the former case, the resource is stored as a separate file in the project and you can edit it from outside Visual Studio; in the latter case, the resource is embedded in a .resx file and can no longer be edited directly from outside Visual Studio. Linked resources (the default option) are usually the best choice, but you might want to use embedded resources if you want to share the resource among multiple projects. Both linked and embedded resources are compiled in the executable's manifest and are accessed in the same way at run time.

Each resource must be assigned a name, and this name must be a valid C# identifier. Such a constraint ensures that the resource can be exposed as a static property of the Properties .Resources type. For example, if you have defined a string resource named CompanyName, you can access it from inside the application as follows:

```
string company = Properties.Resources.CompanyName;
```

Interestingly, you can later change the name of a resource in the designer and have Visual Studio automatically update all references in the current project. Image resources are returned as System.Drawing.Bitmap objects; thus, you can assign them to the Image property of a Picture-Box control:

```
this.pictureBox1.Image = Properties.Resources.CompanyLogo;
```

Even more interesting, in some cases you can assign a resource to a control's property at design time and without writing a single line of code. This is possible, for example, with the Image property of PictureBox controls: switch to the Properties window, click the ellipsis button near the property name, and select the resource among those you have defined on the Resources page of the properties designer. (See Figure 8-11.)

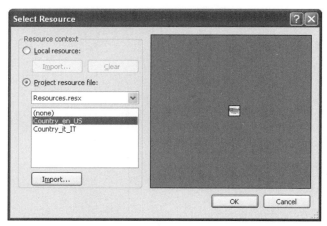

Figure 8-11   Assigning a bitmap resource to the Image property at design time

Icon resources are returned as System.Drawing.Icon objects, which you can assign to Form objects or elements in a TreeView or ListView control:

```
this.Icon = Properties.Resources.MainFormIcon;
```

Text files can be ASCII, Unicode, and RTF files; they are returned as strings and therefore can be assigned directly to the Text property of a TextBox control or the Rtf property of a RichTextBox control:

```
this.richTextBox1.Rtf = Properties.Resources.RegistrationHelpFile;
```

When you add a file that isn't a text file, the corresponding resource is returned as a Byte array, and it's up to you to extract the information contained in the file:

```
byte[] bytes = Properties.Resources.CustomBinaryData;
```

You can switch from binary to text representation of a file resource by modifying its FileType property in the Properties window.

Finally, audio resources are returned as System.IO.UnmanagedMemoryStream objects, which you can pass to the Play method of the System.Media.SoundPlayer object:

```
this.soundPlayer1.Play(Properties.Resources.ShutDownSound, AudioPlayMode.WaitToComplete);
```

The Properties.Resources type exposes two static properties that don't correspond to any resources you've defined in the project designer. The ResourceManager read-only property returns the cached System.Resources.ResourceManager object that is used internally to extract the resource from the assembly; such an object is useful when it's impossible or impractical to access resources in a strongly typed fashion, as in this code:

```
// Read resources from CompanyName1 to CompanyName10.
for ( int i = 1; i <= 10; i++ )
{
    string resName = "CompanyName" + i.ToString();
    string company = Properties.Resources.ResourceManager.GetString(resName);
    …
}
```

The GetResourceSet method of the ResourceManager object enables you to cycle through all the resources defined in the current assembly:

```
foreach ( DictionaryEntry de in Properties.Resources.ResourceManager.GetResourceSet(
    CultureInfo.CurrentUICulture, false, true) )
{
    Console.WriteLine("{0} = {1}", de.Key, de.Value);
}
```

The Culture property is the System.Globalization.CultureInfo object that affects which version of a locale-dependent resource is extracted. You can assign this property to retrieve resources for a locale other than the current one:

```
// From now on, use resources for the Italian culture.
Properties.Resources.Culture = new CultureInfo("it-IT");
```

Manifest Resources

You can embed any data file—including text files and images—in the assembly's manifest by following these simple steps.

1. Right-click the project element in the Solution Explorer window and select the New Folder command from the Add menu to create a project folder to hold your manifest resources—for example, a folder named ManifestResources. This step is optional, but it is recommended to keep manifest resources separated from other source and data files.

2. Right-click the folder you've just created and select the Add Existing Item option to add the file that must be included as a manifest resource, or simply drag the file from Windows Explorer into the Solution Explorer window. If the file is already in the project's directory, click the Show All Files button on the Solution Explorer toolbar, right-click the file icon, and select the Include In Project command.

3. Select the file in the Solution Explorer, press the F4 key (or click the Properties button on the Solution Explorer toolbar) to display the properties of that file, and then change the Build Action property from Content to Embedded Resource (see Figure 8-12).

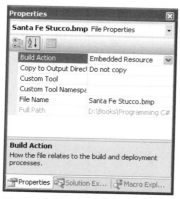

Figure 8-12   The properties of a file, which include the action to be performed at build time (can be None, Compile, Content, or Embedded Resource)

The following code shows how you can programmatically access a text file named Data.txt in the ManifestResources folder from inside an assembly whose default namespace is CodeArchitects.

```
string resFile = "CodeArchitects.ManifestResources.Data.txt";
// Get a reference to the current assembly.
Assembly asm = Assembly.GetExecutingAssembly();
Stream stream = asm.GetManifestResourceStream(resFile);
// Display the contents of the embedded file.
using ( StreamReader reader = new StreamReader(stream) )
{
    string fileText = reader.ReadToEnd();
    MessageBox.Show(fileText, "DATA.TXT");
}
```

The name of a resource is formed by the assembly's root namespace, followed by the name of the folder where the resource resides, the filename, and the extension. An important detail: resource names are compared in case-sensitive mode. You can check the exact names of embedded resources by means of the ILDASM tool or programmatically with the Assembly .GetManifestResourceNames method, which returns a string array that contains all the files you've embedded in the assembly, as well as one .resource file for each Windows Forms class in the application.

In general, manifest resources under Visual Studio 2005 are less important than they were in previous versions because in most cases it is preferable that you access resources in a strong-typed fashion by means of the Properties.Resources type. However, manifest resources can still be useful, for example, when you want to access them as a stream rather than as a self-contained object. For example, a text file can be accessed and processed one line at a time without your having to load the contents of the entire file in memory.

Another minor advantage of manifest resources is that you access them by their name, in a sort of late-bound mode. For example, this mechanism lets you dynamically select a resource whose name matches (or contains) the name or the role of the current user. Also, you might build the name of the resource to be loaded by appending the current culture, which partially remedies the fact that manifest resources aren't localizable:

```
// Load a resource named something like CodeArchitects.ManifestResources.Data.it-IT.txt.
string resFile = "CodeArchitects.ManifestResources.Data." +
    Thread.CurrentThread.CurrentCulture.Name + ".txt";
...
```

Localized Form Resources

Visual Studio gives you the ability to create Windows Forms applications that support multiple cultures, without writing a single line of code. The magic works because Visual Studio generates all the necessary resource files behind the scenes for you and the plumbing code that automatically assigns these resources to controls' properties when the form loads.

Let's take the simple form shown in Figure 8-13 as an example. The first step in localizing a form is to set its Localizable property to true. This is a design-time property that you won't find in the object browser. It tells the designer's code generator that the values of the properties of the form and its controls are to be read from a .resx resource file instead of from what is hard-coded in the source code.

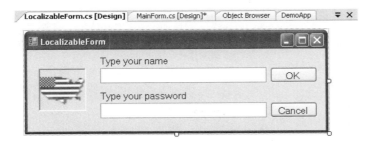

Figure 8-13   A localizable form with captions and one image, as it appears when the Language property is set to (Default)

Next, set the form's Language property to the alternative locale that you want to support. This property is available only at design time, and you can assign to it any of the locales that .NET supports. (See Figure 8-14.) The form designer continues to display the same interface as before, but you can now change all the properties of the form and its controls (including their position, size, visibility, and so on). All the values that you set from now on will be associated with the alternative locale just selected. Figure 8-15 shows how the form might look to an Italian end user. Of course, you can repeat this procedure with any language that you want to support.

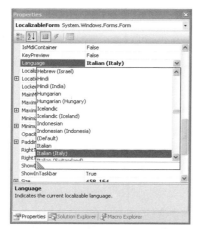

Figure 8-14 Setting the Language property to Italian

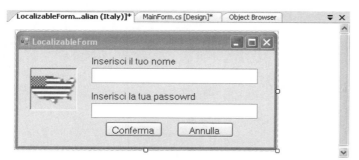

Figure 8-15 The Italian version of the form

> **Note** The localization process can involve more than just changing the visible strings in the user interface or strings used from code. For example, you might need to move a control to a different location or make it invisible under some localized versions. Visual Studio correctly keeps track of different values for properties such as Size, Location, and Visible under different languages. Nevertheless, you should test your form thoroughly before you make it localizable because any change you make to its user interface afterward will require more coding efforts. Unfortunately, not all the properties of all controls are localizable. Most notably, the Image property of the PictureBox control isn't; therefore, you must load images manually through code. See the demo application for a coding technique that you can use to overcome this limitation.

The great thing about localized forms is that in most cases, you can simply forget about them. You run an application containing localized forms as you'd run a regular application. If the current user's culture matches one of the languages you have defined, the form and its controls will use the properties you've set for that language; otherwise, the default language will be used. The fallback mechanism is quite sophisticated: for example, you can create resources with both one-part and two-part locale names, for example, it (for generic Italian) and it-IT (for Italian as spoken in Italy). If the current UI locale is it-IT, the latter resource file is used; if the locale is it-CH (Swiss Italian), it falls back to the it resource file. If it is en-US or fr-FR, it falls back to the neutral language resource file.

Also, Visual Studio uses a space-saving mechanism to avoid unnecessarily large resource files. Only properties with a localized value that is different from the default value are stored in resource files. Also, if you define a localized version for the it (generic Italian), it-IT (Italian as spoken in Italy), and it-CH (Italian as spoken in Switzerland), the it-IT and it-CH resource files will contain entries only for those values for which the Italian and Swiss versions differ.

A minor problem with localized forms is that they require additional testing and debugging. The easiest way to test a localized form is to modify the culture of the UI thread, which you do by creating a suitable CultureInfo object and assigning it to the CurrentUICulture property of the Thread.CurrentThread object. It's essential that you perform this operation before displaying the application's user interface, for example, in the Main method:

```
static void Main()
{
    // Force the UI culture of current thread to it-IT.
    Thread.CurrentThread.CurrentUICulture = new CultureInfo("it-IT");
    …
    Application.Run(new MainForm());
}
```

When you make a form localizable, Visual Studio creates a .resx file for each specified language, including the default one. (See Figure 8-16.) Each file is named after the locale to which it's bound. As I explained previously, a .resx file for a given language contains a resource item only if the resource value for that language is different from the default value.

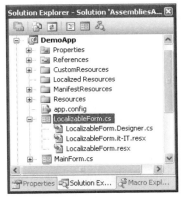

Figure 8-16   The .resx resource files as they appear in the Solution Explorer

When you compile the project, Visual Studio creates a subdirectory of the bin directory, names this subdirectory after the locale for which the resource has been created ("it-IT" in this example), and places there a new DLL named *applicationname*.resources.dll (for example, myapp.resources.dll). You can then XCOPY the bin directory and all its subdirectories to the end user's machine without having to deploy the .resx file. Read the section titled "Probing" later in this chapter for more information about how the CLR locates satellite DLLs.

If you double-click a .resx file in the Solution Explorer, a resource editor window appears. This editor is exactly like the one you use for resources associated with strongly typed resources, so this is known ground for you. The name of each resource is in the *controlname.propertyname* format, for example, btnOK.Text, so you can review and modify localized resources quickly and easily from this editor without having to go through the form's designer. When you attempt to modify a resource value, Visual Studio prompts you to confirm your intention because you might set a wrong value and make the entire form unusable.

Localized Strong-Typed String Resources

Once you understand how Visual Studio names and uses the resource files associated with localized forms, it's easy to duplicate this behavior with your own resource files and have your localized resources appear as properties of the Properties.Resources object. The following technique can be used for strings that can't be assigned directly to a control's property, such as the text you display in a message box:

1. Create a C# project containing a couple of strong-typed string resources, named MsgText and MsgTitle, and use them as the text and the title argument in a Message-Box.Show method. (You can also define other types of resources, if necessary.)

2. Open the Properties folder, select both the Resources.resx and the Resources.Designer.cs files, and drag them to the root folder while pressing the Ctrl key. (This action copies both files in the root folder.)

3. Rename the Resources.resx file you have created so that it matches the culture you want to support. For example, use the name Resources.it-IT.resx for Italian resources. Copy the renamed files back to the Properties folder. (See Figure 8-17.)

Figure 8-17   Creating an Italian version of the Resources.resx file

4. Double-click the renamed .resx file to display the usual resource designer. Translate strings to the language you want to support and change other types of resources as needed. If a value is the same as the default value, you can just delete the item from the localized resource file so that .NET will use the language-neutral resource. When replacing a resource other than a string, you must delete the original item and then add a file with exactly the same name.

You can now run the application as usual, but ensure that you assign the CurrentUICulture of the Thread.CurrentThread object to use the specific locale (Italian, in this example), as I explained in the previous section. If you've performed all steps correctly, you'll see that even strong-typed resources will now refer to the Italian culture.

```
this.PictureBox1.Image = Properties.Resources.MyPicture;
MessageBox.Show(Properties.Resources.MsgText, Properties.Resources.MsgTitle);
```

Custom Resource Files

You don't strictly need to work with strong-typed resources exposed as properties of the Properties.Resources object because you can access resource files directly by means of the ResourceManager object in the System.Configuration namespace. In some cases, this approach can be the only practical one, such as when you have to deal with hundreds of resource names—for example, the localized names of all the countries in the world—and you want to load them in a string array. In this case, the strong-typed feature of the Properties.Resources object is of little use. Another reason for using the ResourceManager directly is for reading a resource associated with a different language without having to switch the UI locale.

To create a custom resource file use the Add New Item command from the Project menu, select the Resources File template, and assign a meaningful name, such as Countries.resx. As usual, I suggest that you put your resource files in a specific folder named CustomResources or something similar. Double-click the .resx file and add strings and other types of resources to it, as you see fit. For example, add the following items:

```
Country001 = "United States of America"
Country002 = "United Kingdom"
Country003 = "Italy"
```

Notice that I used resource names in the format Country*NNN* because the sample code will index them in a for loop, but you can use any meaningful name. You can now create other resource files as needed by copying and pasting the default file in the Solution Explorer and then renaming the file to match the locale. For example, create a Countries.it-IT.resx file for country names in Italian, a Countries.fr-FR.resx for names in French, and so forth. For example, the Italian version might look like the following:

```
Country001 = "Stati Uniti d'America"
Country002 = "Regno Unito"
Country003 = "Italia"
```

Of course, your resource files can contain any kind of resources, not just strings. Next, write the code that reads all resource names into a ComboBox control:

```
// The resource filename is in the format rootnamespace.folder.filename.
string resFile = "CodeArchitects.CustomResources.Countries";
// Create a resource manager that reads the resource file.
ResourceManager manager = new ResourceManager(resFile, Assembly.GetExecutingAssembly());
cboCountries.Items.Clear();
// Read the three country names.
for ( int i = 1; i <= 3; i++ )
{
    // Build the resource name, in the CountryNNN format.
    string resName = "Country" + i.ToString("000");
    // Read the resource value and add it to the combo box.
    string resValue = manager.GetString(resName);
    cboCountries.Items.Add(resValue);
}
```

(Notice that the resource filename is in the format *rootnamespace.foldername.filename* and has no extension.) The ResourceManager object exposes two other methods that let you retrieve a resource value: GetStream (new in .NET Framework 2.0) is used for streamlike resources, whereas GetObject is used for any other type of object. These two methods and the GetString method support an optional CultureInfo argument, which enables you to retrieve a resource for a specific language, even though it isn't currently associated with the UI thread. If there is no resource file for the specified locale, the ResourceManager object falls back to the default resource file:

```
// Read the name of the first country as spelled in French, if possible.
CultureInfo ci = new CultureInfo("fr-FR");
string value = manager.GetString("Country001", ci);
```

Satellite Assemblies

An inconvenience of the techniques I have illustrated in the previous sections is that all localized resource files are part of the main project, and thus you must recompile the entire application to add the support for a new language or change a resource in a language that you support already. Granted, you need to deploy only the *applicationname*.resources.dll files that contain the new or changed resources, but when you support dozens of different languages, recompiling the entire application just to change a typo in a string resource isn't practical.

The .NET Framework supports the concept of satellite assemblies, which are separate DLLs that contain just the resources for a specific culture and no executable code. Satellite assemblies can be deployed separately and can extend the main application with support for additional languages without having to recompile and redeploy the application itself. For example, you should compile resource files separately when you outsource the production of such files to other companies and you don't want to give out your source code together with the resource files. Follow this series of actions to create a satellite project that contains a set of localized resources:

1. Create a new Class Library project, in the same solution as the main application or in a different solution. The name of this project isn't important, but you might want to use a name formed by appending the name of the main project and the culture identifier. (In this example, you might name the project DemoApp_fr_FR because the satellite assembly will contain resources for the fr-FR culture.) Delete the Class1.cs file that Visual Studio creates automatically.

2. On the Application page of the new project, change the assembly name to match the name of the main application (DemoApp, in this example) and change the root namespace to match the root namespace of the main application. In this example, we assume that this namespace is CodeArchitects; in general, .NET guidelines dictate that it should match your company's name.

3. Ensure that version numbers in the main executable and the satellite project match perfectly and that the satellite assembly is signed with the same public key as the main application (or that both of them aren't signed).

4. On the Build page of the project designer, change the Output Path value to point to the subdirectory where the main application's assembly is created. For example, if the main project is stored in the C:\Projects\DemoApp folder, the output directory for both the main application and its satellite assemblies should be C:\Projects\DemoApp\bin\Debug if you compile in Debug mode, or C:\Projects\DemoApp\bin\Release if you compile in Release mode. (You can also use a relative path, such as ..\DemoApp\bin\Debug.)

5. In the AssemblyInfo.cs file, add an AssemblyCulture attribute that specifies the culture of the satellite assembly.

```
[assembly: AssemblyCulture("fr-FR")]
```

You are now ready to add one or more .resx files to the satellite assembly. However, it is essential that all the .resx files you create embed the culture name in their name. For example, a file containing the French name of all countries should be named Countries.fr-FR.resx. In practice, you can drag a .resx file from the main project inside the Solution Explorer window to copy it into the satellite project, and then rename and edit it.

You can now compile the satellite assembly as usual. Visual Studio 2005 recognizes the AssemblyCulture attribute and correctly creates an assembly named DemoApp.resources.dll. This assembly is created in a subdirectory named after the assembly culture, under the folder you have specified in step 2. In this folder, Visual Studio also creates the "standard" DemoApp.dll assembly. This assembly contains no code and no resources and can be deleted before deploying the application or automatically by means of a postcompilation build event.

Attributes for Satellite Assemblies

A couple of attributes become of use when dealing with custom resource files and satellite assemblies, in addition to the AssemblyCulture discussed in the previous section.

As explained in step 3 of the previous section, the version number of a satellite assembly must match the version number of the main executable, and thus it looks like you must redeploy all the satellite assemblies whenever you change the version number of the main application. The SatelliteContractVersion attribute is useful in cases like these because it tells the CLR that the main assembly wants to load satellite assemblies of the specified version:

```
// (Add to AssemblyInfo.cs file in main assembly.)
// Use version 1.0.0.0 of satellite assemblies, even if the
// version of current executable is different.
[assembly: SatelliteContractVersion("1.0.0.0")]
```

It goes without saying that you shouldn't change the version of a satellite DLL; otherwise, the CLR will fail to load it. To keep track of different versions of these DLLs you can increment the FileVersion attribute instead.

The NeutralResourcesLanguage attribute is used in the main project to specify the language associated with the resources in the main executable. This attribute isn't mandatory, but can speed up resource lookup because it tells the CLR that it doesn't need to scan any satellite assembly if the UI language happens to match the neutral resource language (a rather frequent case):

```
// Specify that neutral resources are in English.
[assembly: NeutralResourcesLanguage("en")]
```

Visual Studio 2005 lets you enter this attribute from the Assembly Information dialog box. (See Figure 8-5.)

 Version 2.0 of the .NET Framework supports a new resource model in which even neutral-language resources can be stored in a satellite DLL. Although this model is slightly less robust, because a user might make the program unusable by accidentally deleting its satellite DLLs, it is also more flexible because you can then update resources in the neutral-language DLL without redeploying the main executable. You can enforce this model by passing a second argument to the NeutralResourcesLanguage attribute:

```
// Specify that neutral resources are in English, but these resources
// are held in a satellite DLL.
[assembly: NeutralResourcesLanguage("en",
    UltimateResourceFallbackLocation.ResourceLocation = Satellite)]
```

The Binding Process

When the running application references a different assembly, the CLR must resolve this reference—that is, it must bind the assembly of your choice to the caller application. This portion of the CLR is known as the assembly resolver. The reference stored in the calling assembly contains the name, version, culture, and public key token of the requested assembly if the assembly is strong-named. The version is ignored and the public key is missing if the assembly is private. The process that the CLR follows to locate the correct assembly consists of several heuristic steps:

1. Checks version policy in configuration files

2. Uses the assembly if it has been loaded previously

3. Searches the assembly in the GAC

4. Searches the assembly using codebase hints if there are any

5. Probes the application's main directory tree

These five steps apply to a strong-named assembly. When you're binding a private assembly, the CLR skips step 1 because the CLR ignores version information in private assemblies. Similarly, the CLR skips steps 3 and 4 when binding private assemblies because they can't be stored in the GAC and can't be associated with codebase hints. The following sections describe each step in detail.

Version Policy in Application Configuration Files

You can change the behavior of .NET applications and assemblies by means of configuration files. This mechanism gives both developers and system administrators great flexibility in deciding how managed applications search for the assemblies they must bind to. For example, a configuration file might enable you to specify that requests for version 1.0 of a given assembly should be redirected to version 2.0 of the same assembly. The .NET Framework supports three types of configuration files: the application configuration file, the publisher configuration file, and the machine configuration file.

The application configuration file affects the behavior of a single .NET application. This file must reside in the application's directory and have the same name as the application's main executable plus the .config extension. For example, the application C:\bins\sampleapp.exe should have a configuration file named C:\bins\sampleapp.exe.config.

The publisher configuration file is tied to a signed assembly and affects all the managed applications that use that assembly. Typically, publishers of .NET components provide a configuration file when they release a new version of the component that fixes a few known bugs. The statements in the publisher's configuration file will therefore redirect all requests for the old version to the new one. A component vendor should provide a publisher configuration file only if the new version is perfectly backward compatible with the assembly being redirected. Each major.minor version of an assembly can have its own publisher configuration file. An application can decide to disable this feature for some or all of the assemblies that it uses.

Finally, the machine configuration file affects the behavior of all the managed applications running under a given version of the CLR. This file is named machine.config and is located in the \Windows\Microsoft.NET\Framework\v*x.y.zzzz*\Config directory (where *x.y.zzzz* is the .NET Framework version). The settings in this file override the settings in both the application and publisher configuration files and can't be overridden.

All three types of configuration files are standard XML files that can contain several sections. The outermost section is marked by the <configuration> tag and might contain the <runtime> section (among others), which in turn contains information about the assemblies you want to redirect. Here's an example of an application configuration file:

```xml
<?xml version="1.0" encoding="UTF-8" ?>
<configuration>
   <runtime>
      <assemblyBinding xmlns="urn:schemas-microsoft-com:asm.v1">
         <dependentAssembly>
            <assemblyIdentity name="myAsm" culture="neutral"
                              publicKeyToken="378b4bc89e0bb9a3" />
            <bindingRedirect oldVersion="1.0.0.0" newVersion="2.0.0.0" />
            <publisherPolicy apply="no"/>
         </dependentAssembly>
      </assemblyBinding>
   </runtime>
</configuration>
```

Remember that XML tags and attributes are case sensitive, so you must type the tags exactly as reported in the preceding example.

Each <dependentAssembly> section is related to an assembly for which you want to establish a new version policy. This section must contain an <assemblyIdentity> subsection that identifies the assembly itself, with the name, culture, and public key token attributes. You can determine the public key token of a shared assembly by browsing the GAC from Windows Explorer, by using the GACUTIL command-line utility with the -l switch, or by using the SN utility as follows:

```
sn -T myasm.dll
```

After the mandatory <assemblyIdentity> subsection, the <dependentAssembly> section can contain the following subsections:

- The <bindingRedirect> section redirects one version of the assembly to another. For example, the preceding configuration file redirects all requests for version 1.0.0.0 of the assembly to version 2.0.0.0. The four numbers specified in the oldVersion and newVersion attributes are in the form major.minor.revision.build. The oldVersion attribute can specify a range of versions; for example, the following setting specifies that any version from 1.0 to 1.2 should be redirected to version 1.3, regardless of revision and build numbers:

  ```xml
  <bindingRedirect oldVersion="1.0.0.0-1.2.65535.65535" newVersion="1.3.0.0"/>
  ```

- The <publisherPolicy> section determines whether the publisher configuration file should be applied to this assembly. If you specify a "no" value for the apply attribute, as in the preceding example, the publisher configuration file is ignored and the application is said to work in *safe mode*.

- The <codeBase> section specifies where the assembly is located. This information is especially useful for assemblies downloaded from the Internet or for shared assemblies that haven't been installed in the GAC. (For more information, read the section titled "Codebase Hints" coming up shortly.)

By default, the publisher's policy is enabled for all assemblies. You can disable it for a specific assembly by using a <publisherPolicy> tag inside a <dependentAssembly> section (as shown in the preceding example), or you can disable it for all the assemblies that an application uses by inserting a <publisherPolicy> tag directly inside the <assemblyBinding> section:

```
<assemblyBinding xmlns="urn:schemas-microsoft-com:asm.v1">
    <publisherPolicy apply="no"/>
</assemblyBinding>
```

If you disable the publisher's policy for the entire application, you can't reenable it for individual assemblies. For this reason, the only reasonable setting for the apply attribute is the "no" value, both at the global level and at the individual assembly level.

The <assemblyBinding> section can contain a <qualifyAssembly> element, which specifies how the CLR must handle an Assembly.Load method whose argument isn't a fully qualified assembly name:

```
<assemblyBinding xmlns="urn:schemas-microsoft-com:asm.v1">
    <qualifyAssembly partialName="myasm"
        fullName="myAsm, Version=1.0.0.0, Culture=neutral,
        PublicKeyToken=378b4bc89e0bb9a3"
</assemblyBinding>
```

For more information about the Assembly.Load method, read Chapter 9, "Reflection," and MSDN documentation.

A .NET Framework 2.0 application can depend on an assembly that is platform-specific, that is, an assembly for which two (or more) versions exist, one for 32-bit and one for 64-bit platforms. If you are sure that assemblies for different platforms will always have the same version number (in other words, you always update and deploy new versions for them at the same time), you can use the guidelines described previously in this section because the CLR will always bind to the correct assembly. If you can't be sure that these assemblies always have the same version, you should specify two binding policies, one for each platform you support. (In theory, you might provide two configuration files, one for each platform, but it would be contrary to the principles of XCOPY deployment.) You can do this by means of the new processorArchitecture attribute in the <assemblyIdentity> element, as in this example:

```
<?xml version="1.0" encoding="UTF-8" ?>
<configuration>
   <runtime>
      <assemblyBinding xmlns="urn:schemas-microsoft-com:asm.v1">
         <dependentAssembly>
            <assemblyIdentity name="myAsm" culture="neutral"
                              publicKeyToken="378b4bc89e0bb9a3"
                              processorArchitecture="x86" />
            <bindingRedirect oldVersion="1.0.0.0" newVersion="2.1.0.0" />
         </dependentAssembly>
         <dependentAssembly>
            <assemblyIdentity name="myAsm" culture="neutral"
                              publicKeyToken="378b4bc89e0bb9a3"
                              processorArchitecture="ia64" />
            <bindingRedirect oldVersion="1.0.0.0" newVersion="2.3.0.0" />
         </dependentAssembly>
      </assemblyBinding>
   </runtime>
</configuration>
```

The processorArchitecture attribute can be assigned the values msil, x86, ia64, and amd64. These values are case-sensitive. If the configuration file has two <assemblyIdentity> elements, one with the processorArchitecture attribute and one without this attribute, the former element is used if the attribute matches the current platform, whereas the latter element will be used in all other cases.

You can use the AppDomain.ApplyPolicy method (new in .NET Framework 2.0) to learn which assemblies are going to be loaded by your application. This method takes an assembly name and returns the version of an assembly that will actually be loaded after .NET has applied its binding policy:

```
string oldName = "myAsm, Version=1.0.0.0, Culture=neutral, "
   + "PublicKeyToken=378b4bc89e0bb9a3";
string newName = AppDomain.CurrentDomain.ApplyPolicy(oldName);
// (Assuming the previous configuration file has been used in x86 architecture)
Console.WriteLine(newName);           // => myAsm, Version=2.1.0.0,…
```

Previously Loaded Assemblies and GAC Searches

In the second step of the binding process, the CLR checks whether the specific assembly has been requested in previous calls. If this is the case, the CLR redirects the call to the assembly already loaded, and the binding process stops here.

The CLR uses the assembly's strong name to decide whether the assembly is already in memory. This case can occur even if the application never previously requested the assembly but another assembly in the same process did and the requested assembly can safely be shared among multiple clients. As I've already explained, the strong name is a combination of the assembly's name, version, culture, publisher's public key, and processor architecture. The filename isn't part of the identity of the assembly, so you should never assign the same identity to different files.

If the assembly hasn't been loaded already, the binding process continues by searching the GAC for an assembly with that identity. This step applies only to assemblies with strong names because private assemblies can't be stored in the GAC. First, the CLR searches the GAC folder containing platform-specific assemblies, for example, GAC_32 on a 32-bit computer; if this search fails, it searches in the GAC_MSIL folder that contains assemblies compiled as IL code.

If the assembly is found in the GAC, the binding process stops here.

Codebase Hints

Once the version of the assembly is known and the assembly isn't in the GAC, the CLR has to locate the assembly file. The CLR usually accomplishes this task by means of a search process known as *probing* (described in the next section), but the developer, the publisher of the component, or the system administrator can disable probing by adding a codebase hint to one of the three configuration files. A codebase hint is a <codeBase> tag that appears in a <dependentAssembly> section.

Codebase hints are especially useful and common in browser-based and ClickOnce scenarios to inform the CLR of the location from which a given assembly can be downloaded. For example, the following portion of the configuration file tells the CLR that versions 1.0 through 1.4 of the MathFns assembly can be downloaded from *http://www.dotnet2themax.com/asms/ mathfns.dll* (this is just an example—there is no such assembly at this URL).

```
...
<assemblyBinding xmlns="urn:schemas-microsoft-com:asm.v1">
    <dependentAssembly>
        <assemblyIdentity name="mathfns" culture="en-us"
                          publicKeyToken="378b4bc89e0bb9a3" />
        <bindingRedirect oldVersion="1.0.0.0" newVersion="2.0.0.0" />
        <publisherPolicy apply="no"/>
        <codeBase version="1.0.0.0-1.4.65535.65535"
            href="http://www.dotnet2themax.com/ams/mathfns.dll"/>
    </dependentAssembly>
</assemblyBinding>
...
```

In some cases, you don't even need a codebase hint for every assembly used by an application. For example, if the MathFns assembly references the TrigFns assembly, the CLR automatically reuses the hint for MathFns and assumes that TrigFns can be downloaded from *http:// www.dotnet2themax.com/assemblies/trigfns.dll*.

You can use codebase hints to reference assemblies outside the application's main directory, provided the assembly has a strong name. Either using a codebase hint or installing the assembly in the GAC is the only valid way to reference an assembly located outside the application's main directory, and both techniques work only with assemblies with strong names. For example, you might decide to install an assembly in a separate directory if it is going to be used by multiple applications from your client (and you don't want to deploy all these applications in the same directory). In general, however, strong-named assemblies deployed to a location other than the GAC don't offer any advantages other than a simpler installation; on the con side, they load slightly more slowly than assemblies in the GAC do and aren't protected from accidental deletions.

You can also have codebase hints in the machine.config file. This feature is important when you want to make a new version available to all the applications installed on a computer but for some reason you don't want to install the component in the GAC.

If a codebase hint is provided but no assembly is found at the specified address, or the assembly is found but its identity doesn't match the identity of the assembly the CLR is looking for, the binding process stops with an error.

Probing

Probing is the process by which the CLR can locate an assembly inside the application's directory or one of its subdirectories. As I explained in the preceding section, the CLR begins probing only if no codebase hint has been provided for the assembly. Probing is a set of heuristic rules based on the assembly's name, base directory, culture, and private binpath.

The binpath is a list of directories, expressed as relative names that implicitly refer to subdirectories under the application's main directory. (Absolute paths are invalid.) The binpath is specified as a semicolon-delimited list of directories and is assigned to the privatePath attribute of the <probing> tag, inside the <assemblyBinding> section of an application configuration file:

```
...
<assemblyBinding xmlns="urn:schemas-microsoft-com:asm.v1">
    <probing privatePath="bin;bin2\subbin;utils"/>
</assemblyBinding>
...
```

The sequence of directories searched during the probing process depends on whether the assembly in question has a culture. For assemblies without a culture, the search is performed in each location in the order listed:

1. The application's base directory

2. The subdirectory named after the assembly

3. Each directory in the binpath list

4. The subdirectory named after the assembly under each directory in the binpath list

The CLR scans these directories first looking for a DLL named after the assembly (for example, myasm.dll). If the search fails, the CLR performs the search again in all these directories, this time looking for an EXE named after the assembly (myasm.exe).

For example, let's assume that the CLR is searching for an assembly named myasm.dll and the binpath is the one defined in the previous configuration file. Here are the files that the CLR searches for (assuming that the main application directory is C:\myapp):

```
C:\myapp\myasm.dll
C:\myapp\myasm\myasm.dll
C:\myapp\bin\myasm.dll
C:\myapp\bin\subbin\myasm.dll
C:\myapp\utils\myasm.dll
C:\myapp\bin\myasm\myasm.dll
C:\myapp\bin\subbin\myasm\myasm.dll
C:\myapp\utils\myasm\myasm.dll

C:\myapp\myasm.exe
C:\myapp\myasm\myasm.exe
C:\myapp\bin\myasm.exe
C:\myapp\bin\subbin\myasm.exe
C:\myapp\utils\myasm.exe
C:\myapp\bin\myasm\myasm.exe
C:\myapp\bin\subbin\myasm\myasm.exe
C:\myapp\utils\myasm\myasm.exe
```

For assemblies with a culture, the sequence is slightly different:

1. The application's base subdirectory named after the culture

2. The subdirectory named after the assembly under the directory defined in point 1

3. The subdirectory named after the culture under each subdirectory defined in the binpath

4. The subdirectory named after the assembly under each directory defined in point 3

Again, the CLR searches these directories for a DLL named after the assembly and then for an .exe file named after the assembly. For example, let's assume that an application using the preceding configuration file is requesting an assembly named myasm and marked as Italian culture (it-IT). These are the places where the CLR would search for this assembly:

```
C:\myapp\it-IT\myasm.dll
C:\myapp\it-IT\myasm\myasm.dll
C:\myapp\bin\it-IT\myasm.dll
C:\myapp\bin\subbin\it-IT\myasm.dll
C:\myapp\utils\it-IT\myasm.dll
C:\myapp\bin\it-IT\myasm\myasm.dll
C:\myapp\bin\subbin\it-IT\myasm\myasm.dll
C:\myapp\utils\it-IT\myasm\myasm.dll

C:\myapp\it-IT\myasm.exe
C:\myapp\it-IT\myasm\myasm.exe
```

```
C:\myapp\bin\it-IT\myasm.exe
C:\myapp\bin\subbin\it-IT\myasm.exe
C:\myapp\utils\it-IT\myasm.exe
C:\myapp\bin\it-IT\myasm\myasm.exe
C:\myapp\bin\subbin\it-IT\myasm\myasm.exe
C:\myapp\utils\it-IT\myasm\myasm.exe
```

If even this last step fails, the CLR checks whether the assembly was part of a Windows Installer package; if this is the case, the CLR asks the Windows Installer to install the assembly. (This feature is known as *on-demand installation*.) The Windows Installer program has other important features, such as the ability to advertise the application's availability, use the Add or Remove Programs option in Control Panel, and repair the application if necessary.

The Assembly Binding Log Viewer Utility (FUSLOGVW)

You now know everything you need to know about assembly binding, although in practice you're in the dark when the CLR can't locate one or more assemblies at run time. If you are running the program under the Visual Studio 2005 debugger, you can read a log of failed binding operations in the Debug window, a piece of information that usually lets you spot and fix the problem quickly and easily.

If you have already deployed the application on the user's machine, however, you can't use the Visual Studio debugger. In such a situation, the Assembly Binding Log Viewer can be a real lifesaver. The FUSLOGVW utility is located in the C:\Program Files\Microsoft Visual Studio 8\SDK\v2.0\Bin folder: you can run it from the command line or add it to the Start menu. (See Figure 8-18.)

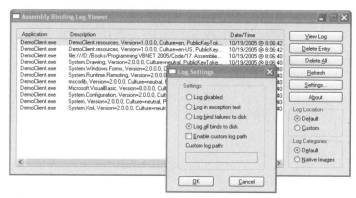

Figure 8-18 The Log Settings dialog box in the FUSLOGVW utility, which lets you log all binds or just failed ones, for all assemblies or only for those in the specified directory

You can specify whether FUSLOGVW should log all binding operations, just the unsuccessful ones, or no binding operations at all in the Log Settings dialog box that you open by clicking the Settings button, and you can also enable a custom log that shows only the failed binding operations that occur in a specified directory. Notice that the logging feature is disabled by default.

The options in the Log Categories panel let you display all bind operations or hide those related to assemblies that were compiled using the NGen tool. (See later in this chapter for more information about this tool.) You can display more details on any entry in the main window by clicking the View Log button or by double-clicking the entry.

Setting the Runtime Version

In general, you should always run a .NET application on a computer where you have (or your customer has) installed the .NET Framework against which the application was compiled. Only in this case can you be sure that all calls to methods in the CLR will work as expected. However, the CLR is able to run an executable compiled under a different version of the .NET Framework. This technique is called *redirection* and can be affected by configuration files.

Let's begin with an important note: an application compiled under Visual Studio 2005 can't run under .NET Framework 1.1. The reason is that the addition of many new features, including generics, asks for a change in metadata format in a way that makes the .NET Framework 2.0 executable incompatible with the .NET Framework 1.1 runtime. This limitation implies that you need to worry only about .NET Framework 1.*x* applications running under .NET Framework 2.0.

If the .NET Framework 2.0 runtime is installed on a computer, it will always attempt to load the .NET version the application was compiled against. This means that you don't need any configuration file to run a .NET Framework 1.1 application on a system where both versions 1.1 and 2.0 of the .NET Framework are installed. (This behavior is new to .NET Framework 2.0 because in the same situation you need a configuration file under .NET Framework 1.1.)

Versions 1.1 and 2.0 of the .NET Framework (but not version 1.0) recognize multiple <supportedRuntime> tags in the configuration file, the order of which dictates which .NET Framework version should be used when more than one version is installed on the end user machine. When you want to run an application compiled under version 1.0 of the .NET Framework on a machine that has either version 1.1 or 2.0 of the .NET Framework (or both), you specify a pair of <supportedRuntime> tags, the first of which points to .NET Framework 1.1 because this version is more similar to version 1.0:

```xml
<?xml version="1.0"?>
<configuration>
   <startup>
      <supportedRuntime version="v1.1.4322"/>
      <supportedRuntime version="v2.0.50727"/>
   </startup>
</configuration>
```

You redirect only the runtime but don't need any <bindingRedirect> tag for the individual .NET assemblies that the application uses because .NET Framework 1.1 or later is able to automatically redirect requests for older assemblies to the assemblies in the current version. This feature is called *unification* and works only for .NET Framework assemblies; third-party assemblies must be redirected manually by means of a <dependentAssembly> element.

Unification rules have changed in .NET Framework 2.0. Starting with this version, the CLR compares the major.minor version of the requested assembly with the major.minor version of the installed .NET Framework and will do the redirection only if the former version number is less than or equal to the latter. This new rule guarantees that a .NET Framework 1.1 application requesting, say, version 1.0.5000.0 of System.dll works well under .NET Framework 2.0 because it will be serviced with version 2.0.50727.0 of this assembly. However, if Microsoft releases a version 2.1 of the .NET Framework, an application compiled under version 2.0 asking for version 2.0.50727.0 of System.dll won't run under this new version, unless the configuration file contains one <dependentAssembly> element for each .NET assembly that must be redirected to the newer 2.1 version.

You can programmatically test which version of the .NET Framework your code is running under by invoking the GetSystemVersion method of the System.Runtime.InteropServices .RuntimeEnvironment class:

```
if ( RuntimeEnvironment.GetSystemVersion == "v2.0.50727" )
{
    // Running under version 2.0 of the .NET Framework
    ...
}
```

You can use this method to selectively disable the portions of your application that use features that aren't supported under the version of the .NET Framework in use.

Let me conclude this section with a warning. Even if the .NET Framework provides the ability to have an application run under different versions of the runtime, this feature comes at a high cost: you must thoroughly debug and test your code under different configurations (and possibly on different machines), which takes a lot of time and effort. Microsoft has done wonders to ensure that .NET Framework 1.1 applications work well under version 2.0 of the .NET Framework; however, version 2.0 is quite different from version 1.1 in many critical ways, so in most cases you can't expect that a program compiled under version 1.1 will run correctly under a newer version. A wiser solution might be to invest your time in recompiling the source code under the most recent version of the runtime and ensuring that your customers have that recent version installed.

The .NET Framework Configuration Tool

Although you should be familiar with the syntax of machine.config and application configuration files, most of the time you can perform your administration chores by using a Microsoft Management Console snap-in. The snap-in offers a simple user interface that lets you browse and modify files using a visual approach. This tool can be used only with Microsoft Windows NT, Windows 2000, Windows XP, and Windows Server 2003. You can launch the .NET Framework Configuration tool from the Administrative Tools submenu of the Start menu.

To interactively change the configuration file of an application you first must add the application to the list of configured applications by right-clicking the Application element and selecting the Add command. You can then right-click the application element and select the

Properties menu command to display a dialog box that enables you to change the most important settings you'd put inside an application's configuration file. (See Figure 8-19.)

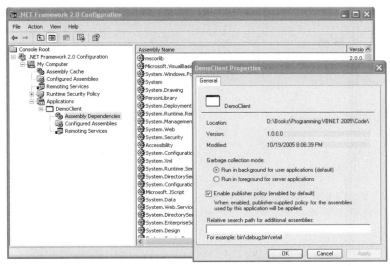

Figure 8-19   Adding an application to the list of configured applications with the .NET Framework Configuration tool

Next, expand the application element, right-click the Configured Assemblies folder, and select the Add command to add a new assembly to the list of those that this application must redirect. When you click Finish, a dialog box like the one shown in Figure 8-20 appears. Here you specify how versions are redirected and the codebase corresponding to each version of the assembly in question. (These settings correspond to entries in the .config file for the specific assembly.)

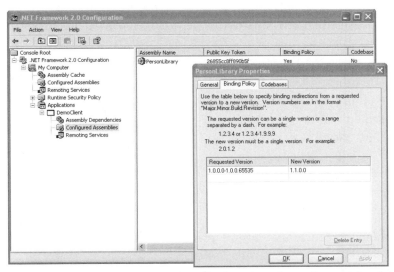

Figure 8-20   Adding an assembly to the list of configured assemblies for a specific application

The NGen Tool

You have read countless times in previous chapters that the CLR compiles the IL code to native code—the process known as Just-In-Time compilation—one instant before running a method for the first time. JIT compilation has a lot of advantages, most of which derive from the exact knowledge of the runtime environment. For example, the JIT compiler can produce a sequence of opcodes that is optimized for the target CPU, can optimize away indirect method calls (which would otherwise require a vtable-lookup operation), and can make some decisions based on the available resources. Several other potential advantages aren't exploited in the current version of the .NET Framework, but might be in the future. For example, the JIT compiler might dynamically recompile a piece of code with more aggressive optimization if that code is executed very frequently.

JIT compilation has several drawbacks, too. First and foremost, the JIT compiler tends to slow the startup step of an application because it has to compile many types and methods before the user can see something on the screen. (Startup time is an issue especially for Windows Forms programs, but isn't a serious problem for server-side applications that are meant to run for days or months.) Also, the JIT compiler must perform its chores while the program is already running; thus, it typically has no time to analyze the entire application's IL code to apply global optimizations, as most traditional compilers do.

To cope with these issues, the .NET Framework includes a tool named NGen, which translates an entire assembly to native code. This step is performed only once, and therefore startup time is dramatically reduced. Unlike traditional compilers, the NGen tool doesn't allow you to compile the application on your development system and then move the native code executable to the customer's machine: an application can be compiled with NGen only after the application has been installed on the target computer and the assembly containing the IL code must be present for proper execution. This detail implies that you can't use NGen as a tool to prevent assembly decompilation. Microsoft itself uses NGen to precompile a few assemblies in the .NET Framework, most notably mscorlib.dll, which in part explains why installing the Framework takes a significant amount of time.

The NGen tool compiles an application's assembly and stores its native code image in a directory known as native image cache, under the C:\Windows\Assembly folder. You don't need to do anything else because the binding process will automatically select this image instead of the IL image (which must always be available). An important warning: .NET runs the native code image only if its version corresponds to the IL image that would be run otherwise. This means that if you recompile the original assembly, you *must* compile it again with NGen; otherwise, the native code version will do nothing but take space on your hard disk. A less evident consequence is that a native code image becomes obsolete even if any of the assemblies it depends on are recompiled. For example, if you have written a custom control and you later update it, you should recompile all the applications that use that control. If you fail to do so, .NET will use the IL version and no error message will inform you of what has happened.

This detail explains why NGen hasn't been very popular among .NET developers, at least until version 1.1.

 The NGen version included in .NET Framework 2.0 has many great new features that make it much more useful:

- When you precompile an application (as opposed to a library DLL), NGen creates a native code image of both the application and all the assemblies it depends on.

- If the application or one of its dependencies is updated, NGen can automatically recompile both the application and all its dependencies. This is possible because .NET Framework 2.0 installs a Windows service process known as .NET Runtime Optimization Service, which checks whether an application compiled with NGen needs to be recompiled. This service works in the background when your CPU is idle, but you can force it to perform all pending tasks if you wish.

- NGen locates dependent assemblies by using the same probing logic described earlier in this chapter; this guarantees that the correct versions of these dependent assemblies are used. (In .NET Framework 1.1, there were a few discrepancies between the logic used by NGen and the one used by the CLR at run time.)

- Assemblies compiled with NGen can be shared among application domains in a process, unlike what happened in .NET Framework 1.1. An important consequence of this improvement is that you can see the benefits of precompiled assemblies also in Microsoft ASP.NET applications.

Note that you need administrative privileges to run NGen.

Using the NGen Tool

The syntax for NGen has changed in .NET Framework 2.0, even though the old syntax is still supported. According to the new syntax, you specify the command for NGen in its first argument. For example, the INSTALL command generates a native code image for the executable file passed in the second argument (known as the *root executable*) and all the assemblies it depends on:

```
NGEN INSTALL myapp.exe
```

Then NGen utility is stored in the C:\Windows\Microsoft.NET\Framework\v2.0.50727 directory, and thus the preceding command works only if you have added this directory to the system path. Here's an easy tip: add a command on the Tools menu so that you can invoke the NGen utility on the current executable directly from inside Visual Studio 2005.

If the assembly to be precompiled is in the GAC, the command syntax is slightly different and requires that you specify the assembly's strong name, as in this code:

```
NGEN INSTALL "myapp, Version=1.0.0.0, Culture=neutral,
    PublicKeyToken=ab349f12fe3a234e, ProcessorArchitecture=x86"
```

By default, NGen compiles both the main application and all its dependencies, as they appear in the assembly's manifest. This implies that assemblies that are loaded dynamically through the Assembly.Load method must be compiled separately. You can limit the number of dependent assemblies that are compiled by NGen by using the /NODEPENDENCIES option:

```
NGEN INSTALL myapp.exe /NODEPENDENCIES
```

You use the UNINSTALL command to remove all the native code images related to a root executable and all its dependent assemblies (unless these assemblies are used by other applications compiled with NGen):

```
NGEN UNINSTALL MyApp.exe
```

You can also specify a strong name to have NGen look in the GAC for the root assembly. The strong name you provide might lack some elements: for example, if you omit the Culture attribute, NGen uninstalls all the assemblies with the given name, regardless of their culture. If you provide just the assembly name, all the native code images of that assembly will be removed.

The UPDATE command tells NGen to recompile all the native code images that need to be updated, that is, the images that correspond to assemblies that have been updated or that depend on assemblies that have been updated since the last time this command was invoked:

```
NGEN UPDATE
```

Depending on how many assemblies need to be refreshed, this command can take several seconds or even minutes to complete. In the next section, you'll see how to mitigate this issue by means of the new asynchronous features of NGen.

The last basic command I want to cover is DISPLAY, which simply lists all the items in the native image cache, subdivided into two sections containing only the root assemblies and all the native images:

```
NGEN DISPLAY
```

You can pass an assembly name or an assembly path, which restricts the output to that assembly and all the roots that depend on it. For example, the following command shows cache information about a specific executable:

```
NGEN DISPLAY c:\myapp.exe
```

whereas the next command displays information about System.dll and all the roots that depend on it:

```
NGEN DISPLAY System
```

As usual, you can specify a complete or a partial strong name if the assembly is stored in the GAC.

Using the NGen Service

Some NGen commands support the /QUEUE switch, which causes the command to be scheduled for later execution through the .NET Runtime Optimization Service. This service doesn't start automatically with the Windows operating system and is launched indirectly when a queued command is invoked; when there are no more commands in the queue waiting to be carried out, the service goes to sleep again. By default, this service performs its chores only when the system is idle, even though you can assign a higher priority to a specific command and you can tell the service to complete all the pending commands.

To generate a native code image asynchronously you append the /QUEUE option to the INSTALL command:

```
NGEN INSTALL myapp.exe /QUEUE
```

The /QUEUE switch can be optionally followed by a priority, in the range of 1 to 3, where 1 is the highest priority. (The default value is 3.) A priority is sometimes necessary to ensure that an assembly is compiled before another one. Commands with priority 1 or 2 don't wait for system idle time:

```
NGEN INSTALL myapp.exe /QUEUE:1
```

You can schedule a system-wide update by applying the /QUEUE option to the UPDATE command:

```
NGEN UPDATE /QUEUE
```

You can display which commands are pending by issuing the following command:

```
NGEN QUEUE STATUS
```

The PAUSE command has two more subcommands, for pausing and restoring the activity of the background service. For example, to avoid conflicts it is recommended that you pause the service before compiling two or more assemblies in the background:

```
NGEN QUEUE PAUSE
NGEN INSTALL myapp.exe /QUEUE
NGEN INSTALL myapp2.exe /QUEUE
...
NGEN QUEUE CONTINUE
```

Finally, you can force the background service to complete all pending recompilations by means of the EXECUTEQUEUEDITEMS command, which optionally takes a priority number in the range of 1 to 3. For example, the following command forces all pending updates with priority equal to 1:

```
NGEN EXECUTEQUEUEDITEMS 1
```

If you omit the priority number, the preceding command returns only when all pending recompilations are completed.

Debugging Native Images

You must use the /DEBUG switch of the INSTALL command if you plan to debug the native code version; this option tells NGen to generate debug symbols and everything that is needed by the debugger. If you omit this switch and attempt to debug an assembly, the IL image is used instead:

```
NGEN INSTALL MyApp.exe /DEBUG
```

You can also specify an option that generates native images that can be used under a profiler:

```
NGEN INSTALL MyApp.exe /PROFILE
```

Interestingly, the native image cache can contain the versions compiled with and without this switch at the same time, so you don't have to worry about running NGen with a different setting to test the debug and the release version. You can check whether a native code image version of a DLL is used by means of the FUSLOGVW I described earlier in this chapter, which has a special log category for native images.

When you compile a DLL that will eventually be compiled with NGen, it is essential that you select a correct base address in the Advanced Build Settings dialog box, which you can display by clicking the Advanced button on the Build page of the project designer. (See Figure 8-21.) Ideally, all the managed and native DLLs used by an application should have a different base address and their addresses should be separated enough to let the operating system load the DLLs in memory at their base address. If a DLL can't be loaded at its base address because those memory locations are already taken, the Windows operating system has to *rebase* the DLL (that is, patch the DLL in memory to change the target of all jump and call opcodes). Rebasing is a relatively slow process, but what is more important is that a rebased DLL can't be shared among processes and therefore doesn't make optimal use of memory. You can check the base address for any DLL by means of the DUMPBIN tool.

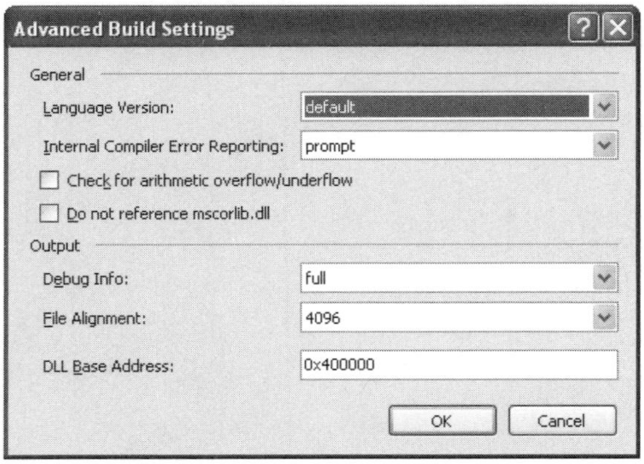

Figure 8-21   The Advanced Build Settings dialog box

Attributes for NGen

You can control a couple of important NGen features by means of attributes in your source code.

Domain-Neutral Assemblies

A domain-neutral assembly is an assembly that can be shared among different AppDomains in a process. The assembly is JIT-compiled only once and it takes a fixed amount of memory even if used by multiple AppDomains, two features that make domain-neutral assemblies improve performance. For example, the mscorlib is always loaded as a domain-neutral assembly.

Domain-neutral assemblies have a few drawbacks, too. First, a domain-neutral assembly is never unloaded from memory, even if all the AppDomains using it have been unloaded. Second, access to static fields is slightly slower than usual because it must go through an indirection level. (Such an indirection level is needed because the CLR must ensure that each AppDomain sees its own set of static fields.)

The great news is that the NGen tool is now able to compile domain-neutral assemblies, a definite improvement over the version provided with earlier .NET versions. For example, you can compile assemblies used by Microsoft ASP.NET 2.0.

You decide whether your application can load domain-neutral assemblies by decorating its Sub Main method with a LoaderOptimization attribute:

```
[LoaderOptimization(LoaderOptimization.MultiDomain)]
static void Main()
{
    …
}
```

(This attribute is ignored when applied to any method other than Main.) You have three possible values for the attribute's argument:

- **LoaderOptimization.SingleDomain**   The assembly is optimized to work with single AppDomains, and it won't load domain-neutral assemblies except mscorlib (which is always loaded in a domain-neutral mode). This is the default setting.

- **LoaderOptimization.MultiDomain**   The assembly is optimized to be shared among multiple application domains, all of which run the same application, and will load domain-neutral assemblies.

- **LoaderOptimization.MultiDomainHost**   The assembly is optimized to be shared among multiple application domains, which don't necessarily run the same application, and will load strong-named assemblies from the GAC in domain-neutral mode. This is the setting used for ASP.NET.

Remember that this attribute is just a hint for the assembly loader; depending on specific circumstances, the CLR can ignore the optimization you have requested and load the assembly using the default mode.

Hard Binding

Hard binding is an NGen feature that improves performance and reduces the amount of memory (the working set) used by a native image. Hard binding is especially useful when all or most dependent assemblies are usually loaded when the main application runs. If an application is hard bound to one or more dependent assemblies, the native images of all these assemblies are loaded when the application is launched. The downside is that the startup time can increase and make native image optimization less evident.

You can control which dependent assemblies are hard bound to an application by means of two attributes: DependencyAttribute and DefaultDependencyAttribute. You use the Dependency attribute in the main application to specify how likely a dependent assembly will be loaded:

```
// (Inside the main application...)
// The MathFunctions assembly will always be loaded.
[assembly: Dependency("MathFunctions", LoadHint.Always)]
// The FinancialFunctions assembly will be loaded sometimes.
[assembly: Dependency("FinancialFunctions", LoadHint.Sometimes)]
// Use the default load hint for the StringFunctions assembly.
[assembly: Dependency("StringFunctions", LoadHint.Default)]
```

When the Dependency attribute uses the LoadHint.Default value, the actual hint is taken from the dependent assembly, where it must have been specified by means of a DefaultDependency attribute:

```
// (Inside the StringFunction assembly...)
// This assembly is likely always to be loaded by clients.
[assembly: DefaultDependency(LoadHint.Always)]
```

Assemblies that are more likely to be loaded by the main application are also more likely to be hard bound by NGen. However, remember that the Dependency attribute provides a hint, not a command, and NGen can decide to ignore such a hint.

Chapter 9
Reflection

Reflection is a set of classes that allow you to access and manipulate assemblies and modules and the types and the metadata that they contain. For example, you can use reflection to enumerate loaded assemblies, modules, and classes and the methods, properties, fields, and events that each type exposes. Reflection plays a fundamental role in the Microsoft .NET Framework and works as a building block for other important portions of the Common Language Runtime (CLR). The CLR uses reflection in many circumstances, such as to enumerate fields when a type is being serialized or is being marshaled to another process or another machine. Some .NET compilers also use reflection behind the scenes; for example, Microsoft Visual Basic transparently uses reflection whenever your code accesses an object's member through late binding.

Reflection code typically uses the types in the System.Reflection namespace; the only class used by reflection outside this namespace is System.Type, which represents a type in a managed module. The .NET Framework also contains the System.Reflection.Emit namespace, whose classes let you create an assembly dynamically in memory. For example, the .NET Framework uses the classes in this namespace to compile a regular expression into IL code when the RegexOptions.Compiled option is specified. Because of its narrow scope, I won't cover the System.Reflection.Emit namespace in this book.

Note To avoid long lines, code samples in this chapter assume that the following using statements are used at the top of each source file:

```
using System;
using System.CodeDom.Compiler;
using System.Collections;
using System.Collections.Generic;
using System.ComponentModel;
using System.Diagnostics;
using System.IO;
using System.Reflection;
using System.Runtime.InteropServices;
```

Working with Assemblies and Modules

The types in the System.Reflection namespace form a logical hierarchy, at the top of which you find the Assembly class, as you can see in Figure 9-1. All the classes in the hierarchy shown in the figure belong to the System.Reflection namespace, except System.Type. FieldInfo, PropertyInfo, and EventInfo inherit from the MemberInfo abstract class, whereas MethodInfo and ConstructorInfo inherit from the MethodBase abstract class (which in turn derives from MemberInfo).

In this section, I describe the Assembly, AssemblyName, and Module classes.

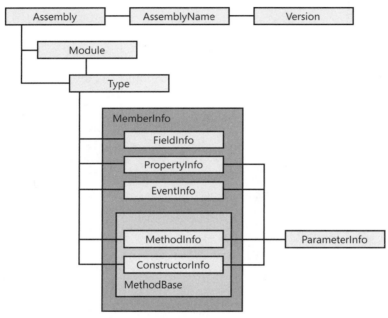

Figure 9-1   The Reflection logical hierarchy

The Assembly Type

As its name implies, the Assembly type represents a .NET assembly. This type offers no constructor method because you never actually create an assembly, but simply get a reference to an existing assembly on disk or in memory. There are many ways to perform this operation, as described in the following section.

Loading an Assembly

The Assembly type exposes several static methods that return a reference to an assembly, either running or not (that is, stored on disk but currently not running):

```
// Get a reference to the assembly this code is running in.
Assembly asm = Assembly.GetExecutingAssembly();

// Get a reference to the assembly a type belongs to.
asm = Assembly.GetAssembly(typeof(System.Data.DataSet));
```

```
// Another way to reach the same result.
asm = typeof(System.Data.DataSet).Assembly;

// Get a reference to an assembly given its display name.
// (The argument can be the assembly's full name, which includes
//  version, culture, and public key.)
asm = Assembly.Load("mscorlib");

// Get a reference to an assembly given its filename or its full name.
asm = Assembly.LoadFrom(@"c:\myapp\mylib.dll");

// Another way to get a reference to an assembly given its path. (See text for notes.)
asm = Assembly.LoadFile(@"c:\myapp\mylib.dll");
```

Microsoft .NET Framework version 1.1 supports the LoadWithPartialName method, which is now obsolete and causes a compilation warning. Along the same lines, version 1.1 of these Load*Xxxx* methods ignores any unknown or incorrect attribute in the display name; in the same circumstances, the Microsoft .NET Framework version 2.0 throws an exception.

A few subtle differences exist among the Load, LoadFrom, and LoadFile methods, and also a few minor changes from .NET Framework 1.1 might affect the way existing applications behave, as explained in the following list. These differences lie in how the assembly is located and the binding context in which the assembly is loaded. The *binding context* works like a cache for loaded assemblies so that the CLR doesn't have to locate the same assembly again and again each time the application asks for it. (See the section titled "Previously Loaded Assemblies and GAC Searches" in Chapter 8, "Assemblies and Resources.")

- The Load method takes the assembly name, either the short name or the fully qualified name (that includes version, culture, and public key token). If a fully qualified name is provided, this method searches the GAC first and, in general, it follows the same probing sequence that the CLR applies when loading an assembly because your code references one of its types. (See Chapter 8 for details about the probing process.) Assemblies loaded with the Load method become part of the execution context; the main advantage of assemblies loaded in this context is that the CLR is able to resolve their dependencies. You can enumerate assemblies in the execution context with this code:

  ```
  foreach ( Assembly refAsm in AppDomain.CurrentDomain.GetAssemblies() )
  {
      Console.WriteLine(refAsm.FullName);
  }
  ```

- The LoadFrom method takes either a relative or an absolute file path; if relative, the assembly is searched in the application's base directory. An assembly loaded with this method becomes part of the LoadFrom context. If an NGen image for the assembly exists, it won't be used, but if an assembly with the same identity can be found by probing or is already loaded in the LoadFrom context, the method returns that assembly instead, a behavior that can be quite confusing. When an assembly in the LoadFrom context is executed, the CLR is able to locate its dependencies correctly only if they are under the application's base directory or are already loaded in the LoadFrom context.

■ The LoadFile method also takes a file path. It works similarly to LoadFrom, but the assembly is loaded in a different context, and the CLR is unable to find its dependencies, unless they are already loaded in the Load context or you handle the AssemblyResolve event of the AppDomain object. (See the next section for more details about this event.)

To make things more complicated, the behavior of these methods has changed slightly in .NET Framework 2.0. First, both LoadFrom and LoadFile apply the probing policy (which they ignored in .NET Framework 1.1). Second, these methods check the identity of the assembly and load the assembly from the GAC if possible. There is a small probability that these minor changes may break your existing code, so pay attention when migrating your reflection-intensive applications to Microsoft Visual C# 2005.

Another minor difference from version 1.1 is that if loading of an assembly fails once, it will continue to fail even if you remedy the error, until that AppDomain exists. In other words, you can't just trap the exception and ask the user to install the requested assembly in the GAC or in the application's base directory. Instead, you'll have to restart the application or at least load the assembly in a different AppDomain.

.NET Framework 2.0 has the ability to load an assembly for inspection purposes only, using either the ReflectionOnlyLoad or the ReflectionOnlyLoadFrom method:

```
// Load the System.Data.dll for reflection purposes.
asm = Assembly.ReflectionOnlyLoad(
   "System.Data, Version=2.0.0.0, Culture=neutral, PublicKeyToken=b77a5c561934e089");

// Load a file for reflection purposes, given its path.
asm = Assembly.ReflectionOnlyLoadFrom(@"c:\myapp\mylib.dll");
```

You can enumerate members and perform most other reflection-related operations when you load an assembly in this way, but you can't instantiate a type in these assemblies and therefore you can't execute any code inside them. Unlike the LoadFrom and LoadFile methods, you are allowed to load the assembly even though code access security (CAS) settings would otherwise prevent you from doing so.

Another difference from other load methods is that the ReflectionOnlyLoad and Reflection-OnlyLoadFrom methods ignore the binding policy. Thus, you can load exactly the assemblies you are pointing to—you can even inspect assemblies compiled for a different process architecture—except if you load an assembly with the same identity as one that is already loaded in the inspection context, the latter assembly is returned.

Assemblies loaded with these two methods become part of yet another context, known as the inspection context. There is exactly one inspection context in each AppDomain, and you can enumerate the assemblies it contains with this code:

```
foreach ( Assembly refAsm in
   AppDomain.CurrentDomain.ReflectionOnlyGetAssemblies() )
{
   Console.WriteLine(refAsm.FullName);
}
```

The Assembly object has a new read-only property, ReflectionOnly, which returns true if the assembly is loaded in the inspection context.

AppDomain Events

When the CLR successfully loads an assembly, either as the result of a JIT-compilation action or while executing an Assembly.Load*Xxx* method, the AppDomain instance that represents the current application domain fires an AssemblyLoad event. You can use this event to determine exactly when an assembly is loaded, for example, for diagnostics purposes:

```
void AppDomainLoadAssemblyEvent()
{
    // Subscribe to AppDomain event.
    AppDomain appDom = AppDomain.CurrentDomain;
    appDom.AssemblyLoad += new AssemblyLoadEventHandler(AppDomain_AssemblyLoad);

    // This statement causes the JIT-compilation of DoSomethingWithXml method,
    // which in turns loads the System.Xml.dll assembly.
    DoSomethingWithXml();
    Console.WriteLine();

    // Unsubscribe from the event.
    appDom.AssemblyLoad -= new AssemblyLoadEventHandler(AppDomain_AssemblyLoad);
}

void DoSomethingWithXml()
{
    // This statement causes the loading of the System.Xml.dll assembly.
    System.Xml.XmlDocument doc = new System.Xml.XmlDocument();
}

void AppDomain_AssemblyLoad(object sender, AssemblyLoadEventArgs e)
{
    Console.WriteLine("Assembly {0} is being loaded", e.LoadedAssembly.Location);
}
```

Notice that methods in applications compiled in Debug mode are JIT-compiled earlier; therefore, the previous code snippet delivers the expected results only if compiled in Release mode.

When the CLR isn't able to load an assembly, the current AppDomain instance fires an AssemblyResolve event. By handling this event, you can tell the CLR where the assembly is located. For example, let's suppose that you want to force an application to search for dependent assemblies—either private or strongly named—in a given folder. As you might recall from Chapter 8, by default weakly typed assemblies must be located in the application's folder or one of its subfolders, but the AssemblyResolve event enables you effectively to override the .NET standard binding policy. The syntax of the handler for this event is peculiar: it is implemented as a method that returns an Assembly instance (the assembly that our code loaded manually) or null if the load operation must fail:

```csharp
void AppDomainAssemblyResolveEvent()
{
    // Subscribe to AppDomain event.
    AppDomain appDom = AppDomain.CurrentDomain;
    appDom.AssemblyResolve += new ResolveEventHandler(AppDomain_AssemblyResolve);

    // Attempt to load an assembly that isn't in the private path.
    Assembly asm = Assembly.Load("EvaluatorLibrary");
    Console.WriteLine("Found {0} assembly at {1}", asm.FullName, asm.Location);

    // Unsubscribe from the event.
    appDom.AssemblyResolve -= new ResolveEventHandler(AppDomain_AssemblyResolve);
}

Assembly AppDomain_AssemblyResolve(object sender, ResolveEventArgs e)
{
    // Search the assembly in a different folder.
    string searchDir = Path.GetFullPath(@".\..\..\..\EvaluatorLibrary\bin\Debug");
    foreach ( string dllFile in Directory.GetFiles(searchDir, "*.dll") )
    {
        try
        {
            Assembly asm = Assembly.LoadFile(dllFile);
            // If the DLL is an assembly and its name matches, we've found it.
            if ( asm.GetName().Name == e.Name )
            {
                return asm;
            }
        }
        catch
        {
            // Ignore DLLs that aren't valid assemblies.
        }
    }
    // If we get here, return null to signal that the search failed.
    return null;
}
```

The AssemblyResolve event lets you do wonders, if used appropriately. For example, you might load an assembly from a network share; or you might store all your assemblies in a database binary field and load them when needed, leveraging the Assembly.Load overload that takes a Byte array as an argument.

 The AppDomain type also exposes the ReflectionOnlyAssemblyResolve event. As its name suggests, this event is similar to AssemblyResolve, except that it fires when the resolution of an assembly fails in the reflection-only context, that is, when the ReflectionOnlyLoad or the ReflectionOnlyLoadFrom method fails. The ReflectionOnlyAssemblyResolve event also fires when the CLR successfully locates the assembly you're loading for reflection-only purposes but fails to load one of the assemblies that the target assembly depends on.

Properties and Methods

Once you have a valid reference to an Assembly object, you can query its properties to learn additional information about it. For example, the FullName property returns a string that holds information about the version and the public key token (this data is the same as the string returned by the ToString method).

```
// This is the ADO.NET assembly.
asm = typeof(System.Data.DataSet).Assembly;
Console.WriteLine(asm.FullName);
   // => System.Data, Version=2.0.0.0, Culture=neutral, PublicKeyToken=b77a5c561934e089
```

The Location and CodeBase read-only properties both return the actual location of the assembly's file, so you can learn where assemblies in the GAC are actually stored, for example:

```
Console.WriteLine(asm.Location);
   // => C:\WINDOWS\assembly\GAC_32\System.Data\2.0.0.0__ b77a5c561934e089\System.Data.dll
```

When you're not working with assemblies downloaded from the Internet, the information these properties return differs only in format:

```
// ...(Continuing previous example)...
Console.WriteLine(asm.CodeBase);
   // => file:///C:/WINDOWS/assembly/GAC_32/System.Data/2.0.0.0__
   //    b77a5c561934e089/System.Data.dll
```

The GlobalAssemblyCache property returns a Boolean value that tells you whether the assembly was loaded from the GAC. The ImageRuntimeVersion returns a string that describes the version of the CLR stored in the assembly's manifest (for example, v.2.0.50727). The EntryPoint property returns a MethodInfo object that describes the entry point method for the assembly, or it returns null if the assembly has no entry point (for example, if it's a DLL class library). MethodInfo objects are described in the section titled "Enumerating Members" later in this chapter.

The Assembly class exposes many instance methods, the majority of which enable you to enumerate all the modules, files, and types in the assembly. For example, the GetTypes method returns an array with all the types (classes, interfaces, and so on) defined in an assembly:

```
// Enumerate all the types defined in an assembly.
foreach ( Type ty in asm.GetTypes() )
{
   Console.WriteLine(ty.FullName);
}
```

You can also list only the public types that an assembly exports by using the GetExported-Types method.

The Assembly class overloads the GetType method inherited from System.Object so that it can take a type name and return the specified Type object:

```
// Next statement assumes that the asm variable is pointing to System.Data.dll.
Type ty2 = asm.GetType("System.Data.DataTable");
```

If the assembly doesn't contain the specified type, the GetType method returns null. By passing true as its second argument, you can have this method throw a TypeLoadException if the specified type isn't found, and you can have the type name compared in a case-insensitive way by passing true as a third argument:

```
// This statement doesn't raise any exception because type name
// is compared in a case-insensitive way.
Type ty3 = asm.GetType("system.data.datatable", true, true);
```

Finally, two methods of the Assembly class return an AssemblyName object, which is described in the next section.

The AssemblyName Type

The AssemblyName class represents the object that the .NET Framework uses to hold the identity and to retrieve information about an assembly. A fully specified AssemblyName object has a name, a culture, and a version number, but the CLR can also use partially filled AssemblyName objects when searching for an assembly to be bound to caller code. Most often, you get a reference to an existing AssemblyName object by using the GetName property of the Assembly object:

```
// Get a reference to an assembly and its AssemblyName.
Assembly asm = Assembly.Load("mscorlib");
AssemblyName an = asm.GetName();
```

You can also get an array of AssemblyName objects using the GetReferencedAssemblies method:

```
// Get information on all the assemblies referenced by the current assembly.
AssemblyName[] anArr;
anArr = Assembly.GetExecutingAssembly().GetReferencedAssemblies();
```

Most of the properties of the AssemblyName type are self-explanatory, and some of them are also properties of the Assembly type (as is the case of the FullName and CodeBase properties):

```
Console.WriteLine(an.FullName);
   // => mscorlib, Version=2.0.0.0, Culture=neutral, PublicKeyToken=b77a5c561934e089

// The ProcessorArchitecture property is new in .NET Framework 2.0.
// It can be MSIL, X86, IA64, Amd64, or None.
Console.WriteLine(an.ProcessorArchitecture.ToString());   // => X86

// These properties come from the version object.
Console.WriteLine(an.Version.Major);                      // => 2
Console.WriteLine(an.Version.Minor);                      // => 0
Console.WriteLine(an.Version.Build);                      // => 0
Console.WriteLine(an.Version.Revision);                   // => 0
// You can also get the version as a single number.
Console.WriteLine(an.Version);                            // => 2.0.0.0
```

A few methods of the AssemblyName object return a Byte array. For example, you can get the public key and the public key token by using the GetPublicKey and GetPublicKeyToken methods:

```
// Display the public key token of the assembly.
foreach ( byte b in an.GetPublicKeyToken() )
{
    Console.Write("{0} ", b);
}
```

The CultureInfo property gets or sets the culture supported by the assembly, or returns null if the assembly is culture-neutral.

Unlike most other reflection types, the AssemblyName type has a constructor, which lets you create an AssemblyName instance from the display name of an assembly:

```
AssemblyName an2 = new AssemblyName("mscorlib, Version=2.0.0.0, Culture=neutral, "
    + "PublicKeyToken=b77a5c561934e089, ProcessorArchitecture=x86");
```

The Module Type

The Module class represents one of the modules in an assembly. You can enumerate all the elements in an assembly by using the Assembly.GetModules method:

```
// Enumerate all the modules in the mscorlib assembly.
Assembly asm = Assembly.Load("mscorlib");
foreach ( Module mo in asm.GetModules() )
{
    Console.WriteLine("{0} - {1}", mo.Name, mo.ScopeName);
}
```

The preceding code produces only one output line:

```
mscorlib.dll - CommonLanguageRuntimeLibrary
```

The Name property returns the name of the actual DLL or EXE, whereas the ScopeName property is a readable string that represents the module. The vast majority of .NET assemblies (and all the assemblies you can build with Microsoft Visual Studio 2005 without using the Assembly Linker tool) contain only one module. This module is the one that contains the assembly manifest, and you can get a reference to it by means of the Assembly.ManifestModule property:

```
Module manModule = asm.ManifestModule;
```

In general, you rarely need to work with the Module type and I won't cover it in more detail in this book.

Working with Types

The System.Type class is central to all reflection actions. It represents a managed type, a concept that encompasses classes, structures, interfaces, and enums. The Type class provides all the means to enumerate a type's fields, properties, methods, and events, as well as set properties and fields and invoke methods dynamically.

An interesting detail: a Type object that represents a managed type is unique in a given App-Domain. This means that when you retrieve the Type object corresponding to a given type (for example, System.String) you always get the same instance, regardless of how you retrieve the Type object. This feature allows for the automatic synchronization of multiple static method invocations, among other benefits.

Retrieving a Type Object

The Type class itself doesn't expose any constructors because you never really create a Type object; rather, you get a reference to an existing one. You can choose from many ways to retrieve a reference to a Type object. In previous sections, you saw that you can enumerate all the types in an Assembly or a Module:

```
foreach ( Type t in asm.GetTypes() )
{
    Console.WriteLine(t.FullName);
}
```

More often, you get a Type object using the C# typeof operator, which takes the unquoted name of a class:

```
Type ty = typeof(string);
Console.WriteLine(ty.FullName);              // => System.String
```

If you already have an instance of the class in question, you can use the GetType method that all types inherit from System.Object:

```
double d = 123.45;
ty = d.GetType();
Console.WriteLine(ty.FullName);              // => System.Double
```

The Type.GetType static method takes a quoted class name, so you can build the name of the class dynamically (something you can't do with the typeof operator):

```
// Note that you can't pass Type.GetType a C# data type,
// such as short, int, or long.
ty = Type.GetType("System.Int64");
Console.WriteLine(ty.FullName);              // => System.Int64
```

The Type.GetType method looks for the specified type in the current assembly and then in the system assembly (mscorlib.dll). Like the Assembly.GetType instance method, the Type.GetType static method returns null if the specified type doesn't exist, but you can also pass true as its second argument to force a TypeLoadException in this case, and you can pass true as its third argument if you want the type name to be compared in a case-insensitive way. If the type you want to reference is neither in the caller's assembly nor in mscorlib.dll, you must append a comma and the name of the assembly in which the type resides. For example, the following code snippet shows how you get a reference to the System.Data.DataSet class, which resides in the assembly named System.Data. Because the GAC might contain many assemblies with this friendly name, you must pass the complete identity of the assembly after the first comma:

```
string typeName = "System.Data.DataSet, System.Data, "
    + "Version=2.0.0.0, Culture=neutral, PublicKeyToken=b77a5c561934e089";
ty = Type.GetType(typeName);
```

The .NET Framework 2.0 adds a variant of the previous method, which loads a type for inspection purposes only (similar to the Assembly.ReflectionOnlyLoad method):

```
// Second argument tells whether an exception is thrown if the type isn't found.
// Third argument tells whether case should be ignored in the search.
ty = Type.ReflectionOnlyGetType(typeName, false, true);
```

The TypeResolve Event

When the CLR isn't able to load a type successfully, it fires the TypeResolve event of the AppDomain object that represents the current application domain. As it happens with the AssemblyResolve event, the TypeResolve event gives you the ability to override the .NET Framework's default binding policy. The following example shows how you can use this event:

```
void TypeResolveEvent()
{
    // Subscribe to the event.
    AppDomain appDom = AppDomain.CurrentDomain;
    appDom.TypeResolve += new ResolveEventHandler(AppDomain_TypeResolve);

    // Get a reference to the Form type.
    // (It should fail, but it doesn't because we are handling the TypeResolve event.)
    Type ty = Type.GetType("System.Windows.Forms.Form");
    // Create a form and show it.
    object obj = ty.InvokeMember("", BindingFlags.CreateInstance, null, null, null, null);
    ty.InvokeMember("Show", BindingFlags.InvokeMethod, null, obj, null);

    // Unsubscribe from the event.
    appDom.TypeResolve -= new ResolveEventHandler(AppDomain_TypeResolve);
}

private Assembly AppDomain_TypeResolve(object sender, ResolveEventArgs e)
{
    if ( e.Name == "System.Windows.Forms.Form" )
    {
        string asmFile = Path.Combine(RuntimeEnvironment.GetRuntimeDirectory(),
            "System.Windows.Forms.dll");
```

```
        return Assembly.LoadFile(asmFile);
   }
   // Return null if unable to provide an alternative.
   return null;
}
```

The TypeResolve event fires when you fail to load a type through reflection, but it doesn't when the CLR has located the assembly and the assembly doesn't contain the searched type. (If the CLR isn't able to locate the assembly, an AppDomain.AssemblyResolve event fires.) For example, the following statement doesn't cause the TypeResolve event to be fired because the CLR can locate the mscorlib.dll even though that assembly doesn't contain the definition of the Form type:

```
Type ty2 = typeof(object).Assembly.GetType("System.Windows.Forms.Form");
```

Exploring Type Properties

All the properties of the Type object are read-only for one obvious reason: you can't change an attribute (such as name or scope) of a type defined in a compiled assembly. The names of most properties are self-explanatory, such as the Name (the type's name), FullName (the complete name, which includes the namespace), and Assembly (the Assembly object that contains the type). The IsClass, IsInterface, IsEnum, and IsValueType properties let you classify a given Type object. For example, the following code lists all the types exported by mscorlib.dll, specifying whether each is a class, an enum, a value type, or an interface:

```
Assembly asm = Assembly.Load("mscorlib");
foreach ( Type t in asm.GetExportedTypes() )
{
    if ( t.IsClass )
    {
        Console.WriteLine(t.Name + " (class)");
    }
    else if ( t.IsEnum )
    {
        // An enum is also a value type, so we must test IsEnum before IsValueType.
        Console.WriteLine(t.Name + " (enum)");
    }
    else if ( t.IsValueType )
    {
        Console.WriteLine(t.Name + " (struct)");
    }
    else if ( t.IsInterface )
    {
        Console.WriteLine(t.Name + " (interface)");
    }
    else
    {
        // This statement is never reached because a type
        // can't be anything other than one of the above.
    }
}
```

The IsPublic and IsNotPublic properties return information about the type's visibility. You should use these properties only with types that aren't nested in other types: the IsPublic property of a nested type is always false.

If the type is nested inside another type, you must use the following IsNested*Xxxx* properties to deduce the scope used to declare the type: IsNestedPublic (public), IsNestedAssembly (internal), IsNestedFamily (protected), IsNestedFamORAssem (protected internal), IsNestedPrivate (private), and IsNestedFamANDAssem (protected and visible only from inside the assembly, a scope you can't define with C#). You can also use the DeclaringType property to get the enclosing type of a nested type; this property returns null if the type isn't nested.

While we are on this subject, notice that the FullName property of a nested type includes a plus sign (+) to separate the name of the class and the name of its enclosing type, as in this code snippet:

```
MyNamespace.MyEnclosingType+MyNestedType
```

A couple of properties are new in .NET Framework 2.0: IsNested returns true if the type is nested in another type (regardless of its scope), whereas IsVisible lets you determine whether the type can be accessed from outside the assembly; it returns true if the type is a public top-level type or is a public type nested inside a public type.

You can get information about inheritance relationships by means of the BaseType (the base class for a type), IsAbstract (true for abstract classes), and IsSealed (true for sealed classes) properties:

```
// (The asm variable is pointing to mscorlib…)
foreach ( Type t in asm.GetExportedTypes() )
{
   string text = t.FullName + " ";
   if ( t.IsAbstract )
   {
      text += "abstract ";
   }
   if ( t.IsSealed )
   {
      text += "sealed ";
   }

   // We need this test because System.Object has no base class.
   if ( t.BaseType != null )
   {
      text += "(base: " + t.BaseType.FullName + ") ";
   }
   Console.WriteLine(text);
}
```

You can get additional information on a given type by querying a few methods, such as IsSubclassOfType (returns true if the current type is derived from the type passed as an argument), IsAssignableFrom (returns true if the type passed as an argument can be assigned to the current type), and IsInstanceOfType (returns true if the object passed as an argument is an instance of the current type). Let's recap a few of the many ways you have to test an object's type:

```
if ( obj is Person )
{
   // obj can be assigned to a Person variable (the C# way).
}

if ( typeof(Person).IsAssignableFrom(obj.GetType()) )
{
   // obj can be assigned to a Person variable (the reflection way).
}

if ( typeof(Person).IsInstanceOfType(obj) )
{
   // obj is a Person object.
}

if ( typeof(Person) == obj.GetType() )
{
   // obj is a Person object (but fails if obj is null).
}

if ( obj.GetType().IsSubclassOf(typeof(Person)) )
{
   // obj is an object that inherits from Person.
}
```

Enumerating Members

The Type class exposes an intimidatingly large number of methods. The following methods let you enumerate type members: GetMembers, GetFields, GetProperties, GetMethods, GetEvents, GetConstructors, GetInterfaces, GetNestedTypes, and GetDefaultMembers. All these methods (note the plural names) return an array of elements that describe the members of the type represented by the current Type object. The most generic method in this group is GetMembers, which returns an array with all the fields, properties, methods, and events that the type exposes. For example, the following code lists all the members of the System.String type:

```
MemberInfo[] minfos = typeof(string).GetMembers();
foreach ( MemberInfo mi in minfos )
{
   Console.WriteLine("{0} ({1})", mi.Name, mi.MemberType);
}
```

The GetMembers function returns an array of MemberInfo elements, where each MemberInfo represents a field, a property, a method, a constructor, an event, or a nested type (including delegates defined inside the class). MemberInfo is an abstract type from which more specific types derive—for example, FieldInfo for field members and MethodInfo for method members.

The MemberInfo.MemberType enumerated property lets you discern between methods, properties, fields, and so on.

The GetMembers method returns two or more MemberInfo objects with the same name if the class exposes overloaded properties and methods. So, for example, the output from the preceding code snippet includes multiple occurrences of the Format and Concat methods. You also find multiple occurrences of the constructor method, which is always named .ctor. In the next section, I show how you can explore the argument signature of these overloaded members. Also note that the GetMembers method returns public, instance, and static members, as well as methods inherited by other objects, such as the GetHashCode method inherited from System.Object.

The GetMembers method supports an optional BindingFlags enumerated argument. This bit-coded value lets you narrow the enumeration—for example, by listing only public or instance members. The BindingFlags type is used in many reflection methods and includes many enumerated values, but in this case only a few are useful:

- The Public and NonPublic enumerated values restrict the enumeration according to the scope of the elements. (You must specify at least one of these flags to get a nonempty result.)

- The Instance and Static enumerated values restrict the enumeration to instance members and static members, respectively. (You must specify at least one of these flags to get a nonempty result.)

- The DeclaredOnly enumerated value restricts the enumeration to members declared in the current type (as opposed to members inherited from its base class).

- The FlattenHierarchy enumerated value is used to include static members up the hierarchy.

This code lists only the public, nonstatic, and noninherited members of the String class:

```
MemberInfo[] minfos = typeof(string).GetMembers(BindingFlags.Public |
    BindingFlags.Instance | BindingFlags.DeclaredOnly);
foreach ( MemberInfo mi in minfos )
{
    Console.WriteLine("{0} ({1})", mi.Name, mi.MemberType);
}
```

The preceding code snippet produces a list that includes the ToString method, which at first glance shouldn't be in the result because it's inherited from System.Object. It's included because the String class adds an overloaded version of this method, and this overloaded method is the one that appears in the result array.

To narrow the enumeration to a given member type, you can use a more specific GetXxxxs method. When you're using a GetXxxxs method other than GetMembers, you can assign the result to an array of a more specific type, namely, PropertyInfo, MethodInfo, ConstructorInfo,

FieldInfo, or EventInfo. (All these specific types derive from MemberInfo.) For example, this code lists only the methods of the String type:

```
foreach ( MethodInfo mi in typeof(string).GetMethods() )
{
   Console.WriteLine(mi.Name);
}
```

The GetInterfaces or GetNestedTypes method returns an array of Type elements, rather than a MemberInfo array, so the code in the loop is slightly different:

```
foreach ( Type itf in typeof(string).GetInterfaces() )
{
   Console.WriteLine(itf.FullName);
}
```

All the GetXxxxs methods—with the exception of GetDefaultMembers and GetInterfaces—can take an optional BindingFlags argument to restrict the enumeration to public or nonpublic, static or instance, and declared or inherited members. For more sophisticated searches, you can use the FindMembers method, which takes a delegate pointing to a function that filters individual members. (See MSDN documentation for additional information.)

In many cases, you don't need to enumerate a type's members because you have other ways to find out the name of the field, property, methods, or event you want to get information about. You can use the GetMember or other GetXxxx methods (where Xxxx is a singular word) of the Type class—namely, GetMember, GetField, GetProperty, GetMethod, GetEvent, GetInterface, GetConstructor, and GetNestedType—to get the corresponding MemberInfo (or a more specific object):

```
// Get information about the String.Chars property.
PropertyInfo pi2 = typeof(string).GetProperty("Chars");
```

If you're querying for an overloaded property or method, you need to ask for a specific version of the member by using GetProperty or GetMethod and specifying the exact argument signature by passing an array of Type objects as its second argument:

```
// Get the MethodInfo object for the IndexOf string method with the
// following signature: IndexOf(char, startIndex, endIndex).

// Prepare the signature as an array of Type objects.
Type[] argTypes = { typeof(char), typeof(int), typeof(int) };
// Ask for the method with given name and signature.
MethodInfo mi2 = typeof(string).GetMethod("IndexOf", argTypes);
```

The method signature you pass to GetMethod must include information about whether the argument is passed by reference or is an array. Two new methods of the Type class make this task simpler than it is in .NET Framework 1.1:

```
// This code shows how you can build a reference to the following method
//     void TestMethod(ref int x, string[,] arr)
Type argType1 = typeof(int).MakeByRefType();
```

```
Type argType2 = typeof(string).MakeArrayType(2);
Type[] arrTypes = { argType1, argType2 };
MethodInfo mi3 = typeof(TestClass).GetMethod("TestMethod", arrTypes);
```

Speaking of arrays, notice that the name of array types ends with a pair of brackets:

```
Type arrTy = typeof(int[]);
Type arrTy2 = typeof(int[,]);
Console.WriteLine(arrTy.FullName);        // => System.Int32[]
Console.WriteLine(arrTy2.FullName);       // => System.Int32[,]
```

Also, the name of a type that represents an argument passed by reference has a trailing ampersand (&) character; therefore, you need to process the value returned by the FullName property if you want to display a type name using C# syntax:

```
string typeName = argType1.FullName.Replace("&", "");
```

Finally, your code can easily get a reference to the MethodBase that describes the method being executed by means of a static member of the MethodBase type:

```
MethodBase currMethod = MethodBase.GetCurrentMethod();
```

Exploring Type Members

After you get a reference to a MemberInfo object—or a more specific object, such as FieldInfo or PropertyInfo—you can retrieve information about the corresponding member. Because all these specific XxxxInfo objects derive from MemberInfo, they have some properties in common, including Name, MemberType, ReflectedType (the type used to retrieve this Member-Info instance), and DeclaringType (the type where this member is declared). The values returned by the last two properties differ only if the member has been inherited.

The following loop displays the name of all the members exposed by the string type, together with a description of the member type. To make things more interesting, I'm suppressing constructor methods, multiple definitions for overloaded methods, and methods inherited from the base Object class:

```
// We use this ArrayList to keep track of items already displayed.
ArrayList al = new ArrayList();
foreach ( MemberInfo mi in typeof(string).GetMembers() )
{
    if ( mi.MemberType == MemberTypes.Constructor )
    {
        // Ignore constructor methods.
    }
    else if ( mi.DeclaringType != mi.ReflectedType )
    {
        // Ignore inherited members.
    }
    else if ( ! al.Contains(mi.Name) )
    {
```

```
        // If this element hasn't been listed yet, do it now.
        Console.WriteLine("{0}  ({1})", mi.Name, mi.MemberType);
        // Add this element to the list of processed items.
        al.Add(mi.Name);
    }
}
```

Exploring Fields

Except for the members inherited from MemberInfo, a FieldInfo object exposes only a few properties, including FieldType (the type of the field), IsLiteral (true if the field is actually a constant), IsInitOnly (true if the field is marked as readonly), IsStatic (true if the field is marked as static), and other Boolean properties that reflect the scope of the field, such as IsPublic, IsAssembly (internal), IsFamily (protected), IsFamilyOrAssembly (protected internal), IsFamilyAndAssembly (protected but visible only from inside the same assembly, a scope not supported by C#), and IsPrivate:

```
// List all the nonconstant fields with Public or Friend scope in the TestClass type.
foreach ( FieldInfo fi in typeof(TestClass).GetFields(
    BindingFlags.Public | BindingFlags.NonPublic | BindingFlags.Instance) )
{
    if ( ( fi.IsPublic || fi.IsAssembly ) && ! fi.IsLiteral )
    {
        Console.WriteLine("{0} {1}", fi.FieldType.Name, fi.Name);
    }
}
```

A new method in .NET Framework 2.0 allows you to extract the value of a constant:

```
// List all the constants in the TestClass type.
foreach ( FieldInfo fi in typeof(TestClass).GetFields() )
{
    if ( fi.IsLiteral )
    {
        Console.WriteLine("{0} = {1}", fi.Name, fi.GetRawConstantValue());
    }
}
```

Exploring Methods

Like FieldInfo, the MethodInfo type exposes the IsStatic property and all the other scope-related properties you've just seen, plus a few additional Boolean properties: IsVirtual (the method is marked with the virtual keyword), IsAbstract (abstract), and IsFinal (sealed). The IsSpecialName property returns true if the method has been created by the compiler and should be dealt with in a special way, as is the case of the methods generated by properties and operators. If the method returns a value, the ReturnType property returns the type of the return value; otherwise, it returns a special type whose name is System.Void and that you can compare with typeof(void). This snippet uses these properties to display information on all the methods in a class, exposed in a C#-like syntax:

```
// List all methods of the Array class.
foreach ( MethodInfo mi in typeof(Array).GetMethods() )
{
   // Ignore special methods, such as property getters and setters.
   if ( mi.IsSpecialName )
   {
      continue;
   }
   else if ( mi.IsFinal )
   {
      Console.Write("sealed ");
   }
   else if ( mi.IsVirtual )
   {
      Console.Write("virtual ");
   }
   else if ( mi.IsAbstract )
   {
      Console.Write("abstract ");
   }
   if ( mi.ReturnType == typeof(void) )
   {
      Console.WriteLine("void {0}", mi.Name);
   }
   else
   {
      Console.WriteLine("{1} {0}", mi.Name, mi.ReturnType.FullName);
   }
}
```

The ConstructorInfo type exposes the same members as the MethodInfo type (not surprisingly because both these types inherit from the MethodBase abstract class, which in turns derives from MemberInfo), with the exception of ReturnType (constructors don't have a return type).

Exploring Properties

The PropertyInfo type exposes only three interesting properties besides those inherited from MemberInfo: PropertyType (the type returned by the property), CanRead (false for write-only properties), and CanWrite (false for read-only properties). Oddly, the PropertyInfo type doesn't expose members that indicate the scope of the property or whether it's a static property. You can access this information only indirectly by means of one of the following methods: GetGetMethod (which returns the MethodInfo object corresponding to the get accessor block), GetSetMethod (the MethodInfo object corresponding to the set accessor block), or GetAccessors (an array of one or two MethodInfo objects, corresponding to the get and/or set accessor blocks):

```
// Display instance and static public properties.
foreach ( PropertyInfo pi in typeof(TestClass).GetProperties(
   BindingFlags.Public | BindingFlags.Instance | BindingFlags.Static) )
```

```
{
    // Get either the get or the set accessor methods.
    string modifier = "";
    MethodInfo mi;
    if ( pi.CanRead )
    {
        mi = pi.GetGetMethod();
    }
    else
    {
        mi = pi.GetSetMethod();
    }
    // Add the static qualifier if necessary.
    if ( mi.IsStatic )
    {
        modifier = "static ";
    }

    // Display the C# syntax.
    Console.WriteLine("public {0}{1} {2}", modifier, pi.PropertyType.FullName, pi.Name);
}
```

If you need to retrieve a property accessor only to determine its scope or whether the property is static, you can use the GetAccessors method. For example, you can replace all the code in bold type in previous listing with this statement:

```
// Get the first property accessor, even if it's private.
MethodInfo mi = pi.GetAccessors(true)[0];
```

By default the GetGetMethod, GetSetMethod, and GetAccessors methods return only public accessor methods; if the accessor method doesn't exist or isn't public, the return value is null. However, these methods are overloaded to take a Boolean argument: if you pass true, they return the accessor method even if it doesn't have a public scope.

Exploring Events

Getting information about an event is complicated by the fact that the EventInfo type has no property that lets you determine the scope of the event or whether it's static. Instead, you must use GetAddMethod to return the MethodInfo object corresponding to the method that adds a new subscriber to the list of listeners for this event. (This is the method that the += operator calls for you behind the scenes.) Typically, this method is named add_*Eventname* and is paired with the remove_*Eventname* hidden method (the method called by -= and whose MethodInfo is returned by the GetRemoveMethod). The C# compiler creates these methods for you by default, unless you define a custom event.

You can query the MethodInfo object returned by either GetAddMethod or GetRemoveMethod to discover the event's scope, its arguments, and whether it's static:

```
// Get information on the SampleEvent event of the TestClass object.
EventInfo ei = typeof(TestClass).GetEvent("SampleEvent");
// Get a reference to the hidden add_SampleEvent method.
MethodInfo mi2 = ei.GetAddMethod();
// Test the method scope and check whether it's static.
...
```

Exploring Parameters

The one thing left to do is enumerate the parameters that a property or a method expects. Both the GetIndexParameters (of ParameterInfo) and the GetParameters (of MethodInfo) methods return an array of ParameterInfo objects, where each element describes the attributes of the arguments passed to and from the member.

A ParameterInfo object has properties with names that are self-explanatory: Name (the name of the parameter), ParameterType (the type of the parameter), Member (the MemberInfo the parameter belongs to), Position (an integer that describes where the parameter appears in the method signature), IsByRef (true if the parameter is marked with either the ref or out keyword), IsOut (true if the parameter is marked with the out keyword), IsOptional (true for optional parameters, which are supported by Visual Basic but not by C#), and DefaultValue (the default value of an optional parameter). The following code shows how to display the calling syntax for a given method:

```
MethodInfo mi = typeof(TestClass).GetMethod("MethodWithRefArgs");
Console.Write(mi.Name + "(");
foreach ( ParameterInfo pi in mi.GetParameters() )
{
    // Display a comma if it isn't the first parameter.
    if ( pi.Position > 0 )
    {
        Console.Write(", ");
    }

    // Notice that IsOut must be tested before IsByRef.
    string direction = "";
    if ( pi.IsOut )
    {
        direction = "out ";
    }
    else if ( pi.ParameterType.IsByRef )
    {
        direction = "ref ";
    }

    // Process the parameter type.
    string tyName = pi.ParameterType.FullName;
    // Drop the & character (included if parameter is passed by reference).
    tyName = tyName.Replace("&", "");
    Console.Write("{0}{1} {2}", direction, tyName, pi.Name);
}
Console.WriteLine(")");
```

Getting the syntax for an event is more complicated because the EventInfo object doesn't expose the GetParameters method. Instead, you must use the EventHandlerType property to retrieve the Type object corresponding to the delegate that defines the event. The Invoke method of this delegate, in turn, has the same signature as the event:

```
EventInfo ei = typeof(TestClass).GetEvent("SampleEvent");
Type delegType = ei.EventHandlerType;
MethodInfo mi2 = delegType.GetMethod("Invoke");
```

```
foreach ( ParameterInfo pi in mi2.GetParameters() )
{
   ...
}
```

Exploring the Method Body

Version 2.0 of the .NET Framework introduces a new feature that, although not completely implemented, surely goes in a very promising direction: the ability to peek at the IL code compiled for a given method. The entry point for this capability is the new MethodBase .GetMethodBody method, which returns a MethodBody object. In turn, a MethodBody object exposes properties that let you list the local variables, evaluate the size of the stack that the method uses, and explore the try...catch exception handlers defined in the inspected method.

```
// Get a reference to the method in a type.
MethodInfo mi = typeof(TestClass).GetMethod("TestMethod");
MethodBody mb = mi.GetMethodBody();
// Display the number of used stack elements.
Console.WriteLine("Stack Size = {0}", mb.MaxStackSize);

// Display index and type of local variables.
Console.WriteLine("Local variables:");
foreach ( LocalVariableInfo lvi in mb.LocalVariables )
{
   Console.WriteLine("  var[{0}] of type {1}", lvi.LocalIndex, lvi.LocalType.FullName);
}

// Display information about exception handlers.
Console.WriteLine("Exception handlers:");
foreach ( ExceptionHandlingClause ehc in mb.ExceptionHandlingClauses )
{
   Console.Write("  Type={0}, ", ehc.Flags.ToString());
   if ( ehc.Flags == ExceptionHandlingClauseOptions.Clause )
   {
      Console.Write("{0} ex, ", ehc.CatchType.Name);
   }
   Console.Write("Try off/len={0}/{1}, ", ehc.TryOffset, ehc.TryLength);
   Console.WriteLine("Handler off/len={0}/{1}", ehc.HandlerOffset, ehc.HandlerLength);
}
```

The list of exception handlers doesn't differentiate between catch and finally clauses belonging to distinct try blocks, but you can group them correctly by looking at elements with identical TryOffset properties. The Flags property of the ExceptionHandlingClause object helps you understand whether the clause is a filter (corresponding to a When expression in Visual Basic), a clause (catch block), or a finally block. The type of the Exception object is exposed by the CatchType property. For example, given the following method:

```
public void TestMethod(ref int x, string[,] arr)
{
   try
   {
      ...
   }
```

```
        catch ( NullReferenceException ex )
        {
            ...
        }
        catch ( Exception ex )
        {
            ...
        }
        finally
        {
            ...
        }

        try
        {
            ...
        }
        catch ( NullReferenceException ex )
        {
            ...
        }
        catch ( OverflowException ex )
        {
            ...
        }
        catch ( Exception ex )
        {
            ...
        }
}
```

Here's the information that might be displayed in the console window. (The actual offset and length information varies depending on the actual executable statements in the method.)

```
Stack Size = 1
Local variables:
  var[0] of type System.NullReferenceException
  var[1] of type System.Exception
  var[2] of type System.OverflowException
Exception handlers:
  Type=Clause, NullReferenceException ex, Try off/len=1/15, Handler off/len=16/16
  Type=Clause, Exception ex, Try off/len=1/15, Handler off/len=36/16
  Type=Finally, Try off/len=1/50, Handler off/len=51/14
  Type=Clause, NullReferenceException ex, Try off/len=66/15, Handler off/len=81/16
  Type=Clause, OverflowException ex, Try off/len=66/15, Handler off/len=97/16
  Type=Clause, Exception ex, Try off/len=66/15, Handler off/len=113/16
```

Notice that the list of local variables is likely to include variables that you haven't declared explicitly but that are created for you by the compiler to store intermediate results, such as the Exception variables in catch clauses or the upper limit of a for loop.

The only method of the MethodBody object of interest is GetILAsByteArray, which returns an array containing the raw IL opcodes. These opcodes are fully documented, so you might use this method to disassemble a .NET executable. As you can guess, this isn't exactly a trivial task, however.

Reflecting on Generics

Reflection techniques in .NET Framework 2.0 fully support generic types, and you must account for them when exploring the types that an assembly exposes.

Exploring Generic Types

You can distinguish generic type definitions from regular types when enumerating all the types in an assembly by checking their IsGenericTypeDefinition method. The full name of a generic type definition contains an inverse quote character (`) followed by the number of type arguments in the definition. Therefore, given the following code:

```
// List all the generic types in an assembly:
Assembly asm = typeof(object).Assembly;
foreach ( Type ty in asm.GetTypes() )
{
   if ( ty.IsGenericTypeDefinition )
   {
      Console.WriteLine(ty.FullName);
   }
}
```

This is the kind of results you'll see in the console window:

```
System.Collections.Generic.List`1
System.Collections.Generic.Dictionary`2
System.Action`1
...
```

The names of the generic parameters in the type definition don't appear in the type name because they aren't meaningful in the composition of a unique type name: as you might recall from Chapter 4, "Generics," you can have two generic type definitions with the same name only if the number of their generic parameters differs. The syntax based on the inverse quote character becomes important if you want to retrieve a reference to the generic type definition, as in this code:

```
Type genType = asm.GetType("System.Collections.Generic.Dictionary`2");
```

There is no built-in method or property that returns the signature of the generic type as it appears in source code, and thus you have to manually strip the inverse quote character from the name and use the GetGenericArguments method to retrieve the name of type parameters:

```
// Display the name of a generic type (including name of type parameters).
string typeName = genType.FullName;
// Strip the inverse quote character.
typeName = typeName.Remove(typeName.IndexOf('`')) + "<";
// Append the name of each type parameter.
foreach ( Type tyArg in genType.GetGenericArguments() )
{
   // The GenericParameterPosition property reflects the position where
   // this argument appears in the signature.
```

```
    if ( tyArg.GenericParameterPosition > 0 )
    {
        typeName += ",";
    }
    typeName += tyArg.Name;
}
typeName += ">";
Console.WriteLine(typeName);       // => System.Collections.Generic.Dictionary<TKey,TValue>
```

Exploring Generic Methods

You must adopt a similar approach when exploring the generics methods of a type. (Remember that a method with generic arguments can appear in both a regular and a generic type.) You can check whether a method has a generic definition by means of the MethodInfo .IsGenericMethodDefinition method and explore its generic parameters by means of the MethodInfo.GetGenericArguments method. For example, the following loop displays the name of all the methods in a type using the <...> clause for type parameters of generic methods:

```
// List all the generic methods in the ArrayType.
foreach ( MethodInfo mi in typeof(Array).GetMethods() )
{
    if ( mi.IsGenericMethodDefinition )
    {
        string methodName = mi.Name + "<";
        foreach ( Type tyArg2 in mi.GetGenericArguments() )
        {
            if ( tyArg2.GenericParameterPosition > 0 )
            {
                methodName += ",";
            }
            methodName += tyArg2.Name;
        }
        methodName += ">";
        Console.WriteLine(methodName);       // => IndexOf<T>, ...
    }
}
```

When you explore the parameters of a method, you must discern between regular types (for example, System.String) and types passed as an argument to a generic type or method (for example, T or K). This is possible because the Type class exposes a new IsGenericParameter property, which returns false in the former case and true in the latter. It is essential that you test this method before doing anything else with a Type value because some properties of a type used as a parameter in a generic class return meaningless values or might throw an exception. For example, this is the most correct way to assemble the signature of a method:

```
// (The mi variable points to a MethodInfo object.)
string signature ;
Type retType = mi.ReturnType;
if ( retType == typeof(void) )
{
    signature = "void ";
}
```

```
else
{
    signature = GetTypeName(retType) + " ";
}
signature += mi.Name + "(";

foreach ( ParameterInfo par in mi.GetParameters() )
{
    if ( par.Position > 0 )
    {
        signature += ", ";
    }
    signature += GetTypeName(par.ParameterType) + " " + par.Name;
}
signature += ")";
Console.WriteLine(signature);     // => T TestMethod(K key, V[] values, System.Int32 count)
```

where the GetTypeName function is defined as follows:

```
public static string GetTypeName(Type type)
{
    if ( type.IsGenericParameter )
    {
        return type.Name;
    }
    else
    {
        return type.FullName.Replace("&", "");
    }
}
```

Exploring Members That Use Generic Types

A slightly different problem occurs when you are dealing with a member of a type (either a regular or generic type) and the member takes or returns a generic type that has already been
bound with nongeneric arguments, as in the following case:

```
public Dictionary<string,double> Convert(List<int> x)
{
    …
}
```

When you reflect on the argument and the return type of the previous method, you get the following types:

```
System.Collections.Generic.List`1[[System.Int32, mscorlib, Version=2.0.0.0,
    Culture=neutral, PublicKeyToken=b77a5c561934e089]]

System.Collections.Generic.Dictionary`2[[System.String, mscorlib, Version=2.0.0.0,
    Culture=neutral, PublicKeyToken=b77a5c561934e089],
    [System.Double, mscorlib, Version=2.0.0.0, Culture=neutral,
     PublicKeyToken=b77a5c561934e089]]
```

Three details are worth noticing:

- The type name uses the inverse quote character syntax and is followed by the names of all the types that are bound to the generic type.

- Each argument consists of the type's full name followed by the display name of the assembly where the type is defined, all enclosed in a pair of square brackets.

- The entire list of argument types is enclosed in an additional pair of brackets.

You can easily extract the name of a generic type and its argument types by parsing this full name, for example, by using a regular expression. Alternatively, you can use the IsGeneric-Type method to check whether the type is the bound version of a generic type, and, if this is the case, you can use the GetGenericTypeDefinition method to extract the name of the original generic type and the GetGenericArguments method to extract the type of individual type arguments:

```
// (The mi variable points to a MethodInfo object.)
Type retType = mi.ReturnType;
string typeName = retType.GetGenericTypeDefinition().FullName;
typeName = typeName.Remove(typeName.IndexOf('`')) + "<";
string sep = "";
foreach ( Type argType in retType.GetGenericArguments() )
{
    typeName += sep + ReflectionHelpers.GetTypeName(argType);
    sep = ", ";
}
typeName += ">";
Console.WriteLine(typeName);
    // => System.Collections.Generic.Dictionary<System.String, System.Double>
```

In practice, you can gather all the cases that I've illustrated so far in an expanded version of the GetTypeName function (which I introduced in the previous section):

```
public static string GetTypeName(Type type)
{
    string typeName = type.FullName;
    if ( type.IsGenericTypeDefinition )
    {
        // It's the type definition of an "open" generic type.
        typeName = typeName.Remove(typeName.IndexOf('`')) + "<";
        foreach ( Type targ in type.GetGenericArguments() )
        {
            if ( targ.GenericParameterPosition > 0 )
            {
                typeName += ",";
            }

            typeName += targ.Name;
        }
        typeName += ">";
    }
    else if ( type.IsGenericParameter )
```

```
    {
        // It's a parameter in a <...> clause.
        typeName = type.Name;
    }
    else if ( type.IsGenericType )
    {
        // This is a generic type that has been bound to specific types.
        typeName = type.GetGenericTypeDefinition().FullName;
        typeName = typeName.Remove(typeName.IndexOf('`')) + "<";
        string sep = "";
        foreach ( Type argType in type.GetGenericArguments() )
        {
            typeName += sep + GetTypeName(argType);
            sep = ", ";
        }
        typeName += ">";
    }
    else if ( typeName == null )
    {
        // Use short name if full name is null.
        typeName = type.Name;
    }

    // Account for byref types.
    typeName = typeName.Replace("&", "");
    return typeName;
}
```

Thanks to its being recursive, this function is able to deal correctly even with contorted cases such as these:

```
public List<Dictionary<string,double>> MyList;
public Dictionary<string, Dictionary<string, List<int>>> MyDictionary;
```

Binding a Generic Type

At times you might need to bind a generic type with a set of one or more specific type arguments. This is necessary, for example, when you want to retrieve the Type object that corresponds to List<string> or Dictionary<string, int>. The key for this operation is the Type.MakeGenericType method:

```
// Retrieve the type that corresponds to MyGenericTable<string,double>.
// First, get a reference to the "open" generic type.
Type tableType = Assembly.GetExecutingAssembly().GetType("MyApp.GenericTable`2");
// Bind the "open" generic type to a set of arguments, and retrieve
// a reference to the GenericTable<string,double>.
Type type = tableType.MakeGenericType(typeof(string), typeof(double));
```

A bound generic type can be useful on at least a couple of occasions. First, you can use it when you need to create an instance of a specific type. (I cover object instantiation through reflection later in this chapter.) Second, you can use it when you are looking for a method with a signature that contains an argument of a specific type. Say you have the following class:

```
public class TestClass
{
    public void TestSub(List<int> list, int x)
    {
        ...
    }

    public void TestSub(List<string> list, string x)
    {
        ...
    }
}
```

How can you build a MethodInfo object that points to the first TestMethod rather than the second one? Here's the solution:

```
// First, get a reference to the List "open" generic type.
string typeName = "System.Collections.Generic.List`1";
Type openType = typeof(object).Assembly.GetType(typeName);
// Bind the open List type to the int type.
Type boundType = openType.MakeGenericType(typeof(int));
// Prepare the signature of the method you're interested in.
Type[] argTypes = { boundType, typeof(int) };
// Get the reference to that specific method.
MethodInfo method = typeof(TestClass).GetMethod("TestSub", argTypes);
```

When you bind an open generic type to a set of argument types, you should ensure that generic constraints are fulfilled. Reflection enables you to extract the constraints associated with each argument by means of the GetGenericParameterConstraints method, whereas the GenericParameterAttributes property returns an enum value that provides information about the New, Class, and Structure constraints:

```
Type genType = Assembly.GetExecutingAssembly().GetType("MyApp.GenericList`1");
foreach ( Type argType in genType.GetGenericArguments() )
{
    if ( (argType.GenericParameterAttributes &
        GenericParameterAttributes.DefaultConstructorConstraint) != 0 )
    {
        Console.WriteLine("  new() (default constructor)");
    }
    if ( (argType.GenericParameterAttributes &
        GenericParameterAttributes.ReferenceTypeConstraint) != 0 )
    {
        Console.WriteLine("  class (reference type)");
    }
    if ( (argType.GenericParameterAttributes &
        GenericParameterAttributes.NotNullableValueTypeConstraint) != 0 )
    {
        Console.WriteLine("  struct (nonnullable value type)");
    }
```

```
    // Get the constraints for this argument.
    foreach ( Type constraint in argType.GetGenericParameterConstraints() )
    {
        Console.WriteLine("  {0}", constraint.FullName);
    }
}
```

Reflecting on Attributes

.NET attributes provide a standard way to extend the metadata at the assembly, type, and member levels and can include additional information with a format defined by the programmer. Not surprisingly, the .NET Framework also provides the means to read this attribute-based metadata from an assembly. Because the attributes you define in your code are perfectly identical to the attributes that the .NET Framework defines for its own purposes, the mechanism for extracting either kind of attributes is the same. Therefore, even though in this section I show you how to extract .NET attributes, keep in mind that you can apply the same techniques for extracting your custom attributes. (You'll find many examples of the latter ones in Chapter 10, "Custom Attributes.")

Exploring Attributes

You can use several techniques to extract the custom attribute associated with a specific element.

First, you can use the IsDefined method exposed by the Assembly, Module, Type, Parameter-Info, and MemberInfo classes (and all the classes that inherit from it, such as FieldInfo and PropertyInfo). This method returns true if the attribute is defined for the specified element, but doesn't let you read the attribute's fields and properties. The last argument passed to the method is a bool value that specifies whether attributes inherited from the base class should be returned:

```
// The second argument specifies whether you also want to test
// attributes inherited from the base class.
if ( typeof(Person).IsDefined(typeof(SerializableAttribute), false) ) {
   Console.WriteLine("The Person class is serializable");
}
```

(See the companion code for the complete listing of the Person type.) Second, you can use the GetCustomAttributes method (note the plural) exposed by the Assembly, Module, Type, ParameterInfo, and MemberInfo classes (and all the classes that inherit from it). This method returns an array containing all the attributes of the specified type that are associated with the specified element so that you can read their fields and properties, and you can specify whether attributes inherited from the base class should be included in the result:

```
// Retrieve the Conditional attributes associated with the Person.SendEmail method.
MethodInfo mi = typeof(Person).GetMethod("SendEmail");
// GetCustomAttributes returns an array of Object elements, so you need to cast.
ConditionalAttribute[] miAttrs = (ConditionalAttribute[])
   mi.GetCustomAttributes(typeof(ConditionalAttribute), false);
```

```
// Check whether the result contains at least one element.
if ( miAttrs.Length > 0 )
{
   Console.WriteLine("SendEmail is marked with the following Conditional attribute(s):");
   // Read the properties of individual attributes.
   foreach ( ConditionalAttribute attr in miAttrs )
   {
      Console.WriteLine("   [Conditional(\"{0}\")]", attr.ConditionString);
   }
}
```

Third, you can use an overload of the GetCustomAttributes method exposed by the Assembly, Module, Type, ParameterInfo, and MemberInfo classes (and all the classes that inherit from it) that doesn't take an attribute type as an argument. When you use this overload, the method returns an array containing all the custom attributes associated with the element:

```
// Display all the attributes associated with the Person.FirstName field.
FieldInfo fi = typeof(Person).GetField("FirstName");
Array fiAttrs = fi.GetCustomAttributes(false);
// Check whether the result contains at least one element.
if ( fiAttrs.Length > 0 )
{
   Console.WriteLine("FirstName is marked with the following attribute(s):");
   // Display the name of all attributes (but not their properties).
   foreach ( Attribute attr in fiAttrs )
   {
      Console.WriteLine("   " + attr.GetType().FullName);
   }
}
```

To further complicate your decision, you can achieve the same results shown previously by means of static methods of the System.Attribute type:

```
// Check whether the Person class is marked as serializable.
if ( Attribute.IsDefined(typeof(Person), typeof(SerializableAttribute)) ) {
   Console.WriteLine("The Person class is serializable");
}

// Retrieve the Conditional attributes associated with the Person.SendEmail method,
// including those inherited from the base class.
MethodInfo mi = typeof(Person).GetMethod("SendEmail");
ConditionalAttribute[] miAttrs = (ConditionalAttribute[])
   Attribute.GetCustomAttributes(mi, typeof(ConditionalAttribute), true);
// Check whether the result contains at least one element.
if ( miAttrs.Length > 0 )
{
   …
}

// Display all the attributes associated with the Person.FirstName field.
FieldInfo fi = typeof(Person).GetField("FirstName");
Array fiAttrs = Attribute.GetCustomAttributes(fi, false);
```

```
// Check whether the result contains at least one element.
if ( fiAttrs.Length > 0 )
{
   …
}
```

The System.Attribute class also exposes the GetCustomAttribute static method (note the singular), which returns the only attribute of the specified type:

```
// Read the Obsolete attribute associated with the Person class, if any.
ObsoleteAttribute tyAttr = (ObsoleteAttribute)
   Attribute.GetCustomAttribute(typeof(Person), typeof(ObsoleteAttribute));
if ( tyAttr != null )
{
   Console.WriteLine("The Person class is marked as obsolete.");
   Console.WriteLine("  IsError={0}, Message={1}", tyAttr.IsError, tyAttr.Message);
}
```

> **Important**   You should never use the Attribute.GetCustomAttribute method with attributes that might appear multiple times—such as the Conditional attribute—because in that case the method might throw an AmbiguousMatchException object.

All these alternatives are quite confusing, so let me review when each of them should be used:

- If you just need to check whether an attribute is associated with an element, use the Attribute.IsDefined static method or the IsDefined instance method exposed by the Assembly, Module, Type, ParameterInfo, and MemberInfo classes. This technique doesn't actually instantiate the attribute object in memory and is therefore the fastest of the group.

- If you are checking whether a single-instance attribute is associated with an element and you want to read the attribute's fields and properties, use the Attribute.GetCustomAttribute static method. (Don't use this technique with attributes that might appear multiple times—such as the Conditional attribute—because in that case the method might throw an AmbiguousMatchException object.)

- If you are checking whether a multiple-instance attribute is associated with an element and you want to read the attribute's fields and properties, use the Attribute.GetCustomAttributes static method or the GetCustomAttributes instance method exposed by the Assembly, Module, Type, ParameterInfo, and MemberInfo classes. You must use this technique when reading all the attributes associated with an element, regardless of the attribute type.

Although all the techniques discussed in this section are available in .NET Framework 1.1 as well, there is a new important change in how you use them to query some special CLR attributes, such as Serializable, NonSerialized, DllImport, StructLayout, and FieldOffset. To improve performance and to save space in metadata tables, previous versions of the .NET

Framework stored these special attributes using a format different from all other attributes. Consequently, you couldn't reflect on these attributes by using one of the techniques I just illustrated. Instead, you had to use special properties exposed by other reflection objects, for example, the IsSerialized and IsLayoutSequential properties of the Type class or the IsNonSerialized property of the FieldInfo class. A welcome addition in .NET Framework 2.0 is that you no longer need to use any of these properties because all the special .NET attributes can be queried by means of the IsDefined, GetCustomAttribute, and GetCustomAttributes methods described in this section. (However, properties such IsSerializable and IsLayout-Sequential continue to be supported for backward compatibility.)

The CustomAttributeData Type

Version 1.1 of the .NET Framework has a serious limitation related to custom attributes: you could search attributes buried in metadata, instantiate them, and read their properties, but you have no documented means for extracting the exact syntax used in code to define the attribute. For example, you can't determine whether an attribute field or property is assigned in the attribute's constructor using a standard (mandatory) argument or a named (optional) argument; if the field or property is equal to its default value (null or zero), you can't determine whether it happened because the property was omitted in the attribute's constructor. For example, these limitations prevent a .NET developer from building a full-featured object browser.

In addition to this limitation inherited from .NET Framework 1.1, you run into another problem under .NET Framework 2.0 when you want to extract custom attributes from assemblies that have been loaded for reflection-only purposes. In fact, both the GetCustomAttribute and the GetCustomAttributes methods instantiate the custom attribute and therefore would run some code inside the assembly, which is prohibited.

Both issues have been solved by means of the new CustomAttributeData type and the auxiliary CustomAttributeTypedArgument class (which represents a positional argument in the attribute's constructor) and CustomAttributeNamedArgument class (which represents a named argument).

You create an instance of the CustomAttributeData type by means of the GetCustomAttributes static method that the type itself exposes. Each CustomAttributeData object has three properties: Constructor (the ConstructorInfo object that represents the attribute's constructor being used), ConstructorArguments (a list of CustomAttributeTypedArgument objects), and NamedArguments (a list of CustomAttributeNamedArgument objects):

```
// Retrieve the syntax used for custom attributes in the TestClass type.
IList<CustomAttributeData> attrList =
   CustomAttributeData.GetCustomAttributes(typeof(TestClass));

// Iterate over all the attributes.
foreach ( CustomAttributeData attrData in attrList )
```

```
{
   // Retrieve the attribute's type, by means of the ConstructorInfo object.
   Type attrType = attrData.Constructor.DeclaringType;
   // Start building the C# code.
   string attrString = "[" + attrType.FullName + "(";
   string sep = "";

   // Include all mandatory arguments for this constructor.
   foreach ( CustomAttributeTypedArgument typedArg in attrData.ConstructorArguments )
   {
      attrString += sep + FormatTypedArgument(typedArg);
      // A comma is used as the separator for all elements after the first one.
      sep = ", ";
   }

   // Include all optional arguments for this constructor.
   foreach ( CustomAttributeNamedArgument namedArg in attrData.NamedArguments )
   {
      // The TypedValue property returns a CustomAttributeTypedArgument object.
      CustomAttributeTypedArgument typedArg = namedArg.TypedValue;
      // Use the MemberInfo property to retrieve the field or property name.
      attrString += sep + namedArg.MemberInfo.Name + "=" + FormatTypedArgument(typedArg);
      // A comma is used as the separator for all elements after the first one.
      sep = ", ";
   }
   // Complete the attribute syntax and display it.
   attrString += ")]";
   Console.WriteLine(attrString);
}
```

The FormatTypedArgument method takes a CustomAttributeTypedArgument object and
returns the corresponding C# code that can initialize it:

```
// Return a textual representation of a string, date, or numeric value.
public static string FormatTypedArgument(CustomAttributeTypedArgument typedArg)
{
   if ( typedArg.ArgumentType == typeof(string) )
   {
      // It's a quoted string.
      return "\"" + typedArg.Value.ToString() + "\"";
   }
   else if ( typedArg.ArgumentType.IsEnum )
   {
      // It's an enum value.
      return typedArg.ArgumentType.Name + "." +
         Enum.GetName(typedArg.ArgumentType, typedArg.Value);
   }
   else
   {
      // It's something else (presumably a number).
      return typedArg.Value.ToString();
   }
}
```

Creating a Custom Object Browser

All the reflection properties shown enable you to create a custom object browser that can solve problems that are out of reach for the object browser included in Visual Studio. Creating a custom object browser isn't a trivial task, though, especially if you want to implement a sophisticated user interface. For this reason, in this section I focus on a simple but useful object browser implemented as a Console application.

The sample application I discuss here is able to display all the types and members in an assembly that are marked with the Obsolete attribute. I implemented this utility to keep an updated list of members that are in beta versions of .NET Framework 2.0 but would have been removed before the release version, as well as members that were present in .NET Framework 1.1 but have been deprecated in the current version. You can pass it the path of an assembly or launch it without passing anything on the command line: in the latter case, the utility will analyze all the assemblies in the .NET Framework main directory.

The program displays its results in the console window and takes several minutes to explore all the assemblies in the .NET Framework, but you can redirect its output to a file and then load the file in a text editor to quickly search for a type or a method. Here are the core routines:

```csharp
using System.IO;
using System.Reflection;
using System.Runtime.InteropServices;
using System;
using System.Collections;

public class App
{
   public static void Main(string[] args)
   {
      if ( args.Length == 0 )
      {
         ShowObsoleteMembers();
      }
      else
      {
         ShowObsoleteMembers(args[0]);
      }
   }

   // Process all the assemblies in the .NET Framework directory.
   public static void ShowObsoleteMembers()
   {
      string path = RuntimeEnvironment.GetRuntimeDirectory();
      foreach ( string asmFile in Directory.GetFiles(path, "*.dll") )
      {
         // Call the other overload.
         ShowObsoleteMembers(asmFile);
      }
   }
```

```csharp
// Process an assembly at the specified file path.
public static void ShowObsoleteMembers(string asmFile)
{
   try
   {
      Assembly asm = Assembly.LoadFrom(asmFile);
      ShowObsoleteMembers(asm);
   }
   catch ( Exception ex )
   {
      // The file isn't a valid assembly.
   }
}

// Process all the types and members in an assembly.
public static void ShowObsoleteMembers(Assembly asm)
{
   Type attrType = typeof(ObsoleteAttribute);

   // This header is displayed only if this assembly contains obsolete members.
   string asmHeader = string.Format("ASSEMBLY {0}\n", asm.GetName().Name);

   foreach ( Type type in asm.GetTypes() )
   {
      // This header will be displayed only if the type is obsolete or
      // contains obsolete members.
      string typeHeader = string.Format("   TYPE {0}\n", GetTypeName(type));

      // Search the Obsolete attribute at the type level.
      ObsoleteAttribute attr = (ObsoleteAttribute) Attribute.GetCustomAttribute(type,
         attrType);
      if ( attr != null )
      {
         // This type is obsolete.
         Console.Write(asmHeader + typeHeader);
         // Display the message attached to the attribute.
         string message = attr.IsError ? "ERROR" : "WARNING";
         Console.WriteLine("      {0}: {1}", message, attr.Message);

         // Don't display the assembly header again.
         asmHeader = "";
      }
      else
      {
         // The type isn't obsolete, let's search for obsolete members.
         foreach ( MemberInfo mi in type.GetMembers() )
         {
            attr = (ObsoleteAttribute) Attribute.GetCustomAttribute(mi, attrType);
            if ( attr != null )
            {
               // This member is obsolete.
               string memberHeader = string.Format("      {0} {1}",
                  mi.MemberType.ToString().ToUpper(), GetMemberSyntax(mi));
               Console.WriteLine(asmHeader + typeHeader + memberHeader);
               // Check whether using the member causes a warning or an
```

```
                    // error, and display the message.
                    string message = attr.IsError ? "ERROR" : "WARNING";
                    Console.WriteLine("            {0}: {1}", message, attr.Message);
                    // Don't display the assembly and the type header again.
                    asmHeader = "";
                    typeHeader = "";
                }
            }
        }
    }
}
```

The main program uses a few helper routines, for example, to assemble the name of a type or the signature of a method using C# syntax. I have explained how this code works in previous sections and I won't do it again here, but you can browse their complete listings in the book's companion code.

As provided, the utility displays output in a purely textual format. It is easy, however, to change the argument of String.Format methods so that it outputs XML or HTML text, which would greatly improve the appearance of the result. (The complete demo program contains modified versions of this code that outputs HTML and XML text.)

Reflection at Run Time

So far I've shown how to use reflection to enumerate all the types and members in an assembly, an activity that is central to applications such as object browsers or code generators. If you write mostly business applications, you might object that reflection doesn't have much to offer you, but this isn't correct. In fact, reflection also enables you to actually create objects and invoke methods in a sort of "late-bound" mode, that is, without you having to burn the type name and the method name in code. In this section, I show a series of techniques based on this capability.

Creating an Object Dynamically

Let's start by seeing how you can instantiate an object given its type name. You can choose from three ways to create a .NET object using reflection: by using the CreateInstance method of the System.Activator class, by using the InvokeMember method of the Type class, or by invoking one of the type's constructor methods.

If the type has a parameterless constructor, creating an instance is simple:

```
// Next statement assumes that the Person class is defined in
// a namespace named "MyApp."
Type type = Assembly.GetExecutingAssembly().GetType("MyApp.Person");
object o = Activator.CreateInstance(type, null);
// Prove that we created a Person.
Console.WriteLine("A {0} object has been created", o.GetType().Name);
```

To call a constructor that takes one or more parameters, you must prepare an array of values:

```
// (We reuse the type variable from previous code...)
// Use the constructor that takes two arguments.
object[] args2 = { "John", "Evans" };
// Call the constructor that matches the parameter signature.
object o2 = Activator.CreateInstance(type, args2);
```

You can use InvokeMember to create an instance of the class and even pass arguments to its constructor, as in the following code:

```
// Prepare the array of parameters.
object[] args3 = { "John", "Evans" };
// Constructor methods have no name and take null in the second to last argument.
object o3 = type.InvokeMember("", BindingFlags.CreateInstance, null, null, args3);
```

Creating an object through its constructor method is a bit more convoluted, but I'll demonstrate the technique here for the sake of completeness:

```
// Prepare the argument signature as an array of types (two strings).
Type[] types = { typeof(string), typeof(string) };
// Get a reference to the correct constructor.
ConstructorInfo ci = type.GetConstructor(types);
// Prepare the parameters.
object[] args4 = { "John", "Evans" };
// Invoke the constructor and assign the result to a variable.
object o4 = ci.Invoke(args4);
```

Regardless of the technique you used to create an instance of the type, you usually assign the instance you've created to a System.Object variable, as opposed to a strongly typed variable. (If you knew the name of the type at compile time, you wouldn't need to use reflection in the first place.) There is only one relevant exception to this rule: when you know in advance that the type being instantiated derives from a specific base class (or implements a given interface), you can cast the object instance to a variable typed after that base class (or interface) and access all the members that the object inherits from the base class (or interface).

The new MakeArrayType method of the Type class makes it very simple to instantiate arrays using reflection, as you can see in this code:

```
// Create an array of Double. (You can pass an integer argument to the MakeArrayType
// method to specify the rank of the array, for multidimensional arrays.)
Type arrType = typeof(double).MakeArrayType();
// The new array has 10 elements.
Array arr = (Array) Activator.CreateInstance(arrType, 10);
Console.WriteLine("{0} {1} elements", arr.Length, arr.GetValue(0).GetType().Name);
```

When you work with an array created using reflection, you typically assign its elements with the SetValue method and read them back with the GetValue method:

```
// Assign the first element and read it back.
arr.SetValue(123.45, 0);
Console.WriteLine(arr.GetValue(0));                    // => 123.45
```

Accessing Members

In the most general case, after you've created an instance by using reflection all you have is an Object variable pointing to a type and no direct way to access one of its members. The easiest operation you can perform is reading or writing a field by means of the GetValue and SetValue methods of the FieldInfo object:

```
// Create a Person object and reflect on it.
Type type = Assembly.GetExecutingAssembly().GetType("MyApp.Person");
object[] args = { "John", "Evans" };
// Call the constructor that matches the parameter signature.
object o = Activator.CreateInstance(type, args);

// Get a reference to its FirstName field.
FieldInfo fi = type.GetField("FirstName");
// Display its current value, and then change it.
Console.WriteLine(fi.GetValue(o));          // => John
fi.SetValue(o, "Robert");

// Prove that it changed, by casting to a strong-type variable.
Person pers = (Person) o;
Console.WriteLine(pers.FirstName);          // => Robert
```

Like FieldInfo, the PropertyInfo type exposes the GetValue and SetValue methods, but properties can take arguments, and thus these methods take an array of arguments. You must pass null in the second argument if you're calling parameterless properties.

```
// Get a reference to the PropertyInfo object.
PropertyInfo pi = type.GetProperty("Age");
// Note that the type of value must match exactly.
// (Int32 constants must be converted to Int16, in this case.)
pi.SetValue(o, (short)35, null);
// Read it back.
Console.WriteLine(pi.GetValue(o, null));    // => 35
```

If the property takes one or more arguments, you must pass an Object array containing one element for each argument:

```
// Get a reference to the PropertyInfo object.
PropertyInfo pi2 = type.GetProperty("Item");
// Prepare the array of parameters.
object[] args2 = { 1 };
// Set the property.
pi2.SetValue(o, "Tell John about the briefing", args2);
// Read it back.
Console.WriteLine(pi2.GetValue(o, args2));
```

A similar thing happens when you're invoking methods, except that you use the Invoke method instead of GetValue or SetValue:

```
// Get the MethodInfo for this method.
MethodInfo mi = type.GetMethod("SendEmail");
// Prepare an array for expected arguments.
```

```
object[] arguments = { "This is a message", 3 };
// Invoke the method.
mi.Invoke(o, arguments);
```

The Invoke method traps all the exceptions thrown in the called method and converts them into TargetInvocationException; you must check the InnerException property of the caught exception to retrieve the real exception:

```
try
{
    mi.Invoke(o, arguments);
}
catch ( TargetInvocationException ex )
{
    Console.WriteLine(ex.InnerException.Message);
}
catch ( Exception ex )
{
    Console.WriteLine(ex.Message);
}
```

The InvokeMember Method

In some cases, you might find it easier to set properties dynamically and invoke methods by means of the Type object's InvokeMember method. This method takes the name of the member; a flag that says whether it's a field, property, or method; the object for which the member should be invoked; and an array of Objects for the arguments if there are any. Here are a few examples:

```
Type type = Assembly.GetExecutingAssembly().GetType("MyApp.Person");
object[] arguments = { "John", "Evans" };
// Member name can be null when using BindingFlags.CreateInstance.
object obj = type.InvokeMember(null, BindingFlags.CreateInstance, null, null, arguments);

// Set the FirstName field.
object[] args = { "Francesco" };                // One argument
type.InvokeMember("FirstName", BindingFlags.SetField, null, obj, args);
// Read the FirstName field. (Pass null for the argument array.)
object value = type.InvokeMember("FirstName", BindingFlags.GetField, null, obj, null);

// Set the Age property.
object[] args2 = { (short) 35 };                // One argument
type.InvokeMember("Age", BindingFlags.SetProperty, null, obj, args2);

// Call the SendEmail method, create the argument array on the fly.
type.InvokeMember("SendEmail", BindingFlags.InvokeMethod, null, obj,
    new object[] { "This is a message", 2 });
```

It is very important that you pass the correct value for the BindingFlags argument. All the examples shown so far access public instance members, but you must explicitly add the Non-Public and/or Static modifiers if the member is private or static:

```
// Read the m_Age private field.
object age = type.InvokeMember("m_Age", BindingFlags.GetField |
    BindingFlags.NonPublic | BindingFlags.Instance, null, obj, null);
```

When you invoke a static member, you must pass null in the second to last argument. The same rule applies when you use InvokeMember to call a constructor method because you don't yet have a valid instance in that case.

The InvokeMember method does a case-sensitive search for the member with the specified name, but it's quite forgiving when it matches the type of the arguments because it will perform any necessary conversion for you if the types don't correspond exactly. You can change this default behavior by means of the BindingFlags.IgnoreCase (for case-insensitive searches) and the BindingFlags.ExactBinding (for exact type matches) values.

InvokeMember works correctly if one or more arguments are passed by reference. For example, if the SendEmail method would take the priority in a ref argument, on return from the method call the args2[1] element would contain the new value assigned to that argument.

Even though InvokeMember can make your code more concise—because you don't have to get a reference to a specific FieldInfo, PropertyInfo, or MethodInfo object—it surely doesn't make your code faster. In fact, the InvokeMember method must perform two distinct operations internally: the discovery phase (looking for the member with the specified signature) and the execution phase. If you use InvokeMember to call the same method a hundred times, it will "rediscover" the same method a hundred times, which clearly adds overhead that you can avoid if you reflect on the member once and then access the member through a FieldInfo, PropertyInfo, or MethodInfo object. For this reason, you shouldn't use InvokeMember when repeatedly accessing the same member, especially in time-critical code.

The StackTrace Object

The code you place inside a method can learn which method called it (and which called its caller, and so on) by means of the StackTrace type in the System.Diagnostics namespace. As its name suggests, the StackTrace object keeps track of all the procedures that are pending waiting for the current one to complete. Strictly speaking, the StackTrace object isn't a reflection object; however, you need reflection to leverage its full potential.

You can create the StackTrace object in many ways. In its simplest form, you pass no arguments to its constructor and you get the complete stack image as a collection of StackFrame objects, which you can enumerate by their index:

```
StackTrace st = new StackTrace();
// Enumerate all the stack frame objects.
// (The frame at index 0 corresponds to the current routine.)
for ( int i = 0; i < st.FrameCount; i++ )
{
    // Get the ith stack frame and print the method name.
    StackFrame sf = st.GetFrame(i);
    Console.WriteLine(sf.GetMethod().Name);
}
```

Another occasion for creating a StackTrace object is when an exception is caught. In this case, you can pass the exception object to the first argument of the StackTrace constructor so that the StackTrace object contains the stack state at the time the exception was thrown, rather than when you create the StackTrace object itself. The following code creates a chain of calling procedures, with the innermost procedure causing an exception that's trapped in the outermost one:

```csharp
static void TestStackFrameFromException()
{
    try
    {
        // This causes an exception.
        TestStackFrameFromException_1(1);
    }
    catch ( Exception e )
    {
        DisplayExceptionInfo(e);
    }
}

static void TestStackFrameFromException_1(int x)
{
    TestStackFrameFromException_2("abc");
}

static void TestStackFrameFromException_2(string x)
{
    TestStackFrameFromException_3();
}

static void TestStackFrameFromException_3()
{
    // Cause an exception (null reference).
    object o = null;
    Console.Write(o.ToString());
}
```

DisplayExceptionInfo is a reusable routine that displays error information:

```csharp
static void DisplayExceptionInfo(Exception e)
{
    // Display the error message.
    Console.WriteLine(e.Message);
    string res = "";
    StackTrace st = new StackTrace(e, true);
    for ( int i = 0; i < st.FrameCount; i++ )
    {
        // Get the ith stack frame and the corresponding method.
        StackFrame sf = st.GetFrame(i);
        MemberInfo mi = sf.GetMethod();
        // Append the type and method name.
        res += mi.DeclaringType.FullName + "." + mi.Name + " (";
        // Append information about the position in the source file
        // (but only if Debug information is available).
```

```
         if ( !string.IsNullOrEmpty(sf.GetFileName()) )
         {
            res += string.Format("{0}, Line {1}, Col {2},",
               sf.GetFileName(), sf.GetFileLineNumber(), sf.GetFileColumnNumber());
         }
         // Append information about offset in MSIL code, if available.
         if ( sf.GetILOffset() != StackFrame.OFFSET_UNKNOWN )
         {
            res += string.Format("IL offset {0},", sf.GetILOffset());
         }
         // Append information about offset in native code and display.
         res += " native offset " + sf.GetNativeOffset() + ")\n";
      }
   Console.WriteLine(res);
}
```

The code inside the DisplayExceptionInfo procedure shows how you can use other methods of the StackFrame object, such as GetFileName (the name of the source file), GetFileLineNumber and GetFileColumnNumber (the position in the source file), GetILOffset (offset in IL code from the top of the module), and GetNativeOffset (offset in JIT-compiled native code). By using all these pieces of information, the DisplayExceptionInfo routine can provide a more informative error report than you usually get inside the IDE. For example, you can use the value returned by the GetILOffset to launch ILDASM and see the individual MSIL opcode that threw the exception. Note that the source code's filename, line, and column are available only if the program was compiled with debugging information. If you compiled the executable for Release configuration, these properties return a null string or zero.

Because the GetMethod method of the StackFrame object returns a MethodInfo object, you can leverage reflection to learn more about that procedure, including its argument signature, which is useful when there are overloaded versions of the same procedure or any custom attribute associated with it.

Here's another case when the StackTrace object can be useful. Let's say that you discover that a given method A delivers incorrect results, but only when it's being called by another method B, either directly or not. Here's a reusable method that solves this problem:

```
public bool CheckCaller(string methodName, string typeName, bool immediateOnly)
{
   // Create a stack trace, skipping both current method and the method that invoked it.
   StackTrace st = new StackTrace(2);
   for ( int i = 0; i < st.FrameCount; i++ )
   {
      // Retrieve the MethodInfo object describing the calling method.
      StackFrame sf = st.GetFrame(i);
      MethodBase mi = sf.GetMethod();
      // Exit if method name matches. If typeName was provided, check it as well.
      if ( mi.Name == methodName && (typeName == null || mi.ReflectedType.FullName ==
         typeName) )
      {
         return true;
      }
```

```
      // Exit and return false if only the immediate caller had to be checked.
      if ( immediateOnly )
      {
          break;
      }
   }
   return false;
}
```

Here's how you can use the CheckCaller method:

```
void OpenFile(string fileName)
{
    // Break if called directly by the PrintReport method in the MyApp.DataReport type.
    if ( CheckCaller("PrintReport", "MyApp.DataReport", true) )
    {
        Debugger.Break();
    }
    …
    // Break if called by the EvalData method (in any type),
    // regardless of whether it's the direct caller.
    if ( CheckCaller("EvalData", false) )
    {
        Debugger.Break();
    }
}
```

The CheckCaller method is also useful in other situations. Let's say that you have the following handler for the TextChanged event of the txtName control:

```
private void txtName_TextChanged(object sender, EventArgs e)
{
    …
    // Oops: this causes a recursive call to this method!
    txtName.Text = txtName.Text + " ";
    …
}
```

You can prevent the recursive call by defining a class-level bool field, as follows:

```
bool runningTextChanged;

private void txtName_TextChanged(object sender, EventArgs e)
{
    // Exit if this is a recursive call.
    if ( runningTextChanged )
    {
        return;
    }
    try
    {
        runningTextChanged = true;

        …
        // Oops: this causes a recursive call to this method!
```

```
        txtName.Text = txtName.Text + " ";
        ...
    }
    finally
    {
        // Use a try...finally block to ensure that the flag is reset before exiting.
        runningTextChanged = false;
    }
}
```

You'll probably agree that it's a lot of code for just a simple task. In fact, you can simplify it significantly with the CheckCaller method:

```
// (Insert at the top of the txtName_TextChanged method...)
// Exit if this is a recursive call.
if ( CheckCaller("txtName_TextChanged") )
{
    return;
}
```

One last note about visiting the stack with the StackTrace object: some methods might not appear in the list because they've been inlined by the JIT compiler. If your program depends on the contents of the StackTrace object, you should disable inlining optimization by marking the method in question with the MethodImpl(MethodImplOptions.NoInlining) attribute.

Creating a Universal Comparer

As you might recall from Chapter 3, "Interfaces," you implement the IComparer interface in auxiliary classes that work as comparers for other types, whether they are .NET types or custom types you've defined. The main problem with comparer types is that you must define a distinct comparer type for each possible sort criterion. Clearly, this requirement can soon become a nuisance. Reflection gives you the opportunity to implement a *universal comparer*, a class capable of working with any type of object and any combination of fields and properties and that supports both ascending and descending sorts.

Before discussing how the UniversalComparer type works, let me show you how you can use it. You create a UniversalComparer instance by passing its constructor a string argument that resembles an ORDER BY clause in SQL.

```
Person[] persons;
// Init the array here.
...
// Sort the array on the LastName and FirstName fields.
UniversalComparer<Person> comp = new UniversalComparer<Person>("LastName, FirstName ");
Array.Sort<Person>(persons, comp);
```

You can even sort in descending mode separately on each field:

```
UniversalComparer<Person> comp = new UniversalComparer<Person>("LastName DESC, FirstName DESC");
Array.Sort<Person>(persons, comp);
```

Not surprisingly, the UniversalComparer class relies heavily on reflection to perform its magic. Here's its complete source code:

```csharp
public class UniversalComparer<T> : IComparer<T>
{
    private SortKey[] sortKeys;

    public UniversalComparer(string sort)
    {
        Type type = typeof(T);
        // Split the list of properties.
        string[] props = sort.Split(',');
        // Prepare the array that holds information on sort criteria.
        sortKeys = new SortKey[props.Length];

        // Parse the sort string.
        for ( int i = 0; i < props.Length; i++ )
        {
            // Get the Nth member name.
            string memberName = props[i].Trim();
            if ( memberName.ToLower().EndsWith(" desc") )
            {
                // Discard the DESC qualifier.
                sortKeys[i].Descending = true;
                memberName = memberName.Remove(memberName.Length - 5).TrimEnd();
            }
            // Search for a field or a property with this name.
            sortKeys[i].FieldInfo = type.GetField(memberName);
            if ( sortKeys[i].FieldInfo == null )
            {
                sortKeys[i].PropertyInfo = type.GetProperty(memberName);
            }
        }
    }

    // Implementation of IComparer.Compare
    public int Compare(object o1, object o2)
    {
        return Compare((T) o1, (T) o2);
    }

    // Implementation of IComparer<T>.Compare
    public int Compare(T o1, T o2)
    {
        // Deal with simplest cases first.
        if ( o1 == null )
        {
            // Two null objects are equal.
            if ( o2 == null )
            {
                return 0;
            }
            // A null object is less than any nonnull object.
            return -1;
        }
```

```
else if ( o2 == null )
{
   // Any nonnull object is greater than a null object.
   return 1;
}

// Iterate over all the sort keys.
for ( int i = 0; i < sortKeys.Length; i++ )
{
   object value1 = null;
   object value2 = null;
   SortKey sortKey = sortKeys[i];
   // Read either the field or the property.
   if ( sortKey.FieldInfo != null )
   {
      value1 = sortKey.FieldInfo.GetValue(o1);
      value2 = sortKey.FieldInfo.GetValue(o2);
   }
   else
   {
      value1 = sortKey.PropertyInfo.GetValue(o1, null);
      value2 = sortKey.PropertyInfo.GetValue(o2, null);
   }

   int res = 0;
   if ( value1 == null & value2 == null )
   {
      // Two null objects are equal.
      res = 0;
   }
   else if ( value1 == null )
   {
      // A null object is always less than a nonnull object.
      res = -1;
   }
   else if ( value2 == null )
   {
      // Any object is greater than a null object.
      res = 1;
   }
   else
   {
      // Compare the two values, assuming that they support IComparable.
      res = ( (IComparable) value1 ).CompareTo(value2);
   }

   // If values are different, return this value to caller.
   if ( res != 0 )
   {
      // Negate it if sort direction is descending.
      if ( sortKey.Descending )
      {
         res = -res;
      }
      return res;
   }
```

```
        }
        // If we get here, the two objects are equal.
        return 0;
    }

    // Nested type to store detail on sort keys
    private struct SortKey
    {
        public FieldInfo FieldInfo;
        public PropertyInfo PropertyInfo;
        // True if sort is descending.
        public bool Descending;
    }
}
```

As the comments in the source code explain, the universal comparer supports comparisons on both fields and properties. Because this class uses reflection intensively, it isn't as fast as a more specific comparer can be, but in most cases the speed difference isn't noticeable.

Dynamic Registration of Event Handlers

Another programming technique you can implement through reflection is the dynamic registration of an event handler. For example, let's say that the Person class exposes a GotEmail event and you have an event handler in the MainModule type:

```
public delegate void GotEmailEventHandler(object sender, GotEmailEventArgs e);

public class Person
{
    public event GotEmailEventHandler GotEmail;
    ...
    // A method that fires the GotEmail event
    public void SendEmail(string text, int priority)
    {
        ...
        // Raise the event if it has any subscribers.
        if ( GotEmail != null )
        {
            GotEmailEventArgs e = new GotEmailEventArgs(text, priority);
            GotEmail(this, e);
        }
    }
}

class App
{
    void GotEmail_Handler(object sender, GotEmailEventArgs e)
    {
        Console.WriteLine("GotEmail event fired");
    }
    ...
}
```

Here's the code that registers the procedure for this event, using reflection exclusively:

```
// (obj and type initialized as in previous examples…)
// Get a reference to the GotEmail event.
EventInfo ei = type.GetEvent("GotEmail");
// Get a reference to the delegate that defines the event.
Type handlerType = ei.EventHandlerType;
// Create a delegate of this type that points to a method in this module.
Delegate handler = Delegate.CreateDelegate(handlerType, typeof(App), "GotEmail_Handler");
// Register this handler dynamically.
ei.AddEventHandler(obj, handler);
// Call the method that fires the event using reflection.
object[] args = { "Hello Joe", 2 };
type.InvokeMember("SendEmail", BindingFlags.InvokeMethod, null, obj, args);
```

A look at the console window proves that the EventHandler procedure in the App class was invoked when the code in the Person.SendEmail method raised the GotEmail event. If the event handler is an instance method, the second argument to the Delegate.CreateDelegate method must be an instance of the class that defines the method; if the event handler is a static method (as in the previous example), this argument must be a Type object corresponding to the class where the method is defined.

The previous code doesn't really add much to what you can do by registering an event by means of the AddHandler operator. But wait, there's more. To show how this technique can be so powerful, I must make a short digression on delegates.

Delegate Covariance and Contravariance in C# 2.0

.NET Framework 2.0 has enhanced delegates with two important features: covariance and contravariance. Both features relax the requirement that a delegate object must match the signature of its target method exactly. More specifically, delegate covariance means that you can have a delegate point to a method with a return value that inherits from the return type specified by the delegate. Let's say we have the following delegate:

```
// A delegate that can point to a method that takes a TextBox and returns an object
delegate object GetControlData(TextBox ctrl);
```

The GetControlData delegate specifies object as the return value; the covariance feature indicates that this delegate can point to any method that takes a TextBox control, regardless of the method's return value, because all .NET types inherit from System.Object. The only requirement is that the method actually returns something; therefore, you can't have this delegate point to a C# void method. For example, a GetControlData delegate might point to the following method because the String type inherits from System.Object:

```
// A function that takes a TexbBox control and returns a string
string GetText(TextBox ctrl)
{
    return ctrl.Text;
}
```

Delegate contravariance means that a delegate can point to a method with an argument that is a base class of the argument specified in the delegate's signature. For example, a GetControl-Data delegate might point to a method that takes one argument of the Control or Object type because both these types are base classes for the TextBox argument that appears in the delegate:

```csharp
// A function that takes a Control and returns an Object value.
public object GetTag(Control ctrl)
{
    return ctrl.Tag;
}
```

It's important to realize that covariance and contravariance allow a delegate to point to methods with a signature that doesn't exactly match the delegate's signature, but they don't make the code less robust because no type mismatch exception can occur at run time.

An interesting, and somewhat undocumented, detail is that covariance and contravariance are supported at the CLR level, and therefore you can create a delegate that leverages both of them through reflection. Let's say you have the following delegate and the following method in a Microsoft Windows Forms class:

```csharp
public delegate object GetControlData(TextBox ctrl);

public string GetText(Control ctrl)
{
    return ctrl.Text;
}
```

Let's see how you can create a MethodInfo object that points to the GetText method and then pass this object to the Delegate.CreateDelegate static method:

```csharp
// The target method
MethodInfo method = this.GetType().GetMethod("GetText");
// Build the delegate through reflection.
GetControlData deleg = (GetControlData) Delegate.CreateDelegate(
    typeof(GetControlData), this, method);
// Show that the delegate works correctly.
Console.WriteLine(deleg(this.TextBox1));      // Displays the TextBox1.Text property.
```

This code is only marginally slower than the "pure C#" counterpart is, but this isn't a serious issue because you typically create a delegate once and use it repeatedly.

The most interesting application of this feature is the ability to have an individual method handle all the events coming from one or more objects, provided that the event has the canonical .NET syntax (sender, e), where the second argument can be any type that derives from EventArgs. Consider the following event handler:

```csharp
// (Inside a Form class)
public void MyEventHandler(object sender, EventArgs e)
{
    Console.WriteLine("An event has fired");
}
```

The following code can make all the events exposed by an object point to the "universal handler":

```
// (Inside the same Form class...)
// The control we want to trap events from
Control ctrl = TextBox1;
foreach ( EventInfo ei in ctrl.GetType().GetEvents() )
{
    Type handlerType = ei.EventHandlerType;
    // The universal event handler method
    MethodInfo method = this.GetType().GetMethod("MyEventHandler");
    // Use contravariance to create a delegate that points to the method.
    Delegate handler = Delegate.CreateDelegate(handlerType, this, method);
    // Use reflection to register the event.
    ei.AddEventHandler(ctrl, handler);
}
// Prove that it works by causing a TextChanged event.
ctrl.Text += "*";
```

This code proves that it is technically possible to use reflection to have all the events of an object point to an individual handler, but this technique doesn't look very promising. After all, the MyEventHandler method has no means for understanding which event was fired. To get that information, we need to do more.

A Universal Event Handler

What we need is an object that is able to "mediate" between the event source and the object where the event is handled. Writing this object requires some significant code, but the result is well worth the effort. The EventInterceptor class exposes only one event, ObjectEvent, defined by the ObjectEventHandler delegate:

```
public delegate void ObjectEventHandler(object sender, ObjectEventArgs e);

public class EventInterceptor
{
    // The public event
    public event ObjectEventHandler ObjectEvent;

    // This method is invoked from inside the EventInterceptorHandler auxiliary class.
    protected void OnObjectEvent(ObjectEventArgs e)
    {
        if ( null != ObjectEvent )
        {
            ObjectEvent(this, e);
        }
    }
    ...
```

The ObjectEventArgs class exposes three fields: EventSource (the object that raised the event), EventName (the name of the event), and Arguments (the arguments passed to the event). See the book's companion code for its source code.

The EventInterceptor class uses the nested EventInterceptorHandler type to trap events coming from the object source. More precisely, an EventInterceptorHandler instance is created for each event that the event source can raise. The EventInterceptor class supports multiple event sources; therefore, the number of EventInterceptorHandler instances can be quite high: for example, if you trap the events coming from 20 TextBox controls, the EventInterceptor object will create as many as 1,540 EventInterceptorHandler instances because each TextBox control exposes 77 events. For this reason, the AddEventSource method supports a third argument that enables you to specify which events should be intercepted:

```csharp
public void AddEventSource(object eventSource, bool includeChildren, string filterPattern)
{
    foreach ( EventInfo ei in eventSource.GetType().GetEvents() )
    {
        // Skip this event if its name doesn't match the pattern.
        if ( !string.IsNullOrEmpty(filterPattern) &&
            !Regex.IsMatch(ei.Name, "^" + filterPattern + "$") )
        {
            continue;
        }

        // Get the signature of the underlying delegate.
        MethodInfo mi = ei.EventHandlerType.GetMethod("Invoke");
        ParameterInfo[] pars = mi.GetParameters();
        // Check that event signature is in the form (sender, e).
        if ( mi.ReturnType == typeof(void) && pars.Length == 2 &&
            pars[0].ParameterType == typeof(object) &&
            typeof(EventArgs).IsAssignableFrom(pars[1].ParameterType) )
        {
            // Create a EventInterceptorHandler that handles this event.
            EventInterceptorHandler interceptor =
                new EventInterceptorHandler(eventSource, ei, this);
        }
    }
    // Recurse on child controls if so required.
    if ( eventSource is Control && includeChildren )
    {
        foreach ( Control ctrl in (eventSource as Control).Controls )
        {
            AddEventSource(ctrl, includeChildren, filterPattern);
        }
    }
}
    ...
}       // End of EventInterceptor class
```

The EventInterceptorHandler nested class does a very simple job: it uses reflection to register its EventHandler method as a listener for the specified event coming from the specified event source. When the event is fired, the EventHandler method calls back the OnObjectEvent method in the parent EventInterceptor object, which in turn fires the ObjectEvent event:

```
private class EventInterceptorHandler
{
   // The event being intercepted
   public readonly EventInfo EventInfo;
   // The parent EventInterceptor
   public readonly EventInterceptor Parent;

   public EventInterceptorHandler(object eventSource, EventInfo eventInfo,
      EventInterceptor parent)
   {
      this.EventInfo = eventInfo;
      this.Parent = parent;
      // Create a delegate that points to the EventHandler method.
      MethodInfo method = this.GetType().GetMethod("EventHandler");
      Delegate handler = Delegate.CreateDelegate(
         eventInfo.EventHandlerType, this, method);
      // Register the event.
      eventInfo.AddEventHandler(eventSource, handler);
   }

   public void EventHandler(object sender, EventArgs e)
   {
      // Notify the parent EventInterceptor object.
      ObjectEventArgs objEv = new ObjectEventArgs(sender, EventInfo.Name, e);
      Parent.OnObjectEvent(objEv);
   }
}
```

Here's how a Windows Forms application can use the EventInterceptor object to get a notification when any event of any control fires:

```
public EventInterceptor Interceptor = new EventInterceptor();

private void Form_Load(System.Object sender, System.EventArgs e)
{
   Interceptor.AddEventSource(this, true, "");
   Interceptor.ObjectEvent += new ObjectEventHandler(Interceptor_ObjectEvent);
}

private void Interceptor_ObjectEvent(object sender, ObjectEventArgs e)
{
   string msg = String.Format("Event {0} from control {1}",
      (e.EventSource as Control).Name, e.EventName);
   Debug.WriteLine(msg);
}
```

You can limit the number of events that you receive by passing a regular expression pattern to the AddEventSource method:

```
// Trap only xxxChanged events.
Interceptor.AddEventSource(this, true, ".+Changed");
// Trap only mouse and keyboard events.
Interceptor.AddEventSource(this, true, "(Mouse|Key).+)");
```

For more information, see the source code of the complete demo program. (See Figure 9-2.)

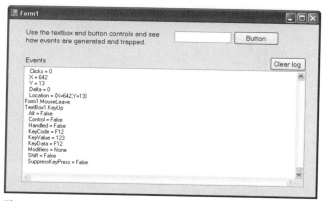

Figure 9-2   The EventInterceptor demo application

Scheduling a Sequence of Actions

Reflection enables you to implement techniques that would be very difficult (and sometimes impossible) to implement using a more traditional approach. For example, the ability to invoke methods through MethodInfo objects gives you the ability to deal with call sequences as if they were just another data type that your application processes. To see what I mean, let's say that your application must perform a series of actions—for example, file creation, registry manipulation, variable assignments—as an atomic operation. If any one of the involved actions fails, all the actions performed so far should be undone in an orderly manner: files should be deleted, registry keys should be restored, variables should be assigned their original value, and so forth.

Implementing an undo strategy in the most general case isn't a simple task, especially if some of the actions are performed only conditionally when other conditions are met. What you need is a generic solution to this problem, and you'll see how elegantly you can solve this programming task through reflection. To begin with, let's define an Action class, which represents a method—either a static or an instance method:

```csharp
public class Action
{
    public readonly string Message;       // Description of the action
    public readonly object Object;         // Instance on which the method is called
    public readonly MethodInfo Method;     // The method to be invoked
    public readonly object[] Arguments;    // Arguments for the method

    // Second argument can be an object (for instance methods) or a Type (for static methods).
    public Action(string message, object obj, string methodName, params object[] arguments)
    {
        this.Message = message;
        this.Arguments = arguments;
```

```
    // Determine the type this method belongs to.
    Type type = obj as Type;
    if ( type == null )
    {
        this.Object = obj;
        type = obj.GetType();
    }
    // Prepare the list of argument types, to call GetMethod without any ambiguity.
    Type[] argTypes = new Type[arguments.Length];
    for ( int index = 0; index < arguments.Length; index++ )
    {
        if ( arguments[index] != null )
        {
            argTypes[index] = arguments[index].GetType();
        }
    }
    // Retrieve the actual MethodInfo object, throw an exception if not found.
    this.Method = type.GetMethod(methodName, argTypes);
    if ( this.Method == null )
    {
        throw new ArgumentException("Missing method");
    }
}

    // Execute this method.
    public void Execute()
    {
        this.Method.Invoke(this.Object, this.Arguments);
    }
}
```

Instead of performing a method directly, you can create an Action instance and then invoke its Execute method:

```
// Create c:\backup directory.
Action act = new Action(@"Create c:\backup directory",
    typeof(Directory), "CreateDirectory", @"c:\backup");
act.Execute();
```

Of course, executing a method in this way doesn't bring any benefit. You see the power of this technique, however, if you define another type that works as a container for Action instances and that can also remember the "undo" action for each method being executed:

```
public class ActionSequence
{
    // The parallel lists of actions and undo actions.
    private List<Action> Actions = new List<Action>();
    private List<Action> UndoActions = new List<Action>();
    // This delegate must point to a method that takes a string.
    private System.Action<string> DisplayMethod;

    // The constructor takes a delegate to a method that can output a message.
    public ActionSequence(Action<string> displayMethod)
```

```
    {
        this.DisplayMethod = displayMethod;
    }


    // Add an action and an undo action to the list.
    public void Add(Action action, Action undoAction)
    {
        Actions.Add(action);
        UndoActions.Add(undoAction);
    }


    // Insert an action and an undo action at a specific index in the list.
    public void Insert(int index, Action action, Action undoAction)
    {
        Actions.Insert(index, action);
        UndoActions.Insert(index, undoAction);
    }


    // Execute all pending actions, return true if no exception occurred.
    public bool Execute(bool ignoreExceptions)
    {
        // This is the list of undo actions to execute in case of error.
        ActionSequence undoSequence = new ActionSequence(this.DisplayMethod);

        for ( int index = 0; index < Actions.Count; index++ )
        {
            Action act = Actions[index];
            // Skip over null actions.
            if ( act == null )
            {
                continue;
            }

            try
            {
                // Display the message and execute the action.
                DisplayMessage(act.Message);
                act.Execute();
                // If successful, remember the undo action. The undo action is placed
                // in front of all others, so that it will be the first to be executed in case
                //     of error.
                undoSequence.Insert(0, UndoActions[index], null);
            }
            catch ( TargetInvocationException ex )
            {
                // Ignore exceptions if so required.
                if ( ignoreExceptions )
                {
                    continue;
                }

                // Display the error message.
                DisplayMessage("ERROR: " + ex.InnerException.Message);
                // Perform the undo sequence. (Ignore exceptions while undoing.)
                DisplayMessage("UNDOING OPERATIONS...");
```

```
            undoSequence.Execute(true);
            // Signal that an exception occurred.
            return false;
        }
    }
    // Signal that no exceptions occurred.
    return true;
}


// Report a message by using the delegate passed to the constructor.
private void DisplayMessage(string text)
{
    if ( this.DisplayMethod != null )
    {
        this.DisplayMethod(text);
    }
}
}
}
```

The constructor of the ActionSequence type takes a System.Action<string> object, which is a delegate to a void method that takes a string as an argument. This method will be used to display all the messages that are produced during the action sequence: it can point to a method such as the Console.WriteLine method (to display messages in the console window), the WriteLine method of a StreamWriter object (to write messages to a log file), the AppendText method of a TextBox control (to display messages inside a TextBox control), or a method you define in your application:

```
// Prepare to write diagnostic messages to a log file.
StreamWriter sw = new StreamWriter(@"c:\logfile.txt");
ActionSequence actionSequence = new ActionSequence(sw.WriteLine);
…
// Close the stream when you're done with the ActionSequence object.
sw.Close();
```

The following code shows how you can schedule a sequence of actions and undo them if an exception is thrown during the process:

```
// Schedule the creation of c:\backup directory.
ActionSequence actionSequence = new ActionSequence(new Action<string>(Console.WriteLine));
Action act = new Action(@"Create c:\backup directory", typeof(Directory),
    "CreateDirectory", @"c:\backup");
Action undoAct = new Action(@"Delete c:\backup directory",
    typeof(Directory), "Delete", @"c:\backup", true);
actionSequence.Add(act, undoAct);

// Create a readme.txt file in the c:\ root directory.
string contents = "Instructions for myapp.exe...";
act = new Action(@"Create the c:\myapp_readme.txt", typeof(File), "WriteAllText", @"c:\myapp
_readme.txt", contents);
// Notice that this action has no undo action.
actionSequence.Add(act, null);
```

```
// Move the readme file to the backup directory.
act = new Action(@"Move the c:\myapp_readme.txt to c:\backup\readme.txt",
    typeof(File), "Move", @"c:\myapp_readme.txt", @"c:\backup\readme.txt");
undoAct = new Action(@"Move c:\backup\readme.txt to c:\myapp_readme.txt",
    typeof(File), "Move", @"c:\backup\readme.txt", @"c:\myapp_readme.txt");
actionSequence.Add(act, undoAct);

// Execute the action sequence. (false means that an exception undoes all actions.)
actionSequence.Execute(false);
```

After running the previous code snippet, you should find a new c:\backup directory containing the files readme.txt and win.ini. To see how the ActionSequence type behaves in case of error, delete the c:\backup directory and intentionally cause an error in the sequence by attempting to copy a file that doesn't exist:

```
// (Insert the lines in bold type before the call to the Execute method.)
...
// Copy the c:\missing.txt file to the c:\backup directory.
// THIS ACTION WILL CAUSE THE ENTIRE SEQUENCE TO BE ROLLED BACK.
act = new Action(@"Copy c:\missing.txt to c:\backup", typeof(File), "Copy",
    @"c:\missing.text", @"c:\backup\missing.txt");
actionSequence.Add(act, null);

// Execute the action sequence. (false means that an exception undoes all actions.)
actionSequence.Execute(false);
```

The intentional error causes the ActionSequence object to undo all the actions before the one that caused the exception, and in fact at the end of the process you won't find any c:\backup directory, as confirmed by the text that appears in the console window:

```
Create c:\backup directory
Create the c:\myapp_readme.txt
Move the c:\myapp_readme.txt to c:\backup\readme.txt
Copy c:\missing.txt to c:\backup
ERROR: Could not find file 'c:\missing.text'.
UNDOING OPERATIONS...
Move the c:\backup\readme.txt file back to c:\myapp_readme.txt
Delete c:\backup directory
```

In this example, I used the ActionSequence type to undo a sequence of actions that are hard-coded in the program, but I could have used a similar technique to implement an Undo menu command in your applications. Or I could have read the series of actions from a file instead, to implement undoable scripts.

You can expand the ActionSequence type with new features. For example, you might have the series of actions be performed on a background thread (see Chapter 11, "Threads," for more information) and specify multiple undo methods for a given action. You might add properties to the Action type to specify whether a failed method should abort the entire sequence. Also, you might extend the Action class with the ability to create new instances (that is, to call constructors in addition to regular methods) and to pass instances created in this way as arguments to other methods down in the action sequence. As usual, the only limit is your imagination.

On-the-Fly Compilation

Earlier in this chapter, I mentioned the System.Reflection.Emit namespace, which includes classes that let you create an assembly on the fly. The .NET Framework uses these classes internally in a few cases; for example, when you pass the RegexOptions.Compiled option to the constructor of the Regex object (see Chapter 6, "Regular Expressions"). Using reflection emit, however, isn't exactly the easiest .NET programming task, and I'm glad I've never had to use it heavily in a real-world application.

Nevertheless, at times the ability to create an assembly out of thin air can be quite tantalizing because it opens up a number of programming techniques that are otherwise impossible. For example, consider building a routine that takes a math expression entered by the end user (as a string), evaluates it, and returns the result. In the section titled "Parsing and Evaluating Expressions" in Chapter 6, I show how you can parse and evaluate an expression at run time, but that approach is several orders of magnitude slower than evaluating a compiled expression is and can't be used in time-critical code, such as for doing function plotting or finding the roots of a higher-degree equation (see Figure 9-3). In this case, your best option is to generate the source code of a C# or Visual Basic program, compile it on the fly, and then instantiate one of its classes.

Figure 9-3   The demo application, which uses on-the-fly compilation to evaluate functions and find the roots of any equation that uses the X variable

The types that allow us to compile an assembly at run time are in the Microsoft.CSharp namespace (or in the Microsoft.VisualBasic namespace, if you want to generate and compile Visual Basic source code) and in the System.CodeDom.Compiler namespace, so you need to add proper using statements to your code to run the code samples that follow.

In this particular example, I show how to generate Visual Basic code because the syntax of this language is more similar to standard algebraic expressions than C#'s is and the Visual Basic Imports statement works with types as well, unlike C#'s using statement, which works only with namespaces. In this case, both these features are quite valuable because users of our evaluator can enter expressions such as

```
Min(5, Sqrt(32)) ^ 2
```

rather than the more verbose (and obscure, for users who aren't .NET developers)

```
Math.Pow( Math.Min(5, Math.Sqrt(32)) , 2)
```

Of course, even if the evaluator generates and compiles Visual Basic code, the evaluator itself is written in C#. The demo program includes a compilation constant that allows you generate code either in Visual Basic or in C#.

The first thing to do is generate the source code for the program to be compiled dynamically. In the expression evaluator demo application, such source code is obtained by inserting the expression that the end user enters in the txtExpression field in the middle of the Eval method of an Evaluator public class:

```
string source = @"
Imports Microsoft.VisualBasic
Imports System.Math

Public Class Evaluator
    Public Function Eval(ByVal x As Double) As Double
        Return @@@
    End Function
End Class
";
// Replace the Return expression with the contents of the txtExpression field.
source = source.Replace("@@@", txtExpression.Text);
```

Next, you create a CompilerParameters object (in the System.CodeDom.Compiler namespace) and set its properties; this object broadly corresponds to the options you'd pass to the VBC command-line compiler:

```
CompilerParameters parameters = new CompilerParameters();
// Generate a DLL, not an EXE executable.
// (Not really necessary because false is the default.)
parameters.GenerateExecutable = false;
// Generate the assembly in memory, don't save to a file.
parameters.GenerateInMemory = true;
#if DEBUG
// Include debug information and keep temporary source files.
parameters.IncludeDebugInformation = true;
parameters.TempFiles.KeepFiles = true;
parameters.GenerateInMemory = false;
// params.OutputAssembly = "c:\out.dll"
#else
// Treat warnings as errors, don't keep temporary source files.
parameters.TreatWarningsAsErrors = true;
parameters.TempFiles.KeepFiles = false;
// Optimize the code for faster execution.
parameters.CompilerOptions = "/Optimize+";
#endif
// Add a reference to necessary strong-named assemblies.
parameters.ReferencedAssemblies.Add("System.Dll");
parameters.ReferencedAssemblies.Add("Microsoft.VisualBasic.Dll");
// Create the Visual Basic compiler.
VBCodeProvider provider = new VBCodeProvider();
```

If you want to compile C# code on the fly, the only differences are that you must instantiate a Microsoft.CSharp.CSharpCodeProvider instead of a Microsoft.VisualBasic.VBCodeProvider object and you don't need to add a reference to the Microsoft.VisualBasic.dll assembly.

The preceding code snippet shows the typical actions you perform to prepare a Compiler-Parameters object, as well as its most important properties. The statements inside the #if block are especially interesting. You can include debug information in a dynamic assembly and debug it from inside Visual Studio by setting the IncludeDebugInformation property to true. To enable debugging, however, you must generate an actual .dll or .exe file (GenerateInMemory must be false) and must not delete temporary files at the end of the compilation process (the KeepFiles property of the TempFiles collection must be true). If debugging is correctly enabled, you can force a break in the generated assembly by inserting the following statement in the code you generate dynamically:

```
System.Diagnostics.Debugger.Break();
```

You are now ready to compile the assembly:

```
CompilerResults compRes = provider.CompileAssemblyFromSource(parameters, source);
// Check whether we have errors.
if ( compRes.Errors.Count > 0 )
{
    // Gather all error messages, display them, and exit.
    string msg = "";
    foreach ( CompilerError compErr in compRes.Errors )
    {
        msg += compErr.ToString() + "\n";
    }
    MessageBox.Show(msg, "Compilation Failed", MessageBoxButtons.OK,
        MessageBoxIcon.Error);
}
else
{
    // Compilation was successful.
    …
}
}
```

If the compilation was successful, you use the CompilerResults.CompiledAssembly property to get a reference to the created assembly. Once you have this Assembly object you can create an instance of its Evaluator class and invoke its Eval method by using standard reflection techniques:

```
Assembly asm = compRes.CompiledAssembly;
object evaluator = asm.CreateInstance("Evaluator");
MethodInfo evalMethod = evaluator.GetType().GetMethod("Eval");
object[] args = { (double) 123)};                // Pass x = 123.
object result = evalMethod.Invoke(evaluator, args);
```

Notice that you can't reference the Evaluator class by a typed variable because this class (and its container assembly) doesn't exist yet when you compile the main application. For this reason, you must use reflection both to create an instance of the class and to invoke its members.

A tricky thing to do when applying this technique is to have the dynamic assembly call back a method in a class defined in the main application by means of reflection, for example, to let the main application update a progress bar during a lengthy routine. Alternatively, you can define a public interface in a DLL and must have the class in the main application implement the interface; being defined in a DLL, the dynamic assembly can create an interface variable and therefore it can call methods in the main application through that interface.

You must be aware of another detail when you apply on-the-fly compilation in a real application: once you load the dynamically created assembly, that assembly will take memory in your process until the main application ends. In most cases, this problem isn't serious and you can just forget about it. But you can't ignore it if you plan to build many assemblies on the fly. The only solution to this problem is to create a separate AppDomain, load the dynamic assembly in that AppDomain, use the classes in the assembly, and finally unload the AppDomain when you don't need the assembly any longer. On the other hand, loading the assembly in another AppDomain means that you can't use reflection to manage its types (reflection works only with types in the same AppDomain as the caller). Please see the demo application in the companion code for a solution to this issue.

Performance Considerations

I have warned about the slow performance of reflection-based techniques often in this chapter. Using reflection to invoke methods is similar to using the late-binding techniques that are available in script languages such as Microsoft Visual Basic Scripting Edition (VBScript), in Visual Basic 6 when you use a Variant variable, or even in Visual Basic 2005 when you invoke a method using an Object variable and Option Strict is Off.

In general, invoking a method by using reflection is many times slower than a direct call is, and therefore you shouldn't use these techniques in time-critical portions of your application. In some scenarios, however, you need to defer the decision about which method to call until run time, and therefore a direct call is out of the question. Even then, reflection should be your last resort and should be used only if you can't solve the problem with another technique based on indirection, for example, an interface or a delegate.

If you decide to use reflection and you must invoke a method more than once or twice, you should use Type.GetMethod to get a reference to a MethodInfo object and then use the MethodInfo.Invoke method to do the actual call, rather than using the Type.InvokeMember method, because the former technique requires that you perform the discovery phase only once.

Don't use the BindingFlags.IgnoreCase value with the Get*Xxx* method (singular form), if you know the exact spelling of the member you're looking for, and specify the

BindingFlags.ExactBinding value if possible because it speeds up the search. The latter flag suppresses implicit type conversions; therefore, you must supply the exact type of each argument:

```
// This code doesn't work—the GetMethod method returns null.
// You must either use int instead of short in the argTypes signature
// or drop the BindingFlags.ExactBinding bit in the GetMethod call.
Type[] argTypes = {typeof(char), typeof(short)};
MethodInfo mi = typeof(string).GetMethod("IndexOf", BindingFlags.ExactBinding |
    BindingFlags.Public | BindingFlags.Instance, null, argTypes, null);
```

.NET Framework 2.0 improves performance in many ways. For example, in previous versions of the .NET Framework, a call to the Type.Get*Xxxx* (singular) adds a noticeable overhead because all the type's members are queried anyway, as if Type.GetMembers were called. The results from this first call are cached, so at least you pay this penalty only once, but this approach has a serious issue: if you reflect on many types, all the resulting MemberInfo objects are kept in memory and are never discarded until the application terminates.

In .NET Framework 2.0, a Type.Get*Xxxx* method (singular form) doesn't cause the exploration of the entire Type object, and therefore execution is faster and memory consumption is kept to a minimum. Also, the cache used by reflection is subject to garbage collection; therefore, type and member information is discarded unless you keep it alive by storing a reference in a Type or MemberInfo field at the class level.

An alternative technique for storing information about a large number of types and members without taxing the memory is based on the RuntimeTypeHandle and RuntimeMethodHandle classes that you can use instead of the Type and MemberInfo classes. Handle-based objects use very little memory, yet they allow you to rebuild a reference to the actual Type or Member-Info-based object very quickly, as this code demonstrates:

```
// Store information about a method in the Person type.
RuntimeTypeHandle hType = typeof(Person).TypeHandle;
RuntimeMethodHandle hMethod = typeof(Person).GetMethod("SendEmail").MethodHandle;
...
// (Later in the application…)
// Rebuild the Type and MethodBase objects.
Type ty = Type.GetTypeFromHandle(hType);
MethodBase mb = MethodBase.GetMethodFromHandle(hMethod, hType);
// Use them as needed.
...
```

Security Issues

A warning about using reflection at run time is in order. As you've seen in previous sections, reflection enables you to access any type and any member, regardless of their scope. Therefore, you can use reflection even to instantiate private types, call private methods, or read private variables.

More precisely, your code can perform these operations if it is fully trusted or at least has ReflectionPermission. All the applications that run from the local hard disk have this permission, whereas applications running from the Internet don't. In general, if you don't have ReflectionPermission, you can perform only the following reflection-related techniques:

- Enumerate assemblies and modules.

- Enumerate public types and obtain information about them and their public members.

- Set public fields and properties and invoke public members.

- Access and enumerate family (protected) members of a base class of the calling code.

- Access and enumerate assembly (internal) members from inside the assembly in which the calling code runs.

You see that code can access through reflection only those types and members that it can access directly anyway. For example, a piece of code can't access a private field in another type or invoke a private member in another type, even if that type is inside the same assembly as the calling code. In other words, reflection doesn't give code more power than it already has; it just adds flexibility because of the additional level of indirection that it provides.

This discussion on reflection is important for one reason: never rely on the private scope keyword to hide confidential data from unauthorized eyes because a malicious user might create a simple application that uses reflection to read your data. If the application runs from the local hard disk, it has ReflectionPermission and can therefore access all the members of your assembly, regardless of whether it's an EXE or a DLL. (If you also consider that decompiling a .NET assembly is as easy, you see that the only way to protect confidential data is by means of cryptography.)

The ability to invoke nonpublic members can be important in some scenarios. For example, in the section titled "The ICloneable Interface" in Chapter 3, I show how a type can implement the Clone method by leveraging the MemberwiseClone protected method, but in some cases you'd like to clone an object for which you don't have any source code. Provided that your application runs in full trust mode and has ReflectionPermission, you can clone any object quite easily with reflection. Here's a reusable routine that performs a (shallow) copy of the object passed as an argument:

```csharp
public static T CloneObject<T>(T obj)
{
   if ( obj.Equals(default(T)) )
   {
     // Cloning a null object or an empty structure is easy.
     return default(T);
   }
   else if ( obj is ICloneable )
   {
     // Take advantage of the ICloneable interface, if possible.
     ICloneable iclone = (ICloneable) obj;
     return (T) iclone.Clone();
   }
```

```
        else
        {
            // Use reflection if everything else failed.
            // (Throws if application doesn't have ReflectionPermission.)
            MethodInfo mi = obj.GetType().GetMethod("MemberwiseClone",
                BindingFlags.ExactBinding | BindingFlags.NonPublic | BindingFlags.Instance);
            return (T) mi.Invoke(obj, null);
        }
    }
}
```

Assuming that you have a Person type—with the usual FirstName, LastName, and Spouse properties—the following code tests that the CloneObject method works correctly:

```
// Copy a Person object by using reflection.
Person joe = new Person("Joe", "Evans");
Person ann = new Person("Ann", "Beebe");
joe.Spouse = ann;
ann.Spouse = joe;
// We need no cast, thanks to generics.
Person joe2 = ReflectionHelpers.CloneObject(joe);
// Prove that it worked.
Console.WriteLine("{0} {1}, spouse is {2} {3}", joe2.FirstName,
    joe2.LastName, joe2.Spouse.FirstName, joe2.Spouse.LastName);
// => Joe Doe, spouse is Ann Beebe
```

Chapter 10
Custom Attributes

In Chapter 9, "Reflection," I illustrate how you can use it to enumerate the Microsoft .NET Framework attributes associated with code entities, for example, to determine programmatically whether a class is serializable. In this chapter, I focus on how you can write your own custom attributes and use them to implement advanced programming techniques.

Applying .NET attributes is vaguely similar to assigning properties to a Microsoft Windows Forms or Web Form control. When you assign a value to the Location and BackColor properties, you know that a piece of code in the .NET Framework will eventually read those properties and change the position and the background color of that control. Properties promote *declarative programming*, by which you state what you want to achieve and let another piece of code process the property and run the actual instructions that carry out the assignment. Similarly, when you label a type or a class member with an attribute, you declare how that type or that member should be processed and let another piece of code perform the actual action.

This description holds true with all the .NET attributes I illustrate in earlier (and later) chapters, and it's also true with the custom attributes that you write. The ability to define and apply custom attributes is among the most underestimated of .NET features. That's why I devote an entire chapter to this topic.

> **Note** To avoid long lines, code samples in this chapter assume that the following using statements are used at the top of each source file:
>
> ```
> using System;
> using System.CodeDom.Compiler;
> using System.Collections;
> using System.Collections.Generic;
> using System.Diagnostics;
> using System.IO;
> using System.Reflection;
> using System.Runtime.Serialization.Formatters.Binary;
> using System.Text;
> using System.Text.RegularExpressions;
> using System.Windows.Forms;
> using System.Xml.Serialization;
> ```

Introducing Custom Attributes

As you learned in previous chapters, attributes are pieces of metadata that you attach to code entities—assemblies, classes, methods, or individual fields—to affect the behavior of the Microsoft C# compiler, the JIT compiler, or other portions of the .NET runtime.

Most of the time, you'll use only attributes that are defined in the .NET Framework and documented in the .NET software development kit (SDK). Attributes are simply .NET classes, though, and nothing prevents you from designing your own attribute types. The main difference between your custom attributes and predefined .NET attributes is that custom attributes require that you write the code that discovers and uses them.

Building a Custom Attribute Class

A custom attribute is a class that inherits from System.Attribute. Its name must end with *Attribute* and it is marked with an AttributeUsage attribute that tells the compiler to which program entities the attribute can be applied: classes, modules, methods, and so on. A custom attribute class can contain fields, properties, and methods that accept and return values only of the following types: bool, byte, short, int, long, char, float, double, string, object, System.Type, and public Enum. It can also receive and return one-dimensional arrays of one of the preceding types. A custom attribute class must have one or more public constructors, and it's customary to expose constructors that let developers specify the mandatory arguments to be passed to the attribute.

> **Note** Custom attributes must be visible to at least two assemblies: the assembly where you apply the attribute and the assembly that reads and processes the applied attributes. For this reason, custom attribute types are usually defined in DLL assemblies. For simplicity's sake, all the sample attribute types I illustrate in this chapter are gathered in a demo DLL named CustomAttributes and are contained in a namespace also named CustomAttributes. You should add a reference to this DLL in all the projects where you apply or process these custom attributes.

The following example shows a custom attribute class that lets you annotate any class or class member with the name of the author, the source code version when the member was completed, and an optional property that specifies whether the code has been completely tested.

```
// The AttributeTargets.All value means that this attribute
// can be used with any program entity.
[AttributeUsage(AttributeTargets.All)]
public class VersionAttribute : System.Attribute
{
   // The Attribute constructor takes two required values.
   public VersionAttribute(string author, float version)
   {
      m_Author = author;
      m_Version = version;
   }

   // Private fields
   private string m_Author;
   private float m_Version;
   private bool m_Tested;

   public string Author
   {
      get { return m_Author; }
   }

   public float Version
   {
      get { return m_Version; }
   }

   public bool Tested
   {
      get { return m_Tested; }
      set { m_Tested = value; }
   }
}
```

Microsoft guidelines dictate that all the values accepted in the attribute constructor be implemented as read-only properties, whereas arguments that can't be set through the constructor must be implemented as read-write properties because they can be assigned only through named parameters, as in the following code:

```
[Version("John", 1.10F, Tested = true)]
public class TestVersionClass
{
   ...
}
```

An attribute can expose fields, but in general encapsulating a value inside a property is preferable. Attribute classes can also include other kinds of members, but in practice this happens infrequently: an attribute is just a repository for metadata values that are read by other programs; therefore, fields and properties are all you need most of the time. Attributes are meant to be discovered by a piece of code running in a different assembly, and therefore these classes typically have a public scope.

The argument passed to the AttributeUsage attribute specifies that the VersionAttribute attribute—or just Version, because the trailing Attribute portion of the name can be omitted—can be used with any program entity. The argument you pass to the AttributeUsage constructor is a bit-coded value formed by adding one or more elements in this list: Assembly (1), Module (2), Class (4), Struct (8), Enum (16), Constructor (32), Method (64), Property (128), Field (256), Event (512), Interface (1,024), Parameter (2,048), Delegate (4,096), ReturnValue (8,192), or All (16,383, the sum of all preceding values).

The AttributeUsage attribute supports two additional properties, which can be passed as named arguments in its constructor. The AllowMultiple property specifies whether the attribute being defined—VersionAttribute, in this case—can appear multiple times inside angle brackets. The Inherited attribute tells whether a derived class inherits the attribute. The default value for both properties is false.

The Conditional attribute is an example of an attribute that supports multiple instances and is also an example of an attribute that's inherited by derived classes. If the Conditional attribute were implemented in C#, its source code would be more or less as follows:

```
[AttributeUsage(AttributeTargets.Method, AllowMultiple = true, Inherited = true)]
public class ConditionalAttribute : System.Attribute
{
    private string m_ConditionString;

    // The constructor method
    public ConditionalAttribute(string conditionString)
    {
        this.ConditionString = conditionString;
    }

    // The only property of this attribute class
    public string ConditionString
    {
        get { return m_ConditionString; }
        set {m_ConditionString = value; }
    }
}
```

Notice that the ConditionalAttribute type violates Microsoft's own guidelines because the ConditionString writable property can also be set through the constructor.

Let's go back to the Version attribute. You can apply it to a class and its members:

```
[Version("John", 1.01F)]
public class TestVersionClass
{
    [Version("Robert", 1.01F, Tested = true)]
```

```
    public void MyProc()
    {
        ...
    }

    [Version("Ann", 1.02F)]
    public long MyFunction()
    {
        ...
    }
}
```

Compile the class in a Console project named TestApplication and read on to see how you can discover the attribute.

Reflecting on a Custom Attribute

As I emphasized previously, an attribute is a piece of information stored somewhere in its assembly's metadata tables, waiting for a program—let's call it the *agent*—to extract it and use it. When you apply .NET standard attributes, the agent program is the C# compiler, the JIT compiler, or the CLR; when you apply a custom attribute, you must write the agent code yourself. Such an agent code can be in the same DLL where the attribute is defined (if it's meant to be invoked from other assemblies) or in a separate EXE file (if it runs as a stand-alone program).

In our first example, the agent program can be as simple as a piece of code that scans an assembly and displays a report that lists which types have been authored by whom and which code members have been tested. Create another Console application, name it ShowVersion, add a reference to the CustomAttributes DLL, and type the following code:

```
using System;
using System.Reflection;
using AttributeLibrary;

namespace ShowVersion
{
    sealed public class App
    {
        public static void Main(string[] args)
        {
            // Read the assembly whose path is passed as an argument; error if not found.
            Assembly asm = Assembly.LoadFile(args[0]);
            // Display the header.
            Console.WriteLine("{0,-40}{1,-12}{2,-10}{3,-6}", "Member",
                "Author", "Version", "Tested");
            Console.WriteLine(new string('-', 68));

            // Iterate over all public and private types.
            foreach ( Type type in asm.GetTypes() )
            {
                // Extract the attribute associated with the type.
                VersionAttribute attr = (VersionAttribute)
                    Attribute.GetCustomAttribute(type, typeof(VersionAttribute ) );
```

```
        if ( attr != null )
        {
            Console.WriteLine("{0,-40}{1,-12}{2,-10}{3,-6}",
                type.FullName, attr.Author, attr.Version, attr.Tested);
        }

        // Iterate over all public and private members.
        foreach ( MemberInfo mi in type.GetMembers(BindingFlags.Public
            | BindingFlags.NonPublic
            | BindingFlags.Instance | BindingFlags.Static) )
        {
            // Extract the attribute associated with each member
            attr = (VersionAttribute) Attribute.GetCustomAttribute(mi,
                typeof(VersionAttribute)) ;
            if ( attr != null )
            {
                Console.WriteLine("    {0,-36}{1,-12}{2,-10}{3,-6}",
                    mi.Name, attr.Author, attr.Version, attr.Tested);
            }
        }
    }
  }
 }
}
```

(You might want to refer to Chapter 9 to read about the many techniques you can adopt to reflect on a custom attribute.) Compile the application and run it, passing the path of the TestApplication.exe assembly as an argument on the command line. You should see this report in the console window:

```
Member                              Author    Version   Tested
--------------------------------------------------------------
TestApplication.TestVersionClass    John      1.01      False
    MyProc                          Robert    1.01      True
    MyFunction                      Ann       1.02      False
```

Thanks to reflection and custom attributes you now have a report utility that lets you quickly display the author, the version, and the tested status of all the methods inside a compiled assembly. Sure, you can author a similar utility that reads special remarks in source code, but such a utility wouldn't work on compiled assemblies and, if your team works with other programming languages, you would be forced to write a different parser for each distinct language.

You can extend the ShowVersion utility to spot outdated or untested code quickly, and you can extend the VersionAttribute type with other properties, such as DateCreated and Date-Modified. You might automatically run ShowVersion at the end of your compilation process—for example, as a postbuild compilation step—to ensure that only fully tested code makes its way to your customers.

A Custom Attribute for CSV Serialization

The .NET Framework offers great support for serializing an object instance to and from XML, by means of the XmlSerializer type:

```
// Create a Person object.
Person pers = new Person();
pers.FirstName = "John";
pers.LastName = "Evans";

// Serialize it to a file.
XmlSerializer ser = new XmlSerializer(typeof(Person));
using ( FileStream fs = new FileStream(@"c:\person.xml", FileMode.Create) )
{
    ser.Serialize(fs, pers);
}

// Read it back. (Reuses the same serializer object.)
using ( FileStream fs = new FileStream(@"c:\person.xml", FileMode.Open) )
{
    Person p = (Person) ser.Deserialize(fs);
    Console.WriteLine("{0} {1}", p.FirstName, p.LastName);    // => John Evans
}
```

At the end of the serialization process, the person.xml file contains the following text:

```
<?xml version="1.0"?>
<Person xmlns:xsd="http://www.w3.org/2001/XMLSchema"
      xmlns:xsi="http://www.w3.org/2001/XMLSchema-instance">
  <FirstName>John</FirstName>
  <LastName>Evans</LastName>
</Person>
```

As you can see, each property of the Person type is rendered as an XML element named after the property itself. When you import XML data produced by another program, however, you have no control over the XML schema adopted during the serialization process; to solve this potential problem, you can change the default behavior of the XmlSerializer type, for example, change the names of XML elements and decide that properties be rendered as XML attributes rather than as elements, as in this XML fragment:

```
<PersonalData xmlns:xsd="http://www.w3.org/2001/XMLSchema"
      xmlns:xsi="http://www.w3.org/2001/XMLSchema-instance"
      first="John" last="Evans">
</PersonalData>
```

As you might have guessed, you can exert this degree of control on the XML serialization process by applying attributes to the members of the Person class. For example, you can produce the previous XML file by defining the Person type as follows:

```
[XmlRoot("PersonalData")]
public class Person
{
    [XmlAttributeAttribute("first")]
```

```
      public string FirstName;
      [XmlAttributeAttribute("last")]
      public string LastName;
   }
```

Unfortunately, not all the world out there speaks XML. This is especially true for legacy applications running on mainframes, which often exchange data in a simple comma-separated value (CSV) format. In this chapter, I show you how to implement CSV serialization by means of a powerful and elegant technique based on a CsvSerializer type and the CsvField custom attribute.

Let's start by defining the CsvFieldAttribute type, which can be applied to individual fields and properties of a class to affect how instances of that class are rendered in CSV format. This custom attribute has three properties: Index is the position of the field in the output; Quoted is a Boolean property that specifies whether the field or property's value must be enclosed in double quotation marks; Format is an optional format string, which gives you better control over how dates and numbers are written to the CSV file. The index value is mandatory, and therefore the Index property is marked as read-only and must be assigned from inside the attribute's constructor; the other two properties are optional and can be assigned by means of named arguments.

```
[AttributeUsage(AttributeTargets.Field | AttributeTargets.Property)]
public class CsvFieldAttribute : Attribute, IComparable

      // These would be properties in a real-world implementation.
{
   public readonly int Index;
   public bool Quoted = false;
   public string Format = "";

   public CsvFieldAttribute(int index)
   {
      this.Index = index;
   }

   // Attributes are sorted on their Index property.
   public int CompareTo(object obj)
   {
      return this.Index.CompareTo((obj as CsvFieldAttribute).Index);
   }
}
```

Unlike most attribute types, the CsvFieldAttribute class exposes an interface, IComparable, and its Compare method. The reason for this design decision will be clear shortly. Let's now define an Employee class that uses the CsvField attribute:

```
using AttributeLibrary;

public class Employee
{
   [CsvField(1, Quoted = true)]
   public string FirstName;
```

```
   [CsvField(2, Quoted = true)]
   public string LastName;
   [CsvField(3, Format = "dd/M/yyyy")]
   public DateTime BirthDate;

   public decimal m_Salary;

   [CsvField(4, Format = "######.00")]
   public decimal Salary
   {
      get { return m_Salary; }
      set { m_Salary = value; }
   }

   // Constructors and other methods...
   public Employee()
   {}
}
```

The Employee class requires a default constructor for the CsvSerializer to work correctly. (The XmlSerializer has a similar requirement.) I have included an explicit parameterless constructor, in case you wish to add other constructors later.

The toughest part is writing the CsvSerializer class, which uses reflection to read the CsvField attribute associated with each field and property exposed by the type being serialized. By implementing the CsvSerializer class as a generic type you can write more concise and efficient code:

```
public class CsvSerializer<T> where T : new()
{
   private Type type;
   private string separator;
   private SortedDictionary<CsvFieldAttribute, MemberInfo> attrList =
      new SortedDictionary<CsvFieldAttribute,MemberInfo>();
   private string rePattern;

   // Constructors
   public CsvSerializer() : this(",")
   { }

   public CsvSerializer(string separator)
   {
      this.type = typeof(T);
      this.separator = separator;
      BuildAttrList();
   }
   ...
}
```

The CsvSerializer class assumes that the field separator is a comma, but it offers an alternate constructor that enables you to specify a different separator, for example, the semicolon. While inside the constructor, the CsvSerializer class parses all the members of the T type and creates a list of (CsvFieldAttribute, MemberInfo) pairs to speed up the actual serialization and deserialization process. Such a list is stored in a SortedDictionary object and is sorted on the attribute's Index property. (Here's why the CsvFieldAttribute type implements the IComparable interface.) In addition to creating the sorted dictionary, the BuildAttrList procedure creates a regular expression that can parse individual lines of a data file in CSV format. I won't describe this regular expression in detail because I explain a similar technique in the section titled "Parsing Data Files" in Chapter 6, "Regular Expressions."

```csharp
// Build the sorted list of (attribute, MemberInfo) pairs.
private void BuildAttrList()
{
    // Create the list of public members that are flagged with the
    // CsvFieldAttribute, sorted on the attribute's Index property.
    foreach ( MemberInfo mi in type.GetMembers() )
    {
        // Get the attribute associated with this member.
        CsvFieldAttribute attr = (CsvFieldAttribute)
            Attribute.GetCustomAttribute(mi, typeof(CsvFieldAttribute));
        if ( attr != null )
        {
            // Add to the list of attributes found so far, sorted on Index property.
            attrList.Add(attr, mi);
        }
    }

    // Create the Regex pattern and format string output pattern.
    StringBuilder sb = new StringBuilder();

    foreach ( KeyValuePair<CsvFieldAttribute, MemberInfo> de in attrList )
    {
        // Add a separator to the pattern, but only from the second iteration onward.
        if ( sb.Length > 0 )
        {
            sb.Append(separator);
        }
        sb.Append(" *");

        // Get attribute and MemberInfo for this item.
        CsvFieldAttribute attr = de.Key;
        MemberInfo mi = de.Value;

        // Append to the Regex for this element.
        if ( !attr.Quoted )
        {
            sb.AppendFormat("(?<{0}>[^{1}]+)", mi.Name, separator);
        }
        else
        {
            sb.AppendFormat("\"(?<{0}>[^\"]+)\"", mi.Name);
        }
        sb.Append(" *");
    }
    // Set the pattern.
    rePattern = sb.ToString();
}
```

The CsvSerializer type exposes two Serialize methods, one that works with files and the other that works with any StreamWriter object. (The former method delegates its job to the latter.) Both methods take an ICollection<T> generic collection in their second argument, so you can serialize entire arrays and collections of T instances.

Serializing an individual object is easy. The list of serializable members is already in the attrList dictionary and is sorted in the correct sequence, so it's just a matter of reading the corresponding field or property, outputting its value to the stream, and applying the correct format string if one has been specified by means of the CsvField attribute:

```
// Serialize to text file.
public void Serialize(string fileName, ICollection<T> col)
{
   using ( StreamWriter writer = new StreamWriter(fileName) )
   {
      Serialize(writer, col);
   }
}

// Serialize to a stream.
public void Serialize(StreamWriter writer, ICollection<T> col)
{
   foreach ( T obj in col )
   {
      // This is the result string.
      StringBuilder sb = new StringBuilder();

      foreach ( KeyValuePair<CsvFieldAttribute, MemberInfo> kvp in attrList )
      {
         // Append the separator (but not at the first element in the line).
         if ( sb.Length > 0 )
         {
            sb.Append(separator);
         }
         // Get attribute and MemberInfo.
         CsvFieldAttribute attr = kvp.Key;
         MemberInfo mi = kvp.Value;

         // Get the value of the field or property, as an object.
         object fldValue = null;
         if ( mi is FieldInfo )
         {
            fldValue = ( mi as FieldInfo ).GetValue(obj);
         }
         else if ( mi is PropertyInfo )
         {
            fldValue = ( mi as PropertyInfo ).GetValue(obj, null);
         }

         // Get the format to be used with this field/property value.
         string format = "{0}";
         if ( attr.Format != "" )
         {
            format = "{0:" + attr.Format + "}";
         }
```

```
                    if ( attr.Quoted )
                    {
                        format = "\"" + format + "\"";
                    }
                    // Call the ToString method, with a format argument if specified.
                    sb.AppendFormat(format, fldValue);
                }
                // Output to the stream.
                writer.WriteLine(sb.ToString());
            }
        }
```

Deserializing from a file or a stream is only marginally more difficult. The Deserialize method uses the regular expression that was built when the CsvSerializer object was instantiated, and it extracts the value of each regular expression's Group. The Deserialize methods take an optional argument that specifies whether the first line should be ignored: this feature enables you to process data files in which the first line contains a header that lists the names of fields:

```
// Deserialize a text file.
public T[] Deserialize(string fileName, bool ignoreFieldHeader)
{
    using ( StreamReader reader = new StreamReader(fileName) )
    {
        return Deserialize(reader, ignoreFieldHeader);
    }
}

// Deserialize from a stream.
public T[] Deserialize(StreamReader reader, bool ignoreFieldHeader)
{
    // The result array
    List<T> list = new List<T>();
    // Create a compiled Regex for best performance.
    Regex re = new Regex("^" + rePattern + "$", RegexOptions.Compiled);

    // Skip the field header, if necessary.
    if ( ignoreFieldHeader )
    {
        reader.ReadLine();
    }

    while ( !reader.EndOfStream )
    {
        string text = reader.ReadLine();

        Match m = re.Match(text);
        if ( m.Success )
        {
            // Create an instance of the target type.
            T obj = new T();
            // Set individual properties.
            foreach ( KeyValuePair<CsvFieldAttribute, MemberInfo> de in attrList )
            {
                // Get attribute and MemberInfo.
                CsvFieldAttribute attr = de.Key;
                MemberInfo mi = de.Value;
```

```
                        // Retrieve the string value.
                        string strValue = m.Groups[mi.Name].Value;

                        if ( mi is FieldInfo )
                        {
                            FieldInfo fi = (FieldInfo) mi;
                            object fldValue = Convert.ChangeType(strValue, fi.FieldType);
                            fi.SetValue(obj, fldValue);
                        }
                        else if ( mi is PropertyInfo )
                        {
                            PropertyInfo pi = (PropertyInfo) mi;
                            object propValue = Convert.ChangeType(strValue, pi.PropertyType);
                            pi.SetValue(obj, propValue, null);
                        }
                    }
                    // Add this object to result.
                    list.Add(obj);
                }
            }
        // Return the array of instances.
        return list.ToArray();
    }
```

Using the CsvSerializer is simple:

```
// Create and fill a sample array of Employee objects.
Employee[] arr;
...
// Serialize all the objects to a file.
CsvSerializer<Employee> ser = new CsvSerializer<Employee>();
ser.Serialize("employees.txt", arr);
...
// Deserialize them from the file back to a different array.
Employee[] arr2 = ser.Deserialize("employees.txt", false);
```

The CsvSerializer type and its CsvField companion attribute enable you to serialize an object to the CSV format by writing very little code. You might achieve the same result by adopting a technique that isn't based on attributes, but you can hardly reach the same degree of code reusability and ease of maintenance. For example, if the order of fields in the CSV file changes, you simply need to edit one or more attributes in the Employee class without changing code elsewhere in the application and without having to worry about side effects.

> **Note**   Often you can replace, or complement, custom attributes burnt in source code with an external file that holds the same kind of information. In this particular case, you might use an XML file that contains the order of fields and the field format so that you simply need to provide a different XML file when the file format changes, without having to recompile the application. Both solutions have their pros and cons. XML files often give you more flexibility—for example, they can store hierarchical information—whereas custom attributes ensure that the metadata always travels with the code it refers to. Also, attributes are a more natural choice when the metadata doesn't change often and when, if the metadata changes, you need to recompile the code anyway. In this particular case, for example, if a new version of the CSV file has additional fields, you need to recompile the project anyway, and therefore custom attributes can be the preferred approach to store the metadata.

Building a Benchmark Tool

Microsoft Visual Studio 2005 offers many tools for testing your applications. However, when it's time to write benchmarks, the .NET Framework gives you the Stopwatch type, and that's it. If you need to benchmark multiple routines, compare and sort their results, and write a little report, you have to write all the plumbing code. You *had* to, at least.

Writing a tool that automates the production of your benchmarks requires very little effort. First, you need an attribute to mark the methods that you want to benchmark. For simplicity's sake, this version uses public fields instead of properties:

```
[AttributeUsage(AttributeTargets.Method)]
public class BenchmarkAttribute : Attribute, IComparable<BenchmarkAttribute>
{
    public BenchmarkAttribute(string group)
    {
        if ( group == null )
        {
            group = "";
        }
        this.Group = group;
    }

    // In the companion code, these are properties.
    public readonly string Group = "";
    public string Name = "";
    public double NormalizationFactor = 1;

    public int CompareTo(BenchmarkAttribute other)
    {
        int res = this.Group.CompareTo(other.Group);
        if ( res == 0 )
        {
            res = this.Name.CompareTo(other.Name);
        }
        return res;
    }
}
```

This class implements the IComparable<T> generic interface because instances of the attribute will be used as keys in a SortedList collection, as you'll see shortly. You can apply the Benchmark attribute only to a void or nonvoid static method that takes no arguments, for example, methods in a static class:

```
public static class TestBenchmarkModule
{
    [Benchmark("Concatenation", NormalizationFactor = 100)]
    public static void TestStringBuilder()
    {
        StringBuilder sb = new StringBuilder();
        for ( int i = 1; i <= 1000000; i++ )
        {
            sb.Append(i);
```

```
      }
   }

   [Benchmark("Concatenation")]
   public static void TestString()
   {
      string s = "";
      for ( int i = 1; i <= 10000; i++ )
      {
         s += i.ToString();
      }
   }

   [Benchmark("Division", Name = "Integer division")]
   public static int TestIntegerDivision()
   {
      int res = 0;
      for ( int i = 1; i <= 10000000; i++ )
      {
         res = 1000000 / i;
      }
      return res;
   }

   [Benchmark("Division", Name = "Long division")]
   public static long TestLongDivision()
   {
      long res = 0;
      for ( int i = 1; i <= 10000000; i++ )
      {
         res += 1000000 / i;
      }
      return res;
   }

   [Benchmark("Division", Name = "Double division")]
   public static double TestDoubleDivision()
   {
      double res = 0;
      for ( int i = 1; i <= 10000000; i++ )
      {
         res += 1000000 / i;
      }
      return res;
   }
}
```

The only mandatory argument of the Benchmark attribute is its Group property: benchmark methods that must be compared with each other must have the same Group name, and the tool you're going to build sorts results by their Group name. In the previous example, two benchmark groups, Concatenation and Division, contain two and three benchmarks, respectively. A benchmark also has a name, which defaults to the method name: this name identifies the individual benchmark in the report, and thus you should select a descriptive text for this property.

To see when the NormalizeFactor property can be useful, consider the TestString method, which appends 10,000 characters to a regular string. You'd like to compare this method with TestStringBuilder, but adding just 10,000 characters to a StringBuilder takes too little time to be measured by means of a Stopwatch object. The solution is to have the TestStringBuilder method perform one million iterations and to set the NormalizeFactor property to 100 so that the benchmark code knows that the result time must be divided by 100.

The structure of the benchmark tool is also simple. It scans the assembly passed to it on the command line, looking for methods flagged with the Benchmark attribute. (Only static methods with zero arguments are considered.) It sorts all benchmarks by their Group property, and then invokes each method in each group, sorts the results, and displays a report.

```
sealed public class App
{
    public static void Main(string[] args)
    {
        // Parse the assembly whose path is passed as an argument.
        Assembly asm = Assembly.LoadFile(args[0]);
        // Search all methods marked with the Benchmark attribute, sorted by their Group.
        SortedDictionary<BenchmarkAttribute, MethodInfo> attrList =
            new SortedDictionary<BenchmarkAttribute, MethodInfo>();

        // Iterate over all public and private static methods of all types.
        foreach ( Type type in asm.GetTypes() )
        {
            foreach ( MethodInfo mi in type.GetMethods(BindingFlags.Public |
                BindingFlags.NonPublic | BindingFlags.Static) )
            {
                // Extract the attribute associated with each member.
                BenchmarkAttribute attr = (BenchmarkAttribute)
                    Attribute.GetCustomAttribute(mi, typeof(BenchmarkAttribute));
                // This must be a void method that takes no arguments.
                if ( attr != null && mi.GetParameters().Length == 0 )
                {
                    // Benchmark name defaults to method name.
                    if ( attr.Name.Length == 0 )
                    {
                        attr.Name = mi.Name;
                    }
                    attrList.Add(attr, mi);
                }
            }
        }

        string lastGroup = null;
        SortedDictionary<long, BenchmarkAttribute> timingList =
            new SortedDictionary<long, BenchmarkAttribute>();
        // Display the report header.
        Console.WriteLine("{0,-20}{1,-30}{2,14}{3,12}", "Group", "Test", "Seconds", "Rate");
        Console.Write(new string('-', 78));
```

```csharp
        // Run all tests, sorted by their group.
        foreach ( KeyValuePair<BenchmarkAttribute, MethodInfo> kvp in attrList )
        {
            BenchmarkAttribute attr = kvp.Key;
            MethodInfo mi = kvp.Value;

            // Show a blank line if this is a new group.
            if ( attr.Group != lastGroup )
            {
                DisplayGroupResult(timingList);
                Console.WriteLine();
                lastGroup = attr.Group;
                timingList.Clear();
            }

            // Invoke the method.
            Stopwatch sw = Stopwatch.StartNew();
            mi.Invoke(null, null);
            sw.Stop();
            // Remember total timing, taking normalization factor into account.
            timingList.Add(Convert.ToInt64(sw.ElapsedTicks / attr.NormalizationFactor), attr);
        }
        // Display result of the last group.
        DisplayGroupResult(timingList);
    }

    // Helper routine that displays all the timings in a group
    static void DisplayGroupResult(SortedDictionary<long, BenchmarkAttribute> timingList)
    {
        if ( timingList.Count == 0 )
        {
            return;
        }

        long bestTime = -1;
        foreach ( KeyValuePair<long, BenchmarkAttribute> kvp in timingList )
        {
            // The first timing in the sorted collection is also the best timing.
            if ( bestTime < 0 )
            {
                bestTime = kvp.Key;
            }
            double rate = System.Convert.ToDouble(kvp.Key) / bestTime;
            Console.WriteLine("{0,-20}{1,-30}{2,14:N4}{3,12:N2}", kvp.Value.Group,
                kvp.Value.Name, System.Convert.ToDouble(kvp.Key) / 100000000, rate);
        }
    }
}
```

Groups in the final report are sorted alphabetically, whereas benchmarks in each group are sorted by their timings, after normalizing them if necessary. (Faster benchmarks come first.) The rightmost column, Rate, compares each timing with the best time in its group. For example, this is the report produced on my computer by running the tool against the five benchmarks listed previously:

```
Group              Test                    Seconds      Rate
-------------------------------------------------------------------
Concatenation      TestStringBuilder        0.1435      1.00
Concatenation      TestString              17.8863    124.66

Division           Double division          3.8228      1.00
Division           Integer division         5.8769      1.54
Division           Long division            6.1644      1.61
```

You can improve this first version of the benchmark tool in many ways. For example, you might save benchmark reports and automatically compare timings against a previous run of the tool to check whether some key methods of your application are performing slower than they did previously.

Writing Plug-ins for Windows Forms Applications

Most business applications must be extensible and customizable to meet specific requirements of different customers. For example, one customer might require additional fields on a data entry form; another customer might want to delete or add menu commands, and so forth. Typically, developers respond to these requirements by interspersing tons of if and switch statements in code, but this approach is clearly unsatisfactory and can quickly lead to maintenance insanity.

Even if customization isn't a requirement, you might want to build your applications from the ground up with extensibility in mind so that you can later release new modules that fit into the main application without forcing users to reinstall a completely new version. If your application can be extended and customized without having to recompile its source code, expert users might create their own modules, without putting your support team under pressure.

The first and most delicate step in building extensible and customizable applications is designing a plug-in infrastructure. In this section, I show you how to implement a powerful and flexible mechanism that enables you (or your users) to create plug-ins that are notified when a form in the main application is created so that each plug-in can add its own controls and menu commands or even replace the original form with a completely different form. Not surprisingly, the technique I am about to illustrate is based on custom attributes. It is a simplified version of the extension mechanism we use for Code Architects' Windows Forms applications that need to be extensible.

The PluginLibrary Project

Create a new blank solution and add a Class Library project named PluginLibrary. This project contains only two classes: FormExtenderAttribute and FormExtenderManager.

The FormExtenderAttribute Type

For simplicity's sake, the listing for the FormExtender custom attribute class uses fields instead of properties. (The companion code for this book uses property procedures that validate incoming values, though.)

```
[AttributeUsage(AttributeTargets.Class)]
public class FormExtenderAttribute : Attribute
{
    public readonly string FormName;
    public readonly bool Replace;
    public bool IncludeInherited;

    // Constructors
    public FormExtenderAttribute(string formName) : this(formName, false)
    {}

    public FormExtenderAttribute(string formName, bool replace)
    {
        this.FormName = formName;
        this.Replace = replace;
    }
}
```

You can use the FormExtender attribute with two different kinds of classes. You can use it either with a plug-in (nonvisual) class that must be notified when a form in the main application has been created or with a plug-in form class that replaces a form in the main application. In the former case, you set the Replace argument to false (or omit it); in the latter case, you assign it the true value. In both cases, *FormName* is the complete name of a form in the main application that is being instantiated; if IncludeInherited is true, the plug-in works with both the specified form class and all the forms that inherit from that form class. These three properties enable you to create several plug-in flavors:

```
[FormExtender("MainApplication.MainForm")]
public class MainForm_Extender
{
    public MainForm_Extender(MainForm frm)
    {
        // This plug-in class is instantiated when the MainForm is loaded.
        …
    }
}

[FormExtender("System.Windows.Forms.Form", IncludeInherited = true)]
public class GenericForm_Extender
{
    public GenericForm_Extender(Form frm)
    {
        // This plug-in class is instantiated when any form in the main application is
        // loaded because it specifies a generic form and sets IncludeInherited to true.
        …
    }
}
```

```
[FormExtender("MainApplication.MainForm", true)]
public class OptionForm_Replacement :
System.Windows.Forms.Form
{
   // This form replaces the main application's OptionsForm class.
   …
}
```

Plug-in classes that don't replace a form (Replace argument is false) are instantiated immediately after the form in the main application and a reference to the form is passed to their constructor so that the plug-in has an opportunity to add one or more user interface elements. (Read on for examples.)

The FormExtenderManager Type

The FormExtenderManager class exposes three important static methods. The Initialize-Plugins method parses all the DLL assemblies in a directory that you specify, looks for types marked with the FormExtender attribute, and stores information about these types in a generic Dictionary for later retrieval. If the main application doesn't call this method explicitly, it will be executed anyway when any of the next two methods is invoked. (In this case, you can't specify a path and InitializePlugins automatically looks for plug-ins in the main application's folder.)

```
public static class FormExtenderManager
{
   // All the FormExtenders known to this manager
   private static Dictionary<string, FormExtenderInfo> extenders;

   // Initialize the list of form extenders when the type is referenced.
   public static void InitializePlugIns()
   {
      string dirName = Path.GetDirectoryName(Application.ExecutablePath);
      InitializePlugIns(dirName);
   }

   // Create the list of form extenders.
   public static void InitializePlugIns(string dirName)
   {
      extenders = new Dictionary<string, FormExtenderInfo>();
      // Visit all the DLLs in this directory.
      foreach ( string dllName in Directory.GetFiles(dirName, "*.dll") )
      {
         try
         {
            // Attempt to load this assembly.
            Assembly asm = Assembly.LoadFile(dllName);
            ParseAssembly(asm);
         }
         catch ( Exception ex )
         {
            // Ignore DLLs that aren't assemblies.
         }
      }
   }
```

The extenders Dictionary contains instances of the FormExtenderInfo nested type. This dictionary is built inside the ParseAssembly private method:

```
private static void ParseAssembly(Assembly asm)
{
    Type attrType = typeof(FormExtenderAttribute);
    // Check all the types in the assembly.
    foreach (Type type in asm.GetTypes() )
    {
        // Retrieve the FormExtenderAttribute.
        FormExtenderAttribute attr = (FormExtenderAttribute)
            Attribute.GetCustomAttribute(type, attrType, false) ;
        if ( attr != null )
        {
            // Add to the dictionary.
            FormExtenderInfo info = new FormExtenderInfo();
            info.FormName = attr.FormName;
            info.Replace = attr.Replace;
            info.IncludeInherited = attr.IncludeInherited;
            info.Type = type;
            extenders.Add(info.FormName, info);
        }
    }
}

// A nested class used to hold information on form extenders
private class FormExtenderInfo
{
    public string FormName;
    public bool Replace;
    public bool IncludeInherited;
    public Type Type;
}
```

The Create method takes a form type as a generic parameter, creates an instance of that form type, and then notifies all plug-ins that the form has been created. However, if a plug-in class has a FormExtender attribute whose FormName property matches the form's name and whose Replace property is set to true, the Create method creates an instance of the plug-in form rather than the original form.

```
public static T Create<T>() where T : Form
{
    // The private CreateForm method does the real job.
    return (T) CreateForm<T>() ;
}

private static Form CreateForm<T>() where T : Form
{
    // Initialize plug-ins if necessary.
    if ( extenders == null )
    {
        InitializePlugIns();
    }
```

```
            Type formType = typeof(T);
            string formName = formType.FullName;
            bool mustNotify = true;

            // Check whether this form appears in the dictionary.
            if ( extenders.ContainsKey(formName) )
            {
                FormExtenderInfo info = extenders[formName];
                // If form must be replaced, instantiate the corresponding type instead.
                if ( info.Replace )
                {
                    formType = info.Type;
                    mustNotify = false;
                }
            }

            // Create the form.
            Form frm = (Form) Activator.CreateInstance(formType, true) ;
            // Notify all extenders, if necessary, and then return form to the caller.
            if ( mustNotify )
            {
                NotifyFormCreation(frm);
            }
            return frm;
        }
```

NotifyFormCreation takes a form type as an argument and instantiates all the plug-in classes that have been declared as extensions for the specified form.

```
        public static void NotifyFormCreation(Form frm)
        {
            // Initialize plug-ins if necessary.
            if ( extenders == null )
            {
                InitializePlugIns();
            }

            string formName = frm.GetType().FullName;
            Type extenderType = null;

            // Check whether this form appears in the dictionary.
            if ( extenders.ContainsKey(formName) )
            {
                // Don't notify forms that would replace the original one.
                if ( ! extenders[formName].Replace )
                {
                    extenderType = extenders[formName].Type;
                }
            }
            else
            {
                // Check whether there is an extender that applies to one of the base classes.
                Type type = frm.GetType();
```

```
      do
      {
         type = type.BaseType;
         if ( extenders.ContainsKey(type.FullName) )
         {
            FormExtenderInfo info = extenders[type.FullName];
            // We can use this extender only if the IncludeInherited property is true.
            if ( info.IncludeInherited && !info.Replace )
            {
               extenderType = info.Type;
               break;
            }
         }
         // Continue until we get to the System.Windows.Forms.Form base class.
      }
      while ( type != typeof(Form) );
   }

   if ( extenderType != null )
   {
      // Invoke the extender's constructor, passing the form instance as an argument.
      // (This statement fails if such a constructor is missing.)
      try
      {
         object[] args = { frm };
         Activator.CreateInstance(extenderType, args);
      }
      catch ( Exception ex )
      {
         // This should never happen.
         Debug.WriteLine("Constructor not found for type " + extenderType.FullName);
      }
   }
  }
 }
}   // End of FormExtenderManager class
```

Notice that this version of the PluginLibrary supports only one plug-in for each form. A more complete implementation would manage a list of all the plug-ins that want to be notified when a given form is created. (Clearly, only one plug-in class can replace a form, though.)

The MainApplication and MainApplicationStartup Projects

Applications that are extensible through plug-ins must be built by following a couple of criteria. First, the application is actually split into two assemblies: a DLL that contains the bulk of the application, including all its forms, and a simple EXE that displays the application's main form (and therefore indirectly bootstraps the DLL). It is necessary to have all the forms in a separate DLL because plug-ins might need to inherit from one of the forms in the main application. (You can reference a type in another EXE assembly, but you can't inherit a form from a form defined in an EXE.) The second criterion requires that you instantiate a form by means the FormExtenderManager.Create method rather than by using the New keyword, as I explain shortly.

The Startup Project

Let's create the startup assembly first. Create a Windows Forms application containing this code:

```
// (This code assumes that you've imported the PluginLibrary namespace.)
public static void Main()
{
    Application.EnableVisualStyles();
    Application.Run(PluginLibrary.FormExtenderManager.Create<MainApplication.MainForm>());
}
```

The current project requires a reference to both the PluginLibrary project and the Main-Application project, which I illustrate in the following section.

The MainApplication Project

Next, create a Class Library project named MainApplication, and add a reference to the PlugioLibrary project and to any other .NET assembly you use, including the System.Windows .Forms.dll assembly. Also, the code that follows assumes that a using statement for the Plugin-Library namespace has been added at the top of each source file.

Start adding forms to this project and the code that uses these forms as you'd do normally, with one exception: use the FormExtenderManager.Create method rather than a plain New keyword to instantiate a form. For example, the MainForm class can have a menu, as shown in Figure 10-1. The Sample Form command on the View menu should display a form named SampleForm, and thus you should display such a form using the following code:

```
Form frm = FormExtenderManager.Create<SampleForm>();
frm.Show();
```

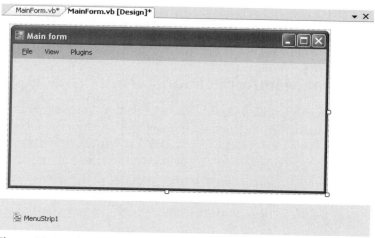

Figure 10-1   The application's main form

Alternatively, if you are sure that a form is never replaced by a plug-in form, you can create the form normally and then use the NotifyFormCreation method to let plug-ins know that the form has been created. You can call this method from inside the overridden OnLoad method:

```
protected override void OnLoad(EventArgs e)
{
    base.OnLoad(e);
    FormExtenderManager.NotifyFormCreation(this);
}
```

Creating Inheritable Forms

If the main application accesses one or more public members of a form, you can't simply replace the original form with another form defined in the plug-in DLL. For example, notice how the following code accesses the Total public property of the CalculatorForm:

```
CalculatorForm frmCalc = PluginLibrary.FormExtenderManager.Create<CalculatorForm>();
if ( frmCalc.ShowDialog() == System.Windows.Forms.DialogResult.OK )
{
    // Read the Total public property of the CalculatorForm type.
    MessageBox.Show(frmCalc.Total.ToString(), "Total", MessageBoxButtons.OK,
        MessageBoxIcon.Information);
}
```

The only way for a plug-in to replace the CalculatorForm type with a different form without making the previous code fail is by having the plug-in form inherit from CalculatorForm. (Because of this requirement you had to define all the application's forms in a DLL rather than in a plain EXE.) If you want to allow plug-ins to do the replacement in a simple way, you should create the CalculatorForm class with inheritance in mind. Basically, this means that you have to adhere to the following guidelines:

- In the Properties window, set the Modifiers property to Protected for all the controls on the form. (Tip: select all controls by pressing Ctrl+A and change the Modifiers property for all of them in one operation.)

- Don't put any "interesting" code inside event handlers; instead, place this code inside public or protected methods marked as virtual and call these methods from inside event handlers.

For example, the CalculatorForm must update all TextBox controls on the right when the contents of any field on the left changes. (See Figure 10-2.) Here's the correct way to update these calculated fields:

```
public partial class CalculatorForm
{
    public decimal Total;

    public CalculatorForm()
    {
        InitializeComponent();
    }
```

```csharp
private void ValueChanged(System.Object sender, System.EventArgs e)
{
    CalculateTotal();
}

protected virtual void CalculateTotal()
{
    try
    {
        int units = int.Parse(txtUnits.Text);
        decimal unitPrice = decimal.Parse(txtUnitPrice.Text);
        decimal percentTax = decimal.Parse(txtPercentTax.Text);
        decimal total = units * unitPrice;
        decimal tax = total * percentTax / 100;
        decimal grandTotal = total + tax;

        txtTotal.Text = total.ToString("N2");
        txtTax.Text = tax.ToString("N2");
        txtGrandTotal.Text = grandTotal.ToString("N2");
    }
    catch ( Exception ex )
    {
        // Clear result fields in case of exceptions.
        txtTotal.Text = "";
        txtTax.Text = "";
        txtGrandTotal.Text = "";
    }
}
}
```

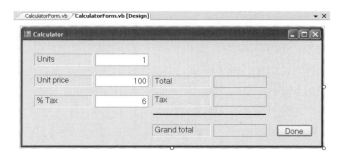

Figure 10-2   The CalculatorForm, which lets you perform simple calculations

Before proceeding, make MainApplicationStartup the startup project in the solution and run the application. You haven't defined any plug-in so far, and thus the PluginLibrary should do absolutely nothing.

The SamplePlugin Project

You're now ready to create your first plug-in. Add a new Class Library project, name it Sample-Plugin, and add a reference to the PluginLibrary and the MainApplication projects. The sample plug-in project contains three types: SampleForm_Replacement is a form that replaces the SampleForm form; MainForm_Extender adds a menu command to the application's main form; CalculatorForm is a form that replaces the CalculatorForm class.

Replacing a Form with a Different Form

The first class is very simple indeed. Just create a form named SampleForm_Replacement, mark it with the FormExtender attribute, and add controls as you'd do in a regular form:

```
[PluginLibrary.FormExtender("MainApplication.SampleForm", true)]
public class SampleForm_Replacement
{
   …
}
```

In this case, the replacement form doesn't need to have any relation to the original form because the main application never references a method, a field, or control from outside the form class itself.

Extending a Form with User Interface Elements

The MainForm_Extender class extends the MainForm class without replacing it; thus, you must flag the MainForm_Extender class with a FormExtender attribute whose Replace property is false. The plug-in infrastructure will pass a MainForm instance to this class's constructor when the main form is loaded so that code in MainForm_Extender can add new elements to the form's Controls collection or, as in this case, to the DropDownItems collection of a StripMenu component:

```
[PluginLibrary.FormExtender("MainApplication.MainForm")]
public class MainForm_Extender
{
   public MainForm_Extender(MainApplication.MainForm frm)
   {
      // Add an entry to the Plugins menu.
      ToolStripMenuItem item = new ToolStripMenuItem("Show Date", null, MenuClick);
      frm.mnuPlugins.DropDownItems.Add(item);
   }

   private void MenuClick(object sender, EventArgs e)
   {
      MessageBox.Show(DateTime.Now.ToString(), "Current Date/Time",
         MessageBoxButtons.OK, MessageBoxIcon.Information);
   }
}
```

Notice that the previous code assumes that the mnuPlugins ToolStripMenu object on the application's MainForm is declared as public; otherwise, the code in the plug-in DLL can't add new elements to it.

Replacing a Form with an Inherited Form

The CalculatorForm_Replacement form both inherits from and replaces the main application's CalculatorForm type. To create this form, select the Add New Item command from the Project menu, select the Inherited Form template, click the Add button, select the Calculator-Form element inside the Inheritance Picker dialog box, and then click OK.

Next, make the form taller and move the two bottommost rows of fields down to make room for new controls that let you define a discount percentage. (See Figure 10-3.) Finally, add this code to make the form perform as intended:

```
[PluginLibrary.FormExtender("MainApplication.CalculatorForm", true)]
public partial class CalculatorForm_Replacement
{
    public CalculatorForm_Replacement()
    {
        InitializeComponent();
    }

    private void txtPercentDiscount_TextChanged(System.Object sender, System.EventArgs e)
    {
        CalculateTotal();
    }


    protected override void CalculateTotal()
    {
        if ( !this.Visible )
        {
            return;
        }

        try
        {
            int units = int.Parse(txtUnits.Text);
            decimal unitPrice = decimal.Parse(txtUnitPrice.Text);
            decimal percentTax = decimal.Parse(txtPercentTax.Text);
            decimal percentDiscount = decimal.Parse(txtPercentDiscount.Text);

            decimal total = units * unitPrice;
            decimal discount = total * percentDiscount / 100;
            decimal discountedTotal = total - discount;
            decimal tax = discountedTotal * percentTax / 100;
            decimal grandTotal = discountedTotal + tax;

            txtTotal.Text = total.ToString("N2");
            txtDiscount.Text = discount.ToString("N2");
            txtDiscountedTotal.Text = discountedTotal.ToString("N2");
            txtTax.Text = tax.ToString("N2");
            txtGrandTotal.Text = grandTotal.ToString("N2");
        }
        catch ( Exception ex )
        {
            // Clear result fields in case of exceptions.
            txtTotal.Text = "";
```

```
            txtDiscount.Text = "";
            txtDiscountedTotal.Text = "";
            txtTax.Text = "";
            txtGrandTotal.Text = "";
        }
    }
}
```

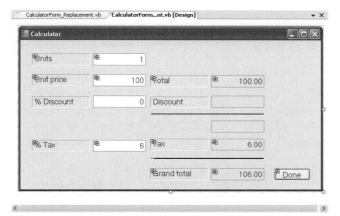

Figure 10-3   The new SamplePlugin project, which extends the CalculatorForm to account for a discount percentage

Notice that you need to handle the TextChange event only for the txtPercentDiscount control because the original CalculatorForm class in the main application takes care of the other input controls. When the original form invokes the CalculateTotal method, the overridden version in CalculatorForm_Replacement runs and you have an opportunity to take a discount into account.

Compiling and Testing the SamplePlugin Project

By default, The FormExtenderManager.InitializePlugins method looks into the main application's folder for plug-in DLLs. In our example, this folder is the folder where the MainApplicationStartup EXE file is located; therefore, you should manually copy the SamplePlugin.dll file into this folder whenever you recompile the SamplePlugin project. Alternatively, you can define a postcompilation build step that automates the copy operation or, even better, modify the Output Path setting (on the Build page of the project's designer) so that the SamplePlugin.dll file is compiled right in the main application's folder.

Another simple solution to this minor issue is to have the MainApplicationStartup project include a reference to the SamplePlugin project. The code in the main application's project never references the plug-in project, but this reference forces Visual Studio to copy the plug-in DLL into the application's folder whenever you recompile the solution.

Once all the executables are compiled and stored in the correct folders, you can run the application, check that the new user interface elements have been created, and check that they react as intended.

One final note: the PluginLibrary enables you to extend or replace any form defined in the main application, but the concepts it relies on can be applied to any kind of class, not just forms. In the last section of this chapter, you'll learn more about using custom attributes to affect the way objects are instantiated and used in your applications.

A Framework for *n*-Tiered Applications

The last example in this chapter is also the most complex code sample in the entire book. It is a completely functional, though simplified, framework that promotes the creation of data-centric applications that can be expanded, modified, and customized at will. In this section, I refer to this framework as the CAP framework because it's a (very) stripped-down version of Code Architects Platform, a product that my company has built and refined over the years and that is the heart of many real-world data-centric applications used in Italian government agencies that serve tens of thousands of clients simultaneously. (Contact me if you need information about the real thing.)

An *n-tiered application* is an application that makes a clear distinction between objects that generate the user interface, objects that represent real-world entities (the *business objects*), and objects that take care of reading and writing data on a database or another persistent medium (the *data objects*). All the data objects used in an application make up the Data Access Layer, or DAL. Keeping the three kinds of objects completely distinct makes programming more complex, but it offers an unparalleled degree of flexibility. For example, if your *n*-tiered application has a DAL that works with Oracle, you might replace it with a DAL that is tailored for Microsoft SQL Server. If the user interface, business, and data layers are completely distinct, this change doesn't affect either the user interface or the business tier.

Having distinct data and business tiers offers additional advantages. For example, in some cases you can change the structure of the database with minimal or no impact on the user interface. Even better, you can deploy the data objects on a remote computer, where they can interact with the database in a more efficient way. (In this case, the data objects must have a way of communicating with the business tier or the user interface tier by means of a remoting technique supported by .NET, such as Web Services, serviced components, or .NET remoting.) If the *n*-tiered application is designed correctly, you can change the deployment configuration of individual data and business objects to match a specific network configuration, again with minimal impact on other tiers.

The example I illustrate in this section is a simplified *n*-tiered application, which has only the user interface tier (a Windows Forms client) and the data tier. For simplicity's sake, no business tier is included. Also, in an attempt to make the code as concise as possible, DAL objects move data from the database to the application and back by means of typed DataSet objects. Some Service Oriented Architecture (SOA) purists might dislike this design choice, but—again—I wanted to simplify the code to make the important details stand out. If you don't like using DataSets in this fashion, you can modify the CAP framework to use custom collections. This replacement is relatively simple, thanks to generic collections. (See Chapter 4, "Generics.")

Despite its simplicity, the CAP framework supports a couple of advanced features. First, the client application never instantiates a data object directly; instead, it uses a factory class named DataObjectFactory, which returns a data object that is specific for a given configuration and the specified database table. This approach enables you to use different data objects for different configurations transparently—such as "SqlServer," "Oracle," "Access," "Demo," and so forth—without changing the code in the client application. Different configurations can correspond to different databases, different application versions, different network topologies, and so on.

> **Note**   In this chapter, I use the term *database table* to indicate the entity that a data object reads from and writes to. A data object can interact with sources other than database tables—for example, text or XML files, or a Web Service—therefore, you shouldn't take this term literally in this context. Think of it more as an abstract "data entity" than a physical database table.

Second, and more interesting, you can associate one or more companion objects with each data object. A *data object companion* is an object that attaches itself to a data object and can take part in commands that read or write data to the database. The job of a companion object can be as simple as logging all database operations to a trace file or as complex as filtering the data being read from or written to the database. Near the end of this chapter, I show you how to build a companion object that extends a data object with caching abilities.

The DataObjectLibrary Project

All the interfaces, custom attributes, and helper types that make up the CAP framework are gathered in the DataObjectLibrary.dll assembly. (See Figure 10-4.) This assembly must be referenced both by the client application and the DLLs that contain data objects and companion objects. In the remainder of this chapter I assume that a using statement for the DataObject-Library namespace has been added at the file or project level where necessary.

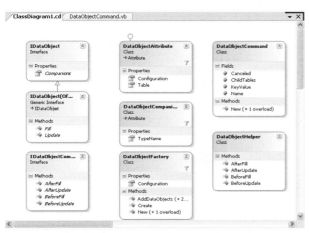

Figure 10-4   All the types in the DataObjectLibrary project, the core of the CAP framework

Interfaces

The CAP framework defines three interfaces. The IDataObject and IDataObject<T> interfaces define the methods that a data object must expose, whereas the IDataObjectCompanion interface defines the data commands a companion object can take part in:

```
public interface IDataObject
{
   List<IDataObjectCompanion> Companions { get; }
}

public interface IDataObject<TDataSet> : IDataObject where TDataSet : DataSet
{
   TDataSet Fill(TDataSet ds, DataObjectCommand command);
   TDataSet Update(TDataSet ds, DataObjectCommand command);
}

public interface IDataObjectCompanion
{
   void BeforeFill(IDataObject obj, DataSet ds, DataObjectCommand command);
   void BeforeUpdate(IDataObject obj, DataSet ds, DataObjectCommand command);
   void AfterFill(IDataObject obj, DataSet ds, DataObjectCommand command);
   void AfterUpdate(IDataObject obj, DataSet ds, DataObjectCommand command);
}
```

Notice that the IDataObject<T> interface derives from the nongeneric IDataObject interface and defines data objects that work with a strong-typed DataSet object. The role of these interfaces will be clear shortly.

Custom Attributes

The DataObjectLibrary project contains two custom attributes: DataObjectAttribute is used to mark data objects, whereas DataObjectCompanionAttribute is used to mark companion objects. Here's an abridged definition of these attributes, where I have replaced properties with fields to keep the listing as concise as possible. (See the companion code for the complete definition of these classes.)

```
[AttributeUsage(AttributeTargets.Class | AttributeTargets.Struct, Inherited = true)]
public class DataObjectAttribute : Attribute, IComparable<DataObjectAttribute>
{
   public DataObjectAttribute(string configuration, string table)
   {
      this.Configuration = configuration;
      this.Table = table;
   }

   // The configuration in which the data object is valid
   public string Configuration;
   // The database table this data object applies to
   public string Table;
```

```
   // Support for the IComparable<DataObjectAttribute> interface
   public int CompareTo(DataObjectAttribute other)
   {
      int res = this.Configuration.CompareTo(other.Configuration);
      if ( res == 0 )
      {
         res = this.Table.CompareTo(other.Table);
      }

      return res;
   }
}

[AttributeUsage(AttributeTargets.Class, AllowMultiple = true)]
public class DataObjectCompanionAttribute : Attribute
{
   public DataObjectCompanionAttribute(string typeName)
   {
      if ( typeName == null )
      {
         typeName = "";
      }
      this.TypeName = typeName;
   }

   // The type of the data object. Use "" for all data objects.
   public string TypeName;
}
```

The DataObjectCompanionAttribute can be applied multiple times to the same class: in other words, a companion object can serve multiple data objects.

The DataObjectFactory Type

The DataObjectFactory type is a key component of the CAP framework. Client applications use this type to instantiate the data object that corresponds to a given configuration and a given database table.

```
public class DataObjectFactory
{
   // This dictionary holds all data objects found so far.
   public readonly Dictionary<string, Type> DataObjects = new Dictionary<string, Type>();
   // This dictionary holds all validator objects for a given data object.
   public readonly Dictionary<string, List<Type>> DataCompanions = new Dictionary<string,
      List<Type>>();

   // Constructors
   public DataObjectFactory(string configuration, Assembly assembly)
   {
      this.Configuration = configuration;
      AddDataObjects(assembly);
   }
```

```
public DataObjectFactory(string configuration, string dataObjectsDirectory)
{
    this.Configuration = configuration;
    AddDataObjects(dataObjectsDirectory);
}

// The Configuration string
public readonly string Configuration;
```

The AddDataObjects method is where the DataObjectFactory type parses an assembly and records all the data objects and the companion objects it finds:

```
// Add all the DataObjects of this assembly to the list.
public void AddDataObjects(Assembly assembly)
{
    foreach ( Type type in assembly.GetTypes() )
    {
        // Look for types marked with the DataObject attribute.
        DataObjectAttribute doAttr = (DataObjectAttribute)
            Attribute.GetCustomAttribute(type, typeof(DataObjectAttribute), false);
        // Ensure that type implements IDataObject and that it's suitable
        // for this configuration (or current configuration is null).
        if ( doAttr != null && typeof(IDataObject).IsAssignableFrom(type) &&
            ( string.Compare(this.Configuration, doAttr.Configuration, true) == 0
            || this.Configuration.Length == 0 ) )
        {
            // Add to the dictionary only if not there already.
            if ( !DataObjects.ContainsKey(doAttr.Table.ToLower()) )
            {
                DataObjects.Add(doAttr.Table.ToLower(), type);
            }
        }

        // Look for types marked with the DataObjectValidator attribute.
        // (This attribute allows multiple instances.)
        DataObjectCompanionAttribute[] coAttrs =
            (DataObjectCompanionAttribute[])Attribute.GetCustomAttributes(type,
            typeof(DataObjectCompanionAttribute), false);
        if ( coAttrs != null && coAttrs.Length > 0 )
        {
            // Iterate over each instance of the attribute.
            foreach ( DataObjectCompanionAttribute coAttr in coAttrs )
            {
                // Create an item in the DataValidators dictionary, if necessary.
                if ( !this.DataCompanions.ContainsKey(coAttr.TypeName) )
                {
                    this.DataCompanions.Add(coAttr.TypeName, new List<Type>());
                }
                // Add this validator to the list.
                this.DataCompanions[coAttr.TypeName].Add(type);
            }
        }
    }
}
```

The Create method is invoked by client applications when they need a data object for a specific database table:

```csharp
// Create a data object for a given database/table.
public IDataObject Create(string table)
{
    if ( !this.DataObjects.ContainsKey(table.ToLower()) )
    {
        throw new ArgumentException("Table not found: " + table);
    }
    // Create an instance of the corresponding data object.
    Type type = this.DataObjects[table.ToLower()];
    IDataObject dataObj = (IDataObject) Activator.CreateInstance(type, true);

    // Add all data companions associated with this specific data object.
    if ( this.DataCompanions.ContainsKey(type.FullName) )
    {
        // Create an instance of each companion associated with this data object,
        // and add the instance to the Companions collection.
        foreach ( Type coType in this.DataCompanions[type.FullName] )
        {
            IDataObjectCompanion compObj = (IDataObjectCompanion)
                Activator.CreateInstance(coType, true);
            dataObj.Companions.Add(compObj);
        }
    }

    // Add all the generic companions (associated with all data objects).
    if ( this.DataCompanions.ContainsKey("") )
    {
        // Create an instance of each companion associated with this data object,
        // and add it to the Companions collection.
        foreach ( Type coType in this.DataCompanions[""] )
        {
            IDataObjectCompanion compObj = (IDataObjectCompanion)
                Activator.CreateInstance(coType, true);
            dataObj.Companions.Add(compObj);
        }
    }
    return dataObj;
}
}       // End of DataObjectFactory type
```

In practice, a client application must create an instance of the DataObjectFactory type for a given configuration and then invoke the Create method when a new data object is needed. The Create method instantiates the data object associated with the configuration/table combination, creates all the data companions that should be associated with that data object, and finally returns the data object to the client:

```csharp
// (In a client application...)
// Prepare a list of all data objects in the application's folder.
DataObjectFactory factory = new DataObjectFactory("Access", Application.StartupPath);
```

```csharp
void PerformQuery()
{
   // Create a data object for the Customers database table that
   // knows how to deal with NWINDDataSet objects.
   IDataObject<NWINDDataSet> doCustomers =
      (IDataObject<NWINDDataSet>) factory.Create("Customers");
   ...
}
```

If you have your data objects spread in more than one DLL, you can call the AddDataObjects method multiple times, once for each DLL.

The DataObjectCommand Type

The DataObjectCommand type is a repository for storing information about an operation that a data object must perform. It contains only fields and one constructor.

```csharp
public class DataObjectCommand
{
   // The name of this command
   public readonly string Name;
   // The list of child tables to be included in the fill/update command
   public readonly List<string> ChildTables = new List<string>();
   // The value of key column. (This version supports only one key column.)
   public readonly object KeyValue;
   // True if this command has been canceled (by a data companion)
   public bool Canceled;

   public DataObjectCommand(string name, object keyValue, params string[] childTables)
   {
      this.Name = name;
      this.KeyValue = keyValue;
      if ( childTables != null )
      {
         this.ChildTables.AddRange(childTables);
      }
   }
}
```

The DataObjectCommand type adds a lot of flexibility to the CAP framework. Thanks to this type, data objects simply need to expose two methods, Fill and Update, which can execute virtually all the operations you typically perform on a database. Each method can behave differently, depending on the values you pass through the DataObjectCommand argument. For example, the Fill method can read an entire table or just one row, depending on whether you've assigned a value to the KeyValue property, and might return the rows in child tables as well, if you have passed the name of one or more child tables.

```csharp
// (In a client application...)
// Create a data object for the Customers database table that
// knows how to deal with NWINDDataSet objects.
   IDataObject<NWINDDataSet> doCustomers =
      (IDataObject<NWINDDataSet>) factory.Create("Customers");
```

```
// Create a command that reads the entire Customers table (no key specified)
// and also retrieves the Orders child table.
DataObjectCommand command = new DataObjectCommand("GetCustomers", null, "Orders");
// Use the data object to fill a local DataSet.
doCustomers.Fill(this.NwindDataSet1, command);
```

A crucial feature of the CAP framework is that all companion objects can inspect the Data-ObjectCommand that has been passed to the Fill or Update method, both before and after the actual data operation is performed. In the "before" phase, a companion object can set the command's Cancel property to true and indirectly prevent the command from being carried out. Later in this chapter, I show you how you can use this feature to implement a caching mechanism: in that case, the companion object fills the DataSet with data taken from the cache, and then sets the Cancel property to false to notify the data object that it doesn't have to actually extract data from the database. A common operation you can perform either in the "before read" or in the "after read" phase is setting a filter on the data being read to ensure that each user can see only the data he or she is allowed to see. You often use the "before write" phase to validate all data one instant before it is written to the database.

The DataObjectHelper Type

The last type in the CAP framework is simply a container for static helper methods. You can use this helper object to reduce the amount of code inside individual data objects.

```
public static class DataObjectHelper
{
    public static bool BeforeFill(IDataObject obj, DataSet ds, DataObjectCommand command)
    {
        foreach ( IDataObjectCompanion companion in obj.Companions )
        {
            companion.BeforeFill(obj, ds, command);
        }
        return !command.Canceled;
    }

    public static bool BeforeUpdate(IDataObject obj, DataSet ds, DataObjectCommand command)
    {
        foreach ( IDataObjectCompanion companion in obj.Companions )
        {
            companion.BeforeUpdate(obj, ds, command);
        }
        return !command.Canceled;
    }

    public static bool AfterFill(IDataObject obj, DataSet ds, DataObjectCommand command)
    {
        foreach ( IDataObjectCompanion companion in obj.Companions )
        {
            companion.AfterFill(obj, ds, command);
        }
        return !command.Canceled;
    }
```

```
public static bool AfterUpdate(IDataObject obj, DataSet ds, DataObjectCommand command)
{
    foreach ( IDataObjectCompanion companion in obj.Companions )
    {
        companion.AfterUpdate(obj, ds, command);
    }
    return !command.Canceled;
}
}
```

In practice, each method in this class notifies all the companions of a data object that a
Before*Xxxx* or After*Xxxx* step has been reached, and it returns true if no companion object has
canceled the command. Thanks to this helper class, the code in the data object can be simplified remarkably:

```
// (Inside a data object...)
public NWINDDataSet Fill(NWINDDataSet ds, DataObjectCommand command)
{
    // Notify all companion objects that the Fill command is about to be executed.
    if ( DataObjectHelper.BeforeFill(this, ds, command) )
    {
        // Execute the Fill command. (No companion object has canceled it.)
        …
    }
    // Notify all companion objects that the Fill command has been completed.
    DataObjectHelper.AfterFill(this, ds, command);
    return ds;
}

public NWINDDataSet Update(NWINDDataSet ds, DataObjectCommand command)
{
    // Notify all companion objects that the Update command is about to be executed.
    if ( DataObjectHelper.BeforeUpdate(this, ds, command) )
    {
        // Execute the Update command. (No companion object has canceled it.)
        …
    }
    // Notify all companion objects that the Update command has been completed.
    DataObjectHelper.AfterUpdate(this, ds, command);
    return ds;
}
```

The DataSets Project

The next step in building a data-centric application based on the CAP framework is creating
a separate DLL project where you define one or more strong-typed DataSet types. Keeping
your DataSets in a separate project is necessary because both the main application and the
various DLLs that contain data objects and companion objects must have a reference to these
shared DataSet types.

The demonstration solution contains an assembly named DataSets, which contains one DataSet type named NWINDDataSet, which is shaped after the NWIND.MDB Microsoft Access database. (I use this database because chances are that you already have it on your computer; if not, it comes with the companion code for this book.) I use Access only for the sake of simplicity: *n*-tiered applications typically work with enterprise-sized database engines such as SQL Server or Oracle.

Code in the companion project assumes that the NWIND.MDB file resides in the C:\ root directory, and thus you should move it there before running the samples. If you want to store the file in a different directory, you must change the value of the NWINDConnectionString setting in all the projects that make up the solution.

The whole point in using data objects is the ability to keep the code in the main application completely separate from the data access code so that you can easily migrate this sample application to use a different database engine. For this reason, you should look at the NWINDDataSet type only as a container for data, not as a sort of in-memory database that exactly mirrors the structure of a real database. As I noted previously, a data object doesn't necessarily interact with a database and can read from and write to other data stores, such as XML files.

You can create the NWINDDataSet type in Visual Studio 2005 very simply. Select the Add New Data Source command from the Data menu to open the Data Source Configuration Wizard. In the first step, select the Database option and click Next; in the second step, click the New Connection button to create a new OLE DB connection that points to the NWIND.MDB file. When you click Next, Visual Studio asks whether you want to include the .mdb file in the project folder: answer No because the NWINDDataSet type should have no direct relation to the database you're using, as I just emphasized. In the next step, accept that you want to save the connection string in the application's configuration file. (See Figure 10-5.) In the fourth and last steps, select which tables you want to include in the DataSet. In this demonstration, you can just select the Customers, Orders, and Order Details tables.

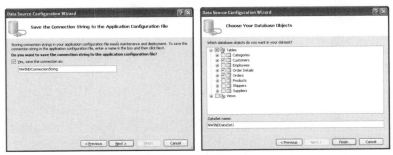

Figure 10-5 Two steps in the Data Source Configuration Wizard

When you click the Finish button, Visual Studio creates the file NWINDDataSet.xsd, which contains the schema of the new DataSet. You can double-click this file in the Solution Explorer to view the graphical representation of all the tables in the DataSet and their relations. (See Figure 10-6.) In Microsoft Visual Studio .NET 2003, you had to create table relationships by hand.

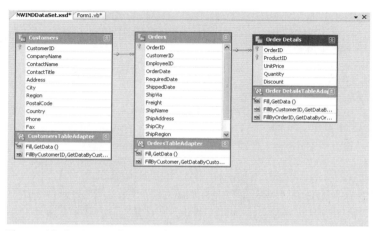

Figure 10-6   For each DataTable in the DataSet, you can define one or more custom commands, such as FillByCustomerID.

Each DataTable type in the DataSet has a companion TableAdapter object, which enables you to read data from and write data to that table by means of methods named Fill, GetData, and Update. In addition to these standard methods, you can define your own queries by right-clicking a table in the .xsd schema, pointing to Add, and selecting Query. For example, the sample code requires that you add a query named FillByCustomerID. In the first step of the TableAdapter Query Configuration Wizard, you decide whether you want to retrieve data using an SQL statement or a stored procedure; if you're using an Access database, only the first option is available. In the second step, you select which type of query you want to perform; for this demo, choose the Select Which Returns Rows option. In the next step, type the SQL statement that returns data, for example, a parameterized query that returns a single record:

```
SELECT CustomerID, CompanyName, ContactName, ContactTitle, Address, City,
    Region, PostalCode, Country, Phone, Fax FROM Customers WHERE CustomerID=?
```

(Use an argument name prefixed with the at sign (@) if you're accessing a SQL Server database.) In the fourth step, assign a name to the Fill*Xxxx* and GetData*Xxxx* commands you are creating (FillByCustomerID and GetDataByCustomerID in this specific example). Finally, click the Finish button to generate the custom TableAdapter commands. (See Figure 10-7.)

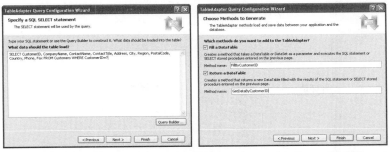

Figure 10-7   Two steps of the TableAdapter Query Configuration Wizard

> **Note**   Although I love the power of TableAdapters and their custom commands, I can't help but notice that the Microsoft decision to generate TableAdapter types in the same assembly as the DataSet type they refer to is a rather questionable design choice that makes TableAdapters less useful in enterprise-level *n*-tiered applications. In such applications, TableAdapter objects shouldn't be located in the same assembly where the DataSet is defined because this arrangement prevents each data object from using a TableAdapter object that is specific for a given database.
>
> In this demonstration program, we leave the TableAdapters as nested classes of the NWIND-DataSet type. In a real application, however, you should cut the TableAdapter code from that type and paste it into the same assembly where the data objects for that specific database are located. Of course, you'll also need to update all the using statements to ensure that all the TableAdapter commands continue to work correctly even if they now reference a DataSet in a different assembly.

The DemoClient Project

Even if you haven't defined any data objects so far, already you can create a client application that will use them. In fact, the client application doesn't need any direct reference to the assembly that contains your data objects. More precisely, the application should *not* have such a reference because clients must be completely independent of the actual data objects. If you don't create a dependency between the client and a specific data object, you can later replace a new set of DAL objects to match a different database or network configuration.

Create a Windows Forms project named DemoClient and ensure that it has a reference to the DataObjectLibrary and DataSets projects. Open the Data section of the Toolbox, drop a DataSet component onto the form's designer, specify DataSets.NWINDDataSet as the typed DataSet, and name it NwindDataSet1. Next, drop two BindingSource components onto the form, name them bsCustomers and bsCustomersOrders, and set their properties as follows:

```
bsCustomers.DataSource = NwindDataSet1
bsCustomers.DataMember = Customers
bsCustomersOrders.DataSource = bsCustomers
bsCustomersOrders.DataMember = CustomersOrders
```

Create a very simple user interface by dropping a couple of buttons and two DataGridView controls on the main form, as shown in Figure 10-8. Set the DataSource property of the topmost DataGridView equal to bsCustomers and the DataSource property of the bottommost DataGridView equal to bsCustomersOrders. Finally, enter this code in the form's class:

```
// Look for all the data objects in the application's folder.
DataObjectFactory factory = new DataObjectFactory("Access", Application.StartupPath);

private void btnFill_Click(System.Object sender, EventArgs e)
{
    IDataObject<NWINDDataSet> doCustomers =
        (IDataObject<NWINDDataSet>) factory.Create("Customers");
    DataObjectCommand command = new DataObjectCommand("GetCustomers", null, "Orders");
    doCustomers.Fill(this.NwindDataSet1, command);
}

private void btnUpdate_Click(object sender, EventArgs e)
{
    IDataObject<NWINDDataSet> doCustomers =
        (IDataObject<NWINDDataSet>) factory.Create("Customers");
    DataObjectCommand command = new DataObjectCommand("UpdateCustomers", null, "Orders");
    doCustomers.Update(this.NwindDataSet1, command);
}
```

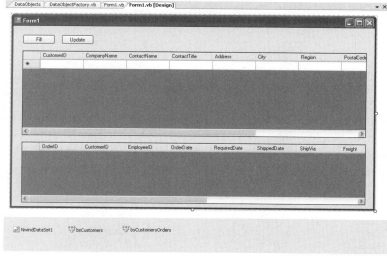

Figure 10-8 The main form of the DemoClient project

I commented on this code in the section titled "The DataObjectCommand Type" earlier in this chapter. Just notice that the client code has no direct reference to the actual data object: it uses a DataObjectFactory to get a data object that works with the specified configuration/table combination, it specifies a data command in a generic way, and finally it interacts with the data object by means of the IDataObject<T> generic interface.

Compile the DemoClient project to ensure that everything is in place, but don't run it yet because it won't work until you define at least one data object for the "Access" configuration.

The DataObjects Project

Create a new Class Library project named DataObjects and ensure that the output directory for this project matches the output directory of the main application. This build configuration simulates what happens in a real-world application when you deploy a DLL holding one or more data objects in the main application's folder.

The DOCustomers Type

A data object is a class that implements the IDataObject(Of T) generic interface and that is marked with the DataObject custom attribute. For example, the following data object is used under the configuration named "Access" and can access the database table named "Customers":

```
[DataObject("Access", "Customers")]
public partial class DOCustomers : IDataObject<NWINDDataSet>
{
    // The IDataObject interface

    private List<IDataObjectCompanion> m_Companions = new List<IDataObjectCompanion>();

    public List<IDataObjectCompanion> Companions
    {
        get { return m_Companions; }
    }

    // The IDataObject<TDataSet> interface

    public NWINDDataSet Fill(NWINDDataSet ds, DataObjectCommand command)
    {
        …
    }

    public NWINDDataSet Update(NWINDDataSet ds, DataObjectCommand command)
    {
        …
    }
}
```

The main application invokes the Fill method to read one or more database tables into the DataSet. The DOCustomers object is expected to read data from the database and fill one or more tables of the DataSet passed in the first argument. The data object learns which child tables to read, if any, by looking at the ChildTable collection of the DataObjectCommand passed in the second argument. (Corresponding statements in the following listing are in bold type.) Before actually reading any data, however, the data object notifies its companion objects that an operation is about to be performed:

```csharp
public NWINDDataSet Fill(NWINDDataSet ds, DataObjectCommand command)
{
    if ( ds == null )
    {
        ds = new NWINDDataSet();
    }

    if ( DataObjectHelper.BeforeFill(this, ds, command) )
    {
        DataSets.NWINDDataSetTableAdapters.CustomersTableAdapter taCustomers =
            new DataSets.NWINDDataSetTableAdapters.CustomersTableAdapter();
        taCustomers.Fill(ds.Customers);
        if ( command.ChildTables.Contains("Orders") )
        {
            DataSets.NWINDDataSetTableAdapters.OrdersTableAdapter taOrders =
                new DataSets.NWINDDataSetTableAdapters.OrdersTableAdapter();
            taOrders.Fill(ds.Orders);
        }
    }
    DataObjectHelper.AfterFill(this, ds, command);
    return ds;
}
```

You can easily enhance the DOCustomers type to support additional commands. For example, this data object might be able to read data about individual customers and their orders:

```csharp
// (Replace the bold type section of the previous listing with this code.)
string customerId = "";
if ( command.KeyValue != null )
{
    customerId = command.KeyValue.ToString();
}

DataSets.NWINDDataSetTableAdapters.CustomersTableAdapter taCustomers =
    new DataSets.NWINDDataSetTableAdapters.CustomersTableAdapter();
if ( customerId.Length == 0 )
{
    taCustomers.Fill(ds.Customers);
}
else
{
    taCustomers.FillByCustomerID(ds.Customers, customerId);
}

if ( command.ChildTables.Contains("Orders") )
{
    DataSets.NWINDDataSetTableAdapters.OrdersTableAdapter taOrders =
        new DataSets.NWINDDataSetTableAdapters.OrdersTableAdapter();
    if ( customerId.Length == 0 )
    {
        taOrders.Fill(ds.Orders);
    }
```

```
            else
            {
                taOrders.FillByCustomerID(ds.Orders, customerId);
            }
        }
```

Typically, the Update method is simpler and has fewer options. Here's an implementation of this method that writes the Customers table and, optionally, the Orders child table. This code splits in two parts the updates to the Customers table—first it inserts the new records and then it removes the deleted records—to not break the referential integrity of the records that take part in the Customers_Orders relation:

```
public NWINDDataSet Update(NWINDDataSet ds, DataObjectCommand command)
{
    if ( DataObjectHelper.BeforeUpdate(this, ds, command) )
    {
        DataSets.NWINDDataSetTableAdapters.CustomersTableAdapter taCustomers =
            new DataSets.NWINDDataSetTableAdapters.CustomersTableAdapter();
        // Send new and modified rows to the database.
        taCustomers.Update(ds.Customers.Select(null, null,
            DataViewRowState.Added | DataViewRowState.ModifiedCurrent));

        // Update the child table, if so requested.
        if ( command.ChildTables.Contains("Orders") )
        {
            DataSets.NWINDDataSetTableAdapters.OrdersTableAdapter taOrders =
                new DataSets.NWINDDataSetTableAdapters.OrdersTableAdapter();
            taOrders.Update(ds.Orders);
        }
        // Remove deleted records from the database.
        taCustomers.Update(ds.Customers.Select(null, null, DataViewRowState.Deleted));
    }
    DataObjectHelper.AfterUpdate(this, ds, command);
    return ds;
}
```

A more robust implementation should account for other relations that exist in the database. For example, you can't delete a row in the Orders table if you don't delete all the rows in the Order Details table that are related to that specific order. Also, a real-world data object should perform all the updates under a transaction so that all changes can be rolled back if an error occurs during the process.

At this point, you can compile the entire solution and run the DemoClient application. If you didn't make any mistakes, the application should be able to view and modify any record in the Customers and the Orders tables. Once you're sure that everything is working as expected, you can begin building a few companion objects for the DOCustomers type.

Data object companions can be located in the same assembly as the data objects they refer to or in a separate assembly. In the demonstration solution, I opted for the first approach to keep the number of projects as low as possible, but in most real-world cases you should put them in their own assembly.

The Tracer Companion Type

The simplest data object companion you can build is a tracer component, which displays details of all the operations being performed on data. Such a tracer component can work with any data object; thus, the first argument in the DataObjectCompanion attribute that marks it can be an empty string:

```
[DataObjectCompanion("")]
public class Tracer : IDataObjectCompanion
{
    public void BeforeFill(IDataObject obj, DataSet ds, DataObjectCommand command)
    {
        Console.WriteLine("[{0}] BeforeFill - Command:{1}",
            (obj as object).GetType().Name, command.Name);
    }

    public void BeforeUpdate(IDataObject obj, DataSet ds, DataObjectCommand command)
    {
        Console.WriteLine("[{0}] BeforeUpdate - Command:{1}",
            ( obj as object ).GetType().Name, command.Name);
    }

    public void AfterFill(IDataObject obj, DataSet ds, DataObjectCommand command)
    {
        Console.WriteLine("[{0}] AfterFill - Command:{1}",
            ( obj as object ).GetType().Name, command.Name);
    }

    public void AfterUpdate(IDataObject obj, DataSet ds, DataObjectCommand command)
    {
        Console.WriteLine("[{0}] AfterUpdate - Command:{1}",
            ( obj as object ).GetType().Name, command.Name);
    }
}
```

Recompile the DataObjects.dll, run the DemoClient again, and test the read and update commands: you should see the various diagnostic messages in the Visual Studio console window. (Needless to say, a real tracer object should send its output to a debugger or a file.)

The CustomerCache Companion Type

The second companion type in the DataObjects project is far more interesting in that it enables you to cache the result of a query on a local file transparently so that the actual database isn't accessed too often. Thanks to the CAP framework's infrastructure, such a caching feature can be achieved with very little code. First, define a user-level setting named CacheFile and assign it the path to the cache file you want to create, for example, c:\CustomersCache.xml. Next, enter this code:

```
[DataObjectCompanion("DataObjects.DOCustomers")]
public class CustomerCache : IDataObjectCompanion
{
```

```csharp
// The location of the cache file is stored in the application's config file.
public string cacheFile = Properties.Settings.Default.CacheFile;

public void AfterFill(IDataObject obj, DataSet ds, DataObjectCommand command)
{
    if ( command.ChildTables.Contains("Orders") & !command.Canceled )
    {
        SaveToCache(ds);
    }
}

public void AfterUpdate(IDataObject obj, DataSet ds, DataObjectCommand command)
{
    if ( command.ChildTables.Contains("Orders") & !command.Canceled )
    {
        SaveToCache(ds);
    }
}

public void BeforeFill(IDataObject obj, DataSet ds, DataObjectCommand command)
{
    // If the cached file has already been saved today, use cached data.
    if ( File.Exists(cacheFile) && File.GetCreationTime(cacheFile).Date == DateTime.Today )
    {
        LoadFromCache(ds);
        // Let the data objects know that the command has been canceled.
        command.Canceled = true;
    }
}

public void BeforeUpdate(IDataObject obj, DataSet ds, DataObjectCommand command)
{
    // Nothing to do.
}

// Save and load from the cache.

private void SaveToCache(DataSet ds)
{
    Console.WriteLine("Dataset is being saved to {0}", cacheFile);
    ds.RemotingFormat = SerializationFormat.Binary;
    using ( FileStream fs = new FileStream(cacheFile, FileMode.Create) )
    {
        BinaryFormatter bf = new BinaryFormatter();
        bf.Serialize(fs, ds);
    }
}

private void LoadFromCache(DataSet ds)
{
    Console.WriteLine("Dataset is being loaded from {0}", cacheFile);
    ds.RemotingFormat = SerializationFormat.Binary;
    using ( FileStream fs = new FileStream(cacheFile, FileMode.Open) )
```

```
        {
            BinaryFormatter bf = new BinaryFormatter();
            DataSet ds2 = (DataSet) bf.Deserialize(fs);
            ds.Merge(ds2);
        }
    }
}
```

The companion object checks the creation date of the cache file in the BeforeFill method, and then, if the cache file has been created on the same day, the DataSet is filled with data taken from the local file and the command is canceled. Other companion objects can check the command's Canceled property and decide whether they should perform their intended action. For example, the Tracer companion might output a message that makes it clear that the default command has been canceled.

The CustomerFilter Companion Type

The last companion type I show is a filter that automatically removes from the DataSet all the records that the current client shouldn't see and that ensures that records being written to the database meet specific criteria. In this particular example, the CustomerFilter class displays only customers who are located in Germany (see Figure 10-9), but of course you can expand the code as you prefer:

```
[DataObjectCompanion("DataObjects.DOCustomers")]
public class CustomerFilter : IDataObjectCompanion
{
    public string Country = "Germany";

    public void AfterFill(IDataObject obj, DataSet ds, DataObjectCommand command)
    {
        NWINDDataSet ds2 = (NWINDDataSet) ds;
        // Remove all companies not in the right country.
        for ( int i = ds2.Customers.Rows.Count - 1; i >= 0; i-- )
        {
            if ( ds2.Customers[i].Country != Country )
            {
                // Remove this row from the result.
                ds2.Customers.Rows.RemoveAt(i);
            }
        }
    }

    public void AfterUpdate(IDataObject obj, DataSet ds, DataObjectCommand command)
    {}

    public void BeforeFill(IDataObject obj, DataSet ds, DataObjectCommand command)
    {}

    public void BeforeUpdate(IDataObject obj, DataSet ds, DataObjectCommand command)
    {
        NWINDDataSet ds2 = (NWINDDataSet) ds ;
        foreach ( NWINDDataSet.CustomersRow custRow in ds2.Customers.GetChanges().Rows )
```

```
        {
            if ( custRow.Country != Country )
            {
                throw new Exception("Records must have Country = " + Country);
            }
        }
    }
}
```

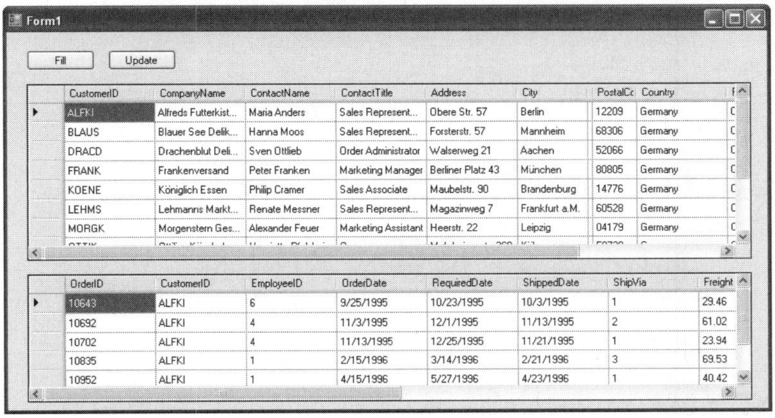

Figure 10-9 The demonstration application filtering customers by their country

You can improve the CustomerFilter type to support a filter based on an SQL clause that the type would use to modify the Select command. This approach would be far more efficient than reading all the data and discarding those pieces you aren't interested in is.

The GenericFilter Companion Type

The CustomerFilter type always filters in only customers that reside in Germany, which is a rather unrealistic assumption. A more useful filter class should let client applications decide which filter to apply. In general, a companion object might require that the client application provide one or more values to its constructor. In this case, the client application should instantiate the companion object directly, initialize its properties, and then add it to the data object's Companions collection:

```
IDataObject<NWINDDataSet> doCustomers = (IDataObject<NWINDDataSet>)
    factory.Create("Customers");
// Add a companion filter that filters in only customers whose City is Berlin.
doCustomers.Companions.Add(new GenericFilter("Customers", "City", "Berlin"));
```

Obviously, the previous code works only if the main client has a reference to the assembly where the GenericFilter type is defined.

A companion object meant to be instantiated directly by the client application shouldn't be marked by a DataObjectCompanion attribute because this attribute would force the CAP framework to instantiate the attribute directly, and such instantiation would fail if the constructor takes one or more arguments. The following code shows how such a companion object can be implemented:

```csharp
public class GenericFilter : IDataObjectCompanion
{
   public readonly string TableName;
   public readonly string FieldName;
   public readonly object FieldValue;

   public GenericFilter(string tableName, string fieldName, object fieldValue)
   {
      this.TableName = tableName;
      this.FieldName = fieldName;
      this.FieldValue = fieldValue;
   }

   public void AfterFill(IDataObject obj, DataSet ds, DataObjectCommand command)
   {
      DataTable dt = ds.Tables[TableName];
      // Remove all rows that don't match the condition.
      for ( int i = dt.Rows.Count - 1; i >= 0; i-- )
      {
         if ( !dt.Rows[i][FieldName].Equals(FieldValue) )
         {
            // Remove this row from the result.
            dt.Rows.RemoveAt(i);
         }
      }
   }

   public void BeforeUpdate(IDataObject obj, DataSet ds, DataObjectCommand command)
   {
      DataTable dt = ds.Tables[TableName];
      // Check that all rows match the filter condition.
      foreach (DataRow row in dt.GetChanges().Rows )
      {
         if ( ! row[FieldName].Equals(FieldValue) )
         {
            throw new Exception("Record doesn't match the filter criteria");
         }
      }
   }

   // AfterFill and AfterUpdate methods contain no statements.
   …
}
```

By now you should be convinced that companion objects can add a nearly unlimited degree of flexibility to your data-centric applications. Here are a few suggestions:

- Use the BeforeUpdate method to fix values that are out of the valid range.

- Implement sophisticated security and audit rules, for example, to prevent certain users from accessing data outside the normal working hours, and log all such attempts.

- Keep a log of queries that take longer so that you can later fine-tune the application or add new indexes to the database structure.

- Send an e-mail to a supervisor when data with exceptionally high or low values is entered, for example, when an employee enters an order with a value higher than a given threshold.

- Build more sophisticated caching policies than those adopted by the sample Customer-Cache type.

You might also consider the opportunity to extend the CAP framework with more features. For example, the DataObjectCommand type might support additional properties to specify whether a transaction is requested or already exists, whether data pagination is requested, and so forth.

Chapter 11
Threads

If you don't look closely at the Microsoft Windows architecture, you might think that the operating system allocates CPU time to processes so that they can execute at the same time, even on single-CPU systems. The truth is, CPU time is allocated to threads, not processes. You can think of threads as independent execution paths, which can access resources such as memory. Processes, on the other hand, are passive containers for running threads, even though they have many other interesting features, such as the ability to allocate resources and provide a linear address space where you can store your variables and arrays.

 Note To avoid long lines, code samples in this chapter assume that the following using statements are used at the top of each source file:

```
using System;
using System.Collections;
using System.Collections.Generic;
using System.ComponentModel;
using System.Diagnostics;
using System.IO;
using System.Reflection;
using System.Runtime.CompilerServices;
using System.Runtime.Remoting.Messaging;
using System.Security.AccessControl;
using System.Security.Principal;
using System.Threading;
```

Threading Fundamentals

The Windows operating system allows *preemptive multitasking*, which means a thread can be suspended at almost any time and another thread can be given CPU time. This contrasts with *cooperative multitasking*, allowed by versions of the Windows operating system through 3.1, in which each thread must explicitly ask for suspension. As you can imagine, cooperative multitasking makes the operating system more fragile because a thread crash affects the entire system.

When to Use Threads

Each thread maintains a private set of structures (the thread context) that the operating system uses to save information when the thread isn't running, including the values of CPU registers at the time when the thread was suspended and the processor was allocated to another thread. A thread also maintains its own exception handlers and a priority level. For example, you can assign higher priority to threads that manage the user interface (so that they're more responsive) and lower priority to threads for less urgent tasks, such as background printing. In all cases, the time slice allocated to each thread is relatively short, so the end user has the perception that all the threads (and all the applications) run concurrently.

The thread scheduler—that is, the portion of the operating system that schedules existing threads and preempts the running thread when its time slice expires—takes some CPU time for its own chores. Moreover, the operating system consumes some memory to keep the context of each thread, be it active or temporarily suspended. For this reason, if too many threads are active at the same time, this scheduling activity can take a nonnegligible amount of time and can degrade the overall performance, leaving less spare time for worker threads (the threads that do something useful). So, you should never create more threads than is strictly necessary, or you should use threads taken from the thread pool, as I explain later in this chapter.

You might want to create additional threads to perform operations such as asynchronous file or database I/O, communication with a remote machine or a Web server, or low-priority background jobs. You make the most of multithreading when you allocate distinct threads to tasks that have different priorities or that take a lot of time to complete. Before opting for a multithreading application, you should consider available alternatives, such as using timers to schedule recurring tasks or taking advantage of the Application.Idle event in Windows Forms applications.

The main problem with threads is that they can compete for shared resources, where a resource can be as simple as a variable or as complex as a database connection or a hardware device. You must synchronize access to such resources—otherwise, you can get into trouble, for reasons that will be clear shortly. Microsoft Visual C# provides the lock keyword to help you deal with these problems, and the Microsoft .NET Framework offers several synchronization objects. The key to effective multithreading is learning how to use these features properly.

Creating Threads

The System.Threading.Thread class offers all the methods and properties you need to create and manage threads. To create a new thread, you simply instantiate a new Thread object and then invoke its Start method. The Thread type's constructor requires one argument, a ThreadStart delegate object that points to the method that runs when the thread starts. In Microsoft .NET Framework version 1.1, such a method had to be a void method without any arguments; in .NET Framework version 2.0, the method can have zero or one object argument.

The following C# application spawns a second thread that prints some messages to the console window:

```
public static void RunThread()
{
    // Create a new thread and define its starting point.
    Thread t = new Thread(new ThreadStart(RunThread_Task));
    // Run the new thread.
    t.Start();

    // Display some messages in the console window.
    for ( int i = 1; i <= 10; i++ )
    {
        Console.WriteLine("Msg #{0} from main thread", i);
        // Wait for 0.2 seconds.
        Thread.Sleep(200);
    }
}

private static void RunThread_Task()
{
    Thread.CurrentThread.Name = "Worker thread";
    for ( int i = 1; i <= 10; i++ )
    {
        Console.WriteLine("Msg #{0} from secondary thread", i);
        // Wait for 0.2 seconds.
        Thread.Sleep(200);
    }
}
```

The console window will contain intermixed messages from both the main and the secondary threads, evidence that they are running independently. You can omit the explicit instantiation of the ThreadStart delegate because the C# 2.0 compiler can infer the delegate type by looking at the signature of the target method:

```
    // Create a new thread and define its starting point.
    Thread t = new Thread(RunThread_Task);
```

The Start method is asynchronous in the sense that it might return before the spawned thread has actually started its execution. A thread terminates when its main method (RunThread_Task, in this case) exits, when an unhandled exception occurs, or when the thread is programmatically killed by a Thread.Abort method. The application as a whole terminates only when all its threads terminate. You can check how many threads an application has created by using the Windows Task Manager utility, which you can run by using the Ctrl+Shift+Esc shortcut. You must use the Select Columns command on the View menu in the Processes tab and select the Thread Count check box to see this information. (See Figure 11-1.) Interestingly, this utility shows that .NET applications might have additional threads—for example, the thread that manages garbage collections and finalizers—over which you apparently have no control.

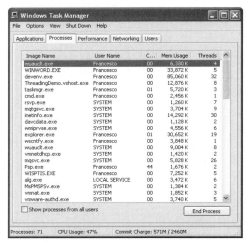

Figure 11-1   The Windows Task Manager utility

Passing Data to and from a Thread

In version 1.1 of the .NET Framework, passing data to a thread and receiving a result from it requires that you write some code because the ThreadStart delegate that the Start method takes as an argument must point to a void method without arguments. Version 2.0 fixes this serious issue by defining a new delegate named ParameterizedThreadStart, which points to a void method that takes an object argument.

The following code shows how the main thread can pass the other thread a value—in this case, the number of iterations of the for loop:

```csharp
public static void RunParameterizedThread()
{
   Thread t = new Thread(new ParameterizedThreadStart(RunParameterizedThread_Task));
   // Specify that we want 20 iterations.
   t.Start(20);

   // Display some messages in the console window.
   for ( int i = 1; i <= 10; i++ )
   {
      Console.WriteLine("Msg #{0} from main thread", i);
      // Wait for 0.2 seconds.
      Thread.Sleep(200);
   }
}
```

```
private static void RunParameterizedThread_Task(object obj)
{
   int number = (int) obj;
   for ( int i = 1; i <= number; i++ )
   {
      Console.WriteLine("Msg #{0} from secondary thread", i);
      // Wait for 0.2 seconds.
      Thread.Sleep(200);
   }
}
```

If you need to pass multiple arguments to the other thread, you can pass an array of values, or, even better, you can define a class that carries all the values. The latter technique makes for more readable code and is recommended if the secondary thread must return a value to the main thread, as in this case:

```
private class ThreadData
{
   // Input values
   public int Iterations;
   public string Message;
   // Output values
   public int CurrentIteration;
   public bool Done;
}

public static void RunThreadWithObjectArgument()
{
   // Create an instance of the ThreadData class and initialize its fields.
   ThreadData data = new ThreadData();
   data.Iterations = 20;
   data.Message = "Msg #{0} from secondary thread";

   // Run the secondary thread.
   Thread t = new Thread(new ParameterizedThreadStart(RunThreadWithObjectArgument_Task));
   t.Start(data);
   …
}

static void RunThreadWithObjectArgument_Task(object obj)
{
   ThreadData data = (ThreadData) obj;
   for ( int i = 1; i <= data.Iterations; i++ )
   {
      Console.WriteLine(data.Message, i);
      data.CurrentIteration = i;
      Thread.Sleep(200);
   }
   // Set the Done flag.
   data.Done = true;
}
```

The ThreadData instance is accessible from both threads, and therefore it can be used to exchange information in the two directions. In this specific example, the main thread can query the CurrentIteration to learn how many messages the other thread has displayed in the console window and can test the Done field to check whether the other thread has terminated its execution:

```
// (In the main thread…)
// Wait until the other thread has reached the 10th iteration.
while ( data.CurrentIteration < 10 )
{
   Thread.Sleep(100);
}
```

Unfortunately, this code might not work well in all circumstances because whenever an object can be accessed by multiple threads—as is the case with the ThreadData object—race conditions might arise. You can read more about this topic in the section titled "Storing and Sharing Data" later in this chapter.

Working with Threads

To manipulate a Windows thread, you need a reference to the corresponding Thread object. This can be a reference to a new thread or a reference to the current thread—that is, the thread that is running the code—which you get by using the Thread.CurrentThread static method. Once you have a reference to a Thread object, you can read or set its properties or abort it using members of the Thread class.

```
// Define and start a new thread.
Thread t = new Thread(TheTask);
t.Start();
…
// Abort the thread.
t.Abort();
```

As I explained earlier, a thread naturally terminates when it exits its main procedure, but it also can be aborted by another thread (or by itself) by means of the Abort method. Like the Start method, the Abort method is asynchronous in the sense that it doesn't abort the thread immediately (unless you call the method for the current thread). In fact, threads can be aborted only when they reach a safe point. In general, a *safe point* is a point in time when it's safe to perform a garbage collection—for example, when a method call returns.

The CLR has several ways to control when a thread reaches a safe point for a garbage collection. It can, for example, *hijack* the thread: when the thread is making a call to a class in the framework, the CLR pushes an extra return address (which points to a location in the CLR itself) onto the call stack. Then, when the method call completes, the CLR can take control and decide whether it's time to perform a garbage collection or to abort the thread if there's a pending Abort method.

There's another reason the Abort method doesn't immediately halt a thread. Instead of killing the thread immediately—as is the case with the ExitThread and TerminateThread Windows API functions—the Abort method causes a ThreadAbortException to be thrown in the target thread. This exception is special in that managed code can't catch it. However, if the target thread is executing inside a try block, the code in the finally clause is guaranteed to be executed and the thread is aborted only at the completion of the finally clause. A thread might even detect that it's being aborted (by means of the ThreadState property, described in the next section) and might continue to run code in the finally clause to postpone its death. (Trusted code can also cancel an Abort method using the ResetAbort method—see the SDK documentation for additional details.)

The Thread class also exposes the Suspend and Resume methods, for suspending a thread and resuming the execution of a suspended thread. In .NET Framework 2.0, however, these methods have been deprecated. If you need to synchronize two threads, you should resort to .NET types, such as Mutex or Semaphore, which I illustrate later in this chapter. The reason the Suspend method (and, consequently, its Resume counterpart) has been deprecated is that if a thread is suspended while it is performing a critical section, while it is holding a lock, or while it is executing the static constructor of a type that is also used elsewhere in your application, your entire application might be compromised.

A thread can suspend itself temporarily by using the Thread.Sleep static method, which takes a timeout in milliseconds:

```
// Pause for half a second.
Thread.Sleep(500);
```

The Sleep method works only on the current thread. Using this method is similar to calling the Windows API Sleep function. You can use the special 0 timeout value to terminate the current time slice and relinquish control to the thread scheduler, or you can use the Timeout .Infinite value (−1) to suspend the current thread indefinitely until another thread wakes it up. You can also pass a TimeSpan object to specify the length of the timeout.

It's quite common to wait for a thread to terminate; for example, the main thread can start a worker thread and then continue to execute to the point at which it must ensure that the worker thread has completed its task. You can use the Join method to easily achieve this behavior, as you can see in the following snippet:

```
Thread t = new Thread(TheTask);
t.Start();
// Do something else here.
…
// Wait for the other thread to die.
t.Join();
```

The Join method can take an optional timeout, expressed in milliseconds or as a TimeSpan object. The method returns true if the thread died within the specified timeout; it returns false if the method returned because the timeout elapsed:

```
// Wait for the other thread to die, but print a message every second.
while ( !t.Join(1000) )
{
    Console.WriteLine("Waiting for the other thread to die...");
}
```

An important note: never call Join on the current thread because this action would cause the current thread to stop forever. If you are in doubt, compare the Thread instance with the current thread before proceeding:

```
// Join a thread only if it's alive and isn't the current thread.
if ( t.IsAlive && t != Thread.CurrentThread )
{
    t.Join()
}
```

When a thread calls Sleep on itself or Join on another thread, the calling thread enters the WaitSleepJoin state (see Table 11-1 in the following section). A thread exits this state when the timeout expires or when another thread invokes the Interrupt method on it. When the Interrupt method is called, the target thread receives a ThreadInterruptedException, which must be caught or the thread will be killed. Thus, the following is the typical code that you should write for threads that go to sleep and are waiting for another thread to wake them up:

```
try
{
    // Go to sleep for 10 seconds or until another thread
    // calls the Interrupt method on this thread.
    Thread.Sleep(10000);
    // We get here if the timeout elapsed and no exception is thrown.
    …
}
catch ( ThreadInterruptedException ex )
{
    // We get here if the thread has been interrupted.
    …
}
```

Thread Properties

You can test whether a thread is active—that is, it has started and isn't dead yet—using the IsAlive read-only property. When it's applied to the current thread, this property always returns true, for obvious reasons.

You can also check the state of any thread—including the current one—by using the Thread-State enumerated property, whose values are summarized in Table 11-1. This is a bit-coded value because a thread can be in more than one state at any given time, so you should test individual bits with the & operator:

```
if ( (Thread.CurrentThread.ThreadState & System.Threading.ThreadState.StopRequested) != 0 )
{
    // The current thread is being stopped.
}
```

Table 11-1   The Possible Values for the ThreadState Property

State	Description
Aborted	The thread has been aborted.
AbortRequested	The thread is responding to an Abort request.
Background	The thread is running in the background. (Same as the IsBackground property.)
Running	The thread is running. (Another thread has called the Start method.)
Stopped	The thread has been stopped. (A thread can never leave this state.)
StopRequested	The thread is about to stop.
Suspended	The thread has been suspended.
SuspendRequested	The thread is responding to a Suspend request.
Unstarted	The thread has been created, but the Start method hasn't been called yet.
WaitSleepJoin	The thread has called Monitor.Wait or Thread.Join on another thread.

The IsBackground property tells whether a thread is a low-priority background thread. Interestingly, you can change the background state of a thread by assigning true or false to this property before the thread starts:

```
// Make a thread a background thread before starting it.
t.IsBackground = true;
t.Start();
```

An important detail: background threads don't keep an application alive, so if your application has created one or more background threads, it should check the IsAlive property of all of them before exiting the main thread. Otherwise, those threads are mercilessly killed, regardless of what they're doing at that moment.

The Priority property offers a different way to affect a thread's priority without making it a background thread. This property sets or returns one of the ThreadPriority enumerated values, which are Normal, AboveNormal, BelowNormal, Highest, or Lowest:

```
// Supercharge the current thread.
Thread.CurrentThread.Priority = ThreadPriority.Highest;
```

The Windows operating system can adjust the priority of threads automatically—for example, when an application becomes the foreground application—but changing the priority of a thread through code isn't recommended, so you should do it only for a good reason, for example, to ensure that enough CPU time is assigned to your code even if it runs in the background.

All threads have a Name property. This property is usually a null string, but you can assign it a value for the threads you create. The Name property doesn't change the behavior of a thread, but it turns useful during the debugging phase, as you'll read in the next section. For example, the thread name is reported in the message that the Microsoft Visual Studio 2005 debugger displays when a thread terminates.

The Thread class doesn't expose any property that returns the ID of the underlying Windows physical thread. The reason: a managed thread might map to a Windows fiber (also known as a lightweight thread), in which case it wouldn't have a stable thread ID. This is the case today when a .NET assembly runs inside Microsoft SQL Server and might happen under a future version of the operating system. Under the current version of the Windows operating system, you can retrieve the physical thread ID with a call to the GetCurrentThreadId Windows API function or, even better, by calling the AppDomain.GetCurrentThreadId static property:

```
int currThreadId = AppDomain.GetCurrentThreadId();
```

However, neither technique is recommended, and the GetCurrentThreadId method has been marked as obsolete in .NET Framework 2.0. In the current version of the framework, you can use the Thread.ManagedThreadID read-only property as a thread ID that is stable and is guaranteed not to change during the life of the thread:

```
int id = Thread.CurrentThread.ManagedThreadId;
```

Storing and Sharing Data

Whenever you have multiple threads that share data you also need a way to synchronize access to that data. If two threads can access the same variable, you might ensure that they don't change it at the same time because the result isn't a pleasant one. Data sharing and synchronization are always two facets of the same issue.

Variables and Fields

The scope of a variable determines whether multiple threads can share it. Threads never share local dynamic variables—that is, variables defined inside a procedure—even if the threads happen to be executing inside that procedure at the same moment. The reason is simple: local variables are allocated on the stack. Each thread maintains its own private stack and keeps its own copy of all local dynamic variables, which means that you can't share data among threads using local dynamic variables. The good news is that you don't have to worry about synchronizing access to such variables.

By default, threads share all types of type fields. You can use these fields to make data visible to all the running threads. Unfortunately, you also have to provide a way to synchronize access to this data. Consider this simple code:

```
// The globalVar field should never be negative.
if ( globalVar > 0 )
{
   Console.WriteLine("About to change globalVar");
   globalVar -= 1;
}
```

If access to the globalVar field isn't arbitrated and synchronized in some way, a thread might execute, test the value of globalVar, find that it's 1, and enter the if block. The first statement in this block is a call into the .NET runtime, which gives the thread manager a chance to perform a thread switch and activate another thread. What happens if the other thread enters the same block of code? As you might expect, it finds that the globalVar variable is still 1, and the other thread (incorrectly) enters the block. As a result, the variable is decremented twice and becomes negative, which you probably don't want and which might cause an error later in the application. Logic errors of this kind are problematic because they occur in random fashion, are rarely reproducible, and therefore are very difficult to debug.

Even if you decide not to explicitly create new threads in your applications, you might have to worry about arbitrating access to fields anyway, if your class has a Finalize method. In fact, by default the Finalize method of your objects runs on a different thread than your application's main thread does; therefore, you should ensure that either you don't access any shared variables from Finalize methods or you protect these variables by using synchronization blocks (which I explain later).

Finally, you have to worry about how fields are shared between threads if you use objects that create secondary threads and fire their events on these secondary threads, as is the case with the FileSystemWatcher component (which I describe in Chapter 7, "Files, Directories, and Streams"). This situation is especially problematic if you are calling a multithreaded object from inside a Windows Forms application because code in form objects must run in the same thread that created the form itself—or the application might crash. You can read more about this issue in the section titled "The ISynchronizeInvoke Interface" near the end of this chapter.

The ThreadStatic Attribute

To understand the kinds of problems you have to watch out for when you're working with multithreaded applications, consider this simple class:

```
class SampleClass
{
  public static string ThreadName;
  …
}
```

Suppose that this class can be used by multiple threads but that each thread wants to store and retrieve a distinct value for the ThreadName static field. Unfortunately, being static, the ThreadName variable is shared among all the instances of the class and hence all the threads, so each thread will override the current value with its own ThreadName.

To obviate this problem, the CLR supports the concept of thread-relative fields, which are static fields that are shared among all class instances but not among threads. You create a thread-relative static field by marking the declaration of a static field with the ThreadStatic attribute:

```
// The ThreadName variable isn't shared among threads.
[ThreadStatic()] public static string ThreadName;
```

Threads and Unhandled Exceptions

When a thread—either the main thread or a secondary thread—throws an exception and your code doesn't catch it, an AppDomain.UnhandledException event is fired. The event receives an UnhandledExceptionEventArgs object, which exposes two properties, ExceptionObject and IsTerminating. The former is of course the exception being thrown, but it returns an Object value, and you must cast it to an Exception variable before you can read the usual properties such as Message and StackTrace, as the following code example demonstrates:

```
public static void TestThreadException()
{
    // Prepare to trap AppDomain events.
    AppDomain.CurrentDomain.UnhandledException +=
        new UnhandledExceptionEventHandler(AppDomain_UnhandledException);
    // Cause an exception on a secondary thread.
    Thread t = new Thread(new ThreadStart(TestThreadException_Task));
    t.Start();
    t.Join();
    // This line will never be reached.
    Console.WriteLine("Application terminated normally");
}

private static void TestThreadException_Task()
{
    throw new DivideByZeroException();
}

static void AppDomain_UnhandledException(object sender, UnhandledExceptionEventArgs e)
{
    // Show information about the current exception.
    Exception ex = (Exception) e.ExceptionObject;
    Console.WriteLine(ex.Message);
}
```

An important note about this event: you can trap it correctly only when the application isn't running under the Visual Studio debugger, so you must start the program by choosing Start Without Debugging from the Debug menu or by pressing the Ctrl+F5 shortcut.

In .NET Framework 1.1, the value of the IsTerminating property (and therefore the effect of the exception on the application's life) depends on the kind of thread being terminated. An exception on a secondary thread—for example, a thread used by the garbage collector to call the Finalize method, a thread created with the Thread class, or a thread taken from the thread pool—isn't fatal for the application (even if it might cause error messages to appear, depending on the type of the current application). Only uncaught exceptions thrown by the main thread or an unmanaged thread—for example, a thread running in a COM object called by a .NET assembly—terminate the application.

In .NET Framework 2.0, an unhandled exception on any thread will terminate the application. This is clearly a breaking change that might force you to rewrite and retest old applications being ported to the new version of the .NET Framework, and thus Microsoft correctly decided that letting exceptions silently kill your secondary thread was just too dangerous. You can, however, revert to the .NET Framework 1.*x* behavior by adding the following entry to the application's configuration file:

```
<configuration>
   <runtime>
      <legacyUnhandledExceptionPolicy enabled="1"/>
   </runtime>
</configuration>
```

Although the UnhandledException event can be useful, keep in mind that you can't catch and solve every unhandled exception using this technique. In practice, you only can save any unsaved data, log the exception somewhere (for example, in the system event log), and display a dialog box to inform the user that the application is closing. Regardless of whether you're handling the UnhandledException event, .NET applications display a message box that asks whether you want to debug the application or send Microsoft a report of the error. (See Figure 11-2.) If you decide not to debug the application, a complete error message is displayed in the command window (if there is one) and the application is terminated.

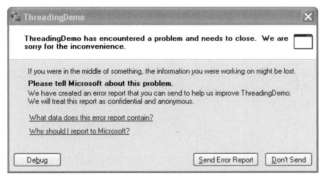

Figure 11-2   The dialog box that .NET applications display by default when an unhandled exception occurs

Debugging Threads

You can see the name of the running thread—as well as other information such as the application name and the stack frame—by activating the Debug Location toolbar inside Visual Studio 2005. (You can activate any toolbar by right-clicking any Visual Studio menu or toolbar.) This data is especially useful when you want to determine where a thread is executing when you hit a breakpoint. You can display this toolbar by right-clicking any toolbar and clicking Debug Location on the shortcut menu. (See Figure 11-3.)

```
Process: [596] ThreadingDemo.v ▼ Thread: [4280] <No Name ▼ Stack Frame: ThreadingDemo.exe!ThreadingD ▼
App.cs
ThreadingDemo.App              ▼  SyncLockStatement_Task(object obj)
               {
                        // Split the output line in two pieces.
                        Console.Write(" ");
                        Console.Write(number);
               }
```

Figure 11-3   The Debug Location toolbar, which displays the thread name and other information about the running process

The Thread window in Visual Studio 2005 lets you list all the running threads, the method being executed, and the name, status, and priority of each thread. You activate this window by pointing to Windows on the Debug menu and clicking Threads. (The current program must be in break mode for you to see this menu command.) The yellow arrow on the left identifies the current thread, and you can switch to another thread by right-clicking it. (See Figure 11-4.) You can also freeze a thread, which is then displayed with two vertical blue bars, and restart (thaw) it.

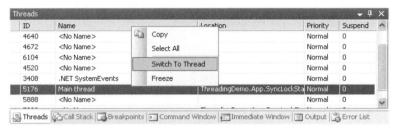

Figure 11-4   The Threads window, which lists all threads and lets you freeze and restart them

Visual Studio 2005 supports the ability to define per-process and per-thread breakpoints, which is a great bonus when debugging applications that use many threads. To make a breakpoint active only for a given thread, take note of the thread's ID (from the Threads window), right-click the red breakpoint icon in the left margin of the code editor, and select the Filter command. This command brings up the Breakpoint Filter dialog box (see Figure 11-5), where you can type an expression such as this:

```
ThreadId = 1234
```

Even better, assign the thread a name from code, and then use this name in the Breakpoint Filter dialog box as follows:

```
ThreadName = "Worker thread"
```

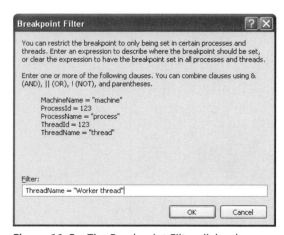

Figure 11-5   The Breakpoint Filter dialog box

The Performance utility offers a way to monitor threads and the performance bottlenecks they might create. (See Figure 11-6.) The .NET Framework has a performance object named .NET CLR LocksAndThreads that exposes several counters, the most important of which are the following:

- **# of current logical threads**   The current number of threads known to the CLR in a given application.

- **# of current physical threads**   The number of native Windows threads created and owned by the CLR.

- **# of current recognized threads**   The number of threads that were created outside the CLR (for example, in a COM component) that the CLR has recognized.

- **contention rate/sec**   Rate at which threads in the CLR fail to acquire a managed lock— for example, when reaching a lock block. A high number for this counter is a symptom indicating that the application isn't well designed for multithreaded operations.

- **total # of contentions**   The total number of times threads in the CLR have failed to acquire a managed lock.

- **current queue/sec**   The average number of threads waiting to acquire a lock; a high value means that most threads spend most of their time waiting for a lock to become available.

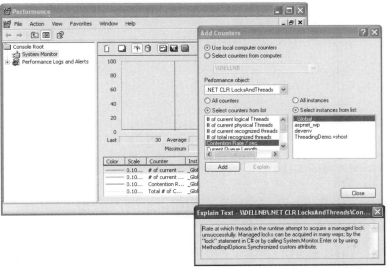

Figure 11-6   The Performance utility, which lets you see several statistics regarding CLR threads

The meaning of some of these counters—most notably, those related to contention and locks— will become evident later in this chapter.

Thread Synchronization

Now that you know how a thread can share data or prevent data from being shared, you're ready to tackle synchronization issues related to concurrent access to variables and objects accessible by multiple threads at the same time.

The lock Statement

As you know, a thread can be preempted at any time, usually at the completion of a call to an object's method. The following example demonstrates what can happen when a piece of code isn't guaranteed to execute atomically:

```csharp
public static void SynchronizationProblem()
{
    // Create 10 secondary threads.
    for ( int i = 0; i <= 9; i++ )
    {
        Thread t = new Thread(SynchronizationProblem_Task);
        t.Start(i);
    }
}

static void SynchronizationProblem_Task(object obj)
{
    int number = (int) obj;
    // Display a lot of information in the console window.
    for ( int i = 1; i <= 1000; i++ )
    {
        // Split the output line in two pieces.
        Console.Write(" ");
        Console.Write(number);
    }
}
```

A glance at the console window shows some interruptions of a thread between the Console.Write statements, which result in scrambled output. (See Figure 11-7.)

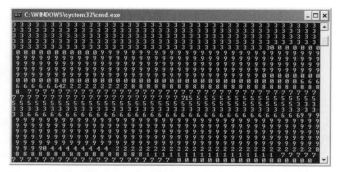

Figure 11-7 The console window, which clearly shows that typing a space plus the thread number isn't an atomic operation

The CLR offers no means of ensuring that a group of statements behaves as an atomic, uninterruptible operation. This would be too stiff a requirement in an operating system that must guarantee multitasking to all applications. However, most of the time you would be satisfied to have atomicity at the application level (rather than at the system level). In the preceding code, for example, it would be enough to ensure that only one thread in the current application can execute a specific block of statements at a time. You can achieve this by enclosing those statements in a lock block. The lock block requires a variable as an argument, and this variable must satisfy the following requirements:

■ It must be a variable shared by all the threads (typically, an instance field or a static field without the ThreadStatic attribute).

■ It must be a reference type, for example, a string or an object variable. (Using a value type causes a compilation error.)

■ It must not have a null value. (Using a null value causes a runtime error.)

Here's the code shown before, which has been revised to take advantage of the lock block (additions are in bold type):

```csharp
// The lock object. (Any nonnull reference value will do.)
static object consoleLock = new object();

static void SyncLockStatement_Task(object obj)
{
    int number = (int) obj;
    // Display a lot of information in the console window.
    for ( int i = 1; i <= 1000; i++ )
    {
        lock ( consoleLock )
        {
            // Split the output line in two pieces.
            Console.Write(" ");
            Console.Write(number);
        }
    }
}
```

The preceding code uses the consoleLock variable to arbitrate access to the Console object, which is the only resource that all threads share in this trivial example and is therefore the only resource for which you need to provide synchronization. Real-world applications might contain many lock blocks; such blocks can share the same object variable or use different variables for finer granularity. As a rule of thumb, you should have a distinct object variable for each shared resource that must be synchronized or for each group of statements that must be executed by one thread at a time.

Each lock block implicitly uses a hidden try block because C# must ensure that the lock is correctly released if an exception is thrown. (A lock release requires a Monitor.Exit method.)

If the lock block is placed inside an instance method of a class and all threads are running inside a method of that instance, you can pass this to the lock statement because this object surely satisfies all the requirements. It's accessible by all threads, it's a reference value, and it surely is nonnull.

```
class TestClass
{
    public void TheTask()
    {
        lock ( this )
        {
            // Only one thread at a time can access this code.
            …
        }
    }
}
```

> **Note**   You can use the this keyword in this fashion only if you need to synchronize on a single resource, for example, the console window or a specific file. If you have multiple synchronization blocks that protect multiple resources, you'll typically use different variables as the argument of the lock block. Even more important, you should use this as the argument of a lock block only if the class isn't visible outside the current assembly; otherwise, another application might use the same instance in a different lock block and would therefore prevent your threads from executing a block of code without any real reason. In general, you should never use a public object visible to other assemblies as the argument for a lock keyword.

Also notice that some code samples you can find on the Internet use the typeof operator to retrieve a Type object that is then used as a lock object to protect a static method. Using a Type object in this fashion is strongly discouraged by Microsoft and should be avoided.

When you use nested lock statements to synchronize access to multiple objects, it's essential that you follow the identical nesting sequence everywhere in your application. Acquiring locks in identical order avoids deadlocks among different portions of your application. This rule of thumb also applies to those cases when code in a lock block calls a method containing another lock block.

```
// Always use this sequence when locking objLock1 and objLock2.
lock ( objLock1 )
{
    lock ( objLock2 )
    {
        …
    }
}
```

The Thread class in .NET Framework 2.0 supports two new methods named BeginCritical-Section and EndCriticalSection. The names of these methods suggest that you can use them to mark an uninterruptible block of code, but this isn't the case. Instead, these methods have been introduced to make .NET applications more reliable in critical conditions: they tell the CLR that a block of code won't suffer from unanticipated exceptions deriving from JIT compilation errors. For more information, read the MSDN documentation.

Performance Considerations and Lazy Instantiation

Putting a lock block around all the pieces of code that access a shared variable can be overkill and can degrade your application's performance, especially when it runs on a multiprocessor computer. (Locks on multiple-CPU computers can be quite time-consuming.) If you can avoid a lock block without compromising the integrity of your data, you should absolutely do it.

For example, consider the problem of correctly implementing the Singleton pattern using lazy instantiation in a multithreaded environment. (Singletons are types for which only one instance can exist at any time. An example of a singleton is the Console object or the Application object in a Windows Forms project.) The first version of such a class might look like this:

```
public class Singleton
{
    private static Singleton m_Instance;
    private static object sharedLock = new object();

    public static Singleton Instance
    {
        get
        {
            lock ( sharedLock )
            {
                if ( m_Instance == null )
                {
                    m_Instance = new Singleton();
                }
                return m_Instance;
            }
        }
    }
}
```

The problem with the previous code is that most accesses to the Instance property don't need synchronization because the m_Instance private variable needs to be instantiated only the first time the property is read. Here's a better way to implement the requested behavior:

```
public class Singleton
{
    private static Singleton m_Instance;
    private static object sharedLock = new object();

    public static Singleton Instance
    {
        get
        {
            // In most cases this test fails and the lock block is avoided.
            if ( m_Instance == null )
            {
                lock ( sharedLock )
                {
                    if ( m_Instance == null )
```

```
                {
                    m_Instance = new Singleton();
                }
            }
        }
        return m_Instance;
    }
}
```

Volatile Fields

Many developers incorrectly believe that they can avoid a lock block if a field is simply read or written to. After all, these operations correspond to a single opcode at the CPU level, and therefore no thread can ever interrupt them, right?

Unfortunately, things aren't so simple. Although it's true that reading a field or storing a value in a memory location can be considered an atomic operation, it's also true that most compilers, including the C# compiler, can optimize code by enregistering a variable or a field. *Enregistering* means that the variable or field's value is cached in a CPU register and written back only when the method exits or when the compiler detects that the variable is no longer accessed. Accessing CPU registers is significantly faster than accessing memory is; thus, this optimization technique is very effective, actually among the most effective optimization techniques applied by the C# compiler.

However, this technique is also dangerous if the field can be accessed by another thread at the same time. (Enregistering a local variable is never a problem because local variables are never shared among threads.) In fact, if a thread holds the value of a field in a CPU register, it won't see any changes applied by other threads. This situation can almost always lead to malfunctioning and intermittent problems that are quite difficult to diagnose. Consider this code:

```
private bool Done = false;

void TheTask()
{
    // Exit the loop when another thread has set the Done flag
    // or when the task being performed is complete.
    while ( this.Done == false )
    {
        ...
        if ( nothingMoreToDo )
        {
            this.Done = true;
            break;
        }
    }
}
```

The problem: if the code produced by the C# compiler causes the Done field to be enregistered, a thread A might never realize that thread B has already set the Done field to true, and therefore would continue to run longer than expected, possibly causing other problems.

The C# language offers a solution to this problem in the form of the volatile keyword. If you mark a field as volatile, the compiler will never cache that field in a CPU register:

```
// Change this line in the previous example.
private volatile bool Done = false;
```

You can use the volatile keyword with all reference types, and most numeric types, including sbyte, byte, short, ushort, int, uint, char, float, and bool. (Notice that long, ulong, double, and decimal aren't included in this list.) Volatile Enum types are supported, except when their base type is long or ulong, as are IntPtr and UIntPtr values.

Once again, keep in mind that the volatile keyword ensures that a field is read from and written to main memory directly, but it doesn't guarantee that operations on the field are carried out atomically. To achieve that, you need a lock block or another synchronization technique, such as those I describe in the remainder of this chapter.

Synchronized Objects

Another problem related to threading is that not every .NET object can be shared safely among threads. In other words, not all .NET objects are *thread-safe*. When you're writing a multithreaded application, you should always check the documentation to determine whether the objects and the methods you're using are thread-safe. For example, all the static methods of the Regex, Match, and Group classes are thread-safe, but their instance methods aren't and shouldn't be invoked by different threads at the same time. Some .NET objects—most notably, Windows Forms objects and controls—pose even more severe limitations in that only the thread that created them can call their methods: these objects are said to require *thread affinity*. (Read the section titled "Threading in Windows Forms Applications" later in this chapter for more information about accessing Windows Forms controls from a different thread.)

Synchronized .NET Types

Several objects that aren't thread-safe natively—including ArrayList, Hashtable, Queue, SortedList, Stack, TextReader, TextWriter, and regular expression Match and Group classes—expose a Synchronized static method, which returns a thread-safe object that's equivalent to the one you pass as an argument. Most of these classes also expose the IsSynchronized property, which returns true if you're dealing with a thread-safe instance:

```
// Create an ArrayList object, and add some values to it.
ArrayList al = new ArrayList();
al.Add(1); al.Add(2); al.Add(3);
// Create a synchronized, thread-safe version of this ArrayList.
ArrayList syncAl = ArrayList.Synchronized(al);
```

```
// Prove that the new object is thread-safe.
Console.WriteLine(al.IsSynchronized);        // => False;
Console.WriteLine(syncAl.IsSynchronized);    // => True;
// You can share the syncAl object among different threads.
...
```

Keep in mind that accessing these synchronized objects is typically slower than accessing the corresponding nonsynchronized object because each method call goes through a series of internal tests. In most cases, you can write more efficient code if you use regular arrays and collections and you synchronize access to their members by means of standard lock blocks.

The Synchronization Attribute

Using the System.Runtime.Remoting.Contexts.Synchronization attribute is the simplest way to provide synchronized access to an entire object so that only one thread can access its instance fields and methods. That is, any thread can use that instance of the class, but only one thread at a time can execute one of the methods. If a thread is executing code inside the class, any other thread that attempts to use that class has to wait. In other words, it's as if there were lock blocks enclosing every method of that class, with all these blocks using the same lock variable.

The following code shows how you can synchronize a class using the Synchronization attribute. Also notice that the class must inherit from ContextBoundObject to be marked as a context-bound object:

```
[System.Runtime.Remoting.Contexts.Synchronization()]
public class Display : ContextBoundObject
{
    ...
}
```

The Synchronization attribute automatically synchronizes access to all instance fields, properties, and methods, but it doesn't provide synchronization for static members. The attribute can take an optional argument, which can be either true or false (to indicate whether reentrant calls are permitted) or one of the constants exposed by the SynchronizationAttribute class itself: NOT_SUPPORTED, SUPPORTED, REQUIRED, REQUIRES_NEW. For more information, read the MSDN documentation.

The MethodImpl Attribute

In most cases, synchronizing an entire class is overkill, and protecting just a few of its methods from concurrent accesses is often satisfactory. You can apply this sort of protection by wrapping the body of such methods in a lock block. Or you can use a simpler technique based on the System.Runtime.CompilerServices.MethodImpl attribute:

```
public class MethodImplDemoClass
{
    // This method can be executed by one thread at a time.
    [MethodImpl(MethodImplOptions.Synchronized)]
```

```
    void SynchronizedMethod()
    {
        ...
    }
}
```

Applying the MethodImpl attribute for multiple methods in the class provides the same effect as wrapping the body of those methods with lock blocks that use the this instance as the lock variable. In other words, a thread calling a method marked with the MethodImpl attribute will block any other thread calling the same or a different method marked with this attribute.

Interestingly, you also can use the MethodImpl attribute for static methods. The object variable implicitly used to lock static methods is different from the object variable used for instance methods, so a thread invoking a static method marked with the MethodImpl attribute doesn't block another thread calling an instance method marked with the same attribute. (More precisely, static methods marked with the MethodImpl attribute use the System.Type object that identifies the current type.)

Volatile Read and Write Operations

When a variable is shared among multiple threads and the application runs on a multiprocessor computer, you should take into account another potential cause of malfunctioning. The problem with multiprocessor systems is that each processor has its own cache; therefore, if you write to a class field from one thread, the new value is written to the cache associated with the current CPU and isn't automatically "published" for all the CPUs to see it. A similar problem can also occur with 64-bit CPUs, which can rearrange the order of execution of a block of statements, including reads and writes from memory: such a rearrangement never has a visible effect as long as only one thread is accessing a given portion of memory, but it might cause problems when memory is accessed by multiple threads.

The .NET Framework offers two solutions to this issue: the VolatileRead and VolatileWrite pair of methods, and the MemoryBarrier method, all exposed by the Thread type.

The VolatileWrite method enables you to write a variable and ensure that the new value is automatically written in the memory shared by all processors and is not kept in a CPU register (where it would be hidden from other threads). Likewise, the VolatileRead method enables you to read a variable in a safe way because it forces all the caches in the system to be emptied before the read operation is carried out. Both methods are overloaded to take a primitive variable (numeric or Object) by reference, as in this code:

```
class TestClass
{
    private static int sharedValue;

    public int IncrementValue()
    {
        int value = Thread.VolatileRead(ref sharedValue);
        value += 1;
```

```
        Thread.VolatileWrite(ref sharedValue, value);
        return value;
    }
}
```

The VolatileRead and VolatileWrite methods are OK as long as a numeric or an object value is accessed, but they can't be applied when another kind of type is used. (You can't just use the overload that takes an Object variable because you can't rely on casting when a by-reference argument is involved.) This consideration leads us to the MemoryBarrier method.

The MemoryBarrier method flushes the contents of all caches and CPU registers to the main memory, and thus it ensures that variables contain the most recent data that was written to them. For example, the following code ensures that the Singleton pattern—which I illustrated in the section titled "Performance Considerations and Lazy Instantiation" earlier in this chapter—is absolutely bullet-proof even on multiple-CPU systems:

```
public class Singleton
{
    private static Singleton m_Instance;
    private static object sharedLock = new object();

    public static Singleton Instance
    {
        get
        {
            if ( m_Instance == null )
            {
                lock ( sharedLock )
                {
                    if ( m_Instance == null )
                    {
                        Singleton tempInstance = new Singleton();
                        // Ensure that writes related to instantiation are flushed.
                        Thread.MemoryBarrier();
                        m_Instance = tempInstance;
                    }
                }
            }
            return m_Instance;
        }
    }
}
```

You should place a call to MemoryBarrier just before the assignment that "publishes" a new value for all the other threads to see; in the preceding example, this call ensures that the instantiation of the Singleton object and the assignment to tempInstance are completed before trying the assignment to the variable that is going to be shared among threads.

The Monitor Type

The lock block provides an easy-to-use method for dealing with synchronization issues, but it can be inadequate in many situations. For example, a thread can't just test a lock code block and avoid being blocked if another thread is already executing the lock block or another lock block that is associated with the same object.

Blocks using the lock keyword are internally implemented using Monitor objects. Interestingly, you can use a Monitor object directly and gain more flexibility, although at the expense of somewhat more complex code.

You never instantiate individual Monitor objects, and in fact, all the methods I illustrate are static members of the Monitor type. The most important method is Enter, which takes an object as an argument. This object works exactly like the argument you pass to a lock block and undergoes the same constraints—it must be a nonnull reference variable that's shared by all the threads. If no other thread owns the lock on that object, the current thread acquires the lock and sets its internal lock counter to 1. If another thread currently owns the lock, the calling thread must wait until the other thread releases the lock and the lock becomes available. If the calling thread already owns the lock, each call to Monitor.Enter increments the internal lock counter.

The Monitor.Exit method takes the lock object as an argument and decrements its internal lock counter. If the counter reaches 0, the lock is released so that other threads can acquire it. Calls to Monitor.Enter and Monitor.Exit must be balanced, or the lock will never be released. If the statements between Monitor.Enter and Monitor.Exit are likely to raise an exception, you should put all the code in a try block because it's imperative that you always release the lock:

```
// A nonnull module-level object variable
object objLock = new object();
…
try
{
   // Attempt to enter the protected section;
   // wait if the lock is currently owned by another thread.
   Monitor.Enter(objLock);
   // Do something here.
   …
}
finally
{
   // Release the lock.
   Monitor.Exit(objLock);
}
```

If a thread calls the Interrupt method on another thread that is currently waiting inside a Monitor.Enter method, the thread receives a ThreadInterruptedException, which is another good reason for using a try block.

The Enter and Exit methods of the Monitor type let you replace a lock block but don't bring you any additional advantages. You see the extra flexibility of the Monitor class when you apply its TryEnter method. This method is similar to Enter, but the method exits and returns false if the lock can't be acquired in the specified timeout. For example, you can attempt to get the monitor lock for 10 milliseconds and then give up, without blocking the current thread indefinitely. The following code rewrites a previous example based on the lock, this time using the Monitor object, and also displays the failed attempts to acquire the lock:

```
try
{
    while ( !Monitor.TryEnter(consoleLock, 10) )
    {
        Debug.WriteLine("Thread " + Thread.CurrentThread.Name
            + " failed to acquire the lock");
    }
    // Split the output line into pieces.
    Console.Write(" ");
    Console.Write(number);
}
finally
{
    // Release the lock.
    Monitor.Exit(consoleLock);
}
```

The Mutex Type

The Mutex type provides yet another synchronization primitive. A *mutex* is a Windows kernel object that can be owned by one thread at a time and is said to be in a *signaled* state if no thread currently owns it.

A thread requests ownership of a mutex by means of the Mutex.WaitOne static method (which doesn't return until the ownership has been successfully achieved) and releases it by means of the Mutex.ReleaseMutex static method. A thread requesting the ownership of a Mutex object that it owns already doesn't block itself, but even in that case it must call Release-Mutex an equal number of times. This is how you can implement a synchronized section using a Mutex object:

```
// This Mutex object must be accessible to all threads.
Mutex m = new Mutex();

public void WaitOneExample()
{
    // Attempt to enter the synchronized section, but give up after 0.1 seconds.
    if ( m.WaitOne(100, false) )
    {
        // Enter the synchronized section.
        …
        // Exit the synchronized section, and release the Mutex.
        m.ReleaseMutex();
    }
}
```

In a real application, you should use a try block to protect your code from unhandled errors and place the call to ReleaseMutex in the finally block. If you pass WaitOne an optional timeout argument, the method returns the control to the thread when the ownership is successfully achieved or the timeout expires. You can tell the difference between the two results by looking at the return value: true means ownership was acquired, false means the timeout expired.

```
// Attempt to enter the synchronized section, but give up after 0.1 seconds.
if ( m.WaitOne(100, false) )
{
    // Enter the synchronized section.
    …
    // Exit the synchronized section, and release the Mutex.
    m.ReleaseMutex();
}
```

When used in this way, the Mutex type provides a mechanism equivalent to the Monitor .TryEnter method, without offering any additional features. You see the added flexibility of the Mutex type when you consider its WaitAny and WaitAll static methods. The WaitAny method takes an array of Mutex objects and returns when it manages to acquire the ownership of one of the Mutex objects in the list (in which case, that Mutex becomes signaled) or when the optional timeout expires. The return value is the array index of the Mutex object that became signaled or the special value 258 if the timeout expired.

You typically use an array of Mutex objects when you have a limited number of resources, such as communication ports, and you want to allocate each one to a thread as soon as the resource becomes available. In this situation, a signaled Mutex object means that the corresponding resource is available, so you can use the Mutex.WaitAny method for blocking the current thread until any of the Mutex objects become signaled. (The Mutex type inherits the WaitAny method from its WaitHandle base class.) Here's the skeleton of an application that uses this approach:

```
// An array of three Mutex objects
static Mutex[] mutexes = { new Mutex(), new Mutex(), new Mutex() };

public static void WaitAnyExample()
{
    // Wait until a resource becomes available.
    // (Returns the index of the available resource.)
    int mutexNdx = Mutex.WaitAny(mutexes);
    // Enter the synchronized section.
    // (This code should use only the resource corresponding to mutexNdx.)
    …
    // Exit the synchronized section, and release the resource.
    mutexes[mutexNdx].ReleaseMutex();
}
```

The WaitAll static method (also inherited from the WaitHandle base class) takes an array of Mutex objects and returns the control to the application only when all of them have become signaled. This method is especially useful when you can't proceed until all the other threads have completed their jobs:

```
// Wait until all resources have been released.
Mutex.WaitAll(mutexes);
```

A minor problem with the WaitAll method is that you can't call it from the main thread of a Single Thread Apartment (STA) application, such as a Console application or a Windows Forms application. If the main thread of an STA application must stop until a group of mutexes is released, you should invoke the WaitAll method from a separate thread and have the main thread call the Thread.Join method on that thread to stop the main thread until the WaitAll method returns.

The new SignalAndWait static method, which the Mutex type inherits from the WaitHandle base class, enables you to signal one Mutex object and wait on another Mutex object (in general, any object that inherits from WaitHandle) as an atomic operation:

```
// Signal the first Mutex and wait for the second Mutex to become signaled.
Mutex.SignalAndWait(mutexes[0], mutexes[1]);
```

Unlike other synchronization objects covered so far, Mutex objects can be assigned a name, which brings up one of the most important features of these objects. Mutex objects that have the same name are shared among different processes. You can create an instance of a named Mutex using this syntax:

```
Mutex m = new Mutex(false, "mutexname");
```

If a Mutex with that name already exists in the system, the caller gets a reference to it; otherwise, a new Mutex object is created. This mechanism lets you share Mutex objects among different applications and therefore enables these applications to synchronize their access to shared resources.

A new constructor added in .NET Framework 2.0 enables you to test whether the calling thread was granted the initial ownership of the Mutex:

```
bool ownership ;
Mutex m = new Mutex(true, "mutexname", out ownership);
if ( ownership )
{
   // This thread owns the mutex.
   …
}
```

A common use of named mutexes is to determine whether the running application is the first (or the only) instance being loaded. If this is not the case, the application might exit immediately or wait until the other instance has completed its chores, as in this code sample:

```
static void Main()
{
   bool ownership;
   Mutex m = new Mutex(true, "DemoMutex", out ownership);
```

```
      if ( ownership )
      {
         // Carry out the task; then release the mutex.
         …
         m.ReleaseMutex();
      }
      else
      {
         // Another application is running. Display a message and exit.
         …
      }
   }
}
```

The OpenExisting static method, also new in .NET Framework 2.0, offers an alternative way to open a named system-wide Mutex object. Unlike the Mutex constructor, this method enables you to specify which degree of control you need to exert on the mutex:

```
try
{
   // Request a mutex with the right to wait for it and to release it.
   MutexRights rights = MutexRights.Synchronize | MutexRights.Modify;
   Mutex m2 = Mutex.OpenExisting("DemoMutex", rights);
   // Use the mutex here.
   …
}
catch ( WaitHandleCannotBeOpenedException ex )
{
   // The specified object doesn't exist.
}
catch ( UnauthorizedAccessException ex )
{
   // The specified object exists, but current user doesn't have the
   // necessary access rights.
}
catch ( IOException ex )
{
   // A Win32 error has occurred.
}
```

The most important new feature of the Mutex type is the support for access control lists (ACLs), in the form of the System.Security.AccessControl.MutexSecurity object. You can specify an ACL when you instantiate a new Mutex object, use the GetAccessControl method to retrieve the MutexSecurity object associated with a given mutex, and enforce a new ACL with the SetAccessControl method:

```
bool ownership;
Mutex m = new Mutex(true, "DemoMutex", out ownership);
if ( ! ownership )
{
   // Determine who is the owner of the Mutex.
   MutexSecurity mutexSec = m.GetAccessControl();
   NTAccount account = (NTAccount) mutexSec.GetOwner(typeof(NTAccount));
   Console.WriteLine("Mutex is owned by {0}", account);    // => MYSERVER\Administrator;
}
```

Review the section titled "Working with Access Control Lists" in Chapter 7 for more information about ACLs in version 2.0 of the .NET Framework.

The Semaphore Type

The Semaphore type is new in .NET Framework 2.0 and maps on the Win32 semaphore object. Unlike all other threading objects (which are found in mscorlib.dll), this type is implemented in System.dll.

A semaphore is used in situations when you want no more than *N* threads to execute in a given portion of code or to access a given resource. A semaphore has an initial count and a maximum count, and you must pass these values to its constructor:

```
// A semaphore that has an initial count of 1 and a maximum count of 2.
Semaphore sem = new Semaphore(1, 2);
```

A thread can attempt to take ownership of a semaphore by calling the WaitOne method; if the current count is higher than zero, the count is decremented and the method returns immediately; otherwise, the WaitOne method waits until another thread releases the semaphore or until the optional timeout expires. A thread releases a semaphore by calling the Release method, which increases the count by 1 (or by the specified amount) and returns the *previous* count value.

```
Semaphore sem = new Semaphore(2, 2);
// Next statement brings count from 2 to 1.
sem.WaitOne();
…
// Next statement brings count from 1 to 2.
sem.Release();
// Next statement attempts to bring count from 2 to 3, but
// throws a SemaphoreFullException.
sem.Release();
```

You typically use a Semaphore object as follows:

```
// Initial count is initially equal to max count.
Semaphore sem = new Semaphore(2, 2);

void Semaphore_Example()
{
   // Wait until a resource becomes available.
   sem2.WaitOne();
   // Enter the synchronized section.
   …
   // Exit the synchronized section, and release the resource.
   sem2.Release();
}
```

(Remember to use a try...finally block to ensure that the semaphore is released even if the code throws an exception.) Like mutexes, semaphores can have a name and be shared among processes. When you try to create a Semaphore object that already exists, the initial and maximum count values are ignored:

```
bool ownership;
Semaphore sem3 = new Semaphore(2, 2, "semaphoreName", out ownership);
if ( ownership )
{
   // Current thread has ownership of the semaphore.
   …
}
```

The Semaphore object supports ACLs, which you can pass to the constructor, read with the GetAccessControl method, or modify with the SetAccessControl method. See the section titled "The Mutex Type" earlier in this chapter for more details about ACLs.

It's important for you to notice that the Mutex and the Semaphore types (as well as the AutoResetEvent, ManualResetEvent, and EventWaitHandle types that I cover in a later section) all inherit from the WaitHandle base class and therefore can be passed as arguments to the WaitAny, WaitAll, and SignalAndWait static methods of the WaitHandle type. This means that you can easily synchronize resources that are protected with any of these objects, as in this code:

```
// Wait until two mutexes, two semaphores, and one event object become signaled.
WaitHandle[] waitHandles = {mutex1, mutex2, sem1, sem2, event1};
WaitHandle.WaitAll(waitHandles);
```

The ReaderWriterLock Type

Many resources in the real world can be either read from or written to. Often these resources allow either multiple read operations or a single write operation running in a given moment. For example, multiple clients can read a data file or a database table, but if the file or the table is being written to, no other read or write operation can occur on that resource. You can create a lock that implements single-writer, multiple-reader semantics by using a ReaderWriterLock object.

Using this object is straightforward. All the threads intending to use the resource should share the same instance of the ReaderWriterLock type. Before attempting an operation on the resource, a thread should call either the AcquireReaderLock or the AcquireWriterLock method, depending on the operation to be performed. These methods block the current thread until the lock of the requested type can be acquired (for example, until no other thread is holding the lock if you requested a writer lock). Finally, the thread should call the ReleaseReaderLock or ReleaseWriterLock method when the read or write operation on the resource has been completed.

The following code example creates 10 threads that perform either a read or a write operation on a shared resource:

```
ReaderWriterLock rwl = new ReaderWriterLock();
Random rnd = new Random();
```

```
public void TestReaderWriterLock()
{
    for ( int i = 0; i <= 9; i++ )
    {
        Thread t = new Thread(ReaderWriterLock_Task);
        t.Start(i);
    }
    ...
}

void ReaderWriterLock_Task(object obj)
{
    int n = (int) obj;
    // Perform 10 read or write operations. (Reads are more frequent.)
    for ( int i = 1; i <= 10; i++ )
    {
        if ( rnd.NextDouble() < 0.8 )
        {
            // Attempt a read operation.
            rwl.AcquireReaderLock(Timeout.Infinite);
            Console.WriteLine("Thread #{0} is reading", n);
            Thread.Sleep(300);
            Console.WriteLine("Thread #{0} completed the read operation", n);
            rwl.ReleaseReaderLock();
        }
        else
        {
            // Attempt a write operation.
            rwl.AcquireWriterLock(Timeout.Infinite);
            Console.WriteLine("Thread #{0} is writing", n);
            Thread.Sleep(300);
            Console.WriteLine("Thread #{0} completed the write operation", n);
            rwl.ReleaseWriterLock();
        }
    }
}
```

If you run this code, you'll see that multiple threads can be reading at the same time and that a writing thread blocks all the other threads.

The AcquireReaderLock and AcquireWriterLock methods can take a timeout argument, expressed as a number of milliseconds or a TimeSpan value. You can test whether the lock was acquired successfully by means of the IsReaderLockHeld or IsWriterLockHeld read-only property if you passed a value other than Timeout.Infinite:

```
// Attempt to acquire a reader lock for no longer than 1 second.
rwl.AcquireWriterLock(1000);
if ( rwl.IsWriterLockHeld )
{
    // The thread has a writer lock on the resource.
    ...
}
```

A thread that owns a reader lock can also attempt to upgrade to a writer lock by calling the UpgradeToWriterLock method and later go back to the reader lock by calling Downgrade-FromWriterLock.

The great thing about ReaderWriterLock objects is that they are lightweight objects and can be used in large numbers without affecting performance significantly. And because the AcquireReaderLock and AcquireWriterLock methods take a timeout, a well-designed application should never suffer from deadlocks. Nevertheless, a deadlock can still occur when you have two threads and each thread is waiting for a resource that the other thread won't release until the operation completes.

The Interlocked Type

The Interlocked type provides a way to perform the simple atomic operations of incrementing and decrementing a variable shared among multiple threads. This class exposes only static methods (not counting members inherited from Object). Consider the following code:

```
// Increment and Decrement methods work with 32-bit and 64-bit integers.
int lockCounter = 0;
...
// Increment the counter and execute some code if its previous value was zero.
if ( Interlocked.Increment(ref lockCounter) == 1 )
{
   ...
   // Decrement the shared counter.
   Interlocked.Decrement(ref lockCounter);
}
```

The Add method is new in .NET Framework 2.0; it enables you to increment or decrement a 32-bit or 64-bit integer by the specified quantity:

```
if ( Interlocked.Add(ref lockCounter, 2) <= 10 )
{ ... }
```

The Interlocked class exposes two additional static methods. The Exchange method lets you assign a value of your choosing to an int, long, float, double, or IntPtr variable and return its previous value, as an atomic operation. In .NET Framework 2.0, the Exchange method has been overloaded to take an object argument; therefore, in practice you can make this method work with any reference type, for example, the String type:

```
string s1 = "123";
string s2 = Interlocked.Exchange(ref s1, "abc");
Console.WriteLine("s1={0}, s2={1}", s1, s2);
```

The CompareExchange method works similarly, but it does the swap only if the memory location is currently equal to a specific value that you provide as an argument.

The ManualResetEvent, AutoResetEvent, and EventWaitHandle Types

The last synchronization technique I illustrate in this chapter is based on three types that work in a similar way: ManualResetEvent, AutoResetEvent, and EventWaitHandle. The last type is the base class for the other two and has been added in version 2.0 of the .NET Framework. Even if the ManualResetEvent and the AutoResetEvent types haven't been made obsolete, in practice you can replace them with the new EventWaitHandle type, which actually gives you even more flexibility.

The ManualResetEvent and AutoResetEvent types are most useful when you want to temporarily stop one or more threads until another thread says it's OK to proceed. You use these objects to wake up a thread much like an event handler can execute code in an idle thread, but don't be fooled by the "event" in their names. You don't use regular event handlers with these objects.

An instance of these types can be in either a signaled or an unsignaled state. These terms don't really have any special meaning; just think of them as on and off states. You pass the initial state to their constructor, and any thread that can access the object can change the state to signaled (using the Set method) or unsignaled (using the Reset method). Other threads can use the WaitOne method to wait until the state becomes signaled or until the specified time-out expires.

```
// Create an auto reset event object in unsignaled state.
AutoResetEvent are = new AutoResetEvent(false);
// Create a manual reset event object in signaled state.
ManualResetEvent mre = new ManualResetEvent(true);
```

The only difference between ManualResetEvent and AutoResetEvent objects is that the latter ones automatically reset themselves (that is, become unsignaled) immediately after a thread blocked on a WaitOne method has been restarted. In practice, an AutoResetEvent object wakes up only one of the waiting threads when the object becomes signaled, whereas a ManualResetEvent object wakes up all the waiting threads and must be manually reset to unsignaled, as its name suggests.

As I mentioned previously, you can always replace an AutoResetEvent or a ManualResetEvent object with a proper EventWaitHandle object, as follows:

```
// These statements are equivalent to the previous code example.
EventWaitHandle are = new EventWaitHandle(false, EventResetMode.AutoReset);
EventWaitHandle mre = new EventWaitHandle(true, EventResetMode.ManualReset);
```

Event objects are especially useful in producer–consumer situations. You might have a single producer thread that evaluates some data—or reads it from disk, a serial port, the Internet, and so on—and then calls the Set method on a shared synchronization object so that one or more consumer threads can be restarted and process the new data. You should use an AutoReset-Event object (or an EventWaitHandle object with the AutoReset option) if only one consumer thread should process such data; you should use a ManualResetEvent object (or an EventWait-Handle object with the ManualReset option) if data should be processed by all consumers.

The following example shows how you can have multiple threads (the producer threads) performing file searches on different directories at the same time but a single thread (the consumer thread) collecting their results. This example uses a shared AutoResetEvent object to wake up the consumer thread when new filenames have been added to the List<string> object, and it also uses the Interlocked class to manage the counter of running threads so that the main thread knows when there's no more data to consume.

```
// (These fields are defined in a class named App.)

// The shared AutoResetEvent object
public static AutoResetEvent are = new AutoResetEvent(false);
// The list where matching filenames should be added
public static List<string> fileList = new List<string>();
// The number of running threads
public static int searchingThreads;
// An object used for locking purposes
public static object lockObj = new object();

public static void TestAutoResetEvent()
{
   // Search *.zip files in all the subdirectories of C:
   foreach ( string dirname in Directory.GetDirectories(@"C:\") )
   {
      Interlocked.Increment(ref searchingThreads);
      // Create a new wrapper class, pointing to a subdirectory.
      FileFinder sf = new FileFinder();
      sf.StartPath = dirname;
      sf.SearchPattern = "*.zip";
      // Create and run a new thread for that subdirectory only.
      Thread t = new Thread(sf.StartSearch);
      t.Start();
   }

   // Remember how many results we have so far.
   int resCount = 0;
   while ( searchingThreads > 0 )
   {
      // Wait until there are new results.
      are.WaitOne();

      lock ( lockObj )
      {
         // Display all new results.
         for ( int i = resCount; i <= fileList.Count - 1; i++ )
         {
            Console.WriteLine(fileList[i]);
         }
         // Remember that you've displayed these filenames.
         resCount = fileList.Count;
      }
   }
   Console.WriteLine("\nFound {0} files", resCount);
}
```

Each producer thread runs inside a different FileFinder object, which must be able to access the public variables defined in the preceding code.

```
public class FileFinder
{
   public string StartPath;        // The starting search path
   public string SearchPattern;    // The search pattern

   public void StartSearch()
   {
      Search(this.StartPath);
      // Decrease the number of running threads before exiting.
      Interlocked.Decrement(ref App.searchingThreads);
      // Let the consumer know it should check the thread counter.
      App.are.Set();
   }

   // This recursive procedure does the actual job.
   public void Search(string path)
   {
      try
      {
         // Get all the files that match the search pattern.
         string[] files = Directory.GetFiles(path, SearchPattern);
         // If there is at least one file, let the main thread know about it.
         if ( files != null && files.Length > 0 )
         {
            // Ensure found files are added as an atomic operation.
            lock ( App.lockObj )
            {
               // Add all found files.
               App.fileList.AddRange(files);
               // Let the consumer thread know about the new filenames.
               App.are.Set();
            }
         }

         // Repeat the search on all subdirectories.
         foreach ( string dirname in Directory.GetDirectories(path) )
         {
            Search(dirname);
         }
      }
      catch
      {
         // Do nothing if any error.
      }
   }
}
```

 Using an EventWaitHandle in lieu of an AutoResetEvent or ManualResetEvent object gives you one important feature: the ability to create a system-wide named object that you can share with other processes. The syntax for the EventWaitHandle constructor is similar to the one exposed by the Mutex class:

```
// Create a system-wide auto reset event that is initially in the signaled state.
bool ownership;
EventWaitHandle ewh = new EventWaitHandle(true, EventResetMode.AutoReset,
   "DemoEvent", out ownership);
if ( ownership )
{
   // The event object was created by the current thread.
   …
}
```

You can also use the OpenExisting static method to open an existing event object.

```
// This statement throws a WaitHandleCannotBeOpenedException if the specified
// event doesn't exist, or an UnauthorizedAccessException if the current
// user doesn't have the required permissions.
ewh = EventWaitHandle.OpenExisting("DemoEvent", EventWaitHandleRights.FullControl);
```

The second important new feature of event objects in .NET Framework 2.0 is the support for ACLs by means of the SetAccessControl and GetAccessControl methods, which take and return an instance of the EventWaitHandleSecurity type. You can use these methods in much the same way you use the SetAccessControl and GetAccessControl methods exposed by the Mutex object and all other .NET objects that support ACLs, and thus I won't provide any code samples.

Using the Thread Pool

Creating too many threads can easily degrade system performance, especially when the additional threads spend most of their time in a sleeping state and are restarted periodically only to poll a resource or to update the display. You can often improve the performance of your code significantly by resorting to the .NET thread pool, which permits the most efficient use of thread resources. Some objects in the System.Threading namespaces, such as Timers, transparently use the thread pool (see the following sections for more details about timers).

The ThreadPool Type

The thread pool is created the first time you invoke the ThreadPool.QueueUserWorkItem method or when a timer or a registered wait operation queues a callback operation. The pool has a default limit of 25 active threads; each thread uses the default stack size and runs at the default priority. The thread pool is available in all Windows versions.

You can borrow a thread from the pool by using the ThreadPool.QueueUserWorkItem method, which requires a WaitCallback delegate and an optional object that holds the data you want to pass to the thread. The WaitCallback delegate must point to a void method that receives one object argument (whose value is either the optional object passed to the

QueueUserWorkItem method or null). The following code shows how you can use a large number of threads to call an instance method of a class:

```
for ( int i = 1; i <= 20; i++ )
{
    // Create a new object for the next lightweight task.
    LightweightTask task = new LightweightTask();
    // Pass additional information to it. (Not used in this demo.)
    task.SomeData = "other data";
    // Run the task with a thread from the pool. (Pass the counter as an argument.)
    ThreadPool.QueueUserWorkItem(task.Execute, i);
}
```

The next block is the LightweightTask class, which contains the code that actually runs in the thread taken from the pool:

```
public class LightweightTask
{
    public string SomeData;

    // The method that contains the interesting code
    // (Not really interesting in this example)
    public void Execute(object state)
    {
        Console.WriteLine("Message from thread #{0}", state);
    }
}
```

The running thread can determine whether it has been taken from the thread pool by querying the Thread.CurrentThread.IsThreadPoolThread property. You can retrieve the highest number of threads in the pool by invoking the ThreadPool.GetMaxThreads static method, and the number of the threads that are currently available by invoking the ThreadPool.GetAvailableThreads static method.

A new method in .NET Framework 2.0 enables you to change the maximum number of threads in the pool:

```
// Maximum 30 worker threads and maximum 10 asynchronous I/O threads in the pool
ThreadPool.SetMaxThreads(30, 10);
```

You might sometimes be puzzled about whether you should create a thread yourself or borrow a thread from the pool. A good heuristic rule: use the Thread class when you want to run the associated task as soon as possible or when you perform a time-consuming task that doesn't run often. In the majority of cases, you should use the thread pool for more scalable server-side tasks.

The Timer Type

The .NET Framework offers several types of timers, each one with its strengths and limitations. For example, you should use the System.Windows.Forms.Timer control inside Windows Forms applications. If your application doesn't have a user interface, you should use either the System.Threading.Timer class or the System.Timers.Timer class. These two classes are broadly equivalent in their functionality, so I describe only the first one.

The Timer class in the System.Threading namespace offers a simple way to create a timer that calls back a given procedure. You can use this class to schedule an action in the future, and this action can be performed with whatever frequency you decide, including just once. The Timer's constructor takes four arguments:

- A TimerCallback delegate pointing to the procedure that's called when the timer's time-out elapses. The callback procedure must be a void method that takes a single object as an argument.

- An object that will be passed to the callback procedure. This object can be an individual number or string, an array or collection (or any other object) that holds additional data required by the callback method. (This data might be necessary because one callback procedure can serve multiple timers.) Use null if you don't need to pass additional data to the callback procedure.

- A TimeSpan value that specifies the due time—that is, when the timer must invoke the callback routine for the first time. This argument can be specified as a long or uint value, in which case the elapsed time is measured in milliseconds. Pass Timeout.Infinite to prevent the timer from starting, or pass 0 to activate it immediately.

- A TimeSpan value that specifies the timer's period—that is, how often the timer must invoke the callback routine after the first time. This argument can be specified as a long or uint value, in which case the elapsed time is measured in milliseconds. Pass –1 or Timeout.Infinite to disable periodic signaling.

The values that you pass to the Timer's constructor aren't exposed as properties. After the timer is running, you can change these values only by means of a Change method, which takes only two arguments, the due time and the period. The Timer object has no Stop method. You stop the timer by calling its Dispose method. The following example shows how to use the timer with a callback procedure:

```csharp
public void TestThreadingTimer()
{
   // Get the first callback after 1 second.
   TimeSpan dueTime = new TimeSpan(0, 0, 1);
   // Get additional callbacks every half second.
   TimeSpan period = new TimeSpan(0, 0, 0, 0, 500);
   // Create the timer.
   using ( Timer t = new Timer(TimerProc, null, dueTime, period) )
   {
      // Wait for 5 seconds in this demo, and then destroy the timer.
      Thread.Sleep(5000);
   }
}

// The callback procedure
void TimerProc(object state)
```

```
{
    // Display current system time in console window.
    Console.WriteLine("Callback proc called at {0}", DateTime.Now);
}
```

The callback procedure runs on a thread taken from the thread pool, so you should arbitrate access to variables and other resources used by the main thread by using one of the synchronization features that I describe in this chapter.

Asynchronous Operations

By now, you should be familiar with the Thread class and all the synchronization issues that you have to address when you're creating multithreading applications. At times, however, you'd simply like to execute a method call without blocking the main thread. For example, you might want to perform a long math calculation on a secondary thread while the application's main thread takes care of the user interface. In this case, what you really want to do is make a single asynchronous method call, which runs on another thread while the caller thread continues its normal execution. This programming model is so common that the .NET Framework offers special support for it so that *any* method can be called asynchronously without your having to specifically design the target method to support asynchronous calls.

This generic mechanism is based on asynchronous delegates. In addition, the framework offers more asynchronous support in many specific areas, including file I/O, XML Web services, and messages sent over Microsoft Message Queuing (MSMQ). Thanks to this unified approach, you need to learn the asynchronous programming pattern only once, and you can apply it to all these areas.

Asynchronous Delegates

In this section, I show you how you can use advanced features of delegates to call a method asynchronously. Let's start by defining a method that could take a significant amount of time to complete and therefore is a good candidate for an asynchronous call:

```
// This procedure scans a directory tree for a file.
// It takes a path and a file specification and returns a list of
// filenames; it returns the number of directories that have been
// parsed in the third argument.

static List<string> FindFiles(string path, string fileSpec, ref int parsedDirs)
{
    // Prepare the result.
    List<string> list = new List<string>();
    // Get all files in this directory that match the file spec.
    list.AddRange(Directory.GetFiles(path, fileSpec));
    // Remember that a directory has been parsed.
    parsedDirs += 1;
```

```
    // Scan subdirectories.
    foreach ( string subdir in Directory.GetDirectories(path) )
    {
        // Add all the matching files in subdirectories.
        list.AddRange(FindFiles(subdir, fileSpec, ref parsedDirs));
    }
    return list;
}
```

You call the FindFiles method by passing a starting path, a file specification (which can contain wildcards), and an Int32 variable. On returning from the function, the Int32 variable holds the number of directories that have been parsed, whereas the method itself returns a List object that contains the names of the files that match the specification:

```
int parsedDirs = 0;
// Find *.dll files in the C:\WINDOWS directory tree.
List<string> files = FindFiles(@"c:\windows", "*.dll", ref parsedDirs);
foreach ( string file in files )
{
    Console.WriteLine(file);
}
// Use the output argument.
Console.WriteLine("  {0} directories have been parsed.", parsedDirs);
```

Asynchronous Calls

The first step in implementing an asynchronous call to the FindFiles function is defining a delegate class that points to it:

```
delegate List<string> FindFilesDelegate(string path, string fileSpec, ref int parsedDirs);
```

To call the FindFiles procedure asynchronously, you create a delegate that points to the routine and use the delegate's BeginInvoke method to call the routine as you would use the delegate's Invoke method. The BeginInvoke method—which has been created for you by the C# compiler—takes the same arguments as the procedure the delegate points to, plus two additional arguments that I describe later. Unlike the Invoke method, though, BeginInvoke returns an IAsyncResult object. You can then query the IsCompleted read-only property of this IAsyncResult object to determine when the called routine has completed its execution. If this property returns true, you call the delegate's EndInvoke method to retrieve both the return value and the value of any argument that was passed by using the ref or out keyword (parsedDirs in the following procedure):

```
// Create a delegate that points to the target procedure.
FindFilesDelegate findFilesDeleg = new FindFilesDelegate(FindFiles);
// Start the asynchronous call; get an IAsyncResult object.
int parsedDirs = 0;
IAsyncResult ar = findFilesDeleg.BeginInvoke(@"c:\windows", "*.dll",
    ref parsedDirs, null, null);
```

```
// Wait until the method completes its execution.
while ( !ar.IsCompleted )
{
   Console.WriteLine("The main thread is waiting for FindFiles results.");
   Thread.Sleep(500);
}

// Now you can get the results.
List<string> files = findFilesDeleg.EndInvoke(ref parsedDirs, ar);
foreach ( string file in files )
{
   Console.WriteLine(file);
}
Console.WriteLine("  {0} directories have been parsed.", parsedDirs);
```

You should call EndInvoke only after IAsyncResult.IsCompleted returns true; otherwise, the EndInvoke method blocks the calling thread until the called procedure completes. (And you would lose the advantage of making an asynchronous call.)

The code in the preceding procedure polls the IsCompleted property to determine when the asynchronous call has completed. A less CPU-intensive means to achieve the same result uses the IAsyncResult.AsyncWaitHandle property, which returns a WaitHandle synchronization object. You can then use the WaitOne method of this object to make the main thread wait until the asynchronous call completes:

```
ar.AsyncWaitHandle.WaitOne();
```

As you learned earlier in the section titled "The Mutex Type," the WaitHandle type exposes the WaitAny and WaitAll static methods, which are especially useful when you run multiple asynchronous operations in parallel. Both methods take an array of WaitHandle objects: the WaitAny method blocks the calling thread until any of the asynchronous operations complete, whereas the WaitAll method blocks the calling thread until all the asynchronous operations complete. Unfortunately, you can't call these two methods from a thread running in a Single Thread Apartment (STA); thus, you must create a separate thread using the Thread class and run the asynchronous operations from this new thread (unless you're already running in a thread outside an STA).

Asynchronous Callback Procedures

As I explained earlier, the BeginInvoke method takes all the arguments in the original method's signature, plus two additional arguments. The second-to-last argument is a delegate pointing to a callback procedure that's called when the asynchronous method completes its execution:

```
IAsyncResult ar = findFilesDeleg.BeginInvoke(@"c:\windows", "*.dll", ref parsedDirs,
   new AsyncCallback(MethodCompleted), null);
```

The technique based on callback procedures offers a viable alternative to making the main thread use the IsCompleted or AsyncWaitHandle property of the IAsyncResult object to determine when it's safe to gather the return value and any arguments that were passed by reference.

The callback procedure must follow the syntax of the AsyncCallback delegate (defined in the System namespace), which defines a void method that takes an IAsyncResult object as its only argument. The code inside the callback procedure should call the delegate's EndInvoke method to retrieve the return value and the value of any arguments passed by reference. Here's a possible implementation of the callback procedure for the example shown previously:

```
void MethodCompleted(IAsyncResult ar)
{
   int parsedDirs = 0;
   List<string> files = findFilesDeleg.EndInvoke(ref parsedDirs, ar);
   // Display found files.
   // ...(Omitted, same as previous examples)...
}
```

This approach poses two minor problems. First, the callback routine doesn't have any way of knowing why it has been called, so it's difficult to reuse the same callback routine for multiple asynchronous calls. This problem can be solved easily by passing one value in the last argument of the BeginInvoke method:

```
// (In the caller program...)
string msg = @"DLL files in c:\windows";
IAsyncResult ar = findFilesDeleg.BeginInvoke(@"c:\windows", "*.dll", ref parsedDirs,
    new AsyncCallback(MethodCompleted), msg);
```

(If you need to pass two or more values, you can stuff them into an array and pass the array as the argument.) You can extract this argument by querying the AsyncState property of the IAsyncResult argument in the callback method:

```
// (In the callback method...)
string msg = (string) ar.AsyncState;
```

The second problem: the callback method must have access to the delegate variable (find-FilesDeleg, in this particular example); this isn't an issue when both routines belong to the same class (you can simply declare the delegate as a private class-level variable), but it becomes a problem when the callback routine is in another class, possibly located in a different assembly. You can solve this problem by casting the IAsyncResult value to an AsyncResult object and then querying the AsyncDelegate property of the AsyncResult object:

```
// (Inside the callback method...)
FindFilesDelegate deleg = (FindFilesDelegate) ( ar as AsyncResult ).AsyncDelegate;
```

To recap, this is the code you need to write in the method that creates the asynchronous delegate:

```
// Create a delegate that points to the target procedure.
FindFilesDelegate findFilesDeleg = new FindFilesDelegate(App.FindFiles);
// Start the async call, pass a delegate pointing to the MethodCompleted
// procedure, and get an IAsyncResult object.
string msg = @"DLL files in C:\WINDOWS";
int parsedDirs = 0;
IAsyncResult ar = findFilesDeleg.BeginInvoke(@"c:\windows", "*.dll",
    ref parsedDirs, new AsyncCallback(MethodCompleted), msg);
...
```

The callback method must retrieve the data passed in the AsyncState property of the IAsyncResult:

```
private static void AsyncCallbacks_CBK(IAsyncResult ar)
{
    // Extract the delegate.
    FindFilesDelegate deleg = (FindFilesDelegate) ( ar as AsyncResult ).AsyncDelegate;
    // Extract the value.
    string msg = (string) ar.AsyncState;
    // Call the EndInvoke method, and display the result.
    Console.WriteLine(msg);
    int parsedDirs = 0;
    foreach ( string file in deleg.EndInvoke(ref parsedDirs, ar) )
    {
        Console.WriteLine(file);
    }
    Console.WriteLine("  {0} directories have been parsed.", parsedDirs);
}
```

More on Asynchronous Method Invocation

A relevant detail I haven't covered yet is how the asynchronous architecture deals with exceptions. It turns out that both the BeginInvoke and EndInvoke methods can throw an exception.

If BeginInvoke throws an exception, you know that the asynchronous call hasn't been queued and you shouldn't call the EndInvoke method. These exceptions might be thrown by the .NET asynchronous infrastructure—for example, when the target of the asynchronous call is a remote object that can't be reached.

EndInvoke can throw an exception, too; this happens either when the asynchronous method throws an exception or when the .NET asynchronous infrastructure throws an exception—for example, when the remote object can't be reached any longer. The obvious suggestion is that you should bracket EndInvoke calls inside a try...catch block, as you would do for any regular method call that can throw an exception.

Sometimes, however, you don't really care whether the called method actually throws an exception. This might be the case, for example, if the procedure doesn't return a value and doesn't take arguments passed by reference. You can inform the CLR that you aren't interested in the outcome of the method, including any exceptions it might throw, by marking the method with the System.Runtime.Remoting.Messaging.OneWay attribute:

```
[System.Runtime.Remoting.Messaging.OneWay()]
void MethodThatMayThrow(object arg)
{
    ...
}
```

You get no error if this attribute is applied to a method that includes a ref or out argument or a return value, but such an argument or return value isn't returned to the calling application. Here are a few more tips about asynchronous calls:

- The effect of calling EndInvoke twice on the same IAsyncResult object is indefinite, so you should avoid performing this operation.

- Even if BeginInvoke takes a ref or out argument, the .NET asynchronous infrastructure doesn't record the address of this argument anywhere, and therefore it can't automatically update the variable when the method completes. The only way to retrieve the value of an output argument is by passing it to the EndInvoke method.

- If the called method takes a reference to an object (passed either by value or by reference), the method can assign that object's properties. The caller can see those new values even before the asynchronous method completes. If both the caller and the called method can access the same object, however, you might want to provide some form of synchronization of its property procedures.

- The .NET asynchronous infrastructure provides no generic means to cancel an asynchronous method once the BeginInvoke method has been called because in many cases there's no reliable way to cancel a running operation. In general, it's up to the class's author to implement a method that cancels an asynchronous method call.

Asynchronous File Operations

The great thing about asynchronous support in .NET is that once you become familiar with its programming pattern, you can apply it to several classes that expose asynchronous operations natively—that is, without the need of an explicit asynchronous delegate to the method. In this section, I show you how to use the BeginRead, EndRead, BeginWrite, and EndWrite methods of the Stream type to perform asynchronous file I/O. All the stream-based classes, including FileStream, inherit these methods. Other .NET types expose a similar Begin-End pattern, for example, the Web services proxy classes that Visual Studio generates.

The BeginWrite method takes a Byte array that contains the data to be written to the stream, the index of the first element to write, and the number of bytes to write: these are the same arguments that the regular, synchronous Write method accepts. You also pass an Async-Callback delegate and a state object, as you do with all the asynchronous method invocations shown in earlier sections. The callback routine must conclude the write operation by invoking the EndWrite method, and then close the stream.

The BeginRead method has the same argument signature as BeginWrite, with the first three values defining the location at which data read from the stream will be stored. The callback routine must conclude the asynchronous read operation by invoking an EndRead method, and then close the stream. The EndRead method returns the total number of bytes read; a 0 value means that there were no more bytes to read.

The following code shows an example of asynchronous write and read operations on the same file. A single callback routine serves both the write and the read operations: the type of operation is passed as a string in the last argument to BeginWrite and BeginRead. To keep the code simple, both the caller routine and the callback routine share the variable pointing to the Byte array buffer and the FileStream object. In a real-world application, you might want to pack this data into an object and pass it as the last argument to BeginWrite and BeginRead:

```csharp
// The file being read from or written to
private const string FileName = @"C:\TESTDATA.TMP";
// The FileStream object used for both reading and writing
public FileStream fs;
// The buffer for file I/O
public byte[] buffer = new byte[1048576];

public void AsyncFileOperations()
{
    // Fill the buffer with random data.
    for ( int i = 0; i < buffer.Length; i++ )
    {
        buffer[i] = (byte) (i % 256);
    }

    // Create the target file in asynchronous mode (open in asynchronous mode).
    fs = new FileStream(FileName, FileMode.Create, FileAccess.Write,
        FileShare.None, 65536, true);
    // Start the async write operation.
    Console.WriteLine("Starting the async write operation");
    IAsyncResult ar = fs.BeginWrite(buffer, 0, buffer.Length,
        new AsyncCallback(AsyncFileCallback), "write");

    // Wait a few seconds until the operation completes.
    Thread.Sleep(4000);
    // Now read back the file.
    fs = new FileStream(FileName, FileMode.Open, FileAccess.Read,
        FileShare.None, 65536, true);
    // Size the receiving buffer.
    buffer = new byte[System.Convert.ToInt32(fs.Length) - 1];
    // Start the async read operation.
    Console.WriteLine("Starting the async read operation");
    ar = fs.BeginRead(buffer, 0, buffer.Length,
        new AsyncCallback(AsyncFileCallback), "read");
}

// This is the callback procedure for both async read and write.
public static void AsyncFileCallback(IAsyncResult ar)
{
    // Get the state object (the "write" or "read" string).
    string opName = ar.AsyncState.ToString();

    // The behavior is quite different in the two cases.
    switch ( opName )
    {
        case "write":
            Console.WriteLine("Async write operation completed");
```

```
         // Complete the write, and close the stream.
         fs.EndWrite(ar);
         fs.Close();
         break;
      case "read":
         Console.WriteLine("Async read operation completed");
         // Complete the read, and close the stream.
         int bytes = fs.EndRead(ar);
         Console.WriteLine("Read {0} bytes", bytes);
         fs.Close();
         break;
   }
}
```

You get the best benefits from asynchronous file I/O if you also open the FileStream for asynchronous operations by passing true in the last argument of the object's constructor:

```
fs = new FileStream(path, mode, access, share, bufferSize, useAsync);
```

When you open a FileStream in this way, synchronous operations are slowed, but asynchronous operations are completed faster. Keep in mind that read and write operations of less then 64 KB are usually performed synchronously anyway, even if you use BeginWrite or BeginRead, and that the useAsync argument might be ignored on Windows platforms that don't support asynchronous file operations. You can test whether the FileStream was actually opened for asynchronous operation by testing its IsAsync property.

Adding Asynchronous Support to Your Types

Even though the .NET Framework enables you to invoke any method of any type asynchronously, it's a good idea to expose a pair of Begin*Xxxx*/End*Xxxx* methods for any lengthy task that your class can perform. This pattern is especially useful if you can also expose a Cancel*Xxxx* method, which enables clients to abort an asynchronous operation. (As you saw earlier, asynchronous delegates don't expose this feature because, in general, the .NET Framework can't assume that it is safe to cancel a running method without compromising data integrity.)

The following example shows a TextFileReader class that exposes a Read method for reading a text file in a synchronous manner, the BeginRead and EndRead methods to perform the same operation asynchronously, and the CancelRead method to cancel an asynchronous read operation.

```
public class TextFileReader
{
   // This private delegate matches the signature of the Read method.
   private delegate string InvokeRead(string fileName);

   // True if the asynchronous operation has been canceled
   private bool canceled;
   // A delegate that points to the Read method
   private InvokeRead deleg;
```

```csharp
// The object used to control asynchronous operations
private IAsyncResult ar;

// The Read method (synchronous)
public string Read(string fileName)
{
    canceled = false;
    System.Text.StringBuilder sb = new System.Text.StringBuilder();
    using ( StreamReader sr = new StreamReader(fileName) )
    {
        while ( sr.Peek() != -1 )
        {
            sb.Append(sr.ReadLine()).AppendLine();
            if ( canceled )
            {
                return null;
            }
        }
        return sb.ToString();
    }
}

// The following methods add support for asynchronous operations.
public void BeginRead(string fileName)
{
    deleg = new InvokeRead(Read);
    ar = deleg.BeginInvoke(fileName, null, null);
}

public string EndRead()
{
    if ( canceled || deleg == null )
    {
        return null;
    }
    else
    {
        return deleg.EndInvoke(ar);
    }
}

public void CancelRead()
{
    // Cause the Read method to exit prematurely; then return the thread to the pool.
    if ( canceled == false && deleg != null )
    {
        canceled = true;
        deleg.EndInvoke(ar);
    }
}
}
```

You can easily apply the same mechanism to other classes that expose time-consuming operations that can be split into simpler tasks.

Threading in Windows Forms Applications

All the techniques I have illustrated so far were applied in a Console application, and I had a good reason to do so. In fact, you must take into account some constraints when you implement threading in a Windows Forms project; otherwise, your application will almost surely fail at run time.

The problem with Windows Forms objects—both controls and the Form object itself—is that they must be accessed *exclusively* from the thread that created them. In fact, all the Windows Forms objects rely on the STA model because windows and controls are based on the Win32 message architecture, which is inherently apartment threaded. This means that you can create a control or a form from any thread, but all the methods of the control must be called from that same thread.

This constraint can create a serious problem because other .NET portions use the free-threading model, and carelessly mixing the two models isn't a wise idea. Even if you don't explicitly create a thread in your code, you might experience problems anyway, for example, if you access a UI element from the Finalize method of a type. (As you know, the Finalize method runs on a thread other than the main thread.)

The ISynchronizeInvoke Interface

The only members that you can call on a control object from another thread are those exposed by the ISynchronizeInvoke interface: the Invoke, BeginInvoke, and EndInvoke methods and the InvokeRequired read-only property.

The InvokeRequired property returns true if the caller can't access the control directly (that is, if the caller is running in a thread other than the thread that created the control). If this is the case, the caller should invoke the Invoke method to access any member exposed by the control. The Invoke method is synchronous, and therefore the calling thread is blocked until the UI thread completes the method. Alternatively, the calling thread can use the BeginInvoke and EndInvoke methods to perform the operation asynchronously: the pattern for using these two methods is exactly the same as the one I illustrate in the section titled "Asynchronous Delegates" earlier in this chapter. In this section, I focus on the Invoke method only, but you can easily apply these concepts to the BeginInvoke and EndInvoke methods as well.

The Invoke method takes a delegate pointing to a method and can take an array of objects as a second argument if the method expects one or more arguments. The Windows Forms infrastructure ensures that the procedure pointed to by the delegate is executed in the UI thread and can therefore safely access any control on the form.

Let's see how you can use the Invoke method to access a control from a non-UI thread. The following example shows how you can visit all the directories in a directory tree from a secondary thread, while displaying the name of the directory being parsed in a Label control.

The first thing to do is to define a method that performs the intended UI operation; such a method can be as simple as this procedure:

```
// This method must run in the main UI thread.
void ShowMessage(string msg)
{
    this.lblMessage.Text = msg;
    this.Refresh();
}
```

Next, you define a delegate type that can point to the previous method and a variable that can hold an instance of the delegate. This variable is defined at the form level so that it can be shared by all methods in the form:

```
// A delegate that can point to the ShowMessage procedure
delegate void ShowMessageDelegate(string msg);
// An instance of the delegate
ShowMessageDelegate threadSafeDelegate;
```

You need a method that starts the secondary thread. Being a Windows Forms application, this method is likely to be the Click handler of a Button control:

```
// Parse the c:\windows directory when the user clicks this button.
private void btnSearch_Click(object sender, EventArgs e)
{
    Thread t = new Thread(ListFiles);
    t.Start(@"c:\windows");
}
```

Finally, you write the code that runs in the secondary thread. It is essential, however, that this code accesses the lblMessage control only by means of a call to the ShowMessage method, and that this call occurs through the Invoke method of the Form class (or the Invoke method of any control on the form, which is perfectly equivalent). Such calls are highlighted in bold type in the following listing:

```
// (This method runs in a non-UI thread.)
void ListFiles(object arg)
{
    // Retrieve the argument.
    string path = (string) arg;
    // Prepare the delegate.
    threadSafeDelegate = new ShowMessageDelegate(ShowMessage);
    // Invoke the worker procedure. (The result isn't used in this demo.)
    List<string> files = GetFiles(path);
    // Show that execution has terminated.
    string msg = String.Format("Found {0} files", files.Count);
    this.Invoke(threadSafeDelegate, msg);
}

// A recursive function that retrieves all the files in a directory tree
// (This method runs in a non-UI thread.)
List<string> GetFiles(string path)
```

```
{
   // Display a message.
   string msg = String.Format("Parsing directory {0}", path);
   this.Invoke(threadSafeDelegate, msg);

   // Read the files in this folder and all subfolders.
   List<string> files = new List<string>();
   foreach ( string fi in Directory.GetFiles(path) )
   {
      files.Add(fi);
   }
   foreach ( string di in Directory.GetDirectories(path) )
   {
      files.AddRange(GetFiles(di));
   }
   return files;
}
```

The implementation of this technique becomes more complicated if the ShowMessage method is being used by both the UI thread and a non-UI thread. For example, the GetFiles method might be called from a UI thread, in which case making the call through the Invoke method adds an overhead that might and should be avoided. In this case, you should test the InvokeRequired property first and make a regular method call if the property returns false, as in the following:

```
// (Inside the ListFiles and GetFiles methods)
if ( this.InvokeRequired )
{
   this.Invoke(threadSafeDelegate, msg);
}
else
{
   ShowMessage(msg);
}
```

There is an even better approach, though: instead of testing the InvokeRequired property from each caller, test it from inside the ShowMessage method itself:

```
// This method can run in the UI thread or in a non-UI thread.
void ShowMessage(string msg)
{
   // Use the Invoke method only if necessary.
   if ( this.InvokeRequired )
   {
      this.Invoke(threadSafeDelegate, msg);
      return;
   }

   this.lblMessage.Text = msg;
   this.Refresh();
}
```

After this change, any piece of code that must display a message on the lblMessage control can simply call ShowMessage without having to worry about whether the code is running in the UI thread or in a secondary thread.

> **Note** It is crucial that you don't suspend or invoke the Join method on the main UI thread in a Windows Forms application while waiting for the other thread to complete because this action would prevent the main thread from accepting calls from the other thread through the Invoke method.

In some circumstances, a .NET application can access a control from a non-UI thread without causing any problems. For example, it might happen when accessing simple controls (such as a Label) or when performing operations that don't cause a Win32 message to be sent behind the scenes. Also, many properties can be read (but not assigned) without interacting with the underlying Windows control because the property value is stored in a field of the .NET control. It is quite possible that a few .NET Framework 1.1 applications in the real world mistakenly access a control from the wrong thread without causing any noticeable problem. More frequently, however, the application has some sort of random malfunctioning that you can't easily associate with the actual cause.

Microsoft wanted to change this behavior and ensure that these mistakes don't go unnoticed, but at the same time wanted to preserve compatibility with existing applications so that an application compiled using Microsoft Visual Studio .NET 2003 continues to work well under .NET Framework 2.0. Thus, Microsoft adopted the following strategy: Visual Studio 2005 applications that access a control from a non-UI thread cause an exception, but only if compiled in Debug mode. The rationale is that developers won't miss this exception while testing new programs and can fix the problem before releasing the final version.

The BackgroundWorker Component

Although the ISynchronizeInvoke interface enables you to avoid threading problems in Windows Forms applications, most developers need a simpler and less error-prone approach. Also, they need a simple way to cancel an asynchronous method call safely, something that the ISynchronizeInvoke interface doesn't provide automatically.

For this reason, Microsoft has added the BackgroundWorker component to the Toolbox. As you'll see in a moment, using this new component is a breeze and will surely simplify the creation of robust multithreaded Windows Forms applications.

The BackgroundWorker component has only two interesting properties: the WorkerReports-Progress (true if the component raises the ProgressChanged event) and WorkerSupports-Cancellation (true if the component supports the CancelAsync method). The default value for both properties is false, and therefore you must set them to true if you want to take full advantage of this component. (The example that follows assumes that these properties are set to true.) Using the BackgroundWorker component typically requires the following actions:

1. Create a handler for the DoWork event and fill it with the code you want to run in the secondary thread. This code runs when the RunWorkerAsync method is called. The RunWorkerAsync method accepts an argument, which is passed to the DoWork event. The code in the DoWork event handler can't directly access the controls on the form because it runs in a non-UI thread.

2. Use the ReportProgress method from inside the DoWork event handler when you need to access a UI element. This method fires the ProgressChanged event if the Worker-ReportsProgress property is true; otherwise, an InvalidOperationException object is thrown. The handlers for the ProgressChanged event run in the UI thread, and therefore they can safely access the form and its controls.

3. Use the CancelAsync method of the BackgroundWorker control to immediately abort the secondary thread. This method requires that the WorkerSupportsCancellation property be true; otherwise, an InvalidOperationException object is thrown. The code in the DoWork handler should periodically check the CancellationPending property and gracefully exit when this property becomes true.

4. Write a handler for the RunWorkerCompleted event if you need to perform an action when the secondary thread has completed, either naturally or because of a call to the CancelAsync method. Handlers of this event run in the UI thread, and therefore they can access any UI element.

Typically, the code in the DoWork event handler must return a value to the main thread. Instead of assigning this value to a class-level field—a dangerous technique that might lead to race conditions—the code should assign this value to the Result property of the DoWorkEventArgs object. This value is then made available to the main UI thread by means of the Result property of the RunWorkerCompletedEventArgs object passed to the RunWorkerCompleted event.

To recap, here's the typical structure of a form that uses the BackgroundWorker component:

```
// The button that starts the asynchronous operation
private void btnStart_Click(object sender, EventArgs e)
{
    object argument = "abcde";            // The argument
    BackgroundWorker1.RunWorkerAsync(argument);
    // Disable this button, and enable the Stop button.
    btnStart.Enabled = false;
    btnStop.Enabled = true;
}

// The button that cancels the asynchronous operation
private void btnStop_Click(object sender, EventArgs e)
{
    BackgroundWorker1.CancelAsync();
}

// The code that performs the asynchronous operation
private void BackgroundWorker1_DoWork(object sender, DoWorkEventArgs e)
```

```csharp
{
    // Retrieve the argument.
    object argument = e.Argument;
    int percentage = 0;
    ...
    // The core of the asynchronous task
    while ( !BackgroundWorker1.CancellationPending )
    {
        ...
        // Report progress when it makes sense to do so.
        BackgroundWorker1.ReportProgress(percentage);
    }
    // Return the result to the caller.
    e.Result = theResult;
}

// This method runs when the ReportProgress method is invoked.
private void BackgroundWorker1_ProgressChanged(object sender, ProgressChangedEventArgs e)
{
    // It is safe to access the user interface from here.
    // For example, show the progress on a progress bar or in another control.
    ToolStripProgressBar1.Value = e.ProgressPercentage;
}

// This method runs when the asynchronous task is completed (or canceled).
private void BackgroundWorker1_RunWorkerCompleted(object sender,
    RunWorkerCompletedEventArgs e)
{
    // It is safe to access the user interface from here.
    ...
    // Reset the Enabled state of the Start and Stop buttons.
    btnStart.Enabled = true;
    btnStop.Enabled = false;
}
```

The following completed example shows how you can use the BackgroundWorker component to search for files on an asynchronous thread. (See Figure 11-8.) This is the same problem I solved in the section titled "The ISynchronizeInvoke Interface" earlier in this chapter, and thus you can easily compare the two techniques.

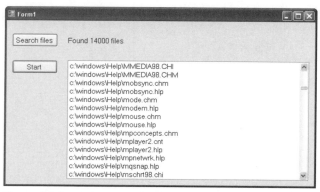

Figure 11-8 A demo application using the BackgroundWorker component to search for files in the background

The new version based on the BackgroundWorker component, however, is slightly more complex because it supports the cancellation of the asynchronous task:

```
public List<string> files;
// We need this variable to avoid nested calls to ProgressChanged.
public bool callInProgress;

// In this version, the same button works as a Start and a Stop button.
private void btnStart_Click(object sender, EventArgs e)
{
    if ( btnStart.Text == "Start" )
    {
        lstFiles.Items.Clear();
        this.BackgroundWorker1.RunWorkerAsync(@"c:\windows");
        this.btnStart.Text = "Stop";
    }
    else
    {
        this.BackgroundWorker1.CancelAsync();
    }
}

// A recursive function that retrieves all the files in a directory tree
public void SearchFiles(string path)
{
    // Display a message.
    string msg = string.Format("Parsing directory {0}", path);
    // Notice that we don't really use the percentage;
    // instead, we pass the message in the UserState property.
    this.BackgroundWorker1.ReportProgress(0, msg);

    // Read the files in this folder and all subfolders.
    // Exit immediately if the task has been canceled.
    foreach ( string fi in Directory.GetFiles(path) )
    {
        if ( this.BackgroundWorker1.CancellationPending )
        {
            return;
        }
        files.Add(fi);
    }
    foreach ( string di in Directory.GetDirectories(path) )
    {
        if ( this.BackgroundWorker1.CancellationPending )
        {
            return;
        }
        SearchFiles(di);
    }
}

private void BackgroundWorker1_ProgressChanged(object sender, ProgressChangedEventArgs e)
{
    // Reject nested calls.
    if ( callInProgress )
```

```
    {
        return;
    }
    callInProgress = true;
    // Display the message received in the UserState property.
    this.lblMessage.Text = e.UserState.ToString();
    // Display all files added since last call.
    for ( int i = lstFiles.Items.Count; i <= files.Count - 1; i++ )
    {
        lstFiles.Items.Add(files[i]);
    }
    this.Refresh();
    // Let Windows process message in the queue.
    // If you omit this call, clicks on buttons are ignored.
    Application.DoEvents();
    callInProgress = false;
}

private void BackgroundWorker1_RunWorkerCompleted(object sender,
    RunWorkerCompletedEventArgs e)
{
    // Display the last message and reset button's caption.
    this.lblMessage.Text = e.Result.ToString();
    btnStart.Text = "Start";
}
```

This code is quite self-explanatory, except for the handler of the ProgressChanged event. This code must contain a call to the Application.DoEvents() method; otherwise, the application can't process clicks on the Stop button (or any other UI action, for that matter). However, calls to this method might cause nested calls to the ProgressChanged procedure itself, and these additional calls might cause a StackOverflowException. The code uses an auxiliary call-InProgress Boolean field to avoid such nested calls.

Also notice that this application doesn't need to report a progress percentage to the main thread, and it uses the ReportProgress method just as a means to execute a piece of code in the UI thread. The actual message to be displayed is passed in the UserState property. If your application uses a progress bar or another indicator of progress, however, you should avoid unnecessary calls to the ReportProgress method because each call causes a thread switch and is relatively expensive in terms of processing time. In such cases, you should store the current percentage in a class field and call the method only if the percentage has actually changed:

```
int currentPercentage = 0;

private void BackgroundWorker1_DoWork(object sender, DoWorkEventArgs e)
{
    const int TotalSteps = 5000;
    for ( int i = 1; i <= TotalSteps; i++ )
```

```
    {
        ...
        // Evaluate progress percentage.
        int percentage = (i * 100) / TotalSteps;
        // Report to UI thread only if percentage has changed.
        if ( percentage != currentPercentage )
        {
            BackgroundWorker1.ReportProgress(percentage);
            currentPercentage = percentage;
        }
    }
}
```

Chapter 12
Object Serialization

Serialization is the act of saving (or *serializing*) an object onto a storage medium—a file, a database field, a buffer in memory—and later *deserializing* it from the storage medium to re-create an object instance that can be considered identical to the original one. Serialization is a key feature in the Microsoft .NET Framework and is transparently used by the CLR for tasks other than simply saving an object to a file—for example, for marshaling an object by value to another application. You should make an object serializable if you plan to send it to another application or save it on disk, in a database field, or in a Microsoft ASP.NET Session object. For example, exception objects should be made serializable if they can be thrown from another AppDomain.

Serialization and *persistence* are often used as synonyms, so you can also say that an object is persisted and depersisted. The SDK documentation makes a distinction, however, and uses *persistence* to mean that the data is stored in a durable medium, such as a file or a database field, whereas *serialization* can be applied to objects stored in nondurable media, such as memory buffers.

Note To avoid long lines, code samples in this chapter assume that the following using statements are used at the top of each source file:

```
using System;
using System.Collections;
using System.Collections.Generic;
using System.Diagnostics;
using System.IO;
using System.Reflection;
using System.Runtime.Serialization;
using System.Runtime.Serialization.Formatters;
using System.Runtime.Serialization.Formatters.Binary;
using System.Runtime.Serialization.Formatters.Soap;
using System.Security.Permissions;
```

Basic Serialization

The .NET Framework knows how to serialize all basic data types, including numbers, strings, and arrays of numbers and strings, so you can save and reload these types to and from a file stream (or any other type of stream) with minimal effort. All you need to serialize and deserialize a basic object is a proper formatter object.

Formally speaking, a *formatter* is an object that implements the IFormatter interface (defined in the System.Runtime.Serialization namespace). You can create your own formatter by defining a class that implements this interface, but most of the time you can use one of the formatter objects provided by the .NET Framework:

- The BinaryFormatter object, defined in the System.Runtime.Serialization.Formatters .Binary namespace, provides an efficient way to persist an object in a compact binary format. In practice, the actual bits in memory are persisted, so the serialization and deserialization processes are very fast.

- The SoapFormatter object, defined in the System.Runtime.Serialization.Formatters .Soap namespace, persists data in human-readable XML format, following the Simple Object Access Protocol (SOAP) specifications. The serialization and deserialization processes are somewhat slower than they are with the BinaryFormatter object. On the other hand, data can be sent easily to another application through HTTP and displayed in a human-readable format.

 The SoapFormatter type has been marked as obsolete in Microsoft .NET Framework version 2.0 and its use has been deprecated in favor of the BinaryFormatter. For this reason, our discussion will revolve mainly around the BinaryFormatter type.

The .NET Framework supports a third form of serialization, based on the XmlSerializer type and known as *XML serialization* (not to be confused with SOAP serialization). I briefly hinted at this type in the section titled "A Custom Attribute for CSV Serialization" in Chapter 10, "Custom Attributes," but I won't discuss this technique any further in this book.

Binary Serialization

The key methods that all formatter objects support are Serialize and Deserialize, whose purpose is quite evident. The Serialize method takes a Stream object as its first argument and the object to be serialized as its second argument:

```
// Create an array of integers.
int[] arr = { 1, 2, 4, 8, 16, 32, 64, 128, 256 };
// Open a stream for output.
using ( FileStream fs = new FileStream("powers.dat", FileMode.Create) )
{
    // Create a binary formatter.
    BinaryFormatter bf = new BinaryFormatter();
    // Serialize the array to the file stream, and flush the stream.
    bf.Serialize(fs, arr);
}
```

The BinaryFormatter (like all other .NET formatters) can complete its task because the .NET Framework uses reflection to inspect any object at run time and discover, read, and assign all the object's fields and properties.

Reading back the file data and deserializing it into an object require the Deserialize function, which takes the input Stream as its only argument and returns an Object value, which must be cast to a properly typed variable:

```
int[] arr2 = null;
// Open a file stream for input.
using ( FileStream fs2 = new FileStream("powers.dat", FileMode.Open) )
{
    // Create a binary formatter.
    BinaryFormatter bf = new BinaryFormatter();
    // Deserialize the contents of the file stream into an Integer array.
    // (Deserialize returns an object that must be cast.)
    arr2 = (int[]) bf.Deserialize(fs2);
}
```

You can indicate the reason you're creating a formatter by passing a StreamingContext object to the second argument of the formatter's constructor. The streaming context object contains information about the serialization and deserialization processes and can be used by the object being serialized. For example, a formatter might opt for a compression algorithm if it's being serialized to a file. Even if you don't know whether the object you're serializing takes advantage of this additional information, specifying the streaming context is a good programming practice. Here's how you define a formatter that's used to serialize an object to a file:

```
StreamingContext sc = new StreamingContext(StreamingContextStates.File);
BinaryFormatter bf = new BinaryFormatter(null, sc);
```

You can simplify the code that serializes and deserializes objects to and from files with a pair of reusable methods exposed by a Functions class:

```
public class Functions
    public static void SerializeToFile<T>(string path, T obj)
    {
        // Open the stream for output.
        using ( FileStream fs = new FileStream(path, FileMode.Create) )
        {
            // Create a formatter.
            BinaryFormatter bf = new BinaryFormatter(null,
                new StreamingContext(StreamingContextStates.File));
            // Serialize the object and close the stream.
            bf.Serialize(fs, obj);
        }
    }

    public static T DeserializeFromFile<T>(string path)
    {
        // Open the stream for input.
        using ( FileStream fs = new FileStream(path, FileMode.Open) )
```

```
        {
            // Create a formatter.
            BinaryFormatter bf = new BinaryFormatter(null,
                new StreamingContext(StreamingContextStates.File));
            // Deserialize the object from the stream.
            return (T) bf.Deserialize(fs);
        }
    }
}
```

Interestingly, the assembly containing the type being deserialized doesn't have to be loaded in memory. By default, the serialized stream contains information about the assembly identity (name, version, culture, and publisher's key if it is a strong-named assembly) and the assembly is searched and loaded as if you were instantiating one of its type with a standard new keyword. In some cases, the fact that the deserialization process preserves type identity can be a problem when the assembly's version changes. Read the section titled "Version-Tolerant Serialization (VTS)" later in this chapter for more information.

SOAP Serialization

You can change the serialization format to SOAP simply by using another formatter object, the SoapFormatter in the System.Runtime.Serialization.Formatters.Soap namespace, which is contained in the System.Runtime.Serialization.Formatters.Soap.dll assembly. This assembly isn't referenced by default by Microsoft Visual C# projects, so you must add a reference to it yourself.

```
// Create a Hashtable object, and fill it with some data.
Hashtable ht = new Hashtable();
ht.Add("One", 1);
ht.Add("Two", 2);
ht.Add("Three", 3);
// Create a soap serializer.
SoapFormatter sf = new SoapFormatter();
// Save the Hashtable to disk in SOAP format.
using ( FileStream fs = new FileStream("hashtable.xml", FileMode.Create) )
{
    sf.Serialize(fs, ht);
}

// Reload the file contents, using the same SoapFormatter object.
Hashtable ht2 = null;
using ( FileStream fs = new FileStream("hashtable.xml", FileMode.Open) )
{
    ht2 = (Hashtable) sf.Deserialize(fs);
}
```

As I noted earlier, the SoapFormatter has been marked as obsolete in .NET Framework 2.0, and thus you should always use the BinaryFormatter. However, the SOAP formatter has one feature that the binary formatter lacks: the serialized stream consists of readable XML text and you can actually browse it. For example, you can double-click the hashtable.xml file from inside Microsoft Windows Explorer to view its contents in a Microsoft Internet Explorer window. This ability is quite handy in the test and debug phase. Even if your applications use the BinaryFormatter object exclusively, you might find it useful to temporarily switch to the SoapFormatter object and persist the serialization stream to a file to understand why your objects aren't serialized and deserialized correctly.

Creating Serializable Types

You've seen how the CLR can serialize and deserialize basic types such as strings and arrays; thus, the next logical step is to understand how you can define a serializable object in your own code. It turns out that, in practice, the only thing you do to make a class serializable is to flag it with the Serializable attribute, whose constructor takes no arguments:

```
[Serializable()]
public class Person
{
    ...
}
```

For this attribute to work correctly, only two conditions must be met: the base class must be serializable and all the fields in the class must be of a serializable type. If these conditions aren't fulfilled, any attempt to serialize an instance of the type results in a SerializationException error.

The first requirement isn't a problem when you inherit from System.Object because the Object class is serializable, but when you derive a class from something else you should ascertain whether your base class is serializable. The Serializable attribute isn't automatically inherited by derived classes and must be applied to them manually. (If it were inherited, all classes would automatically be serializable because they derive directly or indirectly from System.Object.)

If your type includes a public or private field whose type isn't serializable, you can take one of the following approaches: either mark the field with the NonSerialized attribute or use custom serialization. I cover the latter technique in the section titled "Custom Serialization" later in this chapter, so let's focus on the NonSerialized attribute for now. You can apply this attribute to any public or private field:

```
[NonSerialized()] private string m_Password;
```

In general, you should use the NonSerialized attribute for those fields that you don't want to be persisted when the object is serialized. As I explained previously, this attribute is required for fields whose type isn't serializable, for example, a field that points to a Windows Forms control (because the System.Windows.Forms.Control type isn't serializable). This attribute is virtually mandatory also with fields whose value isn't going to be valid when the object is being deserialized. Among such fields are pointers, file handles, and handles to other operating system handles, for example, handles to windows, controls, brushes, and so forth. Other candidates for the NonSerializable attribute are fields whose value can be easily recalculated from other properties, as in the following Person class:

```
[Serializable()]
public class Person : ICloneable
{
   public readonly string FirstName;
   public readonly string LastName;
   private readonly DateTime BirthDate;
   [NonSerialized()]private int m_Age;

   // Note that BirthDate can be set only by means of the constructor method.
   public Person(string firstName, string lastName, DateTime birthDate)
   {
      this.FirstName = firstName;
      this.LastName = lastName;
      this.BirthDate = birthDate;
   }

   // The Age property caches its value in the m_Age private variable.
   public int Age
   {
      get
      {
         // Evaluate Age if not cached already.
         if ( m_Age == 0 )
         {
            m_Age = DateTime.Now.Year - BirthDate.Year;
            if ( BirthDate.DayOfYear > DateTime.Now.DayOfYear )
            {
               m_Age -= 1;
            }
         }
         return m_Age;
      }
   }
}
```

The support for serializable types has been expanded to generic types in .NET Framework 2.0. For example, the following piece of code builds on the SerializeToFile and DeserializeFromFile routines described earlier in this chapter and shows how you can serialize and deserialize a List<Person> object.

```
List<Person> list = new List<Person>();
list.Add(new Person("Joe", " Healy ", new DateTime(1960, 1, 12)));
list.Add(new Person("John", "Smith", new DateTime(1962, 3, 6)));
list.Add(new Person("Ann", "Beebe", new DateTime(1965, 10, 4)));
Functions.SerializeToFile("persons.dat", list);

// Reload the file contents into another list object.
List<Person> list2 = Functions.DeserializeFromFile<List<Person>>("persons.dat");
foreach ( Person p in list2 )
{
   Console.WriteLine("{0} {1} ({2})", p.FirstName, p.LastName, p.Age);
}
```

This result appears in the console window:

```
Joe Healy (45)
John Evans (43)
Ann Beebe (40)
```

The noteworthy detail here is that, although the BirthDate field is private, the deserialization mechanism can restore it correctly from the input stream. (The evidence is the fact the Age property is evaluated correctly.) In other words, the deserialization mechanism can ignore scope rules. Keep this detail in mind when you define a class with a member containing sensitive information, such as passwords and credit card numbers, because this information is included in the serialized stream. If you serialize using a SoapFormatter, a malicious user can find and even modify it by simply loading the file into a text editor; if you use a Binary-Formatter, the information isn't stored in a human-readable format, yet anyone with a bit of knowledge of the .NET deserialization mechanism can retrieve it.

Object Graphs

An object graph is a set of multiple objects with references to one another. You can serialize object graphs as easily as individual objects. The previous listing shows a simple form of object graph because a List<Person> holds references to individual Person objects. As a result, the serialization of the List<Person> object indirectly causes the serialization of all the referenced Person objects. In general, the CLR can serialize all the objects that are directly or indirectly reachable from the object passed to the Serialize method. (Such an object is known as the *root object* of the graph.)

In the simplest cases, when there are no circular references between objects, each object is met exactly once during both the serialization and deserialization processes. Real-world object hierarchies are usually more complex than that, but the serialization infrastructure is capable of dealing with these cases, too. To demonstrate this point, you can add the following field to the Person class:

```
// (Add to the Person class…)
public Person Spouse;
```

Then you can serialize and deserialize an entire object graph with this code:

```
// Create three Person objects.
Person p1 = new Person("Joe", "Healy", new DateTime(1960, 1, 12));
Person p2 = new Person("John", "Evans", new DateTime(1962, 3, 6));
Person p3 = new Person("Ann", "Beebe", new DateTime(1965, 10, 4));
// Define the relationship between two of them.
p2.Spouse = p3;
p3.Spouse = p2;

// Load them into a List<Person> object in one operation.
List<Person> list = new List<Person>(new Person[] { p1, p2, p3 });
// Serialize to disk.
Functions.SerializeToFile("persons.dat", list);
```

```
// Reload into another List<Person> object and display.
List<Person> list2 = DeserializeFromFile<List<Person>>("persons.dat");
foreach ( Person p in list2 )
{
   Console.WriteLine("{0} {1} ({2})", p.FirstName, p.LastName, p.Age);
   if ( p.Spouse != null )
   {
      // Show the spouse's name if there is one.
      Console.WriteLine("   Spouse of " + p.Spouse.FirstName);
   }
}
```

This new version contains a circular reference between p2 and p3 objects, so p3 can be reached from both the root object—the List<Person> object—and the p2.Spouse property. This circular reference might cause an endless loop, but the CLR is smart enough to understand that both references point to the same object, which is therefore persisted only once. (This is one of the most serious limitations of XML serialization.) A look at the Output window can easily prove this point:

```
Joe Healy (45)
John Evans (43)
   Spouse of Ann
Ann Beebe (40)
   Spouse of John
```

Serialization and Events

Serializable types that expose events can pose a special challenge. Events are based on delegates, which in turn are just pointers to a method, possibly defined in another type. When you serialize an object that exposes one or more events, you are actually serializing the entire object graph that includes all the objects that have subscribed to the root object's events. Such a behavior can cause two problems. First, you typically don't want to serialize these subscribers; second, and most serious, if these subscribers aren't serializable, the serialization process fails.

Here's a simple example that proves this point, based on a Widget class that raises a NameChanged event when its Name property changes:

```
[Serializable()]
public class Widget
{
   public event EventHandler NameChanged;

   private string m_Name;

   public string Name
   {
      get
      {
         return m_Name;
      }
      set
      {
         if ( m_Name != value )
```

```
        {
            m_Name = value;
            // Raise the event if there are any subscribers.
            if ( null != NameChanged )
            {
                NameChanged(this, EventArgs.Empty);
            }
        }
    }
}
}
```

Create a form, drop a Button control on it, double-click the button, and type this code:

```
public void Button_Click(object sender, EventArgs e)
{
    Widget w = new Widget();
    // Create a delegate that points to the form instance.
    w.NameChanged += new EventHandler(Widget_NameChanged);
    Functions.SerializeToFile("widget.dat", w);
}

private void Widget_NameChanged(object sender, EventArgs e)
{
    Debug.WriteLine("Name has changed");
}
```

When you click on the button and indirectly execute the code in the Button_Click event handler, the BinaryFormatter.Serialize method throws a SerializationException. The error is caused by the attempt to serialize the current form instance, which is pointed to by the delegate behind the NameChanged event. Alas, forms aren't serializable.

You can solve the problem by marking the delegate as NonSerialized. To do so, you must define all your events as custom events, as in the following example:

```
[Serializable()]
public class Widget
{
    [NonSerialized()]
    public EventHandler m_NameChangedHandler;

    public event EventHandler NameChanged
    {
        add
        {
            m_NameChangedHandler = (EventHandler)
                Delegate.Combine(m_NameChangedHandler, value) ;
        }
        remove
        {
            m_NameChangedHandler = (EventHandler)
                Delegate.Remove(m_NameChangedHandler, value ) ;
        }
    }
    ...
}
```

Alternatively, you might implement a custom serialization mechanism and avoid persisting delegate fields. Read the section titled "The FormatterServices Helper Type" later in this chapter for more details about how you can solve this problem by means of a custom serialization technique.

Deep Object Cloning

As you might remember from the section titled "Shallow Copies and Deep Copies" in Chapter 3, "Interfaces," you can use the protected MemberwiseClone member (inherited from System.Object) to implement the ICloneable interface and its Clone method in any class you define:

```
public class Person : ICloneable
{
    // ...(Variables and methods as in previous example)...

    public object Clone()
    {
        return this.MemberwiseClone();
    }
}
```

This approach to object cloning has two limitations. First, you can clone an object only if you can modify its source code because the MemberwiseClone method is protected and accessible only from inside the class itself. Second, and more important in many circumstances, the MemberwiseClone method performs a shallow copy of the object—that is, it creates a copy of the object but not of any object referenced by the object. For example, the Clone method of the preceding Person class would not also clone the Person object pointed to by the Spouse property. In other words, consider this code:

```
// Define husband and wife.
Person p1 = new Person("Joe", "Healy", new DateTime(1960, 1, 12));
Person p2 = new Person("Ann", "Beebe", new DateTime(1965, 10, 4));
p1.Spouse = p2;
p2.Spouse = p1;
// Clone the husband.
Person q1 = (Person) p1.Clone() ;
// The Spouse person hasn't been cloned because it's a shallow copy.
Console.WriteLine(q1.Spouse == p1.Spouse);      // => True
```

Thanks to object serialization's ability to work with complex object graphs, you can easily solve both problems I mentioned previously. In fact, you can create a generic method that performs a deep copy of any object passed to it. For the best performance, it uses a memory stream and a binary formatter, and specifies that the object is being serialized for cloning:

```
public static T CloneObject<T>(T obj)
{
    // Create a memory stream and a formatter.
    using ( MemoryStream ms = new MemoryStream(1000) )
```

```
    {
        BinaryFormatter bf = new BinaryFormatter(null,
          new StreamingContext(StreamingContextStates.Clone));
        // Serialize the object into the stream.
        bf.Serialize(ms, obj);
        // Position stream pointer back to first byte.
        ms.Seek(0, SeekOrigin.Begin);
        // Deserialize into another object.
        return (T) bf.Deserialize(ms);
    }
}
```

Here's the code that drives the CloneObject routine:

```
// …(p1 and p2 are initialized as in preceding example)…
// Clone the husband. (Notice that the type T can be inferred from the argument.)
Person q1 = (Person) Functions.CloneObject(p1) ;
Person q2 = q1.Spouse;
// Prove that properties were copied correctly.
Console.WriteLine("{0} {1}", q1.FirstName, q1.LastName);        // => Joe Healy
Console.WriteLine("{0} {1}", q2.FirstName, q2.LastName);        // => Ann Beebe
// Prove that both objects were cloned because it's a deep copy.
Console.WriteLine(p1 == q1);                                    // => False
Console.WriteLine(p2 == q2);                                    // => False
```

Version-Tolerant Serialization (VTS)

In version 1.1 of the .NET Framework, you have to face a versioning problem when trying to deserialize an object into a more recent version of the same type. In fact, the Serialize method saves the complete name of the assembly where the serialized type is defined, where the complete name includes the assembly name, version, and public key token if the assembly has a strong name. When the object is deserialized, version 1.1 of the CLR attempts to instantiate an object of the same type and same version. If that specific version isn't available, the CLR throws a SerializationException.

Version 2.0 of the .NET Framework solves the problem in quite a radical way by introducing *version-tolerant serialization* (VTS) and *deserialization*: the version number is ignored when deserializing an object, and only the type's name is taken into account. More precisely, VTS supports the following features:

- Unexpected data is ignored. (This enables older versions of the application to deserialize objects saved by newer versions.)

- Missing optional data is tolerated. (This enables newer versions of the application to deserialize objects saved by older versions.)

The OptionalField Attribute

If the new version of a type being deserialized has a field that was missing in the version that was serialized, you should mark the field with the OptionalField attribute. For example, here's an updated Person class that exposes the new Country field:

```
class Person
{
    [OptionalField()] public string Country;
    // Define all the other members here.
    …
}
```

The OptionalField attribute affects only the deserialization process but doesn't prevent a field from being serialized. If the deserialized stream doesn't contain the value of a field marked as optional, the field retains its default value: zero if numbers, null if string or objects, and so forth. You might believe that you can force a different initial value for these optional fields by using an initializer, as in the following:

```
[OptionalField()] public string Country = "USA";
```

However, initializers and constructors don't run at all during the deserialization process, and therefore these values are ignored. For this reason it is important that the default value be a valid value for a new instance of the class. If this isn't the case, you need to implement the IDeserializationCallback interface or use a deserialization event, as described in a later section.

The OptionalField attribute can take the VersionAdded named argument, as in the following:

```
[OptionalField(VersionAdded=2)]
public string Country;
```

The integer value you pass to the VersionAdded parameter enables you to specify in which version of the class the optional field was added. As I describe in the section titled "The IDeserializationCallback Interface" later in this chapter, you can then use this version number to initialize the optional field with a value that depends on the class version.

The Binder Property

In some cases, you might want to exert more control over which specific type is used to deserialize the saved state of an object. This is possible thanks to serialization binder objects and the Binder property that all formatters expose. Let's suppose that you have moved your objects from one assembly to another, and therefore the namespace and possibly even the name of the type have changed.

The first step is defining a new type that inherits from the SerializationBinder abstract class and overrides the BindToType method. The code in this method can test the name of the type in the serialized stream and returns the Type object corresponding to the object that will actually be deserialized (or null if the CLR's default behavior is OK for you). The following example assumes that you have serialized an object with version 1.0 of the assembly named BOLibrary and you want to deserialize it with the MyApp.Customer object, defined in the current assembly:

```
public class MySerializationBinder : SerializationBinder
{
    public override Type BindToType(string assemblyName, string typeName)
    {
        if ( typeName == "BOLibrary.Customer" )
        {
            // Return the CustomerEx type taken from the current assembly.
            return typeof(CustomerEx);
        }
        else
        {
            // Otherwise, tell the runtime to apply the default binding policy.
            return null;
        }
    }
}
```

Once you have defined your custom binding policy, you simply need to assign an instance of this class to the formatter's Binder property:

```
BinaryFormatter bf = new BinaryFormatter();
bf.Binder = new MySerializationBinder();
// Proceed with deserialization as usual, but create a different
// type of object. (fs is an open stream.)
CustomerEx custEx = (CustomerEx) bf.Deserialize(fs);
…
```

If you force the CLR to deserialize a type that is different from the type that was originally serialized in the stream, it is essential that the old and the new types are similar enough for the deserialization process to make sense. Interestingly, the CLR doesn't throw an exception if the new type has fewer or more members than the original type does; the only condition that must be met is that members with the same name must have the same type, or at least a conversion must be possible. Keep in mind that the CLR uses reflection to discover each field in the new type and then searches for the corresponding value in the stream.

Custom Serialization

When the basic techniques I illustrated so far aren't powerful enough to solve your serialization and deserialization requirements, you should implement a custom serialization technique. You can have trouble, for example, when you want to dynamically decide which information should be persisted or when you need to execute code when the object is deserialized, possibly to recalculate values that are no longer valid.

The IDeserializationCallback Interface

The simplest case of custom serialization is to perform some custom actions when the object has been completely deserialized, for example, to initialize fields marked with the NonSerialized or the OptionalField attribute. For example, say that your Person class opens a FileStream in its constructor and all the other methods in the class rely on this FileStream object to do their chores. As you know, no standard constructor runs when the object is being deserialized, so after deserialization all methods will find the stream closed. You can solve this problem by implementing the IDeserializationCallback interface; this interface has only one method, OnDeserialization, which the .NET Framework invokes when the current object has been completely deserialized:

```
[Serializable()]
public class Person2 : IDeserializationCallback
{
    [OptionalField] public string Country = "USA";
    [NonSerialized()] public FileStream logStream;
    // Define all the other fields here.
    …

    public Person2(string firstName, string lastName)
    {
        // Initialize the FirstName and LastName fields.
        …
        // Open the file for logging.
        OpenLogFile();
    }

    // This method is called when the object has been completely deserialized.
    public void OnDeserialization(object sender)
    {
        // Reopen the file stream when the object is deserialized.
        OpenLogFile();
        // Provide a default value for the Country optional field.
        if ( Country == null )
        {
            Country = "USA";
        }
    }

    // Open a log file just for this instance.
    private void OpenLogFile()
    {
        string fileName = this.FirstName + " " + this.LastName + ".txt";
        logStream = new FileStream(fileName, FileMode.OpenOrCreate);
    }
}
```

Be aware that the .NET Framework invokes the OnDeserialization method when the object graph has been entirely deserialized. This means that you can rely on the fact that all the child objects of the current object have been correctly initialized when this method runs. This detail is important if the fields you must initialize depend on other fields.

As I explained in the previous section, the OptionalField attribute supports the VersionAdded named argument:

```
[OptionalField(VersionAdded = 2)] public string Country;
```

Typically, you use this argument if the initial value of an optional field depends on the version of the class or some other data. For example, let's say that this value should be initialized to "USA" if VersionAdded is equal to 1; otherwise, it should be assigned an empty string. Here's the new version of the OnDeserialization method that implements this behavior:

```
// This method is called when the object been completely deserialized.
public void OnDeserialization(object sender)
{
    // Reopen the file stream when the object is deserialized.
    OpenLogFile();
    // Only if the Country field hasn't been deserialized
    if ( Country == null )
    {
        // Use reflection to read the OptionalField attribute.
        FieldInfo fi = this.GetType().GetField("Country");
        OptionalFieldAttribute attr = (OptionalFieldAttribute)
            Attribute.GetCustomAttribute(fi, typeof(OptionalFieldAttribute));
        if ( attr != null )
        {
            Country = attr.VersionAdded == 1 ? "USA" : "";
        }
    }
}
```

The ISerializable Interface

The ISerializable interface enables you to be in full control of both the serialization and deserialization processes. For example, you might implement this interface if some fields should be persisted or depersisted only if specific conditions are true, or if you want to persist the fields in a nondefault format. The ISerializable interface exposes only one method, GetObjectData, which has the following syntax:

```
public void GetObjectData(SerializationInfo info, StreamingContext context)
{
    ...
}
```

The GetObjectData method is invoked when the object is passed to the formatter's Serialize method. Its purpose is to fill the SerializationInfo object with all the information about the object being serialized. The code inside this method can examine the StreamingContext structure to retrieve additional details about the serialization process, for example, to learn whether the object is being serialized to a file or to memory.

The presence of the ISerializable interface implies the existence of a special constructor method with the following syntax:

```
public TypeName(SerializationInfo info, StreamingContext context)
{
   ...
}
```

The CLR calls this special constructor when the object is deserialized. You won't get a compilation error if you omit this constructor, but you see a runtime error when you try to deserialize the object if this constructor is missing. The scope you use for the GetObjectData method and the special constructor is crucial: these members should have a protected scope if the class can be inherited from because derived classes might (and usually do) invoke them. Because a C# interface member can't have a protected scope, you should implement the ISerializable interface explicitly and have the ISerializable.GetObjectData method delegate to the GetObjectData protected method:

```
[Serializable()]
public class SampleClass : ISerializable
{
   // The method called by the CLR
   void ISerializable.GetObjectData(SerializationInfo info, StreamingContext context)
   {
      // Delegate to the protected method.
      this.GetObjectData(info, context);
   }

   // The method called by inherited classes
   protected void GetObjectData(SerializationInfo info, StreamingContext context)
   {
      ...
   }

   // The constructor called by inherited classes
   protected SampleClass(SerializationInfo info, StreamingContext context)
   {
      Functions.ISerializableConstructorHelper(info, context, this);
   }

   // ...(The remainder of the class)...
}
```

If the class is sealed, you can use a private scope for both the GetObjectData method and the special constructor. Oddly, many .NET types expose either or both of these procedures as public members, but you should avoid doing so in your applications. If the special constructor has private or protected scope, the type must have at least another constructor with public scope; otherwise, you won't be able to instantiate it from your code.

The SerializationInfo object acts like a dictionary object. In the GetObjectData method, you fill this dictionary with one or more values using the AddValue method:

```
// The method called by inherited classes
protected void GetObjectData(SerializationInfo info, StreamingContext context)
{
   // Save all fields.
   info.AddValue("FirstName", this.FirstName);
   info.AddValue("LastName", this.FirstName);
   …
}
```

As you might expect, the object passed to the AddValue method must be serializable, otherwise an exception occurs. You can later retrieve values with the GetValue method, which requires the value name and type, as you see here:

```
protected SampleClass(SerializationInfo info, StreamingContext context)
{
   // Retrieve serialized fields.
   this.FirstName = (string) info.GetValue("FirstValue", typeof(string));
   this.LastName = (string) info.GetValue("LastValue", typeof(String));
   …
}
```

Conveniently, the SerializationInfo object exposes many other Get*Xxxx* methods that return data in a specific format, such as GetString and GetInt32:

```
   // A more concise way to retrieve the FirstName value
   this.FirstName = info.GetString("FirstValue");
```

In all cases, values in the stream are converted to the requested type, or an InvalidCastException is thrown if the conversion isn't possible.

Security Implications

As you know, a formatter can access fields that would otherwise be inaccessible. For this reason, the client code that performs the serialization and deserialization steps requires special permission to do so, namely, the SecurityPermission with the SerializationFormatter flag. By default, this permission is given to fully trusted code but not to code originating from an intranet or the Internet. If your object contains sensitive information, you should protect the GetObjectData method by using an attribute that demands this permission, as in the following code:

```
[SecurityPermission(SecurityAction.Demand, SerializationFormatter= true)]
protected void GetObjectData(SerializationInfo info, StreamingContext context)
{
   // Save all fields.
   info.AddValue("FirstName", this.FirstName);
   info.AddValue("LastName", this.FirstName);
   …
}
```

Remember that, even if you save the object's state by means of the BinaryFormatter, strings stored as clear text can easily be extracted from a stream serialized on a disk file or a database field. Other data types, for example, numbers and dates, aren't human-readable but could be extracted from a serialized stream with just a little more effort. Therefore, if your type contains sensitive data, you should always implement the ISerializable interface and encrypt this data.

A Practical Example: Compressed Serialization

One of the things you can do by implementing the ISerializable interface is compress the serialized stream so that the object can be saved to smaller files or be transferred to another application using .NET remoting in less time. The following CompactArray<T> type behaves like a regular array, except that its serialized version takes fewer bytes:

```csharp
[Serializable()]
public class CompactArray<T> : ISerializable
{
    // Actual elements are stored in this private array.
    private T[] arr;

    // The constructor takes the number of elements in the array.
    public CompactArray(int numEls)
    {
        arr = new T[numEls];
    }

    // The default Item property makes this class look like a standard array.
    public virtual T this[int index]
    {
        get { return arr[index]; }
        set { arr[index] = value; }
    }

    // Compress data when the object is serialized.
    protected virtual void GetObjectData(SerializationInfo info, StreamingContext context)
    {
        // Serialize the private array to a compressed stream in memory.
        using ( MemoryStream memStream = new MemoryStream() )
        {
            using ( DeflateStream zipStream = new DeflateStream(memStream,
                CompressionMode.Compress) )
            {
                BinaryFormatter bf = new BinaryFormatter();
                bf.Serialize(zipStream, arr);
                zipStream.Flush();
                // Save the contents of the compressed stream.
                byte[] bytes = memStream.GetBuffer();
                info.AddValue("bytes", bytes);
            }
        }
    }

    // Implement ISerializable.GetObjectData member explicitly.
    void ISerializable.GetObjectData(SerializationInfo info, StreamingContext context)
```

```
   {
      // Delegate to the protected overload.
      this.GetObjectData(info, context);
   }

   // Decompress data when the object is deserialized.
   protected CompactArray(SerializationInfo info, StreamingContext context)
   {
      // Retrieve the bytes and initialize a memory buffer.
      byte[] bytes = (byte[]) info.GetValue("bytes", typeof(byte[]));
      using ( MemoryStream inStream = new MemoryStream(bytes) )
      {
         // Wrap a DeflateStream object around the compressed buffer.
         using ( DeflateStream zipStream = new DeflateStream(inStream,
            CompressionMode.Decompress) )
         {
            BinaryFormatter bf = new BinaryFormatter();
            arr = (T[]) bf.Deserialize(zipStream);
         }
      }
   }
}
```

Read the section titled "Compressed Streams" in Chapter 7, "Files, Directories, and Streams," for more information about the DeflateStream type.

Custom Serialization and Inheritance

When you inherit from a class that implements ISerializable and the derived class adds new fields that should be serialized, you must create your own version of the GetObjectData method and the special constructor implied by this interface. For example, if you have a CompactArrayEx class that inherits from CompactArray and adds a DefaultValue property, this is the code you should write:

```
[Serializable()]
public class CompactArrayEx<T> : CompactArray<T>
{
   public readonly T DefaultValue;          // A new field in the derived class

   // The standard constructor
   public CompactArrayEx(int numEls, T defaultValue)
      : base(numEls)
   {
      this.DefaultValue = defaultValue;
   }

   // The protected GetObjectData method is overridden.
   protected override void GetObjectData(SerializationInfo info, StreamingContext context)
   {
      // Deserialize the base class; then deserialize any additional field.
      base.GetObjectData(info, context);
      info.AddValue("DefaultValue", this.DefaultValue);
   }
```

```csharp
// The protected constructor
protected CompactArrayEx(SerializationInfo info, StreamingContext context)
    : base(info, context)
{
    // Serialize the base class; then serialize any additional field.
    this.DefaultValue = (T) info.GetValue("DefaultValue", typeof(T));
}
}
```

Notice that the derived class doesn't implement the ISerializable interface because this interface is already implemented by the base class. In the derived class you must override the public or protected GetObjectData method; therefore, it is crucial that this method be marked as virtual in the base class.

You must override the GetObjectData method only if the derived class needs to serialize additional fields; otherwise, the inherited class can rely on its base class's implementation of the ISerializable interface. However, regardless of whether the derived class exposes additional fields, in all cases you must implement the special constructor because this constructor isn't automatically inherited by the derived class. If the derived class doesn't have additional classes, the special constructor simply delegates to the base class's constructor:

```csharp
protected CompactArrayEx(SerializationInfo info, StreamingContext context)
    : base(info, context)
{ /* No code here */ }
```

The FormatterServices Helper Type

The FormatterServices class exposes a few static methods that help you build code that serializes and deserializes an object. For example, the FormatterServices.GetSerializableMembers method returns an array of MemberInfo elements, one element for each class member that must be serialized (in other words, all fields except those marked with the NotSerialized attribute). The FormatterServices.GetObjectData method takes the array returned by the aforementioned method and returns an Object array holding the value of each member. The following procedure builds on these two methods and helps you serialize any object:

```csharp
// Helper procedure meant to be called from inside ISerializable.GetObjectData method.
public static void GetObjectDataHelper(SerializationInfo info,
    StreamingContext context, object obj)
{
    // Get the list of serializable members.
    MemberInfo[] members = FormatterServices.GetSerializableMembers(obj.GetType());
    // Read the value of each member.
    object[] values = FormatterServices.GetObjectData(obj, members);
    // Store values in the SerializationInfo object, and use the member name as the key.
    for ( int i = 0; i < members.Length; i++ )
    {
        info.AddValue(members[i].Name, values[i]);
    }
}
```

The FormatterServices.PopulateObjectMembers method takes an array of MemberInfo and Object values and assigns all the serializable members of a given object. You can use this method in a generic helper routine that initializes a deserialized object:

```
// Helper procedure meant to be called from inside ISerializable's special constructor
public static void ISerializableConstructorHelper(SerializationInfo info,
    StreamingContext context, object obj)
{
    // Get the list of serializable members for this object.
    MemberInfo[] members = FormatterServices.GetSerializableMembers(obj.GetType());
    object[] values = new object[members.Length];
    // Read the value for this member (assuming it's a field).
    for ( int i = 0; i < members.Length; i++ )
    {
        // Retrieve the type for this member.
        FieldInfo fi = members[i] as FieldInfo;
        if ( fi != null )
        {
            values[i] = info.GetValue(fi.Name, fi.FieldType);
        }
    }
    // Assign all serializable members in one operation.
    FormatterServices.PopulateObjectMembers(obj, members, values);
}
```

These two helper methods make implementation of the ISerializable interface a breeze. Assuming that these methods are stored in a type named Functions, this is what a serializable class that uses these routines might look like:

```
[Serializable()]
public class SampleClass : ISerializable
{
    void ISerializable.GetObjectData(SerializationInfo info, StreamingContext context)
    {
        // Delegate to the protected method.
        this.GetObjectData(info, context);
    }

    protected void GetObjectData(SerializationInfo info, StreamingContext context)
    {
        Functions.GetObjectDataHelper(info, context, this);
    }

    protected SampleClass(SerializationInfo info, StreamingContext context)
    {
        Functions.ISerializableConstructorHelper(info, context, this);
    }

    // ...(The remainder of the class)...
    ...
}
```

You can use a variation of this technique to solve the problems caused by events and delegates that point to nonserializable types, which I illustrate earlier in the section titled "Serialization and Events." Instead of invoking the standard FormatterServices.GetSerializableMembers method, you call the following helper method to discard delegate fields:

```
// Get the list of serializable members of a type, except delegates.
public static MemberInfo[] GetSerializableMembersEx(Type type)
{
   List<MemberInfo> list = new List<MemberInfo>();
   foreach ( MemberInfo mi in FormatterServices.GetSerializableMembers(type) )
   {
      // Add this element to the result only if it isn't a delegate.
      FieldInfo fi = mi as FieldInfo;
      if ( fi != null & !typeof(Delegate).IsAssignableFrom(fi.FieldType) )
      {
         list.Add(mi);
      }
   }
   return list.ToArray();
}
```

In the GetDataObjectHelper and ISerializableConstructorHelper procedures, you call this new method instead of the FormatterServices.GetSerializableMembers method:

```
public void GetObjectDataHelper(SerializationInfo info,
   StreamingContext context, object obj)
{
   // Get the list of serializable members for this object.
   MemberInfo[] members = Functions.GetSerializableMembersEx(obj.GetType());
   …
}

public void ISerializableConstructorHelper (SerializationInfo info,
   StreamingContext context, object obj)
{
   // Get the list of serializable members for this object.
   MemberInfo[] members = Functions.GetSerializableMembersEx(obj.GetType());
   …
}
```

You can use the new versions of the GetDataObjectHelper and ISerializableConstructorHelper methods inside any type that exposes public events to ensure that event subscribers aren't serialized when the main object is serialized.

Serialization and Deserialization Events

Version 2.0 of the .NET Framework adds a completely new mechanism for custom serialization and deserialization based on the following four attributes: OnSerializing, OnSerialized, OnDeserializing, and OnDeserialized. You use one of these attributes to mark a void method that takes a StreamingContext argument:

```
[OnSerializing]
private void BeforeSerialization(StreamingContext context)
```

```
{
   // This code runs before the object is serialized.
}

[OnSerialized]
private void AfterSerialization(StreamingContext context)
{
   // This code runs after the object has been serialized.
}

[OnDeserializing]
private void BeforeDeserialization(StreamingContext context)
{
   // This code runs before the object is deserialized.
}

[OnDeserialized]
private void AfterDeserialization(StreamingContext context)
{
   // This code runs after the object has been deserialized.
}
```

An important note: these attributes are honored only when the object is serialized and deserialized by means of the BinaryFormatter and are ignored when the SoapFormatter or another formatter is used. You can mark more than one method with the same attribute, but the usefulness of such a practice is questionable because in this case the CLR calls marked methods in an unpredictable order. If the object implements the IDeserializationCallback interface, the method marked with the OnDeserialized attribute runs after the IDeserializationCallback.OnDeserialization method.

Typically, you use the OnDeserialized attribute in lieu of the IDeserializationCallback interface. For example, here's a different version of the Person class that reopens the log file after deserialization is completed. (Compare this with the code I showed in the section titled "The IDeserializationCallback Interface," earlier in this chapter.)

```
[Serializable]
public class Person3
{
   // The class doesn't implement the IDeserializationCallback interface.
   FileStream logStream;

   // This method is called when the object has been deserialized completely.
   [OnDeserialized]
   private void AfterDeserialization(StreamingContext context)
   {
      OpenLogFile();
   }

   // (Definition of OpenLogFile and other members omitted.…)
   …
}
```

The OnDeserializing attribute is especially useful for assigning an initial value to an optional field: if the field is found in the stream, the serialized value will overwrite the one you assign from code:

```
[Serializable]
public class Person
{
    [OptionalField()] public string Country;

    // This method is called when the object has been deserialized completely.
    [OnDeserialized()]
    private void BeforeDeserialization(StreamingContext context)
    {
        Country = "USA";
    }

    // (Other members omitted.…)
    …
}
```

A clear advantage of the new .NET Framework 2.0 attributes over the ISerializable interface is that you don't need to invoke a method in the base class manually, as you must do inside the GetObjectData method and the special constructor. The CLR runs methods marked with these attributes in the base class first and then it runs the methods marked with these attributes in the current class. (These attributes aren't automatically inherited.) You can't apply these attributes to static methods or instance methods marked as virtual or abstract.

Although you can always use the OnDeserializing and OnDeserialized attributes to replace the IDeserializationCallback interface (provided that the object is serialized with the binary formatter), the four attributes can't really substitute for the ISerializable interface because the methods don't receive the SerializationInfo object and therefore can't manually store data in it and retrieve data from it.

The IObjectReference Interface

In some cases, you might want to implement a singleton object that is also serializable. A few singleton types in the .NET Framework, such as the Console or the GC object, expose only static members and can't be serialized; therefore, they aren't interesting in this discussion. To be serializable, a singleton object must store its state in instance fields and is typically implemented as follows:

```
[Serializable()]
public class Singleton
{
    // The one and only instance is created when the type is initialized.
    public static readonly Singleton Instance = new Singleton();

    // One or more instance fields
    public int Id;
    …
```

```
        // Prevent clients from instantiating this class.
        private Singleton()
        {}
}
```

Unfortunately, this naïve implementation doesn't work well with serialization. For example, if you serialize this type twice and you later deserialize the two instances, they won't point to the same object. The CLR doesn't automatically recognize the singleton nature of this type.

The IObjectReference interface can help solve this problem. This interface exposes only one method, GetRealObject. If a type A implements this interface, you can pass this type as an argument to the SerializationInfo.SetType method inside the ISerializable.GetObjectData method of another type B (the singleton type). When type B is deserialized, the special constructor implied by the ISerializable interface isn't called; instead, the CLR creates an instance of type A and calls its IObjectReference.GetRealObject method, which is expected to return the deserialized object.

In the most general case, A and B are distinct types, and in fact the MSDN documentation shows an example based on the Singleton class (our type B) that uses a nested, private, and sealed class named SingletonSerializationHelper (our type A). However, you can simplify the code remarkably if you make the Singleton class implement the IObjectReference directly, as in the following example:

```
[Serializable()]
public class Singleton : IObjectReference
{
    // The one and only instance is created when the type is initialized.
    public static readonly Singleton Instance = new Singleton();

    // One or more instance fields
    public int Id;
    …
    // Prevent clients from instantiating this class.
    private Singleton()
    {}

    public object GetRealObject(StreamingContext context)
    {
        return Instance;
    }
}
```

This is what happens behind the scenes: when the CLR realizes that an instance of the Singleton type is about to be deserialized, it checks whether the type implements the IObjectReference interface and, if this is the case, it invokes the GetRealObject method instead, which returns the only shared instance of the class. You can check that this implementation works correctly as follows:

```
// Get a singleton instance and serialize it.
Singleton s1 = Singleton.Instance;
Functions.SerializeToFile("singleton.dat", s1);
```

```
// Deserialize it into a different variable and check that both variables
// point to the same object.
Singleton s2 = Functions.DeserializeFromFile<Singleton>("singleton.dat");
Console.WriteLine(s1 == s2);               // True
```

The IObjectReference interface is also useful for types that aren't strictly singleton, yet expose a static factory method instead of a regular constructor. For example, consider the following type:

```
public class IdValuePair : IObjectReference
{
    // This is where all instances created so far are stored.
    private static Dictionary<int, IdValuePair> dict = new Dictionary<int,IdValuePair>();

    // Instance fields
    public readonly int Id;
    public readonly string Value;

    // Private constructor prevents instantiation.
    private IdValuePair(int id, string value)
    {
        this.Id = id;
        this.Value = value;
    }

    // The factory method
    public static IdValuePair Create(int id, string value)
    {
        // Add a new instance to the private table if necessary.
        if ( ! dict.ContainsKey(id) )
        {
            dict.Add(id, new IdValuePair(id, value));
        }
        // Always return an instance from the cache.
        return dict[id];
    }
}
```

Serializing and deserializing an IdValuePair object poses the same challenges that singleton objects pose because you must ensure that serialized objects with the same Id property are deserialized as a single instance. Once again, you can solve this problem by implementing the IObjectReference interface:

```
[Serializable]
public class IdValuePair : IObjectReference
{
    // No need to expose this method as public
    object IObjectReference.GetRealObject(StreamingContext context)
    {
        // The instance has been deserialized, so you can access its properties.
        Debug.WriteLine("GetRealObject method for ID=" + this.Id.ToString());
        return Create(this.Id, this.Value);
    }
}
```

A minor problem with this approach is that the GetRealObject method is invoked three times during the deserialization process, as you can see thanks to the Debug.WriteLine statement. However, these calls don't add a noticeable overhead and don't have other side effects.

The ISerializationSurrogate Interface

The ISerialization interface enables you to define a custom serialization process for a class you create, but it doesn't allow you to intervene in the serialization process of a *different* type, more specifically a type whose source code isn't available or modifiable. For example, you might need to take over the serialization process of a type if that type isn't serializable, or if you are serializing a type that exposes one or more fields that return nonserializable values.

This specific problem can be solved by defining a *surrogate type*, which by definition is a type that implements the ISerializationSurrogate interface. This interface has only two methods, GetObjectData and SetObjectData, that have signatures similar to the ISerializable.GetObject-Data method and the special constructor implied by the ISerializable interface, respectively. To see this technique in action, let's define three types that are related to each other:

```
[Serializable()]
public class PurchaseOrder
{
    public Supplier Supplier;
    public Document Attachment;
}

public class Document
{
    public int Number;
    public string Location;
}

public class Supplier
{
    public readonly string ID;
    public readonly string Name;

    public Supplier(string id, string name)
    {
        this.id = id;
        this.name = name;
    }
}
```

The PurchaseOrder class is marked as serializable, but any attempt to serialize it is going to fail because the types of its Supplier and Attachment fields are nonserializable. However, you can work around this problem by defining two auxiliary surrogate types, one for the Document class and one for the Supplier class:

```
public class DocumentSerializationSurrogate : ISerializationSurrogate
{
    public void GetObjectData(object obj, SerializationInfo info, StreamingContext context)
```

```
      {
         // Save the properties of the object being serialized.
         Document instance = (Document) obj ;
         info.AddValue("Number", instance.Number);
         info.AddValue("Location", instance.Location);
      }

      public object SetObjectData(object obj, SerializationInfo info,
         StreamingContext context, ISurrogateSelector selector)
      {
         // Populate the (uninitialized) object passed as an argument.
         Document instance = (Document) obj ;
         instance.Number = info.GetInt32("Number");
         instance.Location = info.GetString("Location");
         // You can return null if you've populated the object passed as an argument.
         return null;
      }
   }
```

The surrogate for the Supplier class is similar, except that the SetObjectData method can't simply populate the uninitialized object passed in the first argument because the fields of the Supplier type are read-only and can be initialized only by calling a constructor:

```
public class SupplierSerializationSurrogate : ISerializationSurrogate
{
   public void GetObjectData(object obj, SerializationInfo info, StreamingContext context)
   {
      // Save the properties of the object being serialized.
      Supplier instance = (Supplier) obj ;
      info.AddValue("Id", instance.ID);
      info.AddValue("Name", instance.Name);
   }

   public object SetObjectData(object obj, SerializationInfo info,
      StreamingContext context, ISurrogateSelector selector)
   {
      // Ignore the object passed as an argument and create a new instance.
      string id = info.GetString("Id");
      string name = info.GetString("Name");
      return new Supplier(id, name);
   }
}
```

You're finally ready to serialize a PurchaseOrder object:

```
// Create a PurchaseOrder instance and its dependent objects.
PurchaseOrder po = new PurchaseOrder();
po.Supplier = new Supplier("JH", "Joe Healy");
po.Attachment = new Document();
po.Attachment.Number = 11;
po.Attachment.Location = @"c:\docs\description.doc";   // Doesn't need to exist

// Create an empty instance of the standard SurrogateSelector object.
SurrogateSelector surSel = new SurrogateSelector();
```

```
surSel.AddSurrogate(typeof(Document), new StreamingContext(StreamingContextStates.All),
    new DocumentSerializationSurrogate());
// Tell the SurrogateSelector how to deal with Document and Supplier objects.
surSel.AddSurrogate(typeof(Supplier), new StreamingContext(StreamingContextStates.All),
    new SupplierSerializationSurrogate());
// Create the BinaryFormatter and set its SurrogateSelector property.
BinaryFormatter bf = new BinaryFormatter();
bf.SurrogateSelector = surSel;

// Serialize to a memory stream and deserialize into a different object.
MemoryStream ms = new MemoryStream();
bf.Serialize(ms, po);
ms.Seek(0, SeekOrigin.Begin);
PurchaseOrder po2 = (PurchaseOrder) bf.Deserialize(ms) ;

// Prove that the object deserialized correctly.
Console.WriteLine(po2.Supplier.Name);            // => Joe Healy
Console.WriteLine(po2.Attachment.Number);        // => 11
```

The classes for which you provide a surrogate type can appear in multiple places in the object hierarchy, but you still need to define a serialization surrogate for that type only once. For example, suppose that you extend the Supplier class as follows:

```
public class Supplier
{
    ...
    // (Add after all existing members…)
    public Document Description;
}
```

In this case, you must modify the SupplierSerializationSurrogate class to account for the new field, but the code that actually serializes and deserializes the PurchaseOrder object continues to work as before.

Interestingly, you can easily build a "universal" serialization surrogate that can work with simple types that expose fields that don't require any special processing. As you can guess, it's just a matter of using a bit of reflection:

```
public class UniversalSerializationSurrogate : ISerializationSurrogate
{
    public void GetObjectData(object obj, SerializationInfo info, StreamingContext context)
    {
        BindingFlags flags = BindingFlags.Instance | BindingFlags.Public
            | BindingFlags.Public;
        foreach ( FieldInfo fi in obj.GetType().GetFields(flags) )
        {
            info.AddValue(fi.Name, fi.GetValue(obj));
        }
    }

    public object SetObjectData(object obj, SerializationInfo info,
        StreamingContext context, ISurrogateSelector selector)
```

```
    {
        BindingFlags flags = BindingFlags.Instance | BindingFlags.Public
            | BindingFlags.Public;
        foreach ( FieldInfo fi in obj.GetType().GetFields(flags) )
        {
            fi.SetValue(obj, info.GetValue(fi.Name, fi.FieldType));
        }
        return obj;
    }
}
```

Serialization surrogates are quite handy for solving recurring problems related to serialization, but they aren't a remedy in all possible circumstances. In general, surrogates are OK only with simple classes that expose fields of primitive types, such as strings or numeric types. In general, if you don't have the source code of the nonserializable type, you can't be absolutely sure that you are serializing everything correctly; therefore, you should always double-check the behavior of your application when using a surrogate with a class you didn't create yourself.

Inheriting from a Nonserializable Type

A common problem in advanced serialization scenarios occurs when you need to author a serializable type A and this class must derive from a nonserializable type B. In previous sections, you saw that type A must implement the ISerializable interface, but this step doesn't really resolve all the issues you face. In fact, to serialize and deserialize the base type correctly, you must use reflection and read all its fields, including private fields in the base class. There are other problems to solve as well: for example, the (nonserializable) base type B might inherit from a serializable type C, in which case you should rely on type C's serialization code to ensure that data is saved and restored correctly.

To solve this problem once and for all, I wrote a SerializationHelpers type containing a few static methods that you can invoke from types that implement the ISerializable interface and that solve most of the aforementioned issues:

```
public static class SerializationHelpers
{
    // Return True if a type and all its base types are serializable.
    public static bool TypeIsSerializable(Type type)
    {
        while ( type != null )
        {
            // Exit now if the type isn't serializable.
            if ( !type.IsSerializable )
            {
                return false;
            }

            // If this type implements ISerializable, we can assume it's fully serializable.
            if ( typeof(ISerializable).IsAssignableFrom(type) )
            {
                return true;
            }
```

```
      // Continue to analyze its base class.
      type = type.BaseType;
   }
   return true;
}
...
```

The TypeIsSerializable helper method returns true if a type can use default serialization, or false if it requires custom serialization. A type can use default serialization only if it is marked as serializable and all its base types are also serializable, or if any class in the inheritance tree implements the ISerializable interface (in which case the method assumes that the type knows how to deal with its base classes, even if not all of them are serializable).

The SerializeObjectFields method is a bit more complex in that it fills a SerializationInfo object with the value of all the fields of an object, serializes the base object, and serializes all fields whose type isn't serializable by default. The key to this mechanism is using the Path.Combine method to create a hierarchy of keys in the SerializationInfo object.

If a field's type is nonserializable, the SerializeObjectFields method invokes itself recursively to save all the type's fields. In addition, it saves the Type of the object referenced by the field because it can't rely on the field's type. (For example, a field whose type is Control might point to a TextBox object.) The type of such complex fields is stored separately in a SerializationInfo slot named *Type.

To further complicate matters, the SerializationInfo object doesn't provide an enumerator or a method to extract the keys it contains; therefore, for each level in the hierarchy the SerializeObjectFields method must save a list of complex fields that require special treatment; in the following code, this list is maintained in the complexFields ArrayList and is then saved in a slot named *Complex.

```
public static void SerializeObjectFields(SerializationInfo info,
   string key, object obj, Type type)
{
   if ( type == null )
   {
      type = obj.GetType();
   }
   if ( type.BaseType != typeof(object) )
   {
      // First, serialize the base class's fields.
      SerializeObjectFields(info, Path.Combine("*Base", key), obj, type.BaseType);
   }

   // Next, loop over all fields that are declared in this type.
   ArrayList complexFields = new ArrayList();
   foreach (FieldInfo fi in type.GetFields(BindingFlags.Instance | BindingFlags.Public
      | BindingFlags.NonPublic | BindingFlags.DeclaredOnly) )
   {
      // Remember the value of all serializable fields.
      if ( ! fi.IsNotSerialized )
```

```
      {
         // Build the complete field name.
         string fieldKey = Path.Combine(key, fi.Name);
         // Read the actual field value.
         object value = fi.GetValue(obj);

         if ( value == null || TypeIsSerializable(value.GetType()) )
         {
            // Save the directory if the field's type is serializable.
            info.AddValue(fieldKey, value);
         }
         else
         {
            // Remember this is a complex field.
            complexFields.Add(fi.Name);
            // Remember its type.
            info.AddValue(Path.Combine(fieldKey, "*Type"), value.GetType());
            // Store the object value by calling this method recursively.
            SerializeObjectFields(info, fieldKey, value, null);
         }
      }
   }
   // Remember the list of simple fields.
   info.AddValue(Path.Combine(key, "*Complex"), complexFields);
}
```

The DeserializeObjectFields method processes the data stored by the SerializeObjectFields procedure: it reads all the slots of a SerializationInfo object and assigns all the fields of an object passed as an argument, going deep in the inheritance hierarchy to deserialize complex objects manually one field at a time:

```
public static void DeserializeObjectFields(SerializationInfo info,
   string key, object obj, Type type)
{
   if ( type == null )
   {
      type = obj.GetType();
   }
   // First, deserialize the base class's fields.
   if ( type.BaseType != typeof(object) )
   {
      DeserializeObjectFields(info, Path.Combine("*Base", key), obj, type.BaseType);
   }

   // Retrieve the list of complex (nonserializable) fields.
   ArrayList complexFields = (ArrayList) info.GetValue(
      Path.Combine(key, "*Complex"), typeof(ArrayList));

   // Loop over all fields that are declared in this type.
   foreach ( FieldInfo fi in type.GetFields(BindingFlags.Instance | BindingFlags.Public
      | BindingFlags.NonPublic | BindingFlags.DeclaredOnly) )
   {
      // Read the value of all serializable fields.
      if ( ! fi.IsNotSerialized )
```

```
          {
            string fieldKey = Path.Combine(key, fi.Name);
            object value = null;

            if ( ! complexFields.Contains(fi.Name) )
            {
               // Read directly if it's a serializable type.
               value = info.GetValue(fieldKey, typeof(object));
            }
            else
            {
               // Retrieve the type of this field.
               Type fieldType = (Type) info.GetValue(Path.Combine(fieldKey,
                  "*Type"), typeof(Type)) ;
               // Create an uninitialized object of that type.
               value = FormatterServices.GetUninitializedObject(fieldType);
               // Fill this instance by calling this method recursively.
               DeserializeObjectFields(info, fieldKey, value, null);
            }
            fi.SetValue(obj, value);
         }
      }
   }
}   // End of SerializationHelpers class
```

The method uses the FormatterServices.GetUninitializedObject method to create an instance of the type whose fields are all set to the default value (zero or null). This method bypasses any constructor exposed by the class and is also extremely efficient. (It is the same method used by the CLR during the default deserialization step.)

Here's an example that uses the SerializationHelpers module. It shows a serializable Employee type that inherits from the nonserializable PersonalData class. To prove that the mechanism works well even in complex fields—whether serializable or not—the PersonalData class has a Spouse field (of type PersonalData) and the Employee type has a Boss field (of type Employee), and both types have a private field with the same name (m_BirthDate), which apparently can be initialized only through the constructor.

```
public class PersonalData
{
   public string LastName;
   public string FirstName;
   public PersonalData Spouse;
   private DateTime m_BirthDate;        // A private field

   public PersonalData(string firstName, string lastName, DateTime birthDate)
   {
      this.FirstName = firstName;
      this.LastName = lastName;
      this.m_BirthDate = birthDate;
   }
```

```csharp
        public DateTime BirthDate
        {
            get { return m_BirthDate; }
        }
    }


    [Serializable()]
    public class Employee : PersonalData, ISerializable
    {
        public Employee Boss;
        private DateTime m_BirthDate;        // A private field

        public Employee(string firstName, string lastName, DateTime birthDate)
            : base(firstName, lastName, birthDate)
        {
            // Save the birth date in the private field at this hierarchy level.
            this.m_BirthDate = birthDate;
        }

        protected void GetObjectData(SerializationInfo info, StreamingContext context)
        {
            SerializationHelpers.SerializeObjectFields(info, "", this, null);
        }

        // The interface method delegates to the protected overload.
        void ISerializable.GetObjectData(SerializationInfo info, StreamingContext context)
        {
            GetObjectData(info, context);
        }

        // We *must* call the base class's constructor, even if with dummy arguments.
        public Employee(SerializationInfo info, StreamingContext context)
            : base("anyfirstname", "anylastname", new DateTime())
        {
            SerializationHelpers.DeserializeObjectFields(info, "", this, null);
        }
    }
```

Here's a piece of code that tests the serialization features of the Employee type:

```csharp
Employee em = new Employee("Joe", "Healy", new DateTime(1960, 1, 12));
em.Spouse = new Employee("Ann", "Beebe", new DateTime(1962, 4, 6));
em.Spouse.Spouse = em;
em.Boss = new Employee("Robert", "Zare", new DateTime(1965, 11, 7));

Functions.SerializeToFile("employee.dat", em);
Employee em2 = Functions.DeserializeFromFile<Employee>("employee.dat") ;

Console.WriteLine(em2.FirstName);                // => Joe
Console.WriteLine(em2.Spouse.FirstName);         // => Ann
Console.WriteLine(em2.Boss.FirstName);           // => Robert
Console.WriteLine(em2.Boss.BirthDate);           // => 11/7/1965
// Check that circular references are handled correctly.
Console.WriteLine(em2.Spouse.Spouse == em2);     // => True
```

This technique is sophisticated enough to handle circular references correctly, such as the relation that ties two Person objects through their Spouse property. It also deals correctly with object identity. For example, imagine that Joe's spouse is also his boss:

```
Employee em = new Employee("Joe", "Healy", new DateTime(1960, 1, 12));
em.Spouse = new Employee("Ann", "Beebe", new DateTime(1962, 4, 6));
em.Boss = (Employee) em.Spouse ;
// Serialize and deserialize the object graph (as in previous code example).
…
// Prove that object identity has been preserved.
Console.WriteLine(em2.Boss == em2.Spouse);          // => True
```

Chapter 13
PInvoke and COM Interop

The Microsoft .NET Framework is a revolution in the programming world. Managed applications are going to become the most common type of Microsoft Windows software. However, even the most enthusiastic .NET Framework fan can't reasonably expect that unmanaged code will disappear anytime soon, for at least three reasons. First, rewriting all existing software as managed code can be cost-prohibitive, and the advantage of having it running as a managed application might not justify migration costs. Second, many services are available today to Windows programmers only as COM components, such as Microsoft Office Word or Excel object libraries. Third, the .NET Framework encompasses many but not all features of the operating system. You still need unmanaged code to write shell extensions, work with memory mapped files, or perform cross-process window subclassing, just to mention a few Windows features not yet encapsulated in the .NET Framework.

For these and other reasons, Microsoft provides two distinct yet related mechanisms to use unmanaged code from a .NET Framework application: Platform Invoke (also known as *PInvoke*) and COM Interop. PInvoke technology lets .NET code call "traditional" DLLs, such as those that make up the Windows kernel or those written in C or C++, whereas COM Interop lets you reuse COM components from a .NET Framework language or call .NET Framework components from COM applications.

Despite their different purposes, these two technologies have a lot in common, and it makes sense to discuss them in the same chapter. For example, with only a few exceptions, they share the marshaling rules that dictate how data can be moved from the managed world to the unmanaged world and back. PInvoke is the simpler of the two technologies, so I cover it first. I defer COM Interop to the second part of this chapter.

> **Note** To avoid long lines, code samples in this chapter assume that the following using statements are used at the top of each source file:
>
> ```
> using System;
> using System.Collections;
> using System.ComponentModel;
> using System.Diagnostics;
> using System.Reflection;
> using System.Runtime.InteropServices;
> using System.Text;
> using System.Threading;
> using Microsoft.Win32;
> ```

Using PInvoke

Before you can call a function in an external DLL, you must declare the function's name and syntax using the DllImport attribute.

The DllImport Attribute

The DllImport attribute is defined in the System.Runtime.InteropServices namespace and can be applied only to static extern methods. The method marked with this attribute is used only as a blueprint for deriving the type of arguments and the type of the return value (if there is one) and can't have a body. In the simplest case, the DllImport attribute specifies only the name of the DLL that contains the external function:

```
public static class WindowsFunctions
{
    [DllImport("user32")]
    public static extern int FindWindow(string lpClassName, string lpWindowName);

    [DllImport("user32")]
    public static extern int MoveWindow(int hWnd, int x, int y, int nWidth, int nHeight, int bRepaint);
}
```

As you can see, the .dll extension in the DLL name can be omitted. If the path is also omitted, the DLL must be in a system folder or another directory listed in the PATH environment variable.

Once you have declared an external function, you can invoke it as if it were defined in managed code:

```
// Find an instance of the Notepad window, with no document loaded into it.
// (Works only in the English version of the Windows operating system.)
int hWnd = WindowsFunctions.FindWindow(null, "Untitled - Notepad");
if ( hWnd != 0 )
{
    MoveWindow(hWnd, 0, 0, 600, 300, 1);
}
```

```
else
{
   MessageBox.Show("Window not found", "Error");
}
```

The DllImport attribute supports several optional arguments, which let you precisely define how the external procedure should be called and how it returns a value to the caller.

```
[DllImport("filename.dll", CharSet=charsetoption, ExactSpelling=bool,
   EntryPoint="procname", CallingConvention=calloption,
   SetLastError=bool, BestFitMapping=bool, ThrowOnUnmappableChar=bool)]
...
```

The CharSet argument tells how strings are passed to the external routine; it can be CharSet.Ansi (the default), CharSet.Unicode, or CharSet.Auto and dictates how strings are passed to the external DLL. Ansi specifies that strings are passed as ANSI strings (the default behavior); Unicode forces strings to be passed as Unicode; Auto causes strings to be passed as ANSI strings under Microsoft Windows 98 and Windows Millennium Edition (Me) or as Unicode strings under more recent versions of the operating system. In addition, if you specify the Ansi setting and a function with that name isn't found in the DLL, the CLR appends the "A" character to the function name and tries again. If you specify the Unicode setting, the CLR appends the "W" character to the function name before searching for it; if this first search fails, the CLR searches for the name you've provided. Notice the subtle difference between the Ansi and Unicode settings—the latter works as described because the .NET Framework uses Unicode strings, and therefore a function that takes Unicode strings is preferable because it is more efficient than one that doesn't.

The ExactSpelling argument is a bool value that determines whether the method name must exactly match the name in the DLL; if true, the CharSet setting has no effect on the function name being searched. The default setting is false in Microsoft Visual C#.

The EntryPoint argument specifies the actual function name in the DLL, if different from the C# method's name. In practice, you use this argument if the entry point name is an invalid or a reserved name in C#, if it duplicates a name already defined in the application, or if it's an ordinal entry point (such as "#123").

The CallingConvention argument specifies the calling convention for the entry point. Available values are WinApi (the default), CDecl, FastCall, StdCall, and ThisCall. You rarely need to specify this option.

The SetLastError argument indicates whether the called function sets the Win32 last error code. If this argument is true, the compiler emits additional code that saves the last error code; therefore, you should leave this argument false (its default value) if you know that the function you're calling doesn't set the Win32 error because it makes your code slightly faster.

When the CLR converts Unicode strings to ANSI, each Unicode character is translated to the close-matching ANSI character, or to "?" if no close-matching character exists. This approach is usually desirable, but it might cause problems if the close-matching character is a character that might have a special meaning for the called procedure. For example, if the close-matching character is the backslash character, a string representing a path might point to the wrong place. You can disable the default behavior by setting the BestFitMapping argument to false (the default is true), and you can have the CLR throw an exception if a Unicode character in the string has no close-matching character in the ANSI set by setting the ThrowOnUnmappableChar argument to true (the default is false).

The following example shows how you can use the DllImport attribute to call a method named internal in a DLL named myfunctions.dll, which takes Unicode strings and affects the Win32 error code:

```
// We must use an aliased name because internal is a reserved keyword.
[DllImport("myfunctions.dll", EntryPoint = "internal",
   CharSet = CharSet.Unicode, SetLastError = true)]
private static extern int internalFN(string s1, string s2);
```

If the external routine sets the Win32 error code and you passed true to the SetLastError argument, you can read this error code when the call returns by means of the Marshal .GetLastWin32Error method:

```
int res = internalFN("first", "second");
if ( Marshal.GetLastWin32Error() != 0 )
{
    // Deal with the error here.
}
```

You can read the last error code only once.

 A new module-level attribute enables you to specify the character set to be assumed for all the DllImport attributes that lack an explicit CharSet named argument:

```
// Change the default CharSet value from Ansi to Auto.
[module: DefaultCharSet(CharSet.Auto)]
```

Marshaling Data

To invoke a function in an external DLL successfully, you must be familiar with how data is passed from C# to the external DLL, and how results are passed back to C#. This mechanism is known as *data marshaling*.

Most data types can be passed from managed to unmanaged code without much concern on your part because these data types have the same memory representation in the two worlds. These types are known as *blittable types*, a group that includes Byte, Int16, Int32, Int64, Single, Double, and DateTime types, as well as one-dimensional arrays thereof and structures that contain only blittable elements. You should pass blittable types, if possible, because they can cross the boundary between managed and unmanaged code very efficiently.

Nonblittable types are those that have a different representation in the two worlds, or that might have many representations in the unmanaged world, and must undergo marshaling when they cross the border between the managed and unmanaged worlds.

The most common nonblittable types are Boolean, Char, String, Decimal, and Array. The Boolean type is nonblittable because it can be 1, 2, or 4 bytes in the unmanaged world and because the true value can be represented as either 1 or –1. The Char type can be translated to either an ANSI or a Unicode character. The String type can be transformed in a variety of unmanaged formats, including null-terminated strings or length-prefixed BSTRs (each with the ANSI and Unicode variants). The Decimal type must be converted to Currency. Arrays are nonblittable because they can be translated either to SAFEARRAYS or to C-style arrays. You can determine exactly how nonblittable data is passed to or returned from managed code by means of the MarshalAs attribute, which I cover in the next section.

Many Windows API functions that are designed to send a string value back to the caller don't actually return a string in the return value; instead, they take a string buffer as an argument and fill it with zero or more characters, followed by a null character that marks the end of the string. The actual return value is often an integer that specifies how many characters have been placed in the buffer.

When passing a String object to such external methods, you have a problem to solve: .NET Framework strings are immutable, and you wouldn't see a different value in the string when the call returns. To see the actual returned string, you must pass a StringBuilder object instead. Here's an example of how you can define the GetClassName API function:

```
// Add these lines to the WindowsFunctions class.
[DllImport("user32")]
public static extern int GetClassName(IntPtr hWnd, StringBuilder buffer, int charcount);
```

The first argument, a 32-bit integer, is declared as an IntPtr element. Using an IntPtr instead of an Int32 gives you two benefits. First, you can pass the value of a form's Handle property without any conversion. Second, the IntPtr type automatically matches the size of CPU registers and works well under 64-bit versions of the Windows operating system. Here's how you can retrieve the class name of the current form:

```
// This code is meant to run from inside a Form class…
StringBuilder buffer = new StringBuilder(512);
// The last argument is the max number of characters in the buffer.
GetClassName(this.Handle, buffer, buffer.Capacity);
string classname = buffer.ToString();
```

The MarshalAs Attribute

The .NET Framework provides a default marshaling mechanism for each nonblittable type, but you modify the default behavior by means of the MarshalAs attribute. The following code shows how to use this attribute to let the compiler know that the (fictitious) CheckString procedure takes an ANSI null-terminated string and returns a Boolean value as a 2-byte integer that uses −1 to represent the true value:

```
[DllImport("mydll")]
[return: MarshalAs(UnmanagedType.VariantBool)]
private static extern bool CheckString([MarshalAs(UnmanagedType.LPWStr)] string s);
```

You can apply the MarshalAs attribute to parameters, fields, and return values. In most cases, the attribute takes only the UnmanagedType enumerated value that determines how the value is converted during the marshaling operation. Some UnmanagedType values, however, might require additional arguments, such as ArraySubType and SizeConst. See Table 13-1 for more details.

Table 13-1   UnmanagedType Enumerated Values

Value	Description
AnsiBStr	A length-prefixed ANSI character string. (Length is single byte.)
AsAny	A dynamic type that determines the type of an object at run time and marshals the object as that type. (Not valid for COM Interop.)
Bool	A 4-byte Boolean value, corresponding to the Win32 BOOL type. (0 is false; any other value is true.) This is the default way of passing Boolean values for PInvoke.
BStr	A length-prefixed double-byte Unicode character string. (The default way of passing strings for COM Interop.)
ByValArray	A fixed-length array field inside a struct. The SizeConst field must specify the number of elements in the array; the ArraySubType field can specify the UnmanagedType enumerated value that corresponds to the type of the array elements, if array elements aren't blittable.
ByValTStr	A fixed-length string field in a struct. The SizeConst argument must contain the size of the buffer in bytes. The CharSet attribute in the class determines the type of the characters.
Currency	A COM Currency value. (Can be used only with Decimal values.)
I1, I2, I4, I8	A 1-byte, 2-byte, 4-byte, or 8-byte signed integer.
IDispatch	A COM IDispatch interface pointer (same as an Object variable in Microsoft Visual Basic 6).
Interface	A COM interface pointer that specifies the exact interface type or the default interface type when applied to a class. The GUID of the interface is obtained from the class metadata.
IUnknown	A COM IUnknown interface pointer. (Can be used with Object values.)
LPArray	A pointer to the first element of a C-style array. When marshaling from the .NET Framework to unmanaged code, the array length is determined at run time. When marshaling from unmanaged code to the .NET Framework, the array length is determined from the SizeConst or SizeParamIndex arguments, optionally followed by the unmanaged type of array elements if they aren't blittable.
LPStr	A single-byte, null-terminated ANSI character string. (Can be used with String and StringBuilder elements.)

Table 13-1   UnmanagedType Enumerated Values

Value	Description
LPTStr	A platform-dependent character string. ANSI on Windows 98 and Windows Me, Unicode on Microsoft Windows NT and later versions. (Not valid with COM Interop.)
LPWStr	A 2-byte, null-terminated Unicode character string.
R4, R8	A 4-byte or 8-byte floating-point number.
SafeArray	An OLE Automation SafeArray. You can use the SafeArraySubType field to define the default element type.
Struct	A Variant used to marshal a struct or a formatted reference type.
SysInt, SysUInt	A platform-independent signed or unsigned integer. Four bytes on 32-bit Windows, 8 bytes on 64-bit Windows.
U1, U2, U4, U8	A 1-byte, 2-byte, 4-byte, or 8-byte unsigned integer.
VariantBool	A 2-byte OLE Boolean value, also known as VARIANT_BOOL (–1 for true; 0 for false). This is the default way of passing Boolean values for COM Interop.
VBByRefStr	Enables Microsoft Visual Basic 2005 to receive correctly the new value of a string modified in unmanaged code. (Not valid for COM Interop, and not useful in C# applications.)

The following code shows how you can use the MarshalAs attribute to pass a Unicode string to the Windows API function that changes the current directory. This example is for illustration purposes only; you can achieve the same result by using the CharSet.Unicode setting in the DllImport attribute.

```
[DllImport("kernel32", EntryPoint = "SetCurrentDirectoryW")]
private static extern int SetCurrentDirectory(
    [MarshalAs(UnmanagedType.LPWStr)] string lpPathName);
```

The following struct contains two string fields flagged with the MarshalAs attribute. When this struct is passed to an external procedure, the first field is translated to a null-terminated ANSI string, whereas the second field becomes a 256-character fixed-length string.

```
struct MyStructure
{
    [MarshalAs(UnmanagedType.LPStr)] public string f1;
    [MarshalAs(UnmanagedType.ByValTStr, SizeConst = 256)] public string f2;
}
```

Here's another example that uses the SizeConst optional argument:

```
struct Employee
{
    // Marshal the Name string as an ANSI fixed-length string of 100 chars.
    // (We must account for the extra null character.)
    [MarshalAs(UnmanagedType.ByValTStr, SizeConst = 101)] public string Name;
    ...
}
```

The StructLayout Attribute

The .NET Framework defines a couple of attributes that let you control how the elements of a struct block are arranged in memory and how the runtime should marshal them when they're passed to a function in an external DLL.

Fields of a struct are arranged in memory according to the order in which they appear in source code, even though the compiler is free to insert padding bytes to arrange members so that 16-bit values are aligned with word boundaries, 32-bit values are aligned with double-word boundaries, and so on. This arrangement—known as an *unpacked layout*—delivers the best performance because Intel processors work faster with aligned data.

You can finely control where each member of the struct or the class is located by means of the StructLayout attribute. The allowed values for this attribute are StructLayout.Auto (the compiler can reorder elements for best performance—for example, by grouping value types together), StructLayout.Sequential (elements are laid out and properly aligned sequentially in memory), and StructLayout.Explicit.

```
[StructLayout(LayoutKind.Explicit)]
struct ARGBColor
{
   ...
}
```

By default, C# uses the StructLayout.Auto setting for classes and StructLayout.Sequential for structs.

The StructLayout attribute supports three additional fields: CharSet, Pack, and Size. CharSet defines how string members in the struct are marshaled when the struct is passed to a DLL and can be Unicode, Ansi, or Auto. This argument, which defaults to Auto, has the same meaning as the DllImport argument with same name.

The Pack field defines the packing size for the struct and can be 1, 2, 4, 8 (the default), 16, 32, 64, 128, or the special value 0 that uses the default packing size for the current platform. A struct whose LayoutKind is Sequential always aligns elements to this number of bytes; if you omit the StructLayout attribute, elements align to their natural boundary (2-byte words for Int16 elements, 4-byte double words for Int32 and Single, addresses that are multiples of 8 for Int64 and Double, and so forth).

The Size field determines the total length of the struct when passed to unmanaged code; you can use this argument to increase the length of a struct. (You can reach the same goal by appending dummy, unused fields to the struct.)

```
[StructLayout(LayoutKind.Sequential, CharSet = CharSet.Unicode, Pack = 4)]
struct ARGBColor
{
   ...
}
```

By default, the C# compiler is free to arrange class members in a way that optimizes memory usage and performance. This corresponds to the StructLayout.Auto setting. When passing an object—as opposed to a value type—to unmanaged code, you must apply the StructLayout attribute with a different setting, typically StructLayout.Explicit. Classes flagged in this way are known as *formatted classes*. PInvoke supports classes as arguments only if they are formatted classes, with only a few exceptions such as the String and StringBuilder types; conversely, COM Interop doesn't enforce any limitation in passing a reference type.

In practice, you will rarely pass a reference to an object other than String or StringBuilder as an argument to an external DLL using PInvoke. If you do, however, remember that the DLL receives a *pointer* to the data in the object. From the perspective of the called routine, an object reference passed by value is similar to a struct passed using the ref keyword because, in both cases, the routine receives an address. If you pass an object reference to a ref argument, the routine receives the address of a pointer that points to the object's data.

The FieldOffset Attribute

When you opt for an explicit layout, the definition of all the fields in a struct must include a FieldOffset attribute that has an argument specifying the distance in bytes from the beginning of the struct:

```
[StructLayout(LayoutKind.Explicit)]
public struct RGBColor
{
    [FieldOffset(0)] public byte Red;
    [FieldOffset(1)] public byte Green;
    [FieldOffset(2)] public byte Blue;
    [FieldOffset(3)] public byte Alpha;
}
```

The StructLayout and the FieldOffset attributes let you simulate a *union*, a language feature that many languages, such as C and C++, have had since their inception. A union is a struct in which two or more elements overlap in memory. Or, if you prefer, a union permits you to refer to the same memory location in a struct using different names. The key to unions in C# is the support for explicit struct layout. Consider the following example:

```
[StructLayout(LayoutKind.Explicit)]
public struct RGBColor
{
    [FieldOffset(0)] public byte Red;
    [FieldOffset(1)] public byte Green;
    [FieldOffset(2)] public byte Blue;
    [FieldOffset(3)] public byte Alpha;
    [FieldOffset(0)] public int Value;
}
```

The following graphic illustrates how these elements are located in memory:

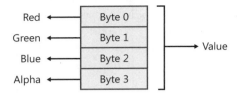

In other words, you can access the 4 bytes as a whole through the Value field or individually through the Red, Green, Blue, and Alpha fields. The following code shows how useful this feature can be:

```
// Split a color into its components.
RGBColor rgb = new RGBColor();
rgb.Value = 0x112233;                          // This is equal to 1122867.
Console.WriteLine("Red={0}, Green={1}, Blue={2}", rgb.Red, rgb.Green, rgb.Blue);
    // => Red=51, Green=34, Blue=17
```

You can also combine the three RGB components into a single color:

```
rgb.Red = 51;
rgb.Green = 34;
rgb.Blue = 17;
Console.WriteLine("RGB color = {0}", rgb.Value);    // => 1122867
```

Unions make it possible to implement some tricky conversion routines far more efficiently than using standard math operators. Consider the following struct:

```
[StructLayout(LayoutKind.Explicit)]
public struct IntegerTypes
{
    // A 64-bit integer
    [FieldOffset(0)] public long Long0;
    // Two 32-bit integers
    [FieldOffset(0)] public int Integer0;
    [FieldOffset(4)] public int Integer1;
    // Four 16-bit integers
    [FieldOffset(0)] public short Short0;
    [FieldOffset(2)] public short Short1;
    [FieldOffset(4)] public short Short2;
    [FieldOffset(6)] public short Short3;
    // Eight 8-bit integers
    [FieldOffset(0)] public byte Byte0;
    [FieldOffset(1)] public byte Byte1;
    [FieldOffset(2)] public byte Byte2;
    [FieldOffset(3)] public byte Byte3;
    [FieldOffset(4)] public byte Byte4;
    [FieldOffset(5)] public byte Byte5;
    [FieldOffset(6)] public byte Byte6;
    [FieldOffset(7)] public byte Byte7;
}
```

This struct takes exactly 8 bytes, but you can refer to those bytes in multiple ways. For example, you can extract the low and high bytes of a 16-bit integer:

```
IntegerTypes it = new IntegerTypes();
it.Short0 = 517;                    // Hex 0205
Console.WriteLine(it.Byte0);        // => 5
Console.WriteLine(it.Byte1);        // => 2
```

This technique works also if the struct fields are declared as private. However, you should use it only with integer member types, such as Byte, Int16, Int32, and Int64; trying to interpret locations as Single or Double values often returns the special NaN (Not-a-Number) value. Trying to map a reference type (such as a String) throws a TypeLoadException error when loading an assembly containing one or more structs in which reference types overlap with other members or aren't aligned properly.

Most of the structs used by Windows API functions are unpacked and don't require any special attribute. Others, most notably those in the Shell32.dll library, might require you to define an explicit layout. One such example is the SHFILEOPSTRUCT struct that you pass as an argument to the SHFileOperation function:

```
[DllImport("shell32.dll", EntryPoint = "SHFileOperationA")]
private static extern int SHFileOperation(ref SHFILEOPSTRUCT lpFileOp);

[StructLayout(LayoutKind.Explicit)]
private struct SHFILEOPSTRUCT
{
   [FieldOffset(0)] public IntPtr hwnd;
   [FieldOffset(4)] public int wFunc;
   [FieldOffset(8)] public string pFrom;
   [FieldOffset(12)] public string pTo;
   [FieldOffset(16)] public short fFlags;
   [FieldOffset(18), MarshalAs(UnmanagedType.Bool)] public bool fAnyOperationsAborted;
   [FieldOffset(22)] public int hNameMappings;
   [FieldOffset(26)] public IntPtr lpszProgressTitle;
   // Was String, only used if FOF_SIMPLEPROGRESS
}
```

By carefully examining the previous struct, you can see that the fFlags field (a 2-byte integer) is immediately followed by a 4-byte Boolean value. If this struct were unpacked, two padding bytes would be inserted between these two fields. Unfortunately, the Shell32.dll library expects a packed struct, so we must resort to explicit layout. Notice also that the last element in the struct is defined as a string in the Windows SDK documentation, but we must use an IntPtr or an Int32 in C# because strings are reference types and must be aligned to the double word.

Here's a procedure that uses the SHFileOperation API function to copy one or more files while displaying the standard Windows dialog box (shown in Figure 13-1). This API function automatically manages name collisions and allows undelete operations.

```csharp
// Copy a file using the SHFileOperation API function.
// It can return 0 (OK), 1 (user canceled the operation), or 2 (error).
public static int CopyFile(string source, string dest)
{
    const int FO_COPY = 0x2;
    const short RENAMEONCOLLISION = 0x8;
    const short ALLOWUNDO = 0x40;
    const short SIMPLEPROGRESS = 0x100;

    // Fill an SHFILEOPSTRUCT structure.
    SHFILEOPSTRUCT sh = new SHFILEOPSTRUCT();
    sh.wFunc = FO_COPY;
    sh.hwnd = IntPtr.Zero;              // No owner window
    sh.pTo = dest;
    // Ensure source file ends with an extra null char. (See SDK docs.)
    sh.pFrom = source + '\0';
    sh.fFlags = ALLOWUNDO | RENAMEONCOLLISION;

    int res = SHFileOperation(ref sh);

    // The API function returns nonzero if there is a problem.
    if ( res == 0 )
    {
        return 0;               // 0 means everything was OK.
    }
    else if ( sh.fAnyOperationsAborted )
    {
        return 1;               // 1 means user aborted the operation.
    }
    else
    {
        return 2;               // 2 means an error has occurred.
    }
}
```

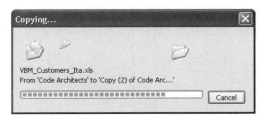

Figure 13-1 The standard window that the SHFileOperation API function displays when copying files

Here's how you can use the CopyFile function to copy all the files in the c:\docs directory to the c:\backup directory:

```csharp
int res = CopyFile(@"c:\docs\*.*", @"c:\backup");
switch ( res )
{
    case 0:
        MessageBox.Show("All files were copied correctly.");
        break;
```

```
      case 1:
         MessageBox.Show("User canceled the operation.");
         break;
      case 2:
         MessageBox.Show("An error occurred.");
         break;
   }
```

Delegates and Callback Procedures

A method in an external DLL can take the address of a *callback procedure*. A callback procedure is a procedure in your program that the external method calls to notify your code that something has happened. For example, the EnumWindows API function enumerates all the upper top-level windows in the system and invokes a callback method for each found window. You can write code in the callback procedure that uses this information—for example, by displaying the name of the window in a ListBox control or by filling an array of structs for later processing. C# enables you to call these Windows API functions in a safe way by means of delegates.

Before you can declare an external procedure that uses a callback mechanism, you must create a delegate class that defines the syntax of the callback routine:

```
// This is the syntax for EnumWindows's callback procedure.
private delegate bool EnumWindowsProc(IntPtr hWnd, IntPtr lParam);
```

In the definition of the API function, you specify the callback argument using the delegate type:

```
[DllImport("user32")]
private static extern int EnumWindows(EnumWindowsProc lpEnumFunc, IntPtr lParam);
```

Finally, you can write the actual callback procedure and pass its address to the external method. The delegate argument forces you to pass the address of a procedure that complies with the delegate's syntax:

```
static void TestAPICallback()
{
   EnumWindows(new EnumWindowsProc(ListWindows), 0);
}

// The second argument to the callback function is ignored in this demo.
// (In a real application, it helps discern the reason why this procedure has been called.)
static bool ListWindows(int hWnd, int lParam)
{
   // Display the handle of this top-level window.
   lstWindows.Items.Add(hWnd);
   // Return true to continue enumeration.
   return true;
}
```

The preceding code snippet displays the 32-bit handle of all the top-level windows in the system in a Windows Forms ListBox control. The complete demo shows how you can display the handle and other pieces of information about all the open windows in the system by using the EnumWindows and EnumChildWindows API functions in a recursive fashion. (See Figure 13-2.)

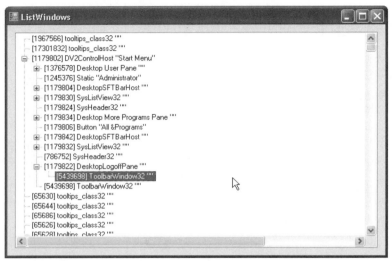

Figure 13-2   The demo program, which uses the Windows API to display the tree of all open windows

The In and Out Attributes

The .NET Framework marshaler always copies a parameter's values from managed code to the unmanaged DLL, but it copies the value back only if the parameter is passed by reference. This means that you see the new value if the callee changes the value of a ref parameter. At first glance, therefore, the semantics of the C# argument-passing mechanism is preserved when working with PInvoke. However, things aren't always so smooth, and you must be prepared to work around a few potential problems you might have with reference types.

As I explained earlier, the PInvoke marshaler can pass a reference type only if the type is a formatted class (that is, it uses an explicit layout), with String and StringBuilder types being among the few exceptions. The PInvoke marshaler copies the fields of a formatted struct to unmanaged memory instead of just passing a pointer to the managed object. (The COM Interop marshaler, however, simply passes the object pointer, as you'd expect.)

As you know, if you pass an object to a C# method that modifies the object's fields, you see the new field values when the call returns, even if the object argument is passed by value. Conversely, the PInvoke marshaler doesn't copy data back to the object when you pass a reference type to an external DLL, to achieve better performance. In other words, by default, reference types are passed as input-only arguments. You can change this behavior by flagging the argument with explicit In and Out attributes, as follows:

```
[DllImport("mydll")]
private static extern void TestRoutine( [In, Out] object objRef );
```

The StringBuilder class is an exception to this rule because the PInvoke marshaler copies it back even if you pass it by value and without the Out attribute. You can omit the In attribute when passing an out argument that doesn't have to be initialized.

In its quest for greater efficiency, under certain circumstances, the marshaler can decide to *pin* the passed argument, a detail that makes matters a bit more complicated. When an argument is pinned, the marshaler passes the address of the original value in the managed heap rather than the address of a copy. (The word *pinning* is used because the object is pinned in memory and doesn't move even if a garbage collection occurs in the meantime.)

For example, under PInvoke, a .NET Framework string passed by value to a Unicode string argument is pinned: the callee receives the address of the internal character buffer, and no copy occurs. If the callee doesn't abide by the by-value semantics and mistakenly changes the passed string, the managed heap might be corrupted. (This happens, for example, if a longer string is assigned.)

Pinning can occur only with strings passed by value. The PInvoke marshaler always copies ref string arguments to a temporary buffer and then passes the address of this buffer to the external procedure. When the call returns, the marshaler creates a new string with the characters found in the buffer and passes the new string back to the caller. (This double copy is necessary to preserve string immutability.)

Pinning occurs also when you pass a blittable formatted class because the marshaler can improve performance by passing a pointer to the object's memory in the managed heap. Pinning happens regardless of whether you use the Out attribute. (In other words, the Out attribute forces a copy of the value back to C# only if the argument isn't pinned.)

Arrays are reference types and can be pinned, too. More precisely, an array is pinned if its elements are blittable and you make either a PInvoke call or a COM Interop call to an object that lives in the same apartment as the caller. Arrays defined as part of a struct are dealt with as other objects, but they can be passed by value by flagging them with a MarshalAs attribute, as follows:

```
[StructLayout(LayoutKind.Sequential)]
struct MyStruct
{
    [MarshalAs(UnmanagedType.ByValArray, SizeConst = 64)]
    public short[] s1;
}
```

The struct in the preceding code takes 128 bytes when it is passed by value on the stack because the MarshalAs attribute specifies that the s1 array has 64 elements. Without this attribute, the array would have been marshaled as any other object reference, and the struct would take only 4 bytes.

The Marshal Class

You've seen that you can affect the behavior of the PInvoke marshaler by means of a few attributes, but in the most intricate cases, you must resort to *manual marshaling* techniques, which require that you manually allocate and deallocate unmanaged memory and copy your data into it.

The basis for manual marshaling is the Marshal class, a container for static methods that let you do virtually anything you might need to do with unmanaged memory. I mentioned this class when I described the Marshal.GetLastWin32Error method in the section titled "The DllImport Attribute" earlier in this chapter.

The SizeOf method takes an object or a struct (or a System.Type that identifies a class or a struct) and returns the number of bytes that object or struct would take when marshaled to unmanaged code:

```
// These statements display the same value.
Console.WriteLine(Marshal.SizeOf(typeof(Person)));
Console.WriteLine(Marshal.SizeOf(new Person()));
```

The OffsetOf method takes two arguments: a System.Type that identifies either a struct or a class flagged with the StructLayout attribute, and the name of one of the type's members. The method returns the offset of the member in the unmanaged representation of the struct or class:

```
Console.WriteLine(Marshal.OffsetOf(typeof(Person), "FirstName"));
```

You can allocate three kinds of unmanaged memory with the methods of the Marshal class; each kind must be deallocated later with a different method.

The AllocHGlobal method allocates memory by invoking the GlobalAlloc API function and returns a pointer to the allocated memory. You can resize the memory block with the ReAllocHGlobal method and release it with the FreeHGlobal method:

```
// Allocates and then releases 10 KB of memory using GlobalAlloc API function.
IntPtr ptr = Marshal.AllocHGlobal(10240);
...
Marshal.FreeHGlobal(ptr);
```

Notice that memory allocated in this way isn't controlled by the garbage collector. If you forget to release it, it will be freed only when the application terminates.

When working with COM, you typically use a different allocating technique based on the CoTaskMemAlloc function. You can deal with this kind of memory through the AllocCoTask-Mem, ReAllocCoTaskMem, and FreeCoTaskMem static methods:

```
// Allocates and then releases 10 KB of memory using CoTaskMemAlloc OLE function.
IntPtr ptr = Marshal.AllocCoTaskMem(10240);

…
Marshal.FreeCoTaskMem(ptr);
```

Once you have allocated a block of unmanaged memory, you usually want to store some data in it before calling an unmanaged function or read data from it when the call returns. If the memory block contains an array of numeric, Char, or DateTime elements, you can use the Copy method:

```
// Pass an array of integers to a procedure that expects a pointer.
int[] values = {1, 3, 5, 9, 11, 13, 15};
int bytes = values.Length * 4;
// Allocate a block of memory and copy array elements into it.
IntPtr ptr = Marshal.AllocHGlobal(bytes);
Marshal.Copy(values, 0, ptr, bytes);
// Call the external unmanaged routine.
TheExternalProc(ptr);
// Copy array elements back to the array and release memory.
Marshal.Copy(ptr, values, 0, bytes);
Marshal.FreeHGlobal(ptr);
```

You often have to allocate a block of unmanaged memory and copy a .NET Framework string into it, possibly after converting the string to ANSI. You can perform this operation in a single step by using one of the following techniques: use StringToHGlobalAnsi, StringToHGlobalUni, and StringToHGlobalAuto when copying a string into a block allocated with the GlobalAlloc API function; or use StringToCoTaskMemAnsi, StringToCoTaskMemUni, and StringToCo-TaskMemAuto when copying a string into a block allocated with the CoTaskMemAlloc function. The last portion of the method name indicates whether the string is converted to ANSI during the copy process:

```
// Use GlobalAlloc to allocate unmanaged memory and copy a string
// after converting it to ANSI if running under Windows 98 or Windows Me.
string s = "A .NET Framework string passed to COM";
IntPtr ptr = Marshal.StringToHGlobalAuto(s);

…
Marshal.FreeHGlobal(ptr);
```

You can also allocate a BSTR—which is the standard format for a COM string—and copy a string into it with the StringToBSTR method; memory allocated in this fashion must be released with the FreeBSTR method:

```
string s = "A .NET Framework string passed to COM";
IntPtr ptr = Marshal.StringToBSTR(s);

…
Marshal.FreeBSTR(ptr);
```

If the unmanaged string contains confidential data, this data will continue to hang in memory until it is overwritten by other information, and other programs—including viruses and Trojan horses—might read it. To reduce this risk, you might want to fill it with zeros before releasing the block by means of the ZeroFree*Xxxx* methods that have been added to the Marshal class in version 2.0 of the .NET Framework, for example, ZeroFreeBSTR or ZeroFreeCo-TaskMemAnsi:

```
ZeroFreeBSTR(ptr);
```

Also, for added security you might decide to work with SecureString objects exclusively. (Read the section titled "The SecureString Type" in Chapter 1, ".NET Framework Basic Types," for more information.)

The Marshal class offers methods that write individual values into a block of unmanaged memory (WriteByte, WriteInt16, WriteInt32, WriteInt64, WriteIntPtr) and that read them back (ReadByte, ReadInt16, ReadInt32, ReadInt64, ReadIntPtr). The first argument to these methods is the IntPtr value returned by an allocation method, and the second (optional) argument is an offset into the memory block:

```
// Write an integer at offset 10 in a block of unmanaged memory.
int oldValue = 1234;
Marshal.WriteInt32(ptr, 10, oldValue);
// Call the unmanaged function.
…
// Read the integer back.
int newValue = Marshal.ReadInt32(ptr, 10);
```

To show what you can do in practice with the allocation methods of the Marshal class, I have prepared an enhanced version of the CopyFile procedure that I introduced in the section titled "The FieldOffset Attribute" earlier in this chapter. As you might remember, the last element of the SHFILEOPSTRUCT struct that the SHFileOperation Windows API function uses is a string field that isn't aligned to the 4-byte boundary. The lack of alignment forces us to declare this element as an IntPtr instead of a string, or the program would throw a runtime exception. This element is used to display a user-defined message in the Copy File dialog box instead of the name of the file being copied. The enhanced version of the CopyFile function takes this user-defined message as an argument (if the passed value is null, the argument is ignored):

```
public static int CopyFile(string source, string dest, string progressText)
{
    const int FO_COPY = 0x2;
    const short RENAMEONCOLLISION = 0x8;
    const short ALLOWUNDO = 0x40;
    const short SIMPLEPROGRESS = 0x100;

    // Fill an SHFILEOPSTRUCT structure.
    SHFILEOPSTRUCT sh = new SHFILEOPSTRUCT();
    sh.wFunc = FO_COPY ;
    sh.hwnd = IntPtr.Zero;                  // No owner window
```

```
    sh.pTo = dest;
    // Ensure source file ends with an extra null char. (See SDK docs.)
    sh.pFrom = source + '\0';
    sh.fFlags = ALLOWUNDO | RENAMEONCOLLISION;

    if ( progressText != null )
    {
        // Allocate an ANSI string somewhere in memory and store its pointer here.
        sh.lpszProgressTitle = Marshal.StringToHGlobalAnsi(progressText);
        sh.fFlags = (short) (sh.fFlags | SIMPLEPROGRESS);
    }

    int res = SHFileOperation(ref sh);

    if ( progressText != null )
    {
        // Release any memory taken for the ProgressTitle string.
        Marshal.FreeHGlobal(sh.lpszProgressTitle);
        sh.lpszProgressTitle = IntPtr.Zero;
    }

    // The API functions returns a nonzero value if there is a problem.
    if ( res == 0 )
    {
        return 0;              // 0 means everything was OK.
    }
    else if ( sh.fAnyOperationsAborted )
    {
        return 1;              // 1 means user aborted the operation.
    }
    else
    {
        return 2;              // 2 means an error has occurred.
    }
}
```

For more details, see the demo program that comes with this book's companion code.

Calling COM Components from .NET

There are three ways to enable a .NET application to call a COM object: you can use the Microsoft Visual Studio Add Reference command, you can run the Type Library Importer utility (TlbImp), or you can code against the TypeLibConverter class. Before looking at the practical details, however, it is important for you to understand what happens behind the scenes when a C# client uses a COM object.

The Runtime Callable Wrapper

Calling a COM component from a .NET Framework application is made possible by an object named the Runtime Callable Wrapper, or RCW. (See Figure 13-3.) This object "wraps" the COM component and makes it look to .NET clients like a regular managed component.

The RCW is in charge of several tasks, all of which are necessary to make the COM component appear to its clients as a .NET Framework component. Such tasks include the marshaling of data, the conversion of COM's HRESULT values to exceptions, and the management of the COM component's lifetime (which is based on reference counting instead of garbage collection).

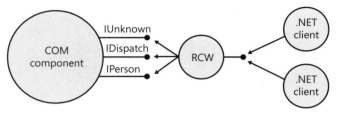

Figure 13-3   The Runtime Callable Wrapper object

The RCW consumes several important COM interfaces—including IUnknown, IDispatch, IDispatchEx, IProvideClassInfo, ISupportErrorInfo, and IErrorInfo—and hides them from .NET Framework clients. For example, a .NET Framework client can use a COM component through late binding because the RCW consumes the IDispatch interface behind the scenes to dispatch these calls to the actual object. The RCW is also responsible for object identity: there is one and only one RCW for each distinct COM object, regardless of how references to the COM object have been returned to the managed client(s). This requirement is necessary for the Object.ReferenceEquals method to work correctly with references pointing to a COM object.

The .NET Framework creates an RCW not only when a managed client explicitly instantiates a COM object, but also when a COM method returns a reference to a new object that isn't already known to the CLR because the COM Interop infrastructure always creates one distinct RCW for each COM object accessed from a managed application, regardless of whether it was created or returned by another method. The COM Interop infrastructure correctly preserves identity even in the most intricate cases. For example, when a managed client passes a .NET Framework object as an argument to a COM method and the unmanaged code later returns that object to the client, COM Interop correctly recognizes that the returned object is actually a managed object and returns a reference to that managed object, without creating an RCW.

A .NET Framework client can create a COM object in two different ways: as an early-bound object or as a late-bound object. You usually create an early-bound object by calling its constructor (with the new keyword) and assigning the result to a specific variable; you create a late-bound object by using Activator.CreateInstance and assigning the result to a generic Object variable.

The difference in how the object is created affects the type of RCW object that COM Interop creates behind the scenes. In the early binding case, the RCW is a well-defined .NET Framework type, and you can invoke its methods using the "dot" syntax, as you do with all .NET types. In the late binding case, the type of the RCW is System.__ComObject, and you can invoke the methods of the wrapped COM object only by using reflection.

The CLR can early-bind a COM component only if metadata is available for it. This metadata must be available both at compile time (to generate the IL code) and at run time (to create the RCW object). The metadata for a COM component is similar to the metadata associated with standard .NET Framework types, except for a few attributes that identify that type as a COM component. In general, this metadata is extracted from the COM object's type library, implicitly as you use Visual Studio or explicitly if you use TlbImp.

Importing a COM Component with Visual Studio

The companion code that comes with this book includes a sample COM component named TestComComponent.dll. This component is written in Visual Basic 6 and exposes a Person class with the usual FirstName, LastName, and CompleteName members. Before proceeding, ensure that the component is registered in the Windows registry by using the regsvr32 tool:

```
REGSVR32 TestComComponent.dll
```

The simplest way to create metadata for a COM component is to let Visual Studio do it for you. Choose the Add Reference command from the Project menu to display the Add Reference dialog box, and then click the COM tab. It might take several seconds to fill this window the first time you run this command because Visual Studio parses the system registry and looks for all the registered COM components. When this process is completed, you see a list of components such as the one shown in Figure 13-4. If the COM component you're looking for doesn't appear in this list, switch to the Browse tab and navigate to the folder where the component DLL resides.

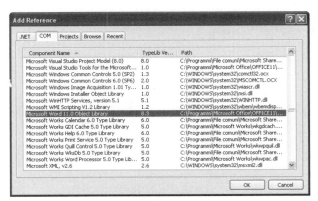

Figure 13-4   The COM tab of the Add Reference dialog box

When you click the OK button, Visual Studio parses the component's type library—which is embedded in the DLL itself in the case of a Visual Basic 6 component—and generates an assembly named Interop.TestComComponent.dll. This DLL is known as *interop assembly*. If you use ILDASM to peek into an interop assembly, you'll see that it contains a lot of metadata but very little executable code.

Using the Imported Interop Assembly

The main goal of COM Interop is to let the developer use COM objects as if they were .NET Framework components. As a matter of fact, the C# code that uses this component looks absolutely similar to the code you'd write to access a standard .NET Framework component:

```
TestComComponent.Person pers = new TestComComponent.Person();
pers.FirstName = "John";
pers.LastName = "Evans";
string res = pers.CompleteName();
```

The preceding code snippet shows that you can use an imported COM object exactly as if it were a .NET Framework object. The only way a programmer could determine whether an object is a COM object is by using the Marshal.IsComObject method or by reflecting on the object's attributes.

If you look at the Interop.TestComComponent assembly with the object browser or at the IL code generated by the previous C# snippet, you can see that it actually isn't as simple as it appears. In fact, COM makes a distinction between a creatable class (a coclass) and the interface that it exposes, and therefore the IL code must account for this difference. When you create an instance with the new keyword, you're actually working with a type named Person-Class; when you invoke a class member, you're actually interacting with an interface named _Person. In some cases you need to account for this distinction, for example, when you work with the class and its members through reflection.

If you know that you're dealing with an imported COM object, often you can optimize your code's behavior and avoid subtle bugs that derive from the different nature of COM and .NET Framework components. The different ways that COM and the .NET Framework manage object lifetime offers an example of what I mean.

A "true" COM component is destroyed as soon as the last variable that points to it is set to null. However, a managed client has a reference to the RCW, which is a .NET object that works as a proxy for the COM component. Even if the managed client sets all the references to the COM object to null, the RCW will not be picked up by the garbage collector until some time afterward. If the COM performs critical cleanup code in its destructor—such as closing a file or unlocking a record—the actual cleanup will occur later, and you might get an error when trying to access that specific file or record.

You can force the immediate release of a COM object by invoking the Marshal.ReleaseCom-Object method just before setting the object reference to null:

```
Marshal.ReleaseComObject(pers);
pers = null;
```

In more advanced scenarios, you can also use the AddRef, Release, and QueryInterface methods of the Marshal class to access the object's IUnknown interface directly and manage its internal reference counter.

The ReleaseComObject method invokes the component's Release method for you and decreases the object's reference counter. If other clients are keeping a reference to the object, the object itself won't be released. In version 2.0 of the .NET Framework, you can use the new FinalReleaseComObject method, which tries to force the release by setting the reference counter to zero and returns the new value of the reference counter. By testing this return value you can detect whether the release operation was successful:

```
int counter = Marshal.FinalReleaseComObject(pers);
if ( counter == 0 )
{
    Console.WriteLine("Object was successfully released.");
}
```

Importing a COM Component with TlbImp

Although the Visual Studio Add Reference dialog box offers a quick-and-dirty method to create metadata for a COM component, in some cases, you need to use the Type Library Importer command-line utility (TlbImp) provided with the .NET Framework SDK. For example, this utility is necessary when you want to perform the conversion by means of a batch or a MAKE program or when you import the COM component as a strong-named assembly. (Strong name is required if you want to reference the interop assembly from another strong-named assembly.) The syntax for TlbImp is simple:

```
TLBIMP source.dll [/OUT:dest.dll]
```

If the /out option is omitted, TlbImp creates a DLL with a name that matches the internal name of the type library, which might be different from its filename. For example, the type library associated with a Visual Basic 6 component is named after the project, not the DLL file (which in fact can be renamed before registering the type library). If the /out option is used, its argument affects both the name of the assembly being created and the namespace of the types inside it. For example, the following command creates a DLL named MyApp.Data.dll that contains types such as MyApp.Data.Invoice:

```
TLBIMP MyApp.dll [/OUT:MyApp.Data]
```

If the internal name of the type library matches its filename, you must use the /out switch because TlbImp correctly refuses to overwrite the source file. If the source DLL contains multiple type libraries (as is the case with the Visual Basic 6 type library, msvbvm60.dll), TlbImp extracts only the first type library, but you can append \N to the filename to extract the Nth type library. For example, the following command imports the VBRUN type library (which is the third type library embedded in msvbvm60.dll):

```
TLBIMP c:\Windows\System32\msvbvm60.dll\3 /OUT:vbrun.dll
```

As I've already mentioned, you must use TlbImp instead of the Visual Studio Add Reference command to generate interop assemblies with a strong name and a version number. Another good reason to use TlbImp is to generate classes in a namespace different from the default one. You can accomplish these tasks with the /keyfile, /asmversion, and /namespace options:

```
TLBIMP source.dll /KEYFILE:c:\codearchitects.snk /ASMVERSION:2.0.0.0
    /NAMESPACE:CodeArchitects
```

Here, the .snk file containing the public/private key pair has been generated previously with the option -k of the SN utility or from the Signing page of the project's designer in Visual Studio. By default, TlbImp recursively imports all the type libraries referenced by the type library you specify. You can avoid this behavior by providing one or more /reference options pointing to other assemblies—in which case, TlbImp will attempt to solve external types in the assemblies you specify before it imports them. You can also specify the /strictref option if you want to cause an error if one or more external references could not be resolved without importing another type library:

```
TLBIMP source.dll /REFERENCE:Interop.Office.dll /STRICTREF
```

You can find additional details on TlbImp and its options in the .NET SDK documentation.

Primary Interop Assemblies

When working with COM Interop assemblies, you might encounter the following problem. Let's say that you create an interop assembly for the Microsoft Office Word type library, and you sign it to obtain a strong-named assembly. As a consequence, all the objects in this assembly have an identity that depends on your assembly's name and version and your publisher key. Let's further suppose that your program interacts with another .NET Framework application that uses Word through COM Interop and that has been created by another company. Here's the problem: if the other company has created *another* interop assembly for Word and has signed it with *their* public key, their Word objects and your Word objects have different identities. For example, if a method in the other application returns a Word.Document object, your code throws a type mismatch exception when it attempts to store the return value to a Word.Document variable.

Microsoft has anticipated this problem and has introduced the concept of Primary Interop Assembly (PIA). A PIA is the "official" interop assembly for a COM component. It should be created by the manufacturer of the COM component itself, and it should be installed in the GAC and registered in the registry. Here's how you can create a PIA for a COM component that you've created:

1. Use the /primary option of TlbImp to create the primary interop assembly, as follows:

    ```
    TLBIMP mylib.dll /OUT:mypia.dll /PRIMARY /KEYFILE:mycompany.snk
    ```

2. Run the AsmReg utility to add the PrimaryInteropAssembly registry key under the HKEY_CLASSES_ROOT\TypeLib\{tlbguid}\Version key related to the COM component:

    ```
    ASMREG mypia.dll
    ```

3. Run the GacUtil tool to install the interop assembly in the GAC:

```
GACUITIL -i mypia.dll
```

4. Copy the assembly file to the C:\Program Files\Microsoft.NET\Primary Interop Assemblies folder to make it appear in the Visual Studio Add Reference dialog box. (This step is optional.)

Visual Studio deals with PIAs in a special way: when you add a reference to a type library for which a PIA exists, Visual Studio doesn't import the type library as it normally would; instead, it uses the PIA installed in the system. Notice that a PIA can reference only other PIAs.

Microsoft provides the PIAs for a few important type libraries, such as adodb, Microsoft.mshtml, Microsoft.stdformat, office, and stdole. Other PIAs might be available on the Microsoft Web site.

Registration-Free COM Components

 A new feature of Visual Studio 2005 dramatically simplifies the deployment of COM components: registration-free COM components. Strictly speaking, this feature is part of the Microsoft Windows XP and Windows Server 2003 operating systems and could be exploited even without Visual Studio 2005. However, it's a new property in the IDE that makes this feature so accessible and easy to use.

A registration-free component is a COM component that resides in its client application's folder and can be accessed without having to register it in the registry with the RegSvr32 program or another similar tool. Even better, these COM components can be used only by the clients that are stored in their folder; therefore, different clients can use different versions of the same COM component. It's obvious that the deployment of these components is much simpler than usual and their setup routines can cause fewer troubles.

Defining a registration-free COM component is very simple in Visual Studio 2005: select the interop assembly in the project's reference list, press F4 to display the Properties window, and change the Isolated property from false (the default) to true, as shown in Figure 13-5. That's it!

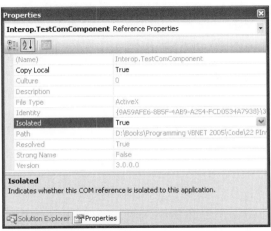

Figure 13-5   The Isolated property of an interop assembly added to the references of a project

Behind the scenes, Visual Studio generates a file named *appname*.exe.manifest, which contains the information that the COM infrastructure uses to locate the component. Keep in mind, however, that this manifest file is used only if COM fails to find the component in the registry. This implies that you need to unregister the component before you can test this feature. To do so, open a command-line window, navigate to the folder where the component is stored, and issue this command:

```
REGSVR32 /U TestComComponent.dll
```

You can now run the application from Windows Explorer and check that the COM component is instantiated correctly. (Running the application from inside Visual Studio would throw an exception because Visual Studio expects that the COM component is registered correctly.) You can double-check that the component runs in registration-free mode by temporarily renaming or deleting the manifest file: any attempt to run the application now throws a COM error.

Registration-free components are especially useful in ClickOnce scenarios, but you can leverage them in any application that uses one or more COM components. When weighing whether you should use these components, consider that you can use them only under Windows XP and Windows Server 2003 operating systems. The component must be an ActiveX DLL (not an ActiveX EXE) and can't be a system component such as msxml6.dll, an Office object library, a Visual Studio add-in, or an ActiveX control meant to be used in Microsoft Internet Explorer or in the Visual Studio Toolbox. When using third-party components, check with their vendors whether they already provide a manifest for their DLLs, and use it if available.

Late Binding and Reflection

In most real-world situations, you will import the metadata for a COM component and use it through early binding, but it's good to know that you don't strictly have to. In fact, managed code can access COM objects by using late binding and reflection techniques without having to import their type library. This technique can be useful when you use a COM object only once in a while, or when you don't know at compile time which objects your application will use.

Creating a COM component in a late-bound fashion requires that you use the Type.GetTypeFromProgID or Type.GetTypeFromCLSID static methods to retrieve the Type object corresponding to the COM component with a given ProgID or CLSID. You can then pass this Type object to the Activator.CreateInstance method to create an instance of the component, which you typically assign to an Object variable. Finally, you use the Type.InvokeMember method to call a method, set a property, or read a property of the object, as you learned in Chapter 9, "Reflection."

The following code shows you how to create an ADODB.Connection object in a late-bound fashion and then query it for its Version property and open a connection to a Microsoft SQL Server database:

```
// Get the Type object for the ADODB.Connection COM component.
Type ty = Type.GetTypeFromProgID("ADODB.Connection");
```

```
// Create a Connection object through late binding.
object cn = Activator.CreateInstance(ty);
// Use InvokeMember to retrieve the connection's Version property.
string version = (string) ty.InvokeMember("Version", BindingFlags.GetProperty, null, cn, null);

// Open the connection. (Open method takes one argument.)
object[] args =
   {"Provider=SQLOLEDB.1;Integrated Security=SSPI; Initial Catalog=pubs;Data Source=."};
ty.InvokeMember("Open", BindingFlags.InvokeMethod, null, cn, args);
```

When you invoke a method through late binding, you are implicitly relying on the COM object's IDispatch interface. This detail has a number of consequences. For example, the method name is case-insensitive because IDispatch works in this way, and all arguments are converted to Variant before being passed to the COM object. All COM components written with Visual Basic 6 support IDispatch and can be accessed in this fashion, but you can't use this technique with vtable-only components written in other languages.

The BinderFlags value passed to InvokeMember is transparently converted to IDispatch flags. For example, BinderFlags.InvokeMethod corresponds to the DISPATCH_METHOD flag, and BinderFlags.GetProperty corresponds to DISPATCH_PROPERTYGET. BinderFlags.SetProperty might pose a problem, however, because it is translated to DISPATCH_PROPERTYPUT or DISPATCH_PROPERTYPUTREF, so it is unclear whether the property being assigned has both a Property Let and a Property Set procedure written in Visual Basic 6. In this case, you can precisely describe which Property procedure you're calling by using either the Binder-Flags.PutDispProperty value (DISPATCH_PROPERTYPUT, for Property Let) or the Binder-Flags.PutRefDispProperty value (DISPATCH_PROPERTYPUTREF, for Property Set).

The System.Type class has a few members that are useful when working with COM objects. You can use the IsComObject read-only property to check whether a .NET type is actually a wrapper for a COM class and the GUID property to retrieve the component's GUID. The BaseType property of a COM object created through late binding is System.__ComObject, whereas the BaseType property of an early-bound COM object is null.

> **Note**   The next two sections assume that you are familiar with advanced COM program-ming topics, such as HRESULTs, VT_* Variant subtypes, and apartments. If you aren't familiar with these concepts, you might want to skip these sections.

COM Interop Marshaling

I covered data marshaling in the section titled "Using PInvoke" earlier in this chapter, but a few issues that concern COM Interop only are left to be discussed.

To begin with, you must learn how COM errors are returned to a managed client. The CLR checks the HRESULT 32-bit value returned from all COM methods: if the COM method returns an error, this value is negative. In this case, the CLR attempts to generate the exception that matches the returned HRESULT value. It can find the matching exception type by looking for a known mapping or by calling methods of the IErrorInfo interface to retrieve additional information about the error, if the COM object supports this interface. If both these attempts fail, the CLR throws a generic COMException object. The ErrorCode property of this COMException object contains the original HRESULT value, so you can use it in a switch block to provide different recovery actions for different error codes.

Variant arguments are another common source of problems. When you import a type library, all arguments and return values of Variant type are converted to Object values by the type library import process. If you pass a value to one of these Object arguments, the CLR dynamically determines the internal type of the Variant that is actually passed to COM. For example, 32-bit integer values are converted to VT_I4 Variants, Boolean values to VT_BOOL Variants, null values to VT_EMPTY Variants, and DBNull values to VT_NULL Variants.

However, not all COM types correspond to .NET Framework types, so you might need to resort to one of the following auxiliary classes to force the marshaler to convert your Object value to a specific VT_* type: CurrencyWrapper (VT_CY), UnknownWrapper (VT_UNKNOWN), DispatchWrapper (VT_DISPATCH), and ErrorWrapper (VT_ERROR). For example, here's how you can pass a .NET Decimal value to a Variant argument that is expected to receive a Currency value:

```
decimal val = 2.5M;
CurrencyWrapper cw = new CurrencyWrapper(val);
obj.MyMethod(cw);
```

Objects passed to Variant arguments pose other problems, too, because the runtime must copy the Object into a brand-new Variant. If the object is passed by value and the COM method changes one or more object properties, these changes can't be seen by the managed client. A similar thing happens when a COM method returns a Variant value that contains an object: in this case, the runtime copies the Variant into a new Object value, but changes to this object's properties aren't propagated to the original Variant seen by the COM component.

Changes in both directions are seen if a managed client passes an object to a Variant argument passed by reference, but keep in mind that the COM method might assign a completely different type of object to the argument. Therefore, you can't assume that, when the method returns, the argument still contains the same type of object it did before the call.

The situation is even more complicated if the Variant returned from COM has the VT_BYREF bit set, which indicates that the Variant contains a 32-bit pointer to the data. (For example, a Variant that contains a VT_BYREF+VT_DISPATCH value is actually a pointer to an object.) If the Variant is passed by value, the marshaler correctly recognizes the VT_BYREF bit and is able to retrieve the object reference, but any changes to this .NET Framework object aren't propagated to the original COM object (unlike what would happen if the client were a true COM application). If the Variant is passed using the ref keyword, however, changes to the .NET object are correctly propagated to the original COM object, but only if the COM method hasn't changed the type of the object. If the COM method has changed the object's type, an InvalidCastException occurs on return from the method.

The bottom line: steer clear of COM objects that take and return Variant arguments, if possible. If you can't avoid them, read the documentation carefully, and use the preceding notes as a guideline for troubleshooting code that doesn't behave as expected.

Threading Issues

One more issue must be taken into account when accessing COM from a .NET Framework client. COM components live either in a Single Thread Apartment (STA) or in a multi-threaded apartment (MTA), even though a few components can live in both apartment types. By comparison, .NET Framework applications run as free-threaded code, don't use apartments, and implement synchronization by other means (for example, synchronized regions and locks).

The CLR must initialize either an STA or an MTA before a managed client can call a COM object. The type of the apartment being initialized affects all subsequent calls: if the apartment isn't compatible with the apartment where the COM component resides, COM has to create a proxy/stub pair between them, which in turn has a serious negative effect on performance. All Visual Basic 6 components can live only in an STA; therefore, calls to these components coming from .NET Framework clients that have initialized an MTA will be slowed by an intermediate proxy/stub.

C# Console and Windows Forms applications initialize an STA by default, but other types of applications initialize an MTA by default. You can affect the apartment type that a managed thread creates by testing the current apartment type with the Thread object's GetApartmentState method and, if necessary, setting it with the SetApartmentState or TrySetApartmentState method. You must call these methods before you make the first call to COM:

```
if ( Thread.CurrentThread.GetApartmentState() == ApartmentState.Unknown )
{
   // Apartment hasn't been created yet.
   if ( Thread.CurrentThread.TrySetApartmentState(ApartmentState.STA) )
   {
      // You successfully managed to set STA mode.
      …
   }
   else
   {
      // For some reason you can't use STA mode. You can decide to emit error
      // or do whatever is more appropriate for the current application.
      …
   }
}
// Now you can call a Visual Basic 6 component.
SampleComponent.SampleObject sc = new SampleComponent.SampleObject();
```

You can't change the apartment type after the thread has initialized the apartment. Further attempts to modify the ApartmentState property are simply ignored, without raising any exception. Another way to tell the CLR which apartment type should be created is by flagging the Main method with either the STAThread or the MTAThread attribute:

```
[STAThread()]
static void Main()
{
    ...
}
```

> **Note**   ASP.NET applications create MTA apartments by default, but you can set the Page.AspCompatMode property or the AspCompat attribute in a @Page directive to true to force the page to execute in an STA. This setting is also necessary to call COM+ objects that access built-in objects such as Request or Response either through the ObjectContext object or through the argument passed to the OnStartPage method. For this property or attribute to work correctly, however, the COM or COM+ object must be created from inside the Page_Init or Page_Load event handler, as opposed to from inside the page's constructor or by means of a field initializer. Setting this property or attribute to true degrades the page's performance, so you should weigh the tradeoff of having an ASP.NET page running in an STA vs. going through a proxy/stub when the page calls an STA-only COM object.

Calling .NET Objects from COM

When porting a large application to .NET, you might decide to leave the bulk of the application as unmanaged code while rewriting selected components as C# classes. In this scenario, roles are reversed: unmanaged COM-based code works as the client of managed components. The COM Interop portion of the .NET Framework makes this scenario feasible.

The COM Callable Wrapper

A COM Callable Wrapper (CCW) works as a wrapper for a .NET Framework component exposed to a COM client. (See Figure 13-6.) It synthesizes any COM interface that clients expect to find, most notably IUnknown ("the mother of all COM interfaces") and IDispatch (which makes the object accessible from languages such as Microsoft Visual Basic Scripting Edition [VBScript] or through late binding in Visual Basic 6 and earlier versions). The CCW is also responsible for the object identity, so there is always at most one CCW instance for each instance of the .NET Framework component, even if multiple clients have a reference to the same object. The CCW also protects the .NET Framework object from garbage collections and morphs CLR exceptions into HRESULT codes when the method call returns to the COM client.

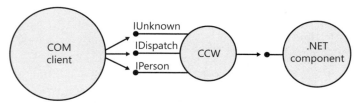

Figure 13-6   The COM Callable Wrapper object

For the .NET Framework to be able to create a suitable CCW object, you should create a type library for each managed DLL you want to expose to the COM world. Providing a type library helps COM developers code against the .NET Framework class—for example, by leveraging the Visual Basic 6 Object Browser and the IntelliSense feature—and allows the .NET Framework object to expose richer information at run time. A type library is also necessary at run time to let OleAut32 marshal remote instances of the objects.

Creating a Sample .NET Component

To see in practice how you can expose a C# component to the COM world, let's create a sample class and see how a COM client can access it. Start by creating a new Class Library project, name it SampleNetComponent, and enter the following code:

```
[ComVisible(true)]
public class Employee
{
    // A creatable COM class must have a public constructor with no arguments.
    public Employee()
    { }

    private string m_FirstName;

    public string FirstName
    {
        get { return m_FirstName; }
        set { m_FirstName = value; }
    }

    private string m_LastName;

    public string LastName
    {
        get { return m_LastName; }
        set { m_LastName = value; }
    }

    public string ReverseName()
    {
        return this.LastName + ", " + this.FirstName;
    }
}
```

The key point in the preceding code is the ComVisible attribute: only public classes with this attribute and with public parameterless constructors are visible to COM clients.

.NET Framework assemblies meant to be used by COM clients are usually registered in the GAC, and for this reason, they should be signed with a strong name. In Visual Studio 2005, you can perform this action on the Signing page of the project's designer. Next, switch to the Build page, and ensure that the Register For COM Interop option is selected. This option forces Visual Studio to create a type library with the same name as the DLL (SampleNetComponent.tlb, in this example) and to register this type library in the system registry.

Build the project, create a DLL named SampleNetComponent.Dll, and then create another project that references and uses the Employee class. This second project can be as simple as a Console application; it serves only to verify that the class works as expected. You'll notice that all the extra attributes in the Employee class don't affect the way the class can be used by a managed client.

Now you can bring up Visual Basic 6, add a reference to this SampleNetComponent.tlb file, and use the .NET Framework class as if it were a standard COM component:

```
' *** Visual Basic 6 code

' Access the object through late binding
Dim o As Object
Set o = CreateObject("SampleNetComponent.Employee")
o.FirstName = "John"
o.LastName = "Evans"
MsgBox o.ReverseName()

' Access the object through early binding.
Set emp = New SampleNetComponent.Employee
emp.FirstName = "John"
emp.LastName = "Evans"
MsgBox emp.ReverseName()
```

A COM client can access all the public fields, properties, and methods of the .NET component, both using either an Object or Variant variable, or a strongly typed variable. However, both these syntax forms internally use a kind of late binding: you can prove this detail by mistyping the name of a member and see that you get a runtime error. (You'd get a compile error if the Visual Basic compiler could use early binding.) In the section titled "The Class-Interface Attribute" later in this chapter, you'll learn how you can build .NET components that support "true" early binding.

Important .NET Framework components undergo all the usual binding and probing rules, even when they are accessed by COM clients. If you don't install the assembly in the GAC, the assembly should be stored as a private assembly in the unmanaged application's directory. If the client is a Visual Basic 6 application running inside the IDE (as opposed to compiled on disk), the application's directory is C:\Program Files\Microsoft Visual Studio\VB98— namely, the directory where the VB6.EXE executable resides. However, when testing a .NET component on a development system that has both Visual Studio 2005 and Visual Basic 6 installed, you don't need to reinstall the component in the GAC because Visual Studio 2005 runs the RegAsm tool with the /codebase option behind the scenes. (Read on for more details.)

The RegAsm and TlbExp Tools

You can also use a couple of utilities in the .NET Framework SDK to export an assembly to a type library. You should become familiar with these utilities because they offer some extra flexibility that you can't achieve solely with the Visual Studio export capabilities.

The Assembly Registration Tool (RegAsm) takes the name of an assembly and registers all the classes it contains in the system registry:

```
REGASM samplenetcomponent.dll /tlb:netcomp.tlb
```

The /tlb switch is optional, but you'll want to use it so that RegAsm produces a type library that COM clients can use to reference .NET Framework objects through early binding. In practice, you can omit the /tlb switch and not create a type library for the component only if COM clients create and use instances of the .NET class exclusively through late binding, that is, by means of Object (or Variant) variables.

You can think of RegAsm as a RegSvr32 utility that works with .NET components instead of COM components. As with the RegSvr32 utility, you can unregister a component from the registry by using the /u option:

```
REGASM samplenetcomponent.dll /u
```

The RegAsm utility supports two more useful switches. The /codebase option adds a Code-Base registry entry and should be used only if the .NET assembly isn't shared or isn't going to be registered in the GAC. (Visual Studio 2005 uses the /codebase option when exporting an assembly.)

```
REGASM samplenetcomponent.dll /codebase
```

The other option is /regfile, which doesn't register the component but creates a .reg file that you can later use to create all the necessary registry keys. (You can't use this option with /u or /tlb, and you can't duplicate its effect from inside Visual Studio.)

```
REGASM samplenetcomponent.dll /regfile:netcomp.reg
```

The .NET Framework SDK offers another tool that you can use to export a type library, the Type Library Exporter utility (TlbExp). TlbExp has the same effect as using the /tlb option with RegAsm, except the component isn't registered:

```
TLBEXP samplenetcomponent.dll /OUT:netcomp.tlb
```

If you omit the /out option, TlbExp creates a type library with the same name as the source DLL but with a .tlb extension. In practice, you'll use TlbExp far less frequently than you use RegAsm.

Conversion Details

.NET Framework assemblies embed more metadata than COM type libraries do; therefore, it is unavoidable that some information is lost in the conversion process from .NET to COM. In most cases, you don't need to care about these details, but you should keep a few things in mind. In this section, I summarize what you should be careful about.

Assembly version information consists of a four-part number, whereas type libraries support only major and minor version numbers. During the conversion process, the assembly's revision and build version numbers are discarded. If the assembly had no version information—that is, the version is 0.0.0.0—the type library is assigned version 1.0; otherwise, it couldn't be loaded correctly by a COM client.

A .NET Framework class or interface is exported to a coclass or interface with the same name. The namespace portion of the class or interface name is discarded: type libraries don't support the concept of nested classes or interfaces, and therefore the conversion "flattens" the object hierarchy. For example, a type named Animal.Mammal.Mouse is exported to a coclass named Animal.Mouse. When a name collision would result—for example, because another class is named Animal.Rodent.Mouse—the type is exported with its full name, but periods are replaced by underscores.

A C# class must be nonabstract and must expose a public parameterless constructor, either explicit or implicit, for it to be converted to a COM creatable class. (COM doesn't support constructors with arguments.) Creatable classes are assigned a ProgID equal to their complete namespace+name path. This ProgID generation process usually works flawlessly because ProgIDs can contain periods, except when the complete class name is longer than 39 characters or contains punctuation symbols other than periods. In such cases, you should specify a ProgID attribute in your C# source code. (See the next section.) Noncreatable classes are marked with the noncreatable attribute in the type library. Only creatable classes are registered by the RegAsm utility.

Any coclass generated by the conversion process is assigned a class identifier (CLSID) calculated using a hash function on the complete class name (including its namespace). This technique ensures that different classes generate different CLSIDs, and therefore each .NET Framework class is converted to a distinct COM class. This technique also ensures that the same CLSID is generated regardless of how many times the conversion process is performed. You can also assign a custom ID if you need to, as explained in the following section.

The conversion process generates one *class interface* for each .NET Framework class. Interfaces generated by the conversion process are assigned an interface identifier (IID) calculated using a hash function on the complete interface name (including its namespace) as well as the signatures of its methods. The hash function ensures that a different IID is generated if the interface name, the order of its methods, or the signature of any method changes. The generation of a new IID is necessary to comply with the immutable interface concept in COM. Notice that method names aren't taken into account by the hash function and that you can control the IID value using the Guid attribute, as explained in the next section.

Only public instance members are exposed through a class interface; static members, constructors with parameters, and members with a scope other than public aren't exported to COM. You can selectively hide one or more public methods to COM by means of the ComVisible attribute, as I explain in the next section.

Methods preserve their name when they are exported to a class interface (or any interface, for that matter). However, C# supports method overloading, whereas COM doesn't. To let COM clients call overloaded versions of a method, RegAsm and TlbExp generate a distinct method for each overloaded variant and decorate the name of additional methods with an ordinal number, starting at 2, so that each method is assigned a unique name. For example, three overloaded versions of a method named MyMethod are exported as MyMethod, MyMethod_2, and MyMethod_3. There is no guarantee that numbers will always be assigned in the same order if you repeat the export process.

Marshaling data from COM to .NET works along the same general guidelines described earlier in this chapter. However, you should be careful about method signatures when working with Visual Basic 6 as a client. A Visual Basic 6 client can't call a .NET Framework method that takes an array passed by value. You should change the method signature so that the array is passed by reference, which is the only legal way to pass array arguments in Visual Basic 6 and earlier versions.

Using Attributes to Control the Conversion

Now that you have a broad view of how the conversion from assemblies to type libraries works, let's see how you can decorate the .NET Framework class with attributes to gain control of the conversion process and solve some of the problems I mentioned in the previous section.

The ComVisible, ProgId, and Guid Attributes

By default, public assemblies, classes, and interfaces are exported and made visible to COM clients. However, you can make a specific public element invisible to COM by using the ComVisible attribute, which can be applied at the assembly, class, or member level. If applied at the assembly level, the attribute affects the visibility of all classes in the assembly, unless a class-level attribute forces a different visibility. Likewise, an attribute at the class level affects all the methods in the class that aren't flagged with a ComVisible attribute. Consider this code:

```
[assembly: ComVisible(false)]

[ComVisible(true)]
public class Person              // This class is visible to COM.
{
    ...
    [ComVisible(false)]
    public void DoSomething()    // This method isn't visible to COM.
    {
        ...
    }
}

public class Employee            // This class isn't visible to COM.
{
    ...
}
```

Interestingly, if a method takes or returns a type that isn't visible to COM, the argument or the return value is exported to COM as an IUnknown value; if a method takes or returns a struct (as opposed to a class) that isn't visible to COM, the method isn't exported at all.

You can explicitly assign a ProgID to a class by using the ProgId attribute in the C# source code. For example, the following code assigns the MouseCollection class a ProgID equal to Animal.Mice:

```csharp
[ProgID("Animal.Mice")]
public class MouseCollection
{
    ...
}
```

You can also assign a specific GUID to a class or an interface by using the Guid attribute. When you apply this attribute at the assembly level, it is taken as the TLBID identifier for the entire type library:

```csharp
// This is the TLBID for the exported type library.
[assembly: Guid("3DC10475-92DB-4E52-A3D2-925AA4E8BA17")]

// This is the CLSID for the class.
[Guid("{E6A2200A-5869-4C89-83A1-D0FE8540020B}")]
public class MouseCollection
{
    ...
}
```

The DispId Attribute

All the members of a COM IDispatch interface must be marked with a DISPID value, and these values are generated automatically in the conversion from .NET to COM. In general, you never see these DISPIDs and don't need to control their generation. The only exception worth mentioning is the special 0 value, which is reserved for the class default member.

If you've ever worked with Visual Basic 6 or other COM-based languages, you might remember that controls and objects can have a default member—for example, the Text property for TextBox controls and the Caption property for Label controls. The default member of .NET classes exported to COM is the ToString method that all classes inherit from System.Object, but you can make any property or method the default class member by applying the DispId attribute, as in the following:

```csharp
[DispId(0)]
public string Name
{
    get { ... }
    set { ... }
}
```

The ClassInterface Attribute

Any public .NET Framework class can be exposed to COM, provided that its source code contains a ComVisible(true) attribute at the class or the assembly level. A class exposed to COM with a ComVisible attribute exports its class interface—that is, the interface that contains all the fields, properties, and methods defined in the class—as an IDispatch interface. This means that COM clients can access the class's members only by means of late binding. Late binding is slow, isn't robust, and doesn't allow you to trap events. Despite these shortcomings, Microsoft decided to make class interfaces accessible through IDispatch by default, mostly because late binding ensures that you don't incur versioning problems.

You can control which type of class interface the export process generates by means of the ClassInterface attribute. This attribute can take one of the following ClassInterfaceType enumerated values: AutoDispatch (the default—methods are accessible through late binding only), AutoDual (methods are accessible through early and late binding), None (no class interface is created and only methods in secondary interfaces can be accessed). Here's how you must decorate a class to offer support for both early binding and late binding:

```
[ClassInterface(ClassInterfaceType.AutoDual)]
public class Employee
{
    …
}
```

All the members of a classed marked as AutoDual are visible in the Visual Basic 6 Object Browser or IntelliSense. However, even such a class doesn't make its events visible to clients. To solve this problem, I need to introduce two more attributes.

The InterfaceType and ComSourceInterfaces Attributes

Let's say that you have the following class:

```
public delegate void NameChangedEventHandler(string newName);

[ClassInterface(ClassInterfaceType.AutoDual)]
public class Person
{
    // Events that are raised when either the FirstName or LastName property changes
    public event NameChangedEventHandler FirstNameChanged;
    public event NameChangedEventHandler LastNameChanged;
    …
}
```

As I've just explained, these events aren't automatically exposed to COM clients. To make events visible to COM clients, you must define a separate interface that contains the event signature and mark the interface with an InterfaceType attribute to make it an IDispatch interface, as follows:

```
[InterfaceType(ComInterfaceType.InterfaceIsIDispatch )]
public interface Person_Events
```

```
{
    void FirstNameChanged(string newFirstName);
    void LastNameChanged(string newLastName);
}
```

Next, you must flag the Person class with a ComSourceInterfaces attribute that informs COM Interop that the class events are defined in the Person_Events interface:

```
[ClassInterface(ClassInterfaceType.AutoDual)]
[ComSourceInterfaces(typeof(Person_Events))]
public class Person
{
    // Events that are raised when the FirstName and LastName properties change
    public event NameChangedEventHandler FirstNameChanged;
    public event NameChangedEventHandler LastNameChanged;
    …
}
```

After these edits, Visual Basic 6 clients can assign an instance of the Person class to a WithEvents variable and correctly trap events:

```
' *** Visual Basic 6 code
Dim WithEvents pers As SampleNetComponent.Person

Private Sub pers_FirstNameChanged(ByVal newFirstName As String)
    MsgBox "New first name for " & pers.ReverseName
End Sub

Private Sub pers_LastNameChanged(ByVal newLastName As String)
    MsgBox "New last name for " & pers.ReverseName
End Sub
```

The ComRegisterFunction and ComUnregisterFunction Attributes

At times, you might need to perform a custom action when the .NET class is registered as a COM component by RegAsm (or by Visual Studio, if you have selected the Register For COM Interop option). For example, you might want to ask the end user for a password or add some keys to the registry (in addition to those added by the registration process). Accomplishing these tasks is as easy as adding a static procedure to the class and marking it with the ComRegisterFunction attribute:

```
private const string COMPANYKEY = @"Software\CodeArchitects\MyApp";

[ComRegisterFunction()]
private static void Register(Type ty)
{
    RegistryKey key = Registry.CurrentUser.CreateSubKey(COMPANYKEY);
    key.SetValue("InstallDate", DateTime.Now.ToLongDateString());
    key.Close();
}
```

If you add a registry key at installation time, you should remove it when the class is unregistered as a COM component. In this case, you create another static procedure and mark it with the ComUnregisterFunction attribute:

```
[ComUnregisterFunction()]
private static void UnRegister(Type ty)
{
    Registry.CurrentUser.DeleteSubKey(COMPANYKEY);
}
```

Both these procedures can be private or public, provided that they are marked with the static keyword and take a System.Type argument; this Type value identifies the class being registered or unregistered.

Working with Exceptions

Most CLR exceptions are automatically translated into the corresponding HRESULT codes when they are marshaled back to COM clients. For example, a DivideByZeroException object is translated to an HRESULT code equal to COR_E_DIVIDEBYZERO.

In those rare cases when you need to return a more specific HRESULT code, you can use a couple of techniques. The first and simplest of these relies on the ThrowExceptionForHR method of the Marshal class:

```
// Throw an exception that has an HRESULT of hex 80001234.
int errcode = (unchecked ((int) 0x80001234));
Marshal.ThrowExceptionForHR(errcode);
```

The second, more elegant technique consists of the definition of a custom exception class that has a constructor that assigns the desired error code to its HResult protected property:

```
public class CustomException : Exception
{
    public CustomException(string message) : base(message)
    {
        this.HResult = (unchecked ((int) 0x80001234));
    }
}
```

Your C# class can then throw an exception with a given HRESULT by throwing this custom exception as it would any standard exception:

```
throw new CustomException("File not found");
```

Writing COM-Friendly .NET Framework Components

.NET Framework components that are meant to be exposed to COM clients shouldn't use features that COM-based clients can't see. Or they should provide alternative ways for COM clients to access those features. Here's a brief summary of the dos and don'ts of COM-friendly components:

- Only public and nonabstract classes can be exposed to COM; use ComVisible(false) for public abstract classes.

- Avoid deep hierarchies in C# classes, such as nested classes or namespaces with more than two levels.

- The class must expose an implicit or explicit parameterless constructor; constructors with parameters can't be accessed through COM Interop.

- The class shouldn't expose static members because they aren't visible to COM clients.

- The class shouldn't expose overloaded members because they can create confusion when used by COM clients.

- If the class exposes events, define them in a separate interface, and use the ComSource-Interfaces attribute to let COM Interop export them correctly.

- Use custom exception classes that set the HResult property for returning nonstandard error codes to COM clients.

The .NET Framework offers superb support for the transition to and from the unmanaged world, thanks to PInvoke and COM Interop. In most cases, these two worlds can communicate quite easily, but you must be familiar with the techniques I have covered in this chapter to solve some of the problems you might bump into when writing real-world applications. However, never forget that a .NET Framework application that relies on COM components inherits many of the issues that have plagued COM programming, for example, the tendency to leak memory.

Index

X-Z

Francesco Balena

Francesco Balena began his software studies in the late 1970s and had to fight for a while against huge IBM mainframes and tons of punched cards while he waited for the PC to be invented. From those good old days—when the word *megabyte* made little sense and *gigabyte* was pure blasphemy—he has retained a taste for writing the most efficient and resource-aware code possible.

In more recent years, Francesco has become a contributing editor and member of the Technical Advisory board of *Visual Studio Magazine* (formerly *Visual Basic Programmer's Journal*), for which he has written more than 80 articles and columns. He's the author of four best-sellers in the Programming Microsoft Visual Basic series, which started in 1999, as well as coauthor of *Applied Microsoft .NET Framework Programming in Microsoft Visual Basic .NET* (with Jeffrey Richter) and *Practical Guidelines and Best Practices for Microsoft Visual Basic and Visual C# Developers* (with Giuseppe Dimauro), all from Microsoft Press. Francesco teaches Visual Basic and C# courses in the United States and Europe and speaks at developer conferences such as VSLive!, WinDev, and WinSummit. He is the founder of the popular .NET-2-The-Max site (*http://www.dotnet2themax.com*), where visitors can find articles, tips, routines, and updates for this book as they occur, and where he maintains his own blog.

Francesco is the lead author of VBMaximizer, a top-seller add-in for Microsoft Visual Basic 6 that has won an award from readers of *Visual Studio Magazine*. He is coauthor of CodeBox for .NET (a code repository tool) and Form Maximizer for .NET (a set of Microsoft Windows Forms controls). He has been Microsoft's MSDN Regional Director for Italy since 2002 and is cofounder of Code Architects, an Italian company that specializes exclusively in .NET Framework programming and training and that consults for many large software companies in Italy, including Microsoft.

Francesco lives in Bari, Italy, with his wife, Adriana, and his son, Andrea, but spends a lot of his time abroad. In a previous life, he had a lot of good times playing his alto sax with big bands and jazz combos until he discovered that computer programming could be just as fun and didn't require him to be awake and blowing until 4 A.M. each and every night. Only later did he realize that to write code and meet deadlines he wouldn't be going to sleep before 4 A.M. anyway—but it was too late to change his mind.

Form Maximizer.NET

Form Maximizer.NET is an innovative component library that extends standard Windows Forms controls with 35 new design-time properties, and enables you to enhance existing applications without replacing any existing control or writing a single line of code. Here's a partial list of what Form Maximizer .NET enables you to do:

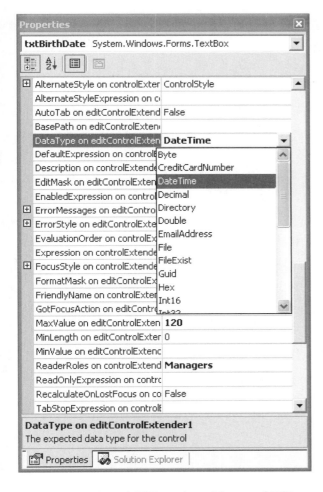

Validate user input: Force a specific data type, a valid range, a validation regex; or specify a custom expression that references other controls, form variables, and methods.

Define the state of a control: Decide when a control becomes visible, enabled, or readonly, depending on the value of other fields or the user's role.

Create calculated fields: Enter an expression in the Properties window and have the field automatically recalculated when other fields on the form change.

Change field appearance: Change the appearance of fields when they receive the input focus, fail to validate, or meet custom condition (e.g. negative numbers, empty fields).

Format data: Automatically format numbers and dates when the focus leaves the control.

Assign common tasks to buttons and menus: Load/save text files and images, show forms and common dialogs, launch applications, without writing code.

…plus auto-tabbing, multiline tooltips, field descriptions, toolbar hotkeys, centralized events, nonrectangular forms, and more.

Form Maximizer.NET works with any .NET programming language. Full C# source code is available (in Form Maximizer .NET Enterprise Edition only).

Read more about Form Maximizer .NET and download a fully functional demo version at **www.dotnet2themax.com/formmaximizer**

Form Maximizer.NET and CodeWall.NET have been authored by Francesco Balena and are distributed by Code Architects Srl, Italy (www.codearchitects.com).

Additional Resources for C# Developers
Published and Forthcoming Titles from Microsoft Press

Microsoft® Visual C#® 2005 Express Edition: Build a Program Now!
Patrice Pelland • ISBN 0-7356-2229-9

In this lively, eye-opening, and hands-on book, all you need is a computer and the desire to learn how to program with Visual C# 2005 Express Edition. Featuring a full working edition of the software, this fun and highly visual guide walks you through a complete programming project—a desktop weather-reporting application—from start to finish. You'll get an unintimidating introduction to the Microsoft Visual Studio® development environment and learn how to put the lightweight, easy-to-use tools in Visual C# Express to work right away—creating, compiling, testing, and delivering your first, ready-to-use program. You'll get expert tips, coaching, and visual examples at each step of the way, along with pointers to additional learning resources.

Microsoft Visual C# 2005 *Step by Step*
John Sharp • ISBN 0-7356-2129-2

Visual C#, a feature of Visual Studio 2005, is a modern programming language designed to deliver a productive environment for creating business frameworks and reusable object-oriented components. Now you can teach yourself essential techniques with Visual C#—and start building components and Microsoft Windows®–based applications—one step at a time. With *Step by Step*, you work at your own pace through hands-on, learn-by-doing exercises. Whether you're a beginning programmer or new to this particular language, you'll learn how, when, and why to use specific features of Visual C# 2005. Each chapter puts you to work, building your knowledge of core capabilities and guiding you as you create your first C#-based applications for Windows, data management, and the Web.

Programming Microsoft Visual C# 2005 Framework Reference
Francesco Balena • ISBN 0-7356-2182-9

Complementing *Programming Microsoft Visual C# 2005 Core Reference*, this book covers a wide range of additional topics and information critical to Visual C# developers, including Windows Forms, working with Microsoft ADO.NET 2.0 and Microsoft ASP.NET 2.0, Web services, security, remoting, and much more. Packed with sample code and real-world examples, this book will help developers move from understanding to mastery.

Programming Microsoft Visual C# 2005 *Core Reference*
Donis Marshall • ISBN 0-7356-2181-0

Get the in-depth reference and pragmatic, real-world insights you need to exploit the enhanced language features and core capabilities in Visual C# 2005. Programming expert Donis Marshall deftly builds your proficiency with classes, structs, and other fundamentals, and advances your expertise with more advanced topics such as debugging, threading, and memory management. Combining incisive reference with hands-on coding examples and best practices, this *Core Reference* focuses on mastering the C# skills you need to build innovative solutions for smart clients and the Web.

CLR via C#, Second Edition
Jeffrey Richter • ISBN 0-7356-2163-2

In this new edition of Jeffrey Richter's popular book, you get focused, pragmatic guidance on how to exploit the common language runtime (CLR) functionality in Microsoft .NET Framework 2.0 for applications of all types—from Web Forms, Windows Forms, and Web services to solutions for Microsoft SQL Server™, Microsoft code names "Avalon" and "Indigo," consoles, Microsoft Windows NT® Service, and more. Targeted to advanced developers and software designers, this book takes you under the covers of .NET for an in-depth understanding of its structure, functions, and operational components, demonstrating the most practical ways to apply this knowledge to your own development efforts. You'll master fundamental design tenets for .NET and get hands-on insights for creating high-performance applications more easily and efficiently. The book features extensive code examples in Visual C# 2005.

Programming Microsoft Windows Forms
Charles Petzold • ISBN 0-7356-2153-5

CLR via C++
Jeffrey Richter with Stanley B. Lippman
ISBN 0-7356-2248-5

Programming Microsoft Web Forms
Douglas J. Reilly • ISBN 0-7356-2179-9

Debugging, Tuning, and Testing Microsoft .NET 2.0 Applications
John Robbins • ISBN 0-7356-2202-7

For more information about Microsoft Press® books and other learning products,
visit: **www.microsoft.com/books** *and* **www.microsoft.com/learning**

Additional Resources for Developers: Advanced Topics and Best Practices

Published and Forthcoming Titles from Microsoft Press

Code Complete, Second Edition
Steve McConnell • ISBN 0-7356-1967-0

For more than a decade, Steve McConnell, one of the premier authors and voices in the software community, has helped change the way developers write code—and produce better software. Now his classic book, *Code Complete*, has been fully updated and revised with best practices in the art and science of constructing software. Topics include design, applying good techniques to construction, eliminating errors, planning, managing construction activities, and relating personal character to superior software. This new edition features fully updated information on programming techniques, including the emergence of Web-style programming, and integrated coverage of object-oriented design. You'll also find new code examples—both good and bad—in C++, Microsoft® Visual Basic®, C#, and Java, although the focus is squarely on techniques and practices.

More About Software Requirements: Thorny Issues and Practical Advice
Karl E. Wiegers • ISBN 0-7356-2267-1

Have you ever delivered software that satisfied all of the project specifications, but failed to meet any of the customers expectations? Without formal, verifiable requirements—and a system for managing them—the result is often a gap between what developers think they're supposed to build and what customers think they're going to get. Too often, lessons about software requirements engineering processes are formal or academic, and not of value to real-world, professional development teams. In this follow-up guide to *Software Requirements*, Second Edition, you will discover even more practical techniques for gathering and managing software requirements that help you deliver software that meets project and customer specifications. Succinct and immediately useful, this book is a must-have for developers and architects.

Software Estimation: Demystifying the Black Art
Steve McConnell • ISBN 0-7356-0535-1

Often referred to as the "black art" because of its complexity and uncertainty, software estimation is not as hard or mysterious as people think. However, the art of how to create effective cost and schedule estimates has not been very well publicized. *Software Estimation* provides a proven set of procedures and heuristics that software developers, technical leads, and project managers can apply to their projects. Instead of arcane treatises and rigid modeling techniques, award-winning author Steve McConnell gives practical guidance to help organizations achieve basic estimation proficiency and lay the groundwork to continue improving project cost estimates. This book does not avoid the more complex mathematical estimation approaches, but the non-mathematical reader will find plenty of useful guidelines without getting bogged down in complex formulas.

Debugging, Tuning, and Testing Microsoft .NET 2.0 Applications
John Robbins • ISBN 0-7356-2202-7

Making an application the best it can be has long been a time-consuming task best accomplished with specialized and costly tools. With Microsoft Visual Studio® 2005, developers have available a new range of built-in functionality that enables them to debug their code quickly and efficiently, tune it to optimum performance, and test applications to ensure compatibility and trouble-free operation. In this accessible and hands-on book, debugging expert John Robbins shows developers how to use the tools and functions in Visual Studio to their full advantage to ensure high-quality applications.

The Security Development Lifecycle
Michael Howard and Steve Lipner • ISBN 0-7356-2214-0

Adapted from Microsoft's standard development process, the Security Development Lifecycle (SDL) is a methodology that helps reduce the number of security defects in code at every stage of the development process, from design to release. This book details each stage of the SDL methodology and discusses its implementation across a range of Microsoft software, including Microsoft Windows Server™ 2003, Microsoft SQL Server™ 2000 Service Pack 3, and Microsoft Exchange Server 2003 Service Pack 1, to help measurably improve security features. You get direct access to insights from Microsoft's security team and lessons that are applicable to software development processes worldwide, whether on a small-scale or a large-scale. This book includes a CD featuring videos of developer training classes.

Software Requirements, Second Edition
Karl E. Wiegers • ISBN 0-7356-1879-8

Writing Secure Code, Second Edition
Michael Howard and David LeBlanc • ISBN 0-7356-1722-8

CLR via C#, Second Edition
Jeffrey Richter • ISBN 0-7356-2163-2

For more information about Microsoft Press® books and other learning products, visit: **www.microsoft.com/mspress** *and* **www.microsoft.com/learning**

Microsoft®
Press

Additional Resources for Visual Basic Developers
Published and Forthcoming Titles from Microsoft Press

Microsoft® Visual Basic® 2005 Express Edition: Build a Program Now!
Patrice Pelland • ISBN 0-7356-2213-2

Featuring a full working edition of the software, this fun and highly visual guide walks you through a complete programming project—a desktop weather-reporting application—from start to finish. You'll get an introduction to the Microsoft Visual Studio® development environment and learn how to put the lightweight, easy-to-use tools in Visual Basic Express to work right away—creating, compiling, testing, and delivering your first ready-to-use program. You'll get expert tips, coaching, and visual examples each step of the way, along with pointers to additional learning resources.

Microsoft Visual Basic 2005 *Step by Step*
Michael Halvorson • ISBN 0-7356-2131-4

With enhancements across its visual designers, code editor, language, and debugger that help accelerate the development and deployment of robust, elegant applications across the Web, a business group, or an enterprise, Visual Basic 2005 focuses on enabling developers to rapidly build applications. Now you can teach yourself the essentials of working with Visual Studio 2005 and the new features of the Visual Basic language—one step at a time. Each chapter puts you to work, showing you how, when, and why to use specific features of Visual Basic and guiding as you create actual components and working applications for Microsoft Windows®. You'll also explore data management and Web-based development topics.

Programming Microsoft Visual Basic 2005 *Core Reference*
Francesco Balena • ISBN 0-7356-2183-7

Get the expert insights, indispensable reference, and practical instruction needed to exploit the core language features and capabilities in Visual Basic 2005. Well-known Visual Basic programming author Francesco Balena expertly guides you through the fundamentals, including modules, keywords, and inheritance, and builds your mastery of more advanced topics such as delegates, assemblies, and My Namespace. Combining in-depth reference with extensive, hands-on code examples and best-practices advice, this *Core Reference* delivers the key resources that you need to develop professional-level programming skills for smart clients and the Web.

Programming Microsoft Visual Basic 2005 Framework Reference
Francesco Balena • ISBN 0-7356-2175-6

Complementing *Programming Microsoft Visual Basic 2005 Core Reference*, this book covers a wide range of additional topics and information critical to Visual Basic developers, including Windows Forms, working with Microsoft ADO.NET 2.0 and ASP.NET 2.0, Web services, security, remoting, and much more. Packed with sample code and real-world examples, this book will help developers move from understanding to mastery.

Programming Microsoft Windows Forms
Charles Petzold • ISBN 0-7356-2153-5

Programming Microsoft Web Forms
Douglas J. Reilly • ISBN 0-7356-2179-9

Debugging, Tuning, and Testing Microsoft .NET 2.0 Applications
John Robbins • ISBN 0-7356-2202-7

Microsoft ASP.NET 2.0 *Step by Step*
George Shepherd • ISBN 0-7356-2201-9

Microsoft ADO.NET 2.0 *Step by Step*
Rebecca Riordan • ISBN 0-7356-2164-0

Programming Microsoft ASP.NET 2.0 *Core Reference*
Dino Esposito • ISBN 0-7356-2176-4

For more information about Microsoft Press® books and other learning products, visit: **www.microsoft.com/books** *and* **www.microsoft.com/learning**

Additional Resources for Web Developers
Published and Forthcoming Titles from Microsoft Press

Microsoft® Visual Web Developer™ 2005 Express Edition: Build a Web Site Now!
Jim Buyens ● ISBN 0-7356-2212-4

With this lively, eye-opening, and hands-on book, all you need is a computer and the desire to learn how to create Web pages now using Visual Web Developer Express Edition! Featuring a full working edition of the software, this fun and highly visual guide walks you through a complete Web page project from set-up to launch. You'll get an introduction to the Microsoft Visual Studio® environment and learn how to put the light-weight, easy-to-use tools in Visual Web Developer Express to work right away—building your first, dynamic Web pages with Microsoft ASP.NET 2.0. You'll get expert tips, coaching, and visual examples at each step of the way, along with pointers to additional learning resources.

Microsoft ASP.NET 2.0 Programming
Step by Step
George Shepherd ● ISBN 0-7356-2201-9

With dramatic improvements in performance, productivity, and security features, Visual Studio 2005 and ASP.NET 2.0 deliver a simplified, high-performance, and powerful Web development experience. ASP.NET 2.0 features a new set of controls and infrastructure that simplify Web-based data access and include functionality that facilitates code reuse, visual consistency, and aesthetic appeal. Now you can teach yourself the essentials of working with ASP.NET 2.0 in the Visual Studio environment—one step at a time. With *Step by Step*, you work at your own pace through hands-on, learn-by-doing exercises. Whether you're a beginning programmer or new to this version of the technology, you'll understand the core capabilities and fundamental techniques for ASP.NET 2.0. Each chapter puts you to work, showing you how, when, and why to use specific features of the ASP.NET 2.0 rapid application development environment and guiding you as you create actual components and working applications for the Web, including advanced features such as personalization.

Programming Microsoft ASP.NET 2.0
Core Reference
Dino Esposito ● ISBN 0-7356-2176-4

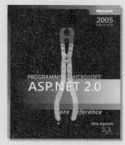

Delve into the core topics for ASP.NET 2.0 programming, mastering the essential skills and capabilities needed to build high-performance Web applications successfully. Well-known ASP.NET author Dino Esposito deftly builds your expertise with Web forms, Visual Studio, core controls, master pages, data access, data binding, state management, security services, and other must-know topics—combining definitive reference with practical, hands-on programming instruction. Packed with expert guidance and pragmatic examples, this *Core Reference* delivers the key resources that you need to develop professional-level Web programming skills.

Programming Microsoft ASP.NET 2.0
Applications: *Advanced Topics*
Dino Esposito ● ISBN 0-7356-2177-2

Master advanced topics in ASP.NET 2.0 programming—gaining the essential insights and in-depth understanding that you need to build sophisticated, highly functional Web applications successfully. Topics include Web forms, Visual Studio 2005, core controls, master pages, data access, data binding, state management, and security considerations. Developers often discover that the more they use ASP.NET, the more they need to know. With expert guidance from ASP.NET authority Dino Esposito, you get the in-depth, comprehensive information that leads to full mastery of the technology.

Programming Microsoft Windows® Forms
Charles Petzold ● ISBN 0-7356-2153-5

Programming Microsoft Web Forms
Douglas J. Reilly ● ISBN 0-7356-2179-9

CLR via C++
Jeffrey Richter with Stanley B. Lippman
ISBN 0-7356-2248-5

Debugging, Tuning, and Testing Microsoft .NET 2.0 Applications
John Robbins ● ISBN 0-7356-2202-7

CLR via C#, Second Edition
Jeffrey Richter ● ISBN 0-7356-2163-2

For more information about Microsoft Press® books and other learning products,
visit: **www.microsoft.com/books** *and* **www.microsoft.com/learning**

What do you think of this book? We want to hear from you!

Do you have a few minutes to participate in a brief online survey? Microsoft is interested in hearing your feedback about this publication so that we can continually improve our books and learning resources for you.

To participate in our survey, please visit:

www.microsoft.com/learning/booksurvey

And enter this book's ISBN, 0-7356-2308-2. As a thank-you to survey participants in the United States and Canada, each month we'll randomly select five respondents to win one of five $100 gift certificates from a leading online merchant.* At the conclusion of the survey, you can enter the drawing by providing your e-mail address, which will be used for prize notification *only*.

Thanks in advance for your input. Your opinion counts!

Sincerely,

Microsoft Learning

Learn More. Go Further.